From Albert Salomon

From Albert Salomon

Essays on Social Thinkers

Edited and introduced by

Duffy Graham and Robert Jackall

Newfound Press
THE UNIVERSITY OF TENNESSEE LIBRARIES, KNOXVILLE

From Albert Salomon: Essays on Social Thinkers

Newfound Press is a digital imprint of the University of Tennessee Libraries. Its publications are available for noncommercial and educational uses, such as research, teaching, and private study.

Newfound Press
University of Tennessee Libraries
1015 Volunteer Boulevard
Knoxville, TN 37996-1000
newfoundpress.utk.edu

Print on demand available through University of Tennessee Press.
DOI: http://dx.doi.org/10.7290/ygtr4qv6

ISBN-13: 978-0-9860803-2-6 (paperback)
ISBN-13: 978-0-9860803-5-7 (PDF)

Names: Salomon, Albert, 1891-1966, author. | Graham, Duffy, editor. | Jackall, Robert, editor.
Title: From Albert Salomon : essays on social thinkers / edited and introduced by Duffy Graham and Robert Jackall.
Other titles: Essays on social thinkers.
Description: Knoxville, Tennessee : Newfound Press, The University of Tennessee Libraries, [2019] | Originally published as individual papers in a variety of journals and monographs between May 1934 and 2008; includes three previously unpublished and undated manuscripts. | Includes bibliographical references.
Identifiers: ISBN 9780986080326 (pbk.) | ISBN 9780986080357 (PDF)
Subjects: LCSH: Salomon, Albert, 1891-1966. | Sociologists. | Socialists. | Sociology—History. | Sociology—Philosophy. | Social sciences—History. | Humanism. | Humanity. | Civilization. | Enlightenment. | Democracy. | Religion.
Classification: LCC HM585.S256 2019 (print) | LCC HM585.S256 2019eb (ebook)

Book design by Jayne W. Smith
Cover design by C. S. Jenkins

Contents

Acknowledgments

The editors wish to thank Frank Salomon, Albert Salomon's son; Elizabeth Janovsky, Lynn Janovsky, Lisa Salomon, and Yana Salomon, Albert Salomon's granddaughters; and the Willmott Family Professorship at Williams College for supporting this project. Special thanks also to Peggy Weyers of Williams College; Jeanne Swadosh, Elizabeth Harrell-Edge, and Wendy Scheir of the New School Archives; and Jayne Smith of Newfound Press for outstanding technical assistance. We also wish to thank Arien Mack, The Alfred J. and Monette C. Marrow Professor of Psychology at the New School for Social Research and Editor of Social Research, and her managing editor, Cara Schlesinger, for generously granting permission to republish several of Albert Salomon's essays.

A Discerning and Generous Scholar

Duffy Graham and Robert Jackall

I

Albert Salomon wastes no time in introducing his essay, "Louis Duc de Saint-Simon: Class Consciousness of the Defeated." By the end of five short paragraphs, the reader has good reason to believe that Saint-Simon is a thinker worth careful consideration and that Salomon will be a worthy guide.

Salomon immediately identifies Saint-Simon as unique, first observing that Saint-Simon's *Mémoires* defy historical, cultural, and stylistic categorization, then calling attention to Saint-Simon's oxymoronic and evocative description of his own work as "contemporary history." Salomon then identifies Saint-Simon's work as "a model of analysis." For the kicker, Salomon ties Saint-Simon's work to an issue that is urgent in the time and place Salomon is writing—mid-twentieth-century America—and that is bedrock for sociology: class consciousness.

The introduction reveals certain of Salomon's own special virtues. To place Saint-Simon in historical and literary context as precisely and elegantly as Salomon does requires erudition. To recognize the humanity, common and rarefied, encompassed in Saint-Simon's

---

term, *contemporary history*, as Salomon does, requires compassion and a cultured mind. To convey so much information so efficiently requires artfulness.

And so, in the introduction to Salomon's essay on Saint-Simon, as in the essay as a whole, and as in all of Salomon's essays, the reader experiences a double thrill. The reader moves from darkness into light, coming into a new understanding of an important social thinker or a remarkable episode of social thought, with all the new collateral awareness that comes with it. The reader marvels, too, at Salomon's critical faculties.

* * *

Saint-Simon's *Mémoires* depict social life in the royal court through the last twenty-five years of the rule of the Sun King, Louis XIV, from 1690 to 1715, and the whole of the Régence of Philippe II d'Orléans, from 1715 to 1723. Salomon notes the diligence with which Saint-Simon, himself a courtier, collected his materials.

> For over twenty years he took notes; every night he wrote in his diaries what he had observed and learned about persons, situations, and events. He exploited the knowledge of his friends in the ministry and in the military. He carefully listened to his wife, questioned his brothers and sisters-in-law, and was on the best terms with the king's physicians and chief valet. He was highly appreciated as a confidant by many ladies at the court, whose stories were a valuable source of information about love, sex, and business at Versailles.

Salomon argues that such recollections have "a greater claim to a rendering of historical reality than the academic constructions of fictitious historical reality." He explained:

> Men of affairs have . . . an advantage over the professors in that they understand how human beings act in their everyday lives. . . . They know, far better than most academicians, the underlying reality beneath the ostensibly harmonious picture most of us have of our world; being informed by their spies and agents about the nature of their opponents, they are able to learn in the most concrete fashion the inner workings of their social milieu.

Salomon notes both Saint-Simon's recognition of the crucial importance of social roles in people's lives and his conviction of "the uniqueness and identity of individual human beings . . . under the pressure of constantly changing circumstances"—that is, the requirements of their social interactions. Salomon extracts Saint-Simon's insight into the provisional character of social behavior:

> Social relationships disclose the precariousness and ambiguity in human action, men living with, for, and against one another. Men pretend and parade, betray and reveal themselves; they 'seem' and 'sham,' 'simulate' and 'dissimulate'; they 'play' public roles and are different in their private lives; their behavior is esoteric and exoteric, overt and closed, according to the requirements of the situation and their own purposes and goals.

In particular, Salomon appreciates Saint-Simon's "portraits." These incomparably rich descriptions of the men and women of the royal court recreate an entire social world. Indeed, Salomon argues that Saint-Simon's "dramatic presentation of human and social situations, whether tragic or comic, and the depth of his imagination make him the Shakespeare of prose." A Saint-Simon portrait differs from a Weberian ideal type—that is, a coherent and logical fictive construct that satisfies some specific scientific concern. Instead, a portrait resembles an Impressionist painting. It usually begins with an account of the subject's physical qualities and proceeds to note his or her acquired qualities: modes of "speaking, moving, and other bodily gestures," poise or lack of it, politeness or rudeness, and self-discipline. Salomon perceives Saint-Simon's fascination with how the "training and education of the young noblemen produced human beings whose bodies and minds were taught to represent a specific way of life, to embody specific social roles every moment of their lives" and how "[t]he educated and cultured classes of the bourgeois patricians had been brought up in the appreciation of graceful conduct rather than mere behavior, in the goods of the *cultura animi* rather than in the virtues of aristocratic conversation[.]" Salomon sees that the portraits stress the power of recollections and the strength of traditions in forming human beings. Salomon singles out Saint-Simon's images of Louis XIV, Mme de Maintenon, Louis Duc de Bourgogne, Mme de Montespan, the Duc d'Orleans, and of the Abbé François Fénelon, Archbishop of Cambrai. Salomon's summary of the portrait of Fénelon is especially arresting:

> The description of Fénelon's physical being is unforgettable: a tall, slim man with a long white face, an aquiline nose, and eyes the flames and spirit of which overwhelmed one like a torrent. This face, while revealing the most contrasting traits, did not disturb the inner harmony and integrity of his mind, but expressed a unity of gravity and charm, of seriousness and joyfulness. It manifested the scholar, the bishop, and the grandseigneur. All these diverse elements and aspects were united and merged into the open stream of a continuously growing personality; it contributed to his greatness and to the halo of saintliness that had taken the blows of destiny and of the intrigues of his enemies. He was

> superior to his fate, however, because he had affirmed it with humility and the creative spirit of spiritual liberation. His greatness was visible even at the surface of his conduct, combining a delicate politeness with genuine depth and integrity, nobility with a radiant mind, and spirituality with the deepest concern for the life of man in the world. Saint-Simon was convinced that this human being embodied the greatest range of human possibilities that he had discovered and presented in the single images of his 'portraits.'

Salomon also emphasized the relationship between Saint-Simon and his master, Cornelius Tacitus. Salomon makes clear that Saint-Simon's *Mémoires* emulate Tacitus's *Annales* in structure and style, but finds a deeper connection: Saint-Simon was a moralist, as was Tacitus, and Saint-Simon perceived that he and Tacitus occupied a parallel moral vantage point. Salomon also specifies that Tacitus helped Saint-Simon understand the transformation of Saint-Simon's world.

> [Saint-Simon] deeply appreciated the Roman's stand against imperial despotism and the absolute majesty of the ruler. He well understood the megalomania of the rulers as the result of prostration and flattery by their courtiers, ministers, and senators. He found the same characteristics in his own society and constantly compared the two patterns of tyranny, finding the same pattern of decadence in both the res publica and the French monarchy. . . . Throughout the *Mémoires*, Saint-Simon recalls the former conditions of the [French] nobles: their indispensable service to the king, the symbolic function of crowning the king at Rheims, their role in government

> during the feudal monarchy, their political activities as compared to the grandees of Spain. But all this was gone: the French feudal elite, the dukes and peers, were in the same situation that the Roman aristocrats were in when the military tyrants overthrew the senatorial patricians.

Salomon distills the crucial and poignant emotional and intellectual implications of this realization for his subject. Saint-Simon felt that Louis XIV's outright alliance with the new rising bourgeoisie, men of commerce and finance, led directly to the decay of the old feudal monarchy and, with it, "the decline of the feudal nobility, politically, socially, and economically." Upon such reflections, Saint-Simon saw his own class as defeated. All that remained to his vanquished class was the "old way of life in its manners, mannerisms, and patterns of behavior." This, in turn, led the old feudal nobility and Saint-Simon himself to become obsessed with the rights and privileges of social etiquette that distinguished them from the new classes. Thus, he led the fight against the aspirations of the bourgeois ministers to wear the suits of noblemen at court instead of their prescribed Parliament robes; he cherished the monarch's kisses, a privilege reserved to dukes and duchesses; he insisted on the privilege of duchesses at court to sit on taborets—armless, backless stools; he guarded the right of dukes to be seated in proper hierarchical order at official dinner parties; and he considered the ducal rights to speak in Parliament while wearing their bonnets and to be addressed there by bareheaded officials a supremely important matter.

Saint-Simon, for all his awareness, cannot fully distance himself from his situation. Salomon is in a position to put the matter in context—and he does so pithily.

> All politically defeated classes tend to maintain their manners, their mannerisms, their attitudes, discipline,

> and ways of life as something they cannot and will not be deprived of. . . . This is precisely the sociological significance of the ardent fights by the dukes and peers against the new wave of the bourgeois. It is a historical and human phenomenon, tragic and comic, bearing at once the depth of human grandeur and misery. The loyalty and allegiance to our traditions, to the training by our ancestors, and to the teaching of our fathers remain a lasting good for those who follow this way of life.

This is the bottom line of Salomon's essay.

Social etiquette gave the court of Louis XIV an appearance of regimented harmony. But, as Salomon notes, Saint-Simon saw that "this harmonious totality was sheer deception, as fictitious as a carnival. Only on the surface was it gay and superior to the routine of everyday life; underneath was a complex of unleashed greed, fear, and combat, merged and united by the demonic pressure of sex." Further, Salomon argues:

> Saint-Simon pointed out in a radical way that the court was in fact the central institution for the production and distribution of power. . . . [It] is a competitive society in which different associations, called machines, struggle with one another for the monopoly of power. The social process is mechanical because it is subject to the law of attraction and repulsion, men moving and being moved. They gather together for realizing their purposes under the pressure of competing machines. The reality of this game is tough and disillusioning as its appearance is aesthetically perfect in a complete, though fictitious, harmony. The courtiers and mistresses, the confessors and generals, the dukes and physicians of the king are the engineers and puppets of the show that seems to be con-

> trolled by the great magician, but is, in reality, directed by the king's associates and agents.

There were three main "machines." First, there were the friends, generals, nobles, and princes who surrounded Monseigneur, Le Grand Dauphin, Louis of France, heir to the throne. This crowd lusted for Monseigneur's ascension to the throne in order to "share in the spoils." Second, there was the machine centered on Françoise d'Aubigné, Madam de Maintenon, the second wife of Louis XIV. A confidant of the king, she controlled the king's ministers by dispensing offices and promotions. Third, there was the crowd of notables who "gambled on a better future." Here, the leaders were François Fénelon; Paul de Beauvilliers, Duke of Saint-Aignan; Charles Honoré d'Albert, Duke of Chevreuse; and Saint-Simon himself. Together, they supported the young and remarkable Louis, Duc de Burgogne, Le Petit Dauphin, who, they hoped, would lead a monarchy that was both less absolute and less centralized.

Salomon underscores Saint-Simon's observation that "men never act as individuals, but as members of a clan." He argues that "it is probably necessary to reconsider many histories and stress neither the importance of individuals nor of collective trends, but of the articulate power of the great families." Certainly, such clan unity was crucial for survival in the court of Louis XIV, "the ideal place for intrigues, conspiracies, and pressure groups [that] formed the social jungle where everyone fought for vested interests." In that world,

> there [was] no human relationship that was not used or abused for social advancement, political power, or economic gain. Almost all social interaction was reduced to 'business,' in a competitive struggle for superiority. Some advanced on the social ladder because the king liked them as champions at billiards; others used their

> charm and wits in the drawing rooms of Mme de Maintenon, in order to gain careers in the army or in the civil service; still others tried to push their way up through love affairs with princesses or mistresses of princes. Husbands became the procurers for their wives in order to achieve great careers.

Only kin loyalty could protect one in such a milieu.

Salomon observes that Saint-Simon made sure also to portray men and women who chose different paths in the social jungle of the court—such as "the ascetic princes of the Church, men of true dedication to God and their parishes, living in the Imitation of Christ" and "great soldiers who do not seek glory for themselves, but cherish victory for the king and perfection in their commands"—and to mention those "nobles and successful courtiers, ministers, gentlemen, ladies, and princesses, men and women who had gained prestigious reputations in politics and love, who suddenly departed the scene of their triumphs and devoted themselves to God in penitent orders, often the Carmelites." Salomon makes the point to honor Saint-Simon's integrity.

Salomon concludes by considering Saint-Simon's preoccupation with the restoration of the political influence of dukes and peers in the face of the "urban and bourgeois advance"—a lost cause and an effort contrary to Saint-Simon's deeper knowledge. Salomon notes aptly that it made Saint-Simon, like the subjects of his portraits, "tragic and comic alike." But Salomon sees more still:

> [T]here is greatness in the man whose sensitivity and imagination, whose penetrating and illuminating eyes, made him conceive of the historical world and of its social patterns as the *comédie humaine*. In his ultimate glory, he is not the historian, sociologist, or psychologist,

> but the great poet who magically resurrected a world of dead men and transformed them into loving and hating people, conspiring with, for, and against one another in their lust, their aspirations for power and recognition by others, and the problem of being themselves. Here was a man whose work was an inspiration to the great French novelists of the nineteenth and twentieth centuries, as it is even now to psychologists, sociologists, and philosophers. It stands today as a major source of aesthetic suggestion and scientific challenge.

II

Across his career, Albert Salomon analyzes the work of an astonishing array of European social thinkers. These include Theophrastus (d. 287 BC), Marcus Tullius Cicero (106–43 BC), Lucius Annaeus Seneca (4 BC–65 AD), Epictetus (55–135), Cornelius Tacitus (56–120), Desiderius Erasmus (1466–1536), Niccolò Machiavelli (1469–1527), Martin Luther (1483–1546), Ignatius of Loyola (1491–1556), Michel de Montaigne (1533–1592), Francis Bacon (1561–1626), Francis de Sales (1567–1622), Hugo Grotius (1583–1645), Thomas Hobbes (1588–1679), René Descartes (1596–1650), Baltasar Gracián (1601–1658), François de La Rochefoucauld (1613–1680), Molière (1622–1673), Blaise Pascal (1623–1662), Samuel von Pufendorf (1632–1694), Richard Cumberland (1632–1718), Nicolas Malebranche (1638–1715), Benedictus de Spinoza (1632–1677), John Locke (1632–1704), Jean de La Bruyère (1645–1696), Pierre Bayle (1647–1706), Bernard Le Bovier de Fontenelle (1657–1757), Bernard Mandeville (1670–1733), Anthony Ashley-Cooper, 3rd Earl of Shaftesbury (1671–1713), Louis de Rouvroy, duc de Saint-Simon (1675–1755), Charles-Louis de Secondat, Baron de La Brède et de Montesquieu (1689–1755), Voltaire (François-Marie Arouet 1694–1778), Francis Hutcheson (1694–

1746), David Hume (1711–1776), Jean-Jacques Rousseau (1712–1778), Étienne Bonnot de Condillac (1714–1780), Paul-Henry Thiry, Baron d'Holbach (1723–1789), Adam Ferguson (1723–1816), Adam Smith (1723–1790), Edmund Burke (1729–1797), John Millar (1735–1801), Nicolas de Condorcet (1743–1794), Johann Wolfgang von Goethe (1749–1832), Claude Henri de Rouvroy, Comte de Saint-Simon (1760–1825), Georg Hegel (1770–1831), Auguste Comte (1798–1857), Honoré de Balzac (1799–1850), Alexis de Tocqueville (1805–1859), Karl Marx (1818–1883), Jacob Burckhardt (1818–1897), Herbert Spencer (1820–1903), Wilhelm Dilthey (1833–1911), Lucien Lévy-Bruhl (1857–1939), Émile Durkheim (1858–1917), Georg Simmel (1858–1918), Henri Bergson (1859–1941), Max Weber (1864–1920), Max Scheler (1874–1928), Edmund Husserl (1859–1938), Maurice Halbwachs (1877–1945), Alfred Weber (1868–1958), Marcel Mauss (1872–1950), Ferdinand Tönnies (1855–1936), Karl Mannheim (1893–1947), Charles Pierre Péguy (1873–1914), Maurice Merleau-Ponty (1908–1961), Georges Gurvitch (1894–1965), and Jacob Taubes (1923–1987). To all of these thinkers and their ideas, Salomon brings the habits of mind exhibited in "Louis Duc de Saint-Simon: Class Consciousness of the Defeated." These are empathy, humility, and appreciation for the unique and the subversive.

Salomon puts these habits of mind in service to an ambitious goal: the reinterpretation of his subjects and their work, to maintain "the heritage of the Western past" as "a living possession, not a pile of dead material," that is, "to preserve the perpetual presence of the living spirit." For Salomon, to make the meaning of social thought of the past our own is vital, a duty owed not only to past thinkers but also to ourselves and to future generations, to further efforts toward human progress, however discouraging and forbidding experience may be, and to resist forces working to dissolve human community.

In any given instance, to achieve his end, Salomon first positions himself in the place of the social thinker at hand. He inhabits the mind, the character, and social and historical milieu of his subject and sees with his subject's eyes. He sets aside, as best he can, his own historical limitations. He resists the temptations to second-guess or censor his subject, misrepresent his subject's thought for his own ends, or assert his own superiority.

Salomon's empathy is not an afterthought or a function of his conclusions, but a precondition to passing judgment and incorporating his subject's thought into a broader historical and intellectual continuum. It is a matter of principle, a form of fairness to the subject and to the reader.

Salomon faithfully articulates his subjects' ideas, even when he disagrees. For instance, his essay "Henri de Saint-Simon, Auguste Comte, and the Origins of Sociology" provides and clarifies his subjects' messianic conception of a wholly planned society under the aegis of the religion of scientific progress, even as Salomon points out the implicit totalitarianism of their vision—an insight that even Émile Durkheim, who was deeply influenced by the Saint-Simonians, misses.

Salomon's capacity to empathize even encompasses the ethnographic ability to enter into religious belief systems wholly different from his own and to grasp their meaning to those invested in them. He is also able to trace the inevitable migration and transformation of religious beliefs. He has keen insights both into Erasmus's project of *Res Christiana* and the international social movement by Erasmians that it produced to hold secular rulers accountable. His reflections on Ignatius of Loyola's *Spiritual Exercises* evince his typical ability to identify with his subject and, at the same time, place his subject's thought in specific historical context.

> Ignatius . . . and the modern Quietism contributed to creating new psychological insights. Loyola discovered the usefulness of mystical techniques for establishing complete control over Self and others by manipulating students who were striving for religious perfection. His technique should enable them to recognize their sins, to confess them, to begin a new life. His *Spiritual Exercises* were the first modern rule and regimentation of psychic training. In contrast to medieval usage, they required a relation between student and trainer, between soldier and officer. The military metaphors are valid because students were never informed about the sequence of the procedure or about the handbook of the *Spiritual Exercises*. No modern psychologist who wishes to train as elite has neglected to study the book and its new theory of asceticism, which neglects the physical asceticism of the past in favor of humiliating the mind and training total obedience.

In reviewing Jacob Taubes's *Abendländische Eschatologie*, Salomon concludes: "This work demonstrates anew that in all fields of history of ideas and of philosophy the quality of the author counts. There will never be an outstanding historian or philosopher who is not, in the sense of William James, capable of the varieties of human experience." Here, as always, the critic's judgment of his subject illuminates the ambition, capacity, and quality of the critic himself.

Salomon does not hesitate to pass judgment, but he measures his judgments with care. His judiciousness is partly a function of his empathy, but also results from a genuine humility, an awareness of the myriad challenges to accomplishing serious social thought. Salomon had the discipline and the temperament to see the greatness in his subjects' ideas. Even in his most forceful judgments, he is never smug. He does not exercise the power he has to elevate himself above his subjects. He does not use his subjects to grind an axe.

Salomon is humble, too, in considering the past. His essays reflect an awareness that current thinking is not inherently superior to past thinking and that the contemporary world is not necessarily superior to past societies, cultures, eras.

In the mid-twentieth century, when sociology enjoys a certain cachet, Salomon displays professional modesty, acknowledging the limitations of his field. He notes, for example, that both the origins and the aims of sociology, contrary to its core claims, are hardly scientific and rational. Further, Salomon regards sociology's estimation of religious experience—as just another commodity for analysis—as foolish. He courageously asserts that religious experience, far more than sociology and the scientific worldview in which it cloaks itself, best enables one to understand the social world.[1]

Salomon's writing style also expresses his humility. He tends not to remind the reader of his role as mediator and expert. His essays place the thinkers and their ideas in the foreground. They typically feature long passages in which Salomon's presence is invisible.

The exception is virtually Salomon's signature: in nearly every one of his essays, Salomon identifies and underscores the particular unique and subversive quality of his subject's mind and ideas. So, for example, one reason to choose Fontenelle as the "genuine image of the Enlightenment" is that Fontenelle "was a writer who dared to popularize philosophical texts in order to stimulate critical thought and a reexamination of traditional ideas about God, the universe, and the place of man in nature." Salomon finds another in a comment by Nietzche—that Fontenelle was "the last aristocratic thinker who knew that esoteric writing is indispensable in a world of total conformism." Similarly, Salomon sees that

> [n]o one fought more passionately than Max Weber for rational knowledge as opposed to all those kinds of sentimental, moralistic, and intellectualistic knowledge that served merely to secure peace of mind and were provisional in character. The best road to genuine knowledge was by way of radical doubt.

To cite one more example: In the poet Charles Péguy, Salomon offers an image of spiritual heroism to the post-Second World War world. "In Péguy's own highly unique way he participated in the vigorous combat that William James and Henri Bergson were waging against the determinism and materialism of their times and for the re-establishment of the character of the actual as dynamic, free, and creative."

Salomon perceives the commitment and bravery of, and the risks taken by, his subjects. Ultimately, his emphasis on the special, radical quality of his subjects and their ideas is an appreciation of moral courage, which Salomon makes explicit in his essay on Alfred Weber.

> [T]he scientific heroism of [Alfred Weber's] approach must be emphasized. Weber had the moral courage to finish this book [*Kulturgeschichte als Kultursoziologie*], knowing very well its weaknesses and imperfections. He is an impressive example of the fact that there are situations in scientific thinking in which the work of pioneers is more fruitful than specialized perfection. As pioneers open the woods and break through the wilderness, so Weber pushes through the tangled mysteries of history with his sociological concepts, finding new perspectives on the intricacies of social causations and conditions.
>
> This moral quality of the book is especially significant in an epoch of growing intellectual mechanization.

> And equally worthy of example is the discrimination that enables Weber to know the borders of empirical analysis and the starting point of ontological problems. Although throughout the book he does not leave the empirical method, he knows very well that the mechanical responses represented by social actions are never able to explain the complexity of social dynamics. He is aware that his own empirical analysis is based upon and constantly recurs to a metaphysical position. His concept of immanent transcendence itself reveals his work to be the sociological and historical aspect of a philosophy of life and existence, and hence his work has to be correlated with this type of philosophy. Because he is so excellent a scholar he reaches the intellectual discipline and modesty that are the characteristics of outstanding thinkers.

Salomon's ability to recognize and convey moral courage is the habit of mind that makes his work—about such potentially static subject matter as thinkers and thought—so unexpectedly dramatic. Yet, in a sense, Salomon's appreciation of subversiveness is unsurprising. All great thinking is original, and all original thinking is subversive. And Salomon devotes himself only to great thinkers.

III

Albert Salomon was born in Berlin in 1891. He studied at the University of Berlin, Freiburg University, and the University of Heidelberg. He launched his sociological career with a paper on Max Weber. He immigrated to the United States in 1935.

Salomon was famously demanding as a professor at the Graduate Faculty of Political and Social Science at the New School for Social Research in New York City. He taught rigorous courses on Weber, Durkheim, Simmel, Tocqueville, Montaigne, Intellectuals, Political

Sociology, Revolutions, the Renascence of Stoicism, German Sociology, Social Roles, and Wilhelm Dilthey,[2] among others, including a 1958 course on the Sociology of Emotions. He also taught an exceptional course called "Balzac as Sociologist."[3] Salomon's student, the sociologist Peter L. Berger,[4] describes his experience in that course:

> I could only afford one course during my first semester—the first course I ever took in Sociology. Taught by Albert Salomon, it was called 'Balzac as a Sociologist.' The idea was brilliant, and Salomon was a brilliant lecturer. It was also a very plausible pedagogical idea: Balzac had intended for his collection of novels, The Human Comedy, to provide a comprehensive picture of French society in the nineteenth century, from the aristocracy to the criminal underworld. And indeed the novels provide a detailed panorama of the many layers of this society. What Salomon did in his course was to use Balzac's opus to introduce students to the major categories of sociology—class, power, religion, social control, social mobility, marginality, [and] crime. I must have read at least ten of Balzac's novels during the semester. . . . At the end of the semester I had become quite familiar with nineteenth-century French society. I knew as little about twentieth-century American society as I had known before my Balzacian adventure. But I had acquired a sense of the excitement of a sociological perspective, which Salomon passionately expounded.[5]

In the best tradition of scholarly work, Salomon's teaching both fueled his own writings and inspired his students to undertake their own creative work.

Returning to Salomon's essay on Alfred Weber: Salomon asserts that situations of "crisis and transformation" put human potentialities at risk, but also provide an opportunity, through creative intelligence, for new thinking that reconciles conflicting experience and knowledge. Given the instability, crisis, and transformations of social experience of the early twenty-first century, as well as the steady passing of generations, the upheaval and uncertainty of Salomon's era tends to fade from view. But Salomon lived and worked in a time of world wars, the rise of totalitarian states, genocide, the advent of nuclear weapons, normalization of bureaucracy, ongoing compartmentalization of knowledge and expertise, alienation, and anomie. Salomon's essay on Alfred Weber reads both as a joyful celebration of individual creativity in "a shaken world of modern crisis" and as a *cri de coeur.* Again, the critic's assessment redounds to the critic: Salomon's work on social thinkers and social thought is an act of moral courage, an act of integration in response to a disintegrating world.

Notes

1. See A. Salomon, "The Study of Man: Prophets, Priests, and Social Scientists," *Commentary*, June 1949, 594–600.

2. Salomon's students, headed by Lester Emery, put together in 1964 a collection of their notes of Salomon's lectures on Dilthey, entitled simply: *Wilhelm Dilthey*. That collection is housed in the Archives of the New School for Social Research in New York City.

3. See Syllabus, "An Introduction to Sociology for Students of the Social Sciences and of the Humanities: Balzac as Sociologist," in this volume.

4. Other notable students of Salomon included Thomas Luckmann, Richard Grathoff, and Bernard Rosenberg.

5. *Adventures of an Accidental Sociologist: How to Explain the World Without Becoming a Bore* (Amherst, New York: Prometheus Books, 2011), 12.

Autobiographical Essay

In the Shadows of an Endless Great Time

Translated from the German by Juliet M. Kelso

> That I may improve myself, and once I have done so,
> give away as soon as possible.
> –Heraclitus

Although I must be thankful for great luck, much beauty, and several insights, I have often asked myself if bravery, perseverance, and love, which one needs in order to develop resistance to the world and the challenges of life, are worth the trouble. Obviously, I have decided to accept such efforts and to say yes to life in defiance of every catastrophe. In great modesty, I would like to adopt what Goethe set as a motto before *Dichtung und Wahrheit*: "The unoppressed person will not be educated."[1]

I have had the luck to encounter many wonderful and distinguished people, to make some friendships, to accept others' harsh criticism and to experience self-contradictions. I have never finished working on myself; thus, I remain a perennial student. With grati-

---

Originally published in Albert Salomon Werke: Band I: Biographische Materialien und Schriften 1921-1933, Peter Gostmann, Gerhard Wagner, eds. (Wiesbaden: VS, 2008). Manuscript located in the Sozialwissenschaftliches Archiv (Social Science Archive), Universität Konstanz. Republished by permission of Sozialwissenschaftliches Archiv (Social Science Archive), Universität Konstanz.

tude, I recognize what my children and students have done for my education.

I am writing these memories down not because I believe that my person or my negligible work justifies an autobiography. It is instead an essay of gratitude for being allowed to live open-mindedly in a time of great teachers and an abundance of new and revolutionary ideas and phenomena. It is an essay of gratitude for the experience of suffering, death and catastrophes, the only way to measure the human ability to transform defeats into victories. The result of such a life is minor. What counts are bravery, integrity, and loyalty, holding onto that which one thinks is right.

It is a story of human beings, in which being a Jew and a German was a continual reason for thought, for constant reorientation, and which caused increased sensibility and emotional tensions. Early on, I tried to understand Montesquieu's idea of *maladie éternelle* as a disciplinary guideline to transform self-glorification and self-hatred as a Jew and a German into a conception of neo-classical humanity.

Born on December 8, 1891, I am proud to come from the nineteenth century and to have experienced 22 years of life before the First World War. I deliberately write "22 years" because for me, bad luck began with the Panther's Leap of the Kaiser: Germany's response to France's challenge to German interests through its interference in the problem of Morocco.[2] Looking back, I remember revering Talleyrand, one of the greatest European statesmen, who disdainfully looked down on the young diplomats of Europe at the 1815 Wiener Congress, who found everything so wonderful. He had only one sentence as commentary: "Whoever hasn't lived before 1789 doesn't know the sweetness of life." I cited the sentence to my American students and used 1914 for 1789.

The sweetness of life was no time for epicurean desire; it existed much more in an unlimited desire to learn and to expand one's horizon because one cannot understand the spirit of people, classes, and nations without understanding theology, philosophy, languages, and literature. My parents were more than generous by adopting a hands-off attitude with me. I shall always remain in debt to them because they made it possible for me to acquire something like a comprehensive education.

I always had mixed feelings while living in my native city of Berlin, although I recognized the humor and sharp self-irony of Berliners as a lively spirit. When Otto Suhr, then mayor of Berlin, was in New York after 1945 and visited the New School, I was the only Berliner and was asked to say a few words. I lauded the qualities of Berliners, which had helped us in the difficult years and afterward: irony and humor, not taking themselves or life so seriously. Out of a very pessimistic outlook on life as a whole, we Berliners still had vitality and the rationality to say yes to life. Berliners were, without knowing it, always in the position to transform their defeats into victories through wit and irony. I remember an example of this humor. At the wedding of the Crown Prince, on the sign of one of the refreshment booths in the middle of Unter den Linden, was written: "Our Crown Prince's Cäcilie now belongs to the family." From the city itself, only Wannsee, the burial site of Heinrich von Kleist, and the Pfaueninsel (*Peacock Island*) are beloved and valuable in memory to me. But otherwise, a cold parvenu determined the climate, and the few patrician streets and private streets, the Tiergarten, and Lützowufer were the only oases in a military business city.

My family had been based in Berlin since 1765. Nobody knew why they moved from Holland to Pomerania and from there to Berlin, but it was probably following business. My grandmother, Anna Salomon, was a born Potocki-Nelken from Breslau. I would like to assume that the Nelkens were Protected Jews of Potocki, who belonged to the Polish nobility. My mother was a born Bunzel from

Hamburg, but my grandfather, Leopold Bunzel, came from a highly distinguished family in Prague and as a young man went to Hamburg in order to build his own business and life. He became one of the most distinguished and honored coffee importers and members of the coffee market. My grandmother Bunzel was also from Prague, from the celebrated Frankl family. She died in 1896, and I have little memory of her.[3]

My first day at school proceeded without tears, but I came home crying and wanted to have the same religion as my Kaiser. After that, I was considered a genius. Unfortunately, I didn't live up to my family's illusions. That is to say, soon after that, I was cast away by the boys of the village school because of my Jewish appearance and was exposed to all possible humiliations. I have never forgotten this shock.

Director Zernecke, a classical scholar, who lived enthusiastically in the world of the ancient Greeks, led the Charlottenburg Reform School at Savignyplatz (Reformgymnasium Charlottenburg am Savignyplatz). I met him twice more during the First World War; he was an infantry captain. Among the teachers, the role of the reserve officers competed with academic education. Nobody has explored the effect of the social prestige of the reserve officers, this invention of the last Kaiser. Our rabbis were named Kroner and Galiner. Kroner received the 4th class Order of the Red Eagle (Babel und Bibel). Among his classmates were both Jews and Christians. After graduation in 1910, there was a collision in Homburg between Jewish Youth and the Kaiser.[4]

Berlin University is unforgettable to me. From seven to eight o'clock in the morning, I attended the lectures of Adolf von Harnack—this Protestant *abbé,* with whom Friedrich the Great himself socialized—who brought forth an encyclopedic and syncretistic theology to a nontheological auditorium with elegant rhetoric. Heinrich Wölfflin from Basel taught on Saturdays in the Baracken Auditorium in Kastanienwäldchen. He became breathless when he interpreted pictures that were dear to him—above all, the early Italian Renaissance. Max and Helene Hermann as well as Georg Simmel were an experience. Later, I came to know Siegbert Elkuß and the Gräfin Schulenburg through Erich Lichtenstein. They opened the door for me to the world of Wilhelm Dilthey. In 1957, I met Dr. Zucker from Zurich in Sils-Baselgia; he was the last assistant in Dilthey's seminar and spoke about the teacher and the father and grandson Graf Yorck with love and warmth.[5] It always depressed me so much that I could do nothing for Lichtenstein in the United States; he was a likable person and had a very sincere courtesy to him that was entirely unmodern. Simmel became a constitutive element of my life, in both a positive and a negative way. He was a true philosophical spirit; his last book is a big book of human wisdom and philosophical rigorousness in the face of impending death. Martin Heidegger spoke in conversation with Hans-Georg Gadamer about the meaning of this book.

One important experience was also the theater: Reinhardt, Brahms, Barnowski. Max Reinhardt's impressionistic performances inspired me and their musical conception fascinated me. His stage directions were scores, his rehearsals of Oedipus: "That must sound like fanfare!" He could chase us for hours through the Circus (*der Zirkus*); other directors never had that effect on us. Some things are unforgettable: the second part of Faust, Nestroy's political satire *Freedom in Podunk (Krähwinkel),* Shaw's Comedies, Don Carlos, *The Prince of Homburg*, Paul Wegener and Tilla Durieux in the *Ibsen-Zyklus* . . . the deep meaning for me, the deep disappointment when I see the same pieces in the United States forty years later. When it comes to music, I remember Joseph Joachim and his quartet, the *Singakademie*, the Philharmonic, Arthur Nikisch and mixed feelings about Ochs's interpretation of Bach. My first opera in the royal opera house was *Mignon*, one of Geraldine Farrar's first roles, which I remember with some gratitude and appreciation. When I read in the *New York Times* a few years ago that she had celebrated her seventieth birthday, I wrote to her how deeply her beauty and grace in the role of Mignon had inspired me and that I wanted to express to her a lifelong gratitude. Naturally, I forgot I had written this letter and suddenly received a handwritten note from the old woman from her house in Connecticut.

At Freiburg University I attended the lectures of Heinrich Rickert. If that even is philosophy. . . .[6]

As for Heidelberg, I think first about Sascha and Ernst Kantorowicz, Friedrich Gundolf, the *Jahrbücher für die geistige Bewegung*, my love for Hugo von Hofmannsthal, Rudolf Borchardt's critique of Stefan George's *The Seventh Ring* and, of course, Dostoevsky. I took all of this very seriously.

I hoped that Friedrich Gundolf, whose *Shakespeare and the German Spirit* was released in 1911, wouldn't deny me his friendship if I explained to him why I could not agree with Stefan George. But he dismissed me as a sterile, barren spirit, who was only capable of negative criticism. It made me unhappy since I had a great personal admiration for him. Friedrich Sieburg began his brilliant career with an imposture. He came to Heidelberg, beautiful and poor, and searched for patrons who were financially generous. He gained entry to the exclusive Stefan George-Kreis (George Circle), made little poems without difficulty—as was common there—and found everything that he sought. In order to improve his success, he committed a colossal mistake. He forged George's handwriting in a dedication to Sieburg in one of his poetry volumes. George's recognition probably should have provided Sieburg with access to George's well-off friends from the Circle. But naturally, it was much too crude and was detected with great consequences: shame and scandal. He was more careful after that: from the *Frankfurter Zeitung* in Paris to Mister Abetz and back to the *Frankfurter Zeitung* after 1945—the Germans are a wise and understanding people with a bad memory.

Through Sunday afternoons in Ziegelhäuser Landstraße 17, I experienced Max Weber. There was something tragic and grand about him that at the same time had something of the greatness, wisdom, and politeness of Don Quixote, if the latter were not possessed by his idée fixe. Weber's vision of resolving conflicts by rationalization (bureaucratization) and his notion of charisma are typical constructions found in extreme situations. His ideas about the plebiscite vote for the president of the Reich in Weimar made the election of Hindenburg and Hitler possible. He was less wise than Tocqueville. In 1926, when Marianne Weber's book about her husband was released, I wrote a short essay about Max Weber, in which I characterized him as a bourgeois Marxist. I was very sorry that Mrs. Weber was so indignant. I have always lived in the shadows of Weber's and Tocqueville's work. The unpublished lectures, "Social Theory of Revolutions," were supposed to be a sign of gratitude; it was supposed to be a draft of the chapter that Weber could no longer write.[7]

Through the Webers, I met Emy and Emil Lederer, with whom I should have established the closest friendship.[8] Emil holds my permanent gratitude in faithful remembrance. I would perhaps never have been in America without his belief in my worth. I also maintained years of intimate contact with Georg Lukács. He also holds my unforgotten gratitude, but also sorrow about the decline of such a great genius: *sacrificio del intellecto* is never a source of *La Vita Nuova*.[9] For a short time, Ernst Bloch fascinated me. His first wife, Else von Stritzky, was unforgettable: she embodied the spirit of utopia. Emil Lask and Erich Frank were true philosophers. Lask was a new, prolific Plato, with a new idea of a *philosophia perennis*. Frank engaged himself with the philosophy of the Romantics, as well as with Kierkegaard, Plato, and Pythagoreans, with the problems of knowledge and beliefs.

With the Webers at Ziegelhäuser Landstraße 17, I also came to know the Jaspers. They invited me to their home. It was very uncomfortable. I always had the feeling that I was a patient with a psychiatrist whom I had not invited to examine me. I spoke enthusiastically about the meaning of Dostoevsky's work for my intellectual and emotional world. Karl Jaspers posed questions about this or some other figure or situation and my interpretation and reacted only with the comment that my answers were interesting. He closed with a sentence that opened my case history of illness. My father used to say: I don't like that sick stuff. Indeed, later, Jaspers's *Psychologie der Weltanschauungen* (1919) had a great effect on me. That led to a philosophy of existence and coupled itself with my slowly growing fascination with such a philosophy through Max Scheler's first edition of *Zur Phänomonologie und Theorie der Sympathiegefühle und von Liebe und Haß* (1913) and *Der Formalismus in der Ethik und die materiale Wertethik* (1913–1916). Jaspers then transferred to the philosophy department. His first seminar was advertised as the philosophy of religion. When he distributed the syllabus, he began to give a lecture on Jesus's epilepsy, Isaiah's schizophrenia, and the mental illnesses of other religious founders and prophets. There I became impudent and said that he invited us to work over the philosophy of religion, but what he encouraged was the pathology of religion. He responded, in his most scathing tone, that I actually claimed to be a student of Max Weber, who always emphasized that nothing was too small or irrelevant for analysis; everything always has a place in the whole. That made me very angry and I said, verbatim, "Yes, Weber said that in his books, but in practice he didn't busy himself with anything minor like the appearance of the capitalistic spirit and what one could do against Marx's critique of capitalism and this historical determinism." That was the end of my relationship with Jaspers. I am completely persuaded that he proved no use to his friend Weber when he turned himself into a philosopher. Weber himself would have negated that. But Jaspers made his ice-cold philosophy from the sullen despair and heroic victories against all of the defeats that represent Weber's greatness. Nevertheless, I was very impressed when the small book *Vernunf und Existenz* (1935) was released. What must be said is that Jaspers never acknowledged that he was guided to Kierkegaard through Erich Frank. This was a turning point in his life, and loyalty to my dead friend and *moral taste* compel me to assert this. Maybe Mr. Jaspers has something to say to this.

It was an honor to be invited by Ernst Robert Curtius to read Plato with him. He lived in Schlossberg 3 with two likable old women, who were named Reiffel and were motherly aunts by nature. They treated their tenants like their own children. Herr Dr. Curtius kept himself very busy, but he enjoyed it. One day, he finally traveled to Straßburg; his grandmother (the widow of an important historian, I think) had died. I knew that he had been very attached to this woman, and I sent him a sign of remembrance. I received it back immediately, with the informative note that I was not entitled to seem so close to him. It hurt, but he was probably right.

In 1912 (or 1913), the Lederers, Lukács, Gustav Radbruch, and I had the adventurous idea to do something for the aesthetic future of film and to regularly release critiques in the Heidelberger Tagespresse. The meetings that we had with the owners of movie theaters and newspapers were themselves film comedies. Back then, there were still no German films. I remember American, French, and Italian films, especially an Italian one, *Quo Vadis*, which seemed entirely weird in its staginess; only the yawning and the honeysuckle-colored tails of lions were cinematically surprising. But there were also the countless sequels to French detective and murder dramas, so that one could always plan a visit to the movie theater. I believe that our weekly critiques, which were the product of our collective discussions, were unwelcome to the owners of the movie theaters and newspapers. After six months, they overcame their timidity toward university folk and lessened the number of free tickets we received. Back then, I already earnestly believed in the great potential of movie theaters to represent the pathos of daily life, the small things that actually define the meaning of life, more clearly than the big things. A flower without 'cause,' the concealment of some songs, inviting a wife or mother to dinner—there are so many possibilities for demonstrating one's shy love for friends and close ones through the heart's imagination. The great achievements of the movie theaters stand out against the traditions of dramas, tragedy, and also intimate plays and novels. The word is no longer the medium of literary works, but the carnal reality of people, their art, to stand by themselves, their walking, swimming, marching, their speaking, tone, melody, the rhythm of a dialog can be punished by false physical expression. Sensual expression as appearance, reality, and symbol can create new opportunities for experiencing humankind's place in the cosmos and in the natural animal kingdom.

Miss Mina Tobler, a Swiss musician, always influenced me most deeply, although I never got to know her. But she had a bit of Wölfflin's integrity and spontaneous beauty about her. She helped Weber with his musical work. I remember the noble Herr von Bubnow well. He was a Russian language and literature administrator, a man of great sensitivity and courtesy, and Willi Salomon-Calvi, my father's uncle, a geologist with a Goethe-esque view of the world of stones in a river, a kind and somewhat naive person, who had fallen in love with a mayor's daughter during a research project in Bergamo and married her. She must have been very beautiful once and was always a very interesting and artistic woman. I was close to his youngest son, Otto, who, if I remember correctly, joined a religious order in Italy. They were, naturally, Catholic. My boyhood friend, Gert Lütkens, also remains in my loyal memory, no different from Max Freiherr from Waldberg, my lifesaver; he guided me to become a sociologist or philosopher, since he would not allow me to work for him. The cult of friendship (a methodical problem of sentimentality) is a topic that still moves me today and that I will never be able to resolve further. There are two ways in Catholic countries: that of Erasmus and François de Sales, *amare magis quam scire* [to love more than to know—Eds.]; and that of Loyola, *gratia lacrimarum* [gift of tears—Eds.]. However, I don't see the source for puritanical sensibility. There are aesthetic traces in Lord Shaftesbury's work on *moral taste* that led toward the work on *moral sentiment* by Francis Hutcheson and Adam Smith.

Alone as I was, I had seen the academic world behind the scenes for so many years that I had no illusions about the human qualities of a university community, which felt like the elite and the navel of the German world. It took itself dead seriously—and there was so much pretension, and emphasis on appearance, and adultery, and divorce, and, quite simply, vulgarity there. When I went into the war [in the Cavalry Medical Corps—Eds.], I was determined not to return to the academic world. It was no better than the worlds of theater, the opera, or of performed music: it was filled with vanity, narcissism, the quest for prestige, and a spirit of competition.

I spent the last night before we positioned ourselves in troops with Gert Lütkens. When I said goodbye to Lukács and Block in Häberlein, they made fun of me; I said, "One cannot bar oneself from a suffering community!" In August 1914 I moved with Reservezug Abt 3 in Spandau. From October until December 1914, I served in the Reservefeldlazarett 73. The doctors were both Jews and Christians, but antisemitism prevailed, especially against Hasidic Jews.

On January 8, 1919, I came to the Gardekavallerie-Schützendivision, where I met Fritz Solmitz, who would later be killed by the Nazis. An observation that I made in 1919 at a get-together was to note the rush of all of the many kinds of Jews into civil service careers: Zionists, Orthodox, agnostics, and liberals. Maybe it would have been beneficial to our strength of character and the integrity of our existence to continue to live in the Ghetto and then we would not have endorsed the illusion that something could have improved our social position.

After the impoverishment of the war and inflation, I had to come to the rapid end of my studies. In May 1921 I was awarded a doctorate in Heidelberg by Lederer, Eberhard Gothein, Gerhard Anschütz, and Rickert. I do not even know now what I provided as my work. Mannheim cited my work as the friendship cult of humanism. This was actually a short introductory chapter. What I really wanted to write was a sociological analysis of changing emotional attitudes and how they functioned. Take an aesthetic and snobbish group in an aristocratic society of Gentlemen and examine the group's *moral taste* as Shaftesbury did. And examine in contrast the intensity of personal love and friendship during a time of revolutionary challenges to all values, an intensity that is only newly experienced and interpreted in mutual relationships. This is a new *Sturm und Drang* emotionality: against static aesthetic, for self-reflection in mutual commitment. This is perceived as the highest value: love as a creative act. This new attitude streamed in the Romantic as a constitutive element of knowledge and fantasy. From the Schlegels and Brentanos, a direct intention guides us to Scheler's conception of the cognitive values of love, to the modalities of sympathy, and the metaphysical value of enthusiasm. I hope that my students will absorb some of my ideas and suggestions.

I cannot express how much I owe my graduation to Karl and Julie Mannheim. Both gave me warmth and geniality, kindness and love.

They always had time for me. It was a great difficulty of my life that we had entirely different opinions about the task of sociology. Károly was as unhappy about my theoretical-contemplative attitude as I was about his pragmatic-political. But here I would like to say clearly and explicitly for the reader, and for Mr. and Mrs. Paul Kecskemeti as well, that I remember with sadness and pain the great love that Julicka and Károly gave me so generously, even though they worried about me. In London, he forced Alvin Johnson to accept me for the University in Exile and waived New York for himself.

The years after my doctorate exams were marked with inflation and deflation. Those were years of uncertain feelings that I had to devote to commercial work in order to earn money. I always say to my students that one cannot learn sociology from a book, but instead one must have walked through many social worlds in order to see with astonishment how differently people behave to each other, how different they are in their views of sexuality, what they consider good in the world and how they come to that opinion, what earns prestige for them and what earns scorn. It was thus good to have served as a common soldier and to have seen with surprise how small and abstract the world of intellectual society was, with its worries and cares. This experience ultimately turned me into a sociologist, if I can even be called one.

I continued to learn such practical sociology when I was a simple accountant for Lipmann Wulf, one of the finest private banks—in the house of the *Frankfurter Zeitung* in Berlin, Potsdamer Straße. When one reads what Simmel writes about inflation in the *Philosophie des Geldes*, we know that we underwent inflation and that one cannot just learn about such phenomena from books. We worked in the last days of every week to 2:00 a.m. or 3:00 a.m., in order to assess the weekly compound interest of our customers, trying at least to build a dam against the flood of daily currency devaluation.

We received pay weekly; the girls immediately bought consumer vouchers, which were often worth no more than two tickets for the electric train. It was ruinous for the largest part of the middle class, who had no property or foreign exchange permit. They were spooky times; I also do not know how long I was there, as the bank house was one of the first victims of deflation. It hit a man who had done what other colleagues also practiced, namely using customers' securities as cover for his own purchases. He had heard nothing about the upcoming conversion, and he shot himself in his office. I was in the next room[.][10]

In one of the inflation years, I was on my way to Rügen and had to spend the night because the boat only went once a day, and I had to ask a woman who was on her own if I could eat at her table. We started to converse. She had lived with her husband in Brazil for a long time, and she explained interesting things about his job. He was an engineer, and she had accompanied him on his trips. I excused myself after the meal and packed my bag again. The boat was delayed. So, I went into the nearest cafe to pass the time. It was empty there, and the woman was the only guest; it would have been foolish of me not to sit at her table. We chatted, and, finally, the cafe filled with travelers from Berlin, who also wanted to take one boat or another. Among them was a small, ugly woman, who was bedecked with jewels and other jewelry. At first glance, she could have been Jewish, or, at least, how Germans imagine Jews. Finally, my friend said, "Look, this horrible Jewess!" I held myself for a second and then said, "You're completely right: the woman is ugly and without taste or tact. One should not walk around so much like a decorated ox. I only wanted to make you aware that I am also a Jew." The woman replied, "You choose to joke!" At that, I said, "I am not in the mood for jokes, and I would recommend that you don't judge all Jews based on unpleasant examples! I also don't paint a picture of all Germans based on color-bearing drunk students in the gutters. I should take my leave." All minorities are exposed to the images that the majorities or other minorities have of them. These are usually negative images that do not stem from personal experiences, but instead from a background of prejudice, to which we are all exposed from our upbringings in our family, school, church, academic connection, the army, the club, and one's profession.

Back then I was also in Davos for a short time. There I met a charming and cultured brother of the Society of Jesus. We moved our deck chairs together and could talk well with each other, above all in evenings after dinner, when nobody else came to the solarium. We often talked about the consequences that strictly political or military events had on spiritual life and on religious customs. I told him how much I was convinced that Luther's real Augustinian experience of German rulers had been misused, in order to achieve the immense gain in power of the state through the secularization of church property and of the property of the order and of the monastery. He was persuaded that German bad luck had already started with the victory of Arminius in Teutoburgerwald.[11] A Roman Germany would have become much better Christianized in the spirit of the Church and of its rights. As it happened, a lot of dark paganism remained in the northern Germans. I often had Catholic students who had been raised in Jesuit schools. They were always surprised by my interpretation of Loyola's *Exercitia spiritualia* (1548), that the members of the order practiced for two weeks, while they as laypeople only practiced for a week and a half.[12] I still believe that Loyola was one of the greatest Christians, and that he—although he himself spoke very negatively of Erasmus—was a post-Luther Erasmus, who wanted to make this bad luck absolutely reversible.

After my apprenticeship in the bank, my father reluctantly took me into his shop. It could have been very interesting, but I obviously did not want to be a businessman. My father was a lambskin importer for glove manufacture. I remember the Meyer Brothers from Guben well, who are now in Gloversville, and Otto Jahn from Brandenburg. My father bought goods in Spain, Algeria, Serbia, and Bulgaria. He was once in Nischnij-Nowgorod, as it was called back then. For a large part of the year, he was traveling, and he was a language genius, through which he revolutionized the business of purchasing. He purchased directly from the slaughterers and, by doing so, did not need to pay the profits to the large trading houses. His competitors tried to imitate him. He was constantly surrounded by observers who informed his competitors of his departures, who then traveled after him and tried to beat him to the draw. During the first war, he was somehow a civilian plenipotentiary in Romania or Bulgaria and was naturally invited to a Christmas party by local commanders. This is memorable to me because the officers' toast impressed me so much: "Our Lord Jesus Christ, hurrah, hurrah, hurrah!"

I was with my father in Spain where there were slaughterers who countersigned contracts with crosses. They were as true as gold! When competitors came twenty-four hours earlier and offered 8–10 percent more, they were dismissed. I did not see Madrid, but I did visit Pamplona, Burgos, Valladolid, Zaragoza, Barcelona, and Salamanca—an intact medieval city with a bridge whose supports dated back to Roman times. There was a plaza where Cisneros taught and Loyola studied and wondered about the spirit of Erasmus. Before Luther's victory and the destruction of the unified Christian world, many Spanish theologians were followers of Erasmus. They had coined a particular word for that: *Erasmista* and *Erasmismo.*

Reflecting back onto my own actions, I would say that I would have been able to serve, but I valued my independence. I had courage, was capable of enthusiasm, dedication, and tenacity, but I had no economic, social, or academic ambition, and no goals. With my naïveté, it borders on the magical that I emerged so lucky without such aspirations, not because I had earned it, but because I had friends.

I didn't make the effort to become a salesman. I used the evenings to work for myself: studying Weber and reading, with emotion, Marianne Weber's book, which was released in 1926. I believed that I understood the intention of Weber's spirit: his liveliness, his wonder that there are people who seek to understand the unspeakable and to turn it into concepts and declarations. His ability always to understand new developments, the stream of consciousness, the concreteness of humanity in history, humanity's for-with-against-each-other ness—all of this fascinated me. Although I knew that this called for an aesthetic lifestyle and poverty, I believed that I could not do anything else. I worked for a long time on my "Weber," which was released in Rudolf Hilferding's 1926 journal *Die Gesellschaft*. That journal was entirely destroyed in Germany in 1933. [See Salomon's essays on Weber in this volume.—Eds.]

When Marianne Weber's book was released, Lederer, who was in Berlin then, asked me what I thought of her presentation of Max Weber. I said, "I find it sublime that she let the philological, skilled reader feel that Max Weber loved another woman." Lederer became entirely pale and told me the story, about which I had no idea. It is good as a sociologist to also be a philologist. My belief in this has only strengthened over the next forty years. Language—communication: the word alone establishes social cohesion. Human reality means intellectual participation. Animals have the pragmatic rationality of their instinct, wiser and more clever than the mechanisms of human vitality. But as strongly as the ruse of our own reason corrupts our vital tendencies, and as much as we degrade the animal kingdom, we can also transcend it. Against all idealism, I still believe that there is a transcendency in total immanence. The great possibilities of a philosophy of existence, which transcend themselves in self interpretation, seem irrefutable to me.

When my essay about Max Weber was published, Hans Simons was the director of the Hochschule für Politik. He was of the opinion that I could become an academic. So he gave my life direction and opened the way for me to a job that seemed meaningful to me. I taught from 1926 to 1931 at this Hochschule, which sought political education for the Weimar Republic and believed in lively debate with opponents from the left and the right. That life brought me together with Simons and his wife Eva, and I enjoyed their friendship—including their hard criticism, which should happen with friends—for many years. I have always regarded and shall always regard our friendship as great luck. His genius was not without tragedy; his ambition and his imagination of complete performance led to a lasting dissatisfaction with his real successes. I still hope that he will one time write about his overflowing, rich thoughts on global politics, the problem of diplomacy in the era of the United Nations, the philosophy of help for the undeveloped parts of the world. I cannot describe what Eva Simons had been with her human warmth and her musical intuition through all those years. She made me happy when she trained my son for the New School's concerts and won his love.

I remember how President Nicholas Murray Butler of Columbia University visited the Hochschule. We had all been introduced and told each other about our fields of work. I said to him that I taught American democracy through Tocqueville. My relationship to Theodor Heuss was very warm; his wife was a good friend of Alice Salomon. I did not feel entirely comfortable with Friedrich Naumann, but I always adored Heuss's liberal humanity. The spirit of the Lutheran Paulskirche in Frankfurt am Main radiated in his person. I was happy that he remembered me well when he served as Bundespräsident from 1949 to 1959.

I got to know Simons through Rudolf Hilferding. I had been a member of the Social Democratic Party since the murder of Walter Rathenau in 1922. I believed then and still believe what I wrote to presidential candidate Adlai Stevenson in 1952: "We have to be liberal in order to be conservative." I no longer remember what I did in the party. My relationship to Rudi Hilferding was a deep and painful friendship. He was a Hamlet-like character. On the one hand, he had spirit, wit, and sensibility. We had unforgettable conversations in the Tiergarten about the gracelessness of Wagner's music, which tried to spiritualize the lasciviousness and nastiness of Teutonic wickedness: deceit, greed, treason, dishonesty. On the other hand, there was Hilferding's laziness and contempt for most of the other members of the Reichstagsfraktion of the Reichstag. He was neither a statesman nor a fat cat of the party. He was a great thinker, not a scholar. I was sick of his blind confidence and his belief in the dependability of the men in the Finance Ministry or of his friend Heinrich Brüning. He introduced me to Léon Blum one time. But by 1931, I was already so disillusioned by the politics of both German and French social democracy that I only spoke with Blum about Stendhal, to whom he had dedicated a book. The party bureaucrats were furious.

When Hilferding was the Finance Minister in Müller's last Cabinet in 1928/29, he asked me to edit *Die Gesellschaft*, the scientific organ of the party. Although I still worked in the Hochschule, I dedicated my time and enthusiasm to this project, without hope, because I was fully disillusioned about the innermost weakness of a bloated party bureaucracy, which lived on Marx's *Kapital*, and about Hilferding's friendship with Brüning and his belief in tactics where everything came down to strategy. Against all outside circumstances, I wanted to rally an elite of radicals among young people that could show all parties that the spirit of Marx was not with the Marxists. It was an inner satisfaction to find such radical thinkers outside of the party and to discover and to publish people who went on to great careers from there: above all Herbert Marcuse, Eckart Kehr, Walter Benjamin, Hans Speier, Hajo Holborn, and Hannah Arendt. I was happy about the help that I received from Ernst Fränkel and Franz Neumann. I was proud to demonstrate to the Conservatives that we had just as little respect for Emil Ludwig as they had, or to publish a collection of essays against the weakening of radical thought through Mannheim's *Ideologie und Utopie.* Someone said to me that our journal won the respect and the greatest attention of the professors and students of the university—not only in Berlin. Otto Bauer once said to Hilferding in my presence that he should have let me continue editing *Die Gesellschaft.* That was the only time that I saw Rudi truly angry: What was wrong with his editorship? I agreed that I would not have been better than him.

In 1931, Hans Staudinger, an old friend from Heidelberg, a statesman and administrator of great style, who had flawlessly driven the socialization of the Prussian electricity works, and now was the state secretary in the Prussian Department of Commerce, invited me to a conference. He planned a university Hochshule for teachers at the vocational schools, which were under his jurisdiction. Such educational institutes should convey to technically specialized teachers a broader view of the universal and historical problems of the world, and with that give them implicitly critical tools against National Socialism. He wanted to send me as a sociologist to Cologne, where one of these schools was planned. But I was not to teach theory primarily, but instead, political sociology, class theory, and so on. I welcomed the idea for various reasons. It was time for me to leave my parents' home and to set up my own. Although from my own experience, I was not optimistic that a teacher could make much headway against radical student elements; I was nonetheless ready to go.

My predictions were pretty accurate. Among the faculty and students there were several open Nazis, though most remained undercover. There were only a few older men who earnestly adhered to the Republic. It was entirely impressive that some of the best students were radical Nazis, and we had animated discussions about the nation, socialism, radical democracy, and the great effort of the Republic and Social Democracy for Germany's rebuilding. But it was entirely unimportant if one was successful and convinced them for a moment. They were dogmatically determined and unwilling to argue, only to convince. But they liked me, and when I recovered from polio, they came in their brown Sturmabteilung uniforms after their exercises in Stadtwald to drink tea with me. Robert Heiss, a brave, fearless anti-Nazi, became my friend in Cologne. He ended our relationship because he could not understand that after the deaths of my mother and brother, whom I could not rescue, I felt no desire to return to Germany. These were the good Germans.[13]

When I was at home during Christmas in 1931, I saw Hilferding. I explained to him how many intelligent and sophisticated young Nazis I had among my students. I said to him that we could still take the wind out of their sails if we explained to them what the party had done for the lower middle class and how difficult and brave it was to really be nationalistic without rhetoric. I cannot forget his response. He said, "That is music." I replied, "If we don't make music, the masses will follow military music." I saw him once more in January 1933. He visited us, held a political meeting, and wrote after his return to Berlin: "This crisis is over and all will go well for you now." His death in 1941 and the horrific circumstances that surrounded it are still an open wound in my life. The end was not necessary; his inactivity and the disastrous influence of Rudolf Breitscheid paralyzed him. He had four passports; the French prefecture was very benevolent. Despite everything, he could not make himself flee. I later saw Rose Hilferding and with bitter sadness said to her, "If you had cared less for the blonde and blue-eyed Germans in Paris and had instilled Rudi with your hard will for life and had simply cared for him, he would still be alive." I never saw her again.

In 1932, I married Dr. Anna Lobbenberg in Cologne, who gave me a new life in body and in spirit. Since I don't have the words to express what this new life meant to me, I do not want to say more about my wife.

Like all non-Aryan officials, I was let go into early retirement with a small pension on April 1, 1933. Leopold von Wiese paid a condolence visit to me, as he did when officials of the wrong race were dismissed. It was a friendly, indeed brave, gesture under the circumstances. He ruined it, however, when he said that we must be objective and acknowledge that Hitler had only meant to block Bolshevism. I could only respond: Wouldn't that be a blunder of formal sociology?

I do not want to pride myself on the fact that I had foreseen the future in the way that it actually happened. I believed that my wife, at the Jewish hospital, and I, with my pension, would have been able to live modestly. But on the same day, a woman friend came with the news that I could receive an invitation to New York through Emil Lederer.

I went to London in July 1933 to meet with Lederer and Dr. Alvin Johnson. It was truly awful. I was speechless and thus fully self-conscious. I did not believe that he would employ me. I would not have done so were I in his place. But after a few weeks, Dr. Johnson sent me the contract. I never learned which friends, who believed in me, had persuaded Dr. Johnson. It was probably both Mannheim and Lederer. I later attended conferences and debates, in which we would choose European scholars to bring to the United States, with dread and trepidation. There were multiple good candidates available for every position and *summum ius* was always *summa inuria.* I was naturally exposed to harsh criticism that I owed my place only to friends while better and more competent scholars would otherwise have earned the position. It was certainly true, and I never knew if I fulfilled the expectations of my friends and Dr. Johnson.

It was like a miracle, and I was terribly frightened. English was entirely beyond my speaking knowledge and ability. I spoke French like it was German, and my love for the French spirit, philosophy, and literature led me to believe that I had only been raised in Germany by accident. In the house of Frederick Augustus Voigt, who back then was working for the *Manchester Guardian* in Berlin and was together with an American author, Margaret Goldsmith (*Nineteenth Century and After*), I met Pierre Viénot, who spent a while with one of the Reparations Commissions in Berlin and wrote a far-sighted book about the German future: *Incertitudes Allemandes.* He was married to one of the liveliest, most spirited, and most independent young women. She was the daughter of Luxembourg's steel king and died in a terrible car accident. I went to Paris because I had to ask Pierre Viénot if there were any opportunities for me to come to France and be accepted there. He said to me something I will never forget: Naturally, we will allow you to hold lectures under the given circumstances. But you will never become a full professor, and probably never a citizen either. And the war will come and we will lose. Go to New York. It was February in 1934. Luckily, Viénot never learned how true his predictions were. He died beforehand. In 1934, I also saw Walter Benjamin for the last time.

We went to New York on the *Europa* on January 18, 1935. I have never looked back since I crossed the bridge to the ship. At the *New School*, I engaged in a shy love affair with the American language.[14] I devoted myself to teaching instead of writing books. I prepared abstracts, which, I hoped, would stimulate some of my students to record their own thoughts. Among these abstracts, there was the contribution on Weber, mentioned earlier. Weber had wanted to write on the social theory of revolution; I worked on this piece for one or two decades. There were also abstracts for the history of sociology, comprehensive studies of the *Foundations of Sociology and Social Psychology*, which begin with Erasmus, Pascal, and Loyola, and which lead to the Scottish philosophy of the 1800s, which were partly published. [See also "Origins of Sociology and Social Psychology (1947)" in this volume.—Eds.] In 1955, I published the book *The Tyranny of Progress: Reflections on the Origins of Sociology.*

I remember my American friends in loving gratitude and sadness: Milton Steinberg, Chaim Greenberg, Shlomo Grodzensky, Elaine and Arthur Cohen, Ludwig and Renate Edelstein, Alfred Schütz, and Kurt Goldstein.

My gratitude also goes to the dead, whose stormy lives shaped me from my youth: Goethe, Kleist, Hofmannsthal, the religious reflections of Erasmus, Pascal, Loyola, Hermann Cohen, and Franz Rosenzweig, the profanity of Montaigne, the historical reflections of Burckhardt and Tocqueville, the natural ones of Lukrez, Montaigne, Simmel, and Scheler. I lived with them more closely and intimately than with most of my contemporaries.

Notes

1. Johann Wolfgang von Goethe, "From my life. Dichtung und Wahrheit. Erster Teil," in Johann Wolfgang von Goethe, *Werke, Hamburger Ausgabe,* Bd. 9: *Autobiographische Schriften 1,* Textkritisch durchgesehen und kommentiert von Erich Trunz (München: C. H. Beck 1998), S. 7–216, hier S. 7; Erich Trunz, "Anmerkungen," in Johann Wolfgang von Goethe, *Werke, Hamburger Ausgabe,* Bd. 9: *Autobiographische Schriften 1,* Textkritisch durchgesehen und kommentiert von Erich Trunz (München: C. H. Beck 1998), S. 640–840, hier S. 641.

2. [Kaiser Wilhelm sent the gunboat SMS Panther to the Moroccan port of Agadir in response to France's deployment of troops in Morocco in April 1911.—Eds.]

3. However, here I wish to start a detailed portrait of Leopold Bunzel and his world. I want to write about the parents and siblings of my parents in a different location. [Not attached.]

4. [Despite an extensive search, the editors are unable to find the incident that Salomon refers to here.—Eds.]

5. [The reference is to Count Hans Ludwig Paul Yorck (1835–1897), a close friend and collaborator with Wilhelm Dilthey, and to his grandson, Peter Graf Yorck von Wartenburg (1904–1944), a distinguished German jurist and a leading conspirator in the failed attempt to assassinate Hitler in 1944.—Eds.]

6. [Heinrich John Rickert (1863–1936) was a leading Neo-Kantian, who greatly influenced the sociologist Max Weber and the philosopher Martin Heidegger. Salomon's skepticism about Rickert's work suggests his attitude toward the work of those influenced by Rickert.—Eds.]

7. [We could not discover any papers or lecture notes in Salomon's scattered *Nachlass* with the title of "Social Theory of Revolutions." But see his essay "Henri de Saint-Simon, Auguste Comte, and the Origins of Sociology" in this volume.—Eds.]

8. Portraits of both and their mother: Frau Seidler from Budapest [*sic*]. [Not attached.]

9. My paper about L is attached. [Not attached.]

10. [Unreadable]

11. [The battle of the Teutoburg Forest took place in 9 A.D. on Kalkriese hill in Osnabrück County in Lower Saxony. An anti-Roman alliance of Germanic tribes led by Arminius, who had won Roman citizenship and received a Roman military education, defeated and destroyed three Roman legions and six auxiliary (noncitizen) troops, led by Publius Quinctilius Varus. The great Roman historian, Theodor Mommsen (1817–1903), considered the Battle of the Teutoburg forest to be a turning point in world history.—Eds.]

12. [Salomon is mistaken in saying that members of the Society of Jesus did Loyola's Spiritual Exercises for two weeks. Until relatively recently, all Jesuits did the Exercises for a full month shortly after their entry into the Society's Novitiate. This was called the Long Retreat. Then, after fifteen years of study, and ordination, they undertook another Long Retreat in their last year of formation known as Tertianship. In the intervening years, Jesuits typically did one or two eight-day retreats each year.—Eds.]

13. [Frank Salomon, Albert Salomon's son, recalls that his father had contracted polio in Germany and was told that he would never walk again. But with great persistence and the unfailing support of his

wife, Anna Lobbenberg Salomon, one of the first female physicians in Germany, Salomon became able to walk again, though with difficulty. He had to use a cane. He usually came to concerts quite early. He would put his coat and hat on his seat and then stand in the lobby, stretching his legs, until a few minutes before concert time. Because of the angular shape of his head and his slightly curved back, he was often mistaken for the composer, Igor Stravinsky. Salomon visited his son in Vermont at the Marlboro Music Festival one summer weekend when the Festival was performing a work by Aaron Copland. Frank relates that, as usual, his father was waiting in the lobby for the concert to begin when a patron approached and said, "Excuse me, sir, aren't you Aaron Copland?" Albert Salomon replied that he was sorry, but that was not the case. Thinking that the famous composer just did not want to be bothered, the patron insisted: "But I know that you are Aaron Copland." To which my father responded: "No, I'm Igor Stravinsky."—Eds.]

14. [Frank Salomon also recalls this father saying that he was not worried about life after death because his first year in the United States was pure hell, trying to teach graduate courses in a language that he had not fully mastered.—Eds.]

PART I
Essays

1

Crisis, History, and the Image of Man

Man is explicable by nothing less than all his history.
—Emerson

In his address at the 200th convocation of the University of Chicago, June 11, 1940, President Robert Maynard Hutchins [1899–1977] invited American youth to reexamine the principles that make life worth living. This enterprise is most urgently necessary in removing the intellectual unpreparedness of the nation. Far worse than the military and economic deficiencies in equipment and armament, are the spiritual dissensions among the various groups of our time. In the universal conflict, those nations will prevail whose unity results from spontaneous and free devotion to values that are recognized as worth living and dying for. We can reintegrate the nation, when we succeed in breaking the continuous secularization that, parallel to the rapid industrialization after the Civil War, is undermining the ethos of American life. The ethos that made this commonwealth great was the fighting spirit of enlightenment. The backbone of the political principles of the Constitution is the spirit of the Christian Law of Nature; that means political freedom as the fulfillment of the rules of the Almighty. This unity between the three spheres: nature, man, and God was discarded by the process of secularization. The

---

Published originally in a slightly different form in *The Review of Politics* 2 (October 1940), 415–37.

ethics of enlightenment shifted to the demand for universal comfort and for good living. The attitude of a boundless optimism prevailed that considered history an unending process of perfection. It was thought that this state of continuous improvement would result from the scientific organization of social and political institutions; their progress would eliminate eventually what the less scientific past had ascribed to the finiteness and sinfulness of man. Thus, scientifism was the dogmatism of secularized times. It is defined as the belief that man is completely determined by environment. It was thought that scientific analysis would make possible the thorough construction and planning of the institutional world according to the scientific principles that disclosed the conditions most favorable to human adjustment. This optimism has destroyed the image of man inherent in the minds of the founders of the commonwealth. It has suffocated the idea of a being capable of human freedom, a freedom to achieve the rules and commands of God. These optimists are proud of having discovered human persons functioning like precise instruments.

Such an idea of history and man causes much confusion. Is not a tremendous success still the sign of justification even for the most secularized Puritan? Are not some of the opinion that, after all, Hitler represents progress, while Great Britain is the reactionary party in this war? And does not Hitler point out that he masters and controls that scientific idea of man? For this reason, it is worthwhile to reconsider the idea of history and the image of man. This reconsideration implies a discussion of optimism and pessimism as fundamental attitudes of man in action, a discussion that might support a real understanding of American life in the very moment when the destiny of man is at stake.

The victor always writes history to justify his successes. That is the reason why the advancement of liberal society has emphasized the growth of philosophies of progress, evolution, and secularized eschatology. It is the privilege of intellectuals in times of crisis to glance at the broken structure of social relations, human standards, and spiritual values to be aware of all aspects of life and its completeness, even though it appears in scattered fragments. They are not biased by subjective prejudices and by stabilized conventions, for everything becomes problematic in a crisis.

Throughout the eighteenth and nineteenth centuries, the optimistic philosophers of progress and evolution flourished side by side with philosophies that held just an opposite view of the historical process and man's destiny. From Vico and Goethe on, there was a never-interrupted chain of interpretations of man in history. This school of interpreters challenged the dynamism of the philosophies of progress that regarded man as instrumental to the general principle of history. They made transparent the wisdom of conservative thinking and contributed in a manner to the knowledge of future trends. The very reason for this positive achievement is that these men are primarily concerned with the completeness of human existence and the range of its potentialities in a specific situation. They see clearly the destructive and leveling tendencies in new conditions that unchain individuals and deprive them of the restricting, but nevertheless protecting, frame of social limits. The radical reformer abstracts and isolates one single element from the complete unity of life. He does not imagine its complex context and trusts his principle of salvation like magic. He thinks as a utopian. The conservative liberal or liberal conservative is realistic. He has a vision of man's completeness. Edmund Burke [1729–1797], Juan Donoso Cortés [1809–1853], Joseph von Görres [1776–1848], Friedrich von Gentz [1764–1832], Johann Adam Müller [1769–1832], Klemens von Metternich [1773–1859], and Alexis de Tocqueville [1805–1859] knew the dangers of democratic revolutions in their coincidence with the industrial revolutions because they had definite ideas of the wealth and strength of human personality. They had realistic pictures of the implications of political and social changes for the character and standard of man; they were aware of the price mankind was to pay for the enlargement of political and social rights. Among these men have been scholars and philosophers whose disinterested pursuit of truth cannot be explained away as an ideological device through psychological explanations that reveal their reactionary character.

I

Almost a century ago, Jacob Burckhardt [1818–1897] visualized the forthcoming debacle of European civilization. His experience and vision brought into existence a new-old idea of history and of man's place and destiny in it. His analyses of the trends towards decadence, and his reflections on man in this crisis, may challenge and support the reintegration of man at the present time in which our very existence is called into question.

Burckhardt was a professor of history and art in his native Basel, but he was an unusual type of professor and historian.[1] He is known to the general public as the author of *The Civilization of the Renaissance in Italy*, but, as a perspicacious reviewer of the American translation of his book noted in the *New York Herald* in 1878, labeling this book "historical" is somewhat in error. Burckhardt deals with a description and analysis of an individual historical situation, but he approaches this particular civilization not with historical intention. Burckhardt's interest centers on the varieties of human experience and the diverse types of man manifesting the richness and the range of human spontaneity. This is certainly not the attitude of the average historian.

The basic and lasting purpose of Burckhardt's work is to reinvestigate the positive and concrete actuality of man apart from all pseudometaphysical a prioris. It results from his fundamental experience of the dynamic course of political and social movements that will eventually end in a terrible catastrophe. For this reason, all his books—except those devoted to art—are confessions of this experience. He himself explicitly stated that his main interest lay in epochs of fundamental transformation and crisis. These convey the power and strength of human personality at its highest and lowest. Simultaneously, they show the continuity of the spirit through all revolutions and crises. His *Civilization of the Renaissance in Italy* analyzes the disintegration of the mediaeval civilization and the origin of modernity in Renaissance and Humanism. His work on *Constantine* describes the end of ancient civilization and the rise of the Christian Roman Middle Ages. *The History of Greek Civilization* is mainly concerned with the forces that destroyed the flowering of the finest civilization created by free and completely human citizens in Athens.

These parts of a great confession verify and clarify the primary experience of his own position in the modern world. They contribute to an idea of history that is just opposite to the dynamic theories of progress. Burckhardt's idea of history is tied up with his idea of man; history becomes a category of human existence, an ontological category. Man is the center of historical reflection, not the mask in the play of an impersonal and dehumanized spirit. Burckhardt has included the scientific results of his experience and his historical verifications of it in a book that deals with power, religion, and culture, as the constitutive elements of man's historicity that is his necessary connection with a specific place in time. The book's title might well be: *On the study of history as determining and determined by human existence.*[2]

These books do not contain the whole sum of his experiences. He was very careful in his public utterances and hated to express ideas that might hurt or confuse the student or the reader. He still felt that scholarship is a moral responsibility and that the thinker who has no comfort to offer, but only the destructive and disenchanting analyses of the disintegrating modern world, had better withdraw from teaching and educating. For this reason, the volumes that contain his correspondence with various friends are an invaluable source for the true expression of his experience and for the realism of his terrific visions.

A religious experience gave him the first opportunity for disclosing the disintegrating character of the historical period in which he lived. Burckhardt was descended from patrician Swiss families that for centuries had supplied loyal ministers to the Protestant faith. He was supposed to follow this tradition but shifted to the study of history when he visualized the discrepancy between his actual religious piety and the pseudodogmatism of the Protestant Church. This experience was typical among Protestants of his time. His protestation against the Divine character of Christ is based on what he perceived to be the fundamental misunderstanding of the Christian religion that results from the opposition to the hardening patterns of Lutheran and Calvinistic orthodoxies.

> I have voluntarily quitted the Church, because I do not know what it is all about. Like many others I do not feel tied up with the Church and my conscience works quite independently; that's natural in a period of disintegration. The spontaneous individual piety beyond the pale of the Churches always indicates a period of crisis and transition. . . . I shall express what the distinguished scholars think, but care to hide: Christianity has entered for our historical thought the purely human epochs of history. It has brought about the people's moral maturity and finally their intellectual strength and independence

> which eventually made them bold enough to reconcile themselves with their own innermost self without needing the mercy of God. Times will teach what pattern of thought Europeans will develop for approaching again a personal God. People will gladly believe in His personality as soon as He will reappear as a human being. . . . As God, Christ is incomprehensible to me. . . . [A]s human being, He illuminates my soul, because He is the most beautiful phenomenon of history. (Letter to Beyschlag, January 14, 1844)

This experience was common to other outstanding young Protestant theologians, such as Karl Wilhelm Justi [1767–1846] and Wilhelm Dilthey [1833–1911]. It gave rise to attempts to reconsider a human world that contains in its very nature the longing of man and his participation in a universal spiritual power; spirit and matter, phenomenon and mind, which in idealistic doctrines were conceived of as constituting the original dualism of the world, are interpreted in these new approaches as constitutive elements of human nature. All these secularized theologians start with realistic and positivistic enmity against metaphysics and theologies. Burckhardt explicitly remarks, with irony worthy of his contemporary Søren Kierkegaard [1813–1855], that, unfortunately, we are not familiar with the Divine intentions and that all philosophers of history who pretend to know something about the destiny of men are subject to errors and problematic hypotheses, challenging the work of Georg Hegel [1770–1831]. Burckhardt asserts time and again that religion as an expression of a fundamental quality and need of the human soul is a constitutive element of human nature.

It is the inherent metaphysical need of overcoming the finiteness and the fragmentary character of the human person that establishes the participation in and the protection by a universal spirit.

This awareness of a spiritual element in human nature as the lasting source of religious acts makes Burckhardt insist on the thesis that religion and the quest for the meaning of the world are the roots of every civilization. All spontaneous acts of the human mind—like poetry, philosophy, art—were primarily parts of the religious interpretations of man. A new world will come into existence after the decline of Europe through a new religion,[3] "for we never will get rid of the whole militaristic and economic business without a transcendental super-worldly orientation." Granting the eternity of religion as a constitutive and an invariable element of the human soul, he refuses to admit the eternity of any particular religious form, for every religion originates in history and is subject to the destiny of historical phenomena to harden in its institutions and to lose contact with human reality. For Burckhardt, because religions are both changing and eternal, the diverse types of religion like supernatural-transcendental, mystic-pantheistic, and magic-ritualistic correspond to different types of human beings. They are determined by the social character of the groups that form the elite. They are conditioned by the standards of societies that carry on the message of a religious genius. Burckhardt's analysis of the sociological implications of Mohammed's religion discloses his all-embracing analytical spirit. This religion is a terrible simplification of Christian and Jewish ideas, intended to satisfy the needs of predatory tribes at the lowest spiritual level.

Burckhardt carefully distinguishes between the historical rise of religion and the origins of higher religions. He does not study the historical rise of religion completely because the material knowledge will always remain haphazard. Furthermore, a genetic analysis of religion from the primitives on will never teach us the nature and character of a phenomenon that is evident without this kind of positivistic genealogy. He lovingly studies the origins of higher religions, for they disclose the spontaneity and the freedom of expanding above and beyond the empirical world, either in the patterns of asceticism and martyrdom, or in those of wisdom and mystical holiness. The nature of the religious aims is evident in these origins. It is the eternal quest for subduing the secular world of power, pride, and vanity. This original situation cannot last. The inescapable pressure of compromising with this world in order to establish a continuous institution will jeopardize the pursuit and the tradition of the original messages. In particular, the close relationship or the unification with the body politic has never failed to harm and corrupt the integrity of the gospel.

It is not incidental that his first book, *The Epoch of Constantine the Great*, verifies historically this religious experience. He describes the process of the waning of Ancient Civilization, the rise of Christianity and its integration into the Empire. It was a fateful moment in the history of the Christian Church. The terrible persecutions under Diocletian had the positive effect, according to Burckhardt, of having united and organized the various conflicting groups into one strong and powerful hierarchical body of the church. It was this well-functioning body with its thorough hierarchical organization all over the Empire that made it attractive to Constantine, as best fitted for taking care of the administration of the Empire. There was no actual administration after the unending military revolutions and the economic bankruptcy. Burckhardt analyzes this turning point in the development of the church from all angles.[4] It was first the unique opportunity for spreading the gospel and educating the barbaric invading tribes; second it was a great chance for proving the continuity of ancient civilization in the church; third it was the terrible seduction of being involved in and mixed with the institutions of the state and of sharing in its power activities. The change of an ascetic and transcendental religion of enthusiastic beliefs into a monopolistic institution, which is spiritual and also political, had far-reaching consequences for all spheres of European civilization. Burckhardt thought that this interference with political institutions logically would jeopardize the tradition and the truth of the message. For it would involve the religious institution in the dynamics of the blind and stubborn selfishness of power.

Likewise, he analyzed the paradoxical results of the Reformation, which strove for the religious inwardness of the individual soul and delivered the social and moral existence of man to the political powers. In terms almost identical to those used by John Neville Figgis [1866–1919] and Georges de Lagarde [1898–1967], he pointed out the fatal affinity of Martin Luther [1483–1546] with Niccolò Machiavelli [1469–1527] and his tragic success of having unconsciously promoted the universal secularization. Finally, he remarked that, sociologically, just those groups that enjoyed the prospect of being emancipated from all spiritual ties carried on these movements. In sharp contrast to the intentions of the founders, Protestants played a vital role in developing the idea of the autonomy of all spheres of life.

He turned his sympathetic understanding to the Catholic Church when she was persecuted by Otto von Bismarck [1815–1898]. He knew that this was a blow that illuminated the problematic relations between power and spirit. He was convinced that a religious renascence would reintegrate the modern world. He insisted, however, that only the separation and emancipation from politics and power would help reestablish the genuine and integral metaphysical spirit of religion. Then again, religion would be a manifestation of freedom.

The analyses of religious developments shed light on the character of Burckhardt's conception of history and of man in history. The desire directed toward a superhuman and universal good is a basic trend of human action. It is the act by which man unifies his frailty and finiteness with a sheltering and protecting whole and meets with a universal order. So far, this trend is a part of man's eternity. The communion with the social institution that realizes this fundamental need establishes the very history of the religious forces. The existence of a lag between the subjective longings and the objective services was in Burckhardt's mind the sign of waning civilization. Man's estrangement from his institutions shows the disintegration and disruption of a rightly ordered world.

II

In his second experience that constitutes a new approach toward history and man's place in it, Burckhardt finds, on a larger scale, what he found in the field of religion. It was the disrupting movement in the relations between state and society and the autonomies assumed by both that provoked Burckhardt's vision of a decaying world. As a young scholar he still hoped to contribute to the new liberalism and to maintain a true liberal position between the ruthless absolutism of Russia and Prussia on the one side and the no-less ruthless radicalism of the rising masses on the other. Already in 1845, he was aware that his conservative liberalism was doomed to failure. For nowhere were human forces visible that could make possible the reconciliation between political necessities and social demands. Shaken by the domestic unrest in Switzerland he writes:

> The term liberty sounds beautiful and perfect. Nobody however, is allowed to talk about it, who has not faced the possible slavery which may be exercised by the pressure of crowds and who has not experienced civil revolts. Nothing is more pitiable than a government which is subject to the intrigues of so-called liberal clubs of rascals and scoundrels. I know too much history to expect anything else from the despotism of the masses than a

> future domination of violence which will extinguish all these liberties. (April 19, 1845)

The destruction of the unity between state and society marks the specific character of the modern period originating in the French Revolution. There is no society without state; there is no state without society. Both are aspects of the same human constellation that we call history. Society is the primary phenomenon of social existence. The independent and spontaneous grouping and cooperation aims at the realization of ends and values. The state is the very institution that makes possible the continuity, duration, and security of the human enterprise we call society. This content and task is already imposed on the state by reason of social existence. If society leaves the state, and the state lacks the impact of social obligations and principles, both will unleash the demonic forces inherent in human vitality when not guided and controlled by the power of reason and by the devotion to a spiritual order.

The French Revolution created this situation. It has let loose the negatively privileged and disinherited groups without incorporating them in the structure of society or reestablishing significance and function in their work and position. It is the tragic failure of the French Revolution to have destroyed the system of an organized society without creating a positive principle of social reconstruction. The consequence was the lawless competition of isolated individuals and the explosive expansion of those groups that, by political, social, and economic crises, had lost income, prestige, and social meaning. The tragedy of this revolution lies in opening the gates for the demonic forces, both of these uprooted masses, and of the unleashed coercive power of the state proper. Burckhardt firmly believed that the French Revolution had broken the principle of social unity and order and, for this reason, had unchained the instincts and greeds of the masses and the no less greedy forces for domination and control inherent in the institutions of the state. This outlook made Burckhardt's liberalism helpless.

> I do not expect any thing of the future. Perhaps we will still enjoy some tolerable centuries, a kind of Roman empire. I am of the opinion that in spite of desperate efforts democrats and proletarians will eventually submit to a severe despotism because this placid century is not capable of realizing true democracy. After 1789 it will not be possible any longer to reestablish a true social order in the waning Europe. (September 17, 1849)

Burckhardt never fails to remember parallel situations in the past, and in particular, the Greek and Roman declines. He is aware that Athenian democracy was no less resentful and greedy and eager to extinguish the minorities of noble and educated groups than are the masses of the industrial society. And he visualizes the future regime of terrorism in Europe as like the rules of the barrack-emperors after the destruction and elimination of the Roman society. In his book on Constantine, he describes all patterns and grades of this military domination from the worst to the best. Perhaps the military domination of the past will return, and a tall man with the talent of a noncommissioned officer will rule again. He recommends in this context the imperial system of adoptions as worthwhile remembering, for these despotic rulers will not spring from any dynasty whatsoever. In this sense, he writes to a friend on March 23, 1883:

> There will be no monarchy in France. History runs differently than in the past. I cannot forget my vision of the future military domination. The change from democracies does not occur as individual tyranny which could

> be assaulted by dynamite. The change will take place as a military corporation. Perhaps these people will use means which even the worst despotism would never have dared to apply.

This idea possessed his mind so urgently that it occurs frequently in his letters.

> For a long time I have been aware that the world is pushing forward to the alternative between universal democracy and absolute despotism both without law and right. This new tyranny will not be achieved by dynasties which are too good hearted, but by military commanders with a republican ideology. It is not very pleasant to imagine a world the rulers of which will abstract completely from law, well-being, economic organization and finance and will instead erect a total domination through absolute brutality. Europe will be the victim of such new tyrants as a consequence of unleashing the masses to compete for the key position of control. (April 13, 1882)

It is a remarkable statement by Burckhardt himself that his vision is correct because he knows history so well. Actually, history is not a collection of dead material but the total presence of mankind in his historical consciousness. This historical consciousness is indeed absolutely different from all pragmatic ways of historical thinking, which are concerned either with justifying the evolution and the growth of the victorious cause, or with the romantic transfiguration of the defeated. Nothing like that informs Burckhardt's approach. The existence of man, human being proper, is historical at any moment because the whole of human kind is present in any moment of this process. Burckhardt changes completely the character and nature of the philosophic dynamic concepts of history, like those of Hegel,

Auguste Comte [1798–1857], and Herbert Spencer [1820–1903], into a static or ontological category. We have to deal with this problem later on. Here, it is only important to visualize the total presence of human history in Burckhardt's mind in order to appreciate objectively his terrific vision of the converging trends of the social revolution with the militaristic imperialism of the unleashed state.

After the French Commune, there remains the latent trend of combining the social revolution and the political imperialism. Here again, the recurring historical trend is present in his mind. The Roman Republic had warded off the imminent social revolution by the imperialistic conquest of the Eastern Mediterranean, the exploitation of which suffocated the revolutionary spirit of the Roman farmer and soldier. The same phenomenon occurs again with the growing social conflicts and the problematic political prestige of the ruling powers during the nineteenth century. All European governments transferred their social conflicts and tensions to the field of nationalist conquest, which, for a long time, turned social unrest into nationalism.

In the esoteric remarks of Burckhardt's correspondence, we find the most realistic observations on the identical dynamics in the foreign policy of Louis-Napoléon [1808–1873] and of Bismarck. Both checked revolutions by their military enterprises. Bismarck alone succeeded in his wars of 1864, 1866, and 1870 in transferring social demands to the field of national imperialism. After the war of 1870 and the French Commune, Burckhardt has a vision that, in the future, the inherent revolutionary tendencies of modern society will coincide with the self-preservation of a militaristic imperialism. In particular, the German situation provokes strange ideas revealing the intense clarity and realism of a thought that makes transparent the driving forces in history. He writes to a friend, who is a high German official:

> Bismarck has achieved by himself what in the long run would have happened without or against him. He was aware that the rapid growth of the democratic and social tide sometime would create a situation of total violence either by the democrats or by the government. For this reason he thought: *ipse faciam* and made the wars of 1866, 1870.
>
> But this is only the beginning. All our intellectual activities look queer, arbitrary or dilletantic compared with the highest efficiency of the Prussian military institutions which have been elaborated so carefully in all details. This military efficiency will become the pattern of life. You will be most interested in watching how the political and administrative machine will be transformed according to the patterns of a military efficiency. My interests turn to the changes in education. The strangest changes will occur in the conditions of the workers. I have an idea which sounds like a silly dream but possesses me thoroughly. The militarized state will become the monopolistic industrialist. Furthermore, it will be impossible in the long run to leave the human agglomerations of workers in the large mills to their needs and greeds. A certain planning of their misery and its overcoming through advancement and military uniforms with the sound of drums at the beginning and at the end of the working hours will logically develop one day or the other. (April 26, 1872)

These observations on the forces driving toward catastrophe spring from the primary experience of the vanishing interaction between state and society. Society strives for the expansion, the radiation, and the growth of independent and spontaneous acts that disclose the range of human personality. The state is a function of this society; it shelters and preserves its continuity and duration. This stabilizing force has the monopoly of coercion for this very purpose. The antagonism between spontaneous action and lasting institution is an invariable of historical existence. It is the antinomy between freedom and order, motion and stagnation. It is the dilemma of all power-institutions that, in reality, duration and continuity are likely to coincide with a hardening of institutions that prevents the growth of human spontaneity.

This type of historical situation, already present in Burckhardt's religious experience, finds its most radical and disastrous manifestation in those recurrent conflicts, when society is either disrupted or destroyed, and the unleashed state expands and enjoys its power drive for its own sake. Burckhardt defines this very situation with the phrase: "Power is evil in itself." This formula is not a liberal resentment or a sentimental moralism. Nobody knew better than Burckhardt that freedom and authority, power and spirit, spontaneity and obligation are constitutive elements of human and historical existence, the cooperation of which realizes the development of man's history. For this reason, power by itself deserves no negative connotation a priori. Power as potency directed towards meaningful ends is the nature of man's positive freedom. However, power is evil insofar as it is the narrow and selfish explosion of vital forces for the sake of enjoying their very lust. It is the unleashing of urges and instincts for their own satisfaction, emancipated from the center of human reason and the unifying meaning of the universal spirit. It is the rise of disintegration in man whose very being is disrupted when he separates vital and spiritual forces. The awareness of this possible catastrophe in human history leads Burckhardt, an ironic and sober writer, to use a pathetic phrase: "The master of world is Satanas!"

In disintegrating times, the selfish and egotistic struggle of institutions for their own survival points out this principle of evil, the pseudomythical unleashing of all demonic forces at its highest. It is this prospect that suggests Burckhardt's terms: *Satanas barbarus* for the forthcoming decadence. This is the most terrific and fateful development of modern times and is based on a fundamental confusion regarding the relationship between human logos and human body. The integrating principle of man—reason—was made an instrument for serving biological needs and drives instead of controlling the human animal. Implied in this confusion is the typical modern principle of the assumed goodness of human nature as only corrupted by social and political institutions. This idea resulted in the paradoxical postulate of all modern revolutions: the destruction of authority and the dignity of the state, and the enlargement of the volume of political tasks and functions, until they extend to the universal control of life. For this reason, the terrifying prospect of the unending modern revolution is the selfish exercise of power by military bodies, which present the single element of unified and integrated power in a dying society. This might be a sociological rule. But Burckhardt himself has presented the one historical exception to this rule: in the decay of Rome, not the army but the Christian Church reintegrated the declining Empire. For this reason, Burckhardt insisted on the lasting responsibilities of thoughtful men to establish or reestablish time and again the unity of life and spirit.

III

Burckhardt's ideas on the tasks and responsibilities of the scholar illuminate his image of man that cannot be separated from his concept of history. In his early letters that contain the farewell to his German friends who joined the revolutionary movement of 1848, he already expressed, definitely, his choice of the contemplative life. This choice is not an escapism, but practical and active work for the survival of freedom and human spontaneity.

In Burckhardt's mind, this theoretical life is the last refuge of intellectual and spiritual freedom. The sentimental intellectuals who sincerely believe in fighting for freedom and democracy do not realize that they are instruments of the darkest and demonic powers that lead toward a new slavery. "Today political action means being involved in a disrupting and confused world. I will look for harmonies." This sounds like an aesthetic escapism. It is not, as we will see later on. Here, we have only to remember that harmony in Burckhardt's conception is first of all a principle of spiritual order, the microcosmic reflex of which might be called aesthetic perfection. Burckhardt himself would never tolerate aesthetic harmonies that do not refer to a universal harmony of the all-pervading spirit. He himself explicitly states the moral implication of his decision. Already in 1846, he writes to a radical friend that there is no Epicureanism in his attitude. On the contrary, it is a moral task and the serious responsibility for the continuity of the mind that enforce on him the choice of the contemplative life.

> You all have not the slightest idea what tyranny will be imposed on intellectual freedom with the ideology that intellectual culture and education are the secret allies of capital which must be destroyed. . . . we all may perish. However, I wish to select the principle for which I gladly will die, that is, the intellectual civilization of Old Europe. (May 26, 1846)

This is not an arbitrary subjectivism. There is a definite theory of loyalties involved in this decision. The loyalties to the spontaneous forces of reason and logos are prior to all other norms for the scholar in times of revolution. It was Burckhardt's belief that in the prospective conflagrations, there ought to be men, who beyond the pale of social institutions, take care of the intellectual traditions in order to preserve the continuity of the spirit. It is the task and function of these thoughtful intellectuals not to be involved in the clashing alignments of the conflicting powers, but to remain true to the commitments of scholars to serve the permanent and lasting values, and to protect the actuality of timeless meanings over against the temporal fashions of thinking. The emphasis of modernity is on material well-being and comfort, but the emphasis of the responsible human person is on the loyal devotion to the preservation of the standards and achievements of the human mind. That the chain of intellectual traditions should not be disrupted is a primary interest of life and a metaphysical evidence of its duration.

Reason and consciousness make possible, time and again, the actualization of the spirit as the lasting transcendence of man over his empirical finiteness. This effort is not a formal intellectualism. According to his frequent remarks, nobody despised more the detached and sophisticated scholarship of modern professors than Burckhardt. He took it for granted that specialization is an inescapable destiny of modern pragmatic reason. He suspected, however, that most scientists would be completely satisfied with technical skillfulness and efficient routine. He clearly foresaw the intellectual barbarism of the transformation of the universities into technological institutes, where scholars are content with narrow boundaries, without referring to a universal context and meaning. His preference for dilettantism over specialization is an invitation to remember the original term *philosophy,* and to pursue all scientific investigations in a philosophical spirit. It is valueless, according to Burckhardt's idea, to enlarge and extend the fields of detailed research and to classify documents apart from the efforts toward understanding and interpreting the human factors involved. Only these attempts transform knowledge into wisdom. Like Thucydides, he does not aim at pragmatic prudence for future use; he strives for permanent wisdom that makes transparent the completeness of man and the eternity of man's spiritual and thinking being. This lasting conviction gave Burckhardt strength and power to stand the terrific visions of the forthcoming catastrophes. The rapid growth of the industrial system, the series of imminent wars, and the social revolutions challenged the strongest resistance of his spiritual loyalty. He had no doubt that only this commitment to the traditions of ancient and Christian civilization would make possible the future renascence of the spontaneity and freedom of man as indispensable elements of the permanent working of the mind and spirit.

This unconditioned devotion to genuine scholarship as a way of life pervades his reflections on the relations between politics and history.

> Man in his concrete situation must intend definite ends, as thinker he must remain true to the standards of scientific truth. Life of the West is struggle. In his individual situation the historian might be compelled to take sides and to follow definite purposes. As scholar he ought to strive for a complete and thorough interpretation. (April 16, 1882)

He once advised a young scholar to refrain from modern problems that always involve political prejudices and subjective partisan approaches determined by our own finite thinking and our interests and emotions. He insists on the discipline and disinterested contemplation of the historian.

> What will be the end of scholarship, if we yield to the social pressure of modern society and shift to a branch of political journalism or social pragmatism? It is worthwhile insisting on the opposite position. We will defend and preserve history, philosophy and the humanities as

> the very rocks to which the tides of temporality are not permitted to rise, because they are the ultimate refuge of disinterested pursuit of truth. (November 12, 1876)

Burckhardt calls this approach that of "humanist epigone."

> We humanistic epigoni are destined never to join unconditionally either of the fighting parties, not even the group which is closest to our ideas. The cruelty and bitterness of past conflicts, the furor and passion of destroying enemies makes it impossible for human reflection to stick to any partisan viewpoint. For this reason genuine historical reflection will definitely eliminate those historians who follow partisan lines and write history as a necessary evolution towards a success and victory of their cause. (June 8, 1876)

If we take seriously the term *humanism*, as applied by Burckhardt to a self-interpretation of man, we are compelled to ask: What is the specific character of this humanism compared with the humanisms of the past? It is incompatible with the authoritarian humanism of the renaissance that changed from the truth of the religious traditions to the authorities of the classics. It is likewise far distant from the romantic and aesthetic humanism of Johann Joachim Winckelmann [1717–1768] and his friends who discovered a perfect world in the harmony of noble innocence and serene greatness among the Greek works of art. Burckhardt, the man who exploded cruelly this idea of a golden past in Greek civilization and described the grim reality of Greek passions, ambitions, and resentments, had no romantic image of this or any period. Throughout his works, we find the idea that there never was, there never will be, a golden age—an age that can claim absolute authority and perfection. He even states that there never will be political forms of government that by their very structure guarantee the good life. However, there are constitutions that, administered with the true spirit of virtue and righteousness, can bring into existence the highest possible achievements of human development in all spheres of freedom.

What then remains for justifying Burckhardt's self-interpretation as humanist? He is humanistic in his trend toward the sympathetic understanding of the totality of man beyond and above the restricted viewpoints of the pragmatic historians. The second element that explains the application of the term *humanism* to Burckhardt is in conformity with the use of this word by the pragmatist Friedrich Schiller [1759–1805]. Burckhardt's humanism is, indeed, a spiritual pragmatism and anticipates to some extent the work of William James [1842–1910] and Ralph Barton Perry [1876–1957]. It is a spiritual pragmatism that understands all human manifestations as contributing to extend and enlarge the individual into a general and universal being. The third element of this humanism marks the complex of the contemplative life. It does not refer to an external power of logos. It is the immanent intention of man's reason to attain through knowledge the loving unification with the universe. It is characteristic of Burckhardt's humanism that in his tendency toward the theoretical life, the intellectual eros of Plato coincides with the purifying and illuminating love of Christ. They appear not as a transcendental grace, but as the inherent radiation of the innermost nature of man. This eternity of man in his concrete transcendence of himself, this participation in and cooperation with the absolute, makes Burckhardt's humanism into a spiritual humanism that could be called by nature Christian.

IV

This humanistic approach destroys the hybrid intellectualism and the subjective political implications of the idealistic and positivistic theories. It eliminates the progressivism and optimism of those nineteenth century philosophies that assumed that all epochs passed are strides toward the present, that evolution is identical with progress, and that progress ultimately results in a secular eschatology. In contrast to all these theories, Burckhardt conceives every period of history as the full expression of concrete humanity in all its aspects. Every historical moment, including our own, is existing for itself, for the past, for the future. History is not the evolution toward a subjective intended meaning. It is the life of mankind as a whole; every moment has meaning for this whole and for the unity of the human world.

The lasting center of historical reflection is the concrete man, acting and being acted upon, striving and suffering, the eternal man identical in his changing disguises. However, the diverse and various types of man in different situations are not changing costumes of the same actor. The ideality of man is not a permanent substance. It is a moving constellation of invariables that turns around according to the interaction of challenges and responses. History is the eternity of the constitutive elements of the human being. In every moment, man strives to realize his potentialities that best respond to the changes of his world. Burckhardt has conquered the positivistic dualism of man and environment. There is no gap between the human world and the surrounding world. We ourselves are the wave, the element of the universal sea. There is no basic distinction between man and environmental world, both are aspects of the world as a whole, shifting and interacting according to the destructive or creative powers inherent in any human situation.

Burckhardt is concerned with the typical and recurrent trends of human conduct. The individual and the general, the specific and the typical, convey two aspects of human existence that is inseparably individual and typical as well. Burckhardt's realism does not lead him toward the positivistic conclusion of radical relativism resulting from the eternal change in man's history. Truth and beauty remain absolute values in spite of all changing conditions.

The true unconditional value is the commitment to a general cause, to a sacrifice abolishing all natural egoisms, and to an extinction of vital selfishness. This moral self-transcendence makes for the greatness of an epoch or a cause. In these acts, the empirical individual meets with the general and typical tendencies that are human property. They show man at his highest because they make it possible for every person to realize himself as a whole and complete being.

Frequently, Burckhardt remarks that this achievement is independent of intellectual superiority that often is combined with miserable vanity and selfishness. The coincidence of the individual with the general marks human grandeur as the unification of a determined will with a determined mind. Burckhardt's examples of grandeur enrich his image of man. Political grandeur is based on strength and harshness of souls that enjoy riding on the wings of the storm and that face death and glory. Their limitations, however, are given in the specific nature of political action. They must be necessarily inconsiderate and selfish and exploit all advantages. The greater and rarer human achievement is grandeur of soul. Burckhardt defines this attitude as corresponding to a man who is able to resign secular advantages in favor of moral principles, a human being capable of voluntary restrictions, not because of prudence, but because of inner grace and kindness. This grandeur of the soul is possible only where the individuals consciously experience their responsibilities and their tasks. This was Caesar's grandeur! "The whole range of human potentialities is perfect if there is still the mercy and clemency of character, a lasting contempt of death and again, like Caesar's, the will to gain and to reconcile. A spark of kindness. . . . A complete soul like that of the passionate Alexander!"

The humanistic image of the philosophic historian and the definition of ontological history converge in this image of human grandeur as the highest achievement of human actuality.

V

All these reflections and visions, in spite of their apparent antiphilosophical emphasis, disclose a very definite philosophy of history. According to Burckhardt, history is the passion of man's living in the world without the sheltering protection of a Divine mercy. This human passion reveals the range of man's potentialities for the highest and the lowest, for spirit and despair. If there is no redemption and transsubstantiation in his passion, there is, at least, the underlying and recurrent idea that this world of man's self-realization has a definite significance in a universal order. That is the reason why evil has a definite function in the "Economy" of this human passion. Only real evil makes possible and challenges the radiating growth of disinterested righteousness and goodness. This might be called a relative pessimism.

It is the grandeur of human nature to transcend the concrete empirical individuality in the acts of spiritual, moral, and social commitments that are inherent in our very being. Their intentions disclose the universality of the human spirit. They contribute to the whole of man's unity with history as determining the standards of humankind. The harmony of the universe and its justice and virtue depend on these acts that manifest the spiritual responsibilities of man.

This concrete transcendence of self marks the continuity of the spirit. History as man's historicity is determined by the dynamism of spirit and matter. They interact and meet with each other. All spiritual and intellectual things in all spheres of life have a concrete (i.e., historical) aspect. All material empirical data have, likewise, a spiritual side by which they participate in eternity. Spirit changes, never perishes.

This is relative optimism. It presents a positive response to the world of evil. It is optimistic, however, only regarding the being of man, not with respect to his success in the evolution of mankind. Burckhardt remarks explicitly that it would be trivial to content oneself with this idea of the eternity of the spirit. Nobody can ever foresee what harm violence, terror, and oppression might do to the growth and to the spontaneity of the inner life and to its continuity. Sometimes evil rules for a long time, destroys civilizations forever, and establishes the rule of the lower over against the higher standards.

These philosophical remarks are the cornerstone of a philosophy of man and make possible the realistic and spiritual interpretation of man. The eternity of man as a being capable of general and universal longings indicates his cooperative participation in a universal power. In hesitant words, Burckhardt points to a "Higher Necessity" and to a "Highest Good," the name of which is lost and unknown. "Perhaps the man who aims at the free and spontaneous acts of human culture and the man who strives for power, are both blind instruments in the service of a third unknown power."

Burckhardt's human passion describes the range and the potentialities of man's grandeur and misery. It is correct to say that this passion lacks the Divine Redemption and Mercy. It is, however, permissible to remark that in the self-transcendence, which is possible for man, in the acts of devotion to friends, causes, and values, mercy has given way to the inherent quality of a spontaneous and overwhelming love radiating kindness, comfort, and reconciliation.

This philosophy of man has transcended the categories of optimism and pessimism. It goes to the roots of human being. It tries to reformulate the eternal wisdom of man's Fall and Creation in secular terms. Finiteness and the demonic forces of human desires endanger permanently the growth and the actuality of the spiritual elements of man. This reality must be faced. That is no pessimism. It is pragmatism. The mastery of this positive reality through the no less positive intellectual and spiritual intentions is carried on with hope and belief in the potential victories of converging wisdom and love. That is no optimism. Hope and faith make that mode of thinking a spiritual pragmatism. This is the reconstruction of the image of man trying to combine Greek realism and Christian spiritualism; it is the message of the souls that could be called by nature Christian.

VI

There is no longer anything mysterious or prophetic about this vision of the European crisis. This understanding was accomplished by the integrity of contemplative thinking and by the completeness of a loving soul. It came into existence as a positive interpretation of man. This awareness embraces the lasting contacts and conflicts between man's material and spiritual forces in their changing constellations. This very interpretation made possible the vision of the European decline that is realistic and spiritual as well.

That is the teaching that can meet our requirements: we are aware that what is at stake in the present conflict is not an alternative between different political institutions. At stake is the image of man. The old and eternal image of the finite and spiritual man is opposed by the image of man as a predatory animal. We stand for the elements of ancient and Christian civilizations that made possible a good and perfect life in the freedom that springs from the devotion to basic principles of being. What many call the democratic way of life is just this fighting ideal of the free citizen devoting his efforts to the values of his body politic. It is this ideal of the political pioneer, enriched by the experience of the infinite value of an individual soul, thirsting for its redemption, that determines our image of man. It has created time and again the rise of all possibilities of American greatness. In this universal crisis, the serene wisdom of Burckhardt supports the effort to rediscover the old truth of the image of man.

Notes

1. Burckhardt's collected works appeared in 14 volumes (Basel: Benno Schwabe, 1929–1933). Selected letters by Fritz Kaphan (Kroner Leipzig, 1935). Among many publications dealing with Burckhardt, we mention only two: on the relation of Burckhardt and Nietzsche in Basel, Charles Andler, *Nietzsche, sa vie et sa pensée*, volumes 1 and 2; and a philosophical interpretation, Karl Loewith, *Jacob Burckhardt, Der Mensch inmitten der Geschichte* (Lucerne: Vita Nova, 1936).

2. Strangely enough Burckhardt's *Reflections on Universal History* are not translated into English.

3. This idea of a new religion is again a typical thought recurring among Protestants where the rationalistic and empty dogmatism had estranged the pious souls from faith in their churches. Burckhardt frequently remarks that all these trends will finally strengthen the Catholic Church. Likewise, the philosophical approach toward the church as a secular institution is typically Protestant.

4. Not all historians share Burckhardt's view on Constantine. See, e.g., H. A. Vasilieu, *History of the Byzantine Empire* (Madison: 1928), 1:61.

2

Democracy and Religion in the Work of Erasmus

It is taken for granted that religious motives play a decisive role in determining the frames of reference in which societies are acting and being acted upon. However, it remains an open question what specific effects religious elements have in building the horizons that condition historical structures. These effects can be constructive, preventive, and destructive, as seen from a religious or secular point of view. The messianism of the Franciscan Spirituals [Fraticelli] had consequences that were disastrous for the Church and precarious for the body politic. The intellectuals of the imperial court jubilantly took over the Franciscan radicalism as a most effective tool in their anti-ecclesiastical policy. Frederic II cynically transformed the spiritual messianism into messianic imperialism as the secular ideology of an antipapal international policy. He inaugurated a development that was continued by Charles V and finally came to an end in the secular messianism of modern political and social revolutions. This effect is destructive for church and state alike.

Many religions were strong enough to prevent the growth of secular ambitions for some centuries at least. Religious convictions, in connection with other causes, prevented the complete expansion

---

Published originally in a slightly different form in *The Review of Religion* XIV (March 1950), 227–49. Republished by permission from Frank Salomon.

of political power into the total state at the beginning of the modern era. Religious indoctrination had created habits that prevented the rise of industrial capitalism in Asia and the Near East.

In the rise of modern Western civilization, religion became a constituent element in the foundations of all political and social institutions. However, there was no longer a Christian religion, but Christian religions. The teachings of the various churches had different effects on the attitudes and patterns of conduct in the respective societies. There is no doubt that the German *Untertan*, with all his negative qualifications as citizen and his positive sides as worker, is determined by Luther's social teachings, whatever might have been the political and social causes that made up the German concatenation of conditions. In genuine Calvinistic countries, such as Geneva and the Netherlands after the Treaty of Dordrecht in 1489, a monopolistic aristocracy was the natural form of government.

Perhaps it is a mistake to stress the influence of the churches as most important. Their teachings in sermons and schools and their strict disciplines had a strong and habit-creating influence. However, there were many psychological and spiritual escapes available. Already prior to the so-called "Reformation," there was a widespread lay piety—independent mystical groups and spiritual communions, as well as reform movements—that many monastic orders had attacked spontaneously. It is a statistical problem whether these movements were quantitatively strong enough to be treated with equal attention as the churches. Unfortunately, we cannot answer such questions because there are no statistical data available for movements that could survive only by hiding their actual beliefs. The historian of liberal and democratic ideas, however, will give his complete attention to these movements, because they started from a spiritual vision that made them antagonistic to the authoritarian control of the leading churches.

Among these movements, Erasmus [1466–1536] and the Erasmian movements, for which the Spaniards coined the term *Erasmismo,* have an important contribution to make. This spiritual liberalism, or better liberal spiritualism, was centered around the idea of Christian liberty. This idea implied the principle of social and political democracy and, in its critical aspect, the grim and disillusioned analysis of disintegrating feudalism and rising military despotism.

Erasmus had chosen freedom as the ruling principle of his life. He explicitly stated again and again that he could not serve. He preferred death to intellectual slavery. He refused the offers of popes and kings who implored him to take ecclesiastical or secular positions. He could not be partisan and had to remain alone in order to preserve his intellectual integrity intact. He was keenly aware that his was a precarious position between the hostile alignments of Catholicism and Lutheranism. He was fighting for the indestructible unity of the Church, not for the existing ecclesiastical institutions. He predicted that Luther's revolution would jeopardize spiritual freedom for a long time to come. Intellectual and social independence were one and indivisible to Erasmus. He had left monastic orders to get rid of external pressure by coercive institutions and of inner depression caused by his illegitimate birth. He recognized only one passion, the desire for freedom from established authorities. His was the Eros of liberty for serving Christ and logos independently and freely. He had dedicated his life to this service. This voluntary service made him free.

He could realize such independence because the new and revolutionary invention of the printing press liberated him from the alternative of serving an individual or collective employer or starving. After some years of the usual misery as tutor to boys of noble families, he finally succeeded in winning the friendship of Aldus Manutius [1449–1515] in Venice and of Johann Froben [1460–1527] and Johann Amerbach [1440–1513] in Basel. These printer families were scholars and businessmen alike and let Erasmus share in the profits of his books and editions. In particular, the Basel printers had established their prestige and reputation as Erasmus's publishers and generously shared their wealth with him. They had made the poor and insecure tutor a well-to-do and independent scholar whose works were fascinating to the world of learning at the time. His followers, the Erasmians, said that he had improved them. They felt he had given them the courage to be independent beyond the pale of established institutions. They stated that he had delivered their spiritual spontaneity, which they turned to social and political improvements in the interests of their subjects.

Erasmus was not concerned with philosophical and theological ideas and conceptions. Nevertheless, his religious anti-intellectualism and his moral intellectualism made him a forerunner of some trends in positivistic and pragmatic philosophies. His main concern was, as he frequently stated, a practical one. He desired to prepare the intellectual tools that enabled human beings to become free as Christians by the experience of learning. This principle made his work coherent and logical. It pointed toward a world of free Christian citizens.

He could have formulated his intention in still a different way. He aimed at purifying ecclesiastical, and spiritualizing secular, institutions in a social situation in which all trends indicated the rapid growth of independent political and economic organizations. In such a moment, Christians had to make a tremendous effort to keep the Christian spirit alive against the pressure of unleashed secular powers. The hierarchical and aristocratic Church that prayed for the laymen could not stem the tide. The responsible Christian thinker and teacher had to mobilize Christian people and train them as Christian soldiers. They had to fight the inner enemy of greed and passions and the outer enemy of lust for power with the weapons of Christian ethics and its ascetic requirements. Erasmus had escaped monastic orders for many subjective reasons. Objectively, in the trend of his inner development, he had to leave in order to democratize spiritual aristocracy and the religious division of labor as established by the medieval Church. Erasmus states frequently—most emphatically in his farewell letter to the Abbot of Steyn—that the whole world should become a monastery and that all Christians should live as canons and monks in the world of everyday institutions. Erasmus conceives of the Christian religion as a way of life. It is a universal way of life valid and required for all Christian people. It is an inner-worldly asceticism that permits the control and overcoming of the secular world.

In Erasmus's vision of a spiritual democracy, various trends of religious thinking are merged. He turns the eschatological vision of the Franciscan Spirituals into the theory of inner-worldly asceticism. This was postulated by the historical situation, the corruption of which is admitted by God in order to invite individual souls to improving and proceeding on the road of perfection.

Second, Erasmus shifted the mystical experience of Christ as all-pervading logos into the moral principle of the philosophy of Christ. The philosophy of Christ is the application of Christ's moral teaching to the problems of social conduct as learned experience. It was Erasmus's sincere conviction that we are able to follow Christ's ideals and to imitate Him in truth and spirit if we consciously affirm and understand His yoke as easy. According to Erasmus, charity and science are no alternatives but are interdependent upon each other. Blind love without knowledge is as impotent as science is without spiritual Eros. Erasmus transformed the knowledge of mystical experience into a theory of social and utilitarian piety that is deeply influenced by the moral intellectualism of Socrates and Plutarch.

Erasmus's religion was an effort to ban magic from his path and to establish a religion of pure logos, thus opening the road for Huldrych Zwingli [1484–1531] and Friedrich Schleiermacher [1768–1834]. It seemed to Erasmus that the Church had submitted to the temptations of monopolistic power and had abused the natural inclinations for magic and superstition that will always prevail among the ignorant. The Church was, for Erasmus, the model case for exemplifying his Law of Degeneracy. This states that all social institutions are subject to the pressure of their organization. For this reason, Erasmus invited Christian people to make use of the wonderful invention of the printing press to spread and explain the Gospel and the Epistles. This, he thought, will make possible the creation of spiritual democracy in which everybody is called upon to be a theologian because everybody will be able to read and to understand the basic verities of Christian piety.

Erasmus was aware of the sociological and historical conditions and possibilities of Christianity as a way of life for his times. He understood that *Imitatio Christi* could not mean the external mimesis of the apostolic lives and of the first communion. Under modern conditions, it means inward living: to live in the world as if we did not live in it and to turn to the Spirit that makes transparent our societal relationships and strengthens our acting and suffering for peace and reconciliation as the fundamentals of spiritual life. The mystical road leads toward the inward, says Novalis [Georg Philipp Friedrich Freiherr von Hardenberg (1772-1801)], in a truly Erasmian spirit.

Erasmus was always aware of social and historical conditions of religious attitudes. He objected to Luther's notion that the times of Revelation and of listening to the Holy Ghost are gone. What remains is slow progress in the evolution of the understanding of Christ's truth. Christ did not want us to know His overwhelming truth at once. We gain more and more of His wisdom by continuous interpretation and reexamination of documents and texts. Revelation is one and eternal; however, men's organs for listening and understanding are subject to error and deception. For this reason, we must see to it that the variety of religious experience makes for the whole truth that includes the experience and cognition of the heretics.

Erasmus was striving for a spiritual pluralism founded on a few basic verities taken for granted by the most antagonistic theologians. These verities are the God of Abraham, Isaac, and Jacob, Creator of the Universe, Logos and Holy Ghost, Christ as Incarnation and Logos, both transcendent and immanent; they imply human obligations to participate in and to contribute to the all-pervading spirit of which we are parts. The vision of Erasmus is mystical rather than theological, panentheistic rather than pantheistic. However, the mystical view is not contemplative, but pragmatic and utilitarian. It leads toward a piety of social and democratic action that alone makes it possible to establish Christian liberty.

Erasmus, not Luther, coined the term *Christian liberty*. It indicates the goal of the Christian for which the Christian republic is the indispensable condition. The goal is the spiritual sovereignty of man, control of Self, and overcoming the world by inner superiority. Christian perfection is not different from the ideals of the pagans as practiced and described by Socrates, Epictetus, Epicurus, and Plutarch. For this reason, Erasmus violently rejects Luther's radical condemnation of everything prior to Christ. "Some have been saved under the Natural Law, many under the Law of Moses, most under the Law of the Gospel: but salvation is properly due not to any law, only to God's pity through Christ." Throughout his work, Erasmus attempts to understand the God of Abraham and the Christ not as historical phenomena that split history into two irreconcilable parts.

Erasmus could conceive of religion merely as a universal phenomenon. Religion is natural, not historical. It is a constituent element of nature, mirrored in human thinking and feeling at all times and in all places. It creates everywhere the same ideals and patterns of perfection that must spring from the same and identical source of the all-pervading logos that is God of Creation, God of mercy, and Christ of pity. Erasmus was intrigued by the lives and sublime ideas of men like Socrates, Cicero, and Epicurus. If they can rightly be called saints, they must have enjoyed the mercy of God and the pity of Christ, the Redeemer. For this reason, Erasmus dares to transform a historical religion into the natural religion of all times and places.

Erasmus radically opposed Luther. Nobody has a monopoly on religious truth; none is justified in practicing fanaticism. If we study the true art of piety, we will find that all spiritual roads converge to the divine mansion that is all embracing peace and everlasting reconciliation in all religions. How else could it happen that all religions postulate the same ideal of perfection: gladness of heart, tranquility of mind, and peace of conscience?

Erasmian liberalism is irreconcilable with any kind of Christian orthodoxy. To Erasmus, it was the very essence of Christianity. He could not be a citizen of a national state; he did not want to be a cosmopolitan; he was striving for the citizenship of *Civitas Caelestis*.

From *Antibarbari* [originally published in manuscript c. 1489, print edition 1520—Eds.] to the posthumously published edition of *Origen* [1536—Eds.], Erasmus pursued the idea that the best religion comes to its highest perfection and has its greatest effect when supported by the best learning. Best learning is to Erasmus the humanities, not philosophy, for the humanities deal with God's manifestations as expressed through and as logos; to Erasmus the humanities presented the immediate and spontaneous presence of the Divine. This is the inner meaning of his philology.

Erasmus formulated his position most articulately in the prefaces to the Fathers whom he edited or translated into Latin. His selection is already indicative. He chose those who, like Jerome and Origen, assumed that man is a free intelligence, and that the Eros toward God and the Good is inherent in the natural moral conscience. These Fathers knew that many approaches lead to God; they loved their cotheologians in spite of dissenting opinions. They were keenly aware that dogmatic formulations were the product of a sociological emergency, strengthened by hostile pressure from without and by competing sects from within. Erasmus believed it possible to find in their writings his own conviction that faith was a way of life rather than a conceptual frame. According to Erasmus, the Fathers connected faith and learning in order to be the educators of the Christian people, who had the task of turning faith into living piety of social action. For this purpose, he unified Christian faith with pagan spiritualism as the true synthesis of the good life.

Saint Ambrose [374–397] had established the ideal of the Christian educator whose conduct and work should bring social peace. "Magnum pondus habet morum integritas, magnam habet auctoritatem coniuncta mansuetudini constantia. Plurimum valet eloquentiae copulata prudentia." [He has moral integrity that carries great weight and great authority, coupled with consistent gentleness. He has as well great eloquence coupled with prudence.—Eds.] This was the ideal Erasmus hoped to realize in his life and work.

It is of no avail to investigate whether Erasmus interpreted the Fathers correctly. He certainly did not. He understood them as he wanted himself to be understood. He wished to connect Christ and Epicurus, Socrates and Paul. His concern was to educate free Christian citizens and to make the elite devoted servants to the realization of Christ in the here and now. In this daring enterprise, he stimulated and promoted all trends toward liberal and democratic institutions and patterns of conduct.

Erasmus's religious position implied three postulates. First, he was deeply concerned with the social standards of society and, in particular, with the lot of the poor and suffering classes. Second, his spiritualism makes possible an analysis of the prevailing social institutions that is as grim and disillusioned as that of Niccolò Machiavelli [1469–1527]. Third, his social and utilitarian piety recommends the transfer of monastic rules to social institutions in order to create the conditions under which Christian liberty could be realized.

Erasmus anticipated the theories of political liberalism by recognizing society as the bearer of social evolution. Society is the sum total of the diverse rational activities of man that make possible security, well-being, and peace. Farmers, burghers, and urban citizens in commerce, industry, and crafts work toward these goals. The urban societies are the resources from which the professions draw their best and strongest forces. Among urban groups arose the enthusiasm for the New Learning. In the urban centers, Erasmus found the liberal attitudes that required participation in and restriction of political power. He had studied experimentally the world of patrician and bourgeois societies in London, Antwerp, and other cities. He was intimately associated with the scholar-printers of Venice and Basel, to whom he was friend and business partner. His practical experience enabled him to compare the new economic developments in modern industries, such as printing, with past economic institutions and to reconsider the relationships between economic societies and the state.

It would be as easy as misleading to understand Erasmus's attitudes as determined by his bourgeois interests and his class situation. His piety is, indeed, conditioned by his experience growing up in the lay mysticism of Dutch urban societies. However, his "vested interests" are the growth of spiritual democracy and the progress of intellectual liberty, both united in his Socratic and Christian piety.

In his analyses of various social strata, Erasmus discloses a definite sympathy for the poor and lower middle classes for two reasons. They are the productive classes whose labors produce the wealth of society. There he finds a thoroughly urbanized population, many small and middle-sized towns that are well and intelligently administered, because a steady and moderate well-being prevails in all strata of society. This can easily be explained. They are the markets for the abundant rural products and import just as many goods as are necessary for balancing the prices. Erasmus praises the character of these classes. Labor, being the center of their lives, has constructive effects on their conduct and mutual relationships. Labor has an "influence on discipline of the individual and on the control of his passions." Labor frequently contributes to making man moderate and considerate in his relations to his fellow men. Labor is sacred because it is the tool for building up the family. It is sacred because it maintains the blessing and happiness of a family by the mutual cooperation of husband and wife. Labor is an indispensable device of inner-worldly Christianity. It is as relevant as frugality and thrift for establishing Christian liberty and for avoiding the pitfalls of wealth and luxury for spiritual independence.

Erasmus never ceased to praise such character traits as belonging to the modest middle classes. He was not aware of the political implications of his analyses. Throughout his work, he describes the societal relationships between husband and wife in a family, between friends and partners in business, in such a way that all differences in authority and status are eliminated by the emphasis on cooperative labor for realizing religious values. Erasmus suggests a social democracy that we could easily call Christian Social Democracy.

He was much concerned about the political and social situation of these groups under the control of disintegrating social classes and integrating absolutistic institutions. He was familiar with the plight of the peasants and of the urban proletariat. His sympathies were with the oppressed, although his reasoning was for preserving the status quo. He was of the opinion that a conscientious scholar could not recommend a revolution that would serve the progress of more cruel and oppressive despotism. However, he longed for the renascence of the extinct race of Brutus that had its own distinct function in epochs of despotism. Erasmus even recognized bravely and frankly, against his own preferences, that revolutions might have their own legitimacy in situations of despair.

He watched with deep sympathy the uprising of the peasants and the proletariat. He was personally attacked by a French Carthusian (December 1524) and by the syndic of the Sorbonne, Noël Beda (May 1525), and described as the author of the religious and social revolutions. According to these critics, he was responsibile for the disintegrating society, because he had spread the libertine spirit of humanistic philosophy. He serenely rejected the accusations and clearly hinted at the social and political motives at the roots of such desperate actions. He had rather impeach the rulers than blame the people. He suspected all the time that feudal lords and princes would welcome the uprisings as an opportunity for strengthening their domination and exploitation. He was keenly aware that the German feudal class, in its state of decomposition, would gladly make use of all possibilities for overthrowing the wealthy elite of urban societies and take over their riches. In this connection, as in his analysis of Luther, we find remarkable observations on the German character. There he asked himself why the Germans are so much better in violent punishment of evils than in their prudent prevention.

In contrast to these sympathetic analyses stands Erasmus's extremely critical description of the bourgeois elite, the patrician, the honored rich. Though with Aristotle he recognized that perfect happiness requires a material fortune, he criticized those who praised Roman law because it established security in business by regulating commerce and interest rates. He thought that these commercial societies combined daring and reason. The new forms of interest seemed to him reasonable, and he did not blame the various groups of bankers. He admitted that these men could defend their activities with a clear conscience. Christ has forbidden, not clever activity, but the tyrannical lust for profit. However, he condemned the daring of international commerce as practiced by the patricians of Antwerp, for he could study in detail the effects of these emancipated economic forces on the common people and could observe everywhere the ruthless exploitation of the masses by economic monopolies. He complained no less of the free competition in new industries, where anyone could undertake an enterprise, and where the law failed to protect already existing ones and did not question the need for new establishments.

His attitude toward the new world was characteristic of a conservative liberal. On the one hand, he recognized the positive and constructive elements in the new urban societies, their efforts to control nature and to build a better economic and social world. Anticipating Thorstein Veblen [1857–1929], he remarked that the new branches of financial and commercial speculation are completely independent of the economic needs of the common people, and that they gamble on the urgently needed goods of life. This is, in Veblen's terminology, a new leisure class; in Erasmus's language, it is the most wicked and the most honored group of wealthy people—honored by the political elite because their wealth is needed to stabilize the rising national state.

Erasmus was struck by the interrelationship of state and society. He saw society splitting into the working classes on the one hand, and the strata of economic power joined to the political elites and the princes, on the other. He was haunted by such visions and spoke of the conspiracy between the nobility and the rich to exploit the people and establish an absolute state for the destruction of civil liberties. He was fully aware that this unholy union of power and wealth would have its implications for foreign affairs. There were too many warmongers striving for economic gains and exploiting the ideology of the Crusades for profit, for example, by manipulation of the sugar market. He drew conclusions from these facts, and, in a formula as Marxist as that of Thomas More, he stated that the body politic was nothing but a tremendous business machine.

But in spite of complete disillusionment on the trend of political evolution, he insisted on government interference in economic and social affairs, in order to maintain the lowest level of standards, at least, for the common people. It was a main concern of his to protect consumers from exploitation by tradesmen who manipulated prices in a criminal manner. The state must intervene, for purely utilitarian reasons, to prevent violent rebellion. Throughout his works, Erasmus demanded control of prices, weights and measures, economic combines, market procedures, and quality of food. Without such regulation, the situation of the common people would be disastrous.

Equally important to him was a general reform of taxation. From 1517 to the end of his life, he never ceased to draw the attention of the rulers to the continuous threat of revolution implicit in the unequal distribution of taxes, most of which were paid by the common people. He suggested four expedients for the intelligent ruler: first, limitation of the expenses of crown and court; second, a heavy import tax on luxury goods to be borne by the rich; third, a kind of excess profit tax to prevent the concentration of wealth in the hands of the few; and fourth, light taxation of necessary commodities, such as bread, wine, beer, and clothing because it is the poor who bear the heaviest burden from taxation of consumer goods. And the methods employed by the framers of tax laws to enrich themselves aggravate that burden. Frequently, Erasmus raised his voice against such unjust practices.

Attacked by his enemies for infringing upon the authority of the emperor, he made a distinction between the rights of a ruler and the misdeeds of his administration. He bravely maintained that, in absolute monarchies, the people are completely broken by disastrous taxation, and called attention to the tradition of the Dutch Provinces and Burgundy, where the provincial assemblies must give their consent to all taxes. He recalled the fact that Charles V and his brother, Ferdinand, had never objected to his independent suggestions on tax reform. In his old age, Erasmus extended his ideas of reform still further. In discussing the possibility of war against the Turks, he warned the rulers to redistribute the tax burden. The poor, being completely exhausted already through monopolies and taxes, should not be forced again to bear the entire war tax. This would only increase the spirit of revolt. The rulers can appease the masses only by introducing radical parsimony in their own economy and moderate taxation of ecclesiastical wealth.

Erasmus anticipated modern liberalism by limiting the state to the function of integrating, unifying, and protecting the different groups of society. The state is a necessary aspect of society. Erasmus granted its positive function as long as the body politic remained instrumental to establishing the conditions for spiritual liberty. He was well aware that such postulates derived merely from spiritual hypotheses. He was too well versed in the history of the Roman Empire (he had been the editor of the *Scriptores Historiae Augustae*), as well as that of the Church, to have any doubt about the collective dynamics of institutions of power. As early as the first edition of the *Enchiridion*, he had established the *lex degenerandi* for all social institutions and described how, necessarily, all institutions are subject to the laws of expansion and power in order to maintain themselves. As in many other observations, Erasmus set the pattern for another liberal from Basel, Jacob B. Burckhardt, in his analysis of power.[1]

For this reason, it is not surprising to see Erasmus, like Machiavelli, following the classical tradition of political philosophy as established by Aristotle and carried on by Polybius [c. 200–c. 118 BC] and Cicero (in *De Legibus*), which proclaimed the mixed constitution or the monarchical republic the best political constitution.

The fundamental differences and the final affinities between Machiavelli and Erasmus are obvious in the perennial ambivalence between state and society. The phenomenon of power was the principle of evil for Erasmus, the principle of reality for Machiavelli. The fundamental difference from Machiavelli led, however, to the political ideal of a limited monarchy or of a mixed constitution. Erasmus, the councilor of Charles V, had never failed to express frankly his deep contempt for the rule of an absolute monarch. From the *Adages* [1500][2] until his old age and the essay on the Turkish War [1530],[3] he openly proclaimed the irrationality and self-centered character of monarchs; he ridiculed the so-called heroic kings of Homer and complained of the barbaric temper of modern monarchs who never enjoyed a careful education for their responsibilities. The feudal classes are no better than the kings. Together, both are eager to exploit and destroy the wealth produced by the people's labor. The dynamics of power that do not refer to a frame of spiritual meaning lead again and again to the pursuit of unleashed desires and insatiable greed. For this reason, Erasmus sees the image of the tyrant as the eternal possibility of unlimited monarchies. A tyrant will treat his people as property and make himself absolute master. He will inspire fear and breed mutual suspicion. This is despotism. According to Erasmus, every sort of despotism degrades human beings and destroys human dignity. It is, like anarchy, beyond the pale of political institutions. Political control is administration, never domination. Almost literally, Erasmus presents the thesis of a liberal sociologist, Max Weber, that control means administration.

His proposals for checking arbitrariness and despotic tendencies are sociological rather than political or legal. Erasmus is neither a Machiavelli, nor a Montesquieu, because his main concern is not the world of secular institutions, but *Res Christiana*. Social alliances, however, might create a balance of power in the state. He suggests, first, that the city states should enter an *entente cordiale* with the industrial classes. Such power might enable them to limit the tyranny of the feudal and military classes. Second, he thinks it indispensable to restrict political authority by constitutional bonds. A mixed constitution is the wisest form of government. It is the wisest because it takes into consideration the fundamental mutuality of societal relationships and the lasting social problem of reconciling the individual with collective institutions. He bases the constitution on the mutual consensus of ruler and ruled. Princes and peoples should respect each other and rely on mutual good will. By introducing the idea of mutuality and consensus, Erasmus transfers his idea of spiritual democracy to the political plane. Authority and liberty should be distributed in such a way among the different social strata as to secure the harmony of the whole. For this purpose, intermediary groups should be organized and local self-government should perform political functions.

These suggestions follow classical traditions, as mentioned above. They are, however, not bookish but realistic, as were his debunking analyses of society and political elite. Machiavelli had referred his mixed constitution to the legal institutions of France. Erasmus could have illustrated his idea by describing the autonomous constitution of the Dutch Provinces within the Habsburg Empire, as an almost independent body politic within the Empire. The executive power was in the hands of the Chancellor of Burgundy, who was supported and elected by the Councils of State that represented the noble families. The General Estates represented the people as a whole. They were the delegates of the Provincial states and voted the taxes for the whole body politic. Such a system of checks and balances will prevent anarchy and tyranny. It follows the general pattern of medieval constitutions that are based on the mutual obligations of rulers and Estates. The ruler takes the oath to preserve the liberties and rights of the Estates, and these promise to defend the common good. When the Dutch revolted against Spain, they acted as true Erasmians. Philip II had broken his pledges and, thus, had broken the constitutional bonds.

There is still another source of Erasmus's liberalism. It stems from the religious sphere, which is constituted by the lasting interdependence and interaction of ecclesiastical authority and Christian liberty of the individuals. Both belong together for securing the continuous growth of the spiritual life. Here, again, a mixed constitution of monarchic, aristocratic, and democratic elements in the organization of the ecclesia deeply influenced the thought of Erasmus. The institution should see to it that the human being has a fence and a guide for coming into his own. The individual should watch the objective institutions to prevent their becoming ends in themselves. The individual, of course, is not an end in itself, but the representative of a Divine meaning whose kingdom the person enlarges by establishing spiritual liberty. Erasmus's thought is centered around *Res Christiana*, which sets the pattern for all societal relationships and social institutions. Mixed constitution means to Erasmus exactly the political establishment that makes possible the freedom of the spiritual person in his devotion to the religious goods.

It is a specific aspect of Erasmus's spiritual liberalism that he requests the political ruler to establish a pattern of ascetic life as most appropriate to his secular position. It is appropriate for very pragmatic reasons. The common people have lost respect for the professional asceticism of the orders. Widespread are the movements of mystical lay piety that preach voluntary asceticism to transform Christianity into a general way of life. The prince is the highest representative of society whose conduct establishes the consensus of the people and the unity of the state. He is subject to the same laws that bind his subjects. He is more responsible to the moral laws because it was his duty to protect and improve the lot of the common people. His is a "secular calvary" in the decisions and actions as ruler. For this reason, the Christian prince cannot divide his secular and spiritual behavior. The truth of Christ appears in our conduct. It is the privilege of the prince to set the pattern of the indivisible unity of secular and spiritual life in his ascetic conduct. In his letter to Francis I, Erasmus uses the symbol of the two swords for describing the duties of rulers. However, he applies the term not in the sense of legal delegation. Legal thinking is unfamiliar to Erasmus. He turns it to an interpretation that indicates subjective and objective aspects of participation in Christ. The ruler who carries the blessed sword is obliged to promote the objective goods of Christ as peace, concord, reconciliation, and to defend such status. The foremost example of Christian liberty is the ruler's total devotion and subjection to the obligations of patriarchal care for his people. This is the objective aspect of the spiritual theory of politics.

There remains the subjective side of the Erasmian theory. Erasmus interprets the term as indicating the subjective obligation of the ruler to follow Christ. The political ruler should live the *Imitatio*

Christi in order to direct and unite the consensus of ruler and people to the spiritual meaning of the organized life of society. Against the irrationality of human passions that strive to satisfy individual or collective selfishness, Erasmus creates a barrier in a social spiritualism. The ruler as saint is an Erasmian postulate that indicates a new trend in the relationship between temporal and spiritual spheres. This is no longer the tradition of medieval political philosophy, which carefully distinguished political and ecclesiastical realms. Erasmus inaugurated a new attitude toward the world. His social spiritualism closes the dualism of the medieval world between the spiritual and secular areas. It indicates the indissoluble unity of the religious and temporal as integrated by the practical Christ in all social institutions. Princes, clergy, and the Christian people are one republic, not a hierarchy. This world is a republic because Christ is the center of the social whole and integrates the varieties of functions into the unity of living action of society. All members of the republic should refer their tasks to the living spirit of Christ, which is peace, concord, and reconciliation. It is Erasmus's main concern to point out that peace is the telos of divine creation because it is the inner meaning of Christ and logos alike. Peace is never a social status, but a lasting process, a problem that all groups have to solve again and again. Erasmus has illuminated the condition for peace on all levels of society. He analyses relationships among friends, husband and wife, dissenting clergy, rulers and ruled. In all cases, he comes to the conclusion that peace can be established when enough prudence and wisdom make possible sympathetic understanding. This can be created by that part of the relationship that is capable of the stronger educational Eros.

For this reason, Erasmus turned all social and political analyses to the problems of war and peace as the fundamental problems of individual and collective relationships. He dealt with the problem of war and peace in church, state, and social institutions. He recognized three valid motives for going to war in an emergency situation. He protested violently against the charge of having preached total pacifism. He never ceased investigating the causes and motives that disturb peace and produce wars. In these analyses, he is as cautious and disillusioned as in the analyses of social and political institutions. He admits a strictly defensive war in order to repel invaders. He reluctantly grants the war against the Turks if it serves the purpose of protecting the survival of Christian civilization, or of spreading the Christian religion. For this reason, he develops a third category, which he takes seriously, although he seems to limit it to pre-Christian societies. He speaks of the war of civilized nations against barbarians as legitimate political action. He refers to pagan emperors who fought easy and nonbloody wars and improved the social and economic conditions of the conquered. Sometimes their clemency reconciled the vanquished and raised their standards.

He mentions the last category mainly in order to remark that these three cases did not play any role among the Christian princes during the preceding two decades. He classified the actual motives leading toward military conflict between states.

> 1. There are always personal motives among the rulers that still play an important role. Glory and prestige of the monarchs, personal superiority and pride, inferiority and anger frequently contribute to producing war.
>
> 2. There are vested interests among the advisors of kings to drive toward war; the military and young courtiers who want to make their careers, will always favor war.
>
> 3. There are the legal advisors and the learned statesmen who reinterpret treaties and alliances

again and again. They are possessed by the idea of expansion, which is more an expression of fear and insecurity than of strength and competition. He knows, although he does not formulate it, that these men are subject to the logic of the body politic. They contend that laws of nature, laws of society, custom, and usage compel them to repel force by force and defend life, and money, too, which is, to some persons, as dear as life. Erasmus is willing to grant such arguments as valid for pagan statesmen. He rejects them for the Christian world. He refuses to acknowledge the logic and necessity of expansion. This is a never-ending process if taken as necessary. He wishes to reduce the *pragma* of power to psychological motives of fear, anger, and ambition. However, he sees very clearly that there are motives that cannot be reduced to individual psychology.

4. The elite wage war for social reasons in order to break the unity of society and oppress and exploit it without resistance.

5. Similarly, the establishment of despotism is best secured by a victorious war that increases the material and moral power of the ruler and of the military. These domestic reasons cannot be reduced to individual psychology. They are truly sociological motives.

6. Finally, he sees that rich and prosperous administrations and flourishing societies attract war-loving neighbors, as did France twice in twelve years.

Erasmus derived his critical analysis from a comprehensive observation of his world. He was well acquainted with rulers and their councilors—many Erasmians were in leading positions and gave him information about matters of state that he was eager to receive. This material made him as disillusioned about the ways of politics as the statesmen who have practiced them. Actually, he developed all the sociological theories on military expansion that have been elaborated scientifically since the development of separate social sciences.

Erasmus was not a defeatist, in spite of his conviction that the autonomous state is evil in itself. He was certainly not an optimistic man of the Enlightenment, as he is frequently presented. He was a reformer, nevertheless, though he never believed that his political and social treatises would have any influence on the princes and rulers to whom they were addressed. However, he was well aware that his opinions, made public, would strengthen the position and action of the learned councilors and civil statesmen to come to a fair deal by compromise. The sociologist might remark that one of his evolutionary accomplishments was the establishment of a kind of public opinion among the learned and educated classes, a remarkable contribution to democracy. This is conspicuous in his various suggestions on avoiding war and establishing firm and permanent peace. These ideas range from reconsidering legal and political habits to manipulating public opinion and to elevating the sentiments of the common people.

First, he detests the role of jurists in the conduct of foreign affairs. They abuse the spirit of law by distorting its letter, and they are not afraid of forging documents in making legal claims. They have completely submitted to the political rulers. They applied the legal formulations of treaties to disguise their true purposes and providing for future claims. They rationalize fear and suspicion in such documents. For this reason, Erasmus desires the utmost limitation of treaties and alliances because of their psychological effects on mutual feelings of insecurity. Second, he holds one specific type of treaty responsible for many wars and condemns political marriages. Again and again, these contracts lead to conflict on succession and inheritance rights; hence, he wishes them abolished. Third, he would like to see the princes surrounded by learned and responsible civilians, who would be able to check the influence of ambitious generals and of young courtiers, who are always in favor of war for advancing their careers. Such advisors could turn the royal good will toward the social and economic problems of the people, the improvement of which would have its effect on the economic power of the state. Thus, the princes would discover that inner prosperity is preferable to outer adventure.

Erasmus's most serious proposal is the postulate that no war should be waged that has not the full and unanimous consent of the people. This is most indicative of his political stand that is so frequently misinterpreted. Even if "people" does not mean the modern mass democracy, it means, at least, all political assemblies of the Estates, which would be a democratic device for the sixteenth century anyway. These suggestions are constructive. They are followed by some negative recommendations that imply the positive attitude. If war is inescapable, it should be conducted in such a way that the severest calamities may fall upon the leader of those who gave the occasion. Repeatedly, he states that in war the innocent and peaceful suffer most: landholders and tradesmen, manufacturers and husbandmen. People who have vested interests in war, however, such as courtiers, kings, bankers, remain in safety and get rich. They are eager to forget that one can buy peace if one invests in just causes and compromises with an unjust enemy in order to preserve the wellbeing and the future progress of the people.

Erasmus is aroused by the techniques of propaganda that the warmongers use to incite the common people and to create hatred against enemies. He resents the idol of national glory. He takes it for granted that people everywhere accept their habits and mores as natural and those of the foreigner as funny and strange. But he knows, as well, that people do not necessarily draw the conclusion that they are superior to others. Common people everywhere know that they live in a communion of suffering under the bad will of their rulers. Kings and their courtiers invented the phantom of national glory that is the identification of their vain ambitions with the destiny of peace loving people. Erasmus is too sensitive a scholar of language not to be shocked by its manipulation for inflaming the sentiments of the common people. He mentions one specific case that anticipates Nazi methods against France and England, and was probably used by the Spanish-Dutch bureaucracy for breaking the national unity of France. These warmongers addressed the civil populations of some northwestern French areas and attempted to confuse the inhabitants by recalling their historical origins and calling them Germans. He despises this kind of warfare and demands its abolishment. He revolts against making peace-loving common people the victims of sophisticated official warmongers and propaganda chiefs. His formulation leads to contemporary content analysis:

> Such is the depravity of their minds that they seek occasions of difference where none is afforded either by nature or institution. They would divide France against herself, in verbal and nominal distinctions of the inhabitants, a country which is not divided by seas or mountains, and is one and indivisible, however men endeavor to carve divisions into it by distinctions merely nominal. Thus some of the French they will denominate Germans, lest

> the circumstances of identity of name should produce that unanimity which they diabolically wish to interrupt.

Finally, Erasmus turns his critical suggestions on Church and clergy, whose behavior was the hardest blow to a sincere educator of mankind, as Erasmus was. Popes and high dignitaries of the Church waged war and instigated military conflicts instead of reconciling the adversaries. Young priests, like courtiers, were anxious to become army chaplains in order to be promoted. Without legal coercion, they completely submitted to the state and preached Christ on either side of the fence. Erasmus explains this perverse phenomenon by a sociological analysis. The Church has become the victim of its own imperialistic control over the political world as a body politic. The clergy could not avoid intercourse with the world; it could not escape accumulating and hoarding the goods that the world values. In this process, the men of the Church have gradually adopted the manners of the world, even in the retreat of the monastic orders, where antagonistic "vested interests" clash with each other and raise violent conflicts among Christian institutions. Erasmus never forgot the experience at Bologna when he saw the triumphant entrance of victorious Julius II [1443–1513], the "Warrior Pope," clad in shining armor. The urgent duty of pope and clergy is to relinquish confounding temporal and spiritual values, to work continuously for realizing the Christian League, and to offer their disinterested services as arbitrators. This suggestion refers to the Holy See and the diplomacy of the higher clergy.

Erasmus offered yet two more suggestions that pertain to the national clergy in the independent states. He was convinced that people and rulers would be deeply shocked and would reconsider waging war if the respective clergies would refuse burial in consecrated grounds to those slain in battle, instead of blessing their arms.

The clergy should see to it that they debunk military romanticism and national vanity. They could do it easily if they would refuse religious blessings to the trophies of war.

> Clergy do not hesitate to hang up flags, standards, banners and other trophies of war, brought from the field of carnage as ornaments of churches. . . . These trophies . . . all stained and smeared with the blood of men for whom Christ shed his blood, are hung in the churches among the tombs and images of apostles and martyrs as if in future it were to be reckoned a mark of sanctity not to suffer martyrdom but to inflict it, not to lay down one's own life for the truth, but to take the lives of others for worldly purposes of vanity and avarice. It would be quite sufficient if the bloody rags were hung in some corner of the Exchange.

These propositions indicate Erasmus's will to contribute pragmatically to the fundamental problems of war and peace. He stated time and again that his relativistic pacifism was a constituent of his political thought and of his spiritual doctrine of man. The question of war is primarily a moral and human—not a legal—phenomenon. As compared to an unjust peace, the just war is hell, for war is the most atrocious of all crimes. It corrupts all moral and religious standards among victors and vanquished alike, and it is an economic disaster for both. Finally, it is the most terrible calamity for the common people, for whom Christ shed his blood as much as for the rich and the princes. For this reason, the sublime rulers and sympathetic princes should overlook offenses and injuries in order not to jeopardize the tranquility and well-being of their subjects. They are well aware that, in a Christian world, there is not domination, but patriarchal administration. Ruler and people are united by mutual confidence and trust, because they live in the orbit of Christian liberty to which every human being is called. Spiritual democracy is the basis for political democracy.

The analyses of various social strata illuminate his religious concern. According to Erasmus, it is primarily a *spiritual* responsibility of the ruling elite to secure standards of life for the middle classes that make it possible to realize the Christian way of life. It must be emphasized that Erasmus prescribes as *religious* duty what medieval authors considered *political* obligations. It is, of course, correct to say that all social rules—as they appear in Erasmus—focus on past philosophical treatises. However, the frame of reference has changed. Erasmus rejects the division of labor between laity and ecclesia. Laity will cooperate in establishing Christ's teaching and image in the here and now, and in the routine of everyday life. This implies an organization of society in which elements of democracy are inevitable, whatever may be the distribution of status and authority.

His analyses of the state of societies and of their political institutions led him to the conclusion that they were rushing toward new kinds of coercive organizations. He characterized them as victims of the strongest organized power, such as princes wealthy enough to hire powerful armies with which to establish a military despotism. This will be, he thought, the end of political and civil liberties, of the authority of Estates, and of political consensus. This is not any longer a body politic, because any kind of despotism is, like anarchy, beyond the pale of rational political constitutions. Such a modern type of government can only be compared to the Roman principate [27 BC–284 AD] and the regime of the barrack emperors.

He summarized his findings on the grim logic of the autonomy of social institutions and of collective pressure in a grave statement that is totally different from the serene discovery of this sociological rule in the *Praise of Folly*. It is significant that he made this remark in a theological commentary: "Habet et hic mundus ordinem suum quam non expedit a nobis perturbari." ["This world has an order all its own, which is not good for us to disturb."—Eds.]

Erasmus is never mentioned in textbooks on history of political and social ideas. This can be justified because his main concern was *Res Christiana*, which meant to him the merging and unifying of spiritual and social spheres and the establishment of Christianity as a way of life leading toward Christian liberty. This last heroic effort of the Christian world was finally defeated in the Puritan Revolution. What remained were the elements of political and social thought that are the foundations of modern democracy and liberalism.

For this reason, one regrets that modern histories of social ideas still remain silent on Erasmus and Social Spiritualism. This is a grave omission, for Erasmus makes evident that democratic and individual liberties from despotism are constructive merely as freedom to serve supreme goods and spiritual ideals. Erasmus knew that all social institutions may easily turn to despotic practices when broken loose from a philosophical or spiritual frame of reference. He was imbued with the spirit of social spiritualism. Erasmus's Social Spiritualism was not a pattern of Utopian thinking. Rather was it the proposition of reform—*quand même*! He called upon individual souls to change; he did not trust a general transformation of social institutions.

Hence, Erasmus was not a political philosopher at all. What, then, was his field and contribution? He had refused to be called a theologian, and he was not a philosopher. He wanted to be a philologist and educator. As lover of logos, Erasmus felt himself to be in the service of God and Christ, who are all pervading logos. He served society by preparing youth for listening to the logos in themselves and for taking it as tradition and learning. He explicitly distinguished his calling from that of a scholar. The scholar is concerned with establishing truth for the sake of truth among fellow scholars. The educator is called upon to spread truth for the sake of its effects on our lives. Erasmus considered its improving effects on human minds. He did not mean "moral improvement" in a narrow sense. As lover of logos, the educator should see to it that his students were enlightened on their social obligations and illuminated on their spiritual responsibilities. As a Christian Socrates, Erasmus was convinced that understanding these truths meant realizing them in our very lives. Moral and spiritual learning as a way of life lead to Christian liberty, tranquility of mind, and peace of conscience—ideals of human perfection on which pagans and Christians agree, Epicurus and Christ.

Education opens the avenues to this goal. For this reason, all social institutions are to be transformed into institutes of education. Church, state, and family are schools on various planes of living that should elaborate their respective logoi and stimulate the participation of all who share in the all-pervading logos. Thus, the content of history is the Education of Mankind. From Erasmus, there is a straight road that leads to Gotthold Ephraim Lessing [1729–1781].

However, there is no universal law of progress. Progress remains a lasting tradition of learning and interpretation. It coexists with the lasting *lex degenerandi* in all social institutions. It has no lasting effect in transforming society. Human nature will remain the same: *never* will Pharisee-ism die out; *never* will the freedom of the Gospel not be attacked by ecclesiastics; *never* will the world stop persecuting the saints to the end of the world; *never* will pious and sincere people be more than a tiny flock.

The world of institutions is evil. Perfection is possible for the individual soul dedicated to the imitation of Christ and Socrates, through whom he participates in a larger whole. For those souls, democratic institutions must exist in church and state in order to open the avenues to Christian people who are not afraid to take upon themselves the hardships of learning and the adventures of knowing for the sake of realizing Christian liberty.

Notes

1. [See Jacob Burckhardt, *Die Zeit Constantin's des Grossen* (Leipzig: E. A. Seemann, 1853); *The Age of Constantine the Great*, trans. Moses Hadas (New York: Pantheon Books, 1949).—Eds.]

2. [See *Adagia* in Latine and English (London: Bernard Alsop, 1621).—Eds.]

3. [See *Consultatio de bello Turico* (Antwerp: Mich. Hillen van Hoochstraten, 1530).—Eds.]

3

Humanistic Contributions to Public Health

As soon as the ruling groups of a society are aware of the epidemic character of a disease, they will attempt to prevent its spread in order to protect their society. Since 1936, for instance, the United States Surgeon General has made great efforts to enlighten the American public about the dangers of syphilis.[1] The surgeon general's campaign against the disease led to many practical steps that helped check its spread, especially since the Second World War.

The most important points of the surgeon general's campaign were as follows:

> 1. There should be a public health staff to deal with syphilis.
>
> 2. State laws should require (at a minimum) reporting of cases, follow-up of victims' illness, and the search for the sexual contacts that led to infection.
>
> 3. Premarital medical certificates should be a legal requirement.

Previously unpublished. Undated manuscript located in file on Albert Salomon, Leo Baeck Institute, New York, New York. Published by permission from Leo Baeck Institute.

> 4. Treatment facilities should be of good quality, including providing hospital beds to victims. Every pregnant woman who is infected must be treated to prevent infected offspring.
>
> 5. This public education program must be persistent, intensive, and aimed especially at the age group when syphilis is most frequently acquired.

Men of the Renaissance postulated all of the regulations—both preventive and remedial—contained in the surgeon general's program. This underlines the realistic trend in the Renaissance, a general intellectual movement in the Western world. New realism means to rely on the minutest observation of man in society, instead of relying on traditional authorities, ecclesiastical and philosophical alike. The famous statement by Niccolò Machiavelli [1469–1527]—that we are not interested in knowing what man ought to be, but what he actually is—indicates this trend toward realism. The same realism is conspicuous among some religious thinkers, like Martin Luther [1483–1546] and Desiderius Erasmus [1466–1536], who violently criticized the practical policies and administration of the Church as irreconcilable with its ideas.

Erasmus was not only a religious thinker. All humanists shared in the realistic movement. They all wished to recognize the very nature of human behavior and of societal relationships as they developed out of human nature, not as postulated by theological and moral philosophies. The medical profession could not remain untouched by such general thought. So, it is not strange that we find a lively interest in problems of medicine and public health among the humanists of Italy, France, and the countries around the Rhine. One of the chief concerns was the problem of a new epidemic—whether it was new or had been latent does not concern us here—that had spread within ten years after 1494 all over the world.[2]

The period in which the new realism came into being was similar to our own. It was a time of radical change. Technological inventions (like gunpowder, the printing press, and the discovery of the New World), the claims of sovereignty by the national states, and the resulting wars and the national revolt against the universal Church made possible the state of mind that was critical against all traditions and authorities.

The life and work of Erasmus is one of the liveliest images of this situation in the Renaissance. Erasmus is known as a humanist who dedicated his life to establishing a pattern of Christian piety that stressed religion as a way of life. The truth of religion should be verified by the conduct of men and their mutual relationships. For this reason, Erasmus, who is supposed to have been an ivory-tower humanist, was deeply concerned to investigate the conditions of man in social, political, and economic affairs. Because Erasmus was worried about the gap between his ideas of Christian living and actual social reality, he was one of the few humanists who attacked vigorously the problem of public health in the years in which syphilis spread all over Europe. He does not deal with this problem in a systematic way in his work. But we find over and over again—in *Lingua, Consultatio de bello Turcico*, and in his *Colloquia*—passages that disclose how much he was alarmed by the contagious character of the disease and reflections about its causes, effects, and possible modes of prevention. In particular, there are many passages about syphilis in his *Colloquia*, principally dialogues that look at the same objects from many sides. He used these for teaching Latin to young students because he believed that Latin should be a living, not a dead, language and that the boys should be able to discuss current problems of general interest.

It is thought that Erasmus himself suffered from syphilis.[3] According to his description, only peasants are relatively free from the disease. The ruling groups, who should be especially careful about health concerns, along with the urban population, the military, and the clergy, all think it fashionable to be afflicted with this disease. Because of his exact knowledge of syphilis, Erasmus concludes that it is worse than all other epidemics. He warns that the "pox," as syphilis came to be called, is more infectious and destructive than the worst of leprosy. He notes that the disease invades suddenly and sometimes has a long incubation, and other times kills quickly, while leprosy will allow its victims to live to extreme old age. What illness, besides syphilis, sticks so strongly or repulses more stubbornly the art and cure of the physicians, Erasmus queries in the *Lingua* in 1525. There, he gives a masterly, drastic description of a syphilitic in the tertiary stage: the snub nose, dragging of one leg, itchy hands, stinking breath, heavy eyes, running nose and ears. It is clear to him that the main cause of spreading this disease is dissipation and sexual intercourse, as he says in the Epicurean: "When young men by whoring, as it commonly falls out, get the pox, by which they are often brought to death's door in their lifetime, and carry about a dead carcass."

It is a characteristic feature of Erasmus's minute observations that he understands very well that there are many other ways of getting infected: by kissing, drinking out of the same cup, sleeping in the same bed with an afflicted person, using the sheets in which an afflicted person has lain, by the touch of the finger, and by using the scissors or comb of barbers who have trimmed someone with the disease.

Erasmus is not satisfied to describe the phenomenon but is eager to ask for laws to prevent the spreading of the disease. Although the passages mentioned demonstrate his keen and provoking observations, he indicates that his novel idea is very modest indeed. He simply suggests applying to syphilis rules widely extant in Europe since the epidemics of leprosy and plague in the fourteenth century, some of them going back to Leviticus 13:45. He states that the same care ought to be taken to prevent so fatal an evil as syphilis, as did the Italians in the case of leprosy. "It is an act of piety to take care of the public good at the inconvenience of a few." At the end of the fourteenth century in the Netherlands, one finds in the *Regulae Technicae Contra Pestilentium*: "De quibus patet, quod vestes morientium non debent subito vendi . . . sic securius esset omnia combuere quam vendere, ut saepius fit in Italia in principiis pestilentiae."[4] One also finds the Edict of Aberdeen in 1497: "To avoid the infirmity cumm out of Franche and foreign parts that all licht weman are ordered to desist their vices and sin of venerie, that their houses are closed, that they have to work for their living under the pain of being branded with a hot iron on their cheeks and banished from the town. . . . That diligent inquisition be taken of all infected persons with this strange seiknes of Nappilis for the safety of the town and that the persons infected therwith be chargit to keip them in their houses and out of places from the healthy folks." Another sanitary ordinance forbids the folks infested with "seikenes of Nappilis to be seen at slaughterhouses, butcher-houses, bakeries, breweries, dairies, for the safety of the town. The persones infected should stay quietly in their houses . . . till they are healed, not to infect their neighbors." Also, the Edinburgh edict of 1497 includes the reference: ". . . as all infected persons within the freedom of this burgh brought upon the island of Leith and . . . furnished with victuals till God proved they were healthy."[5]

Erasmus also proposes a constructive program of public health initiatives. In spite of his liberal ideas on political constitution, he remains medieval in his suggestion to make the state the bearer of a public health administration and accompanying legislation. His proposals are perfectly in line with our contemporary thinking. He strongly suggests establishing a law that prevents syphilitics from marrying. In the event that one has knowingly married a syphilitic, he urges both partners to be banished from society. He invites the Holy See to annul such marriages that were based on the lie of one partner that he or she was in good health. He repeatedly insists that states enact such legislation, stating that marriage and procreation are not the private affairs of citizens. Health is indeed a public affair and the state should take care that children born from a union are healthy. He grimly compares the thoughtlessness and carelessness of men, in regard to their offspring, with the painstaking trouble they take to breed noble horses, dogs, and healthy pigs. Erasmus blames and explains such thoughtfulness as deriving from the ineradicable greed of men to advance on the social ladder of status and prestige regardless of the price their children have to pay. In the dialogue, *Unequal Marriage*, he describes as a typical case the tragic lot of a young, beautiful, intelligent girl married to an old, but titled, syphilitic.

Although Erasmus was in the avant-garde on this issue, he was not alone in his fight. His fellow humanist, sometime friend and later enemy, Ulrich von Hutten [1488–1523]—German scholar, poet, and satirist—gave a remarkable description of the symptoms and cure of syphilis. Still more remarkable is his analysis of the reasons that different contemporary groups give for the outbreak of the disease:

> According to the *theologians,* God has disseminated this malady in anger and in order to punish creatures whose vices have outraged His Majesty. The priests have preached these doctrines from the pulpit, as though they have been revealed to them by the Almighty. . . . The conduct of the *physicians* has been similar to that of the

> priests and instead of searching for remedies that might cure, they have fled from the presence of the people who have been stricken with this illness and have restrained from touching them. . . . For a long time, the matter of occult causation has been discussed by physicians and is far from being solved. There is an extreme divergence of sentiment and that they are in accord on one point alone is easy to understand. Some affirm, in these unfortunate times, that the air suddenly charges itself with miasmas and that impure wind has corrupted the waters. . . . The *astrologers,* who pretend to explain everything by the movements of the stars, trace the epidemic to the conjunction of Mars and Saturn. . . . These savants, in particular, who consulted the stars, predicted that the scourge would last only seven years, but they made a profound mistake. Had they announced that over this period the malady would disappear, or at least its symptoms would disappear in an individual who had contracted the disease, they would have been correct. Furthermore, they would not have been wrong had they stated that the virulence and contagion of the disease would lose their initial intensity. . . . The virus persists, still dangerous, but its effects are less rapid. . . . At this moment, no one contracts this malady unless exposed to it directly. The disease in general is *caught by sexual contact* with women who have venomous poison in their secret places, being very dangerous for those who meddle with them. Sickness got by such congress with such infected women is so much the more vehement how much they be inwardly infected. Children and old people are more rarely infected.

Hutten also stated, "This disease not longe after its beginning entered into Germania, where it wandered more largely than in any other place: Which thynge I do ascribe to our intemperance." He continued: "Many physicians advance the theory that the malady was engendered by an internal tainted principle, by corrupted humors, melancholic dissicatedness, by yellow bile or by phlegm that had been burned or salted. . . . Other physicians, without entering into a thorough explanation, are contented to tell us that the scourge is an infection caused by the corruption of the blood." So wrote Hutton in 1519.[6] He died of the disease in 1523.

It is interesting to note that the Italian poet, Girolamo Fracastoro [1478–1553], wrote two works about syphilis. His famous epic poem, *Syphilis sive morbus gallicus* [1530], still clings to the traditions based on the traditions of Hippocrates [460–370 BC], the Arabic physicians, and Galen [Aelius Galenus (129–200)]. Whereas in *De Contagione et Contagiosis Morbis*, Fracastoro saw clearly in 1546 that syphilis was contracted by the union of the sexes and that a suckling would contract the malady from an infected wet-nurse or that a child who happened to have the disease would give it to her.

William Clowes [1540–1604], a well-known London surgeon, attributes part of his knowledge concerning syphilis to Ambroise Paré [1510–1590], the royal surgeon for several French kings.[7] In his *Profitable and Necessarie Booke of Obseruations*,[8] Clowes gives case histories of persons who had no signs of syphilis at those parts of the body that are the most suspicious and most speedily infected. He talks, for instance, about a young girl of twelve years of age with hard swellings and ulcers that corrupted her bones. He ponders whether she got the sickness from infected parents or whether it was caused by sucking the milk of an infected nurse, a correct observation mixed with humoral philosophy. Another remarkable observation of Clowes: three cases of good and honest midwives infected with the disease by bringing abed three infected women. He also reports that one infected wet-nurse gave syphilis to a whole family. The husband had granted his most chaste wife's desire to nurse her newborn child on the condition that a nurse should share in her trouble and pains. The nurse infected the child, the child the mother, the mother the husband, and the two other children whom he had daily at his table and bed.

[Salomon's essay ends with a reiteration of his original argument that humanistic thinkers anticipated the main postulates of the much later public campaign (1936) to combat syphilis. We wish to note that Salomon's main point in making his case is his insistence that the humanistic thinkers that most concerned him were utterly devoted, first and foremost, to immediate social realities as they observed them.—Eds.]

Notes

1. [Thomas Parran Jr., "Syphilis: a Public Health Problem," *American Association for the Advancement of Science*, No. 6 (1936): 187; Thomas Parran Jr., "Why Don't We Stamp Out Syphilis?," *Reader's Digest* (July 1936): 65–73; Thomas Parran Jr., *Shadow on the Land: Syphilis* (American Social Hygiene Association, 1938).—Eds.]

2. [Scientists have long debated the origins of syphilis. The "Columbian theory" argues that Christopher Columbus's crew brought this New World disease back to Europe from his 1493 expedition to the Americas. The "Pre-Columbian theory" argues that syphilis existed in Europe long before the Columbian expedition but was mistaken for leprosy. The tertiary stages of both diseases are quite similar. In any event, there was an outbreak of syphilis in Naples, Italy, in 1494/1495 that quickly spread throughout the continent. For a thorough discussion, see Alfred W. Crosby, *The Columbian Exchange: Biological and Cultural Consequences of 1492* (Westport, CT: Greenwood, 1972).—Eds.]

3. [Andreas Werthemann, *Schädel und Gebeine des Erasmus von Rotterdam* (Basel: Birkhäuser, 1930).—Eds.]

4. [Karl Sudhoff, *Aus der Frühgeschichte der Syphilis: Handschriften- und Inkunabelstudien epidemiologische Untersuchung und Kritische Gänge, mit 6 Tafeln* (Leipzig: J. A. Barth, 1912).—Eds.]

5. [Henry E. Sigerist, *Civilization and Disease* (Ann Arbor: University of Michigan Press, 1915).—Eds.]

6. [*De Guaiaci Medicina Et Morbo Gallico Liber Unus* (Mogutiae: In aedibus Ioannis Scheffer, 1519).—Eds.]

7. [See Ambroise Paré, "Of the Causes of Lues Venerea," in *Workes*, trans. T. Johnson (London: 1634), 724.—Eds.]

8. [(London: Edm. Bollifant for Thomas Dawson, 1596). Appended to this larger work is "a short treatise, for the cure of lues venerea, by vnctions and other approued waies of curing, heretofore by me collected." This was also published separately at London: Printed by Thomas East for Thomas Cadman, Dvvelling in Paules Churchyard, at the signe of the Bible, 1585.—Eds.]

4

Hugo Grotius and the Social Sciences

To commemorate a great scholar and his work does not mean to dust off a statue in the museum of cultural history. Rather, the student's duty is to see to it that the images of scholarship are reinterpreted again and again, in order to preserve the perpetual presence of the living spirit. Such reconsideration of the past makes it possible to examine the active forces in our own scientific efforts.

The social scientist who wishes to contribute to such a reexamination of the work of Hugo Grotius [1583–1645] and to justify his own intrusion into the domain of jurisprudence feels inclined to begin with a famous quotation. This old saying goes: "Boys read Terence one way, Grotius another way." The social scientist may even expand the statement by adding that the readers of Grotius have understood him differently in different periods. It is the variety of these interpretations that permits the social scientist to add to his understanding of the great jurist's achievement, as a modest contribution to the comprehensive character of Grotius and to the origin of the social sciences.

We are accustomed to identifying the name of Grotius with his *On the Law of War and Peace* [De Jure Belli ac Pacis (1625)]. Actu-

---

Published originally in a slightly different form in *Political Science Quarterly* 62 (March 1947), 62–81. Republished by permission from *Political Science Quarterly.*

ally, the man exercised a much wider influence by his book on Dutch jurisprudence (still in use in English law schools), by his theological and exegetic writings, and by his religious poetry, which was dear to Milton. Nevertheless, the social scientist will necessarily restrict his consideration to Grotius's most famous book, which has exercised a powerful influence in the rise of the social sciences.

As a result of this book and of the Thirty Years' War [1618–1648], the Elector of the Palatinate established a chair of Natural Law and the Law of Nations at Heidelberg in 1661. He called Samuel von Pufendorf [1632–1694] to teach this subject. Pufendorf believed himself to be the true successor to Grotius, whom he had called "the founder of natural law." The formula should indicate that Grotius had succeeded in separating the study of moral and social norms from the religious sphere and in establishing a secular science of social behavior. Pufendorf, still close to Grotius's influence, remarkably distorts the meaning of the master's work. He attributes a merit to Grotius that belongs to Thomas Hobbes [1588–1679], whose anthropological theories were shared by Pufendorf. This misinterpretation, however, had both a positive and negative effect. The negative result was the never-ending repetition of Pufendorf's thesis that Grotius had succeeded in secularizing natural law. The positive consequence was that Pufendorf introduced *Law of War and Peace* as a textbook in the classes on natural law. Many rulers followed the example set by the ruler of Heidelberg. Chairs of natural law were established in the Protestant countries, and the professors, imitating Pufendorf, introduced Grotius's book as required reading. Thus, it became a stimulus to the rise of liberal and social thinking. In the reformed Scottish universities, the treatise had suggested the organization of the required courses in moral philosophy as natural theology, natural law, ethics, and politics. Adam Smith gratefully recognized his indebtedness to Grotius. In France,

Grotius was still a living force to Montesquieu and to some authors of the *Encyclopédie.*

During the nineteenth century, the book was restricted to the law schools. It is difficult for us to hear the overtones of deep satisfaction in the statement of the Napoleon of historicism, Hegel, when he wrote: "Nobody reads it any more." In the hands of students of constitutional and international law, the older comprehensive frame of reference was slowly vanishing. The specialized and positive jurists began to complain of puristic deficiencies, of a relapse as compared to Johannes Althusius [1563–1638], and of the ambiguity of Grotius's legal and sociological concepts. In particular, after the end of the First World War, the students of international law believed that they had found a description of international institutions in the treatise. In 1946, after the shock of the Second World War, and equipped with more articulate tools—such as formal and interpretive sociologies, Gestalt psychology, and phenomenology—the social scientist reopens the book and reads the title *On the Law of War and Peace, three books in which the Law of Nature and of Nations and the principles of constitutional law are explained.* Obviously, Grotius has written a book on natural law with the emphasis on the legalization of war.

The social scientist is primarily concerned with the aspect of the book that was lost in the epoch of historicism—all the more when he sees his own task as that of reestablishing natural law with the tools of modern science and philosophy. Purposely, he must exclude the topics that the jurist and the political scientist will emphasize. He has to neglect the theory of sovereignty, the classification of just and unjust wars, and the elaborate systematization of the rules of military action in their positive legal connotation.

The social scientist will refer to the interpretation that Grotius has presented as to the unique character of the book and its meaning for his time. Grotius insists on the novelty and keenness of his enterprise. His is not a theoretical, but a practical, concern. He endeavors to give a thorough and catholic presentation of the patterns and attitudes of man in society as a handbook for the intelligent ruler and statesman. His work is supposed to be a clarification and systematization of a plurality of legal, moral, and theological ways of dealing with human nature. He reproaches the juristic theologians and the theological moralists with having confused the different spheres of the law and with not having distinguished the sequence and order of norms that establish rights and obligations. They have made the mistake, according to Grotius, of having used the positive laws of the state to establish sweeping generalizations and precarious systems. They have failed to see the arbitrary and specific character of most laws that are established by the body politic. On the other hand, they have neglected the tremendous material that history offers to the scholar engaged in the study of the constancy of man in the variety of his historical guises. Grotius will use his encyclopedic, historical, and juristic knowledge to avoid their mistakes. He will rediscover the potential "common sense of mankind" as the enduring sympathetic consciousness of the inner normativity of human nature whatever may be the changing conditions in time and space. He will help to preserve it by illuminating the minds of rulers and ruled.

For this reason, Grotius regards it as his accomplishment to have founded the *ars naturalis et perpetuae jurisprudentiae*, connecting the tradition of moral and spiritual values with the new scientific methods. This is a scientific discipline that has detached itself both from the theological frame of reference and from the arbitrary laws of the state. He calls his enterprise "the most urgent and noble." It is noble because it is a system of universal jurisprudence that will be the indispensable instrument to all rulers in their efforts to extend progressively the rule of law and to limit the sphere of human insecurity. As such, it will enlighten the statesmen and will help to raise the standards of the whole society. He knows that his system is not yet perfect. He humbly admits that he has only laid the foundations upon which future generations might construct a perfect edifice. He has worked out a first draft of a social system for our better understanding of the social forces and human motives that make for the duration and continuity of society at large on the different planes of living. His effort is noble because he offers an intellectual guide to all men who wish to understand the constructive and destructive forces of human nature and the ability of sympathetic human intelligence to know the divine laws and lead men to loftier moral standards and a more perfect social order. The work seems to him noble because it presents the variety of rational and sympathetic experiences so that man may understand that he is still—in spite of the cruelty and wickedness in which life involves him—the animal dearest to God.

The book seems to Grotius urgent as a response to the alarming situation of the times. He does not restrict his complaints to the savagery of warfare, although he could already imagine that the Great War would compete with those of the past in lawlessness and barbarism. He sees a spirit of revolution spreading to all fields of thought and action. His is the vision of a basically revolutionary period. He had experienced a special variant of the general revolution as a member of the federal and patrician party in the Netherlands that was swept away by the cooperation between the popular party and the executive. They had erected a centralized sovereign state that was virtually the dictatorship of Prince Moritz of Oranien. Grotius had been jailed and, after his escape, exiled. As an exile, he visualized the universal state of revolution. As he saw it, the political revolution and civil wars were a logical outcome of the religious revolutions of the Reformation. Although he belonged to the most liberal group of Protestants, he was deeply worried about the final result of the destruction of the universal Church. Everywhere, he observed a growing irrationalism and an intellectual defeatism. He was keenly aware of the growing intellectual, moral, and social insecurity and the impact of brute power and coercion that were everywhere undermining the sense of right and justice, in conquerors and conquered, in rulers and ruled alike. Might was prior to right. Right was a tool of expediency, according to the advantages of the respective parties. This element of the Machiavellian raison d'être was one aspect of the universal nihilism that threatened to destroy civilization at its roots—the roots Grotius held to be classical logos and Christian spirit.

Explicitly, Grotius wrote his treatise against this trend of his times. He hoped that it would help to stem the tide of violent and irrational lawlessness in thought and action. It was his experience that all things become uncertain the moment they depart from law. He desired to reawaken the sense of legality and morality by inducing men to reconsider the basic intelligibility of the requirements of the social ethos. But he was fully aware that even the most perfect state of law is never completely safe. "Human nature exists under such conditions that complete security is never guaranteed to us. For protection against uncertain fears we must rely on Divine Providence, and on a wariness free from reproach, not on force."

Although the book is primarily directed against the negative aspects of his times, it is allied to the constructive thinking of the period. Like the great liberals of the eighteenth and nineteenth centuries, Edmund Burke [1729–1797] and Alexis de Tocqueville [1805–1859], Grotius strives to go beyond the alternatives of the hidebound conservative or progressive. In the tradition of Erasmus's humanism, Grotius remains true to past values and reformulates them in terms of modern thinking. He is in agreement with Machiavelli that nobody has a claim to the Holy Roman Empire of the Middle Ages. He accepts the sovereign states as a matter of course, and he grimly admits the Machiavellian truth that one has to disguise virtues as advantageous in order to sell them to the rulers.

He is too deeply imbued with the moral spiritualism of the Arminians not to reject the idea of a monopolistic church as a universal power. He believes, however, that the destructive effects of the various revolutions can be checked. He is firmly convinced that it is possible to reestablish the unity of modern civilization. It is possible, he thinks, to demonstrate the inner rationality of the social and religious bonds that hold together human civilization.

Grotius's whole work is based on an implicit presupposition. In times when ecclesiastical institutions are absorbed in the vested interests of conflicting churches, the laymen, in particular the jurists and the statesmen, have to shoulder the responsibilities for the survival of the spirit. They have to see to it that religion remains a working principle in everyday life. Thus, it will be possible to reestablish justice and peace. As an exiled statesman and a jurist, Grotius raised his voice for a reunited mankind. He had passed through the Dutch revolution and had observed the revolutionary tension in Richelieu's France, still trembling with the unbroken spirit of Protestant and feudal oppositions. This detachment from subjective interests enabled him to visualize a Western civilization unified by enlightened common sense and a religious spirit of solidarity. "Such association binding together the human race is in need of law." Grotius is convinced that this vision can become true when established in legal institutions that are in harmony with the requirements of common sense and of religion, as manifest in the all-pervading natural law.

We cannot fully understand *Law of War and Peace* without taking into consideration the living interdependence of law and religion in the thinking of Grotius. The book is not an isolated piece of legal and moral systematization, but a scientific instrument designed to transform a vision into a reality.

All his theological and exegetic writings serve the same purpose. He intends that they should be instrumental in actualizing his vision of a reunified world. They should provide the scientific means that would enlighten the conflicting denominations and teach the educated laity as to their fundamental unity in truth and spirit. In contrast to the philosophy of natural deism of Baron Herbert of Cherbury [1583–1648], Grotius's exegetic books point toward a "natural Christianism." This independent attitude is a pioneering effort toward preserving the fundamentals of tradition in the light of scientific reason. In this, Grotius is much closer to Catholic and Socinian [see Faustus Socinus (1539–1604)—Eds.] rationalisms than to Calvinistic and Lutheran theories. His scientific spirit—the philologist Johann August Ernesti [1707–1781] has called him the ancestor of the higher criticism—even forced him to practice a theory of parsimony with regard to verbal inspiration that was critical to this central element of the Protestant dogma. This rational and critical thought pervades all his theological writings and his understanding of the miracles of resurrection and of the cult. He does not question their truth because they have been believed by intelligent and educated people, who were never swept away by emotions, keeping them always under control of their reason. He comes to the conclusion that the fundamental verities of Christianity are intelligible through reason, simple and evident, as is the truth of all basic things. These verities can be experienced and practiced everywhere by the common people when they are educated to be "commonsense people."

This is Grotius's main concern: the *Res Christiana*, the devotion to the loving God of creation and to the Supreme Judge of our conduct in the practice of the spirit of solidarity in Christ. *Res Chris-*

tiana is the Gospel as a living force and as a standard to which conduct is referred. According to Grotius, the experienced and practiced religion of the laity is the very power that can reestablish unity, peace, and justice in a revolutionary situation. The affinity of this attitude to Erasmus's spiritual pragmatism is conspicuous. It makes Grotius seem to be ambivalently poised between a rational theism and a Christian spiritualism. In spite of his emphasis on Christ's mandate and on the higher plane of the norms of the Gospel, his ideas on the religious requirements of human nature are close to a natural theism.

True religion, as common to all ages, rests upon four principles: the oneness of God, His transcendence, His concern about men as Father and Judge, and His being Creator. These four ideas are born with us and brought out by reasoning. They are universal and necessary to the preservation of religion. All other ideas are acquired by tradition. Grotius had the courage to formulate his religious position as lying athwart the Christian theologies and the deistic dogmatisms.

Grotius's subjective venture in religion has led to misleading interpretations with regard to his fundamental attitude. This is, in particular, the case with the passage in which Grotius stated the autonomy of natural law, which is valid *etsi deus non daretur* [even if God did not exist—Eds.]. Scholars who knew better, like Otto von Gierke [1841–1921] and Wilhelm Dilthey [1833–1911], saw in this statement full evidence of Grotius's secularization of natural law. This was to these distinguished scholars an indication of his "progressive" and "modern" attitude. This interpretation, however, is erroneous. It does not mean the separation of the moral from the divine sphere. It is true, indeed, that natural law is intelligible to human reason (*ab intrinseco ex ratione*). We are able to understand the social constitution by intelligent reasoning without taking refuge in divine inspiration. However, this autonomy is relative to the universe of divine creation that is intelligible and rational in itself and has made right reason in man a reflex of His own intelligence. God remains the guarantor of natural law.

There is nothing revolutionary and secular in this statement. It is a scholastic commonplace, frequently used in the struggle against the radical voluntarism that prevailed among the nominalists. Why does Grotius join the scholastics in this matter while, in general, sharing in the Protestant resentment against Catholic theological philosophers? He rejects the radical voluntarism as disastrous to the ideas of right and justice. He opposes Machiavelli and Luther alike because of their antirational attitudes. Yet, this does not mean a romantic Catholicism. It expresses the conviction that the very essence of God the Creator can only be reason. Hence, justice exists because it is an attribute of His very being, not because He has decided so in His sovereign will. Gottfried Wilhelm Leibnitz [1646–1716] has best formulated Grotius's position when rejecting Pufendorf's nominalistic theory of law. "Right is not right because God has willed it, but because God is just."

All the way through, Grotius refers to God as the Supreme Judge beyond all legal institutions and sanctions. His eternal presence supports and strengthens the obligations of natural law and raises them to the higher plane of the norms of the Gospel. All these considerations point out that Grotius's position is anything but deistic or rationalistic. Modern interpreters mistakenly overlook the value connotations implied in all scientific conceptions and disregard their frame of reference. The physicist Isaac Newton [1643–1727], the naturalist Jan Swamerdam [1637–1680], and Grotius were still able to speak of science and reason as the wonderful instruments through which we participate in God's creative reason.

It is not accidental that Grotius's Christian position coincides with the Neo-Stoicism that was fashionable in his times. The modern Stoicism meant the immanence of divinity as creative reason in the world of nature and of society. In most of his fundamental theses, Grotius refers to Seneca, to Marcus Aurelius, and to the Cicero of the *De Officiis* and *De Legibus*. The last recur throughout the book, in the general trend of Grotius's thinking without explicit quotations. Grotius is even eager to support the higher values of the Gospel by adding references to Cicero, Seneca, and Marcus Aurelius to make clear the fundamental humaneness of mankind when completely illuminated and enlightened by the unity of logos and *caritas*. It is possible to label Grotius's position as Christian Stoicism. There is God the Creator, a Divine Reason, but He is real and working in the universe of nature and of society. It has been one of the functions of Stoicism in the rise of modernity to reconcile the philosophical and legal rationalisms of the secular world with the spirit of the Christian religion. This was a humanistic device that permitted one to remain true to the religious traditions and yet preserve the intellectual integrity of the modern scholar.

Grotius's religious and philosophical attitudes merge in his legal ideals. *On the Law of War and Peace* contains their synthesis. The book analyzes the inner structure of the social universe. Grotius was educated in the traditions of Roman law. Roman law was largely composed of that jus gentium that jurists had elaborated by a comparison of the laws of many states and that they identified with natural law as the general consent of enlightened and educated man. This Roman law was as emancipated from the "written reason" (*ratio scripta*) of the traditional Roman law as was Grotius's spiritualism from the tradition of the Roman and from the authority of the Protestant churches. This renascent Roman law is based on reason, the potential rationality of mankind, however, conditioned in time and space. As to its philosophical frame of reference, it follows traditions of Roman Stoicism, which is essentially the pantheism of reason.

Still more important for understanding Grotius is that Renaissance jurists brought a spirit of "humane interpretation" into the exegesis of law, that is, a comprehensive consideration of the circumstances of every case. This pattern remained normative for Grotius's procedure. Grotius did rely on the conceptual frame of the *Corpus Iuris* when he elaborated the rules of groups and constructed a natural system of social institutions. The Roman jurists conceived of legal relationships in terms of relations between individuals. They recognized mutual relationships between individuals, either equals or nonequals, as the center of societal relationships. The notion of *socius*, basic in sociology, is actually a conception of Roman law. The Romans regarded all fundamental concepts as referring to the original reciprocity among *socii*. They did not consider the collective person as a specific concept. They could describe it only as a sum total of individual relationships. This limitation implied a positive insight that has become highly relevant in the rise of formal sociology and of those conceptions of interpretive sociology that are very close to formal sociology such as Max Weber's in the first chapter of *Wirtschaft und Gesellschaft*. This insight made it possible to understand societal relationships and social institutions in terms of a variety of mutual relationships, of give and take, of superiority and subordination, of sympathetic power and the need for protection, and of kindness and sternness. Following the Roman pattern, the reality of natural law means to Grotius the rationality of human purposes and the intelligibility of social values as evident in social action. Grotius was convinced that the enlightened knowledge of natural law as the working of human nature reveals the teleology of social existence and clarifies the elements that make for the continuity and duration of the basic social constitution.

For this reason, the *Law of War and Peace* is a comprehensive study of natural law that presents a systematization of societal relationships in the diverse patterns of social action and on the diverse planes of living. Within this frame, international relations and political institutions have specific functions that do not admit any kind of absolute autonomy of the social spheres as emancipated from the common ground of the merging processes of logos and spirit.

Grotius frequently remarks that natural law should not be confounded with national customs or with the norms of the divine voluntary law. Such customs and norms are established by acts of will—human and divine. They are open to arbitrary decisions and to specific circumstances. Natural law, however, results from and is the manifestation of human nature as innate right reason (*qua recta ratio insita*). This inner rationality appears already as a tendency in the need for society. It is the characteristic trait of the human animal. Usually, the text of this important passage is not fully quoted. Grotius explicitly describes the kind of society for which human beings long. Man desires social life "not of any and every sort, but peaceful and organized according to the measure of his intelligence, with those also of his kind; the Stoics called this trend sociableness." This is the fundamental thesis of Grotius's book. Human nature instinctively points toward peace—its very telos. Grotius has added the limitation in order to show that, because of the character of human reason, no perfect and absolute peace is possible in human affairs. This should not be confused with Augustine's radical dualism between celestial and terrestrial peace. The whole book, in particular the third part, points out that men are capable of establishing human peace when following the rules of natural law. Peace and tranquility are regulative ideas inherent in human nature. The idea of peace is the core of the book. War is a substitute when institutions of law are lacking. It is an instrument of legal action for the reestablishment of justice among nations.

Mutuality is the primary datum of human life, as life in society. Grotius describes this basic societal relationship as composed of two elements: mutual needs and mutual sympathies. Man is an imperfect being, in need of cooperation and overflowing with sympathy. Grotius refers twice to the bond of spontaneous sympathy as a bent of human nature that establishes friendship and communion among men and states in the common devotion to social and moral goods. Natural sympathy should make it impossible that men misuse the lives of other men as means to their own ends, Grotius states in an almost Kantian formulation. This original sociability of man must be maintained and secured in order to make possible the continuity of society. The maintenance of society (*custodia societatis*) is the one source of law. It springs from the social nature of man and is hence called natural law. The principles of natural law are, for Grotius, manifest and clear. Grotius distinguishes between general and evident principles and inferences. A general principle is that one must live honorably or according to reason. Evident is the principle that one is not allowed to seize another's property. Inferences can be evident and nonevident. It is evident that, granted marriage, we cannot admit adultery. It is not evident that vengeance is wicked if satisfied at the price of another's pain. Anticipating Spinoza's famous formula, Grotius speaks of these principles as certain and intelligible as are mathematical axioms.

Natural law works in man through the antagonistic tendencies of his being. Grotius distinguishes between the social and the humane branches of natural law. He repeats the classical theory that all animals strive to preserve their constitution. Men strive for the preservation of life, self, and property. Natural law, as concerned with the needs of the individual in society, is law in the strict sense of the term. It refers to the establishment of the security of man in his relations to his fellow-*socius*. It is restrictive law that prescribes not to hurt and to abstain from foreign property. It gives the individual security in his domain and recognizes the rights of the individual as qualities of the moral person that can be enforced by the established courts. The reciprocity of right and obligation makes the contract the original mode of legal relationships. It implies the central norm of the social law that contracts must be kept. *Socii* realize that mutual relations as expressed in a variety of agreements must be based on good faith. There cannot be any consensus without good faith. Consensus does presuppose a common purpose, a common affirmation of the purpose or end, and the common will to cooperate in its fulfillment. It is the foundation of all legal and social relationships. It implies good faith, as the will to remain true to the hypotheses of social action. Good faith means more than following the rules of the game. It implies the connotation that truth is the sine qua non of social tranquility and security.

Grotius's intention to give a comprehensive analysis of the social phenomenon becomes evident when he reconsiders social attitudes that seem to be at variance with good faith. He examines under what conditions pretense and falsehood are compatible with morality and justice. Grotius mentions six types of falsehood that are permissible because they are morally constructive. For the teacher, it is permissible to use fiction and falsehood in order to adjust to the limited understanding of his pupils. Irony and esoteric suggestions are allowed in a conversation with people familiar with this mode of communication. If a third person is deceived, it is no wrong. Physicians are entitled to deceive a sick person in order to comfort him. Friends are permitted to lie when they can raise the low spirit of friends in despair and depression. The officer can distort facts and manipulate news in order to strengthen courage and raise the morale of the military and civilian population. We can tell a lie when this is the only way to save the lives of innocent persons or prevent a crime. Rulers and men of authority can lie when it benefits their subjects or is used as device for the discovery of the truth. In this survey, Grotius gives a truly sociopsychological analysis of social conditions under which specific attitudes may possess a positive moral justification, while in a general system of ethics, they are incompatible with moral standards. The description of these patterns of conduct implies a relativistic transformation of the absolute system of ethics. What is good and moral depends on the requirements of specific structures or situations.

Grotius speaks of the role of social consensus in collective bodies as compared with the moral choice of the individual. He distinguishes between associations of equals and the subjection of inferiors to their superiors. Their agreements of mutuality and subjection become the sources of civil law that is historical and individual in all cases. The basic types of grouping, however, correspond to natural requirements. They present patterns that are, according to Grotius, so fundamental that they have their parallel in various types of government. Such types of control as the natural relations between parents and children, husband and wife, guardian and ward, master and servant recur in different types of government. Here we see the influence of the study of Roman law upon Grotius's thinking. All legal conceptions refer to the basic types of societal relationships, which constitute the social branch of natural law. To Grotius, legal and sociological categories are identical. As a branch of natural law, social law is restricting and refers to expletive justice. When enforced by the state, it becomes a branch of natural law. Rights, however, can be established only when they give man something that he recognizes as his own. However, they should never be arbitrary, and those who dispense them should be guided by a wise consideration of all claims existing in the particular circumstances at issue.

This leads to the second and larger branch of natural law, that which refers to the moral and humane requirements of society. It deals with the stratification of society and with the norms of justice that give every man what is due to him, what is inherent in every man as a potential right. But it is not law in the strict sense because it cannot be enforced. This most comprehensive branch of natural law varies with the circumstances, and it frequently occurs that our exercise of it must override existing legal rights and bring about a new division of power. The interaction of law proper and the dynamic right of justice continuously join the moral and humane requirements of society with the institutions of statutory law. According to Grotius, the tranquility and concord of society rest upon the reality of moral duties that are the ground for legislative interference. Grotius devotes much effort to the clarification of the interaction between established laws and the moral requirements that are the recognized values of peace and concord. According to Grotius, the constitution of society is founded on the inseparable unity of moral duties and legal norms as inherent in the nature of man. Law is a mode of the Good.

Grotius distinguishes carefully between law proper and natural law at large. The latter includes a hierarchy of duties having larger claims upon us, under certain conditions, than our rights and privileges that are supported by law and custom. Even if we are not hindered from enjoying those privileges, they may deviate from the rule of right. Hence, we are called to renounce them in the name of superior requirements. For the dynamics of natural law comprehends the various spheres of law that extend from legality to morality, from things permissible to things good and better. There is a law of charity in natural law that was the common property of the pagan world as manifested in Cicero and Seneca. This humanitarianism of natural law, finally, coincides with the norms of the Gospel. Grotius intends to show the universality of human sympathies and common sense as the rational normative principles of human nature.

Human nature has such a wide range of potentialities that it is capable of value—attitudes so clearly and distinctly moral as to surpass and supersede the strict laws of natural law. Men have a sense of shame and modesty indicating a regard for what is more just and better than the requirements of law proper. There is a sense of honor, springing from spontaneous sympathy that is associated with justice in legal matters like bequests in trusts. There are many duties that are not in the domain of law proper, but in that of value—attitudes that illuminate and make intelligible our obligations on the higher plane of existence, but still within the orbit of the natural law. Many things are required by kindness, generosity, love of country, kinship with all men (including enemies) that supersede the rules of law proper. "The rules of duty extend more widely than the rules of law." The former present a "logic of the heart" as intelligent and intelligible as are the rules of selfpreservation. In these passages, Grotius has implicitly stated that mutuality means two things: reciprocity between individuals and membership in a whole. This implicit definition of mutuality becomes evident when Grotius deals with the higher requirements involved in the relations between states.

Although Grotius has demonstrated most emphatically that war is only in very rare cases justified, he still considers it more upright and just to abandon one's right for the higher value of the all-embracing peace. Rulers are like fathers and will not easily decide to punish their sons or subjects and neighbors, except by dire necessity and in the name of the highest values of justice. Grotius goes so far as to assume circumstances that make it obligatory to refrain from the exercise of our own right by reason of the love and consideration that we owe to all men. He wishes to extend the area of international relations. However, he cannot imagine international institutions. He can think only of enlightening all nations so that they may become aware of the same right reason and of the same intelligent sympathies in all human beings despite differences in time and space. Such knowledge will establish the common sense of mankind that makes possible the consensus between states as expressed in international law. Because Grotius cannot conceive of international organizations, he must apply what he calls his a posteriori method. He collects tremendous historical material from philosophers, historians, jurists, poets, and rhetoricians in order to show that, actually, there is a universal common sense of educated and thoughtful people regarding the verities of social and human requirements. These verities are simple and self-evident.

From his analysis of the potential rationality and intelligent sympathy of the human race, Grotius draws the following conclusions. If peace is the telos of social action, life is the primary value involved in its realization. Grotius recognizes that God has a higher claim on our lives than we have. He frequently states that life is the very locus and basis of all temporal and eternal goods that are given to us for constructive, not destructive, ends. In emergency cases, he values life higher than the liberty of individuals and the state as an inexhaustible source of potential goods. This is not moral escapism; it is the humane wisdom of a man who has recognized the higher value of the whole and yet cannot forget the potential richness of every human being. This *humanitas Grotiana* has become the prevailing opinion that has nurtured the idea of international affairs in the Anglo-Saxon countries. It has been one trend in American foreign policy since John Jay instructed George Washington in the principles of Grotius.

Peace is the telos of social action. War is a general sociological category comprehending private and public conflict as suggested by Seneca. It is defined as the condition of contending by force. It is permissible in situations in which legal administration is not available as in the case of surprise attacks by gangsters, thieves, and pirates.

In public affairs, war can be admitted as an emergency tool for reestablishing justice, repairing damage, or punishing aggressors. For Grotius, war is a marginal institution of justice, indispensable because there are no international courts and institutions of arbitration that could pass judgment on conflicts between states and enforce these decisions internationally. For Grotius, war is not the continuity of politics with the means of force. Rather, it is a subordinate instrument of justice. Politics means to Grotius the continuously extending growth of legal institutions and their creative evolution in harmony with the new forces that arise in the social process again and again. It is the living spirit of justice in the reexamination of legal establishments and the unending will to abolish wrong and injury done to the smallest minority. There is no security or freedom in the state except under the rule of law.

Grotius reproached Erasmus with being a utopian pacifist. He himself is close to a pacifistic attitude. He wrote to his brother: "But if Christian princes listened to my warnings, there would be no more war among them; they would prefer to abandon some of their rights or to choose upright arbitration." Grotius's pacifistic attitude is founded on his understanding of the humanitarian and cosmopolitan aspects of natural law. It proposes, even when questions of right and wrong are involved, not to go to war, not to revolt against usurpers, and not to make revolutions against unjust rulers. In this attitude, rigid legal conceptions and spiritual and humanitarian concerns coincide. Human lives are so precious that it is preferable to yield in order to avoid bloodshed and to strive to attain desired ends by wise and humane compromise. Grotius recognizes the right to resist rulers only when firmly established by constitutional law as in the seven cases that he mentions when dealing with the diverse types of constitution in the feudal state and in the *Ständestaat*. He affirms a right to revolution logically forfeited by the pact of subjection. Apart from that, it is impossible for the ruled to search for the guilty men among the rulers and their advisers. This seems to Grotius a vicious circle because the social process is so complex and involved that it is almost impossible to establish certain responsibilities. Men have to rely on God as the Supreme Judge of rulers and people.

Grotius's recurrent emphasis on the moral aspect of natural law derives its force from the analysis of the state of nature and of its revolutionary transformation by the establishment of private ownership. In the state of liberty, things belonged to men in common. The primitive state rested on two principles: a simplicity of life and a comprehensive mutual affection among individuals. Both made it possible to preserve that way of life for a long time. But men are restless and strive for more perfect things. Hence, the original state of communal life could be maintained only under hard natural conditions, as among the American Indians, or by religious communions like those of the Essenes, the early Christians, and monastic orders. The general bent of human nature moved toward knowledge, competition, and the enjoyment of more refined goods. This tendency slowly dissolved "natural communism" by separating the owners of large flocks from each other. There remained a limited communism of common pastures. Tribes and families proceeded with the organization of individual property by appropriating lands and wells. Grotius explains this process by the paradoxical character of human nature. Men as rational beings are never satisfied and strive for perfection. Hence, they invent arts, crafts, and industries. Their achievements increase their desires and raise ambition and avarice, which make reason their servant. Desires and reason as destructive and constructive forces abolished the unity of the early communal life. Technical difficulties, such as the lack of transportation facilities, and moral deficiencies, such as the vanishing sense of solidarity, eliminated a fair distribution of labor and its products.

In these circumstances, private ownership came into existence, but not as irrational violence and pressure of the powerful in the sense described by Franz Oppenheimer [1864–1943]. Grotius explains the process as a kind of agreement, that is, a rational compromise and settlement, in the form of occupation and division. Occupation at large takes place by a people; division distributes the occupied whole among the members of the group.

According to Grotius, introducing private ownership has never completely submerged the ancient bonds of solidarity and of community of property. Grotius states that it was never the intention of the progressive innovators to destroy all remnants of communal liberties. On the contrary, their intention was to depart as little as possible from natural equity. For this reason, it is not a religious norm to give to him who is in dire need. *Natural law prescribes* as a moral obligation to the society of owners of private property to see to it that established laws provide shelter and protection to those in need. "Things have been distributed to individual owners with a benign reservation in favor of the primitive right."

This frame of reference is fundamental to Grotius's universal jurisprudence. It enables him to speak of those communal rights that still obtain in the world of individual property. Natural equity requires a relative freedom of passage on land and sea, general freedom of emigration and migration, and common rights to things and acts. These rights remain norms of natural law and have a higher dignity than contradictory regulations by individual states. Among these rights, Grotius considers the elements of freedom and social obligation in the economic sphere regarding prices, monopolies, profits, usury, and the freedom of buying and selling where and how. All such acts are permitted or vetoed, not as a special favor, but as rights deriving from the power of natural liberty that remains the lasting frame of reference of natural law.

This frame of reference is not supposed to be the image of the Golden Age. It presents the naive and sympathetic rationality of the human animal. In times, enlightened by reason and illuminated by spirit, the frame of reference appears as the "common sense of mankind." It can become actual when natural law is commonly understood as a reflection of human nature making possible a world of human peace and of humane solidarity. Grotius's work serves the purpose to promote the growing enlightenment of human society in order to reestablish the past solidarity as a reflected and understood unity of all mankind.

5

Fontenelle

Men who live at a critical distance from their contemporary world naturally praise a past age in which they would like to have lived. Different causes have led people at various times to praise the Enlightenment. Some fifty years ago, Paul Valéry [1871–1945] expressed his preference for that epoch, in which he could have met with Bernard Le Bovier de Fontenelle [1657–1757], Montesquieu [1689–1755], Denis Diderot [1713–1784], and Jean-Baptiste le Rond d'Alembert [1717–1783]. Valéry feared that men would come to be more and more specialized technicians and social engineers, losing all common principles of value. He visualized the forthcoming age as an age of scientific barbarism. In contrast to this reality, he saw the epoch of the Enlightenment, the eighteenth century, as an age of harmony and moderation:

> Europe was then the best of the possible worlds. Despots and libertarians balanced each other. Truth maintained some moderation. Matter and energy did not yet rule everything directly, though they were indirectly felt. Science was already fairly advanced, and the techniques

---

Published originally in a slightly different form under the title, "In Praise of the Enlightenment: In Commemoration of Fontenelle, 1657–1757," in *Social Research* 24 (Summer 1957), 202–26. Republished by permission from *Social Research*.

> refined. Religion still remained. There were enough whims coexisting with considerable rigidity. (*Variété*, 2:6.)

Now, half a century later, other causes impel men to eulogize the Enlightenment. There are enough orthodoxies, fanaticisms, and prejudices—radical and conservative, philosophical and scientific, intelligent and stupid—that need enlightened reexamination. There is the escapism of Arnold Toynbee [1889–1975], the flight from reason into all kinds of behaviorism and existentialism. There are methods and conceptions that we take for granted because their authors have become idols for worship. The desire for enlightened vigilance and praise of the Enlightenment are appropriate in the contemporary age of irrational modes of thinking and acting.

The term *Enlightenment* is a historical category. It indicates a state of mind that penetrated all segments of life in the Western world during the eighteenth century. Immanuel Kant [1724–1804] defined *enlightenment* as the departure of mankind from its self-inflicted immaturity. And he added his praise of Frederick the Great [1712–1786]: "A prince is to be called enlightened who finds it appropriate to speak of his duty not to prescribe anything in religious matters to his subjects. . . . On the contrary, he gives them liberty and rejects the arrogant term of tolerance. He should he praised for having liberated . . . the conscience of his people and having invited them to use their reason."

Thinkers and rulers, theologians and scientists, lawgivers and moralists shared in this state of mind. They firmly believed that they were obliged to spread the results of scientific philosophy to the ignorant in order to liberate them from the inertia of tradition and from the authority of prejudices. The princes and their ministers tried to establish enlightened welfare states. Frederick the Great and Joseph II [1741–1790] were the most outstanding figures in the effort to penetrate legal and administrative institutions with the principles of enlightened reason. They believed that the truth of reason would eliminate the irrational prejudices by which men live, in particular those deeply rooted in religious convictions.

The philosopher of the Enlightenment invited his fellowmen to have the courage to learn and to know. *Sapere aude*! It was an invitation to criticism and an admonition to examine rationally what had been taken for granted. Everywhere, people met in salons, in studies, in laboratories, in order to learn causes and laws, motives and responses. The conduct of the philosopher who dedicated himself to spreading the new philosophy to the ignorant who wished to learn was "enlightened."

As a historical category, the Enlightenment had a beginning and an end in time. The first important works by Fontenelle were published between 1684 and 1688, and the *Second Treatise of Government* by John Locke [1632–1704] appeared in 1690. The end of this period can be fixed definitely: the day that Maximilien Robespierre [1758–1794] turned Notre Dame into the Temple of Reason and inaugurated the first religion of modern revolution. That day—November 10, 1793—marked the apocalypse of the Enlightenment.

"Enlightenment" is a historical ideal type. As such, it is of questionable value because of the extremely subjective elements of its value perspectives. Still today, enlightenment is a curse to some, a blessing to others. For this reason, it may be a methodological necessity to construct different concepts for genuinely historical phenomena. Let us call them ideal images. Ideal images are the concrete and dynamic representations of ideal patterns of philosophizing, of normative modes of politics, and of the types of human perfection. Their selection is often less arbitrary than the hazardous formation of historical ideal types. The Enlightenment can be truly represented by Fontenelle or Montesquieu, Diderot or Baron d'Holbach [1723–1789], Claude Adrien

Helvétius [1715–1771] or D'Alembert. They all are images of the same enlightened attitude, which regards the light of reason as the force of liberation from traditional beliefs, prejudices, and superstitions.

I

I have selected Bernard le Bovier de Fontenelle as the ideal image of the Enlightenment, an honor that is fittingly stressed in 1957, which is both the tercentenary of his birth and the bicentennial of his death. In so regarding him, I have the authority of two of his younger contemporaries who praised his contribution to the popularization of the cosmology of René Descartes [1596–1650]. D'Alembert, in reference to Fontenelle, wrote in the *Discours Préliminaire à l'Encyclopédie*:

> Books on science seem to have gained the attention of the reading public that has been exclusively interested in the literary arts. A respectable author whom our century is happy to have through a long period . . . has taught the savants to get rid of the yoke of pedantry. Superior in the art of clarifying the most abstractideas, he has succeeded in bringing them down to the understanding of the unlearned by his precision, lucidity, and method. He has even dared to equip his presentation of philosophy with the devices of the literary arts, which seem most alien to philosophy. His keenness has been justified by the most general and flattering success. No one has ever reached his great popularity and incomparable success in popularization.

And Helvetius, in dealing with the spirit of the eighteenth century, mentioned Fontenelle's decisive role in the development of the spirit of enlightenment:

> Before M. de Fontenelle the majority of savants found themselves isolated and deprived of all communication with other people once they had reached the peak of scientific achievements. . . . M. de Fontenelle was one of the first who pioneered in building a bridge between science and ignorance.

There are other reasons, more important than the testimony of his contemporaries, for choosing Fontenelle as the genuine image of the Enlightenment. He was a writer who dared to popularize philosophical texts in order to stimulate critical thought and a reexamination of traditional ideas about God, the universe, and the place of man in nature. Students of Descartes know the constructive heresies of this disciple of the master. His scientific theory and philosophy of history are an original contribution to a philosophical anthropology. He was the first Cartesian who objected to the idea of the constancy of the mind, postulating instead its progress and history. He joined philosophical optimism with a Montaignesque pessimism on the *condition humaine*. Fontenelle should be reread because some of his basic ideas are relevant to a particular aspect of the philosophy of life in the contemporary world. He is an image of the Enlightenment, but not a museum piece that we dust off on the occasion of this or that centennial. Like that of all genuine philosophers, his work is both historical and transhistorical. So also is the historical spirit of the Enlightenment part of the perennial enlightenment of philosophy.

We should remember Fontenelle for still another reason. He gave us the image of the philosophical life in an age of ecclesiastical and political domination. Friedrich Nietzsche [1844–1900] praised him as the last aristocratic thinker who knew that esoteric writing is indispensable in a world of total conformism. Nietzsche might have remarked that Johann Wolfgang von Goethe [1749–1832], too, was conscious of the fact that in a bourgeois epoch he could never communicate to his reading public all the terrible verities he had learned in his long life.

Fontenelle lived to be almost a hundred years old. He was born on February 11, 1657, and died on January 9, 1757. When he was born, the physicians found him so weak that they felt it necessary to advise his parents that he would probably not survive. This report later stimulated his love for Michel de Montaigne [1533–1592], in particular Montaigne's criticism of medicine as a scientific discipline. Fontenelle's physical weakness had a lasting effect on his life. To all his friends he seemed absolutely selfish. His egotism, however, was but a strict discipline that he imposed on himself in order to give himself totally to his work. As a philosopher, he needed distance and reserve, the more so as his social role forced him to live in continuous contact with society.

His father belonged to the elite of the legal profession. His mother was a sister of the dramatists, Pierre [1606–1684] and Thomas Corneille [1625–1709]. Fontenelle was a man of many gifts and ambitions. He was eager to emulate his famous uncles and, at the same time, to be a philosopher in his own right. The revolutionary philosophy of Descartes fascinated him. He did not give up his literary efforts, but these brought him back to philosophy. For example, his *Eclogues* led him to philosophical reflections on pastoral poetry, a pioneering effort in applying sociological method in aesthetics. The *New Dialogues of the Dead*, the *Digression on the Ancients and Moderns*, and *The Judgment of Pluto*, 1683–84, merged philosophical reflections with an attractive literary pattern.

In the next four years, 1684–88, Fontenelle engaged in the most intense philosophical activities, both as a theoretical thinker and as a popularizer. His *Conversations on the Plurality of Worlds* and his *History of Oracles* were popular bestsellers, subsequently earning him the title of forerunner of the Enlightenment. The *Origin of*

Fables was a complement to the work on oracles. He had intended to unite the contents of the two books and of other related essays in a work on the philosophy of history, but never attained that goal. This is the more regrettable since Voltaire [1694–1778] was to plagiarize and vulgarize Fontenelle's relevant ideas and deprive them of their uniqueness as the only contribution made by a Cartesian to the philosophy of history.

Fontenelle, without neglecting his poetry, gave much attention to problems of mathematics, to methodology, and to a philosophy of science. He had the daring to write a devastating critique of the conflicting Christian churches, a work that almost brought him to the Bastille. In 1697, his interest turned in still another direction. He was then appointed "Perpetual Secretary" to the Académie des Sciences, and in that capacity, he wrote his history of that institution and later published the eulogies that he had delivered in his official position.

Through all of Fontenelle's writings, there runs one genuinely Cartesian thought: the principle that the main concern of philosophy is the method of reasoning. He turned this principle against Descartes himself and criticized him for having succumbed to the temptations of metaphysics. He made it his task to apply the new method to moral philosophy and to history, examining the structure of history and disclosing the paradox that despite the irrationality of human life, history is intelligible. This was a keen and original conception for a disciple of Descartes. Fontenelle left many fragments pointing to his endeavor to distinguish different patterns of generalization apart from mathematical and logical conceptions. He was fully aware that the generalizations men use in constructing historical processes and social action have a character of their own and deserve particular consideration. But these reflections, in the line of Jean Bodin [1530–1596] and Montaigne's views on the methods of history, Fontenelle did not live to bring to a conclusion.

II

Fontenelle achieved his greatest success with his brilliant popularization of Descartes's cosmological theory. In the *Conversations,* the work of a true disciple, he developed the Cartesian version of the Copernican-Galilean theory of the solar system. What makes the book fascinating today is its imaginative discussion on the plurality of inhabited worlds—an idea that was then revolutionary indeed. If different worlds were possible, it would be logical that there might be different religions, philosophies, and values. This was, of course, a popularization of Montaigne's *Apology of Raymond de Sebond.* Fontenelle chose this theme for popularization because it implied all problems with which laymen were concerned when at all reflective. The topic included the questions of man's place in the universe, the meaning of nature, and the significance of man's acting and suffering. The philosopher seduced his readers into giving thought to these problems. Readers in the highest ranks of society discussed the ideas of the book and derived from such conversations a zeal for knowing the truth. This was a precious result in the world of Louis XIV [1638–1715] and Mme de Maintenon [1635–1719], who maintained a strict authority over religious and political verities, to which men had to conform. Fontenelle's book implemented the rapidly growing criticism of the state of total conformism.

In presenting the cosmological theory of Descartes, Fontenelle remained a loyal disciple of the teacher, but in the greater part of his work, he became heretical. His is the great merit of having introduced the perspective of historical thinking into a philosophy that insisted on the constancy of the mind. Fontenelle, challenging the Cartesian theory, elaborated the thesis that the mind has its history and is a process in time, moving in ascending progress from the primitive state to the scientific age that Descartes inaugurated.

Prior to Locke, Fontenelle stated that experience is the foundation of knowledge. Two fundamental experiences are a common heritage of all philosophers: the progressive movement of the mind, and the resisting movement of intellectual and emotional habits. These make up the dynamics of the history of philosophy.

Fontenelle combined the tradition of Cartesian thought with his new historical perspective. He was the first author to state the position of the moderns in the battle with the ancients, and his analysis was the more revolutionary because he was the first to regard the question as one of historical perspective. Fontenelle rejected the idea that the ancients were physiologically or intellectually better equipped than the rest of mankind. The time process, he thought, has no qualifying powers. He agreed with Bodin and Montaigne that different areas have different influences on the character of society. But though he was willing to admit the influence of geography and climate, he saw that modern mankind had compensated such differences by the equalizing effects of the migration of ideas, techniques, and inventions from civilization to civilization. The scientific philosopher, he held, is always able to explain the individuation of naturally equal mankind by the sum total of historical and physical circumstances.

This scientific procedure made him see the blunder of those who had made of the accomplishments of the ancients an ideal, absolute, and normative good in a historical vacuum. He recognized that it is wrong to deprive the ancients of their historical place and to turn them into idols for worship. They were the founders and, as such, have claim to our lasting gratitude. We have advanced as their disciples; we have learned new things and acquired new and better methods. We are humble before the greatness of their conceptions. But we have no reason for imitating them as the highest authority.

In a radical analysis of the historical process, we find that there are always ancients and moderns in the alignments of historical generations. It is the natural dialectics of human historicity that we change our social roles in the current of our life process from youth to maturity. Today we are the moderns; tomorrow we will be the ancients. In the field of aesthetics, Fontenelle realized, the historical perspective implies new and constructive ideas against the absolutism principle of classic beauty. The theory of the perfect and unsurpassed Greek drama had brought about the theory of imitation that prevailed during the seventeenth century. Fontenelle attacked the classical theory as invalid. It would be valid if the ancients had lived in an ideal space and in an ahistorical time. Since this was not so, it is senseless to expect to find an ideal model of the drama beyond historical time. Since perfection is historical, Greek tragedy cannot be established as an ideal for imitation. The moderns have their own canons of perfection in drama and have invented new literary patterns, such as the novel, the epistolary form, and the short story. Aesthetic perfection is possible in all historical periods. But it has its specific norms appropriate to the historical frame of reference. There is no universal and formal principle of beauty that could be imitated everywhere.

Fontenelle's pioneering in historical method is most noteworthy in his attack on Descartes's thesis of the constancy of the mind. The great contribution of Fontenelle's philosophy consists in his revolt against this theory of the master. Mind in its unfolding as taste, values, and social norms has history. According to Fontenelle, the mind alone has history. What people usually call history—the changes and transformations in political institutions and in the alignments of social roles—should be called perennial sameness. There is no becoming and advancing in the current of historical time; there is nothing but the unceasing identity of human greed, resentments, lusts, and hatreds. Fontenelle called this sameness the Heart. The first philosopher to acknowledge the progress of the mind, he counterbalanced his philosophical optimism with classical pessimism on the characteristics of human nature.

Fontenelle was a disciple of Descartes, but also of Montaigne. The *New Dialogues of the Dead* illustrates the perfect unity of these two discipleships. The dialogue of the dead is an old literary pattern of Hellenic origin, meant to be a device of satire. Fontenelle applied the form in a grim philosophical mood. Though exposing the stupidities, inconsistencies, and vacillations of men, he placed the greatest value on the human capacity for philosophizing. In this fascinating literary form, Fontenelle offered a serious theory of man, anticipating a philosophical anthropology.

Throughout the *Dialogues*, Fontenelle presents images of great philosophers in conversation with their enemies. The philosophers try to defend the nature of philosophy against all opportunistic and utilitarian claims. Fontenelle makes his philosophers assume that philosophical interest is a unique human attitude. Philosophers are the only human beings who by the act of theoretical thinking transcend the expanding life of the organism. The men who dedicate their lives to philosophy are rare examples of genuine disinterestedness. For this reason, there have been only a few philosophers in the current of time because most people are dedicated to the pursuit of their material interests.

One of the main themes of the *Dialogues* is the antagonism between the theoretical attitude and the organic structure of man. Fontenelle was concerned with the nature of philosophy and the philosophy of nature. The philosopher transcends nature, and nature takes her vengeance on the disinterested philosopher who dares to transcend her order. Nature produces organic beings for the purpose of living. Man lives by habits and customs, which are his second nature. Theoretical reflection discloses the emptiness of life's routines, the total irrelevance of daily life. Contemplation makes us see the secret of nature, which is to keep human beings in control by subjecting man to his senses and drives. But men have escaped nature's domination, as philosophers who no longer care for success in social action, and nature hates this challenge to her power. For this reason, she wars against the philosophical life, which transcends the immanence of nature. She schemes to turn the *homo philosophicus* into a *homo faber*, who makes of reason a device by which to realize and satisfy his vital and emotional needs. The idea of the transcendence of immanence is a thesis that Georg Simmel [1858–1918], in his final thinking, made articulate against Henri Bergson [1859–1941].

The philosophical attitude of the homo philosophicus carries him beyond his social environment and beyond his own self. He is ruled by his theoretical vision and never knows where it will direct him in the unfolding of its inner law. The freedom of the philosopher becomes slavery to philosophy. Fontenelle analyzed these complex and hazardous conditions of the philosopher. His Descartes, a very un-Cartesian philosopher, agrees with Socrates as to the universal domination of nature and the minor place accorded to the thinker. Descartes admits that the substance of philosophy is invariable in spite of the changing patterns of philosophy. But in agreeing with Socrates, he sees the philosophical process in the context of the *condition humaine*, as never finished and never coming to an end of its search.

But it is human and philosophical to hope against hope. Moreover, such hopes are counterbalanced by skeptical thoughts in regard to the philosophical process: "I even believe that we sometimes find the truth concerning problems of considerable importance. But the misfortune is that we never know we have found it." Philosophy resembles Blind Man's Bluff, a child's game. The blindfolded philosopher sometimes grasps the truth, but not knowing its name, he has to let it go. This image of the philosopher indicates a truth of grave importance. It is commonly recognized that human beings in the stream of action, and particularly the great men of history, like Caesar, do not know how they have achieved their glory and domination; for this reason, they refer to their good luck. Fontenelle makes the same statement in regard to philosophy and the philosophers. We do not think as philosophers, but we are possessed by philosophy. It is the greatness and misery of man that he is directed toward theoretical truth but becomes subject to the domineering spirit of philosophy. Reflections on the uniqueness of the philosophical attitude in the human situation are a basic theme of the *Dialogues*. Few are the philosophers in the world of history because people are not inclined to give themselves to the disinterested pursuit of truth. Thus, the idea of the progress of the mind is compatible with a profound pessimism as to the nature of man in social action.

Fontenelle analyzed the ways of human action that have made place for the role of human passions in the process of history. Grim nature, in the diversity of her desires, is manifest in all ways of human behavior. All social roles are expressions of the fundamental needs of human beings for recognition. People are ruled by the lust for glory, which satisfies human vanity. People pretend to ideal motives, but these are nothing but ideologies. In his analysis of Hernán Cortés, Fontenelle condemned as cynical ideology the claim of the Spanish Conquistador that he acted lawfully and justly in the occupation of Mexico.

All human motives arise out of desires to satisfy the needs for self-realization and recognition. Fontenelle attempted to establish the uncertain character of all ideal motives. His Plato [c. 428–c. 348 BC] flatly refuses to be a Platonist in matters of love, knowing very well indeed that physical needs are inseparable from love. Love is a complex phenomenon—the physical and the spiritual are interdependent. Love may be incited by the mind, but it will always meet with the passions of the body. Men and women have only two ways of trying to fulfill their desires: ambition and love. The two passions are of parallel shape. Both are infinite; both open up new vistas and endless horizons. Fontenelle ridiculed a princess who believed that the realization of true love would bring a conclusion to the search for peace of mind. There is no limit to the ambitions and the erotic lust of men. The folly of human beings is most conspicuous in the sphere of sex relationships.

In the *Dialogues*, Fontenelle presented a typology of love relationships that illustrates the unromantic reality of human intimacy. First, there is the pattern of destructiveness, the completely selfish and self-centered passion for happiness, pleasure, and adoration. Mary Stuart [1542–1587] sacrificed David Rizzio [1533–1566] to her lust without understanding that she had alienated him from himself and was responsible for his death. There is, second, the type of recognized futility. The Virgin Queen makes it clear, though in veiled terms, that she has passed through all stages of expectation and fulfillment. Elizabeth I [1533–1603] carefully phrases her conception of the futility of sexual pleasure. She states that people should never scrutinize in detail the pleasures of love, for these joys cannot stand a thorough examination. They are like bogs and swamps that we should trespass on with light feet and quick pace in order to reach solid ground. And third, there is the pattern of total ambiguity. The famous mistresses of kings exchange reminiscences of their power over their foolish lovers, recalling the methods they have successfully followed. They all agree that prudence, beauty, and esprit are the necessary tools, with esprit defined as the intellectual discipline that covered their pretense of love. They never knew whether they acted in order to appear lovable or whether they loved as ambitious women who were thirsting for domination and power. They never underestimated the role of chance in their dangerous game of ambiguity. They were safe as long as their lovers took their appearance of love as reality. But not one of them could predict how long she would be lovable in the eyes of the dupe of the comedy. Neither their prudence nor their beauty could give them security. Love, both real and false, is completely irrational in the game of the sexes in which victors and vanquished alike are dupes.

Fontenelle covered in the *Dialogues* the complex human situation that results from man's standing between the opposite poles of the theoretical and the erotic. He pictured the ridiculous situations that have derived from the prevailing irrational motives in social action, the senseless occasions that have led to great historical catastrophes. Such completely inadequate causes of overwhelming events have induced historians to falsify the truth and to invent solemn and grave motivations. Fontenelle portrayed the proud Charles V [1500–1558], who boasted that he was ruler of two worlds in a conversation with Desiderius Erasmus [1466–1536], who tries to break his pride. Erasmus demonstrates that Charles had no personal merit in the acquisition of his empire; everything had come to him through marriage or inheritance. Charles, however, retorts that this is the human lot, that Erasmus himself should consider that his genius was not his own merit either, but the result of an infinite number of causes the combination of which we call chance until we are able to explain them.

Fontenelle was consistent when he described human ideals as chimeras. Chimeras are fictitious, but they have reality in the process of human action. They are the prerequisites of all individual and collective efforts toward some kind of perfection. It was Fontenelle's contention that men accomplish the possible only when they reach for the impossible. Men are always in search of chimeras and spirits that transcend the human sphere. They will always be disappointed and frustrated, but they will start all over again to look for new ideals. Molière [1622–1673] alone cannot be fooled because he has tested his philosophy by experience. When all tragedies have vanished, Molière's work will remain. "One who wishes to work for immortality should picture the world of dupes and fools."

Fontenelle was not alarmed about the *condition humaine*. The world of human folly will never end in a state of anarchy. Nature, which has produced the *homo faber*, has equipped him with enough prudence and instincts to assure his survival. "The natural order of the universe pursues calmly its own way. Nature will always achieve what needs to be done, through our folly if it cannot be got from our reason."

Men never know what they are doing when they act. Caesar could not understand how he had accomplished his deeds and, thus, he ascribed everything to his luck or to his star. Often people strive for specific ends and achieve something completely different. "Everything is uncertain. It seems that fortune is anxious to see to it that the same acts may result in different achievements. Fortune likes to make sport of human reason and to demonstrate its frailty, as it does not admit hardfast rules."

The *Dialogues* contain Fontenelle's philosophy in a nutshell although they do not yet articulate his discovery of the progressive mind. His theory of the stream of nature and of mind's transcendence breaks through his broad analysis of the areas of human folly. This philosophy is a philosophy of life in the tradition of Montaigne's essays. The *Dialogues* picture the human race on the move, always searching for a goal in order to attain satisfaction and recognition. It is the lot of all men and women to be on the march toward something that they are not, and can never be.

Fontenelle's essay on happiness, too, has a specific relevance to his philosophy of life. In contrast to the Stoics, Fontenelle held that only in a minor degree does happiness depend on ourselves. We contribute something by intellectual discipline—we can remove imaginary evils, the drive toward suffering, the urge toward eternal mourning, through reflection on the variable character of man. But most people will never be happy because they are too busy winning or maintaining prestige, wealth, and power. Happy are only the few who are predisposed by their moderation and kindness to accept the advice of their consciences, those who possess themselves in actuality without escaping into the future in hope or fear. This is the ideal of happiness that Montaigne achieved through the practice of philosophy.

Fontenelle seriously considered whether happiness consists in the insignificant goods: a conversation among friends, an eloquent silence between lovers, a lonely walk on a brisk fall day, a spirited hunt in the forest. Such are the gifts of a stingy Fortuna; most people afterward regret that they have not counted them as blessings. Passing pleasures, however, are not happiness. The ups and downs between moments of pleasure, the pains with which we pay for brief enjoyments, suggested to Fontenelle a solution that is in line with his scientific and mathematical philosophy. He invented a calculus of happiness that made it possible to measure the amount of good in our pleasure and the quantity of suffering in our pains. This device would give men direction and a measuring rod for their conduct.

There are only a few simple goods that do not involve painful cost. These, universally recognized as lasting values, are peace of mind, trust in friends, and love of study. Fontenelle concluded that the highest good in the human situation is the happiness of living in complete harmony with oneself. But this true state of happiness can be realized only under one condition of which we are not masters. Between poverty and grandeur, people can achieve happiness in a state of the mean. Avoidance of the vices of power and of poverty is the true condition for happiness of the few who abstain from the temptations of the world and from the seductions of the passions. In this conclusion, Fontenelle appears as a genuine disciple of Descartes and Montaigne.

III

As a heretic Cartesian, Fontenelle made his greatest contribution in his ideas on the philosophy of history, which he developed in two directions. In the *Origin of Fables,* he studied a stage in the progress of the mind, while in the *History of Oracles,* he exhibited man's reasons for attempting to prevent progress. His hope for a continuous, progressive chain of philosophers was closely bound up with his fear of the folly and stupidity of the mob.

The *Origin of Fables* was keen pioneering. This essay on mythical thinking, based on Fontenelle's postulate of the progress of the mind toward a scientific age, is a daring approach to a theory of symbolic forms. It begins with a revolutionary comparison of Greek and American Indian mythologies, both of which arose out of the intellectual state of primitivism. In contrast to most of his contemporaries, Fontenelle held that myths are not pure fiction, but a mixture of the true and the false. The true elements are drawn from recollections of the past, the false elements from distortions of the past in oral traditions, or from pictures of the imagination. Myths—Fontenelle spoke of fables—are modes of knowledge in the age of the primitive mind, specific patterns of causation that explain the workings of nature in terms of superhuman action.

Primitive peoples, Fontenelle held, explain unknown nature by the familiar principles derived from practical experience in maintaining their existence. In order to explain things unknown, they transfer this primitive knowledge of causation to divine beings; they think in terms of a causal process in nature brought about by superhuman acts of the gods. This is the first stage of knowledge. The gods are conceived in the image of supermen; their attributes are force, potency, and violence. They are thought to be cruel, unjust, and ignorant. With the advance of reason, this picture changes and men transform the image of the gods; they are then believed to be wise, just, charitable, and prudent. Finally, mythical thinking conceives of philosophical divinities, and the myth shifts to historical thinking and to its scientific methods of explanation and hypothetical interpretations.

Fontenelle anticipated the perspective later developed by Ernst Cassirer [1874–1945] on Kantian assumptions that elements of mythical thinking do not completely vanish with the advance of scientific thinking. They remain as residues and exert influence on value judgments and the philosophical vision of the universe. Fontenelle explicitly maintained that mythical thinking and religious thinking are natural phenomena of knowledge through which the mind passes in its evolution. More objective than Voltaire, he admitted throughout his works that myth and religion are necessary forms of knowledge, stages in the unfolding of the scientific mind. They express a historical phase in the progress of the mind, though there may come times when mankind will be enlightened by scientific philosophers and will not be in need of past patterns for constructing an intelligible view of the whole.

The growth of scientific explanation implies a decrease of mythical thinking and, thus, a decline of marvels, miracles, and religions. More specifically, history loses the mixture of true and false in its mythical recollections. Historians begin to penetrate into the motives of agents and to understand their characters with reference to the needs of a given situation. Fontenelle considered such interpretations an advance, though limited and uncertain in their scientific validity. He felt that we can never wholly trust the interpretive method. There always remains a flexible element of guesswork that is almost impossible to estimate correctly. The historian remains the author of certain manipulated and artificial constructs that may be called "fables of prejudice."

The historian, Fontenelle saw, benefits from the progress of scientific thinking. It gives him opportunities to refine his construction of the probabilities, hazards, and necessities that make up the whole progress of history. In this evolution, history becomes a truly important discipline, contributing to a science of man and to moral philosophy. Fontenelle was deeply convinced that history is not worth the effort if it does not inform us about the variety of human possibilities in the diversity of human situations. Scientific history is a division of philosophical anthropology, as modern philosophers would say. And, apart from its contribution to moral philosophy, it can become a tool for understanding ourselves in relation to our fellowmen.

Fontenelle, developing his conception of the historicity of man, spoke of the concrete historical man, *l'homme en détail,* and his continuous changing. But he recognized the identity of human nature in spite of the plurality of historical patterns and their continuous transformations. The philosopher stresses the context of meaning, *l'âme des faits,* in the bewildering variety of historical experience. The genuine historian investigates the conditions and the conditioning responses of men that, taken together, make it possible to construct historical forms and images relevant to understanding the greatness and misery of the *condition humaine.*

Scientific history is the analysis of the unfolding mind in all its manifestations. It is necessary to explain the transformations and renovations of ideas, values, tastes, social conventions, and norms of behavior. These changes take place in an almost imperceptible process. They seem to be arbitrary, but Fontenelle knew that there are hidden and necessary relations that are open to explanation. He mentioned the profound changes that had occurred during his lifetime, changes that had affected all patterns of conduct. At the end of the seventeenth century, it was taken for granted that members of society had esprit. Polite and refined conversation was the highest pleasure of sociability. Everyone was concerned with linguistic standards and poetic imagination; tragedy and the novel were the mode; the salon was a forum where men and women displayed their intellectual independence in discussing the new philosophy. But in the eighteenth century, this pattern changed to its extreme opposite. There was then no value in the spirit of conversation; gambling had taken its place. Sentimentalism became a substitute for esprit; the charms of cultivated language and of classical literature had disappeared in favor of romantic and pleasant authors.

Such changes, Fontenelle held, were not the work of chance. He was convinced that a micro-historical analysis would disclose that the movement of the mind is ruled by laws intelligible to scientific inquiry. This trust in the progress of scientific method extended to the political world. He was absolutely sure that the methods developed by mathematics and physics could be applied to the field of politics—that the hidden laws of politics could be disclosed by scientific analysis. Thus, politics, formerly the area of the greatest irrationality, would be liberated, and scientific controls would be established. (Prince Klemens von Metternich [1773–1859] liked to read Fontenelle for his insights into the prudence and folly that people exhibit in their social roles on the world stage.)

Fontenelle was emphatic in asserting that the philosopher needs courage and vigilance. The evolution of reason meets with prejudices and universal inertia, which prevent the thinker from examining traditions and beliefs that are taken for granted. The truly scientific philosopher of history would analyze the lasting conflict between the philosopher and traditional societies that cling to their indoctrinated habits and prejudices. Genuine history would be the scientific discipline that describes and explains the unceasing battle between the advancing mind and traditional beliefs.

Fontenelle recognized this situation as inevitable. He characterized faith, belief, and prejudice by the summary concept of error. As a philosopher, he rejected such beliefs and prejudices, but as a philosopher of history, he praised them. Social life is based on errors. They make life possible and bearable. Fontenelle widened the scope of the idea of error to include everything that is not scientific reason, as Bernard Mandeville [1670–1733] called vice all behavior patterns not in complete harmony with established laws.

Prejudices, beliefs, and superstitions were, in Fontenelle's eyes, errors that are blessings to human beings. They alone assure the continuity and duration of social life. They make possible the respectability of social roles; they satisfy the cravings for recognition; they create the reality of the fictitious carnival that we call society. They strengthen our will to believe, to trust, and to indulge in all kinds of illusions. For this reason, Fontenelle thought it necessary to complement the *Origin of Fables* with the *History of Oracles.* Together, the two works are parts of a project on the philosophy of history for which we have only notes. These notes present the dynamics of history, the impetus of progress, and the elements of resistance. Persistent inertia, the "sleep of the world," imposes unremitting hardships on the progressive mind in its efforts to enlighten men. Fontenelle reflected on the human conditions that produce these continuing antagonisms.

The *History of Oracles* is a popularization of a scholarly book by Antonius Van Dale [1638–1708], a Protestant Dutch writer who attacked and criticized the marvels of the Catholic faith, ridiculing the superstitions prevailing among Catholics. Fontenelle took the risk of using such a book as a stepping-stone and as a disguise for a general inquiry into the miracle, the basic religious phenomenon. The term *oracle* hides his true subject, which was miracles, and their acceptance by individuals and groups.

Fontenelle had been a disciple of the Jesuits, with whom he remained on cordial terms. He was a practicing Catholic all his life, and his brothers were priests or occupied ecclesiastical positions. As a philosopher, however, he was compelled to submit to the demands of his free and independent mind. He was not willing to accept beliefs unquestioningly when he could find causal explanations for the motives that induced men to believe rather than to inquire.

We may see in the *History of Oracles* a remarkable study of the will to believe, an advance critique of William James's [1842–1910] famous book. Here, Fontenelle analyzed the reasons that make it possible for human beings to accept the supernatural or superrational. He tried to find out what it is that impels men to yearn for the occult, the supernatural; he was anxious to know the significance of the longing for the miraculous. The attempt to answer this question involves a prescientific pioneering in collective psychology. It is almost a summary of the reflections on the role of imagination in social behavior and thought that were available to Fontenelle in the works of Niccolò Machiavelli [1469–1527], Erasmus, and Montaigne.

Men, contended Fontenelle, are always carried away by their fears and hopes; people never live in the present because they are never in control of themselves. Being in fear of the present, they hope for a better future. Whether dominated by fear or hope, they escape into unreality, building up chimeras, wish dreams, a belief in superhuman interference. It is this faith in divine or demonic beings superior to man, nature, and history that makes society persist. As a matter of fact, the most elementary human relationships are based on trust—that is, on a belief that our friends, our cherished next of kin, our fellow workers and business partners will live up to our human and moral expectations. Such trust has no scientific basis; it is a blind belief that frequently amounts to a belief in miracles. People would rather believe in miracles than be skeptical as to the trustworthiness of their fellowmen.

In the tradition of Montaigne, Fontenelle knew that such beliefs are the easiest way to conformism. He recognized that habit is man's second nature. People cling to the prejudices with which they have been indoctrinated by their environment. They are satisfied with them because these prejudices relieve them of fear and personal responsibilities. Fontenelle was well aware of the temptations to inertia that tradition and accepted authority foster in the human mind. This kind of docile conformism extends to the world of the unknown and unintelligible, which people are ready to admire and to consider a reality. He emphasized the frailty of the human mind that permits men to believe in the reality of the unreal and in the unreality of the real, as exemplified by ghosts, witches, sorcerers, and mental derangement.

Fontenelle stressed this strange craving for the miraculous by analyzing the history of miracles and oracles as they appear in the documents and traditions of the pagan and Christian past. The Christians had tried to establish a complete break with the pagan tradition of oracles, which they attributed to demons. They believed that they had a monopoly on genuine miracles—that is, those revealed by God. The Christian historians were impelled by their zeal and fanaticism to invent fictitious sources in order to justify their faith in miracles. Fontenelle showed that these sources—such as the falsifications of the Epistles or the Apostles, or the non-authentic gospels—were worthless if pious frauds. He found bad faith, ignorance, and folly at the very foundation of the Christian tradition and concluded that the belief in miracles as one root of religion must be based on a will to believe.

The will to believe arises out of a fundamental human need. Two different desires merge in its formation: first, a wish to recognize an eternal being within the unceasing changes of nature and history, an urge directed toward rest, tranquility, and peace; and second, an infinite curiosity to know what is beyond the process of everyday life and human experience. Men by nature long for the reality of the unreal, the unreality of the real, and the naturalness of the supernatural. This is a necessary attitude of the imperfect, futile, and frail human being; it expresses the true ambiguity of his strength and his weakness.

Fontenelle derived his findings from his analysis of human affections, of fear and hope, wishful thinking and utopian dreaming, imaginative planning and messianic vision. Wherever they clash with reality, the belief in miracles is born, and the fundamental state of mind is the same in all religions. Hence, there never was anything mysterious about the miracles. They were simply a means by which the priests took advantage of the people's will to believe. Eventually, such conspicuous frauds were bound to open the eyes of the educated and the ignorant alike. Thus, with the progress of the mind, the will to believe is bound to give way to the will to find the truth. Yet the belief in miracles will return since the masses will always long for the supernatural and for the fascination of magic.

From his Cartesian position, Fontenelle rejected all grounds for the belief in miracles and regarded nature as totally explainable. From his Montaignesque position, he declared nothing to be surprising once the folly of men is acknowledged, and thus he considered it unnecessary to seek further causes for the universality of superstition, which constitutes an ever-recurring offense to reason. He had no illusions about the power of the irrational in the life of man in history. It will remain a driving force in the drama of mankind. Therefore, the greatest effort is needed in order to advance the light of reason, to work for the progress of the mind. One who dares to philosophize will be able to free himself of ignorance, inertia, and the tedium of everyday life. The person liberated by philosophy will wish to share his happiness with his fellowmen and will enlighten them with the torch of truth.

As a genuine philosopher, Fontenelle was both historical and transhistorical. He dared to be wise. He invited the ignorant to follow him and to gain knowledge and a spirit of criticism. He hoped that philosophic education would be an important stride forward in the liberation of modern society from traditional prejudices. The philosophy of life that he elaborated was in full accord with those later presented to us by Bergson and Simmel. In his radical analysis of the will to believe, he was a forerunner of William James. He opened up a new perspective on mythical thinking, which anticipated Cassirer's theory of symbolic forms. His philosophy of history entitles him to a place beside Jacob Burckhardt [1818–1897], who, indeed, was more limited.

IV

Fontenelle was internationally famous as the encyclopedic writer who delivered the eulogies of his fellow scholars and scientists in his capacity as secretary to the Académie des Sciences. These documents are precious and require mention in any evaluation of Fontenelle. They constitute an indispensable reference source for the history of the sciences in their pre-specialized state. The scholars he praised were all philosophers. As botanists and physicians, mathematicians and physicists, they lived, nevertheless, in a universe of learning; they wished to discover the nature of all living. Equally notable are the eulogies of the associated members of the academy, such as the unforgettable image of Mme de Lambert [1647–1733], who was dedicated to the advancement of learning. Moreover, Fontenelle's eulogies deserve our lasting admiration as manifestations of courage and generosity. He was generous in his treatment of those who committed errors or were mistaken in their friendships or enmities. Throughout the eulogies, he proved himself superior to his fellowmen in courtesy and tenderness of heart and to men of letters in the versatility of his mind.

Fontenelle displayed great courage in his eulogy of Sébastien Le Prestre de Vauban [1633–1707]. The famous engineer and social reformer had written the *Dixme Royale* in order to help the king and his subjects construct an independent tax system that would eliminate the power of the tax farmers. The book was suppressed before publication, and no one was permitted to mention it. Fontenelle, the cautious and prudent conformist, had the courage to speak of the book, though he mentioned neither its title nor its content. At the end of his eulogy, he said of Vauban: "He was passionately attached to the king, a subject of ardent and zealous loyalty. He was never a courtier; he preferred to serve rather than to please. No one has been so often and so courageously the pioneer of truth. He had an almost imprudent passion for the establishment of truth, to which he dedicated himself without any reservations." Fontenelle knew from his own experience that even a prudent passion for truth had its dangers in an age of total conformism.

Finally, the eulogies stress the relevance of the human coefficient to the specific philosophical or scientific achievements of the men remembered. Today, they are still normative patterns for recalling the chain of death and life in which we are the latest links, working toward the progress of the mind in spite of the *condition humaine*.

There have been times when the spirit of enlightenment turned into the tyranny of progress. The spirit of the historical Enlightenment came to an end in the cult of reason. All historical phenomena have their positive and negative aspects, according to their specific historical patterns. But there will be recurrent situations when the spirit of enlightenment and the criticism of religion and traditions will be more pious and constructive than the established and unquestioned authorities of church, state, or philosophical sect. The unfolding of the mind is a dynamic process in which its own objectivations are broken up in order that they may attain to a new constructive power and a new perspective on life and its open stream.

6

Louis Duc de Saint-Simon: Class Consciousness of the Defeated

It is imperative to give Louis de Rouvroy, Duc de Saint-Simon [1675–1755] a place of his own. His *Mémoires* do not fit into any of the historical classifications the political and literary historians have constructed. His work has nothing of the classical style of the seventeenth century, nor has it the sentimentalism of the eighteenth.

Unable to write in the classical style, Saint-Simon felt quite incompetent as an author. But his principle of writing seems to the contemporary reader much richer and more powerful than the rationalism or sentimentalism of his time. Saint-Simon's style was based on a conception of man as a stream of consciousness that moves and is moved in the context of his life, acting, and being acted upon—a strange and wonderful phenomenon in which everything could coexist, the sublime and the vulgar, the heroic and the vile, the ridiculous and the tragic, the proud and the despicable.

The author called his *Mémoires* "contemporary history," indicating the lasting interdependence of the present with past and future, the depth levels of man's historical existence. Furthermore, the term encompasses all human events beyond the routine of everyday life,

---

Published originally in a slightly different form in Albert Salomon, *In Praise of Enlightenment* (Cleveland: Meridian Books, 1963). Republished by permission from Frank Salomon.

everything unusual, rare, tragic, funny, repulsive, attractive, lovely, and grim. All such aspects of life are worth recording. Thus, the *Mémoires* have rightly been called the *Comédie Humaine.* Charles Augustin Sainte-Beuve [1804–1869] referred to the author as "un Tacite à la Shakespeare."

Saint-Simon's description of the patterns of court behavior has become a model of analysis. He portrays a total social situation in change and transition in which most people are completely absorbed in their social roles. In the political and military spheres, however, the author does not render the total structure of social action, but analyzes only specific configurations of men and those character traits that explain their success and failure.

Most relevant to the contemporary reader is the sociological reflection on the social situation of his class. Saint-Simon developed the class consciousness of a defeated elite, demonstrating the thesis that class consciousness comes from the top of society.

Michel de Montaigne [1533–1593] had considered two ways of writing history: academic historiography and the historical description of practical affairs by the men who actually participated in them. The professor of history was, to Montaigne, an intellectual who studied philology and rhetoric and was able to construct an artificial world of historical reality from the study of mere documents. Statesmen and ministers, diplomats and agents, were often impelled to write history in the form of *Mémoires,* or recollections. Their aim was eminently practical. They wanted to justify or defend their own actions, stressing their expectations, plans, and goals in their fields of action (seen from their own subjective perspective). Quite often, they candidly disclosed their errors and frustrations, the miscalculation of their strength and of the forces of their adversaries. The great political "recollections," from Cardinal Richelieu [1585–1642] to Otto von Bismarck [1815–1898] and Harry Truman [1884–1972], however subjective and prejudiced, have, nevertheless, a greater claim to a rendering of historical reality than the academic constructions of fictitious historical reality. Men of affairs have, it would seem, an advantage over the professors in that they understand how human beings act in their everyday lives (as rulers, ministers, ambassadors, and the like). They know, far better than most academicians, the underlying reality beneath the ostensibly harmonious picture most of us have of our world; being informed by their spies and agents about the nature of their opponents, they are able to learn in the most concrete fashion the inner workings of their social milieu. The experience of political life as a continuous struggle between equal and unequal bodies, and as a permanent conflict for supremacy, is an invaluable asset for the statesman who writes his *Mémoires.* He is able to give a dynamic perspective and totality to his history; his candor and discipline enable him to report objectively on men's faults, errors, and miscalculations. Neither success nor failure is necessarily related to true or false expectations or planning, for unpredictable elements can always occur that can change the concatenation of forces.

The seventeenth and eighteenth centuries were heir to a wealth of political *Mémoires.* Written in an age of deep social transformation, they sought to describe a changing world, reporting the current political scene by means of psychological analysis. Richelieu's "Political Testament" and the *Mémoires* of François VI, Duc de La Rochefoucauld [1613–1680] and of Jean François Paul de Gondi, Cardinal de Retz [1613–1679] document the forces that made possible the absolute state, as well as those that provided resistance to this revolutionary innovation.

Among the *Mémoires* that encompass the transition from the seventeenth to the eighteenth century, those by Louis Duc de Saint-Simon are the most remarkable—not because they cover a long period and consist of forty-one volumes, but because they penetrate the last twenty-five years of the rule of Louis XIV [1638–1715] and the Régence from 1715 to 1723 in a sincere effort to lay the foundations for an objective and scientific treatment of his age that assumes the form of a precritical historiography. Saint-Simon lived as a courtier after he resigned from the army in 1702. For over twenty years he took notes; every night he wrote in his diaries what he had observed and learned about persons, situations, and events. He exploited the knowledge of his friends in the ministry and in the military. He carefully listened to his wife, questioned his brothers and sisters-in-law, and was on the best terms with the king's physicians and chief valet. He was highly appreciated as a confidant by many ladies at the court, whose stories were a valuable source of information about love, sex, and business at Versailles. He did not seem to mind that he was not honored with a court office. He had his own assignment—to recount for posterity his world, in its living concreteness and totality. Because he took the conception of scientific history very seriously, he had an insatiable curiosity about everything human. For the same reason, he described everyone in his "Portraits" with a well-balanced impartiality—even those he hated most (such as the king; Françoise d'Aubigné, Marquise de Maintenon [1635–1719]; Louis de France, son of Louis XIV, known as "Le Grand Dauphin" or "Monseigneur" [1661–1711]; and Cardinal Guillaume Dubois [1656–1723]).

History, considered as a discipline, is the scientific treatment of the past. Saint-Simon, however, stated that he intended to write "contemporary history" as a scientific discipline, in spite of the fact that he was personally and profoundly involved in his own proposed subject matter. Though he was never wholly explicit about it, the term *con-*

temporary history meant different things to him. The contemporary is historical because the present is always directed toward the future and carries within itself its own past. The elements making up this stream can be beliefs, recollections, traditions, ways of life—surviving and coexisting along with new patterns of behavior. Saint-Simon was deeply shocked when he regarded himself as an element of the past caught up in the accelerated tempo of social change—he felt old and part of a revered political tradition in a world in which a new society had established a new social system within the framework of the traditional monarchy.

In addition, "contemporary history" meant to him the total social situation—that is, the fact that all human acts, thoughts, feelings, gestures, attitudes, and the like are determined by the dynamic context of the field of forces that constitute in their totality the *condition humaine*. Saint-Simon conceived of the total social situation as an analysis of the depths of social conduct within its specific historical context. First, he described the various social roles. There are the institutional roles that tradition and destiny impose on some men: rulers, slaves, servants, and the like. Some of these identify themselves with their roles; some attempt to escape the normativity of their position; others are forced into playing a role by means of flattery or because of the images of greatness and glory that courtiers and subjects require of their rulers. Other persons arrive at their roles by chance or fortune (e.g., mistresses of the king; the king's grandson, who became king of Spain). Some might acquire their roles through ambition and lust for power (e.g., Louis August, Duc de Maine [1670–1736]). Still others, seeking moral and spiritual integrity, might take leave of every social role.

Saint-Simon carefully distinguished the place of social roles in the self-realization of human beings from the development, beyond their roles, of personal character traits and human passions and whims.

He is deeply convinced of the uniqueness and identity of individual human beings. What constitutes human nature, what has the greatest significance in the structures of the *condition humaine,* is under the pressure of constantly changing circumstances. Saint-Simon is absolutely certain that men are profoundly molded by the requirements of their social interaction. Social relationships disclose the precariousness and ambiguity in human action—men living with, for, and against one another. Men pretend and parade, betray and reveal themselves; they "seem" and "sham," simulate and dissimulate; they "play" public roles and are different in their private lives; their behavior is esoteric and exoteric, overt and disguised, according to the requirements of the situation and their own purposes and goals. Saint-Simon is as deeply critical of the nature of human beings as was Montaigne in the "Apology of Raymond de Sebond." For this reason, his notion of "contemporary history" encompasses the total social situation, thereby illuminating the complexity of being human in the world of here and now. Contemporary history presents men in living social interaction with all its contradictions, ambiguities, and ambivalences. Human beings within and beyond their social roles—as parts of nature, history, and society—are the true subject matter of his work.

Saint-Simon's intention to write about his own world from a detached and scientific standpoint is not quite fulfilled, as he insists on the right of the scientific historian to express value judgments. He did not believe that the critical examination of human social behavior is sufficient when it merely describes in an impartial manner the selfishness and often-vicious acts and attitudes of men. Saint-Simon's moral indignation needed an outlet that he found by explicitly expressing value judgments on such behavior. Selfish and evil men have enough success and pleasure, recognition and glory, during their lifetime; the historian, at least, should be permitted to inform posterity and to deliver moral judgments. Saint-Simon bases his judgments on Christian or philosophical standards of moral behavior.

Men are subject to moral norms that regulate the process of social action and establish social standards. However, most people make their vested interests the guiding ideals of their lives and only pretend to follow the established normative patterns. Only a few men are naturally dedicated to the goals of moral conduct; only a small group will preserve their integrity by giving service to the state, the Church, or by genuinely developing themselves within the framework of their own particular roles. Because this is a universal truth in the historical life of man, Saint-Simon felt that the historian should be entitled to pass judgments on the conduct of man over and above causal or other analyses. For this reason, his "contemporary history" is indeed a radical innovation, emphasizing as it does neither political, social, nor ecclesiastical histories, but rather the total human being. This visionary concept implies a variety of methods that, though "prescientific" (one might better say imperfectly scientific), we would call today psychological, sociological, and even existentialist. Nothing is more revealing about the prescience of this approach than the following passage from the preface to the *Mémoires*:

> To write the history of one's own country and time means to construct with refined reflection everything that one has seen, handled, or learned from unimpeachable sources; it means to report what has happened on the stage of the theater of the world, to recall the diverse interest groups and the obviously tiny irrelevant events which touched upon the configuration of events and produced the greatest impact on future developments. It means to demonstrate to oneself step by step the nothingness of the world, of its fears, of its desires, of its hopes,

> of its disasters, of its accidents, of its labors; it means to convince oneself of the emptiness of everything in the short and rapid duration of all these things and of the life of men. It means to remember that no one has really been happy and that felicity and serenity do not exist in the world; it means to give evidence to the fact that if the many people necessarily mentioned here could have foreseen the success of their efforts, of their sweat, of their intrigues, at least a dozen would have abandoned their views and pretensions[.]

The statement is a most eloquent and articulate description of the author's intentions. Man acting and being acted upon, the total human being as a sociohistorical creature, is the leitmotiv of such a history. It is a position that is closer to our own philosophical and historical methods than to those of the eighteenth century.

Saint-Simon inaugurated the trend toward sociological historiography as it has been lucidly and rigorously developed in our times by Sir Lewis Bernstein Namier [1888–1960] and his disciples. In the analysis of the court of Louis XIV, Saint-Simon performed some remarkable sociological analyses; his "Portraits" are a striking example of the type of descriptive analysis that transforms the subjects into symbols and images of the various types of human action within a continuously changing social context.

Knowledge of Saint-Simon's method is indispensable to understanding the content and style of the *Mémoires.* His selection of subjects was determined by his curiosity for and fascination with the diversity of human patterns of action. The human coefficient in political, military, and ecclesiastical institutions is his chief interest, and not these institutions in their autonomy and irrevocability. He is anxious to stress the condition of his class and its consciousness of itself as such in the precarious situation created by a social revolution. Finally, he regarded those behavior patterns and human situations that were beyond the pale of the routine and average as significant in their own right and worth his concern and description. For this reason, the scope of his analyses and descriptions, the dramatic presentation of human and social situations (whether tragic or comic), and the depth of his imagination make him the Shakespeare of prose. In literary style, Saint-Simon follows the tradition of the *Annales* of his beloved master, Cornelius Tacitus [56–120]. Year by year, he reported, described, and analyzed what seemed to him relevant and significant in the context of contemporary history. He deserves, indeed, to be called the Tacitus of the Empire of Louis XIV.

The Tacitus of Louis XIV's Empire

Tacitus had established nostalgic historiography as a normative pattern. His own hatred of the Principate and of the emperors was as passionate as his love for the nobles and the aristocratic elite of the Roman senate and of the *consulares.* We know today that his account of the Empire from Tiberius to Nero in the *Annales* is partisan historiography. Ronald Syme [1903–1989], who has given perhaps the most detailed interpretation of Tacitus's whole work, points out that the literary style of the *Annales* was a symbol of the tradition of the Roman aristocracy at a time when the classes making up the elite were rapidly changing.

Tacitus was the ideal master for Saint-Simon. He deeply appreciated the Roman's stand against imperial despotism and the absolute majesty of the ruler. He well understood the megalomania of the rulers as the result of prostration and flattery by their courtiers, ministers, and senators. He found the same characteristics in his own society and constantly compared the two patterns of tyranny, finding the same pattern of decadence in both the res publica and the French monarchy. The Roman Republic, under the control of an aristocracy of office and of landed gentry, had ruled the Mediterranean world but had lost its power under the military despotism of the emperors after Tiberius [42 BC–37 AD]. From then on, the rulers of Rome had the support of the wealthy classes and could slowly dissolve the old ruling classes. This was a genuine social transformation and an age of decadence for the traditional nobility.

Saint-Simon read Tacitus as a fellow historian and discovered their common experiences of historical and social decay. Throughout the *Mémoires,* Saint-Simon recalls the former conditions of the nobles: their indispensable service to the king, the symbolic function of crowning the king at Rheims, their role in government during the feudal monarchy, their political activities as compared to the grandees of Spain. But all this was gone—the French feudal elite, the dukes and peers were in the same situation that the Roman aristocrats were in when the military tyrants overthrew the Roman senatorial patricians.

To Saint-Simon, the comparison disclosed a complete parallelism. Tacitus had not started his story of the decadence from the establishment of the Principate by Augustus [63 BC–14 AD], but with Tiberius. So Saint-Simon did not start with Cardinal Richelieu or Cardinal Mazarin [1602–1661], but with the ambitious Louis XIV, who, though wanting to rule by himself, was pushed toward imperialism by his ministers and courtiers, who played on his lust for glory and power.

Saint-Simon described and analyzed the last twenty-odd years of Louis's rule as the decay of his successful imperialism in Europe led to the breakdown of the nation economically, socially, and politically. In particular, the old feudal nobility had given its sons to the king because it was an honor for this class to shed their blood for the sovereign. But this traditional relationship between the king and the nobles existed only on the battlefield. Because of their poverty, most of the country gentry could not afford to live at Versailles. This meant they could never be promoted beyond the rank of colonel because, in order to advance to higher ranks, one had to live at Versailles and be rich as well. Thus, the old feudal families had to intermarry with the new financial and commercial classes in order to move higher in the military, for only then were they able to afford to obtain and maintain a higher rank.

Saint-Simon saw all these trends as a decay of the old structure of the feudal monarchy. He felt, as Tacitus had felt about his own age, that the monarchy of Louis XIV had allied itself with the new classes of commercial and financial wealth. These groups could give their sons the training and education necessary to enable them to buy offices in civilian and legal administration and to serve the king. Saint-Simon examined the ministers of the king—all the men who had established the military and political power of France had been members of the juridical nobility or came from the bourgeois officials in government agencies. Saint-Simon called Louis XIV "the king of the vile bourgeoisie"; he believed that the absolute state was the decadent result of the true feudal monarchy, that it was monarchical only in appearance and actually was the symbol of the bourgeois revolution that would finally destroy even the last remnants of the monarchy itself. Though cursing the revolutionary state, he was candid and sincere enough to admit that the new classes in government and administration were competent, dedicated, and alert. This observation, though, grimly implied a reflection back on his own class. The social transformation of the state marked the decline of the feudal nobility politically, socially, and economically: politically, because under the conditions of modern technological warfare, the king no longer had to rely upon a feudal class of nobles and knights and had no need to share the government with the nobles, since he was rebuilding it by means of the bourgeoisie; socially, because the nobles who wanted some favor from the king were required to live at Versailles (which usually meant they had to marry into the wealthy bourgeoisie to afford the luxury of Versailles); economically, because war taxation had completely bankrupted the nobles. It was this reflection on his class of dukes and peers that produced in Saint-Simon a new class consciousness.

Class Consciousness

In a stratified political system with rigid distinctions in the possible ways of life, an awareness of oneself as belonging to a particular class is simply taken for granted. However, during Saint-Simon's time, the advancing bourgeoisie had not yet developed a class consciousness of itself. The classes established by financial and commercial wealth liked nothing better than to imitate the ways of life of the nobles and to be treated as nobles by the king. Saint-Simon reported that the king succeeded in persuading the most important banker of the time to give a loan to the state after he had refused for a long time to come to terms with the ministers. Members of the bourgeoisie rarely revolted with indignation against the pride and impertinence of the old aristocratic families, who behaved as if they should be humbly and gratefully received by the well-to-do bourgeois when they were good enough to marry their girls. But Saint-Simon is full of indignation when he tells such a story and is full of praise of the bourgeois lady who ironically responded to the impertinence of her groom's family that she could not better demonstrate her respect than by not reciprocating the visit of the noble family.

The new social classes felt protected by the royal authority but had as yet no consciousness of their power over political institutions. In particular, without intellectuals, they could not have constructed a revolutionary ideology.

In spite of the conformism prevalent among the economically powerful, there were responsible men in government service who had drafted the reports designed to inform Louis, Duc de Bourgogne [1682–1712] about the conditions of the different classes in France. They did not hide the misery of the people or the plight of the country gentry. Some authors approved, with keen and critical suggestions, a reform of the social and political systems of France. In 1687, the *Characters* by Jean de La Bruyère [1645–1696] appeared; in 1695, Pierre le Pesant, Sieur de Boisguilbert [1646–1714] printed the *Detail de la France*; in 1699, François Fénélon [1651–1715] published the *Télémaque*, which envisioned a political utopia based on a conservative and constitutional monarchy; and in 1707, Sébastien Le Prestre de Vauban [1633–1707] wrote the *Dixme Royale*. Saint-Simon was certainly well acquainted with these books. He belonged to the small group of noblemen who worshipped the political philosophy of Fénélon, regarding it as the only way to surmount and repress the despotism of the absolute state.

Saint-Simon found that members of his class—the dukes and peers of France—were being defeated by historical circumstances. The king was suspicious of all old feudal families, wanting none of them in his service; and, as Saint-Simon pointed out, Paul Duc de Beauvilliers [1648–1714] was the only nobleman who had served for many years in high governmental office. Since the incident of the Fronde [a series of civil wars in France between 1648 and 1653 in the midst of the Franco-Spanish war—Eds.], the king had resented all noblemen and their clans, but he could not actually control them. When he dismissed them, they merely went back to their castles in the country and there became relatively independent. But he loved to employ bourgeois men of legal training. They were his creatures, so to speak; believing they were his own work that he could create and annihilate at will, he felt like God. He told his ministers that they should feel grateful and humble for being permitted to serve him, and they should never forget that only his grace gave them status and prestige. Saint-Simon saw in the political and social advances of the economic and cultured classes, however, only the decay of his own class. He developed a new concept of his own class as defeated, a class consciousness that started at the top of society, not at its bottom. He was aware that every despotic regime creates a negative equality of all before the tyrant, that the inflated nobilitations of the bourgeois ministers and the favoritism shown to illegitimate children made the situation of the old feudal families precarious by lowering their social prestige.

Saint-Simon belonged to an old family of country gentlemen, his father having but recently been made a duke by Louis XIII. Probably, for this reason, Saint-Simon was more ducal than a duke. He had, indeed, such an interest in the ranks of the nobility, in their pedigrees, that he soon became an expert on them.

Among the dukes and peers themselves, there was a continuous rivalry regarding the ranks of the various clans, for rank among them was regarded as superior to position and function. The hierarchy of rank among the clans depended on when each had been made a vassal of the crown, and their respective pedigrees gave evidence of the length of time each had been a vassal. Some families were quite unscrupulous and ruthless in this respect, attempting to fix their pedigrees to suit themselves, changing their status from a lower to a higher position in the hierarchy by setting back the date of their establishment. Saint-Simon belonged to the thirteenth clan among the established dukes; François Henri de Montmorency, Duc de Luxembourg [1628–1695], who followed him as the fourteenth, wanted to become the second from the top. The old clans fought his claims regarding the purported establishment of his clan, changing the date from 1662 to 1584. Though Luxembourg was supported by some generals and some relatives among the dukes, Saint-Simon conducted the campaign against the famous general before the Parliament of Paris so effectively that the general's claims were rejected. This success made the unknown young Saint-Simon the political pillar of the dukes. As an expert on pedigrees and on establishments, he became the recognized leader of the dukes and peers in maintaining the standards of the old traditions against would-be usurpers, as well as against the anti-feudal policy of the king.

The class consciousness of the defeated cannot produce politically effective changes. What remains to the vanquished is just the old way of life in its manners, mannerisms, and patterns of behavior. Here they take their last stand. This is what the victors, on the other hand, cannot achieve because that way of life is the fruit of old traditions, of indoctrination, emulation, and discipline, practiced for generations; the defeated are driven back on themselves and their own ways by the rise of a new, more powerful class. The aesthetic element of their way of life, their poise, their attitudes as expressed in the rights and privileges of etiquette, is the last position after defeat in the historical process.

The Don Quixote of Etiquette

Saint-Simon saw that this particular kind of class consciousness produced specific patterns of behavior and ways of life among the dukes and peers. These distinguished old families of the nobility experienced a new meaningfulness of their old rights and privileges that distinguished them from the new classes. Their titles were the symbols of their traditional roles in the feudal monarchy, signaling the closed ranks of the nobility, next to the royal family and to the princes of the blood.

Saint-Simon was fascinated by the strict and rigid regulations of the Spanish court ceremonies that both symbolized and governed the rights and duties of the grandees. In particular, he gave his full attention to the rules that regulated the rights of the Spanish nobles to remain covered before the king or to cover themselves when invited by the king. In the historical analysis of this solemn etiquette, he laconically remarked that the balance of power between the feudal vassals and the monarchy was reflected throughout in the establishment and changes of etiquette. The Hapsburg emperors and kings had infringed on the independence of the Spanish nobles, who were accustomed to appear covered before their rulers. In stages, with the increase of their control over the aristocracies, the Austrian kings changed the traditions, finally granting privileges of various kinds to the diverse classes of noblemen, old and new. In spite of such changes, Spain still remained for Saint-Simon rather like a fairy-tale country that still preserved the rigid rituals and ceremonies of a feudal monarchy. For this reason, his journey to Spain as Ambassador of France, to arrange the marriage of Louis XV with the Spanish Dauphine, was one great climax of his life. He wrote about all the details of his reception by the king and queen, the place of the chief of protocol on the stairs when he arrived for the formal audience, the arrangement of the seats in the hall of audiences, and the informal visits with their majesties. He included drawings in his report to emphasize the solemnity and feudal dignity of court etiquette in Spain.

In his digression on the Spanish grandees and their etiquette, Saint-Simon compared their rights with those acquired by the French nobles. It seemed to him that the French nobles had many advantages over their Spanish cousins. They had truly cooperated with the feudal king in building up the greatness of the monarchy. They had raised the crown over the head of the new king at the coronation at Rheims. They had enjoyed the most important offices in the service of the king. Actually, the monarch had been the first among his peers.

He recalled the grandeur of his class in the past when he examined its plight at the court of Versailles. While there was only one nobleman of distinction in the ranks of the ministers, the rest belonged to *la noblesse de robe*, or still worse, to the bourgeoisie itself. Saint-Simon used his ardent debunking of generals and government agents as a scientific device—we would say a device of the sociology of knowledge—in order to verify the thesis that the so-called monarchy was actually a bourgeois revolution concealed behind the splendid façade of the kingdom. There were generals whose fathers had been clerks in Parliament or attorneys of the guilds; there were government officials whose ancestors had been merchants or artisans. The historical process showed conspicuously the rising tide of bourgeois advance and penetration in government. For this reason Saint-Simon was resolutely determined to keep alive the rights and privileges of the dukes and peers, even when they had become social rather than political distinctions. Everywhere the bourgeois ministers claimed the same rights at court as the old noble families. They aspired to wear the same court suits prescribed by the rules of etiquette for noblemen, while they were supposed to come in the official robes they wore in Parliament. For a long time, Saint-Simon and the dukes blocked egalitarian claims.

His concern for the standards and integrity of his class derived from his conception of the total historical context in which a new social world was being born. The trial against Luxembourg was but a symbol for the things he most highly cherished. [Luxembourg got caught up in *L'affaire des poisons* (1677–1682), a sensational criminal investigation and trial. He was acquitted at trial.—Eds.] By means of his leadership among the dukes, Saint-Simon tried to revive the meaning of etiquette as a factor crucial to their unity and distinction. Though his handling of the Luxembourg affair gave him a new reputation with the dukes, it did not impress the court, where the great general had many friends. But Saint-Simon believed he had a worthwhile cause.

Duchesses customarily collected at the King's Mass. Once, two ladies not of the highest ranks of nobility refused to collect and asked to be excused, whereupon Saint-Simon became alarmed and advised Mme de Saint-Simon and the duchesses not to collect either—in a kind of aristocratic sabotage of a privilege that the king considered an honor. Louis XIV became very angry over the incident; Saint-Simon asked for and was granted an audience. He explained to the king that his whole endeavor was to rekindle the awareness of the diverse patterns of etiquette in order to strengthen the dedication of the nobles to the king's service and to close their ranks around him against the onslaught of the bourgeoisie. The king seemed to be satisfied, but really cared little for this cause, and concluded that all the duchesses should collect without any exception.

Although it is impossible to mention all the rules that had been usages, and then codes, for the privileged classes, a few examples should make Saint-Simon's zeal understandable. It was considered an honor, for instance, to be invited by the king to hold the candlestick at his *coucher*. Saint-Simon repeatedly stated that he was asked to hold the candlestick just at the time the king had blamed him for his intervention on behalf of the dukes. Every courtier was anxious to be invited to the intimate and favorite seats of the king, like the Château de Marly or Fontainbleau. They asked when the king came from Mass: "Sire, Marly?" His answer was a sign of favor or disgrace. Saint-Simon was for a long time in disgrace and did not go to Marly.

A distinct privilege of the dukes and duchesses was the kiss by the monarch. Saint-Simon still remembered when he was introduced to the monarch that Louis XIV kissed his father repeatedly (but, of course, the number of kisses referred to the rank of the family, and his own family was thirteenth!). Most important to the duchesses was the privilege of the taboret, or the right to sit on tiny, armless, backless chairs. This was indeed a great honor because there was no alternative for the others except to stand. A duke would be quite willing to renounce his own privileges if he had the chance to obtain the taboret for his duchess. As important as the taboret was the seat of the dukes at the official dinner parties. The Minister of Protocol had to take care of the hierarchy in seating princes and dukes. Madame once scolded Saint-Simon because he dared to take the seat belonging to a German prince. Most conspicuous in these descriptions was the dramatic incident involving the wife of a minister who had, simply by mistake, taken the seat of a noble lady who was right behind her. The wife of the minister was willing to change seats, but the lady asked her simply to forget it. The king was upset and had an outburst in Mme de Maintenon's living room—an event symbolic of his split loyalties. While stating that the bourgeois should be happy and grateful that he had admitted them to his service and even to the court, he insisted that they should never forget the superiority of the nobles to whom they owed respect and obeisance. But Louis XIV knew that the bourgeois ministers had made his greatness and that the conservative and static tradition of privileges and rights belonging to the dukes was not a constructive principle of politics.

Even the prescribed robes and gowns became to Saint-Simon mythical forces that might revive the power of a class without political functions. For example, he was eager to see that the etiquette for mourning and visits of condolence was maintained, that the rules of conduct as to who was obliged to visit whom on these occasions should be observed.

It is a rather nightmarish experience to analyze these enduring concerns of Saint-Simon. Here is a man of intellectual stature and of remarkable sensitivity, who nevertheless makes it his life's work to keep up the rigid standards of social etiquette in order to produce the integration and the reestablishment of meaning and status for his class. It is possible to derive a generalization from such patterns of behavior—a politically defeated class will maintain its social standards and its ways of life, regardless of its political position. The French aristocracies have verified this generalization throughout the revolutions of the nineteenth and twentieth centuries.

Saint-Simon considered Louis XIV the living image of genuine politeness, able to transform stereotypes of etiquette into genuinely gracious and courteous actions. The king made etiquette the manifestation of his own genuine sensitivity:

> He made distinctions for age, merit, and rank, and showed them in his answers, when they went further than the usual "*Je verrai,*" and in his general bearing. Such fine gradations were perfectly displayed in his manner of giving and acknowledging salutations when one approached or left him. . . . But above all, he was unrivaled in his courtesy to women. . . . For ladies he took his hat quite off, but more or less far as occasion demanded. For noblemen he would half-remove it, holding it in the air or against his ear, for a few moments or longer. For landed gentlemen, he only touched his hat. Princes of the blood he greeted in the same way as ladies[.]

For Saint-Simon the most important part of etiquette was the hat (bonnet). The regulation of being covered or uncovered before the Parliament was for him a political fact of greatest significance. It had seemed to him that the defeat of his class was most pronounced in the behavior of the members of Parliament and of their presidents. They had refused to give the dukes and peers the salutations they had given to the princes of the blood and to the members of the royal family—by removing their hats. President Nicolas Potier de Novion [1618–1693] did address the king's representative bareheaded while speaking to the dukes whose heads were covered. This became to Saint-Simon "*L'affaire des Bonnets.*" It seemed to him the most urgent issue of the new government by Philippe II, the Duc d'Orléans [1674–1723] over and above misery, inflation, and taxation. To restore the ducal rights of the bonnet in Parliament was to Saint-Simon a great political issue against the claims of the bourgeois *nobilité de robe.*

Under Louis XIV's regime, the rights of the dukes and peers had been allowed to lapse because the king had allied himself with the subservient Parliament (which had made no objection to the king's urgent request to legitimize his bastard children). Thus it had become a habit for the President of Parliament to remain covered before the dukes, while the dukes had to uncover themselves when speaking. The members of Parliament had made the greatest efforts to reduce the prestige of the dukes; their President, Novion, had thought, for instance, of having a councilor sit on the dukes' bench so as to lower their rank.

The advance of the Parliament, the symbol of bourgeois power promoted by "the king of the vile bourgeoisie," was to Saint-Simon the most humiliating defeat. After the king died, the field was open for the vengeance of the dukes. Saint-Simon urged the Duc d'Orléans to restore the right of the nobles to remain covered when addressing the assembly. But the Regent felt very uncomfortable: "He said several times that the 'affair of the bonnets' was indeed an intolerable infringement of our rights, and the other matters of which we complained not less so, but that we should choose a better occasion." Finally, though, Orléans gave in, and during the first session of Parliament after the king's death, Saint-Simon was allowed to make a point of order. He recounts:

> I said that I was charged by the peers to announce to the assembly that only in consideration of the urgent and vital nature of the matters now to be discussed (the Last Will and Codicil of the late King) would they tolerate the shameless usurpation of the privileges of the *bonnets* and many other abuses of which they had to complain. In so doing they showed their very proper regard for the vital importance of state affairs. Nevertheless, I have made the strongest possible protest in the most formal manner and in the name of the whole body of peers and with the consent of M. le Duc d'Orléans.

It was Saint-Simon's intention to restore the superiority of the dukes in matters of etiquette over the bourgeoisie (which continued to grow in social, as well as political and economic, power all over France). Saint-Simon really believed that such a victory, though only in formal conduct, would give the dukes a renewed prestige and importance in society.

For this reason, he can rightly be called the "Don Quixote of Etiquette." Like Don Quixote, Saint-Simon knew that a new world was in the making. Both wanted to remain true to the ideals of a feudal-knightly past that no longer existed except in their imaginations. Both were wise, sensitive, and imaginative men, except for their respective idées fixes. But these idées fixes gave each a new perspective on the depths of the human being as a creature concretely engaged in the changing constellations of social and historical forces. It is indeed remarkable that a completely mad assumption opened up the use of what became genuinely sociological methods in historiography, as well as a general conception of the total social situation as a field for scientific inquiry.

The general sociological implication is quite relevant for the explanation and understanding of contemporary experiences in an age of almost total revolution. All politically defeated classes tend to maintain their manners, mannerisms, attitudes, discipline, and ways of life as something they cannot and will not be deprived of. The challenge of defeat is the test of human strength—so, for instance, the concentration camps in Nazi Germany presented a challenge to the intellectual, moral, and vital discipline, the courage and endurance of their inmates. Saint-Simon did not anticipate anything approaching this, except for his account of the sadism of the *dragonnades*, but he knew that it was a blessing for human beings to be convinced of the meaning of themselves as a class and of the significance of their traditions for the historical-social process.

It belongs to the dialectics of history to study how old patterns of etiquette and new types of social conduct clash with one another. But etiquette can be a dynamic and living concern, just as it can be a mere sham. In all societies, etiquette is the prerequisite for the functioning of social interaction. It constitutes the ritual for the encounter of men in their various roles and establishes the ceremonies that make articulate and meaningful the routine of everyday life and the solemn interruption of it by the great festivals of life and death. Etiquette is the symbolic expression and manifestation of mutual recognition by men in their social roles, as superiors and inferiors, as coordinated agents, or in hierarchically organized bureaucracies. All lasting social institutions have their etiquette that guides men on their respective roads toward their various goals, whether it be within a family, a military unit, a business office, or an ecclesiastical institution. Everywhere men live according to specific rules—rituals, etiquette, or stereotypes of behavior. At first, all such types of behavior have a specific meaning; they can become irrelevant when new patterns of acting come into being, but they can be revived and receive a new meaning and force as a last resort of defeated classes and groups. This is precisely the sociological significance of the ardent fights by the dukes and peers against the new wave of the bourgeois. It is a historical and human phenomenon, tragic and comic, bearing at once the depth of human grandeur and misery. The loyalty and allegiance to our traditions, to the training by our ancestors, and to the teaching by our fathers remain a lasting good for those who follow this way of life.

The Grim Carnival: The Court as Appearance and Reality

At the court of Louis XIV, the etiquette of the times prescribed rigid social rules. The courtiers, the nobles and their clans, the ministers, the generals, and the bourgeois of the robe had firm guideposts for their behavior within the complex social stratification. The etiquette prescribed the varying degrees of politeness; it established the legality of the courtiers' behavior; its moral content was the work of the individual human beings who made it function. Johann Wolfgang von Goethe [1749–1832] once remarked that politeness has two aspects: the one defensive, constructing fences to preserve distance and aloofness; the other, the politeness of the heart, indicating the deepest sensitivity of a human lover for the independence and inner freedom of the beloved. Saint-Simon knew very well that although the king and Mme de Maintenon could fully control the legality of the norms of etiquette, they rarely realized the morality of the behavior of the courtiers. Appearance and reality often merged in the "carnival" at Versailles, particularly when members of the royal families were born, married, or died. Even in the routine of everyday life that was formed according to the routine of the king, the stereotypes of prescribed behavior made life at the court appear, at least to the outsider, regimented, although harmonious. But to the analytical eyes of a presociological historian, this harmonious totality was sheer deception, as fictitious as a carnival. Only on the surface was it gay and superior to the routine of everyday life; underneath was a complex of unleashed greed, fear, and combat, merged and united by the demonic pressure of sex. Saint-Simon, though often enjoying as an aesthete the amenities of the carnival, was too serious a sociological historian not to see the grim aspect of reality behind the stage of the world.

Saint-Simon distinguished three different social groupings at Versailles, the formation of which was related to the lonely majesty of the king. No one really enjoyed the life at the court but rather feared the whims of the old man who had become the incarnation of *Fortuna* for most men. Even the next of kin were frightened of him. Monseigneur, a man fifty years old, felt the pressure of his father's glory, power, and pride as depressing, his suspicions and jealousies as shocking. The king had driven him into indifference and inertia because he had kept him aloof from all participation in government and politics. What remained to him was just forced leisure that he enjoyed with his mistress, whom he secretly married (in the example of the king and Mme de Maintenon). Monseigneur, however, was to the king and to the courtiers a most important person. In the near future, he would probably be the king of France. For this reason, he maintained his own court at Meudon. He was surrounded by his friends and generals, nobles, and princes who were speculating upon his forthcoming government. But, according to Saint-Simon, the Dauphin and his friends never talked politics or discussed war and peace or the decay of his father's imperialism. All these men and women looked forward to his coming to the throne as the moment to share in the spoils. In spite of the splendor and gracefulness of the appearance, reality was an ill-concealed struggle for personal interest, for the exploitation of lucrative offices, alimonies, or promotions. In a genuinely sociological analysis, Saint-Simon described the "rackets" of Monseigneur, as we would analyze a political administration—the pragmatic and utilitarian "gang" speculating on the future as a business proposition.

Saint-Simon pointed out in a radical way that the court was the central institution for the production and distribution of power. In marvelously descriptive imagery, he revealed the court as a social mechanism. The court, he said, is a competitive society in which different associations—called "machines"—struggle with one another for the monopoly of power. The social process is mechanical because it is subject to the law of attraction and repulsion, men moving and being moved. They gather together for realizing their purposes under the pressure of competing machines. The reality of this game is tough and disillusioning as its appearance is aesthetically perfect in a complete, though fictitious, harmony. The courtiers and mistresses, the confessors and generals, the dukes and the physicians of the king are the engineers and puppets of the show that seems to be controlled by the great magician but is, in reality, directed by the king's associates and agents.

Saint-Simon's analyses of the patterns of reciprocity at Versailles are masterpieces of an applied theory of social interaction. The king, worshipped like a god, is to Saint-Simon the victim and the prisoner of his ministers, his confessors, and his mistresses. His ministers depended upon Mme de Maintenon, who for her part was under the pressure of her friends, whose promotions and support were indispensable for her own position and prestige. Thus, Saint-Simon conceived of a second machine centered around Mme de Maintenon. She was the lasting center for the men who made up the government or aspired to it. This interdependence of the ministers and of Mme de Maintenon was logical and inescapable. The ministers, on the other hand, were superior to Mme de Maintenon and to the king regarding information, learning, and administrative skills. They knew from experience what could and should be done under the conditions of the king's and Mme de Maintenon's minds and attitudes. Such superiority was, however, balanced by the insecurity of the system in which they were constantly exposed to intrigues of all sorts. For this reason, they knew that their superiority could only be secured when granted by Mme de Maintenon. She alone could support them in the end because she needed the ministers for her own security. Being under the pressure of the influential clans, officers, bishops, and personal friends to help them to get offices, promotions, and the like, her reputation depended on her ability to satisfy the requests of the many who implored her support for gaining favor with the king. But apart from her role as confidential adviser to the king, she was anxious to rule and exploit the ministers for her own vested interests. She was mainly interested in the treasury, and in the ministry of war, for distributing funds and offices. She obliged the ministers, who for objective reasons did not comply with her requests to be ruthlessly removed. Most ministers were prudent enough never to object to her demands, for they had their own vested interests. They were eager to bring their sons and relatives into office with the twofold purpose of enriching themselves and of surrounding themselves with relatives whom they could trust. Thus, their relationship with Mme de Maintenon was like that one might have with a mutual insurance company.

Saint-Simon referred to still another machine made up of those who gambled on a better future. They hoped that the young and remarkable Duc de Burgogne might become Dauphin in the event of Monseigneur's death. The prince embodied (to a few thoughtful and imaginative noblemen) the idea of an anti-despotic, reactionary constitutionalism, with the emphasis on the dukes and peers in government and on the Estates as an advisory body. Fénélon was the political and spiritual leader of this small group, to which Saint-Simon also belonged.

The three groups were not organized "rackets," but open associations for specific purposes, and cross-relations were therefore inescapable. At a court where *Fortuna* seemed to rule the lives of everyone, everyone was anxious to have insurance against the accidents of court life. Saint-Simon had friends and relatives in all camps who knew quite well that even an idealist and Christian gentleman needed virtue and prudence.

One of his remarkable observations is contained in the statement that men never act as individuals, but as members of a clan. The great families asked favors even for distant cousins because their dynamic strength increased with their influence on and in government. The new bourgeois families had learned from the feudal clans: One for All and All for One. The king liked such closed ranks in his service, for he had learned from experience that he could rely more on group responsibility than on that of individuals. He felt that a clan could better discipline and control its own members for common solidarity, so as not to bring disgrace upon the whole group. They would serve the king well and would see to it that they enriched themselves in a respectable way. Louis XIV found this tradition of recruitment most satisfactory. After all, he could not forget that the clan of Michel Le Tellier [1603–1685], including Jean Baptiste Colbert [1619–1683], François Michel Le Tellier, Marquis de Louvois [1641–1691], and Louis François Marie Le Tellier Marquis de Barbezieux [1668–1710], had laid the foundations for his own grandeur. Saint-Simon, however, avidly cursed these bourgeois who had destroyed the feudal pattern of the army and had constructed the beginnings of a rational militarism. His emphasis provides a valuable perspective for historians: it is probably necessary to reconsider many histories and to stress neither the importance of individuals nor of collective trends, but of the articulate power of the great families.

Saint-Simon enjoyed analyzing the techniques that men applied for achieving their ends. The court was the ideal place for intrigues, conspiracies, and pressure groups; it formed the social jungle where everyone fought for vested interests. There is no human relationship that was not used or abused for social advancement, political power, or economic gain. Almost all social interaction was reduced to "business," in a competitive struggle for superiority. Some advanced on the social ladder because the king liked them as champions at billiards; others used their charm and wits in the drawing rooms of Mme de Maintenon, in order to gain careers in the army or in the civil service; still others tried to push their way up through love affairs with princesses or mistresses of princes. Husbands became the procurers for their wives in order to achieve great careers.

Saint-Simon was fascinated by the motives of the actors at court. He found that men everywhere are moved to act by their own interests and passions. Honoré de Balzac [1799–1850] and Stendhal [Marie-Henri Beyle (1783–1842)], the genuine Saint-Simonians, have verified the universality of his thesis, at least for the nineteenth century. Saint-Simon concluded that all institutional behavior is primarily determined by social interests, not by ideal postulates. Power, he contended, is the final goal of men in all walks of life; it alone secures independence and freedom of action; in all groups, men yearn to be *first,* superior to all others. Antagonism and competition merge in the lust for power. Thus, he saw the life at court as grim; there men struggle for predominance in the general struggle for survival. The court was but the beautiful picture of the jungle of social action that exists all over the world. Saint-Simon knew from his own experience how sweet vengeance and the bestial triumph over hated enemies can be.

But other human beings in Saint-Simon's presentation set the images of the saint, the hero, the moral human being in the midst of the jungle. There are the ascetic princes of the Church, men of true dedication to God and to their parishes, living in the Imitation of Christ. There are the great soldiers who do not seek glory for themselves, but cherish victory for the king and perfection in their commands. There are Louis-François de Boufflers [1644–1711], Nicolas Catinat [1637–1712], and many others who are dedicated and ascetic men in their fields.

Throughout the *Mémoires*, Saint-Simon mentions nobles and successful courtiers, ministers, gentlemen, ladies, and princesses, men and women who had gained prestigious reputations in politics and love, who suddenly departed the scene of their triumphs and devoted themselves to God in penitent orders, often the Carmelites. For the purely descriptive variety of human destinies, Saint-Simon drew from the tremendous range that presented itself at the end of the seventeenth century. Here he disclosed all the lusts of flesh and of power, the enjoyment of vanity and glory, the beauty of wealth and its possibilities, and, at the same time, the most sublime vision of the divine and the most creative unfolding of the mind. The elements of transition and change and the constituents of eternity were intertwined in this age with pretense and truth, appearance and reality, in the ambiguity and ambivalence of natural, historical man.

Shakespeare of Portraits

Saint-Simon lived by his eyes, agreeing fully with Homer that living should be defined as seeing the light of the sun that gives plasticity and pattern to the living. The light of the sun is a blessing and a curse, illuminating and burning, creative and destructive; but Saint-Simon knew as well the opaqueness of the night, the abyss of sex, and the voluptuousness of love. He had seen the sublime and the vulgar in the intimate relationships of the actors on the stage of the world. In the description and analysis of the social world, he had witnessed continuous change in the fluid structure of the court; he had inaugurated a presociological approach intended to explain the total human-social situation in the interdependence of its constituent parts. For this reason, his "Portraits," being constructs of the total human being, are relevant for the understanding of sociohistorical action.

The method deserves some attention. In contemporary history some scientists, following Max Weber and others, construct ideal types according to their specific scientific interest; these might be political, social, or even economic. This methodological device makes it possible to build a coherent and logical world, a fictive construct that satisfies the scientific concern. We may ask whether the price the scientist pays for his objectivity is too high.

Saint-Simon either constructed images of various human beings in their ongoing action, or he painted their portraits after they died. The former have to be put together like a mosaic, while the latter are always living images of a stream of a total human unfolding.

The pattern of the portrait was initiated not by Saint-Simon, but by the efforts of a defeated class to observe its own way of life and to reflect on its own interaction with other classes. Under the influence of Montaigne, René Descartes [1596–1650], and Bernard Le Bovier de Fontenelle [1657–1757], the former Frondists [Fronde Parlementaire (1648–1649) and the Fronde des nobles (1650–1653)—Eds.] seriously attempted to reflect on themselves and to encounter the others of their time as persons of another class (i.e., as alter egos). Saint-Simon, however, was able to bring the style and form of the portrait to such fullness that we are able to grasp the fact that each human being is a microcosm whose beginning and end merge into the cycle of life itself. Saint-Simon was completely dissatisfied with his portraits, thinking them clumsy and rudimentary fragments of images that he was unable to frame properly, in the classical style. He was indeed not a writer of the eighteenth century, as he rarely displayed balance in punctuation or sentence structure. Yet, it is just this nonclassical style that makes him an almost contemporary writer. The nongrammatical and asyndetic coexistence of terms describing human qualities in the portraits turn them into a true spontaneous experience of another's own inwardness, the expression of an open system of possibilities.

Saint-Simon usually began with the description of his subject's physical qualities. He was most anxious to separate these from the "acquired" qualities: the ways of speaking, moving, and other bodily gestures, poise, politeness, discipline, and the like. For this reason, he can be said to have followed continually a sociological method in describing and interpreting the various persons conceived as images or types of men. The training and education of the young noblemen produced human beings whose bodies and minds were taught to represent a specific way of life, to embody specific social roles every moment of their lives. The educated and cultured classes of the bourgeois patricians had been brought up in the appreciation of graceful conduct rather than mere behavior, in the goods of the *cultura animi* rather than in the virtues of aristocratic conversation, in the achievement of objective values instead of the subjective presentation of a social self. For this reason, too, Saint-Simon's portraits have a depth in the dimension that recognizes the power of recollections, the strength of traditions in the formation of human beings; his description of persons as "bourgeois" is never a value judgment, but a sociological category that explains certain ways of speaking, modes of politeness, and inner independence in social situations, as they are correlated with bourgeois standards. Men have a natural constitution, but their social roles and historical destiny are of the utmost importance for their growth or decay.

The character of Louis XIV became a model case in Saint-Simon's portraits. He had natural charm, poise, and dignity; he had been kept in ignorance but was alert enough to adapt easily to his informed and learned ministers; and he had acquired the will to rule by himself and not to be the puppet either of his mother or of Cardinal Mazarin. But most important in his development were the prostration and flattery of the courtiers, confessors, and mistresses. They were the ones who created the image of the glorious, benevolent, and absolute king, whose power was unshakable in the Western world. His ministers made him believe that his wisdom ruled their own work, while in actual fact, he granted nineteen of twenty decisions submitted to him by the ministers. No one, however, could predict just what decision would be the one rejected by him, in his effort to show his absolute power. The minister of war was most careful not to risk hazards in his field. He kept the king busy with parades, new uniforms, and regulations for garrison duties, and asked him to think of rewards, medals, and the like, for individuals and standards for regimental units that performed with credit.

Saint-Simon anticipated a genuinely sociological problem in his description of the relationships between the king and his courtiers. Louis XIV established an image of his greatness that was accepted by the people at the court. But the courtiers continuously manipulated this image, and the king was willing to adapt himself to their image of him. As a consequence, the image of the "great king" as a social pattern survived the defeats of the last twenty years of his life, the misery of the people, and the plight of the nobles.

In the portrait of Mme de Maintenon, he achieves an admirable completeness and balance in describing her positive and negative qualities. He was, indeed, fascinated by the natural intelligence and alertness of the former Mme Scarron. He had seen that her precarious character could only have been the result of her various social roles. As Mme Scarron, she had learned to please; she had known what love affairs were really like and had been conscious of the transitory character of most human relationships. She had been ready to make the best use of the opportunities that Mme de Montespan [1640–1707], Louis XIV's mistress, had offered her. Mme de Montespan forced the king to appoint Mme de Maintenon as governess to their illegitimate children, although the king initially thought the younger woman to be disgusting and repulsive. But, once in position, she prudently managed to obtain his attention. She wisely advised Mme de Montespan not to embarrass the king with her moods; she talked to him and demonstrated the deepest concern for his feelings. After the death of his queen, Marie-Thérèse of Austria [1638–1683], and his final estrangement from Mme de Montespan, Mme de Maintenon succeeded in gaining his affection by a strange combination of religious piety and sensual warmth, a mixture of fictitious propriety and political scheming.

She persuaded the lonely king to marry her secretly, but she never accomplished her heart's desire to see the marriage publicly declared. She was witty and alert by nature; she had learned to be polite, pleasing, and compliant. Her ambitions made her a conscious planner, a careerist with superior intelligence who intrigued for her own benefit. She was, besides this, a marvelous actress who would play almost any role, having experienced years of servitude during which she had to practice distance and modesty. But, having achieved her goals, she performed all the roles of the carnival with grace and relaxation. She beautifully pretended the virtues of truth and frankness, while dissimulating her lust for power and her ambition to rule the state by controlling the king.

The most dramatic portrait is that of Louis Duc de Bourgogne, the grandson of Louis XIV. Having been very close to him, Saint-Simon gives us a lucid picture of a complex and dynamic human being. In his youth, he had been open to all kinds of passions, thirsting for pleasures with violence. But, being open to everything, he was vulnerable to the spiritual passions and noble enthusiasm of his tutor, the Abbé Fénélon, who had indoctrinated him with a political utopia—*Télémaque*—of a reactionary constitutional monarchy. This old, yet new, monarchy was to be focused around the reestablishment of the political position of the dukes and peers, in order to destroy the despotism of Louis XIV. Fénélon was able to channel the uninhibited desires and passions of the prince into a spiritual discipline of dedication to his duties. He felt the blessings of asceticism in his life, and began to hate the continuous war. Thus, he created many enemies at court and in the army, with the king leading the criticism of his own piety. The young prince had been the hope of all noblemen who longed for a new constitutional regime if and when he would become Dauphin. To Saint-Simon, he was the living image of the transforming power of spirituality—turning the profligate young man into a serious and dedicated statesman of complete integrity. He had taken Saint-Simon's conception of the dukes and peers seriously and was in full agreement with him. The statement on the transforming power of the spiritual is not, therefore, a contradiction of Saint-Simon's reflections on the motives of collective action. But he had seen too many character developments that deviated from the general tendencies of socially approved behavior for him to trust completely this image he had formed of the prince.

The portrait of the man who had been the tutor of the Duc de Burgogne and the revered political thinker who gave hope to Saint-Simon and his class is the most plastic. The portrait of the archbishop Fénélon was written with profound sympathy and devotion; it is a picture of a most complex human being, one whose very contradictions reveal in their unity the greatness of the man. M. de Fénélon had been tutor to the grandson of the king, friend and spiritual adviser of Mme de Maintenon, to whom he had also introduced his mystical friend, Jeanne-Marie Bouvier de la Motte-Guyon [1648–1717]. He was at the height of his influence and power when his colleague and competitor, Jacques-Bénigne Bossuet [1627–1704], and other jealous prelates rallied to destroy him because of his adherence to the mystical pattern of Quietism.

Fénélon never flinched from his belief in the genuineness of the mystic, Mme Guyon. He submitted with humility and sincerity to Mme Guyon's condemnation by Rome. In a move that was supposed to be his exile, he quietly left Versailles for Cambrai. There he exhibited a true spirit of charity; no one harmed the Jansenists, and there everyone in need of physical and spiritual support, regardless of his occupation, found admission to Fénélon. His burning love for the way, the truth, and the life gave him the courage and patience to live up to his own ideals of maintaining himself in devotion to God and to the expectations of his followers at Versailles.

Saint-Simon was right to stress the point that a spiritual flame was burning in Fénélon's heart. Fénélon took his own aristocratic descent as a moral and spiritual obligation; pride and humility were not alternatives to him. And, indeed, he enjoyed the gifts of learning, of mystical vision, and the stream of love that God had given him in His Grace.

The description of Fénélon's physical being is unforgettable—a tall, slim man, with a long white face, an aquiline nose, and eyes the flames and spirit of which overwhelmed one like a torrent. This face, while revealing the most contrasting traits, did not disturb the inner harmony and integrity of his mind, but expressed a unity of gravity and charm, of seriousness and joyfulness. It manifested the scholar, the bishop, and the grand seigneur. All these diverse elements and aspects were united and merged into the open stream of a continuously growing personality; it contributed to his greatness and to the halo of saintliness that had taken the blows of destiny and of the intrigues of his enemies. He was superior to his fate, however, because he had affirmed it with humility and the creative spirit of spiritual liberation. His greatness was visible even at the surface of his conduct, combining a delicate politeness with genuine depth and integrity, nobility with a radiant mind, and spirituality with the deepest concern for the life of man in the world. Saint-Simon was convinced that this human being embodied the greatest range of human possibilities that he had discovered and presented in the single images of his "Portraits."

Throughout the *Mémoires*, many persons are described in a mosaic in various situations and summarized in a portrait as a commemoration of their death. In such interpretations of human beings, men are always open and dynamic systems, streams of experience and consciousness with an infinite number of possibilities. The portraits are dramatic in the highest degree, tragic and comic alike; often the acting and suffering of the persons presented are tragic and comic in the same acts. It is this totality, this complete comprehension of a person in the understanding of his actions that brings Saint-Simon closest to Shakespeare's plenitude.

The drama of Madame [Marie-Thérèse] is displayed throughout the *Mémoires*. As a proud German princess, conscious to the utmost of her own pedigree, she is pictured at the opening of the *Mémoires* lamenting the engagement of her son to an illegitimate daughter of the king. The weakness of her son, who had promised not to comply with the king's wishes, was shocking to her. She felt free to demonstrate her anger before the court and to box the ears of her son when he greeted her with a hand kiss. She knew the Duc d'Orléans well enough to understand his weaknesses. She had once told Saint-Simon that it was most unfortunate that her son had so many remarkable qualities—esprit, wit, intellectual curiosity, poise, tact—but that he never turned those positive traits to any good. He was irresponsible, escaping from the enforced marriage and the unkept promises of the king into a life of debauchery. He could never resist his lusts and moods and ultimately pursued various seductions with pleasure.

Madame had been very much in love with the charming and handsome king before his affairs with Mme de Maintenon. She never forgave him the secret marriage and often wrote to her German relatives about the king's love for this person whom she often dubbed his concubine and whore. She gave a true picture of Mme de Maintenon's power over the king and over France. She never was prudent enough, however, to consider the implications of such sweeping statements on the censorship of the royal family. A censor once found the text of her letters rude enough to warrant sending a package of them to the king. The king never mentioned this to Madame, but his relationship to her became very formal. When Monsieur died, Madame faced an embarrassing dilemma; the marriage contract specified she either enter a convent or retreat to a lonely country house. Madame disliked both possibilities immensely and tried to see the king about it. But he ordered her to visit Mme de Maintenon, who had received the incriminating correspondence from the king. The scene between the two ladies is a model case of catharsis in a tragic and comic sense. Madame complained that their relationship had become extremely formal and that she regretted it. Mme de Maintenon took Madame's letters and showed them to her, upon which Madame broke down, humiliated herself, asked forgiveness, and let Mme de Maintenon enjoy her triumph. It was a genuinely dramatic scene; its greatness for Saint Simon's presentation consisted in the fact that he showed sympathy for Madame and, at the same time, made transparent the objectively comical aspect of the situation. It could be enjoyed in its grim ridiculousness because their conversation turned out well—

Madame was allowed to remain at the court. This final portrait by Saint Simon is a classic example of his style:

> She was strong, courageous, German to the utmost degree: frank, straightforward, good and charitable, noble and great in her conduct—and petty and pedantic in everything that was due to her. She was truly possessed, always writing letters to her family and friends, except for the few hours she had to give to official entertainments. Otherwise she was alone with her ladies, harsh, rude, easily repulsed by people and things, feared for the responses she gave in conversation; no kindness, no alertness, no intellectual dynamism, though not without *esprit*; no flexibility, jealous to the bone, as was said, of everything that was due to her; the figure and boorishness of a Swiss guard and, with all this, capable of a tender and inviolable friendship.

The end of the portrait is the center of the character analysis; the description at the beginning refers to the qualities deriving from her education and social roles, from her loneliness and forlornness. Continuing the analysis, Saint-Simon interpreted her sensitivity and intellectual standards and found them wanting; but finally he came to the basic roots of her existence, which were, he felt, in strong contrast to her physical appearance. Everything is intertwined, logically unintelligible but understandable as the essence of a human being: a unity in contradiction.

The portrait of her son, the Duc d'Orléans, is most revealing because, from their early youth, he had been Saint-Simon's best friend. At the beginning of the *Mémoires*, Saint-Simon described him as insecure and helpless before his mother and the king's sweet coercion. Regardless of his character, everyone would have submitted to the command of the king. The enforced marriage, however, remained without political consequences; no political or military assignment came to him. Much later, he obtained military positions in Spain and Italy. But before that happened, he escaped into a variety of activities that serve to illuminate his intellectual standards. He was fascinated by the sciences, devoted to chemical experimentation and to problems of physics. Later he was attracted to painting and had his daughter model for him in a slightly incestuous relationship. In spite of Orléans's intellectual curiosity, his main escapes were his independent love affairs. He was firmly antireligious, probably following the sophisticated pattern of Fontenelle. On the other hand, he believed that men might know the unknowable and that people could predict the future. Saint-Simon reported in the minutest detail how Orléans listened to a girl who, staring in a glass, correctly described the furniture and equipment of a place she had never actually seen. When he asked her manager about his own future, he was surprised that the man did not see the king's grandsons in the picture of the future, although he let him see a closed crown without the insignia, the meaning of which he could not discern. In spite of such games with destiny, he was highly intelligent and sensitive, but without goals and convictions—drifting where his friends and moods pushed him. He was full of wit and irony, and enjoyed twitting the narrowness of the king. When he was sent to Spain as the commander of an army, he asked the king to give him a friend as his aide. The king refused on the argument that the man was a Jansenist. Orléans corrected the statement: "But the man is an atheist!" This was not objectionable to Louis XIV. Orléans told the story to Saint-Simon with irony and laughter. He was willing to forsake prudence and forget possible political consequences wherever he could express his wit and his secret criticism with irony. In Spain, he ironically toasted the two great ladies who ruled France and Spain. He did not mention their names, however; but this foolish act, nevertheless, earned him the lasting hatred of Mme de Maintenon and Mme des Ursins [Marie-Anne de La Trémoille, princesse des Ursins (1642–1722)].

He was fascinating in his contradictions: sentimental and cynical, alert in thinking and irresponsible in action, a loyal friend, but careless of his enemies. He was a charming and nonchalant weakling, never taking himself or his duties seriously. Saint-Simon and the popular singers of the day called him "*Debonnaire.*" Orléans himself laughed at his own reputation, but respected intellectual standards. He had contempt for vulgar and trivial people. He was sensitive in all his relationships; his manners and attitudes were refined. He never spoke of himself but had definite ideas on the value of others. His greatest weakness was his belief that he resembled Henry IV [1553–1610] in everything he did, and he took to imitating Henry IV's mannerisms and witticisms. Like Henry IV, he was good, human, sympathetic, unwilling to harm anyone. But he shared in his negative aspects of an easygoing character as well. Orléans had no will or intention to act and did not even care for the direction that he should have followed in politics. As Regent, he underwent the routine of government as if it were a nightmarish dream, while his real life began after the sun had gone down (when he gave himself over to his pleasures and mistresses). All his esprit, wit, and intellectual superiority were worthless because he did not care for his social position and was deeply disgusted with his life; a sense of frustration and of melancholy voluptuousness penetrated his cynicism. For this reason, Saint-Simon's picture of the dying Orléans, his decaying body taken as a symbol of what it is to be human, is a summary of the wasted life of a man who could have been something else.

There are many more pictures and portraits of people who did not play significant roles in the political life of the times—the human beings whom Saint-Simon selected for their own unique characteristics, tender or rude, courteous or vulgar. He took notice of kidnappings and elopements, and of comical situations in general. There is the short portrait of a physically small lady-in-waiting, and the most tender words for her: "tout âme tout esprit et charmant, toujours nouveau . . . délicat sur l'esprit et amoureux de l'esprit, quand elle le trouvait à son gré." There is the rich story of Mme de Charlus [née Marie Françoise de Paule de Bethisy (1657–1719)], whose wig caught fire at the dinner table. The Archbishop of Rheims quickly removed the wig in order to save her life. The lady, however, not aware of what had happened to her, was full of wrath and threw her boiled egg into the face of her neighbor. Saint-Simon reported, as well, the robberies by gangsters who had relieved two noblemen of their possessions when traveling in their coach. After the robbers had departed, one of the gentlemen found that they had overlooked some valuables hidden in his clothing and was overjoyed at his good fortune. His friend, however, was so angry that he called the gangsters back to take the rest of his friend's property!

Throughout the *Mémoires*, the portraits illuminate the scope of human possibilities, the *condition humaine* in its infinite variety—but the same human condition that every man carried with himself—in its depth layers, as they result from the acquired and required qualities of man in his historically conditioned social roles. There is no prose writer who comes closer to the imaginativeness and sensitivity of Shakespeare than Saint-Simon. His openness to all human potentialities, whether sensual or spiritual, courageous or fateful, patient or enthusiastic, makes it evident that for him everything human is worth observation and understanding.

Saint-Simon did not provide a portrait of himself. He was the child of aged parents, physically weak, small, unattractive, and nervous. Having been educated and reared among older people, he lived far more in their worlds, in the past of revered traditions, than in his own. He was willing to accept their values, and he grew up with a sense of worship for Louis XIII [1601–1643], the benefactor of his father. To Saint-Simon the image of this king was that of the chaste and virtuous man—a rather precarious yardstick for king's successor. Saint-Simon was not sensual; he praised the pleasures of the mind as superior to the futility of the senses, but he was able to give, nevertheless, a delicate portrait of Anne Ninon de L'Enclos [1620–1705], who was intellectually in control of her love affairs and often took a quite ironic look at her lovers and those who aspired to become her lovers. Though he was not sensual, he was still always seeking, always aware. "See and be radiant" is profoundly true for his genius, for with his eyes he penetrated everything; they were organs of cognition and illumination, constituting the hypersensitivity that made him one of the greatest pre- and postpsychological thinkers of the social and historical world.

He was obsessed and absorbed by an idée fixe—the reestablishment of the political rule of the dukes and peers in a world that was being carried away by the stream of the urban and bourgeois advance. For this reason, he started his reform by infusing meaning and relevance into the rules of etiquette, which he took to be the symbol for noble superiority. The "*Affaire des Bonnets*" became to him a revolutionary deed, one of extreme urgency even while the country was being threatened with financial bankruptcy and human misery. The triumph in the life of the little duke was the *Lit de Justice* after the king's death. Having proclaimed the old rights of the dukes as over against the usurpations of the *noblesse de robe*, he described himself:

> Joy was nearly killing me. I truly felt as though I were going to swoon, for my heart seemed to swell within me and could find no room in which to expand. I did violence to my feelings in order not to betray them, yet the very torrent was a delight. I remembered the long days and years

> of servitude, those unhappy times, when like a victim I was dragged to the Parliament to witness the triumph of the bastards. Now at last my eyes would see the fulfillment of my prophecy. I could rightly congratulate myself that all this has been brought about by me—and that I enjoyed the shining splendor of the hour in the presence of the king and all that august assembly. I triumphed, I was avenged, I rejoiced in my vengeance. I delighted in the satisfaction of my strongest, most eager, and most steadfast desires[.]

He too was tragic and comic alike. But there is greatness in the man whose sensitivity and imagination, whose penetrating and illuminating eyes, made him conceive of the historical world and of its social patterns as the *comédie humaine.* In his ultimate glory, he is not the historian, sociologist, or psychologist, but the great poet who magically resurrected a world of dead men and transformed them into loving and hating people, conspiring with, for, and against one another in their lust, their aspirations for power and recognition by others, and the problem of being themselves. Here was a man whose work was an inspiration to the great French novelists of the nineteenth and twentieth centuries, as it is even now to psychologists, sociologists, and philosophers. It stands today as a major source of aesthetic suggestion and scientific challenge.

Notes

1. The term *total social situation* was coined by Marcel Mauss [1872–1950], the nephew of Émile Durkheim [1858–1917] and a distinguished sociologist and anthropologist in his own right. Saint-Simon anticipates this notion in his own conception of "contemporary history."

7

Montesquieu: The Historical Variables of the *Condition Humaine*

The Personality and His Meeting with Himself

When Charles-Louis de Secondat, Baron de La Brède et de Montesquieu [1689–1755] published his book on Rome [*Considérations sur les causes de la grandeur des Romains et de leur décadence* (1734)—Eds.], he presented the work personally to Louis Duc de Saint-Simon [1675–1755], who lived in retirement at his château. This meeting is symbolic of Montesquieu's political views and his insatiable curiosity for the minutest details that make up a historical-political totality. Montesquieu's visit to Saint-Simon was a political demonstration. Both grand seigneurs were united in violent hatred of the despotism of the absolute state and shared a longing for the constitutional pattern of traditional medieval monarchies. Both could only visualize a reactionary monarchy in which the king shared the government with the estates of nobles, clergy, and patricians. Both were dedicated to the fight for a constitutional conservatism that understood political liberty as the balance between the sovereignty of the monarch and the rights of the Estates in participating in the royal government. Their political attitude was later on taken up by Louis Gabriel de Bonald [1754–1840] and Joseph De Maistre [1753–1821].

Published originally in a slightly different form in Albert Salomon, *In Praise of Enlightenment* (Cleveland: Meridian Books, 1963). Republished by permission from Frank Salomon.

Montesquieu's visit was motivated by still another reason. No one but Saint-Simon could tell him more vividly the minutest details of the functioning of the political mechanism under the rule of Louis XIV and the Régent than the old courtier and friend of the Duc d'Orléans. Saint-Simon had begun to write his *Memoires* after having collected notes and observations for almost thirty years.

Here were two grand seigneurs who were political reactionaries and philosopher-poets. They both had conceptions of the historical worlds as Human Comedies, intelligible though often absurd; they both had their ideas on the providential meaning of history or its meaninglessness; both believed in the identity of human nature that could appear in a variety of social roles and realize itself in conformity with them, in escaping from them, and in revolting against them.

They were philosophers like François de La Rochefoucauld [1613–1680] and Charles de Saint-Evrémont [1613–1703], in spite of being grand seigneurs and noblemen of the highest rank. They transformed their frustrations and failures into illuminating reflections on the causes of grandeur and misery; they succeeded in conquering their defeats and gaining distance and independence because they were philosophers and seers. They had hoped to play roles in public life and were rejected or defeated or exiled.

Montesquieu, who had traveled for years through Italy, Central Europe, England, and the Netherlands, had hoped for a position in the Foreign Office and was not accepted. This disappointment, merged with erotic and other human defeats, led him to scholarship and learning, the best activities for overcoming grief and conquering human suffering and disappointment.

Montesquieu was trained in law. His families belonged to the *noblesse de robe* and to the *noblesse d'*épée. Throughout his works, he stressed the political and juridical concerns of his work. Apart from these social conditions of his life, he was a Southerner from Gascony, like Michel de Montaigne [1533–1592], who had received legal training and was councilor at the same Parliament of Bordeaux. They knew the plight of the individual surrounded and limited by abstract and unfeeling generalizations of law, court procedure, and grim judgments. Both were violently anti-Christian. In Montesquieu's thought, there are many reflections that could have been derived from Montaigne's *Essays.* As a matter of fact, Montesquieu seriously considered writing about Montaigne. Both men knew the complexity of words, how to be sensual and rational in one. Montesquieu's thesis that reason is the noblest of the senses is completely in line with Montaigne's basic idea of the inseparable relationship of nature and reason.

Montesquieu was keenly aware that he was living at a crossroad of history. He stressed that the age of feudal and military patterns of life was vanishing and with it the ideal of the hero; the coming age of commerce and business capitalism would create new types of government, new types of freedom of religion.

Living within the world and in critical distance to it gave him the opportunity for a comparative study of political societies, ancient, medieval, and modern, always directed by this concern: What will human beings look like under the total system of conditions that determine their political governments, and how will they respond to such conditions and determine their determinations? This is still a Montaignesque question as to the variables of the *condition humaine.*

Montesquieu could realize his philosophical and methodological innovations because during his lifetime he experienced the rise of scientific philosophies. John Locke [1632–1704] and Isaac Newton [1643–1727], René Descartes [1596–1650] and Nicolas Malebranche [1638–1715] were as relevant to his complex thought as were Hugo

Grotius [1583–1645] and Samuel von Pufendorf [1632–1694] in the traditions of natural law and Machiavelli in his immanentism.

Montesquieu visualized the totality of the social and human situation. He was convinced that such complexity of historical man needs conceptualizations more dense and imaginative than the abstractions of philosophy could afford. He coined the term *philosopher-poet*, which he applied to Plato, Malebranche, Lord Shaftesbury [1671–1713], and Montaigne. To Montesquieu, the title was one of praise. The Plato of the Socratic dialogues was to him a thinker who grasped the totality of human possibilities. Malebranche had understood the positive working of imagination as a source of logical errors; he attributed the power of imagination to climatic conditions and was often used by Montesquieu for such insights, in particular, in the *Persian Letters* (1721). Lord Shaftesbury belonged to the group as a developer of a theory of moral taste that merged aesthetic and social patterns of thinking, suggesting a theory of gentlefolk's behavior. Montaigne set the pattern for a poetic treatment of the concrete human situation. Experience alone gave him the density and imagery for describing and interpreting love, friendship, social roles, and the opposite affections of suspicion, hatred, resentment, and hypocrisy as they developed in a situation of civil war.

Descartes, Blaise Pascal [1623–1662], and Montesquieu knew that Montaigne was a philosopher-poet. His philosophical concern was Mind, Self, and Society; his poetical concern, the human constitution in love and death. His work was indeed a philosophy of the place of man in the universe of nature and society. Montaigne established the pattern of philosophy that starts from the total immanence of life disregarding all transcendental or a priori elements.

Montesquieu, under the impact of Machiavelli, transferred the conception of total immanence from the process of nature to that of history. Nature remains an important element as a condition for political and historical ways of life, but it is not the totality of the context of meaning that unfolds in the process of history. Montesquieu recognized that there are pre- and posthistorical human possibilities beyond man's historicity. Hegel praised Montesquieu for having discovered the individual character of the historical in contrast to the passing stream of nature. Montesquieu's conception of the total immanence of the historical process implies its total intelligibility to natural and moral causation, pointing out that moral causes always have priority over natural causes.

The emphasis on the total intelligibility of history is a calm, though vigorous, blow to all patterns of providential history. Jacques-Bénigne Bossuet's [1627–1704] *Discours sur l'Histoire Universelle* (1681) was a challenge to Montesquieu's radical immanentism. The book on the considerations of the causes of the grandeur and decay of the Romans is closest to Machiavelli.

Nothing is unintelligible in the history of a society. The Romans followed a certain pattern of behavior in their ascendancy and logically changed to another one when their conditions and fields of action required new patterns of behavior. In historical action, necessary conditions and their concatenations make possible choices at rare occasions of breaking structures.

The Innovator

Montesquieu knew that he was an innovator and at the same time continued the traditions of the philosopher-poets. He was proud of having revolutionized philosophy by his mode of writing and method. His literary style had turned erudition ("docuit quae maximus Atlas") [Virgil, *Aeneid,* I, 741—Eds.] into enlightened communication with the thoughtful reader, in order to enable men to reflect on their political institutions as ways of life and as relatively best establishments. He was keenly aware of the fact that the *Spirit of the Laws* had no predecessors. "Prolem sine matre creatam" [Ovid, *Metamorphoses*, II, 553—Eds.] meant two things: first, the book does not follow any political or legal tradition, though Montesquieu intended to continue the traditions of Grotius and Pufendorf; second, it expresses the pride of a virile reasoning that cuts through the infinite nuances of historical plenitude to make a systematic treatment of the variables of politics possible.

His method was revolutionary in its comparative study of classical, medieval, and modern patterns of government in the entirety of their natural and moral conditions and societies' responses to them: conditioning the conditions or closing the cycle of the historical dynamics in which acting and being acted upon and reacting are intertwined with one another. Equally revolutionary was his method of applying the concept of Newtonian Law to the historical process in which nature is one of the conditions of human behavior. He was, however, too much of a political and legal philosopher not to see that historical men are the junctures of a variety of laws and norms beyond the natural laws and the laws of nature. Men are ruled not only by the diverse laws of nature, but also mores and folkways, statutory laws, ecclesiastical laws, political constitutions, rules of manners, religious laws, and social laws. The diversity of these laws is dynamic and open to various hierarchies according to the natural and moral conditions of people. All laws are relative to the specific conditions of society; the relatively best laws are those that people can accept. For this reason, the lawgiver is to Montesquieu the scientific philosopher who is able to discover from scientific analyses of natural and moral conditions the normative patterns that should regulate behavior and the conduct of concrete societies in concrete time and certain space.

Although Montesquieu directed his work to the construction of basic patterns of political government, in contrast to Montaigne's concern with Self and social roles, he actually took his institutional detour in order to arrive at the Montaignesque question: What will human beings look like who are the products of the basic forms of government, and what kind of men will the political patterns produce or prohibit, stifle, or corrupt?

Montesquieu finally settled the argument dealing with a common denominator of the historical process. The fundamental patterns of government are the frames of reference for the entire fabric of society. The political pattern is basic because a political constitution determines the scope and autonomies of the diverse institutional segments—such as family, education, the military, religion, commerce, mores, and manners—all indispensable for the continuity and duration of any society. Political patterns set the standards of society because governments create the laws according to their nature and principles, including the laws that determine economic behavior.

Montesquieu believed that he gained his basic generalizations on the nature of government from an empirical study of historical states. Actually, his categories of republics, monarchies, and despotisms are a priori constructs of the governments as they appear in the context of a common sense world; they might even be described as eidetic descriptions in Edmund Husserl's [1859–1938] sense. But these categories become total and genuinely social and historical when united with their principles, which indicate the passions and value attitudes that are the foundations of their establishment and make their dynamics possible. Montesquieu implied with the merging of nature and the principle of government that there are no governments that are not ways of life in the development of their reality.

Democracy implies the emotional evaluation of equality of some kind and a genuine sense of dedication and sacrifice that Montesquieu calls virtue. Montesquieu's description of democracy demonstrates his knowledge that this political pattern opens the avenues toward truly human greatness and ways of life that can become imperative for many human situations. Aristocracies are imbued with a sense of moderation in superiority in order to come closest to a democratic republic. Monarchies in constitutional form need the cooperation of the intermediate powers of Estates and a sense of honor among those who make such elaborate mechanisms work. The realm of despotism, though marginal to politics (which is defined by laws and rational organization), is of alarming relevance to Montesquieu because of its duration and frequency, resulting from man's lust for prostration and desire to obey.

The Realm of Despotism

For Montesquieu, despotism, slavery, the subjection of women, and the rule of eunuchs and freedmen were lasting concerns, because the greater part of Asia and Africa, as well as parts of Europe, felt the human effects of such regimes that produce degrading and corrupting qualities in human beings: indifference, inertia, conformism, cowardice, betrayal of kindred and friends, and other viciousness—all to compensate for the basic fears of death and violence. Despotisms may spring from the radicalization of republics and monarchies that have destroyed the moderation and balance of constitutional powers. But there are tyrannies in Asia and Africa that, according to Montesquieu, resulted from the natural conditions of the climate. It is desirable to reflect upon the role of natural conditions in his work. Even though Montesquieu grants that moral conditions always have priority over physical causes, a great part of the *Spirit of the Laws* deals with the effects of climate on political and social conditions. The lawgiver, however, is equipped with the wisdom to check and control the dangers of bad climate, as in China. The question then arises, Why was the same priority of moral principles not possible in other parts of Asia and in Africa?

Montesquieu needed natural conditions to explain realities that were not justifiable morally and were taken for granted by the prejudices of his age, which the philosopher shared. His reference to natural conditions in distant lands is, moreover, a deliberately ironical allusion to the great and petty despotisms still existing in the moderate climate of Europe, making the immoderate excess of despotism more hateful. Despotism is the pure pattern of domination and servitude, as Georg Hegel [1770–1831], a careful and attentive reader of Montesquieu, explains in *Phenomenology of the Mind* (1807). It is the total humiliation of human beings and the abolition of their dignity. It is a pattern of government that is against the rules of natural and moral law.

Among the natural conditions that explain despotisms is the size of the bodies politic. For Montesquieu, space is a tool for explaining despotisms without justifying them. His theory was rather primitive. Republics are possible in small territories like the Greek and Roman polis and their imitations during the Renaissance. Actually, Montesquieu could not imagine democracies as modern political governments at all. (It is moving to think that he mentioned as democratic organizations the Quakers and the State of the Jesuits in Paraguay.) Middlesized territories made enduring monarchies possible, while despotisms were required for continental empires like Russia. This is an explanation of the existence of a historical reality, but Catherine the Great—repressing Montesquieu's advice to transform her realm into a federation of states or a federal state—loved the *Spirit of the Laws* for giving her a good conscience.

The existence of despotism all over the world is a historical, not a moral phenomenon. It is Montesquieu's deepest concern to answer the question: Why do men easily found tyrannies that endure, while moderate and free governments are rare and short lived? His answer is sad and shows his disillusionment. Men prostrate themselves and obey; they like to be relieved of responsibilities and to be permitted to indulge in their own petty interests. Though they might occasionally revolt, they prefer to submit and to believe that their rulers are legally and morally entitled to be their betters. Inertia is a fundamental prerequisite for the rise and duration of tyrannies—the security of misery is better than the misery of insecurity.

The same statement should be made about Montesquieu's attitude toward slavery. Opposing Aristotle's statement that some men are by nature slaves, Montesquieu postulated the equality of human beings. Slavery is against nature and against civil and moral law. A great part of his inquiry into slavery is in reference to and repudiation of Roman and Christian legislators who manipulated legal norms to entitle rulers and citizens to own slaves.

The passage is a model case for one of the leitmotivs of the *Spirit of the Laws*—Montesquieu's war against some prejudices of contemporary society. In his analysis of the assumptions of the legislators, he praises knowledge as making men tender by enlightenment and reason, advancing them toward *Humanitas* (i.e., toward the destruction of prejudices).

Montesquieu acknowledged the general human situation that we all take certain behavior patterns, habits, and values for granted—they are our prejudices. The philosopher shares certain prejudices with his age, but he should not add new ones of his own. No legislator could ever hope to elevate himself above all prejudices, but Montesquieu had enough integrity and sensitivity to demonstrate his indignation and moral superiority over the prejudices of his times. He ridiculed the color taboo of the white man by remarking that the Egyptians were the best philosophers of the world and had dark black hair. In grim irony, he wrote: "Small minds overemphasize the injustice done to the Africans. If such injustice really existed, would it not have come to the attention of the princes of Europe, and would they not have agreed upon a general convention for the sake of charity and pity for the natives of Africa?"

With great fervor, Montesquieu maintained the inefficiency of slave labor, insisting that even the construction of the Pyramids would have been more efficient with free labor. But the economic point of view is inferior to Montesquieu's moral point of view. In a passage related to the question by Jean de La Bruyère [1645–1696] on the meaningfulness of life for the rich and the poor, Montesquieu asked: Who would vote for maintaining slavery in a general referendum? His answer was that only the leisured classes would like to see slavery maintained. All other classes detest slavery because they know from their own experience that social recognition and reciprocity establish genuine happiness and relaxation.

For Montesquieu, the subjection of women is the most conspicuous case of the degrading effects of such a human situation. Montesquieu liked to demonstrate a universal thesis in the context of Islamic and Oriental worlds. Thus, he described a climate of great sensuality and the complete domination of women by men, who are the owners of female human beings as wives or slaves in the seraglio.

The ownership of women—present or absentee—is a symbol for a way of life in which everything depends upon the arbitrariness of the domineering man. He is master of life and death, of the honor and virtue of his women slaves and of his wives, who are actually not in a better position. The seraglio is a model case for the effects of servitude and slavery—it shows the sexual inertia and the mechanisms of sensuality among the female occupants when used for lovemaking by the owners. But the women do not know what love is because they are never given free choice or the opportunity for spontaneous decisions. All slavery, and in particular slavery of women, is the greatest excess of human alienation in which human beings are turned to economic goods and objects.

In the *Persian Letters* (1721), Montesquieu described with keenest realism the relationships of sexual slavery and despotic ownership, anticipating in literary form the theme of human freedom and love in their interrelationships. The sexual relationships between a master who is an absentee owner and the wives whose lusts he inflamed and then left to the care of eunuchs is the prerequisite for the revolt in the seraglio. The despotism of sex, in Montesquieu's profound insight, is as degrading as the ownership of human beings abused as means for ends that are unrelated to the unfolding of their very being. Against sexual despotism in the seraglio, women can fight only by deceit, ruse, and hypocrisy.

Love is suffocated in a world of violence, cruelty, and sensuality—all three despotic and oppressive. Love requires mutual spontaneity, decision, and resolve because human beings encounter one another in and through acts of liberty. Montesquieu condemned the abuse of domination in *all* human relationships—even those beyond political and social roles. He felt that the necessary establishment of super- and subordination in political and social institutions was a grim requirement for the duration of the social fabric. Montesquieu regarded as criminal all domination and domineering beyond these organizations. Human beings should meet one another in freedom and with distance. It was his deepest conviction that the growth of human beings in reciprocity required a lasting rekindling of spontaneity and affection to keep the flame burning in all personal and collective communions.

This basic concern for human independence is conspicuous in Montesquieu's reflections on the meaning of eunuchs from the *Persian Letters* to the *Spirit of the Laws.* The condemnation of slavery implies the rejection of eunuchs. Montesquieu regarded them with some bewilderment as strange symbols of the ambiguity of human nature. They are men alienated from themselves and equipped with power to dominate over healthy and complete men. Montesquieu regarded the eunuchs as phenomena of despotism. Its servants must be alienated from themselves in order to obey all orders by tyrants. This very condition gives them the resentment and hatred against the subjects of domination that assures the despots that these servants will remain the loyal executioners of their will and command. In dealing with despotism and slavery, sexuality and love, Montesquieu built a bridge between political patterns and the loneliness of the human Self.

Despotism as the symbol of lawlessness is, in turn, a symbol of the dark, vital pressures that unleash the diverse types of lusts: lusts for power, lusts for domination and ownership, lusts for sensual pleasures—sexual, sadistic, and murderous. It is the realm of the human animal deprived of the wisdom of instincts that animals enjoy; it is realm of the unredeemed creature, the area of total irrationality. Throughout all these systematic presentations, Montaigne's basic attitudes and ideas are conspicuous. Montaigne, who experienced all possibilities of despotism in a civil war and in unconstitutional monarchies, is alive in Montesquieu in a systematic pattern; the *Persian Letters*, in the analysis of sex, love, and freedom, are as keen as Essay Five, Book Three, of Montaigne's *Essays*, "On some lines of Virgil," dealing with sex, love, and marriage.

The treatment of despotism, sensuality, violence, and arbitrariness is a general theme of the Oriental stories. The short stories that deal with the Greek landscape breathe a different kind of sensuality, one penetrated by love and tenderness with a touch of irony regarding the fictitious character of the eternal unity of love and fidelity.

The Rationality of History and Its Manifestations

Though Montesquieu is inclined to consider despotism as marginal to the realm of politics and laws, he regards it as one of the lasting human possibilities of the will to power and of the lust to prostrate oneself. It expresses the nightmarish abyss of the *condition humaine*, which Montaigne had recognized in the description of a sadistic father who in uninhibited anger beats his son almost to death. Montaigne postulated laws against the upsurge of such bestiality. Montesquieu systematized and elaborated on this suggestion as the true theme of his work. In spite of the negative potentialities of man, the constructive powers prevail in the realm of human historicity.

Montesquieu, with deep insight, remarked that the realm of history is the segment of life in which the constructiveness of reason unfolds through the legal organization of societies. The lawgivers are scientific philosophers who, by analysis of the totality of conditions under which individual societies live, are capable of establishing rules, norms, and laws that enable societies to live with, for, or against one another according to the requirements of their fields of action.

"We must explain history by laws" means to discover the inner rationality of the organization of mankind through the various legal and social systems that men impose upon their total existence for the sake of the duration and continuity of their institutions. Against all irrational and superrational philosophies, Montesquieu maintained the intelligibility of political behavior and social action of historical mankind.

Laws are to Montesquieu the totality of norm systems that direct and control social action within the patterns of politics. Granted the priority of the political patterns, historical societies exist on a variety of autonomous layers within the total constitutional structure. The entirety of norm systems makes historical man the juncture where all normative patterns meet. Societies are subject to all kinds of law: of climate, of religion, of manners, of mores, of constitutions, of civil and family codes, and of commerce and finance. Laws are the symbols of the constructive powers of dynamic and open reason that make possible the development of new norms according to the changing conditions of nature, tradition, and the requirements of the moral standards of society. *The Spirit of the Laws* is the merging of all norm systems in a meaningful totality, constructing and discovering the basic rationality of the historical organizations of mankind in political bodies. Montesquieu wrote the book as a handbook for the statesman and lawgiver.

He had the distance and aloofness to penetrate both the necessary and the foolish prejudices that are taken for granted prior to all rational norm systems. All groups take certain values, behavior patterns, and habits for granted. There are prejudices required for the foundations of social action in all historical societies. But there are also foolish and unintelligent prejudices against which we must revolt as creatures endowed with critical reason.

All lawgivers have two assignments to fulfill: they must secure the laws that permit people to survive in the lasting competition among nations, and they must consider the individualities of the concrete states. This means that men are ruled by general norms concerning the common traits of collective humanity, such as common passions, fears, hopes, pride, and aggressiveness. The communion in finiteness and frustrations, the *passio humana,* is indeed the bond that unifies mankind. But this aspect needs complementing by the consideration of the specific individualities of the single collectivities. Montesquieu spoke of the ends of states; he implicitly suggested that these goals are not decisions or choices, but, instead, the manifestations of a collective subconscious revealing itself in the sequence of one specific concern or value throughout the changing structures of historical developments. The end of Israel was religion; the end of Rome was imperialism; the end of England was liberty. The Jews did not choose to be God's people; they were chosen and understood themselves as such; Montesquieu defines the Roman telos in the first chapter of the book on the Romans—they began to build magnificent temples when the citizens still lived in log cabins. They experienced the urge for a pagan messianism to rule the world with sword and law. The English people did not consciously intend to become free. But their whole history, from the struggle of the nobles and the people against the kings to the religious freedom and tolerance of modern times and to the economic freedom of capitalism, contains a thread moving through their institutional organization of government.

In the historical process, republics and monarchies establish rational institutions by meaningful legislation. As citizens, men are historical. Montesquieu knew that historicity is one segment of human existence—we are products of our own particular histories (i.e., we are shaped by the totality of conditions under which we live and which we influence by our own responses). These conditions and responses are expressed in diverse norm systems that we call laws. The structures of laws differ in republics and monarchies. Republics can be democracies or aristocracies, but they have in common the idea that a majority or minority rules for more or less an egalitarian society. Societies in which subjects and the objects of sovereignty coincide are egalitarian. Military, economic, ethnic, and religious criteria for citizenship determine the scope of a democracy. The institutions that facilitate differentiation among democracies—especially the rights and duties of citizens to vote, to serve in the armies, and to become public servants—fascinated Montesquieu. He clearly saw the range of democratic republics from radically egalitarian to plutocratic and aristocratic republics, in particular on the basis of a slave economy.

Democracies are avenues toward constitutions of liberty in which citizens enjoy political rights, voluntarily submitting to the obligations of political office. Montesquieu felt that the people had the political sensitivity and instinct necessary for selecting trustworthy leaders; he was convinced that they would rarely fail in their choices of men to be nominated for office. But such qualifications do not equip the people for holding political office. He maintained that government is an art that is traditionally learned and transmitted from generation to generation in a political aristocracy. Unrestricted in his admiration for the political wisdom and moderation of the Roman Senate, he praised the esprit d'corps of these gentlemen, their imagination, stubbornness, their ruthlessness in war and diplomacy, their perseverance in adversities; they seemed to him the ideal political elite. Their wisdom and political acumen made possible republican freedom in which the aristocratic and democratic elements balanced, rather than opposed, each other.

The institutions of political freedom were not destroyed by individuals. Montesquieu coined a term that anticipates Max Scheler's [1874–1928] theory of resentment—he spoke of the Eternal Malady that caused the end of political liberty. This illness consisted in the fact that all groups abuse their power by accumulating more and more power in fear of being deprived of it; they are fascinated by the chimera of a monopoly of domination that would permit them to crush competitors and adversaries. It meant, further, that all classes that have been offended and humiliated, when politically recognized, will overcompensate their resentments and hatreds and will abuse their new powers and destroy freedom and democracy. In Rome, he saw the unleashed masses abusing the power of the tribunes of the people, establishing the military dictatorship and with it the end of the freedom of the Republic.

Montesquieu was aware of the dialectics of all political principles. He knew that the corruption of a government begins with its principles. There is an inner logic in all principles to be carried to their extremes. The principle of democracy—emotional dedication to equality—could easily turn into radical resentment against all officers and representatives and result in the surrender of all political functions to the democratic majority (i.e., a collective despotism). Montesquieu analyzed the disintegration of the democratic virtue in Thucydidean terms: "What was maxim is now called rigidity, what was taken for granted as rule is now described as coercion; attention and vigilance is now fear."

On the other hand, Montesquieu believed that democracy could be a most excellent way of life when directed by wise and happy men. Such leaders could set an example and a normative image of unselfishness and happiness for a tiny group of democratic citizens. Montesquieu even granted the possibility of a positive democracy founded on commerce and capitalism when businessmen would recognize the ascetic devotion required by the inner logic of modern economy.

It is the greatness of Montesquieu's description of the rationality and legal organization of political patterns that he understood them as ways of life and historical variables of the *condition humaine.* This great discovery is paralyzed by the fact that democracy as a political pattern is to Montesquieu a historical phenomenon of the ancient world, surviving as a religious or social pattern. In spite of his fascinating anticipation of a new administrative and revolutionary world after the princes of the House of Thurn and Taxis established a European Mail Service, he could not imagine democracy and its dialectics as Tocqueville would a century after *Spirit of the Laws.*

In contrast to democracies, monarchies are symbols of modern times in which neither the polis of antiquity nor its empires are possible. Montesquieu still lived under the shadow of the fateful folly of Louis XIV's attempt to establish a Spanish-French Empire and to turn the old feudal monarchy into an absolute imperial state. The mechanism of monarchies functions without the moral ethos of democracies and the fear of despotisms. Constitutional monarchies are smoothly working machines that achieve great deeds without virtue. The legal structure of monarchies is directed toward distributing and balancing the king's sovereignty with the intermediate powers of the Estates. It was the function of the Estate to build bridges between the monarch and his people and to reconcile the privacy of the subjects with the authority of the king. In a constitutional monarchy, the Estates represent the social forces of the sword, of the cross, and of wealth. The subjects remain private and are not citizens. Monarchies unite the purposive rational ends of an elaborate military and civil administration with the emotional values of glory and prestige for the sovereign. The social space of the monarchy is the court of the king. Montesquieu constructed the pattern of the courtier as the product of this social structure and described him as the most disgusting type of human being. This analysis could have been written by Montaigne as the extreme negative of the *condition humaine.* To Montesquieu, the courtier is the sad experience of a good form of government. He is the parasite of a monarchy. He never lives up to the truth of his role as a loyal servant to the king; instead, he abuses his position for self-aggrandizement and exploits it for vested interests. Pretending zeal for the royal service, he enjoys leisure and inertia except when he is busy receiving economic favors. The debunking of human virtue and the ridicule of integrity demonstrate the open cynicism of a man who abuses allegiance as a business proposition. Montesquieu regarded the courtier as a typical phenomenon of corruption in a monarchy. But the phenomenon is universal; all regimes have their courtiers, regardless of whether they are called lobbies, pressure groups, or rackets.

The laws of the monarchy require an organization of ranks, preferments, and distinctions for the noble classes in their social roles. For this reason, Montesquieu postulated honor as the principle of the monarchy; incentive makes the wheels of the machine move. Honor makes men conscious of social distance and sensitive to privileges. This field of action will always move according to the ambitions for honor and distinction. Whatever the motives of the individuals might be, even the most selfish ambitions for high ranks can produce great deeds. It is the political pattern of the *Fable of the Bees*, where private vices create public virtues.

Monarchies are the schools of honor. Their sociological analysis is a masterpiece of understanding the basic pattern of the modern competitive society. In contrast to democracies or despotisms that require the total presence or absence of human beings, monarchies offer a model case for demonstrating a fundamental law of sociology—the interdependence of appearance and reality, pretending and acting, the identification with social roles or their abuse in favor of vested interests while playing the normative roles.

Aesthetic fiction is the required pattern of this society, which Lord Shaftesbury well described when he coined the term *moral taste* as a criterion for judging a court society of gentlefolk. Social roles played to aesthetic perfection make up the honor of the social ranks and all actions are judged as beautiful, not as good.

Three postulates are indispensable in a monarchy: people should put a certain nobility into their virtues, a certain frankness into their behavior, and a certain politeness into their manners. Montesquieu commented on these ideals. When courtiers speak of virtue, they mean what men owe to themselves, what distinguishes them from their fellow men. In the same way the courtier would interpret the term *frankness* to mean the parading of keenness and the fiction of independence, not the zeal for truth. Politeness means to the courtier total conformity in order to belong and make a career. Montesquieu actually made a sociological analysis of modern competitive society that developed in a monarchical frame of reference. Men act on a stage, performing various roles in diverse plays in changing density and intimacy or distance and aloofness. To compete successfully and advance their social prestige, men are anxious to recognize others so that they might be recognized by society. Everybody accepts mutualities and reciprocal gentleness and sweetness. In such societies, people do not judge human actions as good, but as beautiful; not as just, but as lovely; not as reasonable, but as extraordinary. The transformation of the moral world into an aesthetic and sensual entity is completely understood by Montesquieu by means of a sociological approach to language.

What Montesquieu described as the pattern of monarchy is indeed the way of life of bourgeois society, setting the pattern for Georg Simmel's [1858–1918] theory of sociability. Goethe's *Maskenzüge* and the *Roman Carnival* are in complete agreement with Montesquieu on the fictitious character of the social world and its inescapable domination.

Montesquieu saw the old feudal-military world vanishing and with it the ideal image of the hero. He saw the new society as a capitalistic bourgeoisie with new horizons and values, with more politeness, but with tough individual competition. But he did not see a law of progress in history. In examining the historical worlds of antiquity—the Middle Ages and modernity—he discovered that the requirements of the historical fields of action had demonstrated the creative and dynamic power of human reason to establish a sequence of laws relative to the natural and moral conditions of particular societies.

We explain history by laws. We describe the total immanence of life, the inseparable unity of nature and reason in the diversity of normative systems that create for men the junctures in their historicity where all laws meet and articulate the unfolding of their possibilities.

Montesquieu is still a modern thinker in the radicalism of his philosophy, of his historicity intelligible through explanation and understanding. He succeeded in enlightening history by the creative discovery of logos in the organized legal worlds of history.

History and Laws

Montesquieu clearly understood the mutual interaction of the constructive powers of reason with the totality of moving structures that make up the historical process of concrete time. While dynamic and open logos enlightens, organizes, and articulates the space and time of history, the changing kaleidoscope of historical structures explains the laws and their transformations according to the changing requirements of the fields of action.

"We must illuminate the laws by history" is complementary to "we must illuminate history by laws." In the sixth part of the *Spirit of the Laws,* Montesquieu inserted some historical chapters that deviated from the systematic character of the work. Here he applied the new method of grasping the individuality of a historical phenomenon by examining the general and particular causes that made it unique.

Book XXVII deals with the origins and changes in the Roman laws of succession; it is a brilliant merging of sociological and historical causation. The general causes that explain the origins and changes of this group of laws are definitely political, while the particular causes refer to the place of the female in Roman society. The transformations of these laws cannot be explained as resulting from the inner logic of the problems in the legal context. The historical understanding of the political ideas that made such changes desirable or necessary is decisive.

The original legislation manifested the radical conflict between natural laws and equity on the one hand, and the political-military concerns of a feudal gentry and of soldier citizens on the other. The general spirit and the mores of this fighting nation were ascetic, frugal, and pious. Romans were dedicated to the glory of the Republic; for this reason, they considered wrong the people who did not conform to the spirit of the body politic. The Roman people were hostile to ladies who enjoyed their wealth for the pleasure and luxury it gave them. This social situation had a decisive impact on the first laws of succession.

The original laws excluded all females—widows and daughters alike—the right of inheritance. The male succession assured the inviolability of the estate as the economic background for the military strength of clan or family. In this context, Montesquieu's reason disclosed itself as reason of state, which often must clash with the wisdom of legal reason and with the principle of equity. Such laws will always harm the natural sentiment of human beings. Like Montaigne, Montesquieu experienced and recognized the lasting possibilities of conflict between legal norms and human feelings. Montesquieu was grimly aware of the precarious character of man in his social roles and in his historical status restricting his natural humanity. Like Montaigne, Montesquieu never forgot that men are subject to their political duties and to the norms imposed on them by society, and that they are exposed to all kinds of suffering beyond their social roles. Societies take for granted that the rules of the body politic and the norms of society, class, and office have priority over the claims of man to be human and to live according to the natural sentiment of his own self.

To Montesquieu, the female in the history of Roman legislation was a good example of such a plight. The political, military, and economic interests of the imperialistic republic necessarily wronged women in the laws of succession. But such laws were designed to limit the luxury of women in the interest of the commonwealth. In the perspective of the ruling elite, it was a necessary law, giving higher value to the polis than to any individual. The change of such laws cannot be understood but by a complete transformation of the general spirit and mores. That alone could produce a new evaluation of women in the political and social context.

The Principate of Augustus (which a twentieth-century historian; Ronald Syme [1903–1989], has called *The Roman Revolution*) was to Montesquieu a complete social transformation. The civil wars and the reciprocal killings of nobles and people had reduced marriages and legitimate children. The Principate marked the end of the civil wars and the inauguration of the Roman Peace. Augustus was determined to rebuild the highest ranks of society and to introduce the new social elite of his regime—the new wealthy middle classes. Their mores and general spirit were indeed worlds apart from the old republican spirit. This traditional virtue and the pious mores of the ancestors had vanished; the new elite regarded the present and future without considering the past. Such attitudes were shared by the judges, who were only motivated by equity, moderation, and the ideals of propriety (decorum), a situation that made possible the introduction of "modern" legislation. Augustus promulgated the Papian Laws that encouraged marriages and the procreation of legitimate children. The success of the laws rested with their promise of possible succession, thus ending the discrimination against women. Wives with children could be made successors in the wills of their husbands. Montesquieu commented on the blessing of this law by stating that the laws often achieve great goods that are hidden and small evils that are most sensitive.

From the Emperor Claudius to Justinian, there was continuous progress in the recognition of the legal rights of women to succeed their husbands and fathers. Justinian believed that he followed the reason of nature when he liberated himself of the last residues of the traditional prejudices of the men of the old republic. Actually, this legal and moral revolution was caused by the same reasons that the republican government had applied. Imperial Rome was as much concerned with the social continuity of the political elite as had been the old republic. Both were convinced that the legal stability of the economic foundations of the ruling class gave the state some security for the duration of this class. Montesquieu stressed this social problem as extremely important to the political system. Though he did not emphasize the point, he observed that a new elite was indispensable to the revolutionary state because the old senatorial nobility had either been exterminated in the civil wars and during the first imperial regimes or retired from the public scene. Montesquieu did not state a thesis, but the structure of the chapter implies that every sociopolitical revolution will be forced to establish a new ruling class from which to recruit the office holders and the loyal servants of the new regime.

Most interesting in this section of *Spirit of the Laws* is the sociological method that Montesquieu used to describe the functioning of the old laws of succession. It was an analysis of the tricks fathers and husbands applied in order to escape the rigidity of the laws and to make their daughters or wives succeed. This was possible, Montesquieu rightly stated, because of the purely formal character of the Roman jurisdiction.

Still more important for the enlightenment of the laws by history are the last two books of the sixth part, which deal with the origins of the feudal laws in relation to the monarchy and to its revolutions. The method is historical in the causal analysis of the circumstances that produced and established feudal laws. These laws created infinite goods and evils; they produced norms with a trend toward anarchy and anarchy with a tendency toward order and legal harmony.

What is most important is that these two books are not merely appendices for partisan purposes. They complement the two patterns of the systems of liberty that Montesquieu developed in Book XI, the classical pattern of the Roman Republic and the modern pattern of the constitutional monarchy in England. The last books present the medieval pattern of feudal constitutional monarchy; it is a system of liberty in which king, nobles, clergy, and the free people balance their rights and obligations in freedom and moderation. For this reason, the books belong in the systematic context of the *Spirit of the Laws.* On the other hand, these books are political and partisan and never as aloof and disinterested as the other parts of the work. They were Montesquieu's scholarly answer to the writings of Count Henri de Boulainvilliers [1658–1722] and Jean-Baptiste Abbé Dubos [1670–1742] on the history of the French monarchy. These authors had written learned treatises on the subject, each with a different political purpose.

The nobleman Boulainvilliers used the vast materials from legal and political sources to demonstrate that the true monarchy is the feudal monarchy in which the king is the first gentleman among equals, and the feudals are the main pillars of the government and in charge of the political and administrative offices. The historical analysis was a political critique by the nobility facing the absolute state and the decay of the feudal monarchy. Though Montesquieu was in full agreement with the political goal of Boulainvilliers, he disagreed with his argument that the Franks had made a general legal settlement that put the Romans in a kind of servitude. The aristocrat seemed to Montesquieu to indulge in a conspiracy against the Third Estate.

The Abbé Dubos, on the other hand, attempted to deal a deathblow to the feudal gentlemen by demonstrating the old cooperation between kings and the bourgeois urban classes, of which the absolute state was the true and logical expression. Montesquieu was conscious that his own argumentation, though more learned than the others' (in spite of his admiration for the erudition of Dubos), was determined by his own political position. He took it for granted that all scholars live in and with their prejudices; he only advised them not to add personal ones to those that rule their era, nation, and class.

Montesquieu shared indeed in the prejudices of his class in interpreting French medieval history. He had presented his book on the Romans to the Duc de Saint-Simon, the author of the *Mémoires* and a friend and political follower of Boulainvilliers. Montesquieu was a conservative thinker who, like all genuine conservatives, was in revolt against a despotic and bourgeois regime. He spoke with enthusiasm of the political philosophy of the Archbishop François Fénélon [1651–1715], who had set the pattern for a traditional constitutionalism as the remedy against tyranny of Louis XIV.

Montesquieu's historical investigations convinced him that the system of feudal liberty had resulted from the political traditions of the Franks when they occupied France. They had taken just the lands they needed with moderation and had not entirely deprived the Romans of their estates. Montesquieu concluded that the conquering Franks were not moved by a tyrannical spirit, but by the hope of reconciling the mutual needs of both peoples.

Montesquieu, however, was induced by his methodological discipline to inquire into the mores and laws of the Franks before he could explain their political constitution. He stressed that these conquering people of a violent and brutal mind demonstrated the scope and quality of their reason by their precise and refined laws. Montesquieu was fascinated by their legislation of a criminal code that punished the wrongs and crimes committed in the fury of vengeance. These laws considered in detail the circumstances, the subjective attitude, and intention of the offended; they weighed the demands for satisfaction in the context of the situation. For Montesquieu, such refined laws demonstrated that these barbarian people had left the state of nature and had reached the true state of historicity in which the law-giving power of reason prevailed.

The same laws were used by Montesquieu to analyze the class structure of medieval society. He wanted to show the prominent role of the nobility in the establishment of law and order in the anarchy of civil wars and in revolutions against helpless rulers. He analyzed the fees that the laws had imposed upon the offenders who had killed members of different social classes. The study showed that the vassals or feudals were worth six hundred saigas; a Roman, guest of the king, three hundred; a Frank, two hundred; an ordinary Roman, one hundred; and a Frank freedman or serf, forty-five. This was an ingenious way to construct a theory of stratification and to prove that the nobles were the highest rank in society. Furthermore, it proved Montesquieu's thesis that Franks and Romans lived and worked together despite differences in social rank.

The feudals were, first of all, warriors who had taken an oath of loyalty to one or several seigneurs. They became vassals and, as such, they had received their fiefs. The structure of feudalism is the hierarchy of dependencies from the king to the different ranks of seigneurs. At the same time, it was a political and social system in which personal allegiances and objective functions, economic status and social prestige, were one and indivisible. Montesquieu was aware of all these implications and admired the legal constructiveness of a society in which greed and murder had contributed to the state of anarchy in the early centuries of the Middle Ages.

Montesquieu was fascinated by the idea that the Franks had originally elected the king for his nobility, although, later on, they had made the crown hereditary. But they always elected the Mayor of the Palace for his military virtue as commander of the armies. In the growing anarchy of the political world under incompetent and greedy kings, the feudal lords were compelled to make the Mayor of the Palace a charismatic leader or to grant leadership to a Mayor of the Palace who suggested his role as leader for a specific enterprise. The nobles gave him full powers for all military, civilian, and political matters. Montesquieu saw the sublimity of reason in this feudal and independent society: "One needed to invite rather than to coerce, one needed to give and promise fiefs when vacated, continuously reward and avoid preferences: the administrator should be also the general of the army." This rational organization of the feudal world was to Montesquieu a great experience. While the political world seemed to disintegrate hopelessly, human reason could still find some device for establishing a social order with freedom and moderation, in spite of the cruelty and selfishness of groups and persons.

The interaction between the Mayor of the Palace and the feudal lords brought into being a cautious and moderate government that was to protect feudal society against incompetent kings. The position of the mayor was firm as long as he was protected by the nobles and satisfied their vested interests. The seigneurs used and abused the mayor's power against lawless and despotic rulers in order to receive new fiefs and privileges. To Montesquieu, this was the era of feudal reason, in which the pattern of constitutional and legal freedom was constructed: the hierarchy of vassalages or fiefs and the jurisdictional power of the seigneurs.

In the anarchy of unceasing civil wars, people could rely on the jurisdiction of their seigneurs, not on the fictitious authority of a king. Charlemagne appeared to Montesquieu the ideal pattern of the good feudal monarch. He had founded a system of political liberty by constructing a balance between the clergy, the nobles, and the free men in their relationships to him as king. This liberty consisted primarily in the political and jurisdictional government of the feudals in their regional districts while they remained true to their oath to the king. Charlemagne and Saint Louis seemed to Montesquieu the expressions of moderation, wisdom, and resolution in their political institutions. It was Montesquieu's idea that such rulers proved that the authority of political-legal truth renders the power of a king invincible in penetrating the vested interests of all estates with the political reason that unites the parts of the states with a common purpose. Political reason meant to Montesquieu a system of moderation and liberty in which all elements had a segment of interdependence within a common cause that all took for granted through the oath of loyalty.

Among the successors to Charlemagne, the weak rulers lost the basis of their powers when they gave away their property, their domain, to the nobility or to the clergy. Each group abused its strength in controlling the other and satisfying its infinite greed. The transformation of the feudal system in extending vassalage and fiefs to free men and in the one-sided declaration of the feudals that they would only serve in wars of defense were signs of the decay of feudal constitutionalism.

Montesquieu illuminated the almost unintelligible laws of the early Middle Ages by submitting them to the criteria of historical causation. History had served him to illuminate the laws and to show the constructiveness of legal reasoning and the working of moderation in the legal establishments that made political liberty possible when violence and greed prevailed. Montesquieu, finally, agreed with Boulainvilliers and Saint-Simon—the old feudal monarchy had realized political freedom; the absolute monarchy had destroyed it. It is interesting to note that Montesquieu did not insert the description of the feudal monarchy in Book XI of the *Spirit of the Laws,* where he dealt with Roman and English liberty. Montesquieu's personal values and his political commitment to the system of conservative constitutionalism led him to place the two books at the end of the work. They were, indeed, his last word on the very reality of freedom as a political pattern in France to be remembered in an age of despotism.

But freedom was to Montesquieu an even more fundamental concern than political institutions. These were, indeed, the prerequisite for the unfolding of a man's spontaneity in self-realization.

In the *Thoughts*, there are many remarks testifying to his grim conviction that superordination and subordination, command and obedience, domination and service are inescapable necessities for the continuity of a political and social order. But in all genuinely human encounters, domination, even disguised as love, is unbearable. Meetings of men in mutual intersubjectivity are to Montesquieu the highest human values when reciprocal spontaneities produce the growth of men in affection and love. Montesquieu was fully conscious that people live on various levels of pre- and posthistorical existence for the thinker who attempts a comprehensive examination of the total human situation.

Man in historical action remains part of nature though playing social roles. Montesquieu draws the attention of the reader to the fact that the blessings of law are compensated for by the ills they might convey to the natural sentiments of human beings. It is not by chance that Montesquieu spoke of the law of nature before entering into the analysis of the meaningful context of the laws of politics. All men are inherently equipped by nature with certain sentiments, regardless of their historical and political situation, specifically the feelings of being a human creature. All humans have by nature the desire to belong and live with and for others; they look for peace in order to overcome their fears and they cooperate for shelter and protection. These basic laws of nature are invariables; they are the emotional foundations of happiness, value attitudes, and political organization for the sake of equity. But they often and necessarily conflict with legal institutions based on grim generalizations and abstractions such as in the Roman laws on succession. The normativeness of equity succumbs easily to the social and political pressures of changing historical structures.

Parallel to the natural desire for happiness are the equally natural sentiments of shame, which to Montesquieu is of the highest importance as the emotional reaction to our frustration of human intentions toward perfection and integrity. There is still another pattern of conflict in men when a natural sentiment can be destroyed by another stronger, natural sentiment. Montesquieu explicitly mentioned, with grave seriousness in the phrasing of the statement, that under the conditions of despotism, women are exposed to a heartbreaking antagonism of their feelings. Most women have a deep longing to bear and raise children. But when they live under a system of tyranny that breeds fear, cowardice, and hypocrisy, abortion has a definite human function. Not to bear children who would have to live as slaves becomes an escape into freedom and free will. Under total tyranny, people believe that it is better not to be born than to live as slaves. This is a pattern of thinking that might be the cause for many childless marriages in totalitarian countries. This conflict of sentiments is one of the strongest examples of Montesquieu's profundity of experience of human servitude and is an eloquent statement about the needs for human liberty.

For Montesquieu, the human beings who achieve *Humanitas*—the serenity and moderation of the soul that is beyond the Heart and the Spirit—are posthistorical. The Stoic emperors gave him the courage to love life, in spite of the monsters who followed them. For Montesquieu, they incorporated the reality of historical men transcending themselves: greatness of soul. It is such greatness of soul that gives men the strength to be superior to destiny. Christina of Sweden [1626–1689] resigned her crown for the contemplative life of philosophy, and another queen asked her Estates to associate her husband to her office as ruler—both were moved by eros, and charity passed through their historical and social roles and illuminated their human nature by acts of genuine creativity.

Posthistorical sentiments remain—in the last analysis—creative acts that control reason and virtue. Though reason and virtue seem to Montesquieu the highest goods, they are exposed to radical alienation under the laws of uprooted autonomous developments. Montesquieu has no answer to the question of what human factor creates the moderation required for all balance in political, social, and human relationships. The disaster of the *condition humaine* can be averted only by the wisdom of the soul—its *Humanitas*, the smile of reason over its own folly to be more than human and the positive affirmation of being part of a whole in spite of defeats and the *passio humana*.

8

Adam Smith as Sociologist

Unity, Purpose, Ethos

The classical social sciences developed as a division of philosophy, and classical philosophers devoted their works to the exploration of the truth about the whole. The human world was a specific part of a universe that could be studied, explained, and understood by itself.

The modern social sciences came into existence as a revolt against philosophy—not against philosophy as such, but against a system of philosophy that was imbued with the spirit of Christian theology and spiritual idealism. The authors whom we regard as the founders of the modern social sciences did not intend to construct a new system of sciences. They simply thought to reform the branch of philosophy that dealt with moral conduct. They attempted to use the new methods of psychology to explain the working of moral standards in social action, and, in this effort, regarded the varieties of social structures and of social changes as understandable in terms of the never-ending transformations of social conditions.

The autonomy of the field of their investigations became apparent, however, when they succeeded in explaining the functioning of moral norms in terms of social-psychological and sociological anal-

---

Published originally in a slightly different form in *Social Research* 12 (February 1945), 22–42. Republished by permission from *Social Research*.

yses of human needs, instincts, and passions. This was a comprehensive effort to eliminate all religious and metaphysical presuppositions from the understanding of social action and of societal relationships. It represented a conception that can almost be described as one of total immanence, and yet most of these thinkers tried to preserve the idea of a divine and creative reason. In the psychological dynamics of human nature, they saw the intentions of a wise Intelligence that establishes again and again a universe of harmony and order, despite the many destructive forces. This was in many respects an effort to rehabilitate nature and human nature, long degraded by many writers on Christian philosophy. In this enterprise, many authors were forced to admit the truth of a teleological interpretation of the life of man in the world. Though they did not refer to Aristotle, the moderns who attempted to understand social life by itself were inclined to grant the necessity of regarding a teleological interpretation as the most probable one.

In this development, Adam Smith [1723–1790] had a unique position.[1] His work was a junction where three roads merged: the traditions of the science of *jus naturae*; the trends in British philosophy toward a shifting from reflection on moral goods to the analysis of moral acts; and the religion of nature, or deism. Adam Smith succeeded in unifying these three tendencies into an interdependent system combining sociology, economics, and political science—the social sciences. In his work, the social sciences were still one and indivisible, centered around the idea of a "science of the statesman" that would meet the various requirements of controlling social action in its many aspects. Smith was attracted throughout his life by the science of the statesman. What was this science?

There were no departments of political science or economics in the Scottish universities. Adam Smith held a chair of moral philosophy. He was required to lecture on four subjects: natural theology, ethics, natural law, and practical problems of politics. In a superficial sense, these courses account for the unity of his work: *The Theory of Moral Sentiments*[2] covers the first two courses; the *Lectures on Justice*[3] are a copy of the course on natural law; and the *Wealth of Nations*[4] deals with the practical problems of politics. From within, however, his books are integrated by a never-deviating intention. They all were the preparation for a forthcoming study on natural jurisprudence, the science of the statesman. Smith repeatedly expressed a desire to conclude his investigations on the principles and techniques of society with a theory of natural law, "the most important and least cultivated science of all."[5] A short time before his death, he still expressed a dim hope of summing up his life work with such a system of the principles and rules of social justice.[6]

Time and again, Smith praised Hugo Grotius [1583–1645] as the founder of this science and as its most comprehensive scholar in spite of his shortcomings.[7] Smith was attracted by the ethos of Grotius's scholarship. He shared Grotius's idea that the scholar carries responsibility for the enlightened conduct of the rulers and for the moral standards of society. Between rulers and ruled, the intellectuals—as the torchbearers of wisdom and illumination—have to be concerned with the preservation of justice and of the values of the good life in the disruption of the Christian universe. But while Adam Smith carried on the humanistic ethos of Grotius, he believed that social responsibility is merely one aspect of the scholar's function. A scholar is responsible not only for the enlightenment of his group but also for the truth about the whole. The search for truth implies a continual reexamination of the methods and techniques that make it possible to establish the truth. This constant inquiry becomes a dynamic factor when ends and means do not meet. Then scholars revolt against the presuppositions that bar the approach toward new methods for getting at the truth.

Smith and his friends carried on Grotius's humanistic beliefs concerning the moral character of the interaction between theory and practice in what they considered to be an emergency situation in English society. Smith described the situation in a comprehensive sociological analysis of the institutions of higher learning in his contemporary England.[8] The universities, he held, were hardening in past patterns that were intended to educate theologians and clergymen, not gentlemen. They were corporations in which a few privileged thinkers enjoyed a good life without being concerned about research and teaching. There was no university where a gentleman could be trained into an enlightened politician. Smith and most of his friends and students drew the conclusion implicit in this observation and, as tutors, accompanied young noblemen on their *grands tours*, which were the substitute for adequate academic training of aristocratic youth. This situation contributed to the social disposition of the Scottish thinkers—to their belief that reflection on the principles of the good and just life must be united with analysis of the techniques and means that make it possible to realize those principles in the changing situations of the social process.

Smith repeatedly stated that he recognized only two sciences as useful: ethics and natural jurisprudence.[9] Several times he compared ethics to criticism, and jurisprudence to grammar. He reproached the highly esteemed Stoic and Peripatetic doctrines that ethics, though useful and agreeable, was not precise. On the other hand, his praise of moral philosophy was restricted. Moral and aesthetic philosophy, he contended,[10] may formulate precepts and exhortations that in general and vague terms encourage the practice of virtue, but it does not provide instruction in how to realize the perfect life. A great advantage of the science of natural law is that it can elaborate and define in final terms the general principles of social action and the specific rules for their application. Smith believed that we can teach the elements of the just life, as we can teach the elements of grammar. Both are simple and unambiguous, clear and evident. Everyone is able to use the rules of grammar intelligently and to learn how to read. Everyone may learn to use the rules of natural jurisprudence in order to live a good and just life.

This admiration for the systematic precision and clarity of the science of natural law, and for its easy applicability by rulers, is evident in Smith's frequent references to Hugo Grotius. As mentioned above, however, Smith's thinking contained an element that was lacking in Grotius, who remained in the great juristic tradition and dealt with systems of norms and abstract requirements. This new element, fundamental to the origins of the modern social sciences, is the trend toward the concrete. Thus, Smith spoke violently and indignantly of the contemplative scholar who takes no responsibility for the social problems of his world.[11] Frequently, he referred to the abstract and speculative point of view that levels down the comprehensive character of social reality.[12] He blamed metaphysical and abstract theories for preventing the proper analyses of social action.

This general trend toward a comprehensive explanation and interpretation of social reality reveals the intention to understand human life in society with all its interdependent actions. Grotius's precision and clarity were those of the jurist who systematizes norms. Smith tried to understand and explain social and moral values as tendencies that come into existence in the experiences of man in society and constitute his social being. Grotius located the legal and moral spheres in an all-pervading spirit of Christian spirituality. Smith postulated the social sciences as the science of man in society, the transformed science of natural law that establishes the laws of nature by a scientific analysis of the incentives, interests, and intentions of man in social action. These social sciences are the tools for discovering the criteria of right and just social action, and the instruments for establishing freedom from theology and metaphysics as the fountain of universal knowledge.

Mutuality, Sympathy, Socius

Smith laid the foundations for an empirical science of society in his *Theory of Moral Sentiments.* Its main purpose was to analyze the elements whose interaction makes possible the continuity and duration of society. This science of the social constitution of society does not recognize a conflict between individual and collectivity. It is a study in mutuality. Smith regarded mutuality as the primary datum of societal relationships, and his theory of mutuality is a cornerstone of his sociology. Giving and taking, acting and being acted upon, encroaching upon another and selfrestraint—these are the original elements of the social constitution. They establish a dynamic unity, a whole that can be compared to a kaleidoscope.

These fundamental relationships point to the essential equality of human beings. Smith stressed this point frequently.[13] Giving and taking, acting and being acted upon, are potentialities in every human being. All men are rich and poor. This mutuality is a universal phenomenon, pervading all spheres of social action, and is not restricted to the sphere of economic needs. Smith explicitly stated that by nature all men are equal. What we call the different characters and the diverse talents result from habits, education, and indoctrination. By nature, we all live as potent and productive and also as needy and incomplete beings. By establishing mutuality, we create a whole. But we do not create this unity by reasoning. Smith shared with David Hume [1711–1776] a deep distrust in the power of reason. Smith recognized that the expanding powers of the organism serve and also disclose the immediate ends of man: self-preservation and security. In the certainty and immediacy of his instincts, nature has endowed man with a prerational knowledge of the means to be applied in serving these ends.[14] Self-interest and self-preservation are, however, dialectical concepts. Actually, the self is realized only in social action—that is, in the cooperation, competition, and conflicts of societal relationships.

Thus, man is primarily a socius.[15] His sentiments make him reflect on the effects of his actions on his fellowmen. He cannot establish his own security without considering the situation and the judgments of his fellows. He can never attain individual well-being without thinking of the effects his actions will have on the whole of society. Individual happiness is possible only when it is approved by and in harmony with society. All human beings and all societies strive for happiness. But happiness is a complex phenomenon.[16] On the one hand, there are the requirements of the organism: care of the body, health, and the economic needs whose satisfaction is an indispensable condition for the good life. On the other hand, there are the requirements of one's status in society: a modest security and independence. Finally, there are the requirements that hold both for society and for the individual: peace, tranquility of mind, and a good conscience. Smith declared that nothing can be added to human happiness when these requirements are met.

Smith's theory of society is necessarily a theory of sympathy. But in this context, sympathy cannot be defined as compassion, empathy, or any imitation of feelings. Smith defined his use of the term several times, most clearly in his critique of David Hume.[17] He sharply rejected Hume's usage, in which sympathy was described as pleasure in the technical perfection of a system of usefulness. Smith objected that Hume confused means and ends when he made utility the criterion for the highest virtue. Hume could conceive of the whole only as a perfect machine, but society too is a whole, and one in which means are subordinate to ends and values. Thus, Smith suggested the concept of sympathy as a measuring rod for perfect conduct in societal relationships.

Sympathy, according to Smith, is the cognitive feeling that is constituted by understanding and evaluating. It is, for the socius, the "logic of the heart," if Blaise Pascal's [1623–1662] term may be transferred to the sphere of social action. Smith stated explicitly that sympathy implies a critical understanding of a social situation—evaluation of the motives of the agent, of the object of his action, and of the response of the person acted upon.[18] Sympathy connects the agent and the person acted upon, within the frame of the structured situation. It permits analysis and appreciation of the elements that constitute the types of mutuality.

In every social situation, there are persons acting and being acted upon. Their relationships establish the varieties of social experience. Sympathetic understanding and sympathetic value cognition are the centers that constitute social mutuality, the fundamental interaction of men in social contact. They are the integrating elements of society because their context is the whole of society and their reflection is the harmony of the total structure. Sympathy makes possible, within the focus of the "Impartial Spectator," the unification and integration of the varieties of societal relationships.[19] It establishes the unity of society as a dynamic whole because it is a cognitive intuition, making transparent the value qualities of patterns of conduct that build up a social structure of justice and a frame of decency.

This concept of sympathy necessarily involves analysis of the rise and development of the standards that are required for sympathy on the various planes of society. Mutuality implies that the social whole has a dual character. Thus, Smith distinguished two opposite types of social value attitudes and two opposite social goods. The value attitudes are what he called the respectable and the amiable virtues, and the highest goods are justice and benevolence.[20] This analysis is the more interesting as it shows clearly that Smith attempted to transfer the perennial question of mystical theology—how to reconcile justice and agape, order and love—to the scientific grounds of psychological and sociological analysis. Man is in need of both and capable of both. Both are necessary for achieving the finite happiness of which societies are capable. Smith's formulation was not entirely clear, however, in regard to their equal strength and value. He said, on the one hand, that a society can exist when based on justice. On the other hand, he declared that no society can last without the amiable virtues, such as goodness, devotion, and sacrifice.

Smith was aware that the presence of these opposite virtues and requirements in human beings is an antinomy in human life. He tried to reconcile the opposites by analyzing the sequence and spheres of our social obligations. He violently attacked the philosophers who have described as immoral the virtues of prudence—that is, the tendencies to strive for health, economic security, and social status.[21] They are indispensable though they are the lowest goods of human happiness. They are indispensable as the necessary conditions for peace of mind. They are lowest because they are merely instrumental to the true well-being of the individual or the group. If these activities remain instrumental, they are goods. Then they have a meaning in the higher sphere of justice, the correct and appropriate distribution of the rights and duties of the socii in the frame of society. The best and ultimate situation would be that in which the virtues of prudence, justice, and benevolence merge. A society in which justice and kindness of heart converge would be a perfect one. Such a situation, in which the exactness of justice meets with the radiant and creative power of the heart, Smith called the realization of true wisdom. He knew that this would be a utopia. With human beings as they are, they are capable, as socii, of establishing justice because they reflect on the interdependence of the members of society and know the utility of peace, and, as individuals and friends, they are able to build up intimate relationships in which justice is overshadowed by kindness of heart.

This inquiry into the different aspects of sympathetic cognition brought forth a description of the different stages of social sympathy and social obligation.[22] There is an original sympathy among the members of a family and a habitual sympathy among the members of a clan or of a neighborhood. There is a conventional sympathy of cooperation and of common interests among the members of a profession or of a trade. In social action, these appear as mores or social conventions. They are habits that are taken for granted within any specific group. They make possible the systems of approval and esteem that we call public opinion in a rational society. In discussing these bonds, Smith envisaged society as prescribing the rules of justice and exerting pressure toward the fulfillment of obligations that cannot be enforced by the state.

This sociological trend of thinking is apparent in the descriptions of the "Impartial Spectator."[23] The Impartial Spectator is an image. He mirrors the common standards and evaluations of the socii regarding the welfare and the common good of their lasting relationships. But he is also the individual conscience, as emancipated from the pressure of public opinion. This dualism between a sociological and a personal basis for the continuity and duration of societal relationships is a characteristic feature of Smith's thinking. On the one hand, the Impartial Spectator is Aristotle's *phronimos aner* (the practical, wise man), the image of the general standards that are taken for granted in an individual historical situation. At the same time, he is the image of the human being who comes into his own when devoted to the pursuit of values beyond the pale of social institutions.

Smith thoroughly analyzed the constitution of man as socius, presenting a phenomenology of social attitudes and of patterns of conduct. He did not at all believe that man is completely explained by the habits, values, and opinions of his society. Only the superficial and the vulgar, he maintained, submit to the judgment of the social elite, the lowest tribunal in the establishment of social sympathy and social standards. Thoughtful and responsible men will submit to the judgment of the Impartial Spectator who, as the representative of social consensus, reflects the true public opinion of the whole society. They will comply with it as individuals and identify it with their own conscience.

These judgments are actually those of the higher tribunal within our breast.[24] Man can appeal to this court from the arbitrary and fashionable opinions of a ruling class. Even when he is in conflict with public opinion, he can appeal to the sympathetic intuitions in his own heart. Then the Impartial Spectator becomes both personal conscience and social compliance. Thus, there is still a supreme court to which man can appeal. This court does not, however, judge the conduct of man as a socius. Men who have failed, or been defeated in spite of the noblest motives, can turn to the supreme court of the deity that alone is able to recognize and to judge upon the truth of goodwill. But it is the human being who can be acquitted, not the socius. The socius is always esteemed or despised for his positive or negative contribution to the happiness of society.

Smith knew that man is not completely defined as socius, but he was reluctant to admit it. He described the individual conscience as able to recognize the truth about the happy life and to understand the principles of justice, but he asserted that the individual conscience, which he called "institution," is derived in great measure from the authority of the lower tribunal—society. Moreover, individual conscience frequently reverses society's judgments According to this sociologistic view, the total control represented by society preceded the rise of an understanding of social values. It was the philosophical knowledge of these values, however, that made possible the responsible human being. The conscientious individual alone can achieve whole happiness because only he is capable of achieving tranquility of mind as a creative act of his own. This thesis of Smith's on the origins of moral consciousness has greatly influenced sociological histories of morals, such as Edvard Westermarck's [1862–1939] well-known book.[25]

Smith established in his works a pluralistic theory of mutuality. He described the unity in the variety of the different spheres of society; in his conception of man as both socius and person, he reconciled contradictory requirements.

This general theory is accompanied by a consideration of particular problems that were so important to Smith that he dealt with them in all his books. There is, for example, the problem of consensus and authority in society[26]—a by-product of the theory of sympathy. Sympathy as recognition of superiority can occur in four different ways. Men are willing to submit sympathetically to the physical or to the intellectual powers of individuals. But it is only among primitive societies that military heroes and wise old men are recognized as highest authorities and rulers. Smith shared Pascal's idea that, in modern societies, it is impossible to recognize such personal qualifications by social sympathies. There remain two other sources of authority and superiority: economic power and noble birth. Since men are inclined by nature to sympathize with the light and positive sides of life, they tend to parade their wealth and hide their misery. They consider it easier to stand the atrocities of destiny, in the manner of the Stoic wise men, than to endure the contempt of society.[27] For this reason, people recognize, with sympathy, the owners of wealth and power as their superiors. They admire and serve them without any expectation of their benevolence. They are stirred by their superiority without any belief in their happiness. They admire the potential of their means, the perfection of the social fabric that makes possible such achievements.

Smith set it forth as a sociological rule that men by nature long to recognize authority and superiority as the seals on peace and order. Even when the conditions shape compellingly toward revolution, the socii will not easily give up the traditional consensus.[28] Smith objected to the philosophers of resistance, declaring that nature has taught men to submit to the owners of power and wealth. There is a natural impulse toward respect, an impulse that is profoundly connected with our longings for justice and peace. Thus, socii recognize the place of the powerful as fact and right, as value and example. Men offer this positive sympathy of consensus because they appreciate peace and order. The socii are even willing to sacrifice sympathy with the poor to the primary sympathy with power and authority.

The rulers know of this impulse toward reverence. They have met it with a pattern of external splendor, of politesse, and of refined and delicate manners. They have answered a true social need with a theatrical show. They have responded to a genuine desire with a pattern of fiction. Smith described perfectly the necessity for social images and symbols. Theoretically, he was a republican; actually, he remained true to English political traditions. He declared that love of country is the first obligation in the sequence of social values—first, not because it is a part of mankind, but because it is a microcosm of the whole. He defined love of country as respect for its constitution and the enlightened will to improve conditions within that frame.[29] He remained true to the liberal spirit of reform even after the French Revolution began. In the last edition of his *Theory of Moral Sentiments*, he indignantly rejected the "doctrines of system" and the "men of system" who believe that they alone know the key to social redemption and that the latter can be realized by the illegal violence of revolution.

Smith added still another observation to his analysis of the elite. The British middle classes, he said, had transformed the licentiousness and corruption of the court of Charles II into a model example of the virtues of generosity and liberality. They had transformed the frivolous reality of the courtier into the image of the perfect gentleman[30] and had completed the circuit by ridiculing the ascetic virtues of the Puritan lower classes, regarding them as the vices of hypocrisy and avarice.

Society establishes consensus for its usefulness as much as for its authority. In fact, according to Smith, the two original tendencies in politics referred to a preference for authority or for utility as a basis of consensus. His thesis is applicable to the principles of conservative and liberal politics—Tories believe that the state and its authority are prior to society, while Whigs believe that the state is purely instrumental to the ends of society.[31]

These investigations stimulated an extremely useful analysis of the sociological significance of customs and fashions.[32] To a considerable extent, customs condition social attitudes and patterns of conduct, having the power to transform rational values into social habits. In particular, the trades and professions develop certain patterns of behavior that meet the objective requirements and remain the property of the respective occupations. But society transforms the objective patterns into social images. These can be turned either into heroic transfigurations or into the caricatures of a comic strip. It is a great merit of Smith's that he stressed the difference between patterns and images and suggested a sociological analysis of the role that the mores play in creating images according to the prevailing ethos and its fashions. In an enlightened society, the image of the soldier or of the clergyman will easily be transformed into its ridiculous potentialities, while in a militaristic country, the merchant and the scholar will be in the same situation. In all societies, there are images of age groups, ranks and professions, determined by the standards of the ruling social elite. Changes in social structure revolutionize customs and fashions, for new societies continuously reevaluate the worth and function of the different occupations and attitudes.

Smith's sociological ideas contain the hypotheses of his theory of economic processes and the division of labor. The primary motive of social action is not an economic one, for the laborer is capable of obtaining wages that make possible a tolerable situation. The main motive is a sociological one—the desire to be applauded and to be considered superior. It is this craving for social prestige and social rank that has stimulated all progress toward civilization. Men can easily satisfy their economic needs and attain a modest social security, even in the lower ranks of society. Nature, however, has unleashed the restless and never-ending efforts of men to improve their social status and to build higher and higher the structure of civilization. Nature was wise to deceive man on the value of wealth and power. He always tends to mistake their instrumental character for real values and genuine ends, but this mistake has made possible the progress of mankind in all spheres of civilization.[33] The sphere of social action is subject to the same deceiving trick—even the most avaricious entrepreneur will necessarily share his profits with his tenants and laborers and invest them in his lands, because his own needs are satisfied with a small part of his gains.

Smith took it for granted that this transformation of evil passions into good results would finally establish harmony and justice in society. Thus, his concrete realism was turned into a spiritual naturalism. He knew that needs and desires end when satisfied, while competition is infinite. Mutuality does not necessarily mean harmony; goodness does not mechanically create the response of goodness. Nevertheless, the concept of society as nature postulates the optimistic belief that societal relationships will transform the subjective and selfish passions into the objective goods of a right and happy society when they develop beyond the pale of political institutions. This normative thesis is opposed to Smith's sociological analysis of the nature of society in history.

History, Progress, Nature

Smith applied the insights achieved in his sociological analysis of the natural societal relationships to the social processes in history and of the change in social institutions. In these investigations, his sociological theory became a universal method for understanding social change. In particular, he demonstrated the truth of his theory of reciprocity as a measuring rod of social equilibrium. This is found in his analyses of militarism, academic institutions, and churches,[34] in which he examined the technical, economic, financial, and social conditions that determine the changing aspects of these institutions. He concluded that when the mutuality between give and take, between teacher and student, minister and community, army and society, is broken up, then social institutions have lost their effectiveness and are on the point of decline. When the socii who make these institutions work neglect their social functions and establish bodies of vested interests, the whole of society as an equilibrium of relationships is jeopardized, and social change becomes inevitable. Social change is indispensable for the establishment and reestablishment of social harmony. This general trend in the social process of history is a sociological rule. Men are always inclined to escape their responsibilities toward the whole and to settle down as owners and exploiters of privileged institutions. This selfish escapism disrupts the balance of rights and duties in the whole of society and makes necessary the reestablishment of a genuine mutuality.

In the *Lectures* and in the *Wealth of Nations*, Smith gave much attention to the development of social institutions in history,[35] subjecting to a thorough analysis the conditions that impede progress in agriculture and industry. He explained the slow progress as resulting from the political structure of the feudal ages. The never-ending wars, the instability of governments, and the resulting insecurity of legal protection made it impossible to improve the economic product of the country. The feudal idea of landed property as the basis of political power, and its legal expression in the laws of primogeniture, suppressed all economic considerations. The social conditions of labor were such that no group of agricultural workers could find any incentive for productive labor or for accumulating stocks. Slaves, serfs, and tenants could have no interest, economic or social, in making improvements. Under absolutism, the mistakes of mercantilist policies made it impossible to develop the potentialities of the rural economy. In dealing with these subjects, Smith was fully aware that societies exist on a variety of planes that are interdependent. The economic, legal, and political spheres interact and are interrelated in a lasting mutuality.

He applied the same method in his analysis of urban institutions, insisting on the decisive role that political power played in the organization of the townships as a new center of social importance.[36] Here, however, he introduced a new element as a condition of progress—the ethos of the ruling elite. The noble lord despised barter and exchange as a vulgar and mean business. To him, power was wealth. Powerless farmers and craftsmen could devote their efforts to the miserable business of attaining wealth; gentlemen did not need it, for they had power. As a result of this attitude of the feudal rulers, the progress of urban societies was slow and precarious.

There was a political motive, however, that furthered it. The urban centers were favored by the absolute princes because they supported them against the feudal class and, thus, the urban societies could establish themselves as military-economic citizenries. They introduced order and good government, and made liberty and security the main concern of the constitution. The townships became the center for the surrounding country. As the central market, they opened new economic possibilities for the rural areas, and they established new patterns of behavior that contributed to the economic progress of the whole. The merchants and the industrial classes developed different habits from those of country gentlemen, learning to employ their money in profitable projects and becoming bold in new enterprises. They came to emphasize order, economy and attention, and to expect honesty and reliability in business affairs. Thus, they furthered the institutions of liberty and security among the rural societies. Smith analyzed also, however, the negative aspects of this progressive movement. He saw that increasing industrialization could lead to shocking exploitation of labor; he was aware of the dehumanizing effects of standardization and specialization in mechanized industrial work.

This emphasis on the reciprocity of social conditions, this awareness of the positive and negative effects of changes in social institutions, was fundamental to Smith's ideas on history. While he had no doubt that the urban professional and business classes made possible important progress in modern history, by spreading the spirit of enlightened moderation and wise social equilibrium, he nevertheless insisted that this progress was accidental, not necessary. It happened that historical conditions favored commerce and industry before they made for improvement and cultivation in rural societies—an example of what Smith called the unnatural and retrograde order of history, the perversion of the natural order of things.[37] History, he contended, is primarily conditioned by the vested interests of the ruling elite, by the vanity of the big landed proprietors, and by the ruthless pressure of business interests. History is the concept for the time process in which political development takes place. It is a process of distorted progress, of obscured truth, errors, failures, and miscarried meanings. Historical progress is progress *quand même*, progress in spite of the arbitrary and irrational situations of the historical process.

Progress was a basic concept in Smith's thought. What he meant by it, however, was not the historical process of society but the very telos of societal relations. "From savagery to civilization" could be his definition of progress. This is the natural progress of social mutuality, the very purpose of social self-realization. It is an ever-present potentiality, and also a possibility in the here and now, reflecting the never-ending effort to enlighten the dark forces in nature. It can never be historical evolution. Progress materializes when the processes of civilization have established a lasting harmony between town and country, between the urbanized farmer and the rural citizen. Progress indicates the potential perfection of society according to the nature of man as socius.

Nature, on the other hand, is represented by the creative acts of sympathetic mutuality that establish and reestablish the whole of society as an open system of justice, emancipated from the historical-political process. Socii intend to create happiness in such acts. Individuals are happy when socii are happy. There is a sequence of goods required for happiness. By nature, man needs, first, the means of subsistence; second, economic independence; and last, a good conscience. Hence, it is a principle of natural justice that the improvement of the country, the area that affords subsistence, should come before that of the town that furnishes the means of comfort. It is a natural rule that the surplus product of the country constitutes the subsistence of the town. For this reason, the natural progress of society consists in establishing a lasting harmony and mutuality between country and town.

Societies are happy that have succeeded in satisfying the biological, economic, and moral requirements in their true sequence. In the mutuality of societal relationships, potential perfection is eternally present. Through that mutuality, the passions of competition are reconciled with the longings for peace. Nature's dynamic center is society. The natural drives and the teleological intentions of the socii make it possible to realize the harmony of nature and the justice of society, for the sympathetic attitudes of the socii imply a cognitive intuition of the values that establish the useful cooperation and just organization of the social whole. Thus, in spiritualizing organic nature as carrying the "seals of eternal wisdom," Smith established a unification of utilitarianism and teleology.

According to Smith, the "Author of Nature" has implanted the rules of conduct in man, the socius, in order to make him a responsible judge for his own and society's moral standards: "the Author of Nature has made man the immediate judge of mankind and has . . . created him after his image and appointed him his viceregent upon earth to superintend the behavior of his brethren."[38] Man as socius or society as a whole thus becomes the delegate of God. The social whole is the center of responsible freedom and of just service because the deity has fitted the organic drives to coincide with the true ends of justice and perfection. Through this spiritualization of nature, the deity has made society the creator of its own destiny and the responsible author of social happiness and justice. This nature-society is a universe of intelligible knowledge that can be explained and understood scientifically. Smith regarded the analysis and interpretation of social conduct as the instruments for scientifically establishing the principles and rules of the good and just life, and for grasping an intelligible knowledge of the creative wisdom of the deity.

This praise of nature expresses a scientific ethos that attempts to reject all transcendental factors in explaining the social constitution.

Thus, Smith rejected those theories in which religion is necessary for an understanding of the motives of social conduct. According to his thinking, philosophy and commonsense have made it evident that the sense of duty, not theology, is the ruling principle of conduct. As scholars, we are able to analyze and explain the rules that are valid for this life and that make possible the control and prediction of social action. We cannot explain scientifically our responsibilities toward God, but we can describe objectively our responsibilities as socii. In social action, we can fulfill the creative responsibilities for the happiness of society that the deity has transferred to society as an independent and intelligent agent, as the center of nature.

Smith described this transfer in terms of the religious myth that God has appointed man his vice-regent on earth. The image has a tradition, and Smith was probably the last who applied it in order to describe the place of man in the universe. Pico della Mirandola [1463–1494] was probably the first, who in his *De dignitate hominis* had God say to Adam, "I have put you into the center of the world that you can easily look around you and inspect everything. I created you as a being neither celestial nor earthly, neither mortal nor immortal, so that you may be your own free creator and conqueror. You can degenerate into a beast or elevate yourself into a God-like being." The man of the Renaissance was enthusiastically and grimly aware that he was capable of both the sublime and the cruel in molding his destiny. He knew that he could achieve both self-redemption and self-condemnation, as his own liberator and judge. Life to him was the *passio humana*, the sum total of sufferings and exaltations.

Smith's socius is not disturbed by such radical alternatives. He is not his own creator, but an independent agent of a divine wisdom. He can accomplish a social equilibrium merely because the Author of Nature has turned even the selfish instincts of the individual to the common good of the whole society. Good and considerate conduct will create kind and good responses. There are no alternatives in Smith's nature-society. This nature is a social panentheism,[39] a normative state between organic nature and the world of history.

The myth of the deified society illuminates the criteria for an independent and self-responsible society in history. As reality, however, this historical society is the arena where human passions and interests present the spectacle of human corruptibility and wickedness. What remains is the disillusioned but ever-present courage of the scholar. Being in possession of the true measuring rods of nature, he can explain the failures and deficiencies of the historical process by analyzing its changing conditions and revealing the disrupted equilibrium of societal relationships.

Notes

1. See in particular Adolf Löwe, *Economics and Sociology* (London: 1935); Glenn R. Morrow, "Adam Smith, Moralist and Philosopher," in *Adam Smith, 1776–1926: Lectures to Commemorate the Sesquicentennial of the Publication of "The Wealth of Nations"* (Chicago: University of Chicago Press, 1928); Glenn R. Morrow, *The Ethical and Economic Theories of Adam Smith*, Cornell University Studies in Philosophy 15 (New York: 1915); and Glenn R. Morrow, "The Significance of the Doctrine of Sympathy in Hume and Adam Smith," *Philosophical Review* 24 (March 1923); Gladys Bryson, "Sociology and Moral Philosophy," *Sociological Review* 24 (April 1932); F. H. Giddings, preface to *The Principles of Sociology*, 3rd ed. (New York: 1896); F. H. Giddings, *Studies in the Theory of Human Society* (New York: 1922); Albion W. Small, *Origins of Sociology* (Chicago: 1924); Albion W. Small, *Adam Smith and Modern Sociology* (Chicago: 1907); Harris Laurie, *The Scottish Philosophy in its National Development* (Glasgow: 1902); James McCosh, *The Scottish Philosophy* (Glasgow: 1875); Richard Schuller, *Die klassische Nationalökonomie und ihre Gegner* (Berlin: 1895).

2. 4th ed. (London: 1774), 6th ed. (London: 1789); hereafter referred to as *Theory* 4th ed. or *Theory* 6th ed.

3. Ed. Edwin Cannan (Oxford: 1896); hereafter referred to as *Lectures.*

4. 2 vols., ed. Edwin Cannan (London: 1904).

5. *Theory* 6th ed., pt. 6, ch. 2, 370.

6. *Theory* 6th ed., preface, 3.

7. *Lectures,* pt 1, § 1, 2; *Theory* 4th ed., 436; *Theory* 6th ed., 570.

8. *Wealth of Nations,* vol. 2, book 5, 395–425.

9. *Theory* 4th ed., 193, 243.

10. *Theory* 4th ed., 253 ff., 415 ff.

11. *Theory* 6th ed., pt 6, ch. 3, 401.

12. *Theory* 4th ed., 143, 291, 312.

13. *Theory* 4th ed., 4–9; *Wealth of Nations,* vol. 1, p. 17; *Lectures,* pt. 2, ch. 3, § 2, 57.

14. *Theory* 4th ed., 130 ff.

15. *Theory* 4th ed., 12, 34, 79.

16. *Theory* 4th ed., 63, 74; *Wealth of Nations,* vol. 1, passim.

17. *Theory* 4th ed., 411.

18. *Theory* 4th ed., 10–29 and *passim.*

19. *Theory* 4th ed., 198–243; *Theory* 6th ed., 1–214.

20. *Theory* 4th ed., 30–36, 132–60.

21. *Theory* 4th ed., 379 ff.

22. *Theory* 6th ed., 269 ff.

23. *Theory* 4th ed., 194, 198–243.

24. *Theory* 4th ed., 205 ff.

25. [Salomon surely means Edvard Westermarck, *The Origin and Development of the Moral Ideas* (Macmillan, 1906).—Eds.]

26. *Theory*, 4th ed., 278–89, 332–48; *Wealth of Nations*, vol. 2, 393–425; *Lectures*, 3–10.

27. *Theory* 4th ed., 106–8.

28. *Theory* 4th ed., 87 ff.

29. *Theory* 6th ed., 393–97.

30. *Theory* 4th ed., 73 ff.

31. *Lectures*, pt. 1, § 1, p. 8.

32. *Theory* 4th ed., 303–24.

33. *Theory* 4th ed., 84 ff., 272 ff.

34. *Wealth of Nations*, vol. 2, 314–35, 393–450; *Lectures*, 184–87.

35. *Lectures*, 10–37, 52–112, 156–71; *Wealth of Nations*, vol. 2, 421–35.

36. *Wealth of Nations*, vol. 2, 170 ff.

37. *Wealth of Nations*, vol. 1, 426 ff.

38. *Theory* 4th ed., 203 ff.

39. [For a concise discussion of panentheism, see the *Stanford Encyclopedia of Philosophy* at: plato.stanford.edu/entries/panentheism/.—Eds.]

9

Goethe (1932)

Das Fütreffliche ist unergründlich, man mag damit anfangen, was man will.

I

On March 22, 1832, at the age of eighty-two, Johan Wolfgang von Goethe died in Weimar. He had attained the summit of worldly fame but had not escaped loneliness that, like an aura, seems to surround all great poets. This seeming paradox of fame and loneliness offers a good opportunity to begin these observations. No one saw more clearly the spuriousness of the sort of recognition that we call fame than Goethe himself. In his "Dedication" (Zueignung), and again and again in verse and prose, he equated fame with falsehood, turning upon it his diabolic irony and expecting posterity to be no more than a vacuum.

Wer wohl versteht, was sich so schickt und ziemt,
Versteht auch seiner Zeit ein Kränzchen abzujagen;
Doch bist du nur erst hundert Jahr berühmt,
So weiss kein Mensch mehr was von dir zu sagen.

Published originally in a slightly different form in Albert Salomon, *In Praise of Enlightenment* (Cleveland: Meridian Books, 1963). Republished by permission from Frank Salomon.

Goethe's profound serenity was undisturbed by the fact that Friedrich Schiller [1759–1805] was far more popular and alive among the people than he was, even though, as he once remarked to Johann Peter Eckermann [1792–1854], Schiller's nature and character were incomparably more aristocratic than his own. On the hundredth anniversary of Schiller's birth, November 10, 1859, all Germany celebrated his achievement. There were countless public readings of "Die Glocke" (The Song of the Bell) and many performances of Schiller's plays. Jacob Grimm [1785–1863] was merely being exact when he called the day a public festival. He chose as the most appropriate close to his speech that very praise of fame, in which Schiller expresses his own conception of the highest glory of life.

Von des Lebens Gütern allen
Ist der Ruhm das höchste doch,
Wenn der Leib in Staub zerfallen,
Lebt der grosse Name noch.

They were good words with which to close a joyous memorial to a man whose very name conveyed a free and unified sense of conviction. In swearing allegiance to Schiller, the German middle classes became the bearers and proclaimers of the fame of "their" poet, whose idealistic pathos had raised them above the gray sobriety of everyday life and whose rhetoric of freedom had moved them deeply. His praise of bourgeois existence had conferred worth and self-respect upon an entire class that, in its turn, loyally passed his name from generation to generation, renewing and remodeling itself through his spirit. Genuine fame always binds a man's name to a community. Through his spirit, the community renews the awareness of its own spiritual structure by recognizing and transmitting the fame of the man and his work. Schiller imposed a moral and spiritual form on the German bourgeoisie, which gave it meaning and self-consciousness and justified both its patriotism and love of freedom.

The special relation to a given human community that supports fame is always precarious. When social structures no longer create representative—that is, objective—bases for cohesive relationships, society disintegrates into solitary groups incapable of performing general functions. Thus, the work and achievement of a man may not find the necessary historical factors to transmit his fame. Occasionally, the scope and greatness of a work transcend the available historical media. Both sets of circumstances coincided in Goethe's case with striking clarity. The words at the beginning of Rilke's book on Rodin could easily stand at the head of any Goethe biography: "He was lonely before fame came, and the fame which did come made him lonelier still. For what is fame but a collection of misunderstandings which tend to gather about a great name?" This dissolution of fame in loneliness, indeed its virtual abolition, becomes a convincing reality, if no social groups exist that dare to carry on the tradition of the great man in a manner consistent with his message, and if society is composed of nothing more than solitary individuals and enemy camps.

That is why the modern world cannot be bearers and prophets of Goethe's fame. Any attempt to transmit his name and work as if they were generally known and accepted, no matter under what auspices or with what pathos, is condemned to failure. It is false and fraudulent. Any genuine achievement of historical perfection must, of necessity, break out of the specific confines of its own era. Like Rembrandt, Bach, Shakespeare, and Mozart, Goethe remained tied to the historical circumstances of his particular existence but, at the same time, overcame and outgrew them. He eventually attained almost complete isolation. The hundredth anniversary of Goethe's birth served to emphasize the starkness of his isolation. The ruling classes stood coolly on the sidelines, full of distaste for a man whose religious and political views were thoroughly repellent to them. The free bourgeoisie, fighting its final struggle for an already lost revolution, could see in Goethe nothing but the arch-aristocrat and the parvenu. In many places, violent demonstrations took place against ceremonies in honor of the poet's memory. There remained only a small class of educated men who gathered to honor the poet and to testify to the productive and creative force of his spirit. They could only transmit to one another the mystery of personal cultivation and development through the medium of his wisdom and poetry. They stood for an educational inheritance; they testified to the greatness and loneliness of his life, not to his fame.

At this moment, there will be no hate or violence aroused by memorial ceremonies. The people, torn and wearied, have never been further from unity of will as a nation than at this moment. The masses, through no fault of their own, have been made brutal and incapable of extracting any meaning from such recollections. The educated class, once homogeneous, has been fragmented, dissolved, and buried. Under such conditions, ought not shame, seriousness, and honesty compel us to carry out our memorial without show and in silence? We cannot transmit his fame. We have no living tradition to carry on. Must not every word of remembrance be meaningless and vain?

Yet the very forces of dissolution and destruction call forth their antidotes. "Where there is danger, there is also salvation." [Friedrich Hölderlin (1770–1843) in his poem "Patmos"—Eds.] An hour of recollection removes us from the containment and distraction of our daily lives and confronts us unexpectedly with an awareness of the timeless and the eternal. In this simple act, we hurl the idea and the essence of greatness into the teeth of our age. Greatness is, after all, the only measure of tradition for us today. Jacob Burckhardt [1818–1897], in his *Force and Freedom: Reflections on History*, summed up the essence of historical greatness in one of his characteristically sharp and lucid phrases: "Greatness is what we are not." This formulation seems negative, but it is actually a voluntary recognition of merit and a humble and submissive acceptance of a spiritual hierarchy of values. This awareness of the possibility of fulfillment of human striving contains at the same time the will to keep great men alive. We see in them the embodiment of what alone gives worth and dignity to human existence: the complete development of an entire personality in its relation to the infinite. In unity of personality and meaning, a profound simplicity—one of the special characteristics of greatness—develops. For what is greatness if not the productivity of a pure heart and great thoughts? Greatness can be understood here and now. It is effective everywhere and at all times because it probes the basis of existence itself, as each and every one of us experiences it, be it in love, in moral or spiritual decisions, or in death. If we are not seized by the presence of something eternal in a work, then it can never be more than an incomplete and transitory achievement, exquisite, fine, interesting, perhaps, but always capricious, always an exercise in taste or intellect, and always without binding force. There is nothing more insufferable than the multitude of elevated intellectual and artistic accomplishments that, lacking any sort of objective task, remain a mere expression of private existence.

Western culture has become a monstrous department store in which the customers hurry from counter to counter without being able to choose among the overwhelming number of loudly praised articles being offered. People also need spiritual bread and sacred, sobering water. Only a work and a personality that, in themselves, are simple and true can provide the right sort of sustenance. Greatness alone creates measure, form, and law. As an example and measure of greatness, we call forth the memory of Goethe and hold his image up to the twisted features of our time—not, to be sure, as the image of a hero, nor as a mythical figure (this tendency must always be countered), but as a memory of a great and pure expression of perfection. The process of making his meaning our own, which is, after all, the principal task of all tradition, must be renewed. Goethe himself approved of no other form of memory. In November 1823, when someone proposed a toast to memory, Goethe broke out angrily:

> I do not accept memory in your sense. You are merely expressing yourself incorrectly. When we meet something great, beautiful, or important, we should not recall it afterwards from outside ourselves or hunt it out. On the contrary, from the moment of meeting, it should weave itself into our inner self, become one with it, create a new and better self, and so continue to live on within us shaping and forming. There is no past for which we should yearn. There is only the new, which builds itself from the enlarged elements of the past. Genuine yearning should always be productive and should strive for something new and better.

This is the only way we can think of Goethe today. The shades of great men ought only to be called forth when we have brought our voluntary offering of devoted service into the magic circle of love.

II

Goethe's work occupied a peculiar place in the history of world literature. Most great poets—Dante Alighieri [1265–1321], Pedro Calderón de la Barcs [1600–1681], William Shakespeare [1564–

1616], or Pierre Corneille [1606–1684]—drew their ideas from the surrounding world of human activity. The real, material substance of life became art through the transforming power of their work. German life in Goethe's day offered an artist very little raw material that he could use. The lack of national themes—indeed, the lack of any sort of themes suitable for a poet—remained one of Goethe's loudest and most frequent complaints, most famously and sharply expressed in his autobiography *Dichtung und Wahrheit* (Poetry and Truth). In "Shakespeare and No End," he praises the great playwright's good fortune to live in such a worthy time. Shakespeare's effect would not have been so great if he had not been the spokesman of a vivid, lively era. He portrays Englishmen whose humanity is evident, rather than poetical Romans. Shakespeare had the advantage "that he came at the right time to harvest, that he was able to work in a rich and lively Protestant country, where for a time the madness of bigotry was still. A truly pious son of nature, like Shakespeare, had freedom to develop his pure inwardness religiously without relation to any specific religion." A German poet born about the middle of the eighteenth century found neither in political nor social life any such poetic inspiration. Goethe describes in the seventeenth book of *Dichtung und Wahrheit* the peaceful, comfortable, unpolitical condition of the German classes, their philistinism, and remoteness in their own narrow world. The American Revolution was much too far away to have any great effect, and the beginnings of political unrest in France were taken far more seriously by the cabinets than by the public.

The inner situation reflected the external conditions exactly. The leadership of the literary movement *Sturm und Drang* had passed to Goethe, whose *Götz und Werther*, as well as his campaign against the rococo, epitomized by the work of Christoph Martin Wieland [1733–1813] and the trivial rationalism of the day, effectively demonstrated his supremacy. The movement showed by the direction of its attacks, its realistic tragedies and novels, the first impetus to a new poetic imagination arising from the spirit of bourgeois morality. The awakening middle classes were swelled with the proud conviction that at last they had become the true bearers of culture. The eruption of luxuriant feeling, the overflowing dedication to nature, and the passionate attack on the dullness of the world and its order were not merely the manifestations of a "youth movement," but also the elementary, intellectual, and spiritual stirrings of the growing self-consciousness of the bourgeois spirit. The stable political nature of Germany and the stolid character of the German middle classes forced this first modern German revolution to take place in the domain of literature and condemned it thereby to fail from its inception. The anxious traditionalism and the prudent sobriety of bourgeois commerce reflected a narrow and provincial social situation. Members of the educated middle class (by no means lacking in vision and daring as individuals) formed an entirely self-contained group, which was insulated from other circles, entrenched in the career hierarchy of the civil service, and thoroughly assimilated to the existing social order. Thus, the group itself, whose spiritual and intellectual structure was given exaggerated attention by the young generation of poets, had no meaningful subject for poetic expression. No active and busy world, no beginnings of great deeds, demanded poetic transfiguration and intellectual expression. The world seemed to offer no impetus to the poetic—that is, elevated and meaningful presentation. For all those who felt themselves called to great deeds, the condition was absolutely unbearable. The young men of *Sturm und Drang* felt that they had to break out of the narrow and tranquil circle of the German middle class in order not to suffocate and to remain true to themselves; filled as they were, however, with the intellectual, moral, and spiritual atmosphere of their class, they could only do so by virtue of their own genius, individuality, and art. An emotional return to nature and tearful sentimentality were the means by which they sought to flee the emptiness of their own condition and to attain the elevated and the grand.[1] Although the essential lack of direction of the movement ultimately brought about its failure, it was a turning point for Goethe.

When Goethe decided to go to Weimar, he severed his connection with the bourgeois world and the formlessness of *Sturm und Drang*. His conversion to classicism and humanism represented his final liberation from the emptiness of German existence. By taking a position in the government of the Prince of Weimar, he broadened the scope of both his experience and effectiveness. At the same time, by this dramatic acceptance of the traditional, customary way of life of the upper classes, he altered the subsequent course of German culture. He introduced a quality of humanist quietism that seeks only the personal cultivation of the intellectual and moral faculties while consciously leaving all established social structures untouched. This decision has, in addition, very important consequences for the external and internal form of his poetry.

III

Although I have considered Goethe the leader of the *Sturm und Drang* movement, I have done so with one major reservation. The fight against the existing order was not a destructive activity for Goethe. On the contrary, the struggle against the ordinary, the commonplace, and the weak was really the expression of his own attempt to liberate the great forces within himself. Freedom meant no more than adequate room in which his passionate compulsion to work could unfold. In an Aeschylean mood, he begs God to give him room for the seething and expanding power of his own mind. *Götz* and the large sketches for *Caesar, Mahommet, Prometheus*, and the beginnings of *Faust*, all works of the time before *Werther*, seem to seek a form in which a grand individual and a striving, busy nature can break out of the bonds of a small and narrow world. That is why the works of this period are both lyrical and realistic. They are filled by the pressing need of the poet for freedom, which is to be understood as the possibility of living greatly.

During this phase of Goethe's career, a very strange thing happened. In the following decades, he suddenly reversed himself and plunged into the very heart of the social and national life of Germany, struggling with constantly changing techniques to purify that life's meaning and to raise it to a general and valid form. Thus, the conversion of the natural productive genius of the seventies, as Goethe admits in *Dichtung und Wahrheit*, was completed, and the poet became a self-conscious educator and teacher of his nation. Whereas in all the other Western nations, poetry has been the most exact expression of the essence of the age and the poet has been the voice of his time, Goethe's work—in precisely the opposite direction—was an attempt to infuse into his people a meaning and form drawn from his own personality. The poem was to be the way leading from philistinism to freedom. "Poetic content is the content of one's own life. No one can give it to us; it can, perhaps, be darkened but never impoverished."

This undertaking fixed the outer form and inner content of his poetry. It explains the peculiar quality of remoteness that all his characters have—even when nearest to us. In order to serve as pedagogic devices, his characters must be transparent and must have especially clear outlines. Goethe always admired Shakespeare's capacity to portray full human beings by simply describing the Englishman from head to toe, but he himself could not afford to do the same. All his poetic figures are German in the sense that the spiritual and moral inheritance of German life, transmuted and relived in Goethe's spirit, always shines through. But they are less German than the figures of Shakespeare and Molière [1622–1673] are English or French. They are more like Goethe than the Shakespearean figures are like Shakespeare. For this reason, the works of his classical period have always been unsuccessful as drama. They cannot appeal to a wide public that wishes to be moved and touched by portrayal and interpretation of its own existence. The object of these works was to refine the personality and to lead it by moral reason toward purity of heart and active love. Unfortunately, the great mass of the people simply cannot be gripped by the image of a higher humanity. What does occur in these works is something quite different. The clarity of the presentation of these elevated themes lifts the violence of human conflicts onto a higher plane, one that transcends, in form, the actual dimensions of human life. This image of humanity is present in every age and illuminates the murky atmosphere of historical reality. Indeed, it sometimes transfigures historical reality, standing forth in the timelessness of the "experienced moment." No matter how varied and confused the garb of time may be, there comes for each man an hour when he must shed that garb and "stand bareheaded under God's thunderclouds."

The unavoidability of final decision in the realm of human activity, the treatment of joy and sorrow, fulfillment and destruction, sins of omission and commission, all these things are eternal subjects for poetic presentation. In the *Iphigenia,* the healing power of pure humanity is treated. Since truth and self-denying love make up the inner substance of the work, the characters in the poetic fable are neither Greeks nor Germans, but pure creatures from the mind and the soul of the poet. If one compares *Hermann und Dorothea* with the idyll *Luise* by Johann Heinrich Voss [1751–1826], one recognizes in both works the world of the small German city and its residents. In Goethe's presentation, the narrowness and poverty of that existence disappear because the characters are raised to a purer level through the clarity and tenderness of their emotions and awareness of their deeds. This world of exalted humanity is ultimately the place where all human decisions are made and where the rank and worth of personality is tested. *Hermann und Dorothea* can never lose its contemporary significance because all its human situations are eternal. Their effect and meaning remain unforgettable for those who seek to escape the dullness and compulsion of daily life and to attain the brilliant light of spiritual form and decision. They are unforgettable because they glow from within.

The problem of poetic form can be most dearly observed in a comparison of the two versions of *Wilhelm Meister*. The earlier version, *Wilhelm Meisters Lehrjahre* (Wilhelm Meister's Apprenticeship), is a realistic bourgeois novel with an almost Dutch liveliness and heartiness. In the final version, *Wilhelm Meisters Wanderjahre* (Wilhelm Meister's Pilgrimage), all trace of realism has vanished. The style is delicate and suggestive. By fixing the actual events in a precise relation to the idea of the whole, the real empirical world becomes both transparent and mysterious. The various areas of life, the theater, the home, the palace, and the society of the nobility turn into more or less obvious symbols of a general meaning. Mignon and the Harpist, who represent the polarity of purity and guilt, act as mirrors that reflect the image of the times in a thousand ways. The same principles of style are used in *Faust, West-östlicher Divan* (The Western-Eastern Diwan), and *Die Wahlverwandtschaften* (Elective Affinities). One can best compare the style of those works with the landscapes of Claude Lorrain [1600–1682], who, not by chance, enjoyed Goethe's great affection. In Claude Lorrain, "we see a perfect human being, who thought and felt beautifully and in whose spirit lay a world not easily found elsewhere. These pictures possess the highest truth, but not a touch of reality. Claude Lorrain knew the real world by heart down to the smallest detail and he used it as a means to express the world of his own beautiful soul. True idealism knows how to use real materials in such a way that the truth that emerges creates the illusion that it is real."

Goethe could not have described his own style more aptly. From *Iphigenia* to *Faust II*, all his works have this in common—the highest truth without a touch of reality. They are landscapes of the soul, heroic only in the sense that they depict an enlarged, purer existence. They make things appear real that are in fact the appearance of truth, and through the beauty of illusion, they reconcile us with the world.

IV

Reconciliation means both the settlement of a conflict and its subordination in a higher unity. The moral force of the intellect accomplishes the one, the magic of a loving heart the other. The purity of Goethe's poetry effects such reconciliation in a remarkable manner. He believed that light in the physical world and intellect in the moral world were "the highest conceivable, indivisible energies," but that man could only perceive them indirectly as a reflection on the surface of life. Truth could also be perceived by man's spirit only when reflected in beauty. Thus, the poet and his art were true mediators between man and truth and between the empirically restricted world and the pure forms of the spirit, which Goethe called "the ordinances of the supreme director." "Art is a true intermediary" and "great talents are the most beautiful means of reconciliation." The painful and unhappy conflicts of existence are banished by the presentation of the beautiful, for as Goethe pointed out, "there is no surer way to escape the world than through art and there is no surer way to tie oneself to the world than through art." In art, insoluble problems of existence can be dissolved in beautiful appearances and universal harmony. There is the danger that a flight into poetry may become a means of avoiding decisions that should no longer be postponed. Since, however, the reality of art appears only in a moral relationship (because all reality without such a relation is common and art by its nature is noble), art is able to reenter and influence the world. This is possible only if the poet performs his highest function and "as representative of the most natural of conditions, of the finest style of life, of pure moral endeavor, of the majesty and earnest worship of God, dares to employ common and ludicrous contrasts." Realizing his own function, Goethe would only speak of the task of a poet in allusive terms. "Art rests on a kind of religious sense, upon a deep, unshakeable seriousness, which is why it unites so happily with religion."

As a messenger of truth, the poet has a formative moral task. Goethe revised the traditional theory of the function of poetry that had been transmitted from the ancient world via humanism to the Enlightenment. Although he still regarded poetry as a means to enlighten and improve humanity, its appeal was not to be made necessarily through reason alone. The experience of living beauty would supplant reason. Inevitably, the problem of form and content and the question of the meaning of beauty became major preoccupations. In the characters of both Pandora and Helen, Goethe tries to answer the latter question. Beauty is simultaneously a form of perfection and a mere illusion. It emerges in life only to disappear again. He attempted to arrive at an answer in several ways. Pandora, for example, is not given to the active, busy Prometheus, but to the worried, thoughtful Epimetheus, the sidelines observer. She illumines his existence even after her disappearance because she leaves with him his most valued possession—the knowledge of beauty. In the existing sketch of a sequel to the fragment, Pandora appears as the mediator among the warring factions and restrains them all by her beauty. She becomes the judge who settles all quarrels and, as perfect form, ennobles the coarse manners of the world of affairs. Epimetheus sings her praises:

> Sie steiget hernieder in tausend Gebilden
> Sie schwebet auf Wassern, sie schreitet auf Gefilden
> Nach heiligen Massen erglänzt sic und schallt
> Und einzig veredelt die Form den Gehalt;
> Verleiht ihm, verleiht sich die höchste Gewalt
> Mir erschien sie in Jugend—, in Frauengestalt.

In the above passage, beauty is conceived as pure and ennobling form, not of this world but appearing in it, never granted to the man of action but only to those who have taken the world and humanity into their inmost selves. Pandora is, therefore, an apparition. The Helen whom Faust evokes and who wanders by his side only seems to be real. After the fall of Euphorion, she disappears and leaves her beloved nothing but a veil as a token of remembrance. The veil plays an equally important role in Ottilie's existence, and in "The Dedication" (Die Zueignung), the poet receives the veil of poetry from the hands of truth. The veil is a symbol of something enshrouded, whose glow is barely visible through its fabric. Goethe was deeply convinced that neither the truth nor the sun could be allowed to shine unshaded in the eyes of men. "In the colored reflection, we have life." For him, truth was only visible in reflection, in apparitions, and in illusion. Beauty, one of the many types of illusion in nature, is the most exalted because it has no other purpose than itself. Being pure form, it can express eternally valid truths. Art as illusion is the mediator between time and eternity. In and through it, the contradictions and tensions of this world are reconciled and disappear.

The ennobling moral character of poetry is caused by the appearance of truth in the beautiful, and men are encouraged by it to seek a higher existence, the good, the beautiful, and the true, those eternal, pure forms in which the highest truth manifests itself. Originally, Goethe had set out to infuse significant meaning into the life of his people through the use of poetry and beauty, but, after the French Revolution, he enlarged his task and began to erect a monument to the unchanging and the eternal. While the inherited orderliness of life degenerated into an unparalleled chaos, and everything was relentlessly sucked into the maelstrom of politics, Goethe stood aloof and, out of the purity and greatness of his own spirit, dared to salvage the eternal, inextinguishable features of the human heart for the future. He was never more successful in this endeavor than in the *West-östlicher Divan*, which, like the ever-turning vault of heaven, is always new and wonderful. Here one finds all life's manifestations: dominion and service, love and trust, good will and forceful self-assertion, worth and pride, shadowy happiness and pure reconciliation, elevated to the tenderest level of words. Yet nothing could be more false than to suppose that the geniality and unfettered feeling of the poem arose from a lack of participation in or an alienation from the world. Especially with regard to *The Divan*, he tried to stand beyond all factions, consciously and joyously: "with awareness, so that he shrinks not before the terrible; with joyousness, so that he knows how to present everything delightfully." This joyousness is the expression of inner love through which the poet transforms life into pure image.

Goethe praised Molière for being the judge of his era and not its servant. In such a high function, the poet can only fulfill his task alone and isolated from his age: "the poet as man and citizen will, of course, love his fatherland, but the fatherland of his poetic talents and creativity is bound to no special province or country. It is the Good, the Noble, and the Beautiful which he captures and shapes wherever he finds it." What is the meaning of patriotic activity? "Could a poet who has spent his entire life fighting harmful prejudices, eradicating narrow-minded views, enlightening the spirit of his people, purifying its taste and ennobling its convictions, do something more patriotic than that?" Beauty transmits to his people an awareness of eternal and immutable truth.

Goethe's poetry often recalls the harmony and balance of the classic epic by the way conflicts are reconciled as if by divine intervention. The tragic in life is not overcome; it is avoided. Goethe once confessed that the strain of writing a tragedy would burst his spirit wide open. The reconciliation achieved in his works cannot, therefore, be permanent because it depends entirely on the poet's personality and on the expansive power of his love. It is an illusion that hovers over the abyss and bears no one across it. Its beauty is a clear, inwardly directed magic, which enchants without transforming. It is temporary, a false consciousness.

V

The outer and inner form of Goethe's poetry was conditioned by special historical circumstances: the lack of content in German life, the demonic release of energy in the French Revolution, and the twenty subsequent years of military catastrophes. Although these circumstances have changed, the wisdom and meaning of Goethe's life and work continue to shine brightly.

Hermann Grimm [1828–1901] suspected as early as 1893 that the twentieth century would learn to appreciate Goethe's wisdom but lose the ability to understand his poetry. "Falsehood belongs to the age, truth to the individual." Goethe became ever more sharply aware that truth is granted only to certain important individuals who, as in a solemn procession of blessed souls, pass the torch of life from one to another across time and space. "The Epoch condemned Socrates." Masses and majorities are always the bearers of falsehood, stupidity, and confusion. This attitude led him to a strictly antihistorical worldview in the age of Hegel and Marx, who were busily subordinating man to the world spirit. Goethe had observed enough worldly activity from sufficient proximity to accurately assess the degree of caprice, circumstance, and corruption that went into the decisions of the political world. His disillusionment with the practice of politics remained his private property and never became the sharp and implacable critique of the French moralists. He tended to view the domain of politics as an arena in which certain types of human acts were constantly repeated. Since he watched the affairs of the world with incomparable exactness and sober attention, his observations were always shrewd. He saw the Revolution coming long before most statesmen and believed that both rulers and ruled would bear equal guilt for the disaster. Sovereignty and authority, freedom and protest, misuse of power and revolt, the necessary weakening of the inner legitimacy of the structure of a state and the rise of new orders—all the possible and typical expressions of political life were, in his opinion, perpetually recurrent complications of human affairs.

> The struggle of the old, the established and the conservative against new developments, education, and reform is eternal. Every order gives rise to pedantry and, in attempting to rid themselves of that evil, men destroy the order as well. After a while they become aware that they must create a new order to replace the old. The wise ruler would try to moderate this struggle so that he prevented the defeat of his own side. This has, however, never been granted to men and God would not appear to want it so.

Perhaps even more typical of Goethe's thought is this observation on the possibility of maturity in a nation:

> I would say yes to that question, if all men could be born thirty years old. Since, however, youth always makes too much noise and age too little, the mature man finds himself hemmed in by both and has to help himself in any way he can.

One can, in a certain sense, call this realism, though the concept contains an overtone that does not echo Goethe's fundamental attitude. It is in these remarks, and there are countless others, that one senses an insight that cuts through reality, through the noise and variety of human activity, to grasp eternally recurrent drives and necessities. The need for both authority and freedom in the political sphere, for regulation and order, on the one hand, and resistance and instinct, on the other, became for Goethe the necessary polarities of any analysis of political life. The quest for pure forms may have given him his capacity to trace the future development of Western civilization with almost frightening clarity, as in his remark, "Before the Revolution everything was striving. Afterwards came the demands." During his years of travel, he described with dismay the development of the mechanized age and predicted the emigration and impoverishment of the rural population.

After the July Revolution of 1830, Barthold Georg Niebuhr [1776–1831] sent Goethe the second volume of his *History of Rome*. In its famous introduction, the author predicted the coming of a new age of barbarism. Goethe agreed. Barbarism is, after all, merely the incapacity to recognize excellence.

VI

Goethe's natural theory of history arose from this highly positive idea of man bearing his own greatness, his faith in the possible perfection of man, the unending struggle upward, and the achievement of universality. Wilhelm Meister declared that the highest goal man could reach was a pure heart and good thoughts. It was Goethe's goal as well. His youth had been devoted to a passionate struggle to liberate himself and to assure himself room to expand. The mature man could only work if he were fixed in an ordered existence, regardless of the type of order, and constantly reminded of his own contingency. Goethe's conception of the political-historical man as an original phenomenon was enlarged by the idea of man as a component of cosmic life. This enmeshment in the orderliness of the universe and the growth of all organic life created not only a protection and a home but released his greatest effectiveness:

> How can man face the infinite if he cannot gather all his spiritual faculties, so often distracted by the things around him, if he cannot ask himself, "How dare you ever think of yourself in the midst of this eternal living order, unless that wonderful awareness, circling around a pure center, emerges tangibly within?" Never mind how difficult it may be to find that middle point, you will know it at once because a harmonious, beneficial effectiveness emerges from it and testifies to it.

The remarkable effectiveness of all his active faculties, released by being fixed in an eternal order, characterizes Goethe's development and fulfillment. The Daemon of the first of the Orphic sayings describes it as "fixed form which develops itself in living." Goethe expressed it at another point:

> The highest gift we have received from God and Nature is life, the rotating movement of the Monad about itself, which knows neither rest nor quiet. The drive to protect and cultivate life is born in each of us. Its singularity remains for ourselves and others a mystery. The second favor from the Being which works from above is experience. The living, moving individual grows conscious of, and seeks to influence, his environment. Thus, he becomes aware of his inner limitlessness and outer fixity. Through this lived experience, we can achieve clarity if we have ability, concentration, and much good luck. To others, this too is always a mystery.

Goethe's compulsion for activity, not only as a poet but as an active scholar, natural scientist, botanist, and geologist, caused him to remark that he had never known four weeks of real ease in his entire life. In the last fifteen years of his life, he sat like the magician Merlin in his silent study, always transmuting new knowledge into wisdom. With a shiver, we read the remark in one of his last letters to Carl Friedrich Zelter [1758–1832] that he had uncovered so many new ideas it would really be worthwhile to be young again. Then there is the almost demonic letter in which he closes a memorial to his dead son with the words, "And so over the graves, onward!" In effectiveness and in increasing activity, he found the only way to assert himself in the world of suffering and human complication. For this reason, during his last years, he wanted young poets again and again to concentrate on healthy, elevating, heartwarming themes in their poetry. Anything that stimulated vigorous activity, the exploitation of the moment, or self-preservation, was positive, whereas indulgence in sickness, pampering of weakness, self-reflection, and self-punishment were contemptible. He hated everything that left men entangled without improving or helping them to a higher awareness.

This demonic existence is the key to understanding Goethe's meaning. Once he had begun to accept this law, everything else followed.

VII

Goethe's powerful need for activity compelled him to find ways to express his creativity within the existing order and forced him to solve for himself the eternal conflict between freedom and law. He accepted a position in the bureaucracy of a princely house, but his decision was not motivated by philistinism, as is so often implied by his critics. He wanted to think and create on a grand scale. It was impossible for him to approach the world resentfully or to permit class resentments to enslave him. His passionate affirmation of the world as it is led him to seek a niche in which to nurture his freedom, and he found it at that time in that particular palace. Consequently, he was always inclined, quite apart from any social or political significance, to accord positive value to any extant order as a potential workshop of human testing and development. His remarks on the preservation of dueling and the indissolubility of marriage are, of course, well known. Typically, he disregards any positive justification or meaning in these institutions. They are valuable simply because they exist, regardless of their validity. He once remarked that he would rather put up with injustice than disorder. He submitted fatalistically to existing laws and social structures because they served as the arena for human activity. There is a perfect expression of this view in *Winckelmann*: "We should stick it out where fate, more than choice, has put us. To stand by a people, a city, a prince, a woman: to relate everything to it, to do everything because of it: to put up with everything, that is admirable."

Goethe's profound revulsion to anarchy sprang from the extraordinary regularity of his own existence. His own creative force was an objective law to him, an Entelechy or Monad, which he had to exert and put to work uninterruptedly in great and worthwhile undertakings. All the metaphysical categories under which he sought to comprehend his own existence were always mere descriptions of the innate stream of his own productivity. This was for him the one and only objective category and form for creative and civilized behavior. He hated nothing in the nineteenth century more than its caprice and subjectivity. He differentiated between subjective and objective epochs in history and called the former unbearable and undesirable, the latter fruitful. Nineteenth-century subjectivity was leading to the abyss. It was unwilling to confine itself and unable to accept voluntarily limitation from without. "There is nothing more pitiable than to observe the contemporary striving for liberation from restraint in this thoroughly restrained world: In 1830, it is, perhaps, less fitting than ever before."

His emphatic recognition of the completely conditioned and limited area of human efficacy was the bittersweet result of a life that, step-by-step, had gathered the knowledge of the necessity for circumscribed and conditioned order. The struggle between freedom and law was not only the subject of all his poetry up to the very last verse of *Faust II*, but also his own strongly felt personal task and moral demand. He comprehended ever more deeply this perpetual conflict and followed his mysterious path, which led inward. In his youth, freedom had been a fight for a place in the world. In the classical phase of his existence, the conflict between the great individual and the world was transferred to the arena of the spirit. Tasso, for example, failed in the world because he lacked the strength to submit to the moral law. In Goethe's old age, the conflict has been resolved since the law is now conceived as the innate form of the individual who lives morally. Ottilie, Makarie, the Faust of Part II, live in such a way that freedom and law are reconciled in the individual's own inner law. "On the highest level, there is no freedom." That is the final wisdom of Goethe's fight for freedom. "He alone achieves both freedom and life who must daily conquer it." The apparent contradiction between the two propositions is resolved by the poet's insight that only in law can freedom attain its greatest efficacy. All subjectivity remains fruitless because it is not fixed in an objective connection to an ordered existence. In the eternal unfolding of creative activity, freedom continues to exist as a form of the development of the world itself. Only in the instant of awareness of his limitations can a man feel truly free. "He who early experiences his limits arrives easily at freedom; he who learns it late and unwillingly, finds his freedom bitter." The attainment and maintenance of this awareness is the precondition of all creative and formative work.

VIII

The concept of a reconciliation between freedom and law contains within it the idea of renunciation. Thoas's loving renunciation and the confrontation of Tasso and Antonio are examples of self-denial as the prerequisite of beautiful and moral deeds. Self-denial is an abiding theme of Goethe's poetry and thought. The second part of *Wilhelm Meister* bears the subtitle "Die Entsagenden" (They Who Renounce). The Wilhelm Meister of *The Apprenticeship*, a man seeking to build his own personality, becomes the busy, shrewd surgeon of *The Pilgrimage*, a man who works for the community. In busy, restricted activity, he finds himself. One sees most clearly the importance of self-denial for Goethe's idea of man in his observation that the fundamental axiom in all natural scientific research is renunciation—the border that the scientist uncovers between the realm of the knowable and the unknowable. In *Dichtung und Wahrheit*, he says:

> Our physical and social lives, our mores, customs, worldly wisdom, philosophy, religion, yes, even coincidental occurrences, require that we resign ourselves. What we need from outside ourselves to augment our lives will be taken from us anyway and, in return, we will be compelled to accept much that is alien and burdensome. We are robbed of things that we have painfully acquired and of things amiably granted us. Before we realize our loss, we have to start surrendering our very personalities, first bit by bit and at the last completely. Since it is our common fate, we are right, therefore, not to respect someone who behaves unfittingly as a result of his losses. On the contrary, the bitterer the cup, the sweeter should be our expression when we drain it so that the calm spectator need not be offended by our grimaces. Nature has outfitted man with more than enough force, vigor, and durability to enable him to master this difficult task. A sense of humor is especially helpful and it is always there for us. Through it we can cheerfully surrender one thing at one moment, if only we be allowed to reach for something new in the next. So we give back, unconsciously, our entire lives. We put one passion in place of another. Occupations, inclinations, hobbies, and diversions, we try them all, only to cry at the end, "all is vanity." No one is horrified at this false, yes, blasphemous outcry. Indeed, we think we have said something irrefutable and wise. There are but a few who understand in advance this unbearable truth and, in order to avoid all partial resignation, resign themselves once and for all.

> Such people convince themselves of the reality of the eternal, the necessary, and the lawful, and try to form such conceptions as are indestructible, which do not disappear through observation of the transitory but are, on the contrary, confirmed by it. Because there is something superhuman in this endeavor, people of this sort are usually regarded as inhuman, godless wretches. One can hardly imagine the kinds of horns and claws people fancify for them.

These words shed the clearest and loveliest light on the affirmative, constructive side of Goethe's greatness. He would not with his pure heart accept the wisdom of the Preacher as true, for he was unshakably convinced of the lasting reality of the Good and the Beautiful. The world is not all vanity. There is an eternal connection with the powers of the Good, the Fruitful, and the Beautiful. To resign oneself wholly is to place oneself completely in the service of these powers. Renunciation reveals a fundamental phenomenon of moral life: proportion and inner order enable mankind to make contact with eternity.

IX

We have seen that Goethe considered the border between the knowable and the unknowable to be a fundamental reality (*ein Urphänomen*) of the science of biology. Similarly, he believed that in the world of morality, these fundamental realities indicated the border between fruitful and unfruitful activity. The moral *Urphänomene* may be called "the appropriate" in social convention, "the beautifully harmonious" in art, and "proportion" at the highest stage of perfection:

> The meanest of men can be complete if only he moves within the limits of his capabilities. Even beautiful attributes can be darkened, dissipated, and destroyed, when that essential sense of proportion is lacking. This is an illness which is more and more manifest in the modem era. Who is able to meet the demands of the present with its incredible speed and awful exaggerations?

The limits of fruitful activity are outlined by the concept of proportion. It is not fixed but elastic. It can always be expanded or altered. The only thing about it that we may call fixed is its existence. We must believe in the existence of an ultimate meaning that we can never fully understand. Since there is no limit to the drive to know and to the striving for truth, man becomes a fighter in life and suffers its wounds. He must always live with the perilousness of his daily decisions and his struggle for proportion and direction. This proportion is not the classical doctrine of aesthetic harmony. It is a moral task through which the individual himself guarantees the divine order of existence. "So divinely is the world established that each man at his place, in his home and time, deems all the rest irrelevant." Since the cosmos is divinely ordered and external activity unfolds in it, morality can be revealed in one's very security in this existence. The moral order can be renewed in oneself every day. By contrast, the supernatural world order of the Middle Ages directed man from above. The world of historical idealism, by making man a mere function of the development of a historically clothed world spirit, controls him from within.

Goethe's vision of man stands between these two worlds. It is curious that no one has ever thought of comparing Goethe's conception of the place of man in the cosmos with that of Søren Kierkegaard [1813–1855]. Neither man in history, nor man in the security of a supernatural authority, but man himself, by nature precarious and yet secure, is the eternal figure of Goethe's attention. The wanderer is a recurrent character in all his works. This wanderer always has one goal, not so much the perfection of his own personality, but his inclusion in a whole where he realizes his own creative forces. Romanticism knew only too well that Goethe's idea of man would henceforth be the perennial goal of all progressive culture. In this struggle for proportion, for balance, for reconciliation, Goethe fought for a higher synthesis, not for the vanity of self-expression. The Romantic Movement knew this as well. In the maintenance and fulfillment of Goethe's divine cosmos, everyone, as a participant, had to bear full responsibility for its continuance and growth. This idea of communal responsibility for the maintenance of civilization is, perhaps, Goethe's most important legacy to our times. In its hopes and despairs, in its deification of the state and technology, our era has completely lost all proportion and direction. It has broken out of the eternal order and thus ceased to revere all that can neither be lost nor explained. Lack of proportion and anarchy, barbarism, and the destruction of genuine order have been the necessary consequences. Goethe conceived man as one who, through the daily exertion of his sense of proportion, could build his own compromise with the world and thereby participate in the eternal realization of the divine. He proclaimed the praise of this high humanity:

> Alle Tage und alle Nächte
> Preis ich so des Menschen Los.
> Setzt er ewig sich ins Rechte,
> Ist er ewig schön und gross.

X

The eternal man of Goethe's conception is the one who loves and through loving is included in the life of the human community. Love the basic divine law of eternal creativity, is the true and good in one. Love is the eternally creative expression of being. All striving and seeking is, in the last analysis, "eternal slumber in God, the Lord." This is the existential foundation of life, where love and creative work are merely different modes of expression of the same active nature. This is the essence of Goethe's faith, perfect security in life itself, a joyous awareness of God's Fatherhood from which all the power of creative and loving beings arises. The manifold possibilities of expressing his own existence assure him of the divinity of the world and his portion in it. This is the only way in which to understand the following passage from *The West-Eastern Divan*:

> The one and only theme of world and human history is the conflict between belief and unbelief. All other themes are subordinate. All epochs in which faith ruled, regardless of the form it may have taken, were brilliant, heartwarming, and fruitful for the age and for posterity. The others in which unbelief in any form whatever gained a pitiful and short-lived victory may for a time have glittered with a false splendor, but ultimately they disappeared entirely in the light of posterity. No one wants to discomfit himself with the awareness of sterility.

Since faith is the expression and appearance of a supreme spiritual nature, and since only through faith does the visage of man appear pure and open, the true subject of human history can be seen in the struggle of faith against the powers of sterility, subjectivity, ugliness, and enslavement. This is a theology of history without history. It reflects the utopian world of love that emerges in the conclusion of *Wilhelm Meister* and in the Moses vision of the dying Faust. Even in Iphigenia and *Hermann und Dorothea*, unity in love as moral awareness and liberation of heart is also established.

In the music of Wolfgang Amadeus Mozart [1756–1791], especially in *The Magic Flute* (it is not a coincidence that Goethe undertook at one point to write a second part to this very opera), the world of pure love emerges in harmony and tone, something that no work of language can ever achieve. It is pure love because it seeks not its own but the freedom and unfolding of every soul. It is the magic of the conquering and transforming power of the spirit. It alone bursts the bonds of time and sets man down in the ageless kingdom of eternal forms.

In Goethe's work, love as a genuine expression of a true human community is demanded and presupposed. As such, it retreats into utopian distance but remains, at the same time, the supreme form of human contact. "There is no external sign of courtesy that has not its profound moral basis, and there is a courtesy of the heart that is closely related to love." In the creative man, love is the ability to accept alien life into his own. All orderliness in human behavior is possible only through love. "Voluntary devotion is the loveliest of conditions, and how would it be possible without love?"

In Schiller's famous birthday letter to Goethe, there is a celebrated passage in which the younger poet suddenly abandons his envy of the older man and writes, "there is no other means of salvation against the great advantages of another but love." Goethe rightly numbered this famous sentence among Schiller's most valuable insights and reflections. The only way Goethe could accept the unbearable rigor of Kantian ethics was to define duty in his own way: "Where one loves what one commands oneself to do."

In *Wilhelm Meister*, the wandering hero is surrounded by a loving and attentive society. The lost and misguided Faust, even in his plunge into the abyss, has the vague sense that he will not wholly perish. Love, as grace, accepts the striving human eros into the unique glory of the divine reality. The yearning eros, ever pushing outward toward perfection, and the love pouring forth from that perfection are merely different aspects of the same essence.

No memorial could be more tenderly and lovingly concluded than with Goethe's own words, dedicated to the memory of departed lodge brothers [Goethe was a member of the Amalia Lodge of Freemasonry in Weimar from 1781 until his death—Eds.]:

> We all suffer in life. Who, except for God, will sit in judgment on us? Let us, the survivors, occupy ourselves, not with their sufferings, nor mistakes, but with their deeds and achievements. We knew them as human beings by their faults but as individuals by their virtues. We share the same fates and the same failings; our virtues belong to each of us alone.

Notes

Translated by Jonathan Steinberg. This essay was prepared in 1932 to honor the centenary of Goethe's death.

1. It is important to distinguish between the rationalistic sensitivity of the rococo and the pathos of grand passions, the formless overflowing of the spirit, which characterized the *Sturm und Drang*.

10

Goethe (1949)

To Johann Wolfgang von Goethe [1749–1832], *Bildung* is the sum total of all efforts to "discipline man's natural impulses by assimilating that which is higher than man and that which transpires about him." It is the constructive power of man to shape his individual person into the general context of nature and civilization.[1]

The mark of culture is to be mindful of the deeds and examples that set our standards and enlighten our minds. Such mindfulness implies a voluntary acknowledgment of the truly excellent—a human independence—which Goethe regarded as the distinguishing characteristic of *Bildung* as against barbarism. He thought it the highest quality in man to be able to respond to outstanding superiority with love, eschewing resentment and envy. He made his own bow to this liberating attitude when he incorporated a statement from Friedrich Schiller's [1759–1805] first letter (establishing their fellowship) almost verbatim into his *Maximen und Reflexionen*: "There is no therapy but love against great advantages of another human being. Such attitudes are the characteristic features of the cultivated man."[2]

Goethe objected strongly when friends proposed a toast to Remembrance.

Published originally in a slightly different form in *Social Research* 16 (September 1949), 289–319. Republished by permission from *Social Research*.

> I am no devotee of remembrance in your sense of the word. That is an inept way of putting things. Whatever great, beautiful, or significant experiences have come our way must not be recalled again from without and recaptured, as it were; they must rather become part of the tissue of our inner life from the outset, creating a new and better self within us, continuing forever as active agents of our *Bildung*. I do not acknowledge anything past that we would be warranted in longing to recall; I admit only the existence of what is eternally new as it shaped itself out of the expanded elements of the past. True longing must always be productive and create something that is both new and better.[3]

In the same vein, reflecting on William Shakespeare [1564–1616], he remarked that the mind of genius stimulates creative thought at all times.[4]

In 1949, the bicentennial of Goethe's birth, we must honor Goethe's central postulate of mindfulness. That is, we must consider the elements in him that today stimulate our constructive thinking.

The general trends of modern civilization are directly opposed to Goethe's idea of *Bildung*, and the ill effects of technological civilization justify Goethe's prophetic concern about the future of the human person. On the other hand, there are tendencies in modern thought that revolt against the prevailing trends in civilization. These trends find support in Goethe's theoretical thinking. Goethe was antidogmatic and antiirrational in his efforts to conceive of the totality of life. He understood the process of nature as a dynamic polarity. All phenomena of life have aspects positive and negative, constructive and destructive. Life is complex and dynamic, moving in a variety of polarities. This basic philosophical attitude of Goethe's unites naturalism and spiritualism in a new kind of realism. As such, it has been stimulating to modern efforts to counteract the general trends of positivistic and mechanistic methods and philosophies.

In the field of philosophy, Georg Simmel [1858–1918] attempted to find the prototype of his philosophy of life in Goethe's thinking. Professor Barker Fairley [1887–1986], a student of Simmel's, has verified Simmel's thesis in his *Study of Goethe*, the most remarkable work on Goethe produced since Carl Gustav Carus [1789–1869] wrote his profound books. Fairley explicitly states that Goethe has significant, immediate bearing on the problems of an age of destructive introspectiveness. "The special appeal in our time of abnormally introverted figures like [Rainer Maria] Rilke [1875–1926], [Friedrich] Hölderlin [1770–1843], [Søren] Kierkegaard [1813–1855], [Franz] Kafka [1883–1924], and others reminds us how near we still are . . . to [Young] Werther and [Torquato] Tasso. To this extent Goethe's problem is . . . part of our problem. We cannot affect to ignore it."[5] Professor Fairley clearly discerns the relevance of Goethe, as thinker and a model of *Bildung*, to our age.

Bildung is not a purely aesthetic category in Goethe's theory of conduct. It is not an ivory-tower notion. It is the primary defense of the human personality against the imminent threats of nationalism, statism, ecclesiasticism, Saint-Simonism. It is the only constructive mode of conduct for maintaining the highest standards of Western civilization against all odds. It is the only creative possibility of extending and integrating groups of educated and cultured persons all over the globe, and thus transcending national, political, social, and religious borderlines. Therefore, men of *Bildung* alone can establish a social power that might work for peace, toleration, and sympathetic understanding. This is the function of world literature and of world citizenship. As Professor Hermann J. Weigand [1892–1985] put it in a brilliant phrase: "It was Goethe's fate to be a German; it was his destiny to become a world citizen."[6]

The international celebration of Goethe's bicentennial is itself a milestone in the realization of Goethe's vision of an age of world literature. Goethe coined the term in 1827, at a time when the master and his works had become a center of authority for American and European men of letters and of learning. His books were translated into many languages, and his translators and admirers kept in contact with him by visits and correspondence. Thus, he became familiar with everything that was going on in literature, philosophy, and science in Europe and the United States. He visualized an age in which all open-minded, educated persons would meet, learn from each other, and establish a solidarity of *Bildung* beyond the limitations of tribal, national, social, religious, and professional boundaries.

For Goethe, world literature was involved in the development of modern civilization. It could come into existence only after all nations had met each other in the most terrible wars. When they regained their national frontiers after the peace settlement, they became aware that, in such meetings, unknown intellectual interests and curiosities had arisen. Thus, the various cultures opened their doors to each other, and the methods of laissez faire were effectively applied to literary and philosophical exchange.[7]

Goethe was of the opinion that such exchange of cultural goods would extend sympathetic understanding among nations and increase the number of men of good will who would rejoice in the magnificent intellectual achievements of other civilizations. "The same interdependence between the general and the specific occurs in the practical life and conduct of men. In human action, too, wisdom and moderation result from the sympathetic understanding of poetry and belles-lettres and spread some sparks of light and illumination into the world of malevolence, selfishness, cruelty, and falsehood."[8]

Goethe was too much of a realist and too well trained in Spinoza to have any illusions about the extent of the enlightening influence of *Bildung* on political affairs. He was confident, however, that meetings between *gebildete* persons or groups would lay the foundations for mutual toleration. Toleration meant to him the positive recognition of specific qualities as constructive elements in the progress of *Bildung*, thus raising the standards of human sympathy and creating the communion of a supranational, supraprofessional elite to be centered around the idea and grounded in love.

In the area of *Bildung*, Goethe adhered to the conception of progress. He regarded the contemporary state of individual *Bildung*, with its universalistic implications, as the result of a long historical development. He had touched on this theme in an essay that reads like the first draft of a theory of culture.[9] Goethe distinguishes a number of successive stages in the social development of intercultural *Bildung*. He postulates an initial, idyllic age of *esoteric patriarchalism*. In that era, tiny groups differentiate themselves from the rude and brutish horde; these groups cultivate and praise in song and literature the most intimate relationships. Such esoteric groups must establish a distance from the masses in order to maintain standards of sensitivity and thought. But they compose in their native language.

Goethe calls the second era the "social and civic" stage. New and larger groups come into existence. Society itself becomes dynamic, and the groups of cultured people are receptive to foreign languages and to the works of different civilizations. They remain separate but tolerate others.

In the *general* era, these groups meet with each other and exercise a mutual influence. The final stage, which in Goethe's view the future must achieve, is the universal era, in which occurs the unification of all groups of *Bildung* into an organic entity. All such groups then acknowledge one goal as valid for all those who had experienced the constructive effects of cultural exchange regarding the concrete and ideal issues of the contemporary world—to extend the sway of universal humanization.

In spite of his firm faith in such progress, Goethe was very realistic in his appraisal of the specific forms such progress would take under the conditions of the modern world. He distinguishes between the tendency toward international literary mass production and the supranational trends of genuine poetry and philosophy. The cultural needs, expectations, and requirements of the mass of average people are the same everywhere. Writers and intellectuals will readily supply this market with standardized productions; there will be international writers, just as there are international business relationships. This will cause difficulties for the sincere and serious thinkers and poets. These will not easily find a public if they maintain their standards without yielding to popular demands. On the other hand, the men of the intellectual and literary elite will meet each other all the sooner because they stand apart in dedicating themselves to the highest standards. There are everywhere such sincere and honest people who are concerned about the genuine progress of mankind. These "Happy Few" will carry on their work in esoteric communication. They will devote themselves to the eternal obligation of the man of *Bildung—vitaï lampada tradere* (to secure the continuity of the traditions and standards of philosophy and of *Bildung*). They are conscious that the esoteric tradition is indispensable, because it would be futile to oppose the broad stream of the commonplaces of the contemporary world.

Goethe had hoped that such meetings and experiences would create world literature and world citizens. World literature would consist of literary or philosophical works enriched by the experience and understanding of the works of foreign civilizations. The assimilation and appropriation of these values would transform native writers or thinkers into world citizens.

> As a man and citizen the poet will love his fatherland, but the fatherland of his poetic powers and of his poetic activity is the good, the noble, the beautiful, which is the property of no particular province and no particular land. . . . And what does it mean to love one's fatherland, and what does it mean to be patriotically active? If a poet has endeavored all his life to fight harmful prejudices, to eliminate narrowness, to enlighten the spirit of his people, to purify their taste and to ennoble their sentiments, what is there better for him to do?[10]

And more concisely: "There is no patriotic art and no patriotic science. Like all exalted, good things, both belong to the whole world; and they can be made to prosper only through a general free interaction of all contemporaries coupled with a steadfast regard for that which is left of the past and known to us."[11]

Such communion of world citizens should be distinguished from the Republic of Letters[12] or the Society of Scholars. Although both transcend the boundaries of racial, national, political, social, religious differentiations, they constitute communities determined and integrated by objective ideals. Goethe's communion of World Citizens through World Literature is united in a philosophical and humanitarian hope that the continuous interaction and interdependence of various civilizations in open-minded hearts will contribute to our progress in knowledge and in human standards of *Bildung*. Goethe was always convinced that only the totality of mankind has the complete truth, and that the continuous exchange of intellectual and poetical goods would extend the pluralistic universe of the verities. For this reason, the world citizen, the man of *Bildung*, is the man who realizes *humanitas*—that is, the transformation of the knowledge of nature and man into a way of life. Men who have read as human beings, not as experts, Homer and Hafiz [c.1320–1388], Shakespeare [1564-1616] and Pedro Calderón de la Barca [1600–1681], Menander [342–291 BC] and Molière [1622–1673], Jean Racine [1639–1699] and Sophocles [c. 496–406 BC], Lucretius [99–55 BC] and Immanuel Kant [1724–1804], Plato [c. 428–c. 348 BC] and Benedict de Spinoza [1632–1677], will meet with each other in moderation and friendship. They will meet in the We-relationship of people united in the common pursuit of extending and enriching their own humanity by sympathetic understanding of all possible modes of living.

Goethe hoped modestly and realistically that such esoteric groups would tend to reduce the frictions between nations and societies. He was convinced that this kind of progress was a constructive good in a world in which many other progressive movements were accompanied by deplorable developments. Even the ideal of *Humanität* has its dark prospect for the future: "I look forward with great pleasure to the third part of [Johann Gottfried] Herder's [1744–1803] work. . . . No doubt, he has admirably developed that lovely wish-dream of mankind that some day things will be better. And I must admit I, too, believe that *Humanität* will eventually triumph; only I fear that at the same time the world will become a vast hospital where each will play the role of warden to the other patients."[13]

As for the technological progress of his time, it is fashionable to quote his prescient 1827 remarks on the probability of the construction of the Panama and Suez canals and their consequent revolutionary impacts. It is correct to state his interest in technological progress as a condition for world citizenship. But it is the characteristic feature of Goethe's complexity that he visualized the other side of technical progress as well. We should not forget that he anticipated the fate of the textile workers in the rural districts following the rise of the industrial technology: they were left with the alternative of emigration or starvation.

The most articulate prediction of the shape of the new world occurs in a letter to Carl Friedrich Zelter [1758–1832], who had written Goethe about a performance of a new Beethoven symphony:

> I cannot end the letter without coming back to the overcrowded music (of which you report). Everything, dear friend, is now *ultra*, everything is in a state of transition in thought and action. Nobody knows himself any longer, nobody understands the elements and foundations of life and action, nobody cares to understand the material and elements with which he has to work. No pure simplicity is extant any longer; simpletons, however, abound. Much too early do young people get excited and tense, much too early are they drawn away by the accelerated pace of the times. People admire wealth and velocity. Everybody strives for them. Railroads, the express stage, steamships, and all new facilities of communication are the main concerns of educated society. Here they compete, here they surpass each other, with the result that they persevere in mediocrity. And this is the result of the general trend of the contemporary world toward an average civilization, common to all. This is the goal of the Bible Societies . . . (and of some English methods of teaching). Actually, it is the century of smart and competent minds; it is the age for alert and practical men who, equipped with a certain shrewdness, feel themselves superior to the masses, though they themselves are not qualified to aspire to the highest. Let us persevere as much as possible

> in the spirit in which we came so far. With some few, we will be the last of an age that will not return very soon.[14]

Goethe saw the historical situation as a process in which different tendencies are intertwined, without merging into a single, philosophically significant stream of historical progress. Technological progress has its constructive and destructive aspects; *Humanität* has its positive and negative aspects; and even in *Bildung*, the most constructive element, there is a possible negative aspect through unwarranted pride in sheer quantity of knowledge. Goethe's criterion is the idea of a human being as the highest product of nature and mind. The dynamic harmony of such a person must reconcile antagonistic elements in the heightening and intensification of his individuality. Goethe is not concerned about the developmental process of mankind as a whole. He flatly rejects the idea of an abstract humanity. He scathingly ridicules the theories of Saint-Simonians, who postulate a collective and dynamic mankind in which all individualities are absorbed. For Goethe, groups are simply the unified, merging interactions of a variety of societal relationships between individuals. They present on a higher plane the simple types of relationships of give and take, superiority and inferiority, acting and being acted upon, remaining and wandering, connecting and separating, loving and hating, freedom and servitude, and so on.

Goethe was too free from the hubris of the nineteenth century to believe that there is an objective meaning of history that can be verified philosophically. He remained true to the idea of the continuity of the tradition of *Bildung* and of the growth of truth. This was progress in the real sense.

Goethe made a point of referring to movements of thought to which he was indebted in the historical part of the *Farbenlehre* and in his autobiographies. He held that the history of ideas is an infallible instrument for rectifying the foolish and trivial theories of the contemporary scene.[15]

He was, however, filled with a devastating skepticism in his appreciation of history as a discipline and as an instrument of social action. History as a discipline is ridiculed because its methods are questionable, and the thesis of the historian is no more than the commonplace that humankind had always suffered and that life was miserable anyway. More seriously, he questions history out of his concern for the individual: "The historian is on the lookout for results and we do not blame him; but this involves sacrificing the individual act as well as the individual human being. History . . . always suggests the corpse and the scent of the tomb."[16] Goethe is only interested in the human being who has turned appropriated ideas and beauty of all times into a way of life that we call wisdom and moderation or *Bildung*.

For this reason, he shared the traditional view of the Enlightenment regarding the historical process and historical actions as constituting a sphere of human stupidity, low ambitions, and vanity. He had studied the world of politics closely enough to know that nonsense rather than sense ruled there. Goethe accordingly developed a natural theory of societal relationships that makes it possible to understand the historical process as a recurrent pattern of change.

> The struggle of what is old, established, and set with the forces of development, expansion, and change is always the same. All order, finally, turns into pedantry. To get rid of the latter, people destroy the former, and some time elapses before the need to re-establish order makes itself felt. Classicism versus romanticism, rigid guild rule versus laissez faire, a policy of large estates versus one of small holdings—it is always the same conflict that ultimately generates a new one. The most intelligent policy

> on the part of those who govern would be, therefore, to moderate this struggle so as to effect a compensating swing without the destruction of the one side. But this is not given to man, and it does not even seem to be the will of God.[17]

Goethe himself had been an extremely accurate analyst of the historical situation of prerevolutionary France. On the occasion of the Diamond Necklace Affair (1785), he predicted the downfall of a monarchy that had lost its dignity and respect. He maintained that the ruling classes are always responsible for revolutions because they turn their political obligations into social privileges.[18]

But he treated revolution as the perennial return to the state of nature, lawlessness, and abandonment of restraints.[19] He preferred a state of injustice to a state of disorder. Thus, he endangered his own idea of the independent person in order to maintain the status quo against majorities, masses, revolutions.[20] His deepest reflections relating to a theory of history deal with those aspects of history in which conduct and action are determined by ideas—that is, in which ideal and normative goods are the decisive elements in social change.

"The deepest, the only theme of human history, compared to which all others are of subordinate importance, is the conflict of skepticism with faith. All epochs that are ruled by faith, in whatever form, are glorious, elevating, and fruitful in themselves for posterity. All epochs, on the other hand, in which skepticism in whatever form maintains a precarious triumph, even should they boast for a moment of a borrowed splendor, lose their meaning for posterity because no one can take pleasure in wrestling with the study of what is essentially sterile."[21] This is not a metaphysics of history but a dynamic theory that contains elements of polarity, not of dialectics.

Henri de Saint-Simon [1760–1825] and Auguste Comte [1798–1857] closely followed Goethe's pattern: their dichotomy of organic and critical periods corresponds to Goethe's distinction. Faith for Goethe is contrasted with skepticism. In setting up these opposites, Goethe implicitly defines faith not as pure spiritual commitment but as a firm conviction and consciousness of the good in the human situation. Faith as confidence in the communion of cultured men for realizing the esoteric empire of progressive enlightenment makes possible *Bildung.*

Thus, history has significance only as the progress of *Bildung*, while the concrete process of historical action is a jumble of vile passions and vile interests. There is only one scene in contemporary history where the trend toward *Bildung* and the dynamics of history converge—this is the phenomenon of Napoleon [1769–1821]. To Goethe, Napoleon was the embodiment of the type of demonic ruler, like Frederick the Great of Prussia [1712–1786] or Julius Caesar [100–44 BC]. He was still more to Goethe. Napoleon alone was able to construct the all-embracing frame of a unified Europe and break down the narrow barriers of national prejudice. Thus, at least a European League of World Citizenship and World Literature could come true, and the irrational sphere of politics could once again serve the cause of progress in world citizenship.[22] Goethe's attempt to associate the freedom of *Bildung* with centralized Caesarism is logical and congruous with his philosophy of society.

Having had his experience with political and administrative action and having observed the narrow, personal interests and resentments that dominate that area, Goethe was convinced that the average government agency will always bungle matters. But at the same time, and as a result of the same observations, he attributed the highest importance to the quality of executive action in politics: "In a state everything depends on the executive power. Let the legislative power be ever so enlightened, it avails the state nothing if the executive power is not effective."[23]

Goethe was a perfectionist to the very core of his being. For this reason, he hated bungling wherever it occurred. The young Goethe was in love with Frederick the Great, not as a sovereign of Prussia, but as the demonic ruler. The mature Goethe distinguished between degrading tyranny and despotism as a regime of efficiency and of welfare, attracting characters, able and great.[24] "Despotism produces great characters. A wise, tranquil grasp of affairs, strict administration, firm determination—all qualities required to serve the despots—develop in all individuals and procure for them commanding positions in the state when they learn to become rulers."[25]

In the cases of Alexander, Frederick, and Napoleon, Goethe found proof of the stimulating and constructive potentials of this type of government. Despotic government sets a pattern for independent groups of free fellow workers, who cooperate in creating goods for the community.

Goethe was firmly convinced that men as constructive workers were free in the most humble conditions: the textile workers in the Thuringia Forest, the carpenters at Weimar, were as independent as Goethe or his Duke in achieving works that were beneficial to society. That the act of objectifying work makes human beings free was the most authentic experience and the deepest truth Goethe perceived throughout his life. In fact, Goethe was aware that his perception of this truth was the great divide in his life. He knew that his youth and student years, the periods of *Werther*, *Iphigenie*, and *Tasso*, his love of Charlotte von Stein [1742–1827], had been marked by a completely self-centered emotionalism, introspection, and subjectivism. Italy was the symbol of his change. From 1788 on, he established complete control over his moods, tendencies, and potentialities. He turned his interests in nature, art, society, into objective, scientific theories, his poetical fancy into metaphysical poetry, his attitude of the eternal wanderer into the steady and stubborn pursuits of the scholar.

The symbolical expression of the dual character of his life is the arrangement of his major works—the autobiography, *Wilhelm Meister*, and *Faust*—each of which has two parts indicating articulate changes in personal history. Most revealing is the radical transformation betrayed in the two parts of the autobiography.

Dichtung und Wahrheit contains the history of his youth from his early years to the invitation to go to Weimar. This part of the autobiography begins with a half-serious, half-ironical presentation of the astrological chart of his life—his horoscope. At the end, in connection with the sudden change in his destiny when called to Weimar, comes a significant description of the Demonic. The initial and terminal stories indicate that the author was completely aware of the determining conditions of his life, whose youth had been passed in recording, with the sensitivity of an Aeolian harp, the slightest movements of the world. In contrast, the various divisions of the second part of the autobiography[26] are concerned with the objectifications of his life, in his concern with science, philosophy, philosophical poetry, the relations between philosophy and poetry, the theories of the Human Condition, and the roles of poetry and art in the historical process.

Goethe was conscious that the formation of his life, the image of *Bildung* that he had established in controlling his subjectivity and transforming it into the liberating objectivity of theoretical truth, was a general contribution to setting standards for the intellectuals of his and all future times. At the end of his life, he stated as his conviction: "Those who come to understand my writings and, indeed, what I stand for as a whole, will have to acknowledge that they have attained a certain inner freedom."[27]

This is the meaning of *Wilhelm Meister* and *Faust*. Only those who dedicate themselves to a worthy cause are able to realize true independence. Goethe rejected the escape of the romanticists into the comfortable shelter of the Catholic Church. He constructed in *Wilhelm Meister* a social utopia based on the figure of the early American settler, in which modern subjectivity merges with dedication to the common goal of a welfare communion of independent men. Wilhelm Meister achieves genuine humanity only after he has wandered through the various aesthetic and erotic experiences and recognized the value of a profession that is of objective value to society. Faust achieves complete humanity after his odyssey through the theoretical-esoteric, the social-erotic, the political-exoteric, the individual-erotic-aesthetic, and the despotic landscapes of the soul. He rules as a benevolent despot like Frederick the Great, subject to the temptations of power and victim to the magic implications of organized power. As demonic ruler, he is immune to the experience of guilt; the man of action is always without conscience. But in the final achievement of humanity, Faust turns to a democratic community of free men, which sets free the constructive elements in human nature and controls the elements of resistance, negativity, and worry to which all humans are subject.

Goethe was concerned with the elements that constitute society from the time of his Italian journey, from the moment when the French Revolution had undermined historical society, and he himself had settled into a position marginal to society. He applied his encyclopedic knowledge of human conduct and action to elaborating a theory of the Human Condition. In *Wilhelm Meisters Wanderjahre* he coined the term *symphronistic method*, which indicates a comparative study of the structures of human situations and the typical responses to such conditions.

It sheds light on Goethe's deep distrust of the demands of society that, when he had discovered its reality, he described it in the same terms that he had applied in describing the Demonic—it is complete ambiguity. In his concrete analyses of the Roman Carnival and of the *Rochusfest* in Bingen, he formulates the thesis that the life of society is *Schein*, appearance or illusion—humans are actors who have to play their roles whether they are equipped for them or not. Throughout his mature life, Goethe acknowledged the power and reality of society, to which he submitted with the personal reservation of remaining marginal to it. At the same time, he never gave up the idea that the power of social reality was simply that of appearances—of parading or of pretending. It is the realm of *Schein*: He presents society either as carnival or festival. Or he describes it as worlds in decay, as in *Stella*, in *Die Wahl Verwandtschaften*, in the court in *Faust II*, or in the prerevolutionary society in *Die Natürliche Tochter;* here the people are presented as helpless puppets rather than as complete human beings.

Goethe formulated his analysis most articulately in the *Märchen*. "Three things rule the world: wisdom, appearance, force."

"Appearance" is the conditio sine qua non of political and social organization. We live by playing roles and pretending, says Mephisto in the *Maskenzug* of 1818. All societal relationships are founded on representation and illusion. And is representation not an illusion as well? Goethe explicitly praised the constructive effect of illusion in human action and endurance. Illusion alone makes man capable of taking and preserving life. Illusion constitutes the meaning of conventions, mores, and etiquette. Illusion serves to maintain the established status of society.

Goethe knew that his daughter-in-law was very unhappy with August Goethe, who was a drunkard, beat her when he was drunk, and continually had affairs with other women. He insisted, however, on her maintaining a noble attitude of aesthetic resignation in order to avoid scandal. It is bitterly ironical to see the poet and thinker who had cherished the cause of human *Bildung* and *Humanität* thus submit to the *Schein* of the requirements of society. He preferred to sacrifice a suffering human being on the altar of the idols of society rather than give her freedom from social coercion.

Nonetheless, he remained true to the ideal of the Pure Man, who is within and yet beyond society. The three forces that control the life of man—wisdom, force, appearance—are basic elements in the constitution of society. But there is still another element of constructive activity that is not among the foundations of society. That element is love. When the young, aspiring prince asks the wise man whether love is not an element of social control, the philosopher rejects the suggestion: Love is not a device of social control. "Love is a formative process. This is more." Man lives within and yet beyond society. He is forced to live in a social frame of reference. He must cherish illusions and appearances in order to be an efficient actor on the stage of human life. But he should not let himself be completely absorbed in his social role. Goethe praised Molière's *Misanthrope* as one of the greatest and most human portrayals of the frustration of man who attempts to escape the hypocrisies and illusions of society. The problem is that of Montesquieu's tale in the *Persian Letters.* All the Frenchmen get embarrassed and confused when the Persians dress like Frenchmen. What remains when we lose the specific characteristics of our social lives? What happens when we do not wear the costumes of our role? What does it mean to hold the claim of being simply human?

Montesquieu did not have an answer to the question. Goethe did.

Man is within and yet beyond society. Two modes of conduct and two attitudes make us transcend the *Schein* and the enforced roles of society—one is the intimate relationship of genuine affinity in love and friendship; the other is dedication to truth. Actually, both are the aspects of a single phenomenon: the constructive and formative powers of man, like all creative acts, are in their very essence love.

The notion of love has no romantic or sentimental connotations. It is the objective love of the productive mind that creates out of the fertility of its experiences. It goes without saying that men remain within their social roles when they realize We-relationships of friendship and love and identification with causes worth living and dying for. But at the same time, they succeed in being beyond society; they transcend the climate of *Schein*, when they realize the eternity of genuine love and the perennial being of truth.

The mature Goethe praised Molière as the young Goethe had praised the Greeks and Shakespeare. He calls the *Misanthrope* a tragedy because it brings to our minds what drives us to despair and makes us seek to escape. Molière represents the Pure Human Being who has remained natural although he has acquired the highest standards of *Bildung*. Such a man wishes to be true and sincere to himself and to others. But we see him in conflict with society, which is based on hypocrisy and shallowness.[28]

Goethe's main concern was Pure Man in Divine Nature, the position of man in the universe. For this reason, all his normative conceptions of human enhancement as *Bildung* and *Humanität* are focused on the idea of Pure Man.

Pure Man, however, is neither rational nor primitive man. The man who has transformed learning into a way of life is the human being in whom nature and art merge. This is not primarily an aesthetic category, but a cosmological one. "Nobody will understand that the formative process is the supreme operation, indeed the only one, alike in nature or art."[29] *Gestaltung* is the very center of the universe: what humans strive to achieve as their summum bonum is pure humanity, and the process of achievement is *Bildung*—the pattern of cosmic *Gestaltung* in the human world.

Goethe would have been completely aware of the role that the unconscious played in the rhythm of his life between creative and barren periods. In a letter that answered Schiller's illuminating interpretation of Goethe's nature (the letter of August 27, 1794, that became the basis of their ambiguous friendship), Goethe drew Schiller's attention to the fact that Schiller would "discover at closer acquaintance a kind of obscurity and hesitancy which I cannot control although I am completely conscious of it."[30] Wilhelm von Humboldt [1767–1835] and Carl Friedrich Zelter [1758–1832] remarked on such states of mind occasionally. Humboldt refers to Goethe's complete silence when some of his works were critically analyzed, and Zelter describes in detail the depressing atmosphere when Goethe was moody and aloof.

But Goethe knew that he had to take such breaks from the reign of his sovereign intelligence. This is conspicuous in his description of the Demonic. "The Demonic is that which defies analysis by the understanding and by reason. I am not endowed with it, but I am subject to its influence."[31] As mentioned before, Goethe considered the impact of the Demonic as decisive in shaping his destiny. It is effective in humans, in events, and in nature: a cosmic power. "Although this demonic essence can manifest itself in everything corporeal and incorporeal—it exhibits itself in animals in the most remarkable ways—nevertheless it is pre-eminently in the human sphere that it shows its exceedingly strange workings. It is a power either opposed to the moral order of the universe or at least at cross-purposes with it, so that the one may be regarded as the warp and the other as the woof of the tissue."[32]

Goethe liked to apply the metaphor of the weaving process in order to indicate unity in polarity as the dynamics of life. The process of life is articulated by the continuous interaction of the conscious and the unconscious, by the lasting interplay of the demonic and the intelligent. This is a polarity, not a dualism; it is the very nature of life to be unity in polarity. For this reason, he could say to Heinrich Meyer [1800–1873] that life itself is the only purpose of life. Most explicitly, he told Friedrich Wilhelm Riemer [1774–1845], "Man cannot dwell for long in a conscious state, or in consciousness. He must again take refuge in the unconscious, for that is where his life is rooted."[33]

In the final formulation of his philosophy of life, he describes life as the highest gift we have received from God and Nature, "the rotating movement of the monad about itself, knowing neither pause nor rest. The impulse to nurture this life is ineradicably implanted in each individual, although its specific nature remains a mystery to ourselves and to others."[34]

This is the prose version of the first stanza of the "Urworte, Orphisch" where Goethe spoke of the *Dämon*. In the prose phrasing, he calls it Monas, in other places, in particular, referring to Faust's immortal parts, the entelechy, signifying the individual structure that establishes from the day of birth the very law of the individual's growth: this is the law of enhancement, the continuous heightening and ascending power of the Monas that overcomes the elements of resistance and negativity in its tension toward a summum bonum. In such a description, elements of the conscious and of the unconscious are intertwined and not separated from each other. This applies to the whole complex of these poems as the sum total of his philosophy of life. Necessity and chance (*ananke* and *tyche*) represent the unpredictable and irrational elements of life that press upon the individual from without. In acts of love and hope, however, self-determination and consciousness again appear as constructive elements in the life of men beyond the conditions of nature.[35]

The characteristic feature of Goethe's comprehensive way of life is his ability to turn his theoretical understanding of the interrelationship between conscious and unconscious to practical use. He had learned by dire experience that he could do something about the inner balance of his own life by liberating himself from the continuous pressure of introspection and of recurrent shocks and depressions. The only effective cure, Goethe discovered, was work, transforming his subjective moods and intuitions into objective understanding and knowledge.

He practiced psychotherapy, first of all, on himself. Throughout the autobiographical writings, Goethe stated explicitly that whenever he suffered shocks and disappointments, he took refuge in his scientific or poetical labors in order to liberate himself by objectivication. After the return from Italy, he felt deeply hurt and depressed because he remained alienated from old friends, isolated from familiar society. He overcame his depression by hard, constructive work. But he no longer sought liberation from suffering by expressing it in subjective poetry. On the contrary, he cured himself by devotion to the theoretical study of nature, society, and art. Throughout the mature part of his life he applied such psychotherapy with the utmost energy.

In one specific case, he explicitly recommended his method of objective description and interpretation as effective therapy against the rise of resentment. The Paralipomena to the *Annalen*, the second part of his autobiography, point out that he intended to continue the work. Among these notes, there is one referring to August von Kotzebue [1761–1819]. This man was a famous playwright at the time of Goethe's maturity and during the period when Goethe directed the theater at Weimar. Socially, he was much better liked by producers and the audiences than Goethe. He was shrewd and skillful enough to give the masses what they longed for. The man was considered ruthless and cynical, and without conscience as a producer. Goethe disliked and resented him intensely. But Goethe was keenly aware that Kotzebue should have a place in his autobiography as his antagonist, for Goethe was convinced that he himself had achieved considerable progress in the literary and theatrical standards of the German stage by his influence on its repertory and acting technique. Kotzebue's plays had been an obstacle to Goethe in his effort to raise the taste of the German public. They had strengthened the middle classes in their addiction to a sentimental dream world of harmonious happiness. The note for the *Annalen* presents Kotzebue as the embodiment and mouthpiece of the middle-class taste. Goethe does not refer to his subjective character; he analyzes him as a social power and explores the relationship of his influence on the public and vice versa. He explicitly mentions the insights that he owes to the man as to the needs and requirements of the bourgeois masses, considered as a clientele for the theater. Goethe gives a completely objective explanation of Kotzebue's role and function in the social dimension of the theater. He concludes with a personal remark: "I would enjoy my confession most thoroughly if I could learn that others in a similar situation effectively applied my device. My method is neither moral nor Christian; it springs from an enlightened Egotism. For there is nobody who would not do everything in order to get rid of the most unpleasant of all feelings—impotent resistance and futile hatred."[36]

Goethe also practiced psychotherapy casually as an obligation of friendship. In a letter of September 5, 1785, addressed to Charlotte von Stein after the return from Karlsbad, Goethe writes:

> Last night I played a psychological trick. Frau Herder was still under a most hypochondriacal strain about all the disagreeable things that had happened to her in Karlsbad, particularly the way she had been treated by her companion. I caused her to tell me about them and to report *everything*, the ill behavior of other people and

> her own mistakes with the slightest of details and consequences. Finally I granted her *absolution* and jokingly gave her to understand under that formula that those things were now bygone and thrown into the depths of the sea. She herself became quite cheerful about it and is now really cured.

Among his literary-philosophical works, *Faust* and *Die Wahl Verwandtschaften*, as well as the short stories in *Wilhelm Meisters Wanderjahre*, bear witness to his comprehensive understanding of the unconscious. Faust, under the spell of his youth, renounces suicide. Faust in search of complete humanity understands that neither escape nor repression can achieve the totality of the human being. It is the crucial meaning of Grim Care,[37] the sister of death, to restore Faust's complete humanity. All humans are blind throughout their lives; Faust becomes blind at his end in order to bear the whole burden of a human being, the *passio humana*, without which his death would not be victory in defeat. Being blind, Faust is subject to the anxieties and traumas of human insecurity. But he is keenly aware that there is a remedy against such paralyzing forces—continuous activity for, and disinterested dedication to, a worthy cause. The complete human being builds his dynamic self in his unremitting efforts of his constructive love, which pervades all his relationships and is superior to the dark forces of the unconscious. We gain freedom and life only in unceasing efforts to balance the conscious and unconscious elements in the dynamics of the individual law of the Monas.

Die Wahl Verwandtschaften depicts in the minutest gestures and utterances of the agents the lasting interdependence between pretending and betraying. The natural-choice relationships among the two couples of the plot conflict with the pressure of legal norms, social conventions, and result in psychological repressions and perversions. Thus, the so-called noble renunciations are not a genuine liberation; rather are they the hypocrisy of sacrifice and the pseudo-bravery of endurance for fear of social conventions. They shun the effort of psychological emancipation that involves fighting for genuine human relationships.

The reader of *Die Wahl Verwandtschaften* may not readily observe that Goethe unintentionally pronounced the hardest judgment upon such psychological repressions for the sake of aesthetic and social convention. For he had loved his daughter-in-law, Ottilie, and considered her a saint. He does not seem aware that the short story of the two strange neighbor children incorporated within the novel completely condemns the pseudoliberation of resignation. The story is focused in a parallel to the plot of the novel itself and reveals hidden love relationships that are disguised as conflict and hatred between the youthful lovers.

They liberate themselves from their repressions only when they risk their lives in order to commit themselves to each other for time and eternity. They seek happiness not through elective affinities, not as choice, but as decision. Theirs is the decision to test their will to belong to each other by the sacrifice of life. This is the seal of their mutual sincerity. Combat and constructive action, happiness gained by the spirit of dedication, is the psychological-moral measuring rod that passes judgment on the character of the aesthetic puppets of the main plot.

One should note that Goethe integrated his knowledge of the dynamics of conscious-unconscious into the general theory of polarity and metamorphosis. For this reason, he has no systematic theory of the unconscious. It was his conviction, which Simmel reformulated, that any rationalization of the unconscious destroys its very nature.

This does not mean that the poet and thinker Goethe, the archrealist, was not fully aware of the tremendous power of sexuality. In the most obscene verses among the Paralipomena to the Romantic Walpurgisnight, Satan parodies the Sermon on the Mount and preaches to the he-goats at his right and to the she-goats at his left that sex and money, money and sex, are the only true needs of the deepest nature. Mephisto displays the destructive and nihilistic pattern of bare sexuality when abstracted and emancipated from the totality of human powers. Goethe's analysis goes so far that he even ironically presents Mephisto's claim that he has a key explanation for all human phenomena by imputing everything to the power of sex. The irony is most sublime when Mephisto interprets his own defeat, in the battle against the Lord, in terms of his homo-heterosexual passion for the angels. He forgets completely what he knows—that in the Prologue in Heaven the Lord had already settled the outcome beyond Faust's death.

Goethe is closer than Freud to the truth about human nature because he is closer to the truth about the whole of nature. Goethe grants the lasting interdependence of the conscious-unconscious, the unity of which makes up the dynamics of human life. Because he understands life as the unity in the variety of its various *Gestalten*, he denies any analytical procedure that is not completed by a synthetic one. Analysis per se abstracts from the context of life and destroys its whole by imposing one or another human faculty—whether sex or mind—as the absolute and general denominator, and ascribing to it the role of chief agent in the construction of life. Both abstractions are transcended by Goethe's idea of the dynamic *Gestalten* of the universe of nature.

His spiritual naturalism, which he first formulated in the *Fragment über die Natur* in 1782–1783, still remains in 1828 a paradox seeking its resolution. Goethe rounds out the conception by defining the driving forces of the process of nature as polarity and enhancement. Polarity is the continuous interaction of attraction and repulsion, the polarity of the material substructure. Enhancement is the continuous heightening and ascending power of the mind. Matter and mind are conceptual abstractions. Actually, there is no matter without mind, no mind without matter. For this reason, polarity and enhancement are valid for the totality of life. Polarity or metamorphosis on a higher human plane is freedom and servitude, give and take, gain and loss, conscious and unconscious.

Enhancement is the category that describes the inner dynamics of the demon, of the individual man that strives to realize itself in continuous and ascending activity and to transcend its organic boundaries by the objectifying powers of the human mind. In Homunculus's longing for total humanity, in Faust's striving for immortal spirituality, in the orgiastic hymn on the cosmogenic Eros, and in the meeting of Eros and Agape in the ascending of Faust's immortal parts—there is the concrete image of the movement of enhancement as the very intention of Faust, as the very meaning of his *passio humana*.

It is certainly correct to recall Goethe's statement that Faust is an image of the modern intellectual, not a picture of his own life development. But this very attitude of never-ceasing struggle for *Bildung*, for higher *Gestaltung*, remained Goethe's concern to the last moment of his life. It certainly is evident to those who recall his last letter, written five days before his death at eighty-three years of age. The addressee is Wilhelm von Humboldt. Goethe refers to a question by Humboldt as to the final draft of Faust II. He grants that the forces of consciousness and will had to be mobilized in order to fill the gaps that the failure of the unconscious had left open.

> Undoubtedly it would have given me infinite pleasure to communicate these very earnest jests to my many excellent, deeply appreciated, far-scattered friends while I am still alive. But the day in which we live is so absurd and confused that, according to my conviction, my

> honest and long efforts to build this strange structure would have been ill-rewarded. Driven upon a barren shore, they might have lain there like ruined wreckage and have soon been covered by the sands of the dunes. Confused doctrine leading to confused action rules our world, and I have no dearer purpose than *to heighten what is in me and remains in me* and *to concentrate my very special character* as you, my excellent friend, seek to do in the fortress in which you live.[38]

"To heighten what is in me"—to the last breath, this is Faust's and Goethe's conviction. This act is the inseparable working together of the conscious and unconscious.

In Goethe's reflection on genius it becomes apparent that stressing the role of the unconscious does not mean neglecting the role of the conscious. He writes to Schiller on April 14, 1801: "I believe that all that genius does as genius happens unconsciously. A man of genius can also act reasonably, deliberately, from conviction, but he does so on the side, as it were. No work of genius can be improved or freed from its faults by reflection and its immediate consequences. Action and reflection can serve, however, gradually to refine genius to such a degree that it ends by producing faultless works." His most explicit statement of the constructive power of the conscious is the maxim that says the first and supreme obligation of the genius is the love of truth.

Goethe's sovereign capacity is to balance the relationship between the conscious and unconscious and to see their interaction as a continuously changing structure of the individual personality. Either side may be constructive or sterile, vital or barren. The interaction depends completely on the elements that constitute the human situation. Most emphatically Goethe stressed the role of reason in his reflections on freedom, some of which are genuinely like Spinoza in spirit and letter. He expresses his own experience: "Who learns to understand his conditions in early life, easily achieves freedom; who experiences the pressure of necessity late in life, gains only bitter freedom."[39]

Never was he near to any of the modern positions of irrationalism. On the contrary, precisely, because he understood the working of the unconscious upon the totality of human existence, he knew that the conscious was not a passive element in the *Gestalten* of life. Conscious and unconscious were both acting and both acted upon. Both could be constructive or destructive, both could be fruitful or barren.

The constructive power of working intelligence was of the greatest relevance to Goethe in his militant speculations on the Socratic "Know Thyself." Actually, Goethe was never free of the suspicion that this imperative smacks of false religiosity; it seemed to him a trick of priests to impose introspection, thus paralyzing independent thought and spontaneous action. "If then we examine the significant adage, Know Thyself, we must not put an ascetic interpretation upon it. It does not point to the self-probing of our modern hypochondriacs, humorists, and self- tormentors. It means very simply: Keep a moderate watch upon yourself in order that you may become aware of your relations to your fellow men and the world. For this no psychological self-tormenting is needed. Every worthwhile individual knows and experiences what it means. It is a good piece of advice of the greatest practical benefit to everyone."[40]

Goethe had a special author in mind when referring to the modern hypochondriacs. The famous anatomist and physiologist, Jan Evangelista Purkyně [1787–1869], who had started as a disciple of Goethe's speculative science of colors and of his morphology, had developed a theory of *Heautognosia* of which Goethe disapproved. In 1827, Purkyně made *Heautognosis* axiomatically the conditio sine qua non of every scientific endeavor. The thesis met with Goethe's decided opposition. According to Goethe, radical introspection will eventually lead to self-tormenting. It will paralyze creative thought and action. Only in rare cases will men of sovereign intelligence be able to control introspection so as to make it productive.

"It takes the endowment of a robust constitution to practice introspection without morbidity. To look into oneself soundly without undermining oneself; to venture into the unexplored deep not with illusion and make believe, but with a pure gaze, is a rare gift. But then, too, the results of such exploration for the world and for science constitute a rare good fortune."[41]

Most emphatic are Goethe's statements that only intelligent activity and active intelligence teach us what we are, make us aware of our potentialities, and liberate us from the pressure of resentments. "How can one learn to know oneself? Introspection is a hopeless method whereas action may lead to success. Try to do your duty, and you know your mettle straightway. But what is your duty? The summons of the day."[42]

This is wisdom's last conclusion, indeed. Faust's insight is that maintaining the standards of life and freedom requires the lasting vigilance and constructiveness of the joint action of idea and love, of the conscious and of the unconscious.

We should recall Goethe's concern about the constructiveness of mind as an irreducible element of all-embracing nature. This is not a philosophy of life, as Simmel tries to present Goethe's basic ideas. Neither can the students of Paul Carus [1852–1919] or Carl Jung [1875–1961] use Goethe's name as a pedigree for their philosophies of the irrational. In our constructive reconsideration of what is living in Goethe from our own perspective, we must reject such interpretations. Our understanding of the unique greatness of Goethe for our times is that he was able to maintain the lasting sovereignty of his mind precisely because he had passed through all experiences of being conditioned by irrational, unconscious, and external forces, and because he had recognized that there is only one therapy against all trauma: the unceasing effort to find and establish truth in objective works.

Still another element in his life is relevant to our precarious condition. The mature Goethe lived half of his life under the continuously darkening shadows of the political, of the social, of the technological revolutions of the modern age. But he did not recognize defeatism or submission to destiny as an honest and constructive way of life. A large part of his work was an effort to meet the challenge of the historical situation. He wished to demonstrate that creative individuals and cooperating fellows in social action are capable of combining the positive goods of the independent person and those of the objective society in which the individual comes into his own by fulfilling service to the social whole.

He was never romantic about reality or about the range of human idealism in action. But he was fully content with the idea of a slow progress of world literature, of the esoteric groups of world citizens, and of the humble and modest contribution such meetings could make to the unification and pacification of the world. As intelligence was constructive only when applied to activity, so *Bildung* was creative only when turned toward the good fellowship of world citizens.

In our world of historicism and relativism, Goethe's arrival at a natural theory of conduct and of societal relationships, founded on his encyclopedic historical knowledge and consciousness of his historical situation, is a marvel. We can elaborate his theory by applying his method.

Goethe, gifted with the most sublime sensitivity, with the burden of great passions, and with a sovereign intelligence, was never victim to any partisan doctrine, to any extreme position in thinking and action. Moderation was to Goethe *Bildung* and *Humanität* alike. His philosophy was not Spinoza's; Goethe himself states that he was primarily fascinated by the philosopher's way of life, which achieved serenity and peace of mind.

Goethe was not a man out of classical antiquity. He was convinced that he once had lived under one of the "good emperors," perhaps under Hadrian [76–138], like Epictetus [55–135]. He was brave enough to accept the role of being merely an epigone of Homer. It appears probable that the mature and old man worked with stubborn energy in all the fields of knowledge open to him in order to build up an ark that should contain everything worth preserving for the future. Thus, new generations would have something to live on when the floods of the various revolutions should recede.

But there was neither fear nor resentment in him. There was only the enduring will to act and create to the last moment of his life, remaining true to the end to his voluntary dedication to *Bildung: vitaï lampada tradere.*

Notes

With regard to the translations in the text of this article, the author wishes to express his gratitude for the excellent selection of Goethe's philosophical writings made by Ludwig Curtius and translated and edited by Professor Herman J. Weigand (published under the title, *Goethe: Wisdom and Experience* [London: Routledge & Kegan Paul, 1949]). For all my notes that I was able to find translated in this volume, I have used Weigand's translations. In one instance, I have used a translation by Ludwig Lewisohn; for the rest, the translations are my own, but have been checked with earlier versions.

Quotations from *Maximen und Reflexionen* are cited by number and date as given in Max Haecker's edition, vol. 21 of *Schnittenden Goethe Gesellschaft* (Leipzig-Weimar: 1907). In only a few cases was it desirable to cite the G. von Loeper edition (*Goethes Sprüche in Prosa* [Berlin: Hempel, 1870]), and these have been indicated.

Two abbreviations recur frequently in the following footnotes: JA refers to the *Jubilaumsausgabe*, 40 vols. (Stuttgart and Berlin: 1902–7); Biedermann refers to *Goethes Gesprache, Gesamtausgabe*, ed. von Flodoard Frhr. Von Biedermann, 5 vols. (Leipzig: 1909–11).

1. Biedermann, 2254: *Maximen und Reflexionen* 649 (1829).

2. *Maximen und Reflexionen* 389 (Loeper).

3. Biedermann, 2185; von Müller, November 4, 1823.

4. JA, 37:37.

5. Barker Fairley, foreword to *A Study of Goethe* (New York: 1947).

6. Wiegand, Goethe: *Wisdom and Experience*, 25.

7. JA, 38:212.

8. Ibid.

9. JA, 38:232ff.

10. Biedermann 3051 [March 1832].

11. *Maximen und Reflexionen* 690 [1829].

12. The Republic of Letters (Respublica literaria) was a community of intellectuals in the late seventeenth and eighteenth centuries in Europe and America.

13. Letter of June 8, 1787, *Goethes Briefwechsel mit Charlotte von Stein* (Leipzig: 1923), vol. 2, pt. 2, p. 87.

14. Letter of June 6, 1825, *Briefwechsel zwischen Goethe und Zelter* (Leipzig: 1915) 2:339.

15. *Maximen und Reflexionen* 352 (Loeper).

16. Weimarer Ausgabe, Werke, 28:358 [draft of Preface to *Dichtung und Wahrheit*, III, 1814].

17. *Maximen und Reflexionen* 346 (1826).

18. Biedermann 2214, Eckermann, January 4, 1824. [The Diamond Necklace affair has been the subject of many scholarly and popular books. See, for instance, Jonathan Beckman, *How to Ruin a Queen: Marie Antoinette and the diamond necklace affair* (Boston: Da Capo Press, 2014); Alexandre Dumas, Pere, *Le Collier de la reine* (Paris: La Presse, 1849–50).—Eds.]

19. *Maximen und Reflexionen* 955 (posthumous).

20. *Kampagne in Frankreich*, JA, 28:257.

21. *West-östlicher Divan*, JA, 5:217.

22. Goethe was well aware of the hubris in Napoleon's genius and of the destructive elements in his demonic nature at the same time that he recognized his constructive vision.

23. JA, 16:264.

24. Tyranny is degrading because it destroys the foundations of politics within its legal frame. Despotism is constructive as the effective action of a demonic ruler who promotes the standards of his people by continuous improvements of administration within the framework of right and law.

25. *West-östlicher Divan*, JA, 5:173.

26. *Annalen*; *Italienische Reise*; *Au seiner Reise in die Schweiz 1707, Aus Rhein, Main und Neckar 1814/1815*; *Kampagne in Frankreich*.

27. Fairley, foreword to *A Study of Goethe*.

28. JA, 38:161ff.

29. Letter of October 30, 1808, *Briefwechsel zwischen Goethe und Zelter*, 1:221.

30. *Briefwechsel mit Schiller* (Stuttgart: n.d.), 1:33.

31. Biedermann 2927, Eckermann, March 2, 1831.

32. *Dichtung und Wahrheit*, JA, 25:125.

33. Biedermann 1317, August 5, 1810.

34. *Maximen und Reflexionen* 391 (1822).

35. Notes to "Urworte, Orphisch," JA, 2:357.

36. JA, 20:93ff., 417ff.

37. I wish to express my deep gratitude to Dr. Alvin Johnston who made the suggestion that the traditional translation of "Worry" be changed to "Grim Care," which reconstructs the ambiguous meaning of the German concept.

38. Letter of March 17, 1832; see Ludwig Lewisohn, *Goethe, The Study of a Man* (New York: 1949), 2:447ff. (italics added).

39. *Maximen und Reflexionen* 654, 1020, 388 (Loeper).

40. Ibid., 657 [1829].

41. Weimarer Ausgabe, *Werke*, pt. 2, *Wissenschaftliche Schriften*, 11:269ff.

42. *Maximen und Reflexionen* 2, 3 (Loeper).

11

Henri de Saint-Simon, Auguste Comte, and the Origins of Sociology

The Scope and Structure of Sociology

When the economist Joseph A. Schumpeter [1883–1950] wrote the introduction to his analysis of Karl Marx [1818–1883], he divided it into three parts: Marx as a prophet, as sociologist, and as economist.[1] A similar division is characteristic of the thought of those Frenchmen who personally transformed sociology by combining social science—including hardheaded economic theory—with humanitarian ideals. In breaking out of the traditional European role of the philosopher, Claude Henri de Rouvroy, Comte de Saint-Simon [1760–1825] and Auguste Comte [1798–1857], like Marx, tried to put theory into practice. Their philosophy was not a system, not an *Encyclopédie,* nor was it an additive summation of philosophic knowledge. Rather, it was a summa that contained all aspects of philosophy—epistemology, methodology, ethics, and the theory of history—the hierarchical totality of objective knowledge itself. It was also an intuition that attempted to carry the implications of primitive capitalism to their ultimate conclusion. One should not be misled by the fragmentary nature of the actual writings of these sociologists—leaflets, speeches,

---

Published originally in different form in *The Tyranny of Progress: Reflections on the Origins of Sociology* (New York: Noonday Press, 1955). Republished by permission from Frank Salomon.

articles and essays—into believing that their philosophy itself was occasional or fragmentary. Their vision was, in fact, a future organization of knowledge in which nothing could possibly remain unknowable.

Émile Durkheim [1858–1917], who was always remarkably blind to the totalitarian aspects of the Saint-Simonian approach, did foresee precisely what would happen to philosophy in the hands of these sociologists. He wrote:

> Saint-Simon saw clearly that his work would be a response and challenge to the *Encyclopédie* of the eighteenth century. The old *Encyclopédie* was critical and destructive. His own work would be constructive and integrative. He planned to build a systematic organization of all the sciences for the practical use of reorganizing society. For this reason, philosophy and what Comte was to call "sociology" were merging in a new pattern which was theory and practice at the same time.
>
> The new philosopher was not only a participant observer, but simultaneously a participant agent.
>
> In other words, Saint-Simon was completely aware of the fact that he proposed a new approach to philosophy. The philosopher is, at his peak, contemplative, but his thoughts are fruitful only if he is not merely the disinterested observer, but shares, with sympathetic understanding, in the grandeur and misery of society in its specific moments. Thus Saint-Simon is deeply convinced that from now on every philosophical system should and would be a social system.[2]

Knowledge under this new dispensation would consist of three things: the synthesis of scientific methods, the objectification of the scientific organization of mankind, and the religion of humanity, all of which, taken together, would inspire each man to work in good conscience for the welfare of all. The three elements of this philosophy, inseparable in the minds of its authors, formed a triumvirate of ideas that would challenge all prior philosophic systems and would transform the area of dispute into a true battleground in which these sociologists, like the heroes of old, would be locked in mortal combat with the forces of darkness. As we shall see, it was not by accident that the men who saw philosophy as the work of society interpreting itself within history should have given the world its first taste of totalitarian social theory.

One must remember that Saint-Simon, his disciples, and Auguste Comte were deeply in debt to such "counter-revolutionaries" as Louis de Bonald [1754–1840] and Joseph de Maistre [1753–1821]. If Anne Robert Jacques Turgot [1727–1781] may be said to have laid the foundations for sociology as a philosophy of total progress, Bonald must be given credit for having contributed another basic element—the idea of total order. In his *Introduction aux Travaux Scientifiques du Dix-neuvième Siècle*, Saint-Simon explicitly acknowledged Bonald's influence as follows:

> When I read and reflected on de Bonald, I became convinced that this author had felt profoundly the usefulness of systematic unity. For he suggested to his contemporaries that, in the present state of learning, systematic unity should be the basis and the goal of all scientific and literary research. In this respect, I am in full agreement with M. de Bonald.[3]

"Systematic unity!" Saint-Simon's words plainly show us his deep fascination with the strict organization of the sciences, which Bonald had applied to the social process. Furthermore, he adds:

> If I succeed in demonstrating that the law of universal gravitation is the only cause of all physical and moral phenomena, I will have found the integrating principle for organizing all disciplines of learning.[4]

Like Bonald's, Saint-Simon's interpretation of history was colored by his personal repudiation of the French Revolution. Moreover, both men had discovered the same principle of social unity, the absolute authority of an elite; and both were attracted by the idea of a society in which legal thinking would be considered anachronistic, and all reliance on the traditional divine right of kings would be abandoned for what might be called the inner logic of power. In Bonald, that logic was expressed in his "scientific" law of conservation, the further expansion of what he thought must be natural law of any society to insure its own self-preservation—the relation between the holders of power and the subjects.[5] For Bonald, this relationship was the inner truth of society, the manifestation of the most basic social realities. The sovereign made his wish; the minister carried it out in his name; the subject heard and obeyed. These three indivisible social entities—sovereign power, minister, and subject—made up the essential part of the collective itself. And, according to Bonald, they had a tendency to reach a natural balance, a status created by their interdependence. Consequently, it was the function of the sovereign to establish and maintain power and, thus, preserve the whole structure.

Saint-Simon responded favorably to the implications in the *Théorie Du Pouvoir* that man was, first of all, a part of the whole, which is society; that the formation of his character was the work of society; and that social man always came before individual man. In fact, he was influenced to such an extent that he eliminated the individual from what he considered the "real" social world and made him merely an abstraction. He left no place in his universe for expression of individual conscience—whether it was progressive or reactionary, royalist, constitutional, or liberal. In other words, Saint-Simon believed that his attack on individual reason was confirmed by Bonald's thesis, which replaced the Cartesian authority of evidence with the evidence of authority.

Saint-Simon is said to have kept a statue of Napoleon Bonaparte [1769–1821] standing on his desk, and he again and again repeated, both in his writings and his conversations, his ambition to become the "Napoleon of the sciences."[6] In breaking out of the political framework, he entered the area of social change; he took from the society Napoleon had brought into being the idea of total control, but without Napoleon's use of political domination or military violence. In Saint-Simon's eyes, he—that is, Napoleon—had no true understanding of what he had created. Accordingly, the new sociologists needed to take the experiment upon which he had stumbled and give it its true dimension.

Saint-Simon wished to transfer to a new scientific elite the authority that, under Napoleon, had belonged to a military elite. These most creative minds, along with managers, entrepreneurs, and workers—all unhampered by the prescientific character of politics and metaphysics—would be organized under governing boards who would administer in the "spirit of love." Under their influence, all society would be brought into harmony—something that Napoleon had never been able to accomplish. Above all, Saint-Simon hoped that such a society could bring the poorer classes into position where their relationship to other groups could be constructive, without having to undergo the dreadful shocks of a class struggle.

If this general picture is kept in mind, Saint-Simon's works may be divided into four parts, the first three of which have relevance to our problem: science, industrialism, and the new religion. The essays between 1802 and 1814 are concerned with the application of scientific methods to human experience. He believed that, if modern scientists were permitted to work without political coercion, they would create a society that could enjoy peace and progress through the intelligent management of industry. To his interpretation of Turgot's theory of total progress, Saint-Simon added what is his own extraordinary contribution—that the triumph of science could occur only as a moral revolution. In castigating the scientific specialization of his age, he held that scientists themselves were responsible for the intellectual anarchy that had brought about the crisis of his time. Mankind needed, and had not received, a general synthetic theory that could be verified in every detail—a theory applicable to the worlds both of nature and of history through which scientific men would make rational the meaning of the social process. Such an integration, he believed, occurred only in the "organic periods" of history:

> The new social structure succeeds the diverse periods of crisis which have shaken us for three hundred years. It will come as a result of the law of the development of mankind.
>
> This law, which was revealed by the genius of Saint-Simon, and verified by him in many historical examples, shows us two structural patterns of society, distinct and alternating. We call the one type "organic." In the organic state, all human activities are classified, foreseen, and planned by a general theory of meaning, which defines clearly and articulately the goal of society's actions.
>
> The other pattern should be called "critical." It refers to social situations in which communion of thinking and feeling, all communal action, all coordination, has ceased to exist. In this state all common bonds are gone

> because there is no unity of mankind to integrate them. Society is just an aggregate of isolated individuals who fight one another.[7]

The authors point out that Saint-Simon made an important distinction, one that approximates the Hegelian dialectic of thesis and antithesis. It was later accepted wholeheartedly by the school of Comte, who were fully aware that history had its own logic and that this logic was necessarily dialectic.

Between 1816 and 1824, Saint-Simon elaborated his conception of the organic as it applied to the social organization of the industrial system. His humanitarian scientism would be administered by a "society of industrialists"—managers, scientists, and entrepreneurs (workers all, he considered them)—who would join together in a common quest for victory over nature. He wrote:

> The producers of useful things are the only useful people in society. They alone should have a share in regulating the march of society as they alone should have the sovereign control of social action.[8]

These industrial "societies" would be under the control of boards of competent specialists who would draft the blueprints of what should be done for the welfare of all, later submitting them to an executive planning board for its final decision. Thus, "constructive" scientists, planners, industrialists, and artists would eventually take charge of the actual dynamics of society. As Saint-Simon said:

> The industrial class satisfies the deepest, most primary needs, the physical tastes of all levels of society. It is they who furnish all the instruments which are useful. The industrial class is the fundamental class, the class which nourishes the rest of society.[9]

In the final analysis, the structure of society would be industrial and hierarchical. In contradiction to the variety of social and economic levels of the French society of his day, Saint-Simon believed that the perfect social organization should be stratified according to social function. The following quotation illustrates his point of view:

> In a surprising correspondence to feudal hierarchy, systematization of interests, and governing levels, the elements of the industrial society point toward a merger which produces a parallel type of social structure. The industrial society is going to constitute itself in a well-integrated structure of industrial commanders, functional hierarchies, systematic organization, and common destinies.[10]

In this society, the artist's role would be to appeal to the imagination of the public, to set literary and artistic styles, to manipulate taste, and to improve morale—in other words, to assume all the functions of a full-fledged propaganda ministry. The role of physicians would be to establish health regulations and that of industrialists to make laws and issue administrative decrees. Lastly, control of the executive branch of the government, the planning board itself, would be held exclusively by bankers, those who were accustomed to bear the responsibility for the well-being of society.

One must remember that this was the age of those great private banks, whose social and financial powers had just emerged with the full organization of a workable credit system. For Saint-Simon, as for Vladimir Lenin [1870–1924] a century later, the banks seemed the hand that secretly turned the wheels of production. If one looked closely at political institutions, one found that bankers were the true rulers of society. It was as logical for Saint-Simon to have given bankers the central role in his administrative scheme, as it was for Lenin to have treated the nationalization of the banks as the key to the destruction of the bourgeois class's stranglehold on society. Lenin saw the banks themselves as the very agency through which total planning might take place. He thought that what he regarded as the present anomaly of production

> must give way to the organization of production. Production will not be directed by isolated entrepreneurs, independent of each other and ignorant of the needs of the people. This task will be entrusted to a specific social institution. A central committee of scientifically trained men, who are able to review a broad field of social and economic problems from a higher point of view, will regulate the process of social action in a manner that will be useful to the whole of society. It will transfer the means of production into the hands appropriate for that purpose, and maintain the equilibrium between demands and production. There are institutions which include among their functions a certain organization of economic work: the banks.[11]

Lenin, possibly jealous because Saint-Simon's version of totalitarianism had preceded Marx's, quoted the above passage from a secondary source. And he called it "the guess of a man of genius, but still only a guess."

The contemporary student of the French sociologists will discover in their writings four alternative modes of social organization: the managerial, the technocratic, the planned welfare, and the harmonious "socialist." In Saint-Simon, the choice among these modes is not specifically made. Although the pattern of total organization is clear enough, he was careless in outlining his theory of social control. There are two possible interpretations of his position. The first would suggest a managerial society in which the managers, filled with sympathy for all members of society, would integrate by scientific means all social and economic activity into an overall "plan," which by eliminating the wastes of competitive existence would bring about the welfare of all. The second would emphasize the tendency in his thought toward a technocratic society, since engineers and technicians would run the social machine under the assumption that they would operate it efficiently for the benefit of all classes. In either interpretation, the executive planning board must be accepted as Saint-Simon's repository of final authority.

Saint-Simon saw a society that would be divided into only two classes: the workers and the nonworkers. The former would consist of all varieties of manual and intellectual laborers, even including capitalists, who would contribute their share, both morally and financially, to productive enterprise. One should note here that the Marxist dichotomy between capital and labor was unknown to Saint-Simon; his "industrialists" were not capitalists in the Marxist sense at all, and "capitalism" was not a negatively critical term for any of the French sociologists. When they spoke of "nonworkers," they meant the idle, those who simply lived off their rents, were politically inactive, and in no way contributed to the operation of society. With this in mind, we more easily understand Saint-Simon's vision of a new industrial world, in which it would be impossible to be idle since all men would work for the common good. What is more, Saint-Simon believed that

> society moves toward an organization in which all members will receive an education through society. Such education will enable all men to bring to the fore their potential qualifications. They will be classified according to their merits in order to be rewarded according to their works.[12]

Extreme disproportion in the ownership of goods would disappear from such a world, but not because all men would then be equal. The concept of equality does not belong in Saint-Simon's view of the society of the future. Rather, he has in mind a social organization that is neither democratic nor liberal in the accepted use of these terms. It must be understood as a kind of giant industrial pyramid in which total planning has replaced political government, and where each man is rewarded according to his abilities and use thereof.

Any analysis of Saint-Simon's theory of social organization must begin and end with its totality. Perhaps that is why the very language he uses in his writings seems such a mixture of curiously unscientific ideas and the most hardheaded technical economic theory. His idiom—the words, phrases, rhythms—often makes his words sound like a sermon on redemption. His economic doctrines are stated in the rhetoric of a prophet just because he was so confident that the society of the future need not concern itself with defending that balance of economic power that is guaranteed by political constitutions. Society's interest lay only in a perpetual revelation of the truths about the correct organization of production and distribution. For Saint-Simon, the structure of economics is the only relevant problem for administrators in a universe whose ends are already evident.

On the other hand, he was aware that such economic planning could not be justified on the grounds of efficiency alone. In his last book, he put forth a secular religion that predated Marx's "real humanism" by twenty years. The key to understanding this religion lies in its subtitle, "The True Gospel for the Advance of the Poor." This doctrine of improving the lot of the indigent provided the spiritual content for Saint-Simon's new faith. At one and the same time, he tried to give a religious justification to the drive toward totalitarianism, while he condemned Christian sectarianism. He sounded very much like a vengeful Émile Zola [1840–1902] when, asserting that Christianity neglected to apply science and its development to improving the situation of the great majority of human beings, he stated:

> There is a science much more important for society than the results of natural science—that is the science which constitutes society—its morals. Now morals have progressed in absolute opposition to that of the sciences. Its foundations were laid more than 1800 years ago and since then the greatest thinkers have not been able to discover a principle superior . . . to that given by the founder of Christianity. When society lost sight of that principle . . . it fell always under the yoke of a Caesar . . . I am convinced that I accomplish a divine mission when I recall the people and the princes to the genuine spirit of Christianity.
>
> . . . I dare to tell the Holy Alliance directly: "The supreme European power which rests in your hands is far from being the ideal Christian power that it should have been . . . All the important steps which you have taken point toward a worsening of the lot of the poor, not only for the present but for many generations to come . . . Princes, listen to the voice of God which speaks through my mouth . . . return and become good Christians."
>
> . . . I accuse the Pope and his Church of heresy . . . The instruction which the Catholic clergy gives to its lay people is vicious, it does not direct their conduct towards a Christian way of life. The Christian religion proposes the immediate improvement of the moral and physical existence of the poor as the temporal goal of the faithful . . . The clergy should direct their attention in their sermons, in their education, in their teachings, to the fact that the

> immense majority of the population could enjoy much higher material and moral standards and that the rich could do the same by raising the standards of living for the poor . . . It is a grave irresponsibility to have turned the attention of their flocks towards paradise instead of the sciences.
>
> . . . I accuse the Pope and the Cardinals of heresy . . . They do not possess or care for the knowledge of the sciences which would enable them to direct the faithful toward the road of their temporal salvation.
>
> . . . I accuse the Pope of heresy . . . of conduct more contrary to the moral and material interest of the poor than any secular ruler against the population of his country.
>
> . . . In the Ecclesiastical States there exists no industrial production, although the cheap labor cost would make industrial establishment very successful. All branches of industry are paralyzed or nonexistent. The poor have no work and would die of hunger if charity did not feed them. The poor fed by charity are badly fed . . . and they live in coercive leisure which is the mother of all vices.[13]

Saint-Simon held that in their failure to incorporate science into their doctrines, Christians had forgotten their true mission—to make human beings more human. But his new Christianity would assume responsibility for the entire functioning of society, not merely looking on man's moral life as the sole aspect of the complex social animal that came within its jurisdiction.

"The Saint-Simonians," as his disciples called themselves, have left a perfect example of the way followers rationalize a master's ideas. The members of the school—Barthélemy Prosper Enfantin [1796–1864], Amand Bazard [1791–1832], Olinde Rodrigues [1795–1851], and the rest—gave to Saint-Simon's "systematic unity" the character of a dogma. They looked on their mentor as the founder of a philosophic school and, at the same time, as the promulgator of a gospel that would bring about a new spiritual communion among men. To put it differently, they admired him as the philosopher of industrialism and worshipped him as the philosopher of love.

To be sure, they tried to demonstrate through their analysis of economic life the inevitability of the scientific method, convinced as they were that industrial society would eventually eliminate the antagonisms between working and leisure classes (which, incidentally, they saw as identical with the antagonism between constructive industrial man and destructive political systems). But it was not enough because the Saint-Simonians were not able to derive ideals for human action from science itself. They found it necessary to introduce another element—that of religion. In order to bring love into industrial life, they invented a spurious sort of human affection that would provide the necessary directing force for science. Plato [c. 428–c. 348 BC] and Aristotle [384–322 BC], as well as the bearers of the Jewish and Christian traditions, were aware of the fact that cognition and love are in reality inseparable. What the Saint-Simonians did in artificially regrafting one onto the other was actually to encourage that specifically modern dichotomy between the rationalism of science and the irrationalism of the affections that has destroyed any concept of the unity of human nature. The Saint-Simonians' vision of the scientist was of a man who would pursue his heedless ways unless he were restrained by the power of collective love. This is an indication of the extent to which sociological science had already been alienated from earlier scientific philosophies, such as that of Johann Wolfgang von Goethe [1749–1832], which had been determined by a teleological view of nature.

The Collective Being, which Saint-Simon had seen as the true essence of the philosophy of history, became in the minds of his disciples the basis on which to establish the priority of collective love over scientific method. To them, the historical process itself gave empirical evidence of the success of the new religion. The rhythm of the process expressed itself by three historical "laws": the law of decreasing antagonism and increasing "association" (later socialism); the law of decreasing exploitation and increasing functionalization; and finally, the law of decreasing property rights and increasing socialization. In other words, they drew "socialist" postulates from the dynamics of a planned society in the belief that economic selfishness could be controlled by the manipulation of love.

The Saint-Simonians thought that the first of these laws could be verified by the historical observation that wars were diminishing and that economic rivalries between mercantile states were rapidly being superseded by international agreements. As for the second and third laws, they seemed to be substantiated by the fact that the relationships between master and slave, between patrician and plebian, between the idle and the working, were steadily improving. The Saint-Simonians took all this as scientific evidence that the day could not be far off when exploitation would cease, not because of political revolution but because men would join in a common program for peace that would attempt to solve those genuinely human problems that faced them by the use of technological methods. If industrial man was educated by the Saint-Simonian elite, then it would be possible for the leap to be made from competitive capitalism to a state in which the age-old struggle between exploiter and exploited would be eliminated. This would be accomplished by a functionalism in which all property rights, including those to the means of production, would be transferred to organized society. As Saint-Simon said, "Property is a function; and man is the functionary of production."[14]

In the Saint-Simonian scheme, centralized credit banks would plan and direct production for the benefit of all society, and they would be assigned the task of organizing branch banks for the various specialized areas of agriculture and industry. The bankers themselves would administer the whole project in a "systematization of effort." Saint-Simon said:

> Industry is organized; everything is interrelated; everything is planned and foreseen. The division of Labor is carried out by each according to his ability, every ability according to its achievement. The combination of interlocking industrial productions becomes more and more powerful.[15]

In their approach to the economic aspects of social problems, the Saint-Simonians made one great contribution to socialist theory. Modern societies no longer recognize any privilege of rank or birth with the single exception of property. Hereditary property, this last claim to privilege, is the basis for the development of the two social classes of modern times: the bourgeoisie who hold property, and the proletarians who do not. The Saint-Simonians, who saw this division clearly, were convinced that property owners, who had been prepared by class background and personal inclination to handle the responsibilities of economic administration, should serve the new society as the trustees of production. Property would no longer be an arbitrary right, but a social function pertaining to the managerial elite concerned with the distribution of the means of production for the benefit of all. The Saint-Simonians held that, as long as distribution was on the basis of property rights, rents, and interest, society could not stop the exploitation of one man by another. Incompetent and unequal economic distribution had been the cause for the contemporary crisis, and administration by men with neither the knowledge nor the interest to inquire into the needs of industry or into the desires of men was responsible for the period's anarchy.

Only total organization of all social and economic enterprise could successfully meet the needs of a mass society. Therefore, property could not accrue haphazardly to those who happened to inherit it, but must belong to society itself.

Unfortunately, the Saint-Simonian pattern of social organization has often been misinterpreted as a stepping-stone to Marxist socialism. Actually, it has no connection with the Marxian theory of class struggle. Rather, it is a *spiritual socialism* (not a religious socialism because this term refers to the efforts of such Protestant theologians as Reinhold Niebuhr and Paul Tillich to reconstruct the foundations of socialism in the spirit of Christian responsibility). *Harmonious socialism* might be the best descriptive term of all for the Saint-Simonian state since it attempts to enlist everyone, even capitalists, in the task of increasing the material, moral, and intellectual wealth of industrial society. A socialism based upon the harmonious interaction among the various members of society is possible only if it is mutually agreed that the establishment of a modest level of security for all will release the most constructive potentialities in each human being. Thus, the Saint-Simonians, by founding their spiritual socialism, brought together for the first time science and love.

Just as Bonald provided the inspiration for Saint-Simon to combine the ideas of progress and order, Joseph de Maistre strengthened Comte's early conviction that scientific society must have a spiritual direction. De Maistre, who had served as the Sardinian ambassador to the court of St. Petersburg in 1803, wrote a series of philosophic books in which he dealt with the problems of political power in the post-Revolutionary world. He maintained that no state was secure that was not founded upon the absolute authority of a spiritual power. Although he accepted the fact that a constitutional monarchy could exist, he insisted that the temporal power of even this sort of government was always secondary to the power of the pope. In his essay and in his famous treatise, he developed certain ideas that later fascinated Auguste Comte.

It was de Maistre's thesis that religion was a universal element in the constitution of society, the sovereign power that established the rules of conduct and controlled the passions. Like Bonald, he was primarily interested in power, but, in his case, it was power as it pertained to the Roman Catholic Church, stripped of its supernaturalism, of course, but still authoritarian. Surprising though it may seem, this functional approach to religion came to be incorporated into the social ideas of Saint-Simon's most important disciple.

While still a student, Comte had struggled with the problem of social organization and had become convinced that it could not exist without the binding power of some sort of spiritual ethos. His own mind was that of an engineer for whom scientific truth was indispensable, but, even at that early stage, he had gone further and attacked the validity of subjective experience itself. Since the individual was unable to see himself and his fellow man as subjective human beings, there could be no scientific theory of consciousness. Only society was real, and only the dynamics of the social process were of significance. Comte eliminated from his system the ideas of primary and final causes, of inner observation, and of the experience of the will because he believed that only by denouncing these worn-out concepts could he establish a scientific philosophy. He held that only by the analysis of the invariable relationships between phenomena and their laws could one arrive at certain knowledge. In contrast to traditional philosophy, he found history itself, as well as nature, subject to these laws. In fact, Comte thought he had discovered a basic law of history that would make possible foreknowledge of man's own development. This knowledge was relative in that every situation was conditioned in its entirety by the dynamics of the social process, but it also had to be considered as a specific moment in the unceasing revelation of the truth, for Comte once said that the only absolute possible was the relative.

Comte believed that he qualified as the interpreter of the law of history, not because he was a philosopher but because of his particular position in history itself. Nothing better reveals the revolutionary nature of the break between Comte and traditional philosophers than Émile Durkheim's book.[16] Durkheim, who was very much influenced by the Saint-Simonians and by Comte, pointed out in his book that the sociologist was no longer able to justify his interpretations of political or social philosophy on the grounds of his own status as a philosopher, nor could it be held any longer that he alone was free from bias. For Durkheim, as for Comte, it was inconceivable that a philosopher could establish the verities of social conduct except by serving as the mouthpiece of a specific historical situation. Only history could make it possible for man to understand the variety of conditions that bore upon each individual situation. What distinguished man from the animals was that he was intimately bound up in history, that he was a part of that continuous chain of mutual interactions between generations that is called civilization. Hence, history alone, and not the philosopher's ineffectual "reason," could give the key to the changing structure of the social order.

Furthermore, Comte interpreted civilization as the intrinsic bond between the single man and the whole species, past and future. All the achievements of society seemed evidence to him that the individual was a product of society, for mankind's past was contained in the subconscious of every human being, and man was recognizable as a concrete entity only in his social role.

The intensity with which Comte stated his position did not spring solely from his methodological genius; he was inspired with the fervor of a missionary for a new *communitas.* Convinced that his philosophy was the manifestation of "common sense," he believed that it would appeal to the overwhelming majority of the masses, who would recognize that it was motivated by love. The workers, he was sure, would adopt the doctrine of positivism almost as a matter of course because it was neither science for the sake of science itself, nor an apology for capitalism, but rather an explicit statement of the union of social altruism with science—a doctrine dedicated to the workers themselves whom he considered the only spontaneous element in society during an age of radical transformation. He stated as follows:

> Training in Positivism is primarily directed to the proletariat. The proletariat is open to such a philosophy because they do not share in our refined and sophisticated system of education . . . The positive studies are logically and immediately tied up with the social program of the proletariat.[17]

But Comte's feeling for the "people" was not limited strictly to the proletariat. He mentioned women, as well as philosophers and workers, as the main bearers of his positivism. They alone had kept alive the sources of affection that the outmoded educated classes had dissipated in their misguided intellectual specialization. He wrote:

> The Moral Force rests upon the union of the three elements in society who are excluded from the sphere of politics, strictly speaking. In their combined action lies our principal hope of solving, so far as it can be solved, the great problem of man's nature, the successful struggle of Social Feeling against Self-love. Each of the three elements supplies a quality indispensable to the task. Without women this controlling power would be deficient in purity and spontaneous impulse, without philosophers in wisdom and coherence; and without the people in energy and activity.[18]

When Comte speaks of "people" he means the largest body in society, all the workers—as below:

> The dictatorship which our transitional policy requires as long as the spiritual interregnum lasts must arise in the first instance from the ranks of the people—in a word, The People. There is a fortunate ambiguity which may serve to remind us that the proletariat is not, properly speaking, a class at all, but constitutes the body of society. For it precedes the various classes which we regard as the organs necessary to that body. . . .
>
> The working class is in a better situation than any other with respect to generality of views and generosity of feeling. In knowledge and experience they might be ordinarily deficient and therefore not fit for the work of any special department. But this does not disqualify them for the supreme power, or indeed any of the higher offices for which breadth of views rather than special knowledge is required. These may be filled by working men whose good sense and modesty will at once lead them to choose their agents for special departments from the classes which have usually furnished them before.[19]

The new men of authority, the scientists of humanity, would take up their tasks in the same spirit. When the rule of the competent had overcome the chaos that had resulted from the rule of the politicians, they would direct where feudal lords had dominated; they would treat their subordinates as "associates" where in the past the masses had been only serfs. The function of the new rulers would be to unite the responsible knowledge of the savant with the virtue of the priest. It was not enough simply to govern humanity—one must also love it. Just as the members of society would fall in love with the "process," which carried them along, so the philosopher-scientist would be attracted by that mysterious, wonderful totality of contradictions, the strivings and the longings of mankind as a whole. Out of such love would arise the philosopher's desire to become the spokesman of society itself and his resolve to dedicate himself to its continual improvement.

Comte assumed that the true nature of the emotions was evident and absolute, and that empirical study of them would result in final scientific answers. His work was a crystal-clear examination of the terribly enigmatic structure of nineteenth century society. Comte's analysis was sometimes marvelously simple: the only problem he saw in the destiny of mankind was how moral and social intentions could be united. It is quite clear that his concept of the total organization of human life was closely modelled on that institution that had welded together into a great power a most irrational gospel and a most rational hierarchical organization—the Roman Catholic Church. If one left out of the Catholic system the idea of Christ, then one could imagine how human beings might be controlled on every level of their existence. The function of the sciences when applied to the correct historical moment was to unify mankind in an organization that surpassed even this model.

Actually, Comte's system can be considered a secular imitation of the Augustinian social doctrine, but with the change that, in his case, the *civitas terrena* would have to be understood as identical with the *civitas terrena*. More than this, Comte derived his social organization directly from the techniques of church government. His writing is filled with ecclesiastical phraseology—the final authority of the gospel as against the personal authority of the leader; the role of hierarchy, discipline, and subordination; the spiritual elite; the marginal freedom of the laity to advance through learning and conviction into the ranks of the elite. The scientific planners were not merely managers, but priests of a gospel of redemption of which the truth was not revealed but demonstrated. In the new religion of humanity, those that followed the doctrine would be both rulers and ecclesiastics.

The followers of Comte even went so far as to compare themselves to the apostles of Christ—modern bearers of a message of social regeneration who would call humanity to a new life. Because they had discovered this new "bond of affection" that had the power of reconstituting society, they believed that egoists, beggars, individualists, speculators, and all sorts of human monsters would thereby be transformed into altruists. This indeed was a new church and one with an advantage over the old—the church of the disciples of Comte would replace the Catholic Church's authoritarian structure with one that was totalitarian. The old church prescribed the limits of moral and social conduct permissible to its members. Within those confines, men might enjoy a certain restricted freedom. But the control of the new regime was total because it based its principles upon science rather than upon faith.

Comte's concept of social organization closely followed that of Saint-Simon, merely strengthening the systematization of the original. The society created by positivism would be brought into existence by his disciples, who would serve much like the board of a business corporation to promote the general welfare. In fact, these competents would assume administrative control of something much like what today we would call a "welfare state." Naturally, this would be a positivist society since Comte insisted that all classes should be educated in the spirit of positivism—that is, to concern themselves with the life of man in society rather than with such studies as rhetoric or aesthetics. In this welfare state, the philosophers—in this case, the positivists themselves—would be the elite. Comte had no illusions about the coming men of power, the new captains of industry. He was completely convinced that, only if the scientific-spiritual elite kept all final power in their own hands, could they control the selfish impulses of the industrial lords and compel them to serve society.

It is important that we remember that the sociologists' dream was of the union of mankind in one universal organization and that they believed that the whole progress of the Western world was toward this goal. The development from the isolated tribe, to the city-state, and to the nation seemed to them to indicate a logical progression towards world brotherhood, when man would be the same everywhere, with the same modes of behavior, unseparated by national or political boundaries. Societies which, in the past, had wasted themselves by foolish military ventures would, in the future, be ruled by the fraternal love that would enable men everywhere to recognize one another. Why? Because the ruthlessness that had distinguished personal ambitions, whether in private industry or in international politics, would disappear from a world in which economics would be the province of disinterested human engineers whose only concern would be the improvement of the species.

There is nothing irrational in an attitude toward mankind that tries to increase its interaction and its homogeneity. Moreover, Comte made a most correct prediction of the general direction that a technological world seems to be taking. The Marshall Plan and the Point Four program, apart from their economic and political goals, are both conceived in the humanitarian spirit of the Saint-Simonians. But this philosophy included within it, not only scientific predictions but also a sympathetic treatment of the constructive potentialities of science in an industrial age. As such, it stayed well within the boundaries of intelligent imagination in looking forward to a unified society in which each man would be able to enjoy real, though modest, economic and social security. It almost might be said to have something humane, even middleclass about it—the belief that no man should suffer because of the structure of social life itself.

To remove the residue of serfdom and slavery from a technological world by judicious humanitarianism and to restrain the otherwise autonomous progress of science could easily be part of a very "safe and sane" program.

What is irrational about this sociology, however, is the idea that collective sympathy somehow is the inseparable complement of scientific rationalism, and that modern man should be seen as split into two opposing camps: the scientific-rational and the subjective-irrational. Both these concepts are as abstract as the methods of the natural sciences themselves and offer a fatally misleading methodology for the understanding of man in history. Thus, what was an authentic attempt to revitalize the organization of society tended instead to widen the gulf between social analysis and social gospel.

Many religions have demanded total dedication to their systems of meaning, but the unique contribution of this new religion was that it required complete submission to a philosophy of history that brought together both theory and practice. Honoré de Balzac (1799–1850) called these sociologists the seers who inaugurated the age of the intellectuals. Because they believed that they possessed the final truth of history, they could not feel themselves to be alienated from the day-to-day events in the real world. Their ideas, experiments, quarrels, and decisions took place within the historical moment, not outside of time and space. Their laboratory was society, not the limbo of prescientific thought. Since they were bound by historical interpretation, they could not even have painful disagreements. The end was predestined, and the engineer or the scientist was at liberty merely to question the efficiency of the means. This change in perspective marks the journey from the *universitas literarum* to the institute of technology. Since the scientist was clairvoyant, his job above all else was to be ready for the future historical moment. A new culture-hero had arrived—the competent man.

These French sociologists thought they held the key to the final total organization of society—final because it was scientifically demonstrable; total because it undertook to explain all aspects of social action and thought through a spirituality that would permanently establish the ends of society. Because of the merging of scientific progress with humanitarian sympathy, the last obstacle to the rationalization of mass society had been removed.

The Religion of Progress

Saint-Simon and Comte held that political revolution dealt merely with superficialities, ignoring the real tasks that confronted the modern age, and that only total social revolution could bring about the perfection of mankind. They insisted that these aims could be accomplished peacefully, even though the spirit of revolution is not peaceful, and the total social reconstruction of society is violent. Saint-Simon in particular was never able to reconcile himself to the fact that, if a revolution unites both theory and practice, it cannot be brought about without revolutionary action. On the one hand, he described the future victory of science as if it could not possibly meet any opposition; on the other hand, he stated his position in the polemical language of the militant revolutionary. His description of the contemporary world is filled with hostile epithets and, sometimes, has a nearly apocalyptic tone. He spoke, as did Comte, constantly and continuously of the "anarchy" of his age. They were not speaking simply of Marx's "anarchy of production" but of a more complex and more profound anarchy—the existential chaos that they felt poisoned their world at every level of life.

Anarchy is a key term for these sociologists. It indicated for them a social climate of such moral insecurity that all people must long for the destruction of everything that had gone before. Durkheim might have called it "anomie"—that death of the spirit that lets the savagery lying beneath a superficially peaceful surface erupt. "Anarchy" implies a time when no one of the competing faiths can prevail unless it provides a home for the weak and a guide for the strong. It has other names as well, such as "alienation" and "uprootedness," and it always indicates that the sources of the mind have lost their meaning. Such was the background of these French thinkers. They had grown up in a Europe that had been torn apart by conflict. When the Napoleonic regime broke down, they were abruptly cut off from the ambitions of empire and were left to turn elsewhere for their private ambitions. We must ask in every age what happens to those men who have been engaged in the political and social life of their time if that life is suddenly brought to an end. After Napoleon, the vast numbers of the officer corps and of the intellectuals were set free to become Napoleons themselves, freed to form what we now know to be the fascist potential of any age. These were the men who wanted to reconstruct society in such a final, stable pattern that never again would it return to the state of nature.

Perhaps it is natural that those who had lived through the Napoleonic period were particularly hostile to the world that followed. They were eager to expose that world as being wholly chaotic. They saw disorder everywhere. They listed countless examples of the paralysis of authority. In industry, they pointed to the irrational conflicts that were endemic in a competitive economy. In the sciences, they attacked that specialization that had made each discipline autonomous. In the arts, they were depressed by the lack of concern for spiritual values. All in all, they felt that their own period climaxed a moral crisis that had been growing worse for three hundred years. Since the Reformation and Renaissance—in France since Michel de Montaigne [1533–1592] and René Descartes [1596–1650]—man's concern with the individual consciousness had focused interest on the single self to the exclusion of the general good of society. Individualism, which had caused the "anarchy" of the age, had destroyed the bonds of affection between human beings. The crisis was so pervasive that intellectual and economic selfishness were actually accepted as primary moral values. To Saint-Simon and Comte, the subjectivism of the nineteenth century was a barometer of the increasing anarchy of the contemporary scene.

It is ironic that social scientists trying to establish a scientific society could have made so unscientific a judgment. Nothing that occurred in French society between 1822 and 1848 could realistically be called anarchy. There were the beginnings of finance capitalism, a modest constitutional government, some respectable academic achievements, and a refinement of sensibility in human relationships. A scientist who called this "chaos" was apparently unable to make competent empirical judgments. "Anarchy" simply is not a scientific category. It is an evaluative judgment on history so unrealistic that it obviously bears reference to some system that has no relation to the true state of affairs. Actually, "anarchy" is a mythical category, and "anarchy" as opposed to "science" is a mythical antithesis.

In reality, the process of history is not mythical. All historical events can be understood in terms of objective causes and subjective motives, both rational and irrational. On the other hand, the life of myth takes place in prehistory. There is a respectable body of social and psychological knowledge that has been gathered from the precise examination of the mythical in primitive life—that period of man's experience when he believed himself the son of the gods, living in their service and engaged in combating their enemies, the demons. The mythical world is populated by divine and antidivine powers, whose wars, victories, and defeats make up the destiny of the universe. Categorically, the world of myth is the world of primitivism. How then is it possible to apply the term *mythical* to an analysis of a modern historical situation?

The one time when modern man steps outside his historical situation and relives these ancient mythical conflicts between gods and demons is at the very moment of revolution. Then, and only then, is the world actually divided. Because all revolutionary groups, whether "progressive" or "reactionary," assume that they possess the final and absolute interpretation of the meaning and end of history, whatever stands in their way must be a final and absolute enemy. Only image and counterimage exist during a revolution, and all communication between the two breaks down. The antagonisms of revolution are distinguished from all other types of social antagonism by the extremity of their positions. Revolutionary adversaries see one another in terms of mythical terror—"We are the gods, they are the demons." When sociologists spoke of "anarchy," it was merely the symbol of everything they opposed. In other words, it was demonism.

Modern revolutions have revived mythical thinking in a very specific form and have followed the existential division between the total friend and the total enemy. During the French Revolution, the nobleman struggled with the citizen. Later, the Communists manipulated the polarity between the bourgeois and the proletariat. The French sociologists, as we have seen, divided society into the idle and the workers. In our time, the Aryan has been opposed to the Jew, and, to a lesser extent, there is now a mythical conflict in the ultraconservative American mind between individualism and socialism. Since one qualifies for membership in a revolutionary group by one's belief that it alone possesses the absolute truth, revolutionaries must look with hatred upon those who do not recognize this absolute claim. They see their opponents as depraved, while they themselves are bathed in the light of a holy communion. The French sociologists who held that there was an essential antagonism between the sterility of eclectic philosophy and the creativity of systematic rationalization were acting within this ancient tradition. By giving the aura of myth to totalitarianism, they helped to prepare the way for the full development of the religion of scientific progress.

In his sociology of religion, Max Weber [1864–1920] investigated the relationships between interest-motives and meaning-motives in social action. The same approach must be applied to the revolutionary secular religions that swept through the nineteenth century, paving the way for modern totalitarianism. Since we have grown accustomed to characterizing our world as secular, we have come to believe that the decline of traditional religion in our age is symptomatic of the end of religion in general. But sociologists, who use categories that are not value-determined, must not discard the concept of religion even if the specifically theological has lost its meaning. For this reason, we speak of the religions of progress in the nineteenth century. These spiritual beliefs of the industrial world should be considered as genuine social phenomena, as the dynamic forces of social movement and the vital realities of the totalitarian ideal. We can call the nineteenth and twentieth centuries profoundly religious epochs because the social and economic issues at stake cannot be separated from the religious meanings that men attributed to their revolutionary action.

Karl Wilhelm Friedrich Schlegel [1772–1829] wrote, "The revolutionary desire to realize the Kingdom of God is the flexible element of progressive learning and the beginning of modern history."[20] This remark illuminates, as does no other statement, the Romantic idea that the dominion of God may be established in the here and now, not in the infinity of the historical process. The same remark might very well have been made by any of the more illustrious Romantics—Samuel Taylor Coleridge [1772–1834], Perry Bysshe Shelley [1792–1822], and Novalis [Georg Philipp Friedrich Freiherr von

Hardenberg (1772–1801)]—or by the Romantics of sociology, for all these men identified religion with progress and sought to unify intellectual advance with an emergent spirituality. Actually, this yearning for a new religion is a characteristically Romantic attitude. These men were both enthusiastic about the possible extension of creative thought, and cast down because, as intellectuals, they were lost in a world of philistines and bourgeois. The experience of the modern intellectual has combined the power of the mind with alienation from society, and, in the case of the Romantics, this created a need in them for a messianic religion that they found in the religion of progress.

But the Romantic conception of progress was entirely different from any previous philosophy of progress. During the seventeenth century, intellectual progress was identified with the discovery of the superiority of the modern mind over the classical. The attack on the classics was primarily an attack on authority itself. Even Turgot, whose contribution to a religion of progress was enormous, did not try to endow his theories with religious dignity. By progress, he meant total revolution—in other words, the practical effects of theory on the whole of society. Herbert Spencer's [1820–1903] sociology of progress is not a religion either, despite its influence on the Protestant churches of the Anglo-Saxon world. And the "philosophes" of the Enlightenment were definitely antireligious. But, when Comte spoke of progress, he meant something else entirely. He hoped to recreate a catholic universe of meaning. By reconstructing the patterns of superiority and submission, he wished to provide a new systematic spiritual home for the individual that would take the place of religious sanctity. From the Renaissance to the French Revolution, progress had implied intellectual liberation, independence, and even freedom. But, with the Romantics, the pendulum began to reverse itself, to swing back toward the Middle Ages. The progress of these sociologists was in effect a promise to reconstruct the security of past ages, to build a shelter for the homeless victims of "anarchy." Like no institution that had existed since the medieval church, the new religion of progress offered an escape from all personal responsibility since all decisions would be left to the authorities. The concepts of progress that had preceded the Saint-Simonians could be answered, they felt, in only one way. Something had to assume the functions of a transcendent God; something had to provide an ultimate meaning to history. When that transcendence disappeared in the materialism and the atheism of the seventeenth and eighteenth centuries, it was absolutely necessary that a new ontology be found. This they called Humanity. Some spoke of peoples or nations, but the accepted social reality was Society; and History, for the Romantics, was the demiurge of the world of progress, the bearer of absolute meaning. For Georg Hegel [1770–1831], for Comte, for Saint-Simon, and for Pierre-Joseph Proudhon [1809–1865], the true reality of history was the self-realization of an emerging absolute. If the establishment of the Kingdom of God on earth was one of the primary elements in the new idea of progress, then the social movements of the nineteenth century must be seen as nothing less than religious. For the Saint-Simonians, the gospel was one of pan-humanitarian collectivism; for Comte, it was a secular, scientific, and sentimental catholicism, made harmonious with the total planning of industry. Even the doctrines of the "godless" revolutionaries look very much like negative religions. Marx's atheism has been translated into an unimpeachable theology, interpreted by a body of priests who dictate Holy Writ and proscribe heresy. Whatever Marx's personal attitude toward his own work might have been, the Russian version of Marxism has become a genuine doctrine of progress and meaning, a religious faith and a militant church. And finally, that the atheism of Mikhail Bakunin [1814–1876] and Proudhon is the most radically religious of all can be seen in the fervor of its attack on institutionalized religion. These two men felt deeply that there could be no social questions that were not involved with the theological. They fully recognized that, in the modern world, revolutions were not simply concerned with the organization of society, but instead with refashioning all human institutions in the image of progress itself.

One can find the fundamental principle of religion in all the variety of social programs put forth in the nineteenth century. This is partially the result of the century's political heritage. These men were the spiritual heirs of French Jacobinism, and of the religions of Reason, of the Supreme Being, and of Theophilanthropy. In spite of their opposition to the Revolution itself, all of them shared its messianism. The Jacobins, who began historical messianism as a religion of progress, bequeathed to the nineteenth century the idea that a spiritual power, separate from the temporal, directs the mind and soul, and controls the unending process of human history. It is this principle that made the idea of a perfect world normative in the minds of the Romantics.

No one has expressed more clearly or more beautifully than Proudhon the nineteenth century intellectual's eschatological vision of a dying world. He saw his struggle with constitutionalism as a decisive battle of destruction and spoke frequently of the revolutionary conflict as a Napoleonic encounter. In the decline of the bourgeoisie, he was able to see its sequel—the disappearance of Christianity. Although at this faith's "last hour," as he called it, he remembered what there was to be said in its favor, he felt that it was destined to perish along with the social and political institutions of the modern world. He wrote:

> All traditions are abused, all beliefs abolished, while the new gospel has not yet entered the mind of the masses. That is what I call the dissolution. It is the most atrocious

> moment in the history of society. Everything merges in order to depress the people of good will . . . I have no illusions and I do not expect to see reappearing in our country . . . intelligence among the bourgeois and common sense among the plebians . . . The killings are going to come and they will be followed by a terrifying prostration. We are not going to see the work of the new period. We are going to fight in the dark.[21]

Nowhere in classical writing can one find anything that resembles this description of terror, and there are similar passages in Saint-Simon, Marx, and Comte in which the historical situation is described in eschatological terms. When Thucydides [460–395 BC] described the fall of Athens, he explained it in terms of human motives and social laws. Neither Sallust [86–35 BC], in analyzing the corruption of the Roman nobility, nor Tacitus [56–120], the analyst of the Roman court, ever left the province of historical and sociological understanding. Even when they were most moved at observing the death of what they loved best, they remained within the sphere of human behavior. Perhaps it is necessary for one to have passed through the final phases of Christian dogmatism before one can confuse the *pax terrena* and the *pax coelestis* or allow oneself to indulge in the romantic fantasy that God and society are one.

Among the new religions, Saint-Simonianism deserves special attention for two reasons: first, because most French sociologists passed through this phase in their own development; and second, because all technocratic religions originate in the Saint-Simonian. What is more, Saint-Simonianism has a particular interest because it predates the age in which capitalist antagonism came out into the open. All were welcome in this church: bankers, engineers, professional revolutionaries, labor leaders, social reformers, and capitalists themselves.

Saint-Simonianism completely discarded the principle of a Divine Being, or the substance of a Holy. Its spiritual power did not derive its dignity from any transcendent God; it derived it from the identification of scientific with humanitarian thinking. Since positive science provided a providential plan for the universe, scientists would make up the main body of the new clergy, and they, supported by poets and artists, would take the initiative in sustaining the temporal power of the industrialists. Obviously, religion—that is, the spirituality of the scientists themselves—would be the all-embracing creative factor in the social world, the key to the successful operation of society as a whole.

The "clergy," in the minds of the Saint-Simonians, had a further duty to elaborate the fundamental religious norms, the gospels of labor, of brotherhood, and of the poor. The interesting turn that these sociologists gave to the gospel of labor was that they believed its blessedness lay in its connection with unlimited productivity. Those who worked contributed to society's well-being and would enter into a state of grace; those who did not work would be "atheists."

No matter what may be thought of the Saint-Simonian idea of scientists as part of a new "clergy," this gospel of brotherhood and the religious transfiguration of the poor cannot possibly be justified on scientific grounds—only on the grounds of humanitarian love itself. It was an attempt to transfer the principle of charity to the plane of social reality, as if the improvement of the condition of the poor was a religious requirement that would somehow be met by the gospel of labor. The flaw in Saint-Simon's new Christianity was not, of course, that it held out its hand to society's most impoverished group, but that it insisted that technology itself was a social ethic that would meet the needs of that group. This association of technology and humanitarianism is neither logical nor natural, and those who argued in favor of it were suffering an optimistic delusion.

The Saint-Simonians were convinced that, in the transition from one organic period of history to another, their religion would prove superior to monotheism because they had eliminated from it the last remaining antagonism between spirit and matter. This was truly the doctrine of a materialistic technical society. Their own term for it was *pantheism*—in the words of Saint-Simon, "God is one, He is all that is . . . He manifests Himself under two main aspects, spirit and matter."[22] According to their preaching, however, the foundation of divinity is located in social reality and social progress, and, for this reason, the term *pantheism* is misleading. A possible interpretation is that, instead of a divine substance that pervades the All, there are simply human emotions and human thoughts that in themselves express the complex unity of human nature and the divine. Human nature in itself contains what might be called the "trinity" for Saint-Simonians: truth, usefulness, and beauty—the three facets of knowledge, security, and love.

In the Saint-Simonian creed, there are two blessings: the glorification of labor and the transfiguration of the affections, both of which serve to unite the otherwise separate forces of matter and spirit. This creed expressed itself in various ways: in propaganda for the rehabilitation of the flesh, in efforts to eliminate the rivalry between the sexes, in the introduction of the idea of the "total person," and finally, in a search for the divine mother. One can see that this religion had only one purpose: to give religious dignity to those intellectuals who spread the Saint-Simonian gospel of the total meaning of history and social evolution. Alas, despite the hopes of the Saint-Simonians, this doctrine did not transform the world. However, it did inspire other men to see the infinite possibilities that lay within the idea of total social control.

Comte takes this doctrine up where the Saint-Simonians left off and applies it more insistently and more systematically. From the very beginning, scientific positivism included within it the religion of humanity.[23] In Comte's view, both science and religion unify and bring order: the former by controlling nature, the latter by controlling society. In the positivist religion, there are two levels of expression: the intellectual and the moral. On the first level, intelligence expressed itself in faith and dogma; on the second, in worship, devotion, and service. Comte described faith as the intellectual affirmation of dogma that provides that security—the knowledge of the universe itself—that makes possible the improvement of the state of mankind. The universe is demonstrated, not revealed; and our life within it is distinguished by both fatality and freedom of choice—a *fatalité modifiable*—for our destiny, although already determined, may be manipulated within the limits of the historical moment. On the moral level of existence, however, we can show our belief in the truth of the dogma by living for others, by devoting ourselves to the service of humanity, and by acting out in worship and prayer the blessings of our subordination and our gratitude at our liberation from individual choice.

This was Comte's religion, an industrial version of capitalism and a church that offered a frame of reference within which obedience, subordination, and service would acquire value and meaning. Here was a spirituality superior to politics, a morality superior to men. Since in this way the positivists hoped to convert the human animal into a social animal, morality ranked higher than sociology in the hierarchy of this science.

The religion of humanity was quite literally the self-adoration of mankind, for the absorption of mankind into the process of history (which formed an unbroken continuity from the dead, through the living, to the unborn) was for Comte a religious experience in itself. The positivists believed that the natural sciences had destroyed the classical cosmos by their discovery of the infinite, open character of the universe. Their religion of progress was designed to build a new universe of meaning in place of the old universe of creation and, thereby, to define the religious mission of the industrial classes. Their sociology would transmute the Christian process of salvation into the progress of society, and by social and political developments would then become matters of spiritual concern and, ultimately, areas of absolute action.

Comte's religion of humanity left nothing to the imagination. It was a thoroughly grim affair, controlling all phases of life, omitting no area of intellectual activity from its dogma down to the smallest details of the budget or the press. He even went so far as to draw up a new calendar with positivist saints designated for every day in the year. His early conviction of the negative character of freedom was society.

Marx's system too must be mentioned among the religions of progress, for "scientific socialism" in its revolutionary form is both romantic and eschatological. It attracted millions of workers, not by its scientific truth, but by the religious hopes it encouraged and the spiritual security it seemed to offer. All the simplifications of the *Zukunftsstaat* derived from concepts that Marx inherited from Hegel and never discarded. Even his early categories of "true democracy" and of "true humanism" confused religious concepts with political. The dialectics of freedom and its final achievement became a sort of metaphysical substitute for the theological principles of grace and providence. And one can see the religious element in the writings of all Marxist political leaders. For instance, August Bebel's [1840–1913] language is moving just because of the religious certainty engendered by his socialist faith. Across Bebel's work, religious fervor slowly vanishes in the routine of everyday politics.

Marx's work shows that on one point at least there was a virtual unanimity among the early sociologists. They were all aware that, under the conditions of modern life, religion must be merged with revolutionary action. Neither Christian nor political ideals remained that could guide the revolutionary masses in their work. These ideals had to be created by the revolutionaries themselves. For this reason, all modern revolutions have become religious.

Both Proudhon and Bakunin, in contrast to Saint-Simon and Comte, sought a radical solution for the religious problem. They made the struggle against Christianity one of the main tenets of their revolutionary doctrine. In their effort to abolish supernatural theology, they tried a new approach—what might be called "the piety of heretics."

Bakunin, whose position was one of an extreme naturalism, declared war on organized religion. He deplored the effects of revolutionary sociology on the institutions of control and discipline. His anger was directed chiefly against the categories of original sin, the fall, and the corruption of the world. According to Bakunin, such principles were solely responsible for the patterns of domination and exploitation he found in the world around him—in other words, the ideas of authority and obedience were derived from the traditional Christian pessimism regarding the nature of man. He believed that this was a concept of humanity that distorted its beauty and robbed it of its truth, and that such unnatural thinking could result only in the universal corruption of rulers and ruled alike. Therefore, Bakunin, who saw that all moral values might ultimately be traced to their theological origins, challenged Christian dogma by proclaiming the radical and absolute goodness of man.[24]

Proudhon knew that his personal struggle with God was not simply a part of a larger struggle against the bourgeoisie. When he fought God, he fought him on the spiritual plane; and, because he was a man with a genuine sense of the meaning of despair, his revolt came close to being a new religious insight. This is quite remarkable since he shared many of the general presuppositions of his contemporaries, including the law of progress, and the beliefs that there was a logic inherent in social man to which philosophers must submit in order not to err on the side of arbitrary subjectivism and that only society could safely follow its instincts without fear of falling into absolute error. But Proudhon rejected violently the social pantheism of the Saint-Simonians and the total immanentism of the positivists. He hated the deification of humanity and ridiculed the reintroduction of mysticism under the guise of love; he resented the subjection of the moral world to the authority of custom and the reduction of economy to the rules of basic communism. He saw this creed for what it was—a religious dogmatism that in its effort to escape from freedom would bring more virulent types of authority and exploitation than had ever existed before.

Because Proudhon was opposed to all varieties of domination, he assailed the idea of God as a center of meaning from which flowed the secular principles of domination and servitude by which the state was organized, as well as the idea of the monopoly of academic truth. Despite—or because of—his recognition of the hypothesis of an Infinite Being, he rejected the Catholicism of his socialist colleagues and considered the Infinite Being as a hostile power against which he must struggle to the death.

Proudhon stated that the principle of evil was in God, the principle of good in man. The human and the divine were the two rival powers who would decide what principle would rule the world. He believed that it was man's duty to conquer God, who, as the enslaving principle itself, was man's enemy, and to erect the principle of human goodness in His stead.

Proudhon was vaguely aware of the fact that his battle with God would have to reckon with religion, one of the deepest roots of human society.[25] He knew that religion was a constitutive element in the foundation of all organized societies. Therefore, the more he was willing to grant the principle of an Infinite Being, the more important he knew it was to destroy the principle of Christian transcendence. When this principle itself had been defeated, he would conquer the entire bourgeois world.

Proudhon was wiser than Marx. Of all the social philosophers of the nineteenth century, he understood best that revolution was total and that it must attack the structure of society at its foundation. Convinced that the death of Christianity would provide his own system with transcendence, he challenged the Kingdom of God by proclaiming the Kingdom of Satan. It was Proudhon who first identified the revolutionary struggle with the spreading of the word of Satan.

Only professional historians read Proudhon these days. His ideas are no longer alive. But there does remain one echo of his radical anti-Christianity, not in the writings of a sociologist, but of a poet, Charles Baudelaire [1821–1867], whose enthronement of Satan was in the exact pattern of Proudhon's spiritual class-war. Baudelaire's Satan is the "adoptive father of all those whom God, the Father, in his dark anger had chased from the terrestrial paradise. Satan's kingdom is Cain's, the murderer in revolt against the bourgeois Abel who warms his belly at the patriarchal fireside."[26] Baudelaire perfectly expressed the existential meaning of Proudhon's religious battle when he wrote:

> Race de Cain, au ciemonte
> Et sur la terre jette Dieu.[27]

To Proudhon, as to Bakunin, the God of the churches could not be the true God. If He were, He could not have borne the misery and humiliation of his children. Since God had fled, man himself must take up the battle.

It is an interesting confirmation of the modern revolutionary situation that Proudhon's greatest opponent should have been a Catholic philosopher, Juan Donoso Cortes [1809–1853], who recognized in his work the embodiment of the religious character of modern revolutions—the archenemy, the anti-Christ. He agreed, nevertheless, with Proudhon's estimate of modern liberalism, and he showed his appreciation of his adversary's noble and superior mind when he acknowledged him to be the Church's greatest foe. He wrote:

> The revolutions of modern times have an unconquerable and destructive force which the revolutions of ancient times did not possess; and this force is necessarily satanic, since it cannot be divine.[28]

Just as Satan was a fallen angel, modern societies "fall" from grace, rid themselves of the God of Creation, and turn to adoring themselves as creators. Philosophers are often not aware of what the social scientists find all around them in the modern world—that the gods of industrial creation have become the slaves of their own works and are destined to be slain by them. Social scientists must look upon those religions of progress, which have identified society with the meaning of divine providence, as demonic phenomena. They are demonic because they believe the powers of man to be absolutely meaningful in themselves, and because they do not recognize a frame of reference that transcends the nature of man. The present world is demonic by virtue of its power to control nature. And, in the final analysis, Satanism and demonism coincide.

All the religions of progress show certain affinities to specific types of historical religions. Comte's religion of humanity applies the pattern of the Catholic Church to irenic religion; the Marxist creed might be described as social Mohammedanism; and Proudhon has been called a Manichean.[29] Despite these differences, they all exhibit one great distinguishing feature—the merger of revolution with religion. Religions of progress became the almost inevitable characteristic of a world which forfeited its vision of God in order to limit its perspectives to man's historical progress.

Comte and Hegel

Early sociology was a uniquely French manifestation, but it emerged as a specific instance of the general philosophic growth of the early nineteenth century. The Romantic Movement gave force to many of the same elements that are characteristic of this first sociology, such as the typical Romantic yearning for a unified spiritual cosmos. Romanticism was a complex historical phenomenon—one that expressed itself through all areas of the intellectual life, from philosophy and poetry to politics and social action—but, despite radical differences between English social reformers, German poets, and French novelists, all these Western intellectuals were deeply conscious that they lived in an age of revolution. That passion for "serenity" that permeates Romanticism has a distinct relationship to the sociologists' vision of a world without order. The poets who lament the fate of the individual in a world growing daily more anonymous can be thought of as the obverse side of those men who praised the state, the people, the nation, or the race. The period is contradictory and yet contains a deep unity. After all, it was the conservative Georg Hegel [1770–1831] who every July 14th solemnly lit candles in memory of the French Revolution. And Romanticism created an affinity between two social thinkers of the century: Hegel and Comte. It is merely one element in their work, but it plays a substantial part.

Comte and Hegel were the first great philosophers of the post-Revolutionary age to make history the primary concern of the philosopher because it was the bearer of the progress of the human mind. They claimed, as scientists, that their knowledge of the meaning of history was objective and that it could be demonstrated by analysis and interpretation. They claimed, as Romantics, that their work stood as synthesis of the past and the future. Both were convinced that their respective theories of society could in practice produce a truly perfect organization; both were outstanding examples of the megalomania of modern Romantics for they were the first pagan philosophers of the modern world, men who tried to turn religion into simply one aspect of a philosophical system that combined the metaphysical past with the scientific present. And one of the postulates of Romanticism is that religion is both the expression of progressive learning and the point of departure for history.

It should be stated here that neither of these thinkers can be classified as a pure Romantic. In neither case is their major contribution—Hegel's idealism or Comte's system of positivism—essentially Romantic in character. But both were deeply affected by that movement because they both were children of the era when intellectuals became the elite of the Western world, their status raised by the new prestige accorded to the sciences. With their authority resting on this prestige, intellectuals became available to all groups—conservative or radical. In this sense, Comte and Hegel were among these new experts who could trace the line of historical progress with certainty, or "hear the grass of necessity growing," to use Jacob Burckhardt's [1818–1897] contemptuous phrase.[30]

Comte and Hegel shared more than a connection through Romanticism: their philosophical ideas have certain basic similarities. This is particularly impressive since Comte, who began his philosophical career at a date when Hegel had all but completed his, was not a student of Hegel. To be sure, he quotes the German philosopher in his *Positive Polity* and also in his *Positivist Calendar*,[31] but it cannot be maintained that he was seriously influenced by him. Comte seems to have known Hegel's work up to 1842 through a translation by Gustave D'Eichthal [1804–1886];[32] and Hegel, apparently, had some knowledge of Comte's early work. At any rate, despite the slight contact, they had a lively respect for one another.

It may seem surprising that two men, whose conditioning was so dissimilar, should have shared such novel and extreme attitudes about traditional philosophy. Hegel was a Protestant who began his career as a student of theology, became a philosophic idealist, and was influenced in his social thought by the unfortunate contemporary political organization of Germany. Comte came from a Catholic family, was educated in the sciences, and was greatly influenced by the impact of the Revolution on his country. And yet they are alike in having broken with traditional philosophy on one important point: they made history the concern of the philosopher.

In the post-Renaissance decline of Augustinian philosophy under the onslaught of rationalist inquiry, thinkers from Niccolò Machiavelli [1469–1527] to Adam Smith [1723–1790] characterized the domain of history as the study of the relationship between rulers and ruled. They felt that this interaction between domination and servitude could yield no philosophic meaning for it was simply the manifestation of human animality, devoid of values even when it was full of guile.

Hegel and Comte broke completely with this way of thinking. Both men, shaken by the phenomenon of the French Revolution, grasped the idea that a historical event might have a concrete meaning. Consequently, since the absolute mind that judged history made history itself the center of philosophy, the historicism of both men was distinguished by a union of theory and practice.

Comte used an appropriate term to describe this new approach—one that is as valid for Hegel's work as for his own. He called it *abstract history*—that is, the philosophical treatment of history. What this means is that from the sum total of individual experiences the philosopher abstracts general trends and recurrent tendencies. He does this rather than study the infinite variety of individual historical events in order to establish a causal interdependence that will explain a particular event. Working with such large general trends tends to lead one inescapably to the conclusion that there is a dynamism that moves unceasingly throughout all history. For both Comte and Hegel, this dynamism is the necessary operation of the progressing mind, an operation that can neither be stopped nor reversed.

Naturally the "abstract histories" of Comte and Hegel differed in some ways. A comparison of the way each philosopher treated the development of Western philosophy—Comte in the sixth volume of his *Positive Philosophy*, and Hegel in his *Phenomenology of the Mind*—shows that each of them colored his version of the historical process to correspond with his own version of the truth. "Abstract history" became subjective, partial, and selective. However, both men argued that it was the only presupposition upon which scientific philosophy could be based since it was the only concept that brought together knowledge of the past with the true nature of the whole social process. What is most important is that "abstract history" is the precondition for that unique and radical method that Comte and Hegel discovered independently and called "dialectical."

In its modern form, the dialectical method gave birth to a new type of logic. Both Comte and Hegel became convinced that the traditional varieties of logic—the Aristotelian or Scholastic, for example—were unfitted for the contents of their new philosophy. A dynamic subject required a dynamic logic. Hegel's system of logic, therefore, which moves from affirmation to negation and then to a denial of the negation, creating thereby a new affirmation, makes possible a coherent system of abstract history. In other words, the dialectical method—thesis, antithesis, and synthesis—imitates the movement of history itself. Comte's logic, which was first borrowed from Saint-Simon and later developed by his disciples, is based on a dialectic that unfolds within the organic and the critical periods of historical thought. An illustration of this logic would be the Law of Three Stages. According to Comte, the Mind progresses in a dialectical movement from the theological state, to the metaphysical, and ultimately, to the positive, the final and most perfect accomplishment of man's intellect. At its most primitive, the theological state is organic; the metaphysical state is essentially critical; and the positive state returns to an organic base on a higher synthetic level. Like Saint-Simon, Comte considered the organic state to be typified by its singleness of purpose and belief, and its capacity for giving men the opportunity to release their most constructive powers because they could trust in the truth of their common ideals. In critical ages, men suffer deeply; every belief is questioned; every act of faith is paralyzed or made passive. This is the negativism that necessarily will bring about the renascence of an organic age.

The dialectic developed by the French sociologists is identical with Hegel's. For the French, as for the German, the synthesis (or organic) integrates and makes positive what first appeared as antithesis (or critical). Goethe, incidentally, who was as indifferent to Hegel's thought as he was ignorant of Comte's, voiced the same idea much earlier:

> The only and the most profound theme of the history of the world and men, to which all other topics are subordinate, is the conflict between belief and unbelief. All epochs in which faith prevails, regardless of its symbols, are brilliant, uplifting, and productive for contemporaries and posterity. All ages, however, in which unbelief maintains a precarious victory, even boasts of the illusion of success, disappear in the face of posterity because nobody likes to be tortured by the knowledge of the sterile.[33]

Besides these similarities between the thought of Comte and Hegel—that they both believed progress revealed the meaning of history, that "abstract history" disclosed the contents of progress, and that dialectics was the method by which it might be understood scientifically—there are other indications of the depth of the parallels between them that makes us regard them together as symbols of their age. One of the most extraordinary is the manner in which both dealt with religion. In their early writings, they searched for religious truths that would bear out their own philosophical approach and rejected that theology that dealt with the concept of the Holy—to them an area that was not open to philosophical investigation. Thus, the principles of alienation, and of infinite love and suffering, which Hegel analyzes, are philosophic categories rather than theological. In Hegel's *The Phenomenology of the Mind*, for example, there is a description of the development of religion from the fetishism of primitive societies to that merger of religion and philosophy that constituted his own system. This section bears a remarkable resemblance to Comte's presentation of the Law of Three Stages.

But the most significant similarity between Comte and Hegel is that both of them were certain that they had successfully integrated religion into their philosophies, leaving no place and no function for independent religious thought. Hegel never used the term *religion of humanity*, but his entire work might very well have been so titled.

A student of the philosophy of the nineteenth century must consider the question why two men of genius, separated by nation, tradition, and education should have independently come so close to one another's beliefs. The similarity between the two is not simply a psychological or an intellectual accident, but an expression of the specific historical situation. The common experience of living in a world perpetually in revolution, suspended in possibilities, brought from both Comte and Hegel a common intellectual response. The challenge of the times was so acute that a Frenchman and a German could simultaneously insist that philosophy had outworn its ancient function and must turn elsewhere—that is, to the study of history.

We might call Hegel's image of himself a prophecy in reverse. One of his most famous quotations, usually offered as proof of his megalomania, includes the remark that he thought of himself as "the last philosopher." But this was not the statement of a megalomaniac. Hegel knew, better than any other contemporary observer, the character of his own age. His early reflections on the dynamics of the economic process and on the inescapable clash between the owners of property and the workers anticipated, by a good many years, radical theories of the historical crisis. *The Phenomenology of Mind*, for instance, contains an analysis of the conflicts between domination and servitude that shows an astounding awareness of the potential of total revolution, and of the radical changes that would occur in all modes of thought and action if the traditional reciprocal relationships among the members of society had passed away.[34] He knew that the character of his epoch was revolutionary and that his philosophy would be the true summit of all the great contributions to Western thought. He brought his philosophy to this perfect state by incorporating within it the classical, the Christian, the idealist, and the romantic. According to the necessity of his dialectic, the next phase of philosophy could only be radical nonphilosophy. If he was the last philosopher, he was also, in a sense, the first.

Thus, Hegel's philosophy recognized in its awareness of the coming of the period of revolutions the grim and unalterable logic of dialectics. Naturally, men themselves were nothing but pawns in this cosmos. Like Comte, Hegel held that human beings were simply the servants of advancing progress, obedient missionaries of the Mind. He and Comte considered men not the creators of destiny but responders to the teleology of history. It should be remembered that when Hegel saw Napoleon at Jena, he called him "The World Spirit on horseback."

One might say that what makes a genuine philosopher is which one of the several alternatives he chooses to answer the crisis of his time. Despite the effect that the age of revolution had upon both Comte and Hegel, there are some startling differences between them. Comte understood Mind to be the expansion of scientific methods as applied by the natural sciences, while Hegel interpreted Mind as the totality of man's creative spirit. Where Comte suggested a totalitarian social organization, Hegel postulated a rational authoritarian state administered by philosophically trained civil servants. Both men recognized the sociological determinants that lay at the heart of all knowledge, but Hegel insisted that, despite historical relativity, all knowledge was a manifestation of perennial philosophic tendencies (for example, the types of Stoicism and Skepticism in the famous chapter, "The Unhappy Conscience," in the *Phenomenology*). Perhaps these instances will indicate the basic difference—Hegel always chose the path of contemplation; Comte chose that of scientific manipulation. To Hegel, it seemed that the philosopher's function was to understand the development of Mind in all its manifestations and thereby to preserve the reality of the spirit in the concrete historical situation. In his view, philosophy could never change the law of historical necessity; it could only reconstruct and perpetuate what the human mind kept alive from each succeeding epoch. Philosophy to Hegel was a way of illumination. But Comte chose the other alternative. He felt that, if philosophy was made up of knowledge in a state of temporal progress, then the philosopher was called upon to direct and assist the transformation required by the dynamics of Mind in conformity with its intellectual, social, and spiritual aspects. Comte's whole creative work, from 1822 to his last book in 1856, was a gradually expanding philosophy of progress and total organization, a detailed elaboration of the tasks that philosophers must assume as scientific administrators, directors, and priests. It was through his disciples that the truth of philosophy—the religion of progress—would conquer the world.

Notes

1. Joseph A. Schumpeter, *Capitalism, Socialism, and Democracy*, 2nd ed. (New York and London: Harper & Brothers, 1942).

2. Émile Durkheim, *Le Socialisme*, ed. Marcel Mauss (Paris: Alcan, 1928), 131.

3. Saint-Simon, *Textes Choisis* (Paris: Alcan, 1925), 38–50.

4. Ibid., 48.

5. See Louis de Bonald, *Essai Analytique sur les Lois Naturelles de L'Ordre Social et du Pouvoir des Ministres dans les Sociétés Oeuvres Complètes*, ed. J. P. Migne, 3rd ed. (Paris: 1859).

6. Ibid., ix.

7. *Doctrines de Saint-Simon*, eds. Célestin Bouglé and Élie Halévy (Paris: Marcel Riviere, 1924), 127.

8. Durkheim, *Le Socialisme*, 193 (quoting Saint-Simon, *L'Industrie*, vol. II).

9. Ibid., 199ff.

10. Ibid., 264.

11. E. H. Carr, *Studies in Revolution* (New York: Macmillan, 1950), 8–9.

12. *Doctrine de Saint-Simon*, 244.

13. Ibid., 218–25.

14. Ibid., 257.

15. Ibid., 264.

16. Émile Durkheim, *Montesquieu et Rousseau*, (Paris: Marcel Riviere, 1953).

17. Auguste Comte, *Discours sur L'Esprit Positif* (Paris: 1844), pt. III, chap. 3, 1–5.

18. Auguste Comte, *A General View of Positivism*, trans. J. H. Bridges M.B. (Stanford, CA: Academic Reprints, n.d.), 238.

19. Ibid., 221.

20. Friedrich Schlegel, *Jugendschriften*, ed. J. Minor (Wien: 1906), 239.

21. Proudhon, *Oeuvres Complètés*, New ed. (Paris: 1927), 10:205ff.

22. *Doctrine de Saint-Simon*, 251.

23. Auguste Comte, *System of Positive Polity* (Paris: 1854), vol. 4. The subtitle of the volume is *A Treatise on Sociology, instituting the Religion of Humanity.*

24. Michael Bakunin, *Oeuvres* (Paris: 1895–1912), 5 vols. See especially vols. 1 and 2.

25. See Proudhon, *Système des Contradiction Economiques ou Philosophie de la Misère* (Paris: 1848); *Les Confessions d'un Revolutionaire* (Paris: 1850); *De la Justice dans la Revolution et dans L'Eglise* (Paris: 1861), 3 vols.

26. Baudelaire, *Les Fleurs du Mal*, ed. Paul Valéry (Paris: 1926), 252.

27. Ibid., 249.

28. Donoso Cortes, *An Essay on Catholicism, Authority, and Order* (New York: J. F. Wagner, 1925), 264.

29. Ibid., 111.

30. Jacob Burckhardt, *Force and Freedom* (New York: Pantheon, 1943).

31. Pierre Ducassé, *Methode et Intuition chez Auguste Comte* (Paris: Alcan, 1939), 424.

32. Ibid., 424. See also *Oeuvres Choisis d'Auguste Comte*, ed. Henri Gouhier (Paris: Aubier, 1943).

33. Goethe, *Jubilaumsausgabe* (Stuttgart and Berlin: 1902–7), vol. 5 [*West-östlicher Divan* (1819)], 247.

34. Cf. Alexander Kojève, *Introduction à la Lecture de Hegel* (Paris: Gallimard, 1947), a profound interpretation of the "Domination and Servitude" chapter in the *Phenomenology*.

12

Tocqueville: Moralist and Sociologist

I

In January 1935 a century had passed since the publication of the first part of *Democracy in America.*[1] The extraordinary success of the book, which brought praise and honors to the young writer Alexis de Tocqueville [1805–1859] and prepared the way for his political career, was due to its concentration on the realities of the times. The theoretical and practical formation of modern democratic and liberal society was the burning problem of his epoch. It is therefore no accident that Albert Thibaudet [1874–1936], in an essay on Tocqueville and Arthur comte de Gobineau [1816–1882],[2] attributes the present lack of interest in Montesquieu [1689–1755] and Tocqueville to the breakdown of western liberalism. As a consequence of this breakdown, he asserts, the younger generation is interested only in those new forms of political organization that lie beyond the traditions of Anglo-Saxon and French civilization. These remarks by such an earnest and scrupulous a political philosopher as Thibaudet lead us to consider what the significance of the centenary of Tocqueville's great book may be, apart from the established cultural convention. Is his work really only an expression of his historical and political situation, and, therefore, has it lost its significance for our times?

Published originally in a slightly different form in *Social Research* 2 (November 1935), 405–27. Republished by permission from *Social Research*.

We may question the usual interpretation of Tocqueville as a foremost exponent of liberalism, in view of the fact that his book was praised by conservatives as well as liberals.[3] It appears rather that Tocqueville's thinking does not represent merely the concrete intellectual expression of a definite political tendency of the nineteenth century. Although he sought to effect a compromise between the divergent political groups of his time, his intellectual endeavor essentially transcends any immediate political purpose.

To designate Tocqueville as a moralist indicates that it was a purely personal need that drove him, the thinking man, liberated from scientific and academic traditions, to seek an understanding of the social and political situation and his own place in it. But the designation has a second meaning: in pursuing the consequences of his researches, Tocqueville came inevitably upon the problem of human nature, and his own distinct idea of man became the presupposition and goal of his work, as in the cases of Michel de Montaigne [1533–1592], Blaise Pascal [1623–1662], Thomas Hobbes [1588–1679], and Anthony Ashley Cooper, 3rd Earl of Shaftesbury [1671–1713]. Because he assumed this philosophical attitude, which the seventeenth and eighteenth centuries dubbed that of moralist, Tocqueville's work breaks through the narrow boundaries of political actuality. It was not only that he felt grief over the political and social decline of the nobility, but much more that he was affected by the problematic situation of the forms of personal perfection in moral, intellectual, and spiritual life under the new social order. Hence, the changing of the old society of estates into a democratic order and the resulting transformations of man and his social relations became the center of his thinking. As the spiritual hero or great man was the most intense concern of his life, Tocqueville's historical experience led him to perceive the profound connection of the forms of social and personal life with the totality of the social structure. These are the reasons why we designate Tocqueville as moralist and sociologist. In his experience, there were the elements, preformed, of a new mode of thought—the historical and sociological consciousness. Historical consciousness means the knowledge of the distinctive character of a constellation of political and social forces, conditioned by the past and directed toward the future. Sociological consciousness means the understanding of the dependence of human existence and its social forms on social conditions and the knowledge of the functioning of social institutions and of the rules of social activity. All these existential and intellectual presuppositions of Tocqueville's work indicate that a summary interpretation of it as liberal in the sense of the nineteenth century neglects the philosophical temper of his thinking.

It would not have been surprising if, like Louis de Bonald [1754–1840] or Joseph de Maistre [1753–1821], Tocqueville, as a representative of the politically vanquished nobility, had espoused a traditionalist or counterrevolutionary political theory. On the other hand, he might have followed the example of many men of his class who followed enthusiastically the new political movement. But Tocqueville never became a political partisan, even when he accepted the new social and political order and strove to make the best of it. His intellectual perspicacity and moral sensitiveness lifted him above the plane of the political thinkers of his epoch. He was able to understand the unity of the historical process and the inner continuity of the revolutionary movement, begun in 1789 and not yet finished in 1848. He was one of the first to see that the social revolution was the inner consequence of the political democratic revolution. The same intellectual and moral vision enabled him to understand that the decline of the nobility was an inexorable historical process begun seven hundred years earlier. Tocqueville was himself aware how fruitful the historical perspective of his work was for a fundamental insight. In a note,[4] he remarks that the place, we may say the sociological place, for important and significant intellectual and spiritual achievement is neither within the static framework of a corporate society, nor within the dynamic structure of an egalitarian democracy. Both are in their varying ways equally conventional. It is in periods of transition from a firmly fixed social order to a new structure of existence that the conditions are given for many fertile insights. We may add that these are the epochs of crisis, when the spirit must span the crumbling world like an arch and by the highest power of its knowledge arrive at definite insights into the primordial phenomena of social life and the intellectual connection of antagonistic concepts within a higher spiritual unity.

Tocqueville possessed all the personal qualities necessary to envisage the crisis of his epoch. He was intellectually and morally so detached that he understood in its logical development the historical process and the final defeat of his class, and therefore he regarded the outcome as providential. Moreover, he was so deeply dominated by social morality and the feeling of social justice that he proclaimed the process of economic leveling as a presupposition of the decent existence of the great masses. Nevertheless, in spite of his strong opposition to the nobility as a social class, his family life and personal experience enabled him to perceive that freedom could exist as a form of personal perfection even within the rigid structure and conventions of that order. Quite independently of the political commonplaces of his period, he was aware of liberty as a permanent element in social structure, changing its content with varying historical and social conditions, and remaining correlative to institutional forms and order. His thinking brought him inevitably to a realistic, positivistic, and historical interpretation of political institutions since he felt the need of observing the practical application of political ideas and their functioning under social and historical conditions.[5]

His inner experience and his survey of a troubled world constituted his preparation for his experiences in America, as expressed in his *Democracy in America*. When he stepped on American soil, it was with the full consciousness that the world of his fathers was irrevocably gone. He was also clearly convinced that democracy was the destiny of the Western world. This he accepted not merely because he realized the inexorableness of historical development. He went farther and asserted that democracy offered the means of developing the potentialities of the new situation and of bringing out the permanent forms of life in the new historical world.

II

This attitude leads Tocqueville to his first basic problem—the nature of democracy. He seeks to answer such questions as the following: What does democracy look like? How does it function? What positive forces for the foundation of modern society does it reveal? What dangers does it present in the construction of a social order? The first section of his book, therefore, is a realistic empirical analysis of the political institutions of the United States. But in his interpretation, he looks upon American democracy only as an example of the general form of modern social and political structure.[6] From the observation of a specific historical form as found in the constitution of the United States, he had, therefore, to pass on to general sociological concepts, which comprehend the typical events and movements of modern democracy. Even in the first part of his work, Tocqueville goes beyond mere empirical analysis and attempts to derive some general concepts from his realistic observations and the inner logic of democratic principles. A result of the combination of deductive and inductive methods is that the sociological character of his concepts is not always plainly evident.

The second part of his book is far from being an analysis of American democracy and presents only a few and fairly unimportant American illustrations. In this section of his work, it becomes clear how heavily the transformations in the political and social structure of the Western world weighed upon Tocqueville, and how they cast their shadow on his interpretation of American democracy. Yet this volume reveals Tocqueville at his most profound. He attempts to show the potency of the social structure in fashioning human types and to demonstrate what transformation in types of thought, forms of emotional response, and moral and intellectual attitudes have been brought about by democratic society, as contrasted with a world of estates and aristocracy. Just as in practical life he accepts the trends toward democracy, so in theory he recognizes the interconnection of all the spheres of human existence. He sees that different social structures aim at different forms of realization. Thus, one age will strive for fame and military glory in the social sphere, and for the contemplative life in the intellectual sphere, while another will glorify the civil virtues, human welfare and peace, practical morality, and social sympathy. But whatever the historical transformation of men, the structure of the permanent social functions is always realized even though in varying historical constellations.

Tocqueville entered upon his new approach to reality through history and the sociological consciousness, in response to the obligation imposed upon him by the situation of crisis. His work, therefore, stands beside the works of Auguste Comte [1798–1857], Edmund Burke [1729–1797], Karl Marx [1818–1883], and Jacob Burckhardt [1818–1897], as among the first great attempts at a criticism of western culture on the basis of a new intellectual method, deeply influenced by the political and social situation.

I am aware that this departs from the usual interpretation of Tocqueville. In French literature, particularly, Tocqueville's name appears exclusively in the histories of political theory and works on public law and historiography. I do not wish to enter upon a discussion of the classification of Tocqueville's work, for clearly he must be treated in political science and history as well as in sociology.[7] I desire only to draw attention to the fact that the concepts in *Democracy in America* involve many difficulties of interpretation, rooted in the discrepancy between the content of ideas and their concrete literary formulation. Tocqueville was intimately acquainted with the great French political and social philosophers of the eighteenth century. The influence of Montesquieu, in particular, is evident in Tocqueville's terminology. Nevertheless, the inner content of the book and its place within the framework of his complete works, including his correspondence and conversations, afford the means for a proper interpretation of Tocqueville's rational and formal categories. For example, when at the beginning of *Democracy in America*, he remarks that he considers the equality of conditions a characteristic mark of the new world, he is referring not only to the political equality of all citizens, but rather to the entire social structure of capitalist democratic society. Also, he often uses the political concept democracy when he means the bourgeois social structure of the postrevolutionary world. In other words, the methodological difficulty in interpreting *Democracy in America* consists in the fact that while the outward form of his concepts is political, their content nearly always refers to a sociological structure or relation. Only in his later work did Tocqueville acquire an adequate conceptual form for the content of his ideas.

III

Tocqueville traces out the general laws of the democratic movement. But he is well aware of the special conditions of the historical form of democracy in America. The Pilgrim fathers and the pioneers brought to America the traditions of Anglo-Saxon freedom, a valuable heritage from the traditions of the middle class, deriving from the later Middle Ages. The struggle of the sects for spiritual liberty created a new sense of liberty and voluntary obedience to the law. Furthermore, in addition to these tendencies toward liberty, the equal conditions of the struggle of life, the promise of a virginal world and the common fate of the immigrants created the homogeneity and equality of democracy. Hence, it was possible in the United States to consider liberty and equality a priori, as organic products of the geographical and political situation and the historical heritage. In Europe, on the other hand, the situation was just the reverse, for there it was absolutism which, before the establishment of democracy, had created by its process of levelling the factual presuppositions for the political stand after the memory of medieval liberty had been lost for centuries. Tocqueville is wholly convinced that because of this difference in origin, democracy in the United States was created by the union of the spirit of religion with the spirit of liberty. His personal problem, and the dominant motive of his political career, was to help the French democracy to realize this union of religious content with the form of liberty.

One must know this spiritual presupposition of Tocqueville before one can understand the significance of his grouping of the conditions for the perpetuation of democracy in three classes or on three levels. The highest and most important level is constituted by those conditions that shape the intellectual, moral and spiritual content of the nation, and that alone can give character, rhythm, and form to political institutions and social life. Therefore, for Tocqueville, Christian morality, or at least its conventional observance, is indispensable to the genuine democratic form.[8]

Tocqueville finds the second class of conditions necessary for the functioning of democracy in the laws, by which he means, above all, the constitution and the fundamental laws of democracy. He sees the greatest menace to democracy in an antagonism between these two groups of conditions and the decline of vitality of moral forces. The consequence would be that the majority in parliament might establish an arbitrary reign, endangering not only the rights of minorities, but also the national interests. In this connection, Tocqueville quotes Jefferson in a letter to Madison: "The executive power in our government is not the only, perhaps not even the principal object of my solicitude. The tyranny of the legislature is really a danger most to be feared and will continue to be so for many years to come. The tyranny of the executive will come in its term, but at a more distant period." Tocqueville sees that the danger of despotism by a majority is countered in the United States by three legislative forms. First, the constitution distributes the lawmaking function between the individual states and the federal government. The United States cannot use physical force against the states, nor are the states able to destroy the fundamental political framework of the federal state. The second legislative device for the protection of democracy is seen by Tocqueville in the democratic constitutions of local and county governments. By virtue of their participation in and responsibility for the government of their immediate communities, citizens are educated in politics and political obligations and in the defense of political liberty. The chapters dealing with the townships in *Democracy in America* are probably the most impressive and beautiful section of the first part. Tocqueville treats the township with special affection because to him this municipal democracy appears to be the root out of which the tree of American democracy grew. Here, also, he is influenced by French and other European history, for the municipalities of Western Europe were the birthplace of everything that was to become political liberty and democracy in the Western world. Tocqueville notes another important characteristic of the township constitution—its existence is in itself sufficient to make impossible a bureaucracy administered centrally by either the state or the federal government. Thus, Tocqueville sees in the existence of these municipal and regional democracies a twofold protection against the dangers involved in the new political institutions of America. These little democratic communities will not only create a shelter against demagogical majority revolutions, but they will also be able to resist the developments of state or federal government in the direction of a centralized political administration. The third and most important barrier against the pressure of mass democracy Tocqueville finds in the federal judiciary and, above all, the Supreme Court. He is well aware that the popular election of judges has its dangers, both for justice and for democracy; for this reason, his view of the Supreme Court is all the more impressive. By virtue of its capacity to determine the constitutionality of legislation through interpretation of the spirit of the constitution, the Supreme Court becomes the guardian of the constitution, and thus the most important factor aside from the president. Hence, Tocqueville terms the Supreme Court the aristocratic element in the radical democratic order of America. He regards this aristocratic institutional factor as the basis for creating, by means of political and legislative institution, a balance between the constructive and the destructive forces of democracy, so long as these institutions remain permeated by the moral idealism of the people.

The third class of conditions, which Tocqueville regards as essential to democracy in America, is the peculiar form of economic labor and its spirit in a country that offers such immense possibilities for work and gain. The equal interest in profit and the ambition for acquisition and its chances create a social homogeneity and a common interest in prosperity, which democracy is likely to guarantee. Tocqueville readily admits that economic tendencies and the spirit engendered by them exert a great influence upon the formation of democracy. But on the other hand, he holds fast to a hierarchy of social values that condition life to such a degree that he holds in least esteem the influence of economic tendencies. Tocqueville did not always, however, follow the inner logic of his position that religious and moral forces are powerful enough to shape the world. He realized that it was impossible to found the new idea of political freedom on that of religious freedom; consequently, he sought to base it on the idea of the personal interest of the citizens.

IV

The presuppositions and the direction of Tocqueville's thought come to even clearer expression in the second part of *Democracy in America*. Here, for the first time in the nineteenth century, the attempt is made to show the change in forms of human existence in and through the process of social development. In three great chapters, Tocqueville treats of the change in forms of intellectual, emotional, and ethical life. In this context, he once remarked that he could not imagine anything more barren for the human mind than an abstract idea. Just as Georg Hegel [1770–1831] sought the concrete concept, whereby to comprehend the totality of things, so also Tocqueville aimed at comprehending the totality of the social via an interpretation of political and social reality.

He achieves new insights into that transformation of the emotions of man that has taken place since the abolition of feudal society: under feudalism personal relationships within a family were determined by social norms, the heir of an estate being considered by his relatives as belonging to a higher social stratum, but in modern society the personal relationships among members of a family are shaped by the subjective power of sentiment.[9] With equal clarity

Tocqueville recognizes how the problem of form in poetry is changed by the new psychological interests, and how the close attention to the study of individual souls is a result of the change in the social structure. He declares—a contention that the sociological analysis of literature has since proved—that the pure tale and story is supplanted by the psychological novel, which becomes the typical literary form of the new society. Similarly, Tocqueville notices certain striking changes in the realm of intellectual life.[10] Thus, he believes that the interest in general and abstract concepts in the political and moral sciences, and also in history, may be regarded as a result of modern democracy, in which not individuality and personal effort but general social movements are the forces determining the course of history.[11] Equally astonishing is the following insight, which is in the general direction of the thinking of Hegel and Comte, although there is no trace of direct influence: Tocqueville contends that in times of a static and feudal structure of society religious thinking runs parallel to the forms of social life, and the absolute is thought of as transcendent, as a supreme creative God and director of the world, but that with the rise of modern democratic mass movements a new metaphysical tendency begins, which tends to set this absolute into the process of history itself.[12] Thus, Tocqueville binds a philosophy of immanence into the sociological structure. The second part of *Democracy in America* moves in the direction of a sociology of culture.

V

Among the aphorisms found in Tocqueville's literary remains, there is a remark that every political form contains within the inner logic of its principle the tendency toward its own destruction.[13] We do not know when Tocqueville formulated this idea. It may perhaps have originated while he was writing his *Democracy in America*. For here, by observing the functioning of democratic institutions and by elucidating their possible consequences, he indicates the way whereby democracy could lead to a new form of undemocratic domination. He sees that this new political form cannot be included under any of the earlier concepts of absolutism and despotism since it would develop out of the conditions of modern life. The absolutism of the seventeenth and eighteenth centuries had created the absolute power of the crown, at least in theory. But the technical imperfections of the state administration and the customs and practices of a society organized in estates acted as limitations upon the claim to absolute sovereignty. With the destruction of local and corporate administration and judicial power, democracy started upon a course that made possible not only the centralization of political power, but also a rationally unified and systematized administration. In politics, the general tendency of rational order is toward the creation of a centralized administrative apparatus that, particularly in the hands of a democratic government, is capable of routinizing, directing, and fashioning extensive sections of social life. The sociological significance of this tendency is seen in a rational domination of society by the state and in a new corporate order. In place of the old hereditary aristocracy, a new bureaucratic aristocracy arises. The inner bond to the state will be either the fear of its unlimited power or the ambition to become a member of this aristocracy of functionaries.[14] To this tendency toward rational organization and the leveling process of political administration, there corresponds a growing feeling of privacy and individualism on the part of citizens. For Tocqueville, individualism signifies nothing but subjective egoism. It throws man back to the narrowest interests of his private existence and destroys all forms of community of spirit. If democracy is not in the position to create artificially local and provincial community forms through communal and provincial self-administration, then the centralizing tendencies of rational organization will find no hindrance to a rule of the majority based on the principle of popular sovereignty; and the way will be open for the development of a new form of absolute, rational social domination.[15]

These tendencies naturally are not to be regarded as formal laws of development. They grow out of the particular character of the individual spheres of life within the general historical and social structure. The development of the political organization of a social structure is thus always closely related to the particular character of all the social and spiritual conditions constituting the historical moment. Just as the state makes its first steps toward rationalization when new potentialities of political rule are rendered available by the combination of a money economy and a new military technique, so will new political forms of democracy be crystallized by the interaction of new rational tendencies in the various spheres of life. It must be kept in mind that while Tocqueville affirmed the inner logic of the development of the different spheres of life and considered their possible tendencies as cognizable, he nevertheless believed that there were limits to our understanding. Thus, it was not possible to predict the final decision that a nation might make concerning its destiny. Although no one before Marx had emphasized as strongly as Tocqueville the determination of the intellectual and emotional life by the historical structure of society, Tocqueville was most deeply convinced that in decisions that have to do with the total existence, not only individuals but also nations are capable of mastering and breaking through the determining forces of their existence. Consequently, nothing final can be said about the future of democracy, even though there are many signs of a new rational and absolute form of government.

VI

Tocqueville saw clearly also the antagonism between the political and economic form of democracy. He noted that the state was in a position to make all classes of the population dependent on it as a result of the development of financial economy. By state loans and state organization of savings banks, the state was able to bring the upper and middle classes into such an immediately interested relationship to itself as to guarantee an effective dependence and participation of the citizen in a definite political form of the state.[16] Ten years before the *Communist Manifesto*, Tocqueville recognized the deep opposition between capitalist economy and political democracy and the tendency of the state to regulate economic affairs. Moreover, he observed how profoundly the new economic system began to change and reshape the character of mankind. He described the change in general social relationships, such as the relation between master and servant in the capitalist and democratic order. With the dissolution of the old patriarchal ties, there also disappeared the personal human bonds of devotion and faithfulness on one hand and of paternal care and responsibility on the other. Democracy creates a formal principle of equality between master and servant; the correlate of this in the economic sphere is a purely market relationship.[17] In agriculture, a parallel situation has developed in the transformation of the relationship of manorial lord and tenant to a relationship based simply on economic profit. In agriculture, these new political tendencies combine to make the ownership of land more mobile. This is shown above all in the system of leases that are made only for short periods and oriented solely on the possibility of profits. The laws of inheritance also take cognizance of the new economic conditions in that they permit the equal division of real property among all children and thus further the mobilization of land.

Tocqueville sees, particularly, the antinomy between the general norms of democracy, which formally guarantee to every citizen the right and opportunity of advancement, and the social development of the new industry, especially of large scale industry. He observes that the economic and technical opportunities for large-scale industries will bring about new agglomerations of capital and create a new industrial aristocracy.[18] This aristocracy, however, will share with the old aristocracy only economic power, and in contrast to the latter, will be interested only in economic profit. Tocqueville clearly foresees the dangers presented to the social order by such a concentration and collectivization of economic interests, even though he is inclined to underestimate it. On the other hand, he sees very clearly that the position of the working class in large-scale industries is in insoluble contradiction to the idea of democracy. These workers will constitute the only class or estate—but a negatively privileged one—in this society, which prides itself so much on having abolished the estates. Without savings and without land, the workers are dependent upon the economic situation of the market and upon the wage offers of the entrepreneur. A crisis will bring them unemployment and throw them upon public charity. It is at this point that the state qua state will become interested in economic problems and will intervene in the economic order from the viewpoint of social policy. In this way, the control and regulation of industry in general becomes one of the most important problems in the tendency toward a new absolutism. In the measure in which the individual branches of industry combine and organize, their social policies, production policies, and economic power become matters of general concern to the state. Since the state itself goes into industry, particularly in the field of heavy industry, the development of state direction of industry opens the way to a new and very effective form of state absolutism—"Industry leads us, and it in turn will be led by the state."[19] Thus, it is not only the antagonism between democracy and bourgeois society that leads to a new transformation of the state. But the powerful economic forces toward concentration and rational organization press on and pass beyond the boundaries of economic privacy to become a problem of general social interest, and so of political importance. In addition to these general economic tendencies, Tocqueville sees certain institutional forces that threaten to undermine the democracy of the future.

VII

Tocqueville devoted some penetrating analysis to the relations between a democratic social structure and its army. He observed here an antagonism between democracy and the immanent tendency of an army, which is parallel to the antagonism revealed in capitalist economy. Whereas modern society loves peace and desires an unbroken and calculable political policy in the interest of its economic system, the interests of a democratic army are directed toward war. Tocqueville derives this phenomenon from the social composition of the class of officers and noncommissioned officers. In an aristocratic social structure, military service is a class privilege, and military rank is independent of the position of the different groups of nobility. In a democracy, on the other hand, where the army does not occupy the same social position as in an aristocratic society, the social rank of the officer depends on his position in the service, and his income derived therefrom. Since advancement during peacetime is determined only by length of service, there is always an active spirit of unrest among officers that makes them avid for the opportunities for distinction and advancement in rank that come with success in war. The only counterweight to these political interests of the officers is found in the civilian spirit of the soldiers, who receive their military training as part of the system of general military service. Since the latter group is always changing, while the officers' corps remains constant—for this is their life career—the military and warlike spirit of this core of the army remains a permanent source of danger for the foreign policy and peace of a democracy. With astonishingly keen insight, Tocqueville foresees that wars will become more rare in coming generations in the measure in which economic and political factors become interconnected in a democracy. But, on the other hand, if a war comes, it will plunge into a common ruin the indissolubly interconnected world of modern democracies. It is not only the possible unfortunate outcome of such a war that can be so fateful for democracy. Any protracted war can undermine and destroy the constitution of a liberal democracy, and there is not even any need for a military coup by victorious generals. The gradual centralization of all the institutions important for life and the conduct of the war, combined with the regimentation of the entire population, may even under a civil government prove to be a slow transition to a permanent form of modern state slavery. Tocqueville finds analogies for such a course only in the late Roman period. In the measure in which a modern democracy pursues a rational and peaceful foreign policy and in its domestic policy advances toward political and administrative centralization, the restless spirit of the army may make possible a military dictatorship. Such a dictatorship will be quite different from that of a Caesar or Napoleon. Instead, it will find available a widely ramified and thoroughly rationalized administrative system that is an obedient instrument in the hands of the existing executive power. "I am convinced that in such a case a sort of merging between the attitudes of the clerk and soldier will take place. The administrative system will take on something of the military spirit and the military something of the civilian spirit. The result will be a military government, regular, clear, precise, and absolute. The people will take on the appearance of an army and society of military barracks."[20] Such tendencies need not develop under pressure; they may also be the result of general apathy and lack of interest, which Tocqueville considers the products of a subjective egoism that has deprived men of any sort of communal spirit. The executive power will then without any danger make itself master of the constitution. In the following phase, it will be relieved of its power by a dictator and thirty men, who will take possession of the executive state apparatus. Neither the executive nor the dictator can establish anything permanent.[21] The very reason for the easy success of the dictatorships makes it impossible to believe that they will continue for a long time in power. They are able to seize power because none resists their attempt, but they will fall also because no one will sustain them in their power. Thus, Tocqueville sees in different aspects of modern life parallel tendencies that are pressing on to a new form of absolute sovereignty. In the rational centralized order of the political and social world, in the technical and economic increase of industrial rationalization, certain tendencies are arising that point inevitably to a central, unified, and standardized regulation of our entire life. In addition to this, there is a tremendous danger of the relaxation of the will to freedom and its substitution by a dull indifference. Tocqueville is emphatic in his warning against this attitude, as this adds subjective elements to the objective tendencies toward despotism. In this connection, it is worth repeating Tocqueville's observation that the old expressions of despotism and tyranny are unsuitable for any new form of absolutism emerging out of democracy. This new form of absolutism will differ from all preceding ones in content and structure. It will be the child of modern rationalism, of the leveling process and of antagonisms in the economic world under conditions of opposition between militarism and democracy. For this reason, Tocqueville believes that the only possibility for maintaining democracy lies in citizens' consciousness of responsibility and their deep love of liberty, finding expression in their political rights.

VIII

Tocqueville's idea of freedom leads us to the profoundest part of his thought. On the basis of sociological and historical knowledge, he ventures into the realm of general and permanent forms of human existence. Like Søren Kierkegaard [1813–1855] and Ludwig Feuerbach [1804–1872], the ultimate aim of his knowledge is a doctrine of man and a theory of social and political existence. It is not by chance that this was the inner tendency of his thinking. Ever since the Sophists, we can observe that a time of social change produces a particular type of philosophizing. The conditions of human existence and the general forms of life become the central problem of thinking and the concrete concept the most important need in this intellectual situation. Only in this light can we understand how it is possible to find in Tocqueville's empirical analysis judgments concerning the value of social tendencies and relations for human existence. He was fearful of the stunting of mankind through occupational specialization and increased technical organization. He foresaw the dissolution and the dehumanizing technization of the forms of the economic process under a system of rational direction and administration, and the devitalization and degradation of labor to merely a dull mechanical exertion of force. He envisaged the approach of a time when the state will not only assume the responsibility for social welfare, but will also take over the schools and churches, converting them into political institutions and the clergy into state officials. Since the state will intervene in and fashion the innermost character of man, it will limit, stultify, and destroy the general character of human life. It was this danger—the possibility that in the modern democratic world man will come to exert a more or less mechanical function in an enormous abstract state machine—that determined Tocqueville's idea of freedom. As early as 1836, he wrote to a friend, "I am a liberal of a new kind."[22] In *Democracy in America*, he definitely expressed his mistrust of the political liberals, for he was well aware that his doctrine of freedom was not compatible with contemporary political theories. It is almost symbolic of his inner loneliness and forlornness in this world that the gift of his friend John Stuart Mill [1806–1873], the first edition of *On Liberty*, came to him on his deathbed.

Tocqueville knew that every historical and social structure produces its own form and specific concept of freedom. From his own experience, he knew the very spiritualized form of aristocratic freedom, through which personal courage, moral responsibility, and spiritual definiteness were realized. But this historical form made transparent for him the eternal task of freedom. It is the everlasting function of freedom to make possible and guarantee the spiritual, moral, and intellectual realization of personal perfection. Freedom therefore stands in the service of the highest and ultimate values. It is that form of life by and through which the historical man breaks through the conditions of his existence and participates in an eternal order. In contrast to the negative concept of freedom of political liberalism, Tocqueville's concept may be designated as one of existential freedom. That is, whereas the political idea of freedom merely sets up a relationship between the state and the individual citizen, Tocqueville undertakes the task of showing in a positive way what is the function and meaning of freedom in the totality of man's social existence, no matter how various its historical forms may be. His gravest concern is that every kind of freedom will be eliminated or destroyed in a modern democracy as a result of the growing omnipotence of the state. If social justice is a social goal of the modern democratic world, the corresponding existential concepts must be personal dignity, responsibility, and virtue as forms of the individual realization of the social ideal. Will these ideas, however, be able to assert themselves, find their place and preserve their function in a world that organizes human existence under the rational and inexorable direction of the state? One hundred years before the despairing attitude of Max Weber [1864–1920], Tocqueville raised the identical question that was the basis of Weber's work: How will it be possible in this world to preserve those forms of life in which personal, intellectual, and spiritual realization are possible? For Tocqueville, the future of democracy is dependent on the balance between these forms of intellectual freedom and the institutions of a social democratic order. Because he is fearful that the weight of order will overbalance that of freedom in the modern world, he clings all the more passionately to his idea of freedom as a permanent form of human realization. His optimism concerning democracy is to be explained only as a pedagogic and didactic attempt. The actual content of all his work is deeply pessimistic as to the future of political and social development.

IX

The analysis of democracy and the investigation of its social principles dominated the thinking of Tocqueville even after the great work on the American democracy. In his most beautiful book, the *Mémoires*, he has given a penetrating sociological description of the political and civil society of the bourgeois monarchy and its parliamentarism. Here we find a profound analysis and characterization of the incapacity of the revolutionists of 1848, and also his ideas on the different socialist systems and their possibilities. It was in this connection that he asked himself whether the idea of private property is really a permanent form of human nature or will be dissolved and destroyed by the new social movements. The speech delivered in parliament in January 1848 prophesying the coming revolution is the most famous of his political career. And the portraits of Louis Philippe [1773–1850], Louis-Napoléon [1808–1873], Louis-Eugène Cavaignac [1802–1857], and the radicals of the French parliament are vivid individual characterizations of different political types.

In studying Niccolò Machiavelli [1469–1527],[23] he notes that the Florentine democracy of that time was altogether different from every type of modern democracy and comparable only to that of the ancient world. A particular interest in past and present forms of democracy and in the problems of democratic federalism produced his various remarks and studies on the Swiss democracy. His combination of sociological and political insights enabled him to prophesy its civil war (*Sonderbundskrieg*) and to understand the one constitutional form of Swiss federalism. The Swiss historian Emil Dürr [1883–1934] has praised the profound empirical analysis and the acuteness of his political perspicacity in the treatment of Swiss democracy.[24]

Even *L'Ancien Régime et la Révolution* is dominated by the problems of the new social structure and its political institutions. It was the first introductory volume of a large work planned for three volumes and intended to follow the development of the social and political organization from the ancien régime to the Empire, and to describe the transformation of man in this period.[25]

In the correspondence with Gobineau, especially in the letters reviewing Gobineau's *Inequality of Races*, the spiritual attitude of Tocqueville finds strong and sublime expression. Not only does he reject the content of Gobineau's book, the conclusions of which he regards as questionable, but he revolts particularly against its biological materialism and the political consequences. There are the most important differences between the two friends in the interpretation of human nature. Gobineau knows man only as a biological being; Tocqueville understands man as living in freedom, in every moment experiencing the possible perfection of his personality. Against the materialistic pessimism and vital heroism of Gobineau, Tocqueville sets up confidence in the justice of God and spiritual heroism. Nowhere so much as in these letters do we understand how deeply Tocqueville was influenced by the spirit of Port-Royal, which taught that the greatest tension exists between God and the world and which engendered an almost Calvinistic rigor of moral sentiment.

Romain Rolland [1866–1944] has attempted to describe this conflict as generational, with Gobineau representing the younger generation, which destroyed the liberal ideals of progress, humanity, liberty, and justice after the disillusionment of 1848, and opposed to them a heroic pessimism. Rolland understands the conflict of the friends as a symbol of an eternal movement of the mind. "It is one of the perpetual movements of the human pendulum oscillating between two poles and seeking the point of equilibrium. But the pendulum is too strong and always swings beyond this point. But this strength itself, these oscillations between the opposite poles are but the rhythms of history, the breath of humanity."[26] The metaphor Rolland finds for the movement of the mind is very true and impressive. But he forgets that the thinking of the two men takes place in different spheres. Gobineau writes as a political thinker and is interested only in the political consequences of his ideas. In a sociological analysis, his work can be correlated with the resentment of the vanquished nobility that had to call in question, minimize, and even destroy the biological racial status, the vital value of the ruling class, in order to justify its own pretensions. Although Tocqueville's work contains the most important concrete political analysis, it is a philosophical one, pointing out the conditions of modern life, the political possibilities, and the place of personal perfection in this world. From his view, human life is an incessant striving toward the fulfillment of its obligation to state and nation, and an aspiration toward perfection through spiritual freedom.

This is the legacy of Tocqueville for our times, his actual significance for our day. Therefore, it is impossible to dispose of his work as part of the historical movement of nineteenth-century liberalism. Tocqueville knew very well that his attitude was out of tune with his times and that he was sharing the destiny of all thinkers who transcend their epoch—solitude and misunderstanding. Repeatedly in his letters to different friends are utterances corresponding almost literally to a phrase of the aged Johann Wolfgang von Goethe [1749–1832] to Zelter [1758–1832]: "We are the last of an epoch, which will not return so soon."

These words cannot be interpreted as an expression of a dying class. Rather, they present in an arresting form the consciousness of the solitude of a spiritual existence combined with an understanding of the complexity of human nature and its permanent structural elements in the midst of the political interests of the different groups of his period. Wilhelm Dilthey [1833–1911] wisely considered him the greatest political philosopher after Aristotle and Machiavelli.[27]

Notes

1. An American translation appeared in 1836 with a preface by M. John Spencer, a member of the New York Legislature.

2. *Nouvelle Révue Française,* February 1934, 216–17.

3. Alexis de Tocqueville, *Oeuvres Complètes* (Paris: Michel Lévy, Libraires Éditeurs, 1861), 1:vi.

4. *Oeuvres Complètes,* 3:423, 424.

5. This point has justly been emphasized by Paul Janet, *Histoire de la science politique,* 2:736.

6. James Bryce [1838–1922] has pointed out clearly that Tocqueville's analysis was not complete and could not become an exhaustive work because, as a result of his philosophical and French presuppositions, he was unable to see the complex reality of the United States. See James Bryce, *The Predictions of Hamilton and de Tocqueville* (Baltimore: Johns Hopkins Univ., 1887), 23–24; *Modern Democracies* (New York: Macmillan, 1921); *The American Commonwealth* (London: Macmillan, 1889).

7. Pitirim Sorokin, *Contemporary Sociological Theories* (New York, London: Harper & Brothers, 1928), 720.

8. It is especially important to emphasize that Tocqueville, a Roman Catholic, stated as a conviction not only of his own but of the American clergy as well, that only the separation of church and state makes possible the vital functioning of religion through church institutions.

9. *Oeuvres Complètes,* 3:315ff.

10. *Oeuvres Complètes,* 3:124ff.

11. *Oeuvres Complètes*, 3:140ff.

12. *Oeuvres Complètes*, 3:49ff.

13. *Oeuvres Complètes*, 8:485.

14. *Oeuvres Complètes*, 3:499 footnote.

15. Lord Hewart in his *The New Despotism* is thus to be regarded as a disciple of Tocqueville.

16. *Oeuvres Complètes*, 3:501.

17. *Oeuvres Complètes*, 3:251ff.

18. *Oeuvres Complètes*, 3:285ff.

19. *Oeuvres Complètes*, 3:511.

20. *Oeuvres Complètes*, 3:557.

21. This early formula of the second part of *Democracy in America* appeared in 1840 but recurs in his memoirs written in 1850–51 in the analysis of Louis-Napoléon: "Il ne fondera rien, mais–ça durera."

22. *Oeuvres Complètes*, 5:433.

23. *Oeuvres Complètes*, 8:445ff.

24. Emil Dürr, "Die Demokratie in der Schweiz nach der Auffassung Tocqueville's," *Baseler Zeitschrift für Geschichte und Altertumskunde*, vol. 23, 1925. *Cf. Oeuvres Complètes*, 8:464, 9:83; Correspondence with Gobineau, *passim*.

25. Unfortunately, Beaumont, Tocqueville's friend and the editor of his works, has published only a few fragments of the continuation of

L'Ancien Régime et la Révolution. The family de Tocqueville would place the learned world in its debt by publishing a new and complete edition of the works, including the unknown correspondence of Tocqueville and Mme De Tocqueville, the restored integral text of the published letters, and the preparatory fragments of his last books.

26. Romain Rolland, "Tocqueville and Gobineau," *Europe* (October 1, 1933), 68–80.

27. Wilhelm Dilthey, *Gesammelte Schriften* (Stuttgart: B. G. Teubner Verlagsgesellschaft; Göttingen: Vandenhoeck and Ruprecht, 1961), 7:104.

13

Tocqueville (1959)

It is indicative of the profound personality of Alexis de Tocqueville [1805–1859] that he and his work have gained in stature and relevance since his death in 1859. In 1959 we remember Tocqueville as a philosopher of freedom and as a human being who established an image of human integrity in an age of revolution. We do not celebrate an academic centenary. During the century since his death, he has been classified as historian, sociologist, moralist, and political scientist, as if his work had been in academic fields, but Tocqueville explicitly rejected the idea that he wrote his books as a scholar for the promotion of learning.

Tocqueville was born in July 1805, shortly after Napoleon had made himself emperor. His family remained true to the revered tradition of the old monarchy. His parents and brothers were proud to belong to an old feudal clan of Normandy that had served the kings for centuries, and they continued their loyalty to the dynasty during the period of revolution. Though the Tocquevilles did not belong to the highest ranks of nobility and were of mediocre wealth, they were respected and esteemed by all classes of society. Alexis de Toc-

---

Published originally in a slightly different form under the title, "Tocqueville, 1959," in *Social Research* 26 (Winter 1959), 449–70. Republished by permission from *Social Research*.

queville was loved by the voters in his electoral district, who trusted him for his integrity.

On his mother's side, Tocqueville was related to the Noblesse de la Robe. The great and brave Guillaume-Chrétien de Lamoignon de Malesherbes, his great-grandfather, had been assigned by the Convention to defend Louis XVI [1754–1793] and courageously defied the revolutionaries, fully aware that he would die under the guillotine. From both families, Tocqueville learned the relevance of authority and freedom for the viability of a body politic.

Of his two main books, *De la démocratie en Amérique* and *L'Ancien Régime et la Révolution*, the latter was the first volume of a grandiose project for a general work on the French Revolution. According to Tocqueville, the two books were two aspects of the same problem: the place of man in the age of democratic revolutions and the standards of democratic social classes. Actually, the problem was for him that of human self-interpretation in an age of transformations. Self-interpretation is a philosophical rather than a scientific mode of reflection; for this reason, his friend Gustave de Beaumont [1802–1866] was right when he called Tocqueville a philosopher who was concerned with the place of man in a world of unceasing revolutions. His basic questions were anthropological, historical, and existential.

A Human Image of Greatness

There are two types of authors: one is as a human personality inferior to his books; the other, through the strength of his personality, surpasses the literary or philosophical force of his writings. Tocqueville belonged to the latter type. He showed, indeed, a potential greatness as statesman and a spark of genius as writer and thinker, but his work remained fragmentary. His political career as a constructive minister was disrupted by the rising tide of a new despotism; his literary career was cut off when he succumbed to the slow destruction of tuberculosis.

During his short life, Tocqueville, against all odds, realized the image of a fearless and free human being. He challenged the reactionary principles of his aristocratic family, disgracing them by his liberal-conservative position in politics and, regardless of his reputation, by his writing. He married an English commoner who was as feeble in health as he. With the power of his mind and will he fought his physical organism, his society, and the exigencies of political life.

He made it evident that the test of human greatness is the discipline required to be superior to the vagaries of destiny, and gave us an unforgettable example of a personality able to hope against hope, to have faith in spite of all defeats, and to love life for the sake of unfolding the strength of the mind and its basic potentialities. He was a Stoic thinker who blended the attitude of Epictetus [55–135] with that of a Christian. In 1959 he is to us a normative image of a human being who remained an old-fashioned lover of freedom in a world of conformism and servility. To us who are old-fashioned lovers of freedom under the shadow of totalitarian imperialism and technological standardization, he sets standards of courage and integrity amidst threats of new social, economic, and political despotisms.

When he died, he was mourned by the educated classes in all the liberal societies of the Western world. He was considered by them a liberal in the political and economic sense, as that term was understood in the first half of the nineteenth century. This classification was appropriate. Though he had joined one of the liberal-conservative groups when he was elected to the Chamber of Deputies, he remained true to the principle of constitutional government—regardless of whether it was monarchical or republican—throughout his career and to the end of his life. He was firmly convinced that this pattern of government was the necessary form of politics for all future western societies. The contemporary types of despotism, such as that of Louis-Napoléon [1808–1873], he tended to regard as mere accidents. Likewise, he shared the faith of the liberals in classical economics, repeatedly contending that the laws of economics are eternal, not transitory, and that the radical workers should be indoctrinated with the true teachings of classical economics. Politically and economically, he was in agreement with many of his aristocratic and patrician friends and, in particular, with the great liberal thinkers in England. Tocqueville took his political and economic convictions very seriously. There was a kind of gravity and solemnity around him that induced Amantine-Lucile-Aurore Dupin aka George Sand [1804–1876] to call him a stuffed shirt. That he was an intransigent liberal in an age of revolution may explain why for a time his work and personality fell under the eclipse that later shadowed the period of liberalism.

This liberalism, however, was just the surface of a man who was equipped with creative powers transcending his historical limitations. Like Honoré de Balzac [1799–1850], he had the imagination to visualize the merging of economic, social, and technological transformations into a total revolution; by reflection on his political experiences, he was able to corroborate his vision analytically. He succeeded in penetrating the total social situation and in conceiving its relevance for and effects on the standards of society. He lived consciously through an epoch that he himself called an age of unceasing revolution. To him, a society in the pangs of radical transformations offered a unique opportunity to learn the scope and intensity of human passions—a conviction that implies both his anthropological concerns and his philosophy of history.

Political Elite in a Democracy

In remembering Tocqueville today, on the centenary of his death, we are less interested in him as an historical liberal than as a statesman who was probably the first to ask a challenging question that we still have not answered: How is it possible to construct a political elite in a democratic society?

The French Revolution had destroyed the traditions of a political elite as a class of nobles—those who by virtue of pedigree, education, and wealth filled the king's offices in politics and administration and had a monopoly of office in the army and navy. Social status gave them a fearlessness, independence of judgment, and moral integrity that made the best of them the successors of the great politiques of the sixteenth century. A few, thinking in terms of political responsibility, were alarmed that the government did not recognize the need for reforms of the constitution and of the systems of taxation.

In contrast, Tocqueville's practical experience as a member of the Chamber of Deputies convinced him that democratic government had very poor foundations indeed. The majority rule involved grave dangers to political planning and continuity of policy. It was exposed to the hazards of shifting pluralities that were often the result of regional conflicts or vested economic interests. Tocqueville was alarmed, in particular, by the banking and commercial interests that tried to disguise their concerns as congruent with the welfare of the state. He understood this condition of a bourgeois democracy as a genuine dilemma of the body politic, and the topic of a political elite became a leitmotif of his reflections.

On his second visit to England, in 1835, he compared British, French, and Irish nobilities, seeking the image of a normative elite in an ideal political structure. He gave a grim description of the vicious practices of Anglo-Irish nobles, and condemned their exploitation of a poor, humiliated people. To Tocqueville, such behavior was a disgrace to a true nobility. He had praise, however, for the English aristocrats. These, he believed, would always prefer the duration of political leadership and control to selfish economic advantages. As a political realist, he knew that the English nobility had its vested interests, as did all other classes. To him, however, the problem was how far economic and political advantages were interrelated, or even identical.

Even so, his appreciation of the English nobility is subject to criticism. Tocqueville himself, in his *Letters from England* (1835), described the unbelievable misery of the working classes in Manchester. This is an unforgettably gruesome and somber picture, and, in drawing it, he forgot everything of classical economics and became Marxist, bluntly stating that the misery of the workers was fully explained by the great profits of the manufacturers. The whole analysis anticipates Engels's famous work on *The Condition of the Working Class in England*. There was not the slightest interest in this condition among the members of the nobility.

A contrasting background to Tocqueville's praise of the English nobles as an ideal ruling class was his emphasis on the irresponsible characteristics of the prerevolutionary French nobility. He subscribed to the adverse criticism of the French nobles made by the Abbé Sieyès [1748–1836] in his powerful pamphlet, *What is the Third Estate?*, which regarded the nobles as characterized by a lack of political morality and a greed for economic privileges. They had accepted the privileges that the kings had extended to them, whereas, in Tocqueville's opinion, they should have revolted against their political degradation and elimination from government. They had sold their political birthright for the precarious privilege of exploiting their subjects to the utmost. They had a considerable amount of responsibility for the revolution, even though a politically responsible minority worked feverishly during the years 1787–88 to avert the break in social continuity and to achieve a constitutional government through legal reforms. In stressing the irresponsible element in the conduct of the French nobles, Tocqueville attempted to explain an important cause for the rise of revolutionary resentments.

But he felt strongly that the class that had formerly exercised political control had certain great advantages over the new politicians, certain valuable traditions that were absent in the new society. The nobles in government had been economically independent, an advantage often not possessed by the representatives of the nation in a democratic government. The members of the nobility had carried on traditions of political wisdom, based on the many and various historical situations their forebears had encountered; they remembered the ways of proceeding in certain contexts, and were aware of the alternatives of political decisions; they had learned that government is art rather than science. The democratic leaders, who were expected to represent the regional or occupational interests of their constituents, were mere delegates, rather than responsible statesmen who gave the authority of their convictions to the nation as a whole. The new state had given up the conception of a political elite for the rule of majorities and their representatives. This democratic modus operandi was producing a rapid ascendancy of bureaucracy in governments.

Balzac was the first to understand the power exercised by bureaucracies over democratically elected parliaments in the modern age of specialization. Tocqueville gained the same conception from his experience in politics. He was keenly aware that government bureaucrats could not be a political elite. Indeed, when they were not directed and controlled by a political elite, they were a danger to political constructivism. On the other hand, he recognized the difficulty of building up a political elite when economic power was vested in capitalistic enterprise and only indirectly in political organisms.

No longer did either landed or capitalistic power create independent minds. In an age of revolution, all positions of power were subject to pecuniary prejudices.

In this context, he evolved his concept of the attitude appropriate to the responsible statesman. In a world in which everything has become a commodity, and the economy has made it a business proposition to increase economic desires, the man who wishes to keep his integrity and inner freedom should be ready to withdraw from the temptations of the market society. He should escape into a life of modesty and asceticism in order to remain independent morally and free intellectually. Distance from the labyrinth of the capitalistic world will give men the opportunity to be free.

The same rule is valid for a political elite. The new elite will no longer be a distinct class, as was the nobility. It will be a communion of ascetic people committed and dedicated to the restoration of a body politic; it will unite the variety of group interests into a whole community that transcends the living, the dead, and the unborn. The new elite will take up again the pattern of earlier elites: the tradition of political wisdom, the independence of judgment, and the continual reexamination of political prejudices.

In 1847, Tocqueville joined a group that might have developed into a party that today we would call Christian Democratic. Its members aspired to raise the standards of the working masses materially, socially, and intellectually, within the classical capitalistic system. This group was not strong enough, however, to cope with the problems of the social revolution.

Closer to Tocqueville's conception of what a political elite should look like were the revolutionary parties. They presented a new type of political intellectual, the first men in French politics who were not brought up in the great literary traditions of France. In the past, the most antagonistic political groups had an element of unity through their common roots in the great literary past of the nation. The new radical intellectuals, living by their political journals and social periodicals, were uprooted from and contemptuous of the chain of political and moral thought in France and England. But they were totally dedicated to their ideas.

Thus, though Tocqueville hated all radical ideas and attitudes, he felt that the antirevolutionary classes could learn from the radicals what an elite should look like. He believed that the power of a political party rested with the total devotion of its members, its will to fight and to conquer. Such will requires discipline, selection, and obedience. The conservative and liberal groups, he maintained, had the possibilities of establishing such a forceful party. They were united by a common concern to maintain freedom and the constitution, regardless of their diverse interests, and they trusted one another because all felt that their cause was at stake. This conviction gave them the spirit of sacrifice, the discipline, and subordination indispensable to counteract radical action. Tocqueville hoped that such a response to an emergency situation would create the political elite of modern democracy.

He had seen in the United States that a democratic elite is possible. There he found American patricians in a democratic setting who still enjoyed the authority of the founders of the republic; families devoted to the commonweal and public office; professional groups, such as men of law, ministers, academic people, who enjoyed some independence economically and socially. In all groups was a political and religious conviction that working for the body politic is a responsibility of those who possess wealth, social prestige, and the authority of learning.

Tocqueville saw that all these social classes could contribute to the formation of a political elite in France. He pointed out the importance of the legal professions in politics as a dynamic and flexible group. Though he was distressed that the big economic powers had infiltrated the political area without contributing to the formation of a political elite, he believed that the possibilities of a democratic elite could be actualized by the voluntary service of the educated and professional classes. They would establish the keen independence, the civil courage, and the authority of political tradition that would affirm the pattern of democratic leadership in the new society.

The Ethos of Society

Tocqueville often mentioned in his correspondence that political institutions as patterns of government were not his primary interest. As statesman and "sociologist," he wanted to observe the functioning of the organs of government and administration. It was his genuinely political approach that prompted him to ask: What is the state of mind of the rulers and ruled? What are their attitudes toward each other, and what their habits of heart and belief? He investigated the ethos of society pragmatically and philosophically, seeing that the basic questions concerned the possibilities of human self-realization and endurance. What human beings are willing to achieve and to suffer, what common men and women are willing and able to take, is of compelling concern to the statesman and to the philosopher in the study of human nature. For this reason, his questions were anthropological. What will human beings look like in a rapidly expanding democratic world in which equality will prevail over liberty? Where will we find political convictions in capitalistic societies? Can we raise the intellectual and moral standards of the democratic masses without lowering our own standards?

The anthropological perspective of Tocqueville's thought is one aspect of his philosophical quest for the meaning of history. Like Georg Wilhelm Friedrich Hegel [1770–1831] and Auguste Comte [1798–1857] and many of his contemporaries, he believed, or tried to believe, that a final meaning is visible in the progress of history. He called this evolution "providential history" and endowed it with a spiritual halo of Christian convictions. He bravely admitted the defeat of his own class as a sign of providence, and he accepted the rise of the middle classes as the will of God. The advance of democracy was a providential necessity. In the United States, he had seen that democracy and liberty were compatible with each other. He was heartened to see the freedoms of the American: the democratic freedom that recognizes the interaction of individual and society in ordered liberty, the freedom of the Christian who voluntarily understands democracy as a religious way of life, and the freedom of the frontiersman in face of nature and man. He was doubtful, however, that the well-balanced equilibrium of liberty and democracy, as realized in the United States, could be readily transplanted to Europe. Providential history was undergoing a grave test in the revolutionary world of the European continent.

In probing his anthropological questions, Tocqueville's method was what I will tentatively call "sociological"—sociological because he was not interested in individuals as makers of history. He emphatically declared that there are only classes, with their conflicts, cooperation, and accommodation. Classes are historical phenomena because society and men are by nature historical. In their interaction, historical classes make up the process of history. This is a genuinely Marxist statement. Tocqueville was, indeed, a conservative Marxist. He was conservative because his radical critique of the bourgeois society and of its capitalistic system had as its yardstick the value attitudes of a past political society, and because the critique comes from an aristocratic political class, not from an economic proletariat.

In his *Democracy in America*, he analyzed the changing social relationships between the industrial employer and his worker, comparing them with the patriarchal interaction of the manorial lord and his serfs and dependent agricultural laborers. The modern relationship is a purely contractual arrangement between business partners, one of which is unequal to the other. There are no moral obligations or human affections. The new industrial lords have established a business feudalism, more cruel and exploitative than anything the feudal lords could have imagined.

As a member of the Chamber of Deputies, Tocqueville often addressed the bourgeois parties—the representatives of financial and banking capital—in this spirit. His life as a statesman and parliamentarian gave him ample opportunity to observe the dangerous effect of capitalistic interests on the democratic state. Thus, he emphasized that the state is not a machine that has the function of satisfying the interests of the rich or of any monopolistic class. The state is a political institution—that is, it should unify all special interests of the various social classes in a meaningful solidarity of the whole body politic. Like Thomas More [1478–1535] and Desiderius Erasmus [1466–1536] in the Renaissance, Tocqueville told the businessmen of the capitalistic society that the body politic is a moral institution and not a tool for exploitation.

Even the body politic has, of course, its economic foundations. No state can last if it is not organized around an adequate and equitable system of taxation. And Tocqueville's insight into the economic foundations of the modern state in the modern money economy produced a brilliant thesis on the revolutionary character of the absolute state. He saw the absolute state as the result of a revolution in which the king liberates himself from constitutional institutions, such as estates or parliaments, in order to be free and independent in raising taxes for his own military or domestic projects. In executing the revolution from the top, kings laid the groundwork for the revolution by the masses from the grass roots.

Tocqueville emphasized the pressure of economic interests on the state. In *L'Ancien Régime et la Révolution*, his last book, written after twelve years of political activity, he discussed in detail the unfair distribution of taxes and services among the classes. The high ranks of society were free from taxation, and the middle classes could escape its burden, for they could easily move to the towns when taxes in the countryside were overwhelming. People paid taxes according to their domicile, regardless of their landed wealth, and taxes in the urban areas were less burdensome. Tocqueville thoroughly analyzed the budgetary troubles of Louis XVI. The king and his administration had inaugurated public works projects in agriculture and industry, but they had not covered the costs by appropriate taxation. The result was inflation, which increased the discontent of all classes, business and consumers alike, and antagonized them against the government. It became a unifying revolutionary force, as it has been ever since. And while this economic discontent was spreading the spirit of radical criticism to all classes, the social and economic situation of the peasants became explosive. Tocqueville established this process as a natural development in revolutionary behavior.

The peasants carried the main burden of direct and indirect taxation. In addition, they had to perform services for the nobles who owned the landed property. But many nobles no longer lived in the countryside; their superintendents administered the land and treated the peasants as objects to be exploited. The others, who lived in the countryside because they were poor, also lived off the sweat and labor of their peasants, who were struggling to earn the rents they owed the noble gentlemen. Gone was the patriarchal relationship that had established moral bonds and affections of charity between the nobles and their dependents on the land. No longer was the right of the lords to claim services and receive obedience matched by an obligation of responsibility and of charity to the poor. Tocqueville described at length the process of dehumanization that had taken place when the nobles became owners of privileges. It was one of the causes of the revolution, for the disappearance of traditions of reciprocal service destroyed the bonds between rulers and ruled, without which no state can last. In his interpretation of this process, he coined the term *absenteeism of the heart.* Thorstein Veblen [1857–1929] should have enjoyed the term. It ought to be accepted in the dictionary of a leisure class.

Tocqueville discovered a general social rule that is as valid today as it was at the time of the French Revolution. This is his thesis that all ruling classes indoctrinate the ruled with ideal images of themselves. They teach the subjects that the king is their good and benevolent father, that the ruling groups are the fair and generous guardians of their trust, and that the judges are wise and equitable men who have compassion for the poor. The subjects themselves are the dear, good, innocent people who, it is ordained, must work for their superiors.

Society lives by such images; they make society work. The imagery is taken for granted by rulers and ruled until the ruled begin to be aware of the reality of the social situation. They will then transform the traditional images into counterimages. The patriarchal king becomes the tyrant, the nobleman appears as hawk, and the judge as slave of the mighty. The rulers, however, still maintain the image of the pastoral goodness of the peasant; they continue their games even when the peasants are already in a spirit of revolt. Tocqueville was shaken by this grim spectacle.

The theory of images and counterimages, established by Tocqueville and philosophically elaborated by Max Scheler [1874–1928], is one of the great discoveries that Tocqueville made in reflecting on the rise of the revolutionary spirit. The changes in the adherence to and interpretation of images indicate the degree of solidarity in social interaction. What the classes think of one another, what positive or negative images men have of their superiors and inferiors, is a fundamental problem to the statesman and—today—to the social scientists who advise him.

The Process of History

Conspicuous in Tocqueville's analyses is his continuous application of the comparative method in history, in order to establish generalizations that could enable him to make articulate the specific character of general social phenomena. Long before Max Weber, he compared the mediaeval democracy of Florence and its revolutions with the modern trend toward radical democracies. He saw the analogy between the Napoleonic Empire and the Roman Republic, as democratic despotisms; in both cases, the constitutional institutions remained fictitious. He saw likewise a correspondence between bourgeois society under the regime of Louis-Napoléon and that under the Roman emperors. "There will be highly sophisticated and civilized societies. They will be politically degenerate and leave everything to the rulers and to their bureaucracies. There will be no will to freedom, no desire to make personal decisions, no dedication to the commonwealth." Thus, Tocqueville visualized the future of a formerly free world, tamed by the sweet and soft new despots.

He believed that the period of the absolute state was the happiest time of the French monarchy. The kings were then no longer dependent on the feudal nobility and not yet the prisoners of the bourgeoisie. This thesis shows, however, that he never studied the *Mémoires* of Louis Duc de Saint-Simon [1675–1755], which had been published by 1830. He could have learned from them that the contemporaries of Louis XIV called him "the king of vile bourgeoisie" and recognized the absolute state as part of the bourgeois revolution.

On all levels of political action, Tocqueville discovered economic causes and social motives conditioning behavior patterns.

After the June 1848 revolution, he flatly predicted that the imperial regime of Louis-Napoléon would come. The bourgeoisie of all ranks was shocked by the socialist upheaval and was willing to exchange freedom for economic security and prosperity. They, therefore, supported Louis-Napoléon.

Tocqueville anticipated that the pressures of the modern economy on the state would increase with the accelerated tempo of capitalist development. He found a paradox in this development. The liberal societies proclaimed limitation of the powers of the state to the barest essentials of social order. At the same time, they assigned to the state new areas of legislative and executive power, in order to protect their interests against the rising proletariat and foreign business competitors. By doing so, they continuously increased what, in principle, they wished to weaken.

Tocqueville conceived of the social revolution as a technological one. He understood the general bureaucratization on all levels of military, judicial, and political administration as the opening of an avenue that would lead to all kinds of managerial welfare states and new patterns of planned despotism. Thus, he met with the Duc de Saint-Simon on the crossroads of the social revolution, where economic and technological trends merged. Here, Tocqueville showed himself the founder of a sociology of politics, even if he would have rejected the classification.

To understand the state as administration was a genuinely sociological conception. *L'Ancien Régime et la Révolution* was the first interpretation of a revolutionary process as a technological revolution. The elimination of the feudal nobility as a political element in the state was possible because the technical and financial necessities of the state made bureaucratic administrations indispensable. Tocqueville recognized that the process of history is in itself revolutionary: what appear to be tiny technological inventions often prove to be momentous events that transform the social and political worlds. The absolute state as a military and civilian bureaucracy, controlling a king as a symbol of political unity, prepares the pattern for the modern state. Tocqueville's analysis of the hierarchical bureaucratic institutions and their contact with members of different classes was one of the great illuminations and advances in sociological thinking. But for him, it was simply the art of politics.

The people retain an indoctrinated respect and affection for the ruler and the dynasty, but they are in contact with the state when they see the policeman, when the tax collector comes, and when they are directed by the organs of government to do or to refrain from this or that. The absolute state, as the first stride toward the modern rational state, illustrates the rise of bureaucracies in the armies as well as in financial and juridical affairs. Through the social revolution, the remnants of personal relationships, of traditions of authority and loyalty, of camaraderie and friendship are transformed into rational relationships among experts who work in a hierarchy of offices and assignments. To Tocqueville, the sociologist of politics, this aspect of the revolution meant the destruction of independent social classes and agencies cooperating with one another for their common good. The absolute state, he believed, set the pattern for all forthcoming despotic regimes in France. From the welfare state that Anne-Robert-Jacques Turgot [1727–1781] and the physiocrats tried to construct under Louis XVI to the Napoleonic Empire and the tyranny of Napoleon's nephew, he saw a logical and coherent development.

For Tocqueville's conception of the Napoleonic state, we have only a detailed outline. A book on Napoleon and the empire was to have been the last volume of a comprehensive work on the French Revolution, of which the *ancien régime* was the first. As we see from his notes, the final book would have viewed the Napoleonic state as the first total state in the modern sense of the word. Through its civil and military bureaucracies, the will of the single ruler could be achieved with the utmost efficiency. Furthermore, the widespread organization of the administration manipulated public opinion in such a way as to make the despotism appear to be a democratic institution. The organization of public opinion through a variety of agencies made it possible to produce a total conformism of the subjects by persuasion and threat.

Tocqueville saw these developments as fateful trends in modern political and social processes. In the merging of these tendencies, he found an answer to his basic question: What are human beings going to look like in the new world of democracy and bureaucracy? The answer he found was that men will be ruthless gangsters in the economic competition for infinite power, and they will be servile and shrewd in complying with the wishes of economically strong men. Thus, the population will be divided into two parts: one in front of the counter, and the other behind it. Those in front of the counter will envy the others and will nurse the ideal of becoming experts in a tiny area of bureaucratic specialization, frantically seeking jobs in the lower or higher ranks of the civil service or the courts of law. Here, they will have security and pensions; they can become small rentiers and attain the peace of the little man. Everybody on both sides of the counter will try to get favors for his family and friends.

This dim prediction was in contradiction to Tocqueville's original belief in providential history, the unfolding of the divine principle of Christian religion in the process of the Here and Now. He had seen God's message in the rise of American democracy. In his interpretation of the new American society, he strongly emphasized the positive elements in the equality that released the productive faculties of a great majority of citizens—for themselves and for the commonwealth. He was willing to appreciate democracy as a form of progress in the providential control of history; the new political pattern, he thought, would be a blessing for most people. Democratic political and social conditions would bring about the slow advance of the intellectual and cultural standards of modern societies through education, political action, and the application of religious ethics to the problems of social action—in a necessary relationship between freedom and religion. This was the lesson he derived from the United States.

He was fully aware that the new democratic societies had to pay the price for progress in civilization. The new democratic mankind would be civilized on a much wider scale than the small aristocratic societies of the past, but necessarily on lower levels. It is characteristic of his humanitarian attitude that he considered the positive accomplishment of this progress more important than its negative aspect.

But while he affirmed providential history as he found it in the United States, he was not certain he could take the same attitude in his interpretation of the age of revolution in Europe. What he lived through in Europe was very different from what he found in the United States. As mentioned, he was born in 1805, at about the time Napoleon made himself emperor. He saw the regimes of the Restoration, was a parliamentarian under the monarchy of Louis Philippe [1773–1850], experienced the two revolutions of 1848, served as a minister in the only republican government of Louis-Napoléon, and lived under the new tyranny for eight years. This course of history could appear to him only as a dialectic of democratic revolutions in which the popular phases were negated by despotic though no less revolutionary stages. Could this be the meaning of providence? He could not deny that the age of revolution had an ultimate meaning, but he came to believe that the social and political institutions that would arise from this holocaust might be vastly different from those he had supposed.

For him, the highest human values were the responsibility of the individual, the freedom of self-realization, and the right of property, ideals that had guided much of the action and suffering of western mankind. The new socialist revolutionaries had no conception of these norms as relevant to their human and political philosophies. Still more explicitly, the new radicals questioned the hypotheses on which the traditional value systems were erected.

After July 1848 Tocqueville had the intellectual courage and discipline to ask himself whether the socialist revolutionaries might not be right. Perhaps the traditional prejudices that had ruled the conduct of people for three hundred years would give way to new social philosophies. It seemed to Tocqueville that he lived in an age of decadence in the perspective of the bourgeois society and an age of progress in the view of the working masses. Never had any people understood the historical relevance of their own experiences, or been able to anticipate the role of these experiences in creating new historical frames of reference. There was a time when nobody could imagine a world without slaves; nobody foresaw the role of the Christian sect in the transformation of the Roman Empire, or predicted the structure of the feudal society. Men are poorly equipped to visualize historical worlds beyond the established pattern of their society. Thus, who could affirm with certainty that one pattern of social action is absolutely necessary and that new types are impossible to realize?

Men had taken for granted the right of property; it had seemed the foundation of Western civilization. But the radical thinkers of the socialist revolutions visualized a new civilization in which the right of property disappeared and other norms prevailed. Though Tocqueville fought against the revolutionaries who attacked the bourgeois civilization, the sweep of his historical imagination made him able to understand the new conception. Everything was possible in this age of revolutions, which might last for a century. "I am tired of trusting the mirages of revolutionary expectations. Perhaps it is our destiny to cruise for the rest of our lives the endless sea without reaching an unknown destination."

Thus, after the revolution of 1848, Tocqueville wrestled with his philosophy of providential history. Was historical progress and its necessity really a truth, revealing the ultimate meaning of a divinity? If history was indeed providential, might it be that in ages of revolution, it was impenetrable for those who had suffered defeat? Historical evolution appeared to evince the necessity of democratic justice for all. But Tocqueville tortured himself with questions. Can providence intend to turn democracy into a negative equality of all before a despot? Or is slavery a fair enough price for welfare to all? The representatives of popular democracies are often tyrants, and, as such, they may exterminate the aristocracies of birth, education, and wealth. Could socialism be the medium for establishing the equality that political democracy had failed to achieve? Tocqueville tried to escape into a theory that the necessities he sought in the alternatives of history were open and dynamic: it might be that relative autonomies of historical trends were subject to the decisions of the political agents in the social context of the political structures; that responsible ruling classes would turn the necessary developments into social reforms, while revolutionary classes would establish despotic regimes. But he knew that this was wishful thinking.

Thus, he began to question the truth of providential history and to turn from the philosophy of history to a philosophical anthropology. In history, he could now see only various patterns of egalitarian regimes—whether party, mob, or Caesaristic tyrannies. He continued his fealty to providence, but now in revolt and indignation. From the God of history, he turned to an unknown divinity, which, beyond the horizon of history, should protect the unfolding of human liberty.

Tocqueville had taken for granted man's historicity. He came ultimately to believe that there is an area beyond the historical process, where man challenges the God of history in asserting his freedom as the essence of human existence.

Patterns in Freedom

In his ten years in the Chamber of Deputies, Tocqueville suffered defeats and humiliations because of his unwillingness to adopt the techniques and tricks of the political gamblers. He resented the shallow mediocrity of the procedures and of the debates, and hated the perverse vulgarity and the passions of most of his fellow deputies. Dedicated only to the principles of constitutional reform and to the firm establishment of political liberty, he was unable to share in the petty ambitions and vanities of mediocre parliamentarians, interchangeable with one another, who regarded their offices as a business proposition rather than as a grave moral obligation. Tocqueville blamed himself for his lack of patience with the Chamber, and felt it to be a weakness that he was attracted only to men of rare qualities of mind and affection like himself. It was possible for him to give himself only to those of sincere conviction who shared his search for truth beyond all pragmatic and utilitarian purposes. Like Michel de Montaigne [1533–1592], he condemned himself as a political failure among the politicians, of whom he said: "I honor them because they rule the world; they cause me, however, to suffer profound ennui."

In contrast, there are pages of almost Nietzschean fervor in Tocqueville's description of his coming into his own in the hours of danger that began with the 1848 revolution. The situation that the nation faced then could not be remedied with the skills and tricks of the parliamentary game. Now, when everything was at stake, the highest moral qualities were required: courage, unselfish dedication to the country, complete disinterestedness.

He enjoyed the climate of the National Assembly, where he felt at ease and relaxed. It was a new experience for him to share value attitudes, fighting spirit, and intentions with a majority—a majority determined, as he was, to maintain the republic in a constitutional pattern and to defeat the radicals and socialists for the sake of freedom and human dignity. He maintained that the unfolding of political freedom was the only road by which France could be rescued from the anarchy of a radical revolution. Anticipating that a socialist regime of workers would be a total despotism, he aligned himself with the political groups that were striving for Christian democracy; that is, for raising the social, moral, and intellectual standards of labor within the structure of the capitalist economy. This kind of reform was a goal that he considered worth fighting for. "Perhaps it was a very attractive goal because the road was dangerous and uncertain; for I have a natural inclination to adventures and a spark of danger has always appeared to me as the fascination of all human action."

Tocqueville tested his qualifications as statesman in the six months of 1849 when he was Minister of Foreign Affairs in the republican government of Louis-Napoléon. Relieved of the constraint he had felt as a deputy, he now devoted his energies to constructive work as a responsible and independent minister, with elation comparable to the feeling he had experienced at the outbreak of the revolution. "I breathed more freely than before the catastrophe." His analytical mind did not prevent him from showing resoluteness in action. From his memoirs, which were not published before the end of the century, it is clear that he thrived under the burden of personal responsibility, feeling his strength growing with the resistance of the problems he had to confront. He enjoyed the techniques of action that his aims demanded: placating the heads of the parties in the Chamber while following his own convictions, planning diverse possibilities on the moving chessboard, calculating the possible countermoves of the foreign powers. The self-realization that he found in constructive political action confirmed his qualifications as a statesman and reestablished his self-confidence, after the years of frustration in the Chamber. He candidly admitted that he was an ambitious statesman. His pure dedication and his disinterestedness would give him, he hoped, the position and respect that his attitude deserved.

But he soon learned that neither integrity nor a fundamental concern for the whole nation is necessarily adequate for a successful career in an institution in which vested interests prevail. He was shocked when the National Assembly voted for the direct choice of the president by referendum. This decision made the election of Louis-Napoléon certain. As he had anticipated, the ideals of political freedom were subordinated to the fears aroused by the threat of socialism. A new despotism arose because the bourgeois classes were willing to bow to any ruler, however legally questionable, who would protect their interests against the masses.

Thereafter, Tocqueville lived as an exile in his own country, still an old fashioned lover of political and human freedom. He was certain that the new despot would not be the founder of a dynasty, but he believed that the rule of the tyrant would last a long time, a phase of the continuing revolution.

> We did not see the beginning of the great revolution, we will not see its end. If I had children, I would frequently repeat to them that we live in an age of revolution. That implies that we live in a world in which we must be ready and prepared for everything; for nobody is certain of his destiny. And I still would add that we should not count on any possessions of which we could be deprived. We should think to acquire the goods which we cannot lose but by death; courage, will-power, wisdom, and poise.

Like Nietzsche, Tocqueville valued the passions, which alone accomplish the self-realization of a human being, and proclaimed as genuine freedom the spontaneity of human action in the transformation of the world. Like Jean-Paul Sartre [1905–1980] or Albert Camus [1913–1960], he maintained that freedom is a constitutive element of our very existence. This fundamental attitude, which Tocqueville cherished throughout his life, makes him even today a norm for our own conduct in an age of unceasing revolutions.

Author's Note

The author wishes to express my deep gratitude to my friends Mr. and Mrs. S. Jacobson of Brooklyn College and Professor Bernard Rosenberg of the College of the City of New York, whose inspiration, criticism, and patience were of invaluable help in my preparation of this paper.

14

Jacob Burckhardt: Transcending History

> Das schönste Glück des denkenden Menschen ist das Erforschliche erforscht zu haben und das Unerforschliche ruhig zu verehren.
>
> [A thinking man's greatest happiness is to have fathomed what can be fathomed and to revere in silence what cannot be fathomed.]
>
> —Goethe. *Maximen und Reflexionen*. 1207

The Tyranny of History

An axiom of sociology is that radical trends in human thought provoke equally radical, opposite attitudes. In the field of psychology, the radical insistence on a mechanistic and deterministic psychology brought forth the violent reaction of William James [1842–1910] and Henri Bergson [1859–1941], who sought to vindicate the image of the spontaneous human personality. In sociology, we have witnessed time and again the renascence of voluntaristic theories in reaction to naturalistic and absolutely deterministic systems. Even more illuminating is the case of historiography. For centuries, the universities and the academies have been engaged in the study and

---

Published originally in a slightly different form in *Philosophy and Phenomenological Research* 6 (December 1945), 225–69. Reproduced with permission of Blackwell Publishing Ltd.

interpretation of history, accumulating vast funds of data, a veritable encyclopedia of the past, valuable in many respects. However, very early in history, rulers and ruled began to use or rather abuse these recollections of the past as a means of justifying their own claims for the future. For centuries, individuals and groups had referred their needs and hopes to the perennial law of nature that is supposed to reflect the divine order in the world of man. The revolutionary peasants of the sixteenth century, the revolting feudal lords of the French Fronde [a series of civil wars in France between 1648 and 1653—Eds.], the armored revolutionists in Oliver Cromwell's [1599–1658] army, all based their claims on the intelligible and unquestioned verities of a divine and natural law. With the rise of secular societies and the development of independent political institutions, these ideas began to lose their old potency, making room for the feeling that the life of reason develops in the process of time and has no perennial being of its own. Since the seventeenth century, scientists and philosophers have been fervently proclaiming that truth is the daughter of time and that the moderns are superior to the ancients because of the tremendous progress of the experimental sciences. The idea of progress became the substitute for the tradition of the law of nature. It was first hailed by the scientists and humanists as the characteristic challenge of the intellectual to the prescientific obscurantism of the "dark ages." These intellectuals were the first to assume that the material content of historical time was the steady progress of knowledge and civilization. They praised the process of history as the most effective element in the growth of intellectual and moral enlightenment and regarded their own efforts as decisive contributions towards the progress of "Reason." These ideas were eagerly grasped by political and liberal intellectuals, particularly the American and the French, who applied them to the pressing social problems of their time. They postulated that progress of reason is the true content of the process of time that we call history. They insisted that only when we shall have applied the yardsticks of "reason" to all social problems and institutions shall we succeed in establishing the rule of happiness on earth. History ceased to mean the totality of the past, its deeds and achievements. Instead, its sphere was restricted to the development of pragmatic and scientific reason and to their realization within social and political institutions. History had become the knowledge of those trends that prepare situations favorable to the aims of revolutionary groups in modern societies. This new philosophy of history is the articulate expression of the secular and progressive societies of the modern world, a substitute for those past philosophies in which the human world was a part of the meaningful and intelligible whole of the universe.

History as the philosophy of progress is an expression of the existential attitude of the rising liberal, progressive, and socialist movements of the nineteenth century. Whatever may be the shades of difference between the rationalistic eschatology of Anne-Robert-Jacques Turgot [1727–1781] and the Marquis de Condorcet [1743–1794], the dialectical agnosticism of Georg Hegel [1770–1831], the dialectical economism of Karl Marx [1818–1883], the positivism of Auguste Comte [1798–1857], and the evolutionism of Herbert Spencer [1820–1903]—they all have four features in common. First, all these systems assume to know the rational meaning of history. Second, all are positive about the direction and the end toward which history is moving; they are sure that meaning and social action coincide in the immanence of the social process. Third, all follow the same procedure—they isolate particular tendencies within the universal whole that serve them as the foundation on which to construct the unity of their historical system. They attain order and unity by referring human action and thought to an abstract principle that lends history the character of a purposeful and moving spectacle.

Philosophies and religions, states and mores, economic systems and moral systems appear as manifestations of the same principle in the various stages of history. They all seem to emanate from the universal principle. History thus becomes a sort of philosophical totalitarianism that forces all the actions and thoughts of man into a predestined pattern. Finally, all these systems agree on the merely instrumental role of the individual in this process of history. They all postulate this anonymous and blind destiny; it does not matter much whether they call it absolute mind, forces of production, or spirit of positivism. In all these systems, man is an instrument and a blind tool of those enigmatic meanings that rule the historical process. Man exists only in his functional relationship to those abstract principles. He is the puppet in a show. These systems testify to the rise of new societies and of new types of behavior in the mobile world of technical efficiency. Some of those thinkers who were witnesses of the emergence of this new world were aware of its implications. Reflecting on the modernity of the "overcrowded" music of Ludwig van Beethoven [1770–1827], Johann Wolfgang von Goethe [1749–1832] regards it as a characteristic manifestation of the "new century."

> Today everything is "ultra." Everything is radical in thought and action. Nobody knows himself any more, nobody cares for the elements that constitute his sphere of life, nobody thinks of the materials of his work. We have lost the spontaneity of our way of life; irrational ways of conduct are abundant. Young men are stirred much too early in life and are then carried away by the maelstrom of the times. The world admires wealth and mobility. People are eager to compete for these goals. The different civilizations strain to surpass each other in the building of railroads, docks, and other facilities of com-

> munication. This must eventually lead to a state of universal mediocrity. Indeed, this is the century of the quick mind, of the alert, smart and practical man. These men are equipped with a certain cleverness and deem themselves superior to the crowd though they themselves are incapable of the highest and most sublime achievements. Let us persevere as much as possible in the spirit in which we have been brought up. We and a few others shall be the last of a period that will not return very soon.[1]

Alexis de Tocqueville [1805–1859] describes his times in similar terms. "We belong to a moral and intellectual family that is disappearing."[2]

However, not all contemporaries of the "new times" accepted it in the spirit of elegiac resignation. Søren Kierkegaard[3] was the first to open the attack on the systems of Hegel and Marx. To him these pseudotheologies were death traps threatening the very existence of the spontaneous human being. Socrates and Christ are the true images of the real and complete person as against the outward man whose existence assumes meaning only in terms of his institutions, churches, states, and societies. Kierkegaard raised his voice to protest against the degradation and dehumanization of man to which these modern philosophies of blind and arbitrary fatalism had subjected him. He ardently desired to save and restore the spiritual person, the human being that comes into its own as living in the actual Christ, not the Christ of the churches. Friedrich Nietzsche [1844–1900] had taken up this attack on historicism. He was not concerned with the defense of the Christian person; he fought for the survival of the independent and creative personality. He hated the adoration of progress and viewed with disgust the optimism of a mechanistic and rationalistic philosophy that left no place for the powerful and self-responsible individual. He stormed the fortresses of history in order to liberate man from the paralyzing influence of historical complacency and fatalism.

This situation brought into existence what may be called the specific German contribution to sociology—the interpretative sociology of Max Weber [1864–1920], Georg Simmel [1858–1918], and Ernst Troeltsch [1865–1923]. These efforts, different in scope and power, have one common purpose. They refute the absolute determinism and the abstract necessity of Marx's dialectical philosophy of history. Working as empirical scientists, these men investigated a variety of historical situations and made it evident that human actions and decisions cannot be imputed to the workings of an anonymous historical law. On the contrary, human choices and final decisions in social action can only be understood as expressing fundamental needs of the human constitution. These sociologists strive to replace the systems of historical dogmatism by a theory of social conduct and social action that unites psychological and sociological elements in order to come as near as possible to a science of the human constitution in the concrete world of history.

However, all these men failed to conquer the spirit of historicism. The case of the sociologists is most illuminating. They attacked most violently one system, but they took for granted the hypothesis on which all these systems are built. They accepted the positivistic version of the immanent necessity of history—namely, the absolute relativity of all ideas and conceptions to their historical situations. These scholars did much to discredit the position of Marx, but they did not destroy it. They refined and made more relative the absolute historicism of the past. They questioned the modern eschatological visions of the end of history and substituted for it the endless relativity of each situation. Against the optimism and fatalism of their times, they summoned their enlightened contemporaries to a sober pessimism. But they did not break the chains of historical immanentism and fatalism.

Kierkegaard and Nietzsche succeeded where the sociologists failed. They had broken the chains of modern historicism. However, this positive statement must be qualified. If one may speak of their emancipation, it must be added that it was a merely personal freedom. They were undoubtedly the bitterest critics of their times. This opposition, or rather enmity, is a constitutive and relevant element of their vision. But it was a vision of despair. They could formulate their positive ends only in the negative terms of revolt and despair. There remained the unresolved tension within the mind that is free only to reflect on a historical situation which is unchangeable and inescapable so that the terms and concepts in which these new ideas were expressed still bear the stigma of the "illness of the times."

There was one man who succeeded more than all the others in the battle against the tyranny of history. He transcended historicism because he was never in revolt or despair. This man was Jacob Burckhardt [1818–1897]. He was a professor of history and art in his native Basel.[4] He was proud to be a citizen of one of the last poleis in the world, although this pride was somewhat tinged with irony—for it was obvious that new social strata were gradually wresting control from the hands of the patrician élite to which the Burckhardts, ministers, and professors, had belonged for almost two hundred years. Except for a short interruption at the School of Engineering in Zürich, Jacob Burckhardt spent all his professional life as a teacher in his native university and in the adult education courses in that city. He had made up his mind that his native city was the only spot in the world where he could think and teach whatever he liked without being obliged to comply with the political whims of governments or public opinion. He refused all calls to German chairs, including one to Berlin as successor to Leopold von Ranke [1795–1886]. He was free of academic vanities and ambitions and desired no more than to be an independent thinker and a good teacher. He abstained from all political activity, not because he lived in an ivory tower, but because he felt that one had to make a choice between politics and scholarship. He had started as a liberal journalist who believed that the hope of a free society could be realized by careful steering between the Scylla of brutal absolutism and the Charybdis of fanatical radicalism. In 1845, he had experienced the revolt of the radical nationalists in Lucerne—with tempestuous mass meetings, riots, and armed storm troops. This experience had broken his faith in the future of the liberal movement. Since those days, he had not ceased to warn his radical and revolutionary friends in Germany that the masses they were arousing would quickly push them aside and establish their own rule that would not be liberal at all. They would, on the contrary, defeat the moderate and educated liberalism of the middle classes. Burckhardt had given up politics because he could not see the means of remedying a situation that was to lead in a dangerous direction, very obvious to him. He summarized his experience in a letter to Gottfried Kinkel [1815–1882]:

> The term liberty sounds beautiful and perfect. However, no one should be permitted to speak about it who has not faced the possible slavery which may be brought about by the pressure of the mob and who has not had the experience of civil rebellion. Nothing is more pitiable than a government which is subject to the intrigues of so-called liberal clubs, of pressure groups and political profiteers. I know too much history to expect from the despotism of the masses anything but the rule of violence which will extinguish all these liberties.[5]

Burckhardt rejected the reproach of his revolutionary friends that he wanted to live as a luxurious Epicurean, an amused onlooker and esthete.

> It does not make much difference whether I do or do not serve liberty and the state; they will not lose very much if I abstain. No state is built by such men as I. As long as I live, however, I will be kindly and cooperate with my fellow men. I will try to be a sincere and honest private man. . . . With society at large, I have no longer any direct contact. I cannot but view with irony any social institution unless it have a specific purpose. . . . All of you do not know as yet what the "people" is and how easily it is transformed into a barbarian mob. You still do not realize what tyranny will be imposed upon the mind on the assumption that education is the secret ally of capital which must be destroyed. I am afraid that the intellectuals are fools if they believe that they can control the movement. The latter will emerge as a natural catastrophe. . . . I should like to experience no more of these times, had I not a duty therein, for I wish to help rescue as much as lies within my limited power. . . . We may all go under. I will at least choose the cause for which I shall go under—namely, the culture of old Europe.[6]

Jacob Burckhardt's personal problem was the question of the responsibility of the scholar in a time of revolutionary change. He felt that it was his duty to work for the preservation of intellectual standards and to establish a tradition of that intellectual heritage that might help to build a new world after the revolutionary deluge has subsided. He lived in Basel like a stoic or epicurean philosopher in the Roman Empire or like Tocqueville during a similar period of revolutionary stress. But Burckhardt did not choose this life of a modest teacher in a small Swiss town in the spirit of a grave and rigid asceticism. It was his way of avoiding the social requirements of the academic life; yet, it is an exemplary life of quiet, ironical service—the ideal life of the ideal scholar. It is the purpose of this article to analyze and to interpret how he succeeded in this enterprise. Burckhardt's name is familiar to all students of Nietzsche.[7] When Nietzsche came to teach in Basel, he was already an independent and original scholar. He was longing for the friendship of the man whose conception of history and particularly whose attitude toward modernity had so much affinity with his own. However, Nietzsche never succeeded in overcoming the benevolent distance of the older man. In spite of their common admiration for Arthur Schopenhauer [1788–1860] and their love of Hellas, Burckhardt could not give Nietzsche the friendship Nietzsche desired. Burckhardt disliked the romantic character and was suspicious of a man who could be an ardent follower of the indecent magician of Tribschen, Richard Wagner [1813–1883]. He was shocked by Nietzsche's Teutonic radicalism and watched with uneasiness his inclination toward despotism and absolutism. Nevertheless, Nietzsche was among the few who knew during his lifetime that Burckhardt was more than a professor or a historian, that he was indeed a prophet and a sage.

The professional historians of the time had no appreciation whatsoever for the original and unique character of Jacob Burckhardt's ideas. Those historians who were nationalists or liberals could not forgive Burckhardt his frankly expressed misgivings with respect to the development of the centralized national state and his unpleasant predictions about a future of revolutions, world wars, and tyrannies. It was a common practice to belittle his political insight and praise the "nobility of his vision" and the "perfection of his prose." This was a polite way of disregarding Burckhardt's specific contribution to historical thought.[8]

Only two writers seemed to have grasped the original and new character of Burckhardt's contribution to historical scholarship. One was Wilhelm Dilthey [1833–1911],[9] who was later to follow in many ways the suggestion contained in Burckhardt's *The Civilization of the Renaissance in Italy*. The other author is an anonymous American who reviewed the American translation of Burckhardt's study of the Renaissance in the *New York Herald* of October 1, 1878.[10]

Both reviewers wonder why the Civilization of the Renaissance in Italy is labeled the work of an "historian." Both agree on the definition of a true historian as a scientist who analyzes social causation, and it is obvious to them that Burckhardt is not interested in this approach. Both critics rightly state that he analyzes the diverse aspects of a situation only to the extent that they point to a specific character that integrates the variety of individual attitudes and achievements.

Both emphasize that Burckhardt interprets this situation in the context of Western civilization as a period of transition that fulfills a specific function in this whole. The American author is more articulate. He shows that this period of transition is a period of decline similar to that of the Roman Empire in its last stages. He does not seem to be aware that Burckhardt's first book dealt exactly with the decay of the pagan and the rise of the Christian commonwealth.[11] The book on the Renaissance describes the decline of the medieval world and the dawn of modern civilization with its specific modes of thinking and feeling. The anonymous reviewer rightly points out that Burckhardt connects and confronts this situation with the present. That is, he is interested in the genesis of the modern period because he is gravely concerned with contemporary modernity and its problematic character. The critic feels that Burckhardt wishes to give an objective and comprehensive picture of an epoch whose negative and destructive elements are only too clear both to Burckhardt and to the anonymous writer. The reviewer himself predicts that the antagonistic elements of modern civilization will necessarily bring into being a reaction, a new synthesis that will meet the challenge of the disintegrating modern world. He seems to relish Burckhardt's lucid understanding of the decadent state of the contemporary scene. Burckhardt's study of the Renaissance is both a careful reading of history and a personal document of great value. "Never were the aspects of human life presented in forms so manifold and in hues so particolored as in the kaleidoscope which Burckhardt holds to the eye of the reader and slowly turns in his hand." Indeed, the anonymous reviewer could not have used a better image for describing the specific character of Burckhardt's historical work than that of "kaleidoscope." This is exactly what Burckhardt succeeds in doing. He cuts vertical lines through the Italian society of the fifteenth century and analyzes the new attitudes and patterns of behavior such as the cultivation of the individual self, and the resulting objectification of its societal relationships and its attitude to nature. He is aware of the larger consequences of the separation of state and society and of the general trend toward secularization. He interprets the variety of these phenomena as indicating the emergence of a new type of man, self-reliant and pragmatic, rational and brutal, disillusioned and sympathetic, hard and humble. This new man comes into existence in the urban and secular centers of modern society, both in tyrant-states and democratic states. The reviewer is aware that this is primarily an investigation of human nature as it unfolds in the historical world. It is an empirical work with philosophical intent, if it is philosophical to wonder at the scope of human action and suffering. Burckhardt's historical work is reminiscent of what an English critic once praised as an outstanding feature of Goethe's vision—panoramic ability, a term that corresponds exactly to the "kaleidoscope" of which the anonymous American reviewer speaks.

Burckhardt practiced this new method of research in all his historical studies and particularly in his Reflections on History, a series of lectures published posthumously and containing a ripe summary of his philosophy of history.[12]

The Method

At the very beginning of his reflections, Burckhardt warns that he does not intend to contribute to the epistemological and technical discussion of history as a scientific discipline. He considers the situation of academic historiography to be as critical as that of the contemporary life of which it is a product. In Burckhardt's view, modern historiography suffers from rapidly expanding specialization and the unending accumulation of data. Consequently, political history is very uncertain in both its criteria and conclusions. Political history must continuously be revised and corrected. The specialized historian has lost all initiative to refer his special field of knowledge to a higher and greater whole. He is helpless before the true problem of the historian—interpreting his individual facts with reference to a structure or a whole. And only within such a context can the historian understand and make clear the significance of individual actions or events. This is the most important and most serious drawback of the historian as a specialist. Burckhardt learned from Goethe that we can grasp the universal only in the individual and concrete phenomenon. He realized that every individual fact has a specific form or *morphe*, which is the universal element in the concrete; Goethe's theory of form, an anticipation of the fundamental thesis of the Gestalt-School, is basic to Burckhardt's critique of modern specialization. Burckhardt is not a romantic. Specialization cannot be stopped. However, we must remain lovers of the whole and attempt to understand the unity beneath the variety. Burckhardt's reflections are addressed to the open-minded people who still desire to understand this strange phenomenon of man in the world of history. He warns that modern historiography is beset by many dangers. Subjective interests, provincialism, and narrow patriotism are jeopardizing all efforts to arrive at objective truth. A source of particularly grave harm to genuine scientific research is the vainglory of the modern progressive spirit. The typical modern believes that the whole past was a mere prelude to our time, which is the consummation of the historical process. Burckhardt warns that we must rid ourselves of this parochial vanity if we wish to understand, even if only in a very fragmentary way, the riddle of life that we call history.

In his reflections on history, Burckhardt presents a hypothesis that questions all that his contemporaries, whether historians or philosophers of history, took for granted. For Burckhardt, history is the life of man in the world; this fragment is the field of study beyond whose limits he refuses to venture. We know nothing about the transcendental or immanent meaning of history. We can only present observations and reflections on the way human beings act and are acted upon. We have no knowledge of a divine providence, nor can we take for granted the grandiose generalizations of the philosophers who "hear the grass of necessity growing." Burckhardt refuses to consider origins, climate, and race. Anthropologists are forced to make and to change too many hypotheses. He doubts if the very process of evolution can teach us anything about the phenomena themselves.

This life of history, always unfolding between an origin and an end, in continuous movement and change, is the material to which Burckhardt applies his new historical method. This limited field of research forces Burckhardt to define the general task of the historian and the means of achieving it. "The task of history as a whole is to show its twin aspects, distinct yet identical, proceeding from the fact that, first, the spiritual has a historical aspect under which it appears as change . . . and that, secondly, every event has a spiritual aspect by which it partakes of immortality." In this sense, Burckhardt conceives of history as historicity, as the eternal present and the presence of the eternal. It is Burckhardt's concern to evoke the memory of the past as a spiritual continuum, and he believes that the study of the historical aspects of the spiritual sphere is the most fascinating of themes. This definition of the task of the historian is in itself a historical fact. Burckhardt believes that beginning with the wars of 1864, 1866, and 1870, the world will witness an era of wars and crises, of growing and accelerating catastrophe, against which all that we know of European history will seem petty and insignificant indeed. In this situation, it must be the duty of the responsible historian to protect those values that may be preserved and cultivated even in the face of catastrophe. Burckhardt is not an idealist; he knows that the orders of a single barbarian chieftain can in one stroke dispose of the most precious men and spiritual goods. Still, the historian must help to safeguard the traditions of this heritage and cultivate the consciousness of the eternal present in times of conflagration. As historical human beings, the historians must pay tribute to the antinomies of life that are "the main phenomenon of history." This "main phenomenon" is the interaction of power and spirit in social institutions and their continuous revision, reform, and revolution by the ideal forces of the spirit. This is the fundamental fact of historicity. All human beings are subject to these fateful transformations. It is inevitable that we suffer this being in history. However, we are also capable of transcending our fate through contemplation. Burckhardt is of the opinion that only the spirit of contemplation can save human beings from the danger of being completely conditioned in the situation of history. We are able to attain objective knowledge because we share an identical human constitution, whatever the kaleidoscope of human appearances under the pressure of divergent conditions. We can achieve this "objectivity" and "panoramic ability" only if we rid ourselves of the fears and interests of the self through acts of contemplation. Burckhardt never mentions that this was the genuine philosophical attitude of the ancients. They were capable of genuine and liberating philosophical reflection because they loved the illumination of knowledge more than their own needs and sorrows. Burckhardt wishes to open his students' minds to the proposition that the highest human condition is the pursuit of life in the disinterested spirit of sympathetic understanding. Only such personal purification can make transparent the intellectual and moral aspects of human action. This procedure will allow us to appreciate correctly and with the moderation of scientific insight the price human societies must pay for the realization of some of their values and the destruction of others. This, Burckhardt says, is a "pathological" approach, pathological in the twofold sense that it involves in all its concreteness the dignity and the misery of human existence. This method Burckhardt names "history of civilization." He is aware that this term is ambiguous and imprecise. Burckhardt is not interested in the accumulation of data on cultural achievements and products; he does not care for "antiquities." He is only interested in one aspect of history. He wishes to describe, to the extent that these data express the working of the mind of historical man, the phenomena of human self-realization. He takes up the study of man as the central theme of history in a new and precarious situation. We are ignorant of the objective meaning of the process that we call history. If there is something like a divine providence, it is hidden, and we have not heard the word of redemption. We are only capable of wondering at this strange and fascinating existence that we experience in life, of wondering at man in his elevation and in his suffering. Human history is to Jacob Burckhardt *passio humana*.

Man is no longer protected by a divine grace; he is not sheltered in an all-embracing stream of the universe; he is alone with the powers of his reason and spirit and with his own passions in a concrete situation in the historical world. Only through disinterested contemplation can we hope to understand the wonderful character of this life that transcends itself in the very immanence of existence.

Contemplation is a right, a duty, and a necessity. It is a right of our "higher pragmatism" to understand the place where we are and the velocity of the contemporary dynamics in which we have been living since the French Revolution; it is a duty if we are to preserve the heritage of the mind in times of radical change; it is a necessity to establish inner independence and spiritual freedom in times of universal determination and pressure against the individual. For this reason, the contemplation of history that Burckhardt teaches is a method of transcending history in order to establish freedom. From this point of view, his effort is parallel to the work of William James [1842–1910]. James achieved in the field of psychology what Burckhardt did for history: he reopened the avenue toward the creative and spontaneous freedom of the human personality in times of general determinism. Burckhardt was able to master his "panoramic ability" because he used categories that were different from those of the political historians. He rejects chronological evolution. He directs his attention to the invariable factors in history. These factors can merely indicate fundamental tendencies and basic needs of the human being. This is precisely Burckhardt's problem: to classify and to describe the recurrent, typical, and invariable patterns of human and social behavior that constitute a human situation in historical time. With his unfailing sensitivity, Dilthey understood that Burckhardt's generalizations have nothing in common with the statistical classifications of the natural sciences. Burckhardt maintained a humanistic distrust of the power of abstract conceptions to recreate the living whole of a concrete human phenomenon. Dilthey defined lucidly the frame of reference of Burckhardt's generalizations. Burckhardt's general conceptions, Dilthey writes, refer to the identity and the dynamic unity of the human being; they are categories of historical and social morphology. They present general modes of existence that appear in changing concatenations in all human situations and in all human phenomena. These categories Burckhardt applied only to the most unquestioned source materials, to documents of the highest objectivity that disclose something about the inner life of men placed in a concrete historical situation, presenting typical attitudes and modes of expression of a variety of human standards in their individual concreteness. This unity of the individual and of the general in the existence of historical man is the central theme of Burckhardt's historical writings. He was not satisfied with the term *kulturgeschichtlich*. What he proposed, and to a large extent achieved, is a historical sociology centered around the *passio humana*.

Historical Sociology

Dilthey clearly understood that Burckhardt's so-called "history of civilization" is a phenomenological description of the human situation in a historical setting. This study of human intentions and attitudes is related to a frame of reference constituted by the interdependent structure of invariables that indicate specific acts and intentions. Unfortunately, Burckhardt has described them as social institutions: state, religion, culture. He intends to say that human conduct and social action can be attributed to certain acts that express basic needs and intentions. These acts are power, devotion, and creative intelligence. They are the fundamentals of the spheres of politics, religion, and culture. They are interdependent and antagonistic at the same time. They are antinomies and yet a continuous unity. The concatenation of their forces establishes the frame of reference for every historical situation. There may be epochs in which the one or the other invariable prevails. But we cannot imagine any period that cannot be referred to this fundamental structure. This scheme did not remain a mere theory. Burckhardt tested its productivity in all his historical works. They all start with an analysis of the political institutions within which and in relation to which all social and cultural acts attain their specific, positive or negative, significance. It is even intimated, to cite one case, that the political institutions of the Renaissance have made possible and bred the modern secular and competitive individual, in tyrannies as well as in democratic states.

For Burckhardt, the political sphere is the primary phenomenon of history. It is the synthesis of the brute force of physical or collective superiority with the "sound force" of creative reason. This is a long and terrible process. Burckhardt, a scholar of the historical school, rejects all contract theories of the state. Physical force and violence are certainly the primary factors in the origin of the state. However, once established, the state is, in Burckhardt's terms, "the abdication of the individual," a formulation reminiscent of the seventeenth or eighteenth century rather than of the romanticism of the historical school. The climate of moral and political enlightenment pervades the work of Burckhardt in many respects; it is, if we take the formulation with a grain of salt, the revolt of the lucid and clear reasoning of the moralist against the romantic transfiguration of history. There is still another element implied in this analysis of the foundations of the state. It is a sober Machiavellian realism. The foundations of the state are irrational—it is the imposition of physical superiority of individuals or of collectivities upon the physically weaker, who are often the better, the nobler, the more cultured. Burckhardt states frequently that the institution of the body politic that makes possible the shift from brute force to meaningful strength, lawfulness, and morality can arise only on the basis of this irrational explosion of power. Burckhardt's recurrent emphasis on this terrible and cruel primacy of the state in all societal relationships is a reaction against the "unverifiable optimism" that assumes that society is the primary phenomenon, and the state is merely the protector of law. "Men are quite different." We must take for granted that the dark forces of violence are at play wherever we establish enduring social institutions. We must be content if the established state can function as trustee and guardian of law and security. The basis of the expanding power of our political institutions is the inseparable unity of fear and greed. It is the fundamental manifestation of human vitality that strives for law and security in order to cast off the feeling of insecurity and of the inexhaustible thirst for power. Burckhardt described this phenomenon as a primary empirical fact, the basis of all social action. He shudders, but he does not wish to escape this reality. He simply evaluates it negatively. "Power is evil in itself." This is not an expression of a simple moralism. Burckhardt is too realistic an observer not to be aware that matter and spirit, freedom and authority, power and spirit are interrelated antinomies. However, it seems that the formulation of this thesis is incorrect and needs a careful reexamination. He speaks of the power of an institution, not of an individual potency, of accumulation and of the agglomeration of individual desires and needs into a collective and abstract selfishness that becomes an end in itself because of the never-ending pressure of the mutually supporting individuals who constitute the collective force. This abstract and autonomous desire to expand and to grow is the natural egotism of the individual whose sole end is the enjoyment of his brute power. Burckhardt elevated it to a position of social dignity as the basis of collective existence. Whatever religion or morality may teach to the contrary, this right to egotism is taken for granted. This is a dangerous precedent for all social and moral obligations. For the state has no absolute value nor has it the status of an a priori. When the state is permitted to dispense with the moral law, crime, terror, and violence will spread throughout society. The state will unleash the natural demons of the human race in all political and societal relationships. In his definition of collective power, Burckhardt formulates a secularized version of the idea of "original sin." Burckhardt bravely accepts the pessimistic doctrine without the comforts of transcendental hope. This stand made it possible for Burckhardt to reject the optimism of Hegel and Ranke regarding the logic, harmony, and spiritual meaning inherent in the process of history. Modern historians and philosophers of progress are too eager to forget the terrible price mankind has to pay for all the spiritual values that emerged under the stimulus of the state. It is always wise to remember the paradox of historical life—that good things can come from evil origins and evil may be the consequence of the best deeds. Burckhardt calls the complex of basic acts upon which states are founded, "power." And power is to him "evil in itself." Power indicates the abstract and autonomous pressure of a collectivity that expands for its own sake without purpose or direction. However, there is a different type of power, the radiant strength of the individual that Burckhardt calls "historical greatness." His treatment of this theme shows the careful and perspicacious observer who investigates the strata and attitudes that determine and establish greatness in history. He stresses the point that what we call "historical greatness" is a sociological phenomenon. It presupposes two things: a qualified man and a society in need of saviors. There may be times in which great men are abundant for tasks to which society does not attach any value, and there may be other times that are in need of a specific salvation and cannot find the man for the task. There is no preestablished harmony between historical periods and genius. However, where this meeting does take place, it is a kind of "holy wedding" between man and the historical process. The sociological condition for the recognition of a great man is a disrupted society in which the fundamentals of life are questioned and his leadership needed to recover social unity and help others achieve meaningful lives. These leaders possess certain recurrent qualifications: a fanatical will, a concentration of all energies, the vision of a universal idea of salvation on a political, social, or religious plane, and the subtle control of all details of action. These general faculties may meet with the requirements of a group when the prospective great man succeeds in discovering the cause or the principle, the devotion to which will reestablish the self-reliance and faith of the society in question.

"Great men" are always exceptions, never the highest products of normalcy. Whether they destroy or build (and it is sometimes difficult to determine the significance of their deeds), they are the "whips of destiny."

As in the analysis of political power, Burckhardt, in his reflections on the rôle of "great men" in history, insists that the lust for power is the main incentive for greatness. However, it must merge with an ideal of political, social, or religious perfection, the devotion to which makes possible the emergence of "historical greatness."

Burckhardt considers the existence of "great men" in history an indispensable fact. It is as indispensable as the demonic acts upon which the body politic is founded. However, it is not a fact that we should praise enthusiastically. These men can accomplish their mission only when they are equipped with a hardness of soul that enables them to exploit all chances of success and with strength that will enable them to endure the adversities and misfortunes that may fall upon the keen and daring revolutionist, whether he be the founder of a political commonwealth or of a religion.

There is only one exception that meets with Burckhardt's approval:

> Greatness of soul does not occur frequently among the great men of history. It comes into existence when men are able to renounce advantages in favor of moral goods and to practice self-restraint by virtue of inner kindness, not for the sake of prudence. Political greatness, however, must be selfish and must exploit all advantages. . . . We cannot require greatness of soul *a priori*, because the great man in politics appears as the exception, not as the ideal image. . . . It would be desirable if the great man would betray a conscious awareness of his relation to the spiritual and cultural forces of his times. . . . Such men will achieve a sublimity of genius and will enjoy the true understanding of their historical significance during their lives. Such a man was Caesar.

Greatness of soul may be perfect if a political leader possesses grace of character and a lasting contempt of death, the will to reconcile, and a grain of kindness.

Burckhardt recapitulates the theory of power on the plane of individual potency. To achieve a harmonious and just life, the sound force of creative reason must merge with the forces of brute power. Burckhardt insists on the thesis that the great men who survive as ideal images are of great value for mankind and, in particular, for their nations. They often give them a pathos and a dignity that spread to all strata of society. They raise the standards of a people by their very normality and comfort them in times of emergency.

Burckhardt presented this as a sociological thesis and discusses at length the contemporary efforts to belittle the role of the "great man" in history. "Contemporaries believe that if people will only mind their own business political morality will improve of itself and history will be purged of the crimes of the 'great men.' These optimists forget that the common people too are greedy and envious and when resisted tend to turn to collective violence." He sees everywhere a trend toward centralized and rationalized organization that will lower standards and spread general mediocrity.

In contrast to this trend, Burckhardt sees the recurrent desire for leaders and great men in the political field. He recalls that France was longing for a great man in 1848 and was eventually satisfied with Louis-Napoléon [1808–1873], who was an adventurer and a crook. He predicts that the social conflicts of the time will create situations of emergency in which people will cry for "great men" and will find them among people who correspond to their tastes.

He writes to a friend:

> [March 12, 1883] There will be no monarchy in France. History now runs differently than in the past. The change from democracy to an authoritarian regime no longer takes place through the tyranny of one man. He could easily be disposed of by dynamite. The new tyranny will be the domination of a military corporation. These fellows will apply means which the most terrible despot of the past could not have imagined.

> [April 13, 1882] For a long time I have been aware that we are driving toward the alternative of complete democracy and absolute despotism without right and law. This despotic regime will not be practiced any longer by dynasties. They are too soft and kind-hearted. The new tyrannies will be in the hands of military commandos which will call themselves republican. I am still reluctant to imagine a world the rulers of which will be completely indifferent to law, well-being, profitable labor, industry, credit, etc., and will govern with absolute brutality.

He visualizes the "great men" of the revolutionary military corporations as men with the talents of noncommissioned officers. That is how "historical greatness" will look when the conflict between capital and labor on the continent enters its more violent stages. Burckhardt's analysis of the phenomenon of power in its diverse aspects have made clear that there is an invariable "power" directed toward establishing enduring social institutions and stabilizing deeds of conquest and usurpation into legal property. This invariable meets with the requirements of another invariable that Burckhardt calls "culture." He defines the term as describing all free and spontaneous acts arising out of the material and ideal needs of man—it is the sphere of human independence and of freedom. In sociological terminology, it is the sphere of society, the opposite of coercive power and of the pressure of systematized violence that is embodied in the state.

These two invariables condition each other all the time. The state conditions culture where the body politic prevails, and culture conditions the state when society is the stronger. Burckhardt's analysis of these interacting invariables is a valuable contribution to historical sociology. It is his thesis that even in a democratic city-state such as Athens, not to speak of the rigid institutions of ancient Egypt, the scope and the direction of the cultural acts were determined or, at least, influenced by the political structure. The political institutions of Egypt were a hindrance to any emergence of independent and personal thought, imagination, or feeling. They favored training in technical skill and professional efficiency. It is, therefore, not surprising that ancient Egypt made so distinguished a contribution to mathematics, astronomy, and medicine—science that can be divorced from the personality of the scientist. Even in democratic Athens, the political structure imposed so many social obligations and conventions upon the citizen that this initiative was greatly restricted.

Political societies stimulate and appreciate technical learning and skills in applied knowledge. Societies that are released from political obligations, like those of the Hellenistic world, the Roman Empire, or the absolutistic states between the Renaissance and the French Revolution, are favorable to the idle curiosity of contemplation and to reflection on the fundamentals of life that have no direct bearing upon practical tasks.

The conflict between the invariable trend toward individual independence and the opposite invariable of enduring order in politics is a constant theme of Burckhardt's thought. In his historical studies, the diverse aspects of this conflict and the types of conquest are thoroughly analyzed. The conquest of freedom as against the pressure of changing determinants is the vital problem of his thinking and teaching. Burckhardt states as an empirical fact of human conduct what Aristotle had postulated as a philosopher—that freedom as a true good is a mean between license and submission. Burckhardt was a young man when he wrote to one of his radical friends that even the revolutionary leader, if he wishes to succeed, must learn to think and act with moderation. In Burckhardt's history of Greek civilization, this problem plays a decisive role. Cleon and Alcibiades are presented as men who turned institutions of political liberty into tools of their selfish ambitions. Through their vanity and greed, they have upset the delicate balance that Pericles achieved through devotion to the cause of the Athenian democracy.

In Burckhardt's studies of the Renaissance, Pietro Aretino [1492–1556] plays the role of the perfect villain. Aretino wasted his great gifts in the pursuit of the most vulgar pleasures. As his counterimage, Burckhardt presents the lucid and pure character of Vittorino da Feltre [1378–1446]. He was surrounded by the temptations of the courts and could have accumulated wealth and honors. But he was careful to preserve his independence in his devotion to his school and to his students. He succeeded in convincing the princes that it is the highest privilege of the intelligent ruler to grant all gifted children an opportunity to study. He succeeded in recruiting half of his student body from among the gifted poor. This devotion to a cause Burckhardt praises as an example of true independence under the most adverse conditions of a tyrannical state. Burckhardt constantly returns to the problem of the independent personality and the means of securing such independence in a world of social and political pressure. He describes the attitudes of the Greek and Hellenistic philosophers, from Socrates to the Cynics, Epicureans, and Stoics, as identical in spite of their metaphysical differences. The central problem of their philosophies is the concern with intellectual independence and spontaneity and the search for the means whereby they can be realized in a world of pressure and of philosophical emptiness. Their asceticism anticipates the withdrawal of the last philosophical pagans and of the early eremites who escaped the degradation of their societies to achieve spiritual liberty and intellectual independence.

This emphasis on the independent personality leads us into the center of Burckhardt's human philosophy. Despite the inescapable historicity of human destiny, the reality of freedom always remains as a challenge and source of wonder. Human beings devote their lives and sacrifice themselves for values, ideas, and principles through which they achieve freedom. They know too that these ideal goods are subject to social pressure and change. Nevertheless, they devote themselves unconditionally to conditioned values and causes. This seems to Burckhardt the miraculous element in human fate. For this is what man is, after all: an enigmatic and wonderful being capable of the noble and sublime as well as of the degrading and the cruel. This voluntary obedience to the summum bonum establishes freedom. Next to this conquest of freedom as an absolute truth, there is a second absolute social truth—namely, the royal right of civilizations to conquer the barbarians. But Burckhardt immediately questions his own certainty. "It is questionable indeed whether the conquered barbarians can ever become completely civilized, whether they will not always remain what they are!"

Although Burckhardt admits that the political frame of reference conditions primarily the sphere of society, he devotes much effort to the analysis of the impact of society-culture on political institutions. This is for him the crux of the problem of the crisis of modern civilization and of human independence. He takes for granted that society and the political institutions are two indispensable invariables in the historical constitution of man. He sees that the trend of events on the European continent leads to a situation in which the interdependent action of the two invariables is destroyed. It is the paradox of modern life that the same societies that boast of their civil rights and their freedom from the power of the state are, on the other hand, eager to see the state in control of all the functions of society. Burckhardt defined the state as the "abdication of the individual." As for the future, he predicts the rise of a political Leviathan that will bring about the abdication both of the individual and of society. More than any other philosopher or historian of the nineteenth century, Burckhardt saw the coming of the totalitarian state. Burckhardt was certain that the European society of his time was drifting in the direction of a new tyranny: when society is paralyzed by social conflicts, it is forced to expand the powers of the state to an undreamt-of degree. Furthermore, technical and economic conditions are extremely favorable to the increase of the organized power of the state. This was the future of European society, as Burckhardt saw it, in the midst of the optimistic nineteenth century. The tyrant state will prevail for a long time, although finally there will be a new effort of the "ideal forces" to reestablish freedom and the dignity of the individual person.

Logically, Burckhardt could have limited his constellation of the invariables to the dichotomy of power and spirit. He singles out the religious invariable as an independent factor separate from the church. He speaks of the church as a stabilizing force in society, thus bringing it close to the state. And he is moved to make this assumption based on the experience of the Christian churches that have attempted to establish and enforce a monopoly of the truth. However, he says, "All religions claim to be as eternal as the visible world and each of them possesses an enduring human significance that may partly justify the claim. . . . Every higher religion is perhaps relatively eternal. . . . All ecclesiastical institutions elaborate the spiritual vision of the founders into a dogmatic system and establish its validity by virtue of the authority of the church."

Burckhardt sees the primary phenomenon of religion as an invariable in contrast with the sociological phenomenon of religious institutions. The sources of this "primary phenomenon" are the need of overcoming the finiteness and the fragmentary character of the human person and the devotion to a larger whole. This awareness of a spiritual element in human nature as the lasting source of religious acts makes Burckhardt insist on the thesis that religion and the quest for meaning are the roots of every civilization.

Granted the eternity of the religious intention, he refuses to admit the eternity of any ecclesiastical institution. Every religion originates in history and is subject to the destiny of a historical phenomenon that becomes a social institution. Religions become entangled in relationships of power and of vested interests, in particular, as interacting and interdependent with the body politic. Therefore, religions are both historical and eternal at the same time. The historicity of religion does not mean an evolution of this invariable.

The diverse types of religion—such as supernatural-transcendental, mystical-pantheistic, magical-ritualistic—correspond to different depths of the religious experience and have affinities to different types of societies. The development and the diffusion of religions are primarily sociological phenomena. The material content of the religious message and the moment of its success are determined by the social conditions of the respective groups, in particular, by the character of the elite. For it is the elite that ultimately decides on the positive or negative appreciation of a religious doctrine, the masses easily yielding because they cannot resist when a firm and determined conviction faces their own gloomy, unsettled, and nihilistic opinions. Burckhardt's analyses of the sociological implications of Mohammed's religion are a model of sociological realism at its best. This religion is a "terrible simplification" of Jewish and Christian ideas, intended to satisfy the needs of predatory tribes at the lowest cultural level. Burckhardt similarly subjected some of the paradoxical aspects of the Reformation to a sociological analysis. It is the paradox of the Reformation that it was originally intended to set free the religious inwardness of the individual and actually delivered the moral and spiritual forces of man to the political powers. In terms similar to those used by John Neville Figgis [1866–1919] and Georges de Lagarde [1898–1967], Burckhardt pointed out the fatal affinity of Martin Luther [1483–1546] to Niccolò Machiavelli [1469–1527] and his tragic success in the unconscious promotion of modern secularization. Finally, he remarks that the Reformation was supported by those groups that had reason to expect to benefit by the unloosening of the spiritual and secular ties.

Burckhardt's most important contribution to a sociology of religion is the analysis of the conditions under which the Christian Church became a part of the Roman Empire. The persecutions under Diocletian [244–311] had the positive effect of uniting the conflicting

Christian sects into one strong hierarchical body. It was this well-functioning body with its strict and rigid organization that made it attractive to Constantine the Great [272–337] as the power best fitted to take over the administration of the empire. Furthermore, among the competing religions, the Christian denomination was in possession of an intelligible and simple message of salvation that appealed to many social and religious needs. Burckhardt analyzed this turning point in the history of the Church: first, it was the unique opportunity to spread the Gospel among the pagans and the barbarian tribes; second, it was a great opportunity to merge the ancient civilization into the new religion; third, it was the terrible temptation faced by the church to get involved with the state and its lust for power.

The change from an ascetic and otherworldly religion to a political institution jeopardized the true message of Christianity—that is, the conquest of life and the establishment of spiritual freedom through the ascetic life. Franz Overbeck [1837–1905] and Karl Barth [1886–1968] have taken up Burckhardt's suggestions regarding monasticism and asceticism as the true meaning of the Gospel.

Burckhardt believed that only through separation from power could the genuine spirit of religion be reborn. Only then will religion again be a manifestation of the urge for freedom and an ideal power capable of making its own contribution toward the rebuilding of the world.

Burckhardt takes for granted that religion is a fundamental act of the human constitution; it is interdependent with the invariables of power and culture. Wherever and whenever religions arise, they are bound to limit the scope and the volume of cultural activities. This can be a positive or a negative consequence of the religious expansion. It can be negative, if we assume that human potentialities are completely absorbed and suppressed; it can be positive, if we assume that that which is frustrated in a religious civilization is "destined" to be reborn in future societies as naive and spontaneous human creativity. The impact of religion will always be positive as an indispensable condition for the arts and for poetry. Religion is the only source of the deepest and the simplest truth about the whole; through its absorption in the arts, religion has delivered the souls of men from fear and superstition and gives them an intelligible idea of the tremendous and overwhelming power of the spirit.

The careful and considered weighing of the positive and negative effects of the invariables in human action dictates moderation in all theories about the "necessity" of historical events. Nevertheless, we encounter the term *necessity* quite often in the writings of this most violent critic of the philosophy of history of Georg Hegel [1770–1831]. The Reformation was "necessary"; the modern mind is termed *necessary*; the House of Borgia [1455–1672] is dubbed "necessary," etc. On the other hand, Burckhardt ridicules the historians who hear "the grass of necessity growing." Through his empirical investigations, he questions the belief that each moment possesses a relative necessity, as a preparation for the next stage in the historical process. "Vulgar is the delusion that acts of terrorism and lawlessness can be justified as historical necessities in the name of expected results." In each moment there are accidents, errors, and personal guilt that cannot be removed. There were great potential religious forces in Italy at the time of the German Reformation; but the Italians did not have the "chance."

What is the meaning of these contradictory statements? Revolutionary changes like the Renaissance or the Reformation must evade in detail and in general philosophical deductions regarding their origins and their evolution. There always remains a riddle because we are never capable of learning all the relevant facts. We can speak of necessities only in a hypothetical form. Burckhardt speaks of "necessity" as the diagonal in the concatenations of conditions in a specific situation. In this empirical sense, necessities mean tendencies that probably will prevail when we succeed in measuring correctly the strength and reality of the constituents of the social structure.

A general reflection on Burckhardt's conceptions is in place. Burckhardt was a student of Hegel, Ranke, Schopenhauer, and Eduard von Hartmann [1842–1906]. He never uses their terms in a strict philosophical sense. He feels that what he has to say is "untimely" and goes beyond the limits of academic thought. For this reason, we must never take his words too literally; we must read him with a grain of salt. Burckhardt ascribes revolutionary power to the spontaneous and independent spirit that freely criticizes the established institutions from the point of view of absolute values. This intellectual freedom makes possible social change. While Max Weber [1864–1920] described this invariable as a "historical" form of modern pragmatic rationalism, Burckhardt is well aware that the revolutionary action of reason has two aspects. It can produce social change and it can "conquer earthly things." It is historical and transhistorical at the same time. It makes possible the transcendence of man's historical self because all acts of knowledge and of spiritual insight attain an objective stand beyond the flux of time. A close study of Burckhardt's works can easily demonstrate that he always identifies the ideal and the spiritual forces as the powers that enable man to become free in a world of general determination.

Burckhardt states that the deepest ground of all religion and knowledge is the conquest of "earthly things." Conquest of the "earthly things" is the end of human perfection. Burckhardt's teachings will give the modern student who is bewildered by the pressure of history the intellectual instruments to transcend the limits of historicism. Burckhardt does not recommend any specific doctrine; he practices the intellectual discipline of the ancients. He is convinced that contemplation will make men free.

However, in his inexorable realism he does not forget that this freedom cannot be practiced outside of an established social order the foundations of which are cemented with violence and force. Facing this antinomy, he asks the question to which the agnostic has no answer: "Perhaps both the man who aims at the free and spontaneous acts of culture and the man who strives for power are but blind instruments in the service of a third unknown power."

Burckhardt presents his reader with many such antinomies that seem to be reconciled in the lives of individual men. For this reason, one may say that Burckhardt's historical sociology is an empirical science with philosophical intent.

History and the Arts

There is still another avenue leading to the transcendence of history. Burckhardt opened this road in his writings on art and the history of art.[13] His approach and his intentions in these writings are parallel to those he applied to the study of history. He is mainly concerned with giving his students scientific instruments for the intelligent interpretation of works of art, dwelling on those aspects of art that can be communicated. In these studies, the works of art are interpreted as the ideal expression of a historical situation, as the unending effort of the human generations in the sequence of time to interpret their being in time and space in symbols and images. The analysis of form occupies an important part in these studies, but his main task is to make the reader and student aware that all these works of art manifest certain aspects of human nature and have some bearing on the understanding of man's existence in the world.

As in his historical studies, so in his studies of art, Burckhardt does not care much for anecdotes and dates. Just as in his reflections on history, he subjected the generalizations of the philosophers to a sound skeptical scrutiny; he is equally suspicious of the theories of the "experts" on aesthetics. Burckhardt, the historian of art, teaches that we encounter the riddle of life, which is the historical existence of man, in the ineffable mystery of the great works of art. Through specialized research, we may conquer some of the secrets of nature; we shall never lift the veil of the living spirit residing in the perfect achievements of the great artists. This is neither defeatism nor irrationalism. It simply means that the definitions of the philosophers are most inadequate means of grasping the living totality of a work of art. The scholar can only describe the constituent elements of the beautiful work of art and the criteria of its perfection.

The arts and their history should be taught as an important element of education and of the interpretation of the self in space and time. The arts are a most powerful factor as a historical phenomenon and an effective and constructive force in the lives of societies. In their highest accomplishments, they disclose the paradox of perfection and absolute value in spite of human finiteness in history. Burckhardt insists on the unique character of the plastic and literary arts. In terms similar to those employed by Henri Bergson, he describes the "spiritual surplus" that comes into existence in the course of any material activity. "This spiritual surplus becomes conscious thought and reflection in the work of art." Burckhardt elaborates:

> Before man himself realizes it, there has awakened in him a need totally different from that which led him to begin his work. It is this new need which continues to grow and make itself felt. This new need which we may identify with the platonic eros can be demonstrated most evidently in the works of art. They constitute a reality of their own, a second creation. . . . They arise from mysterious vibrations communicated to the soul. What is released by those vibrations has ceased to be individual and temporal and has become symbolically significant and immortal.

Burckhardt is striving to arouse in the responsible teacher who is concerned with the growth of an individual person an awareness of the ultimate perspectives of art. Precisely for this reason, Burckhardt wishes to give the student the measuring rods that will enable him to recognize what is truly original, powerful, and great in art. This training will shape the student's whole outlook and his philosophy of life. Only through such training can we be prepared for that "blessed hour" of illuminating experience in which we understand the unity and the wholeness of a great work of art. It can help us understand the sphere of art as the realm of pure and disinterested contemplation. It may teach us that the arts are not synonymous with entertainment and relaxation. They are not substitutes for happiness, and yet they sometimes do transfigure the highest moments of human experience and can make transparent and lucid the confusing and unintelligible destinies of man in the world.

More than in his historical studies, Burckhardt in his works on art praises the "otherwise extremely unpleasant nineteenth century" for having made possible the objective understanding of ancient and foreign works of art. This is not a small achievement. It contrasted with those centuries that appreciated only art that complied with the values of their own specific historical situation. The Renaissance and Baroque had no understanding for the positive value of the Gothic arts; the moderns care little for Baroque art. With the breakdown of political, religious, and social monopolies during the nineteenth century, an avenue was opened that permitted the approach to a variety of artistic experiences. Modern open-mindedness made it possible to visualize three different aspects of the works of art: we can understand them as expressing an individual situation; we may appreciate them as a timeless revelation of the human mind in time; and, eventually, we can recognize them as the very phenomena through which men may achieve a mode of knowledge far superior to the technical discoveries of the sciences and the insights of philosophy.

The modern unbiased eagerness to understand the diversity of expressions, forms, and patterns in all civilizations has had positive effects on the very being of man. It has enlarged the horizon of our thinking and raised the level of our experiences. The very fascination of beauty in the work of art releases in the understanding person an unrest leading from the finite and imperfect to the true and perfect being. Burckhardt believes that the teaching of the history of art is capable of transforming the individual, widening his understanding, and increasing the powers that make it possible to live in historical time and to transcend it in the eternal present of the spirit. Under the precarious conditions that are the artist's lot in the modern world, the study of art can demonstrate the power of the desire to achieve works of beauty despite unfavorable social conditions. The teacher can point out the nature of the artistic intention in every type of civilization and its ability to overcome social contempt or indifference. In contrast to the mobility and the revolutionary dynamics of the nineteenth century, Burckhardt's reflections on the meaning of art establish a sphere of contemplation unknown to the past. We learn to take the historicity of art and of man for granted, understanding the pluralistic eternity of artistic accomplishments and the diverse strata of artistic expression as various modes of interpreting the world. In his art studies, Burckhardt is the true teacher educating his reader to understand the works of art as means of communicating knowledge about the truth of the whole.

There is a profound similarity between Burckhardt's conception of the task of historiography and art study. In his conception, history is concerned with the study of civilization. For the study of art, he coined the rather awkward term, *systematic history of art.* What he actually practiced was the sociological analysis of artistic forms and changing patterns. He took for granted that art has an autonomous existence but regarded it as his own task to study the impact of societal relationships on these autonomous problems. "Perhaps I am disenchanting the history of art. . . . I wish to concentrate on the prose elements in the arts." His sober realism revolted against a purely idealistic or spiritual treatment of the works of art. There are societal relationships between the artist and the collector that may be highly relevant for the problems of the artist and their solution. The sense of glory and of social prestige originating in the illegitimate governments of the Italian Renaissance and their regard for the power of public opinion makes it possible to explain the monumental intentions of the Italian architects. The inclinations and preferences of the collectors whether they belonged to the nobility, to the patricians, or to the wealthy middle classes, had bearing on the artistic production, influencing and changing the technical and material problems of the artist. Burckhardt's essays on the collector, on the portrait, and on the altar-piece are unsurpassed models of this sociological approach toward art. It is the great merit of these studies that they make clear different strata of depth in the history of the arts. Burckhardt is clear-sighted enough to realize that the formal and technical problems with which the artist is forced to grapple are as relevant a determining factor as his sociological position. His conception of the systematic and sociological treatment of the arts points exactly to this problem of connecting the historical situation of the artistic and technical problems with the social situation of artist and collector and of elucidating the transhistoricity of the work of art. The focusing element in this science of art remains the interrelationship and interdependence between the changing contents and the perennial forms of art. As in the historical life of man, Burckhardt assumes in the history of art, too, the existence of recurrent and invariable trends and intentions that appear in the patterns of specific forms. Their contact and merging with the technical problems produce the changes in the development of the arts. However, Burckhardt strongly assumes that the conditions of the external and internal world remain only incentives to the artistic intention. "The small pattern of a form is the germ of the sublime and great form, not the wonderful vision of the artist." Burckhardt taught his students that they must first know what the artist was able to express in a given historical situation with its technical, material, and artistic problems. Only when these questions are cleared, can we approach the problems of the historicity and transhistoricity of the works of art.

Burckhardt discriminates very carefully between the diverse levels of art. There are art products whose purpose is solely to entertain; there are works of art that represent the accomplishments of a style. The great and rare works of perfection are beyond these general levels of artistic achievements. In a very formal sense, all works of art are, as objects of human thought and imagination, historical. What Burckhardt calls "historical immortality" is attributed only to works of art that bear the mark of greatness. He defines this term as indicating an achievement that is irreplaceable and unique. It is the manifestation of a human personality that succeeds in unifying a variety of experiences with an integrating intelligence and imagination. Burckhardt is quite positive that the greatness of artists or poets may be defined only in moral terms. There are many men of genius in all ways of life. Most of them spend their gifts without true devotion to a cause. Burckhardt refuses to concede greatness in an artist of the outstanding craftsmanship of Andrea del Sarto [1486–1530] because of his miserable character. He praises Raphael [1483–1520]: "Raphael's supreme personal quality is not of esthetic, but of moral quality: his overwhelming integrity and the iron will he put in his efforts to conquer the highest perfection he could possibly grasp. . . .

He was never satisfied with his achievements." He praises Rubens [1577–1640] in the same terms. His greatness is described as a never-ending education and cultivation of the self, the sincere and naive pursuit of his work in spite of all worldly distractions and complete independence in his work. "There was much of happiness in his life . . . and he left much happiness to posterity."

These men are truly great. And this is the only greatness that Burckhardt considers sublime and normative, in contrast to which historical greatness is a manifestation of the exceptional and the abnormal. These men are great because they devoted their lives to ideal creation and applied their tremendous energies and moral will to its realization. The quest for greatness in the sphere of art corresponds to the quest for wisdom in the sphere of history as an indispensable condition for the transcendence of history.

Burckhardt states frequently that even in the sphere of the arts greatness is never a purely esthetic or formal category. His analyses of esthetic phenomena have clarified the diversity and hierarchy of the human attitudes that find expression in the works of art. However, the very core of Burckhardt's aesthetic conceptions is contained in his studies of Renaissance culture. It is Raphael, Burckhardt maintains, who is the creator of the specific pattern of modern beauty. His work has become the modern image of perfection through harmony. "Raphael lives in a world crowded by holy, mythical, secular characters of an ideal order which the artist seems to have fashioned with a sort of immediate ease. . . . Raphael alone was able to realize great spiritual powers!" Burckhardt's praise of Raphael has often been wrongly interpreted as an epigonic classicism. For Burckhardt, he is the artist who established the image of "sublime humanity." He gave expression to the individual personality that succeeds in conquering the "earthly things" by virtue of his moral and intellectual power, transforming the contradictory and antagonistic elements of life into a wholistic and meaningful order and context. He is historical and modern in so far as he achieves this monumental living unity on the small basis of his moderate and harmonious subjectivity. In the past, the artist simply had to reproduce a universal order that was valid and taken for granted. Esthetic perfection had no autonomous or particular significance; it was merely an element of religious or philosophical contemplation. Raphael was the first to create an artistic cosmos that was his personal universe. This personal achievement of beauty has a profound moral and spiritual significance. Therefore, Burckhardt assumes that Raphael's work is the triumph not of an epigonic, but of a normative classicism. It is the purest and simplest conquest of life through the self-redemption of man by virtue of contemplation and imagination. It establishes in the plastic arts an invariable normative classicism that is an expression of the pure and normal life at its highest. His work is transhistorical in the formal sense and perennial as an expression of the conquest of life.

Burckhardt's praise of Raphaelian classicism can be fully understood only when seen against his judgement of Michelangelo [1475–1564]. Michelangelo is the modern artist kat'exochen [par excellence—Eds.]. To find himself he must oppose tradition, classical and Christian myths, and the conventions of style. He is always restless, straining to discover new and unheard of possibilities of representing the human body. In his relations with others, he is arbitrary, violent, and imposing. He represents the other pole of modernity—the radical, the immoderate element. Raphael is his counterimage, the rational, reconciled, and harmonious personality.

In Michelangelo, with his density and tension, is mirrored the self-dramatization of the modern epoch amidst the insoluble conflicts in which it is caught. Michelangelo aims at the most naturalistic, physiological realism; at the same time, he aspires to express the superhuman that he embodies in excessive attitudes, violent movements, and exaggerated positions. That which was later to degenerate to mere vulgarity and perversity appears in Michelangelo as "restrained monstrosity." It is the opposite of Raphael's "sublime humanity." Raphael gives expression to the invariable of disinterested and pure rationality; Michelangelo tells the story of modern man caught in the coils of his own irrational desires and unable to transcend history. "Michelangelo has neglected all the beautiful attitudes of the soul. There is not much in his work that can be cherished among the highest human values." Burckhardt concedes the grandeur of Michelangelo's genius, but it is the grandeur of a violent, radical, torn soul, incapable of achieving balance and harmony. His work remains the manifestation of a problematic human situation, a record of a tragic period in human history, like Euripides's [480–406 BC] dramas. Raphael and Aeschylus [525–456 BC] mirror their times, but they also transcend their historical moment, whereas Euripides and Michelangelo merely express it. Burckhardt's approach to works of art is always determined by this question whether its author has succeeded in transcending historicity or has merely given expression to it. He praises Rubens for the same reasons as those he mentions in his apotheosis of Raphael. Rubens is the last expression of a world of plenitude and nobility, a man who succeeded in merging the multitudinous images that threatened to overwhelm him into a harmonious cosmos, over which he was master.

Burckhardt's art studies are sometimes regarded as guidebooks. Indeed they are, but not guides for the amateur and collector; they are really guides to the sublime and perfect life. To Burckhardt, the world of forms discloses a variety of basic human tendencies and intentions whose value is measured by the horizon they embrace. The arts have relevance for him only in terms of the search for and the achievement of wisdom. The arts are modes of human knowledge, the ultimate aim of which is to help man transcend his historical perspective, to make his life more transparent, to see it in the light of that magic that appears real because it is conquered by the ideal powers of natural reason and balanced wisdom.

It is not an accident that the man who has extolled the greatness of Raphael and Rubens should speak in the last pages of his Cicerone with the purest admiration of Claude Lorrain [1600–1682]: "His work radiates an ineffable enchantment. . . . Claude, a candid soul of sublime integrity, turns to nature for comfort. In his work reality and ideality seem to coincide as the highest grace, merging nature and mind." Johann Wolfgang von Goethe [1749–1832] spoke of the great French painter in almost the same terms: "There you have a complete man who thought and felt nobly. In his soul dwelt a world that we do not encounter often in the outer world. His paintings possess the highest truth, but not a trace of reality. He knows the real world thoroughly in all its details, but he uses them merely as tools for expressing the world of his beautiful soul. This is the true ideality: to use reality in such a way that the truth of the imagination creates the illusion of reality."

Like Goethe, Burckhardt was of the opinion that the highest achievement of art is not tragic and dramatic genius, but elevated normalcy and wise moderation. These are the human presuppositions for the transcendence of history and of "earthly things"; this is not a monopoly of the scholar or the artist. It is possible wherever a pure and candid soul devotes himself to the contemplative and imaginative understanding of the wonder of human existence in the world. Homer remains for Burckhardt the greatest poet and Goethe's "Nausikaa" fragment—the superb expression of this spirit of "sublime humanity" in an ugly and blasé civilization.

There remains one utterance that contains the core of Burckhardt's teaching. He is speaking of Luca della Robbia [1400–1482]. We know that his work is not the highest artistic achievement. However, it "is perfect beauty of a kind. He teaches us to understand the soul of the fifteenth century at its most beautiful. Naturalism is his presupposition, but he presents it with a simplicity, graciousness, and tenderness, which brings him close to the sublime style. What may seem to us a religious expression is only the manifestation of a profoundly peaceful, serene, and unsentimental humanity."

This is indeed the secret key to the transcendence of history: to devote one's highest efforts to the task of making life transparent through imaginative contemplation. Burckhardt's interpretation of the function of the arts opens an avenue to the conquest of historicity.

Philosophy of Man in the World of History

Burckhardt's pioneering work in historical and cultural sociology questioned and made evident the problematic presuppositions of contemporary philosophies of history. He insisted on the scientific and empirical character of his work. Nevertheless, this work implies a philosophy of its own, as the positive verification of the theories that he refuted by his empirical research. Burckhardt referred to his point of view as "sound skepticism." This must be explained. It is not "debunking." It is the sober realism of empirical investigation that disregards all hypotheses of anthropology and of theology. As students of history, Burckhardt asserts, we do not have knowledge of the origins and the end of history. There is no immanent and no transcendent meaning of history of which we are aware. The origins are dark and uncertain; the field of investigation is only the life of man in the higher civilizations. It is a continuous and mobile process. "This is the whole, the great and serious whole that we call history." It is the continuity and interdependent action of mankind. The process may appear as evolution or as a cyclical movement; it is subordinate to the movement of the whole. The life of mankind is a whole in which every individual exists not for his own sake, but for the sake of the past and all the future. This statement is the more remarkable, since the author was an opponent of the dehumanizing evolutionism that regards each moment merely as the preparation for the next. Burckhardt insists on the eternity of the present. He admits that the single historical moment does possess a functional meaning within the context of the "higher necessity," but what can we know of this "great and serious whole" and its necessity after we have rejected the intellectualism of the philosophies of progress? The answer is that this "whole" is as ineffable as the genuine work of art. This primary philosophical attitude in the face of man's life in the world is as rational and intelligible as the "sound skepticism" of which Burckhardt was so fond. This whole of history is an open and dynamic unity of antinomies. The life of mankind is a continuous development of antagonistic tendencies. Cooperation and strife, the power of vitality and liberation through "sound reason," are intertwined in the dynamic whole. In this context, our responsibilities for the whole can only mean that our choice of a way of life is only one element in the totality of this whole. There is a universal solidarity of suffering and of intellectual responsibility for the whole of mankind; this is the logical interpretation of Burckhardt's statement on the "higher necessity." For life is growth and development, however painful it may be. We *are* life; we eventually decide on the standards and the horizons of this life of the whole. Human beings make history through acting and being acted on, through imposing on fellow men and restricting their movements. History as a whole can mean only the revelation of the grandeur and misery of man under the determinations of his surroundings; it can mean only the never-ending dynamics of the evil and sound forces of man, their interaction, and their effects in shaping the spontaneous action of the human mind. To achieve a true understanding of the human situation in history, we must be aware of the enduring antinomies in human life, the antagonistic forces of vitality and mind, of the "material" and "higher" interests. Social life can take place only when these forces achieve a synthesis and a provisional equilibrium. Civilizations can develop only within the institutions of a body politic. No state has ever been founded, except through usurpation; no great power has ever been established except through crime. Only when the "sound forces" of man are added to the brute force of violence can power shift to strength, law, and order. These cruel, bloody, and mandevouring foundations of civilization make possible the security and continuity of social action without which no material and intellectual achievements are possible. This Machiavellian realism is one aspect of Burckhardt's sound skepticism. Usurpation is the foundation of social institutions. A secure social life will never be possible without the element of coercive force. Burckhardt ridicules the idealist assumption that a regime built on violence, lies, and terror cannot last. "As if states were ever built on anything else but on these evil forces." The political institutions are the frame of every civilization. For this reason, Burckhardt opens all his historical studies with an analysis of the political institutions within which human conduct and human civilization take place. He considers this dilemma of civilization from all angles: the highest civilizations are built upon the despair and the cries of the conquered and its ground is fertilized with the blood and sweat of its subjects. This brings him to the conclusion that "*Satanas*" (he adds: "in Christian terminology, but not in Christian spirit") is the ruler of the world. Violence and coercion show the demoniac selfishness of man who is driven by greed and fear. The original state is only the systematization of violence. In this sense, Burckhardt declares power to be "evil in itself." Power, however, must be distinguished from potency, which is a genuine element of greatness. In the "great man," vital power appears from the beginning as intellectual concentration and control of the will, directed toward a positive cause. But power is evil as the abstract accumulation of collective pressure that cannot control its urge toward expansion and encroachment upon others because desires and greed are infinite and inexhaustible. These powers are at the basis of civilization. It is the characteristic feature of human inertia to forget these dark origins of all culture after law and order have done their work of humanization. Good results do not eliminate the antinomies of human life; they cannot justify crimes and terror. We must never forget the terrible price mankind had to pay for establishing some bases of civilization. No rationalization makes it possible to remove perennial evil from the balance sheet of history. It is the dehumanizing attitude of the moderns to refer the whole historical process to themselves and to take the past for granted as the preparation of their own perfection. Burckhardt rejects this attitude. It is a scientific observation that throughout history the powers of evil have created positive and good things, and good intentions and actions have made possible the rise of dark and evil forces. Political history is the history of irrational and demoniac forces at work. Burckhardt draws the conclusion that we should not esteem this life more highly than it deserves. This attitude should not be confused with pessimism. As a true skeptic and realist, Burckhardt investigates all aspects of human phenomena. He is aware that in the antinomies of life, the evils of power have a lasting function in history. Evil power may rule for a long time, it may devastate civilization and sometimes extinguish the power of the spirit, but there will always be those who will be ready to meet the challenge of power with the quiet heroism of devotion to the values in which they believe. We must be cautious in interpreting this statement. It does not mean that the life of mankind is an equilibrium that is reestablished over and over again in the perennial interaction between the forces of evil and the "sound forces" of reason and spirit. Burckhardt does not imply that there is such harmony and order. He simply states that the pressure of war, revolution, and tyranny, the radical patterns of violence, sometimes make possible the reality of heroism, martyrdom, and righteousness which otherwise would not easily come to the fore. Goodness and greatness of soul, intellectual illumination and wisdom can coexist with the forces of evil and of wickedness. Sublime works of art can thrive on the "foul ground" of criminal and nihilistic politics, as happened in some states during the Italian Renaissance and in Athens in Socrates's time. Burckhardt seems to be astonished again and again by this coexistence of grandeur and misery in the life of man in the world. His theory of the antinomies in the structure of man's life in history has been fully verified in our time by the heroes and martyrs who resisted the Nazis and Fascists in spite of imminent torture and death. There have been outbursts of courage and defiance in our time that must raise our faith in human dignity, but also deepen our humility when we consider the cruelty and bestiality that provoked these acts of human grandeur. The intellectual discipline of Burckhardt's candid realism shows still another aspect that we may call the Epicurean as opposed to the Machiavellian. Not this or that social type, but man proper is Burckhardt's main concern. It is the deep love of man and the admiration of human potentialities that ultimately was behind his efforts to reestablish the image of man in a world unprotected by divine power and driven by the forces of nature; it is man capable of the highest intellectual sublimity and the most delicate tenderness and, at the same time, the possible embodiment of bestiality and greed.

He establishes as the center of human grandeur the unconditioned devotion to a cause that is conditioned in its historicity. This is not an expression of nihilism.[14] Burckhardt believes in the positive potentiality of man to live up to obligations and norms that can appear only in historical forms. Burckhardt takes the historicity of man for granted because he believes him capable of making the historical disguises transparent and becoming aware of the elements of truth, goodness, and beauty. In this, Burckhardt follows the ways of ancient philosophy. The thoughtful man can endure the awareness of the continuous changes and historicity of the mind. They are at the surface and do not touch the very essence of truth and value. We are capable of realizing true insight and the hint of the absolute within the perspective that is given in the historicity of our situation. This is enough to support the positivity of our being in devoting our efforts to a larger whole.

Burckhardt's teaching points to man's possibilities of establishing truth and objective knowledge about the human world if we break away from the narrow interests of our historical position. The aim of his guidebooks—through the labyrinth of historicity and the paradise of wisdom and of art—is to vindicate the idea of truth and knowledge in order to give human beings the opportunity to establish intellectual freedom and independence in a world in which men are increasingly surrounded by determinations. He reestablishes the dignity of contemplation in a rapidly expanding political world. He knows that we transcend the world of history and of its conditions when we rediscover the ancient way of contemplation. In the very acts of knowledge, we learn to control ourselves and establish distance towards the flux of time as well as to evaluate the process of history and its relevance for our being. This contemplation of man in the world is a responsibility. It involves the continuity of the mind. It proclaims the human right to establish freedom in the midst of universal dependence; it is also a necessity, if we are to clarify our own stand in the unending revolution of modern times. Objective thought makes clear the unwise limitation of all subjective approaches. It makes possible a true appreciation and calculation of the price men have to pay for all their achievements in the world of history. Burckhardt calls himself an "epigonus of humanitas." As such, he has taken up the torch of ancient wisdom and has lighted it to clear the dark fatalism of modern history and to overcome the historicism of modern collectivities. Like the Hellenistic epigoni, the Stoics and Epicureans, Burckhardt withdraws from the alignments of societal relationships and embraces human personality as opposed to its institutions. In this attempt, Burckhardt reflects upon being and the ranks of being and the differences of basic attitudes as indispensable elements of a comprehensive study of man.

This study of man in the world of history is for Burckhardt not a logical postulate. It is an existential attitude of a modern man who still feels himself a part of the whole. It is the attitude of a natural spontaneity and completeness that strives for independence. It is the brave and candid awareness of the loneliness of man in the world of history—awareness that in the secular modern world the thinker who investigates human conduct can only describe a variety of types of human grandeur and misery. It is the sublime necessity of the modern mind that it cannot take for granted the idea of a divine providence or any metaphysical theory of human nature. Only from the study of man in his historical world can we learn what and who we are, what we are striving for, and what are our successes and frustrations.

This is the philosophical implication of Burckhardt's historical sociology; it describes the phenomena that constitute the grandeur and misery of man and that disclose the perennial transcendence of man in the immanence of his being in the world. Burckhardt knew well indeed that his attitude was itself the result of a specific historical situation that had arisen in the Renaissance. In a remarkable passage of his *Civilization of the Renaissance in Italy*, Burckhardt quotes Pico della Mirandola [1463–1494], showing that the study of man in his concreteness can come into existence only when the religious belief in a divine guidance is gone. He quotes from Pico's *Oratio de Hominis Dignitate*: "Said God to Adam: I have placed you in the center of the world so that you may easily survey and inspect all that is around you. I created you a being neither celestial nor earthly, neither mortal nor immortal, so that you may be your own free creator and conqueror. You can degenerate into a beast or elevate yourself into a god-like being." This is precisely the origin of the modern situation. Burckhardt's conception of the meaning of man in the world must be understood in this context. Burckhardt described the character of his own work in terms almost identical to those in which Pico had stated the function of a philosophical science of man in the Renaissance.

> In our precarious and strange existence, we spontaneously limit ourselves to knowledge of man as such, to the knowledge of the empirical human race as we encounter it in the world and in history. . . . Are the three epochs of the world like the three day-times in the riddle of the Sphinx? Rather are they the continuous metempsychosis of the acting and suffering man through numberless disguises. Men in quest of genuine wisdom desire to illuminate all these changes and to cast away all partiality for specific periods, the more so, the more they are aware of human frailty. . . . As soon as we have understood that there never have been "golden" and "happy" epochs, nor ever will be, we shall break loose from the romantic transfiguration of any past, we shall rid ourselves of the unwise despair of the present and cease to indulge in wishful hopes regarding the future. We recognize in the contemplation of history one of the noblest concerns of man.

History as a whole is the *passio humana*. This study of man's greatness and humility may be a source of modest happiness in times of cataclysm. "There is happiness in the performance of acts of contemplation, in turning backward to preserve the heritage of the past, in turning cheerfully and serenely towards the future in a period in which one can easily fall victim to the pressure of material forces." Burckhardt was aware of the philosophical implications of his work. He knew that his presentation of the *passio humana* must raise many questions of a metaphysical and spiritual nature. Burckhardt was a modest and humble worker in the human universe which was to him both a labyrinth and a paradise. Whatever else may be the value of his guides to human historicity, there cannot be any doubt that they are windows to eternity. Burckhardt's life work was one long search for a stand "outside" the world in order to endure the human situation "within" the historical world. For this reason, he did not revolt, and he was not in despair. He was well aware that his teaching would help people to conquer "earthly things" without taking refuge in a religious belief, as did the ancient teachings of self-redemption. His teaching of the *passio humana* is a guide to the transcendence of continuously changing historical life and the sympathetic understanding of all manifestations of human self-realizations.

Like Arnold J. Toynbee [1889–1975], Burckhardt did not plead a return to classical or Christian ways of thinking or existence. However, it was an axiom of his analyses of religion that religion is the very root of civilization, and its limitations can only be transcended by a final effort of the ideal and spiritual powers of man. He was deeply convinced that after the new tyrannies have undergone a series of world wars, there will be an ultimate effort of the ideal and spiritual powers that will break the chains of dehumanizing slavery. This is not romantic idealism; it is the conviction that there are requirements of the human constitution that cannot be neglected without destroying the very character of man. Like Rainer Maria Rilke [1875–1926],[15] Burckhardt knew that there is *Unum Necessarium* which is still hidden and whose reappearance cannot be forced. He did not wait for it, and he did not need it personally. As a sociologist, he predicted the renaissance of the intellectual and spiritual powers in order to meet the challenges of a world of absolute determinations and to reestablish the dignity and independence of man.

Francis Bacon [1561–1626] had inaugurated the modern epoch with a philosophy that taught man to control nature and establish "the rule of man." At the end of this epoch, we find a human philosophy that makes it possible to control history and to reestablish the dignity and humility of man in his historical immortality while surrounded by the threats of nihilism and the all-devouring forces of totalitarianism in the social world.

Historiography of Crisis

Historical sociology is a rather recent science. Burckhardt's historical sociology may be described as a historiography of crisis. There are situations in history when the main concern shifts from the analysis of the general process to the empirical description of a single situation as a comprehensive kaleidoscope of the human universe. Tacitus [56–120] had developed a pattern of history that was revived by Burckhardt. Tacitus's work bears the imprint of the rule of tyranny under which he lived. Burckhardt predicted the forthcoming tyrannies of the totalitarian regimes. The actual and predictable realities of despotism produced the same reaction in the ancient and the modern historian. Both took their tragic times for granted; both served the spirit by carrying on the intellectual and moral heritage of the past, guarding those traditions that future generations will need when barbarian despotism will be gone. Both historians created a scientific pattern of historical sociology that analyzes types of human conduct and action in a specific situation. Tacitus lived through the period of Domitian [51–96]; Burckhardt anticipated in his vision the militaristic and radical despotisms of the twentieth-century totalitarian regimes. Both were resigned to the fact that intellectuals could not change the social institutions. Both endured the historical process as an inescapable fate. They did not attempt to escape the social careers that their respective societies offered them. Tacitus, the son of a provincial middle-class family, was eager to follow the traditional pattern of the administrative career, as it was the custom for a student of Law. Burckhardt, the son of a patrician family of Protestant ministers and professors, entered the academic career. These modest adjustments of the two historians did not interfere with their existential attitude toward their moral allegiances and intellectual obligations. This existential attitude meant that in a terroristic situation, in a despotic or revolutionary regime, it is the task of the scholar to preserve the meaning of *humanitas*. He can do that by collecting and describing the human phenomena that constitute the positive meaning of human existence or indicating what can happen with man under the degrading influence of such conditions. In tyrannies and revolutions, the formula of Lucretius [99–55 BC], "*Vitaï lampada tradunt*," imposes a terrific responsibility on the intellectual. In such situations, the intellectual, if he is to remain true to his calling, is forced to live outside the social situation. In such situations, he will cry with Seneca [4 BC–65 AD]: The house is burning!—and he will attempt to save it. In times of great emergency, the scholar will discover that his work is not primarily concerned with technical, logical, or methodological problems. He will realize that questions and approaches that have no final bearing on the intellectual growth and the illumination of the human mind are not the fundamental and crucial task of the scholar. In a situation of grave emergency, the intellectual will not deal any longer with the tricks and the refined techniques of his specific field. He will refer his field of investigation to fundamental human needs and concerns.

Scholars have sometimes rightly refused to classify the works of such authors as historical, referring to them as moralists. However, this is a very poor alternative. These men are not concerned with moral conduct, nor are they interested in social causation. Tacitus is primarily concerned with a variety of characters as they appear in a specific situation. He comments ironically on the archaic pattern of Roman chronological historiography that describes the annual accomplishments of the magistrates. This is a revolt against the pragmatic historians who reluctantly acknowledged the meaningful transformation of Rome into the Principate. This critical attitude indicates a consciousness that there is no immanent reason and significance in the political machine of the Roman Empire. It was merely a tremendously efficient, anonymous machine, which became possible because the republic had lost its aristocratic responsibilities and submitted itself to two groups of exploiting racketeers: the nobles and the knights. The military despotism supported by the middle classes had established a legal and administrative order for these unpolitical groups. Tacitus did not idealize the dead republic, nor did he praise the "new order." Thoughtful and intelligent men knew too well the price they had to pay for social and economic progress. The price was the slow but continuous destruction of the educated and cultured classes of the old republican nobility. Here, again, there was no romantic longing. Tacitus understood with a bitter clarity that with the destruction of those classes, intellectual independence and spiritual bravery were eliminated from the scene. The new ruling elite was the product of despotic regimes: rackets of informers, adventurers, profiteers, bankers, and businessmen. Teaching and education became a business too. Students were taught the most refined and sophisticated techniques of public speaking—but these were tricks, not convictions, dramatic gestures, not tragic spirit. In spite of its legal and economic security, the Rome in which Tacitus lived was a world of inner decay. Thus far, it may seem as though Tacitus's work is historical—a study of the fall and decline of the Roman nobility. However, this would be a superficial view of his work. Tacitus uses his critique of the archaic pattern of the chronological report as a means of discrediting pragmatic history and all philosophies or theologies of history. He presents a variety of human experiences and a diversity of human attitudes in face of an established tyranny. It is not a political accusation of the regime; it is the heartbreaking and breathtaking vision of what human beings are capable of under the conditions of a despotic regime. It is his explicit purpose to report the corruptibility and misery of man when a spark of a better future is visible in the attempts of Nerva [30–98] and Trajan [53–117] to reestablish a constitution. Tacitus presents historical personalities as social types who are molded by their institutions. The imperial court is the focusing center of the informers, the businessmen, the courtiers, the political generals who regard the empire as an opportunity for exploitation and a career. There is the society of the newly rich: bankers, merchantmen from Italy and the provinces who have no interest in politics and are only concerned with economic success. Tacitus does not indulge in wrath or despair. There are still other types of human conduct that come to the fore in this situation. There are the military and civil officers, generals and judges who cling to the traditions and virtues that had made Rome great. It is to their credit that the inner and external peace is preserved and that the legal and administrative machinery of the empire works fairly well. It is due to their quiet perseverance that this world retains some sort of continuity. They remain true to the traditions of service and devotion to the Republic, paying no attention to the tyrant in power. Gnaeus Julius Agricola [40–93] is supposed to be a pattern of living virtue in a world of vice. However, Tacitus is not completely convinced that this is the final form of perfection in a despotic world. There are remarks in *The Agricola* that show that Tacitus is not sure that it is possible to live an immaculate life in a world of license and terror and not to be co-responsible for the murderous acts of the tyrants. Agricola was a member of the senate, and he did not resist the rules of Domitian who ordered the senate to kill the brave and opposing members of this body. Tacitus knows well that the man of action, the citizen or the statesman, cannot indulge in an attitude of moderation and reconciliation in the radical situation of despotism. He is dimly aware that there is a sociological rule that decent and moral characters are forced into taking up the struggle for the principles of radical justice and equity only when the extreme opposites of arbitrariness and expediency are practiced by the tyrants. He entertains no illusions about the workings of this dialectic; it is possible to interpret the essay on Agricola as a defense rather than a praise of his father-in-law.

Tacitus's panoramic picture of the world of tyrants would not be complete if it had not included those men who refused to adjust themselves to this decadent social order. There are the political escapists (i.e., the members of the republican nobility who could not be induced to enter the imperial senate). They had withdrawn into privacy. They knew well that every tyrant would understand this act of nonconformism as an inimical revolutionary gesture. In a despotic regime, one yields or one faces confiscation of property, exile, and death. The defeated elite knew very well that there was no chance of victory for a revolt; nevertheless, they resisted. It was a moral attitude without any political bearing. They preferred death to an ignominious life, exile to servile behavior. This transformation of a supercilious and licentious elite into a nobility of moral and spiritual character is the positive reaction to extreme moral degradation. There is still another type of conduct originating under the rule of despots: the Stoic martyrs are the last type of human perfection that Tacitus describes. He does not speak of "the" intellectuals as a social group. The professors and literati made the best of the new situation. There were, naturally, only a select few who accomplished the highest perfection. They were the lay philosophers, like Seneca, and philosophical-minded laymen whose convictions were transformed into a religious faith. It is the only case in history where it is permitted to speak of philosophical martyrs. They suffered and gladly submitted to death as the ultimate refuge of independence and self-determination. They died for the sake of the human dignity that could eventually be vindicated only through suicide. They sacrificed their lives in order to remain true to the ideals of human integrity and decency. This philosophical religion was so widespread that wives joined their husbands, parents their sons, children their parents, friends each other, in voluntary suicide.

Tacitus presents a typology of human patterns of conduct in the concrete historical situation of a government of tyrants. There is no meaning in the flux of time that we call history, nor is there a divine providence embracing the human world. There are to be found at the same place and in the same moment wickedness and sublimity, meanness and heroism, refined cruelty and simple spirituality, sophisticated systems of terrorism and the commonsense belief in the dignity of man. These antinomies of human attitudes coexist in the radical situation of terrorism and despotism.

Tacitus's phenomenological presentation shows that a situation of violence makes possible the highest and the lowest potentialities of man. Men obviously need the severest stimuli, the blows of war, revolution, and despotism, in order to realize their highest and lowest potentialities in the here and now of the radical situation. There is no sheltering salvation and no celestial reward for the virtuous; there is no comfort of redemption, but the ineffable wonder of man's living in the world. To be humiliated and to humiliate, to control and be controlled, to act and be acted upon—this is man's grandeur and misery. There is no meaning in the immanent process of history, no divine providence, no all-embracing and protecting reason. There is only the hell and the heaven of man's conduct. This is *passio humana*.

Tacitus, the author, was a best seller at the courts of the absolutistic rulers of the sixteenth and seventeenth centuries. He taught them how to make servants obedient, how to organize an efficient secret police. Washington and Jefferson studied Tacitus carefully as a lasting witness of the degradation and corruption of man under the regime of tyrants.

The sociological study of man in history was not resumed until Jacob Burckhardt. Burckhardt developed his historical sociology under conditions very similar to those under which Tacitus lived and worked. Analogous conditions in the lives of the two historians produced a similar vision of historical man. In Burckhardt's time, the religious meaning of the Christian philosophy of life had vanished; the philosophical claims to have discovered the immanent meaning of history could not be verified by empirical research. The kaleidoscope of the variety and diversity of human attitudes and behavior patterns appeared to be more meaningful than the causal investigation in a chronological order. Burckhardt was terrified by the vision of the forthcoming radical tyrannies of the twentieth century and the prospect of a universal lowering of human standards and the abolition of human independence. This vision determined Burckhardt's humanistic efforts. In his historical studies, he did not present man in the situation of despotism in the political sense of the word. He selected periods of transition and crisis or catastrophe that have the same bearing on human conduct and human thinking. In times of radical change, men are no longer guided by principles and values that are taken for granted and that establish the natural evidence of a common way of life in a secure civilization. A general agreement on a set of moral and social principles makes for the continuity of a society—the antithesis of the revolutionary situation, which takes nothing for granted but the power and the determination to eliminate the opposing groups or individuals. In these emergencies, man will behave as in the situations of despotism. He remains alone with himself; he is free to make his choice for good or evil. Burckhardt selected the periods of transition from the pagan to the Christian and from the Christian to the secular modern world in order to show how in these unguided and unprotected periods men have to rely on themselves and to decide what path they choose to follow in face of the shattered fragments of a hollowed scale of values. It was Burckhardt's main task to point out how man meets himself in meeting nature, his fellow men, and the pressure of political institutions. Thus, his work and the work of Tacitus follow the same pattern. They establish a frame of reference within which the human person can move and act. This frame of reference dominates the picture of history. Within this historical frame, a variety of human attitudes and ways of living is possible. Pietro Aretina and Vittorino da Feltre, the noble and wise pagans in their country retreats and the radical and fanatical organizers of the Christianized Empire, the individual and collective tyrannies of Athens and Greece and the free personalities of the philosophers—they all present a panorama of the highest and lowest achievements of human conduct, of *passio humana*.

Burckhardt never mentions Tacitus as a forerunner of his own method and philosophy; he did not care very much for the Romans. Although Tacitus's works accompanied the young Burckhardt on his first voyage to Italy, he refers to this author only once. In the historical perspective, their affinity becomes conspicuous. Burckhardt himself was aware that his mode of living and thinking was nearest to that of the ancient philosophers and historians; he, who repudiated so proudly the grandiose generalizations of Hegel, the intolerable synthesis of power politics and Christian theodicy of Ranke, and the narrow pragmatism of the contemporary political historians, could find his ancestors only in the ancient world.

Explicitly, he claimed Thucydides as the ancestor of his own sociological-historical (*kulturgeschichtlich*) method. He feels himself the kin of Thucydides [460–395 BC] for three reasons. First, the Greek historian had broken with his ancestral mythos just as Burckhardt had relinquished Christian theology and the philosophies of progress. Both men were in full agreement that it is possible to investigate historical catastrophe with the highest degree of evidence and objectivity. Burckhardt praises Thucydides's skillful and cautious conceptions of general tendencies, the interaction of which establishes historical necessity. He admires Thucydides's success in making transparent and intelligible the causes and motives that brought about the debacle of Athens. They are evident for the common man as well as for the educated because Thucydides refers individual actions and situations to the general rules of human behavior in specific situations. Thucydides's reflections on the identity of human nature and its radical and unrestrained possibilities in situations of crisis and catastrophe anticipate Burckhardt's "pathological" hypotheses.

Second, Burckhardt regards the introduction and the first book of Thucydides's history as the source of his method. Thucydides compares typical situations and trends of development that have occurred in different parts of Greece at different times and subsumes these individual facts and actions under general concepts that enabled the historian to recognize general tendencies in individual actions, ideas, and desires. Burckhardt mentions, in particular, how Thucydides has made possible the sociological treatment of the migration trends, the analysis of the foundations of poleis, and the impact of economic and technological problems on domestic and foreign policies.

Third, Thucydides analyzed the inner structure of a situation of catastrophe as Burckhardt did in all historical works. Burckhardt is well aware that Thucydides writes the story of a political decay, not of the transition between different civilizations. Burckhardt is deeply struck by these first strides toward a comparative sociological method and by the insistence of the Greek author on the identity of human nature in the changing kaleidoscope of the historical world. This is the reason that Burckhardt insists on proclaiming Thucydides as the ancestor of his method in spite of his being a political historian.

Thucydides is more than the ancestor of Burckhardt's method. He has established the true image of scholarship in times of emergency. He does not comfort the Athenians; he serves no interest except the search for historical truth. His book was composed not for the applause of his contemporaries, but as a "possession for all time." It will not serve the narrow pragmatism of practical and utilitarian men who read history to learn how to behave in order to be successful. Thucydides strives for what Burckhardt has called the "higher pragmatism." He enlightened his contemporaries and later future generations so that they will remember this situation in analogous cases and will be able to make them transparent by the careful reference to the human constitution and its requirements.

It is indicative of the close affinity between Burckhardt and Thucydides that the latter has described almost in the same words the intention of his own writing and teaching. "Not to become shrewder for the next time, but wise forever," is Burckhardt's credo. It corresponds completely to the great master's "possession for all time." This correspondence makes evident Burckhardt's affinity with the classical world. The Greek tradition was the most precious good of the intellectual heritage which he labored to preserve for the future. It was the only civilization in which human beings had learned to act and to suffer as free and independent beings, and to transcend the narrow desires and needs of the individual. Finally, his civilization has made possible a way of life where human reason succeeded in making transparent the wonder of human existence and in becoming wise. Burckhardt carried on this heritage, and his own life is an image of the wise man: independent, serene, superior to history.[16]

Notes

1. Goethe to Zelter, June 7, 1835, in *Der Briefwechsel zwischen Goethe und Zelter*, ed. Max Hecker (Leipzig: Insel-Verlag, 1915), 2:339.

2. To A. M. Lanjuinais, March 10, 1859, in *Oeuvres and Correspondence inédites*, ed. Gustav de Beaumont (Paris: 1861), 2:484.

3. Karl Löwith: "On the Historical Understanding of Kierkegaard," *The Review of Religion*, (March 1943), 227–41; D. F. Swenson, *Something about Kierkegaard* (Minneapolis: 1941); Jean Wahl, *Études Kierkegaardiennes* (Paris: Aubier, 1938).

4. Jacob Burckhardt was a Swiss, not a German. We must never forget that the Swiss and Austrians have as much a civilization of their own, as have the Dutch or the Flemish, who certainly speak a German dialect.

5. Letter to Gottfried Kinkel, April 19, 1845, in *Selected Correspondence* (Leipzig: 1933), 241.

6. Letter to Eduard Schauenberg, February 28, 1846, in *Selected Correspondence*, 247.

7. See vol. 1 of Charles Andler, *Nietzsche, sa vie et sa pensée*, 6 vols. (Paris: Éditions Bossard, 1920–31). See also Karl Löwith, *Jacob Burckhardt* (Luzern: Vita Nova Verlag, 1936); Edgar Salin, *Jacob Burckhardt und Nietzsche* (Basel: Verlag der universitätsbibliothek, 1938).

8. Benedetto Croce, *Theory & History of Historiography* (New York: Harcourt, Brace, and Co., 1921); James Westfall Thompson with Bernard J. Holm, *History of Historical Writing*, 2 vols. (New York: Macmillan, 1942), 452–55.

9. Wilhelm Dilthey, *Gesammelte Werke* (Leipzig: 1936), 2: 7–76.

10. I wish to express my sincere gratitude to Mr. Robert E. Grayson, Director of Reference of *The New York Herald Tribune*, who was kind enough to inform me that the records do not indicate the name of the author. However, in my opinion, it seems highly probable that the writer who showed a rare mastery of the literature on the Renaissance and realized the unique qualities and the philosophical implications of the book was either Henry Adams or his brother Brooks Adams.

11. *The Times of Constantine the Great, Werke* (Basel: 1929), vol. 2.

12. Burckhardt's *Reflections on History* has been published in an English translation as *Force and Freedom, Reflections on History*, ed. James Hastings Nichols (New York: Pantheon, 1943). The publishing house deserves high praise for having done this pioneering job. The editor has given an excellent introduction, which made it possible to appreciate adequately Burckhardt's contribution to historical scholarship. Unfortunately, the translation is very poor, although it is fair to state that it is a difficult task to translate a Swiss-German author with leanings towards a French and Latin prose style. This is a limitation of a book, the publication of which should be accepted with gratitude.

13. *The Cicerone: an Art Guide to Painting in Italy for the Use of Travellers and Students*, trans. A. H. Clough (London: J. Murray, 1873); *Kunst der Renaissance in Italien*, ed. Heinrich Wölfflin (Stuttgart: Deutsche Verlags-Anstalt, 1932); *Beitrage zu Kunstgeschichte von Italien*, ed. Heinrich Wölfflin (Stuttgart: Deutsche Verlags-Anstalt, 1930); *Antike Kunst, Skulptur der Renaissance, Erinnerungen aus Rubens*, ed. Heinrich Wölfflin (Stuttgart: Deutsche Verlags-Anstalt, 1934).

14. Compare with Martin Heidegger's praise of heroism for the sake of heroism. See Heidegger, *Was ist Metaphysik?* (Frankfurt am Main: Klostermann, 1949), 23.

15. See *The Notebooks of Malte Laurids Brigge* (1910).

16. On Thucydides, see John H. Finley Jr., *Thucydides* (Cambridge: Harvard University Press, 1942). See also Ernst Kapp's review of Wolfgang Schadewaldt, *Die Geschichtsschreibung des Thukydides*, in *Gnomon* (1930), 76–100, esp. 92–95. On Tacitus, see Ronald Syme, *The Roman Revolution* (Oxford University Press, 1939); Cornelius Tacitus, *Dialogus Agricola*, ed. W. Peterson (Cambridge: Harvard University Press, Loeb Library, 1939); *Histories and Annals*, ed. C. H. Moore and J. Jackson (Cambridge: Harvard University Press, Loeb Library, 1925–37), 4 vols. See also Kurt von Fritz, *Aufbau und Absicht des Dialogs de Oratoribus* (Rheinisches Museum für Philologie, 1932).

15

Tönnies

Modern German sociology cannot be thought of without the fundamental work of Ferdinand Tönnies [1855–1936]. There were trends toward sociology during the nineteenth century, in Karl Marx [1818–1883] and Albert Schäffle [1831–1903], particularly, but they combined sociology with the philosophy of history. It was the great achievement of Tönnies to free sociology from this combination and to establish it as a social science of its own. And it is an acknowledgment of the particular character of his work that a few days before his death, in honor of his eightieth birthday, he received a book containing contributions from scholars in Greece, Japan, Italy, Netherlands, England, and Switzerland as well as the German essays.[1] The importance and appreciation of his work in the United States are evident in the contributions of Franz Boas [1858–1942] and Pitirim Sorokin [1889–1968]. And the contributions are not confined to sociologists. Historians, such as Friedrich Meinicke [1862–1954], and philosophers, such as Karl Löwith [1897–1973] and Herman Schmalenbach [1885–1950], point out the philosophical implications of his thought. But this common esteem must not deceive us on the influence of

---

Published originally in a slightly different form under the title, "In Memoriam Ferdinand Tönnies (1855-1936)," in *Social Research* 3 (August 1936), 441–62. Republished by permission from *Social Research*.

his work. Though his sociological concepts have not been neglected either by Max Weber [1864–1920] or by Alfred Vierkandt [1867–1953] and the younger generation (the most outstanding evidence is Schmalenbach's supplement of Tönnies's categories *Gemeinschaft* and *Gesellschaft* by the concept of league or *Bund*),[2] neither formal nor historical sociology has followed the direction and suggestions of his work. Hence, we may say that he dwelt in solitude, even in the last epoch of his glory under the German democracy. Although he suggested a genuine type of sociological thinking, why was he not able to create a sociological school?

He was solitary when he published the first edition of *Gemeinschaft und Gesellschaft* in 1887, with the subtitle *Communism and Socialism as Empirical Forms of Culture.* It was the first attempt at separating the transhistorical and historical elements within the social structure. He gave an analysis of the social process from the agrarian communism of the early historical periods to the modern capitalistic society, pointing out the elements of socialism implicit in this type of society. But he pushed through the realm of history and discovered in community and society transhistorical sociological categories correlated to the historical social concepts of communism and socialism. Both represent general types of social structure. The social ties of *community* are shaped by natural and emotional relationships, which integrate social existence. Hence, this sociological structure is based upon mutual sympathy and interdependence. The general type of *society* means a social structure that combines private and isolated individuals in a collectivity with utilitarian means-end relationships. Tönnies was the first to see and formulate this tension between the historical and the transhistorical within sociological concepts. Later on, he characterized the epistemological structure of his concepts as ideal types, in the sense of Max Weber, but first he emphasized the transhistorical character of sociological concepts.

This stimulating book did not impress anyone when it was published in 1887. Indeed, the general trend of German thought did not accept the sociological approach. *Die Gesellschaftswissenschaft: Ein Kritischer Versuch* [1859], the famous pamphlet against sociology by Heinrich von Treitschke [1834–1896], indicates emphatically the academic opposition to autonomous social sciences, which were believed to belong to political science. On the other hand, there were some productive trends toward genuine sociological methods in the historical school of economics, in Gustav von Schmoller [1838–1917] and Adolf Wagner [1835–1917], especially. In jurisprudence, Otto von Gierke [1841–1921], like Henry Maine [1822–1888] and Frederic William Maitland [1850–1906] in England, created a new type of sociological approach toward law by his *Genossenschafts* theory. Tönnies was profoundly influenced by the first two volumes of this work,[3] published some years before *Gemeinschaft und Gesellschaft*. Gierke represented a trend of thinking similar to Tönnies's. Gierke's profound analysis of the rationalized modern society based upon capitalism and upon the rational social philosophy of the law of nature led him to a description of other types of social organization. These types of association, however, are not linked up by utilitarian ends but have to be understood from within. Hence, it is no accident that later on, in his criticism of the first draft of the German Civil Code, Gierke accepted Tönnies's concept of community as opposed to the Romanistic and rationalized type of society that was at the basis of this plan.

This is only one example of how the disintegrating tendencies of modern industrial society created a general trend toward sociological thinking, quite independent of political questions and regardless of the status of sociology as a science. The question of what has happened to man and his social existence became the true intellectual expression of a situation of social unrest and uneasiness. A critical attitude toward the modern social structure joined the conservative Gierke and the progressive Tönnies in analyzing the trends of social dynamics and the general lines of a new social order. But because these sociological trends influenced the methods of economics, political science, and jurisprudence, there was no appreciation for Tönnies's attempt to establish sociology as a particular science.

Without being discouraged, Tönnies began to approach the problems of social life by a descriptive method that he later called "empirical sociology." Using statistical methods, he analyzed the most important trends in the moral affairs of life (such as marriage, crime, and suicide) in various social structures, emphasizing differences in behavior patterns in the country and in small and large cities. He pursued this type of empirical sociological description throughout his life and enriched the methods of social statistics by some new correlation concepts.

Not until twenty-five years after the first edition of *Gemeinschaft und Gesellschaft* could he publish a new and revised edition. This book had a great success, but this too was due to a misunderstanding. It was the time of the rising youth movement, especially among students, and they greeted Tönnies's book as a scientific expression of their own antirationalistic feelings and their enthusiasm for the vital powers of life. Many years later, he was even reproached by colleagues for having preferred the idea of community to that of society and for having neglected to create objective sociological concepts. Anyone who knows the work of Tönnies will be astonished by this misunderstanding. Almost no one in his epoch was so strong a rationalist and scientist as he, and nothing was stranger to his mind than the emotional drive and the irrationalism of the youth movement.

But what is perhaps more astonishing is the profound lack of comprehension for his work among the socialist intellectuals. Tönnies not only accepted socialism as the logical outcome implicit in the social presuppositions of modern society, but he also accepted the economic and sociological ideas of Marx and integrated them into his work. However, his sociological approach transformed the ideas and suggestions of Marx into a new structure of thinking, strange to the followers of Marx, and it may be that his approach was so strange and subjective that no one was willing to follow his way of thinking. Throughout the nineteenth century, sociology and sociological method were correlated with the social movement of labor and with the social problems involved in the disorganizing forces of industrial society, so that conservatives and progressives had the same critical starting point in the production of a new scientific view toward social life. The fundamental trend of Tönnies's sociological thought can be found in the early writings of Marx—in the idea of genuine democracy, later the idea of a classless society, a concept similar to Tönnies's idea of community, the coincidence of public and private life as in the ancient Greek polis.

And Gierke's *Genossenschafts* theory can be understood only as an attempt to conquer the atomistic and individualistic social theory of modern rationalized and capitalistic society by an organic theory of autonomous social groups as opposed to the mechanical theories of some western sociologists. Also, Émile Durkheim [1858–1917], who reviewed Tönnies's book, gave a striking example of the identity of intellectual movements in the same historical moment.[4] In his *De la Division du Travail Social* (1893), Durkheim described two types of social structure, designating as mechanical the social organization of the primitives, and as organic the rational modern structure with its social differentiation and stratification. Sorokin has pointed out that Durkheim used the concepts of Tönnies reversely, but he does not explain the causes of this difference.[5] It is based upon Durkheim's positivistic idealism, according to which the growing interdependence of modern social life will produce an organic solidarity of mankind opposed to the mechanical relationships in primitive societies. In contrast to Durkheim, Tönnies emphasized that the rational means-end relationships of modern society are mechanical, while the community integrates the individuals into an organic structure, with all its members held together by common transutilitarian values. Hence, the work of Tönnies is not isolated in the historical trend of social thought but is specific in its individual form.

Tönnies himself declared that it was his opposition to the Darwinist sociology of Herbert Spencer [1820–1903] that became the starting point of his sociological work. He agreed that we have to analyze the historical process as sociologists, but he denied the one-sidedness of Spencer's analysis of the different strata of life and their dynamics. What Tönnies was striving for was a genuine understanding of the different types of social structure and the inner ties of the different behavior patterns. They are the product of human nature in its development. And when he spoke of *will-relationships* as the basis of community and society, the term was not quite correct. His "essential will" (*Wesenwille*) and "arbitrary will" (*Kürwille*) are conceptions of two different aspects of the totality of human nature. The one is characterized by the prevalence of the transrational elements in the structure of man, the other by the priority of reason. But he misunderstood the epistemological structure of these concepts when he called them "psychological." They represent the genuine type of phenomenological description (in the sense of Edmund Husserl [1859–1938]), a kind of social phenomenology avant la lettre. This means that at the basis of his sociological analysis was a philosophical knowledge of human nature. It is no accident that as a heading for the chapter treating the forms of will, he chose Benedictus Spinoza's [1632–1677] *Voluntas atque intellectus unum et idem sunt*. This is the typical presupposition of the social philosophers of the seventeenth century. And for scholars he greatly admired, he knew no higher praise than to compare them with Thomas Hobbes [1588–1679], Hugo Grotius [1583–1645], and Samuel von Pufendorf [1632–1694]. Thus, in his sociological thinking, the types of social behavior patterns may change in respect to the shifting conditions of life and the different types of social structure, but human nature is one and the same throughout the change in the historical process. Therefore, sociology has to discover the permanent and natural trends of social relationships. And Tönnies emphatically pointed out that the different types of community and society may exist in the same social structure in different degrees. In his last book, *Geist der Neuzeit*, he applied his concepts to the process of western history. He called this sociological interpretation "applied sociology," as subordinated to theoretical sociology. Here, he reveals the wealth and the fertility of his sociological concepts, in combining the structural concepts of community and society with the formal concepts of social relations, groups, and associations. In correlating the strata of economic, political, and intellectual life to the general sociological ideas of individualism, domination, and associations, he analyzed the social function of these types of behavior throughout the different historical shapes and contents.

These types of behavior express the original social phenomena (*Urphänomene*), based upon the essence of human nature, and they recur throughout the historical process in various shapes and with different contents. This trend of thinking is fundamental to Tönnies's whole work, from *Gemeinschaft und Gesellschaft* to the *Geist der Neuzeit*. It is the attempt to integrate the anthropological, economic, and historical knowledge of his time into a system of sociological concepts and to break through the world of institutions and organizations in order to understand them as types of social behavior. They realize the different functions of human nature and represent as a whole the unity and complexity of human existence. In contrast to the radical agnosticism and nominalism of Max Weber, the sociological work of Tönnies is based upon a philosophical assumption concerning human nature, a starting point that links his work to the great philosophers of the law of nature. It is the meaning of his sociology to discover in empirical analysis the general traits of human nature, whatever may be the shifting forms of the historical types of social relations. The passionate scientific rationalism of Tönnies fought strongly against religion and theology, but he accepted the secularized basis of the law of nature, identifying nature, will, and reason as the unity of human existence, although in a changing constellation of its elements. His broke through historicism and relativism toward a natural system of social behavior patterns. A conception of sociology as the modern scientific type of the law of nature—this was the specific character of his work, and it was this that created the isolation of his thought. His work was really an untimely meditation, for no one of the sociologists who pursued his concepts was able to accept the philosophical background of his sociological approach. The analytical trend in all sciences had destroyed the scientific truth of his ideas on human nature and had dissolved it into a bundle of relations, which no science was capable of integrating to unity. This is the cause of his strange solitude in the midst of the praise and glory by which he was surrounded in the German democracy. The combination of the scientific achievements of the nineteenth century with the spirit of the social rationalism of the seventeenth century and the existential vitality of his Frisian temperament symbolizes the strength of his mind in spite of the disintegrated and abstract trends of the scientific methods of his time.

Tönnies developed the basic ideas found in *Gemeinschaft und Gesellschaft* in all his later books and essays. In his studies on folkways, he analyzed the organs and the expressions of the community structure, and their change as conditioned by the social process, and the same approach to an understanding of the typical forms of society led him to his researches on public opinion, progress, and religion.[6] The fundamental trend of his thinking is evident in the different strata of his intellectual experiences (*Bildungserlebnisse*): Marxism, law of nature, and romanticism.

In the presentation and the analysis of the modern social process and the relations between capital and labor, he followed the ideas Marx had developed in *Das Kapital.* And throughout his work, in describing the structure of either community or society, he acknowledged the basic ideas of historical materialism as the most efficient method of explaining the social process. He accepted historical materialism in the rather simple interpretation that the dynamics of the economic stratum determines the shape of political institutions and the types of intellectual and spiritual life but that there is a mutuality between the strata that constitute social existence. This agreement with the fundamental ideas of Marx does not, however, make Tönnies a Marxist. Nothing is more characteristic of his thinking than his transformation of these ideas. Repeatedly, in introducing the basic ideas of historical materialism, he started with the remark that Friedrich Schiller [1759–1805], the idealistic thinker and poet, knew well that the spiritual and intellectual development of man depends on his material and economic existence. And he often quoted Schiller's famous letter to Christian, Duke of Augustenburg [1798–1869], to wit, that man first needs food before he can progress to higher and more spiritual activities, that the masses are forced to be interested first in their economic and material aims. Thus, he understood the economic sphere as neither an historical nor an abstract isolated denominator of the total social life, but as the natural basis of social existence. This is the empirical sociological concept of anxiety as one natural type of social self-conservation. As an organic and natural function, it is one pillar that supports the house of man and has to be integrated into the frame of human existence. This is the peculiar character of Tönnies's interpretation of Marx: to accept the overwhelming importance of the economic trend in social life, but to treat the economic behavior patterns as a natural function of life. His sociological concepts were of a kind to destroy the economic entity and to dissolve it into natural social relations. While Marx made human nature economic, Tönnies made the economic realm natural. It is to Tönnies's merit that he called attention to the combination of historicism and the law of nature within the structure of Marx's work.

Whatever was the influence of Marx on Tönnies, the kernel of his thought can be understood only from his affinity to Thomas Hobbes [1588–1679] and the secularized type of the law of nature. Throughout his life, he worked at the publication of unknown works of Hobbes and at an edition of his letters.[7] He hoped to revive the ideas of this great social philosopher, who had been the first to give a sociological analysis of the growing capitalistic society.[8] Tönnies was the first to point out that the political works of Hobbes contain a genuine sociological theory of modern society based on an abstract rational law of nature. This natural law has to be correlated to the revolutionary dynamics of modern industrial society and is its outstanding intellectual expression. The theory endeavors to analyze the modern body politic as a rational collective will, integrating the variety of atomic individual wills and utilitarian ends into an order of peace, security, and reason based upon common consent and obedience. Social behavior patterns are linked by utilitarian means-end relationships. Hence, contracts and conventions are the types of these modern social relations, and rational conventions, instead of the folkways of a community, determine the prestige of social groups. Hobbes's strongly individualistic and secularized conception of the law of nature is distinguished from the theological and metaphysical law of nature of the continent. Tönnies contended that Hobbes's sociological approach was historical because his description was valid only for modern industrial and rational society, not for the Middle Ages, for large parts of the ancient world, or for the primitives. It is an achievement of Tönnies to have seen these limitations in the social philosophy of Hobbes. Since Tönnies accepted the general type of law of nature as sociology, he denied that the rational type is the unique one. He suggested that the rational theory of modern society should be completed by a law of nature concerning community (*Gemeinschaftsnaturrecht*). The basis of the sociological theory would be not the struggle of man but sympathy, mutual toleration, and peacefulness. This presupposition involves some consequences for the social norms in this system. There is a correlation of social rights and duties, the responsibility of each member to another corresponding to his function in the social body, with justice understood as the adequate distribution of common rights instead of the formal justice of a society of exchange. This means the coincidence of morals and law, and leads to socialism as the realization of the norms of community. Tönnies was particularly interested in the sociological theory implicit in the law of nature. It represented the great attempt to break through the relativism of the historical world and to establish a system of general concepts of social relations. This system is not a nominalistic classification but an empirical formula of the radiations and stratifications of human nature. The individual and particular trend in Tönnies's sociological thinking was to reestablish the social philosophy of the law of nature with the means of nineteenth-century sciences.

These two elements of Tönnies's thought, Hobbes and Marx, law of nature and historical materialism, have been newly observed by Raymond Aron [1905–1983] in his excellent presentation of modern German sociology.[9] But the complex character of his work can be understood only in the light of a third element. In the famous preface to the first edition of *Gemeinschaft und Gesellschaft,* Tönnies declared that his book was influenced by Marx, Otto von Gierke [1841–1921], Henry Maine [1822–1888], and Lewis Henry Morgan [1818–1881]. In addition to these, he mentioned also Johann Jakob Bachofen [1815–1887] as one who had profoundly influenced and impressed his thinking. Bachofen in *Das Mutterrecht* (1861) was the first to analyze the interrelationships between the economic conditions of primitive agrarian civilizations and those of the matriarchal social order. But this was only one aspect of Bachofen's work. Tönnies was impressed much more by another achievement of this scholar. Throughout his work, Tönnies developed the basic ideas of Bachofen concerning the shaping powers of mother-relations for the foundation of the social order and for a general type of human behavior patterns. Tönnies's chief distinction between real and organic life (community) and ideal and mechanical social structure (society) took Bachofen's definitions of mother-right and father-right as patterns. And Tönnies's profound analysis of the organic natural relations between mother and child, man and wife, brothers and sisters, and of the social behavior patterns deriving from these relationships—natural distance, piety, devotion, and brotherhood—corresponds to the deepest intentions of Bachofen.[10] Tönnies declared that "[t]he family's roots are invisible, metaphysical, as if from under the earth it were descended from a common ancestor."[11] And he used the same approach to organic social processes when he affirmed and accepted the definition of a nation (*Volk*) by Adam Heinrich Müller [1779–1829] as the unity of past and future families in the present generation.

All these ideas are genuine romantic concepts. But nothing would be more absurd than to call Tönnies a romantic. He described and analyzed the natural organic processes that create a type of social behavior quite different in their sociological relevancy from the purely rational means-end relationships, and he affirmed their general social value. But his own thought was independent and beyond the dynamics of these emotional processes; it was the imperturbable will of rational knowledge. This attitude of knowing and understanding the social ties produced by natural and emotional forces is quite opposite to that of a romantic, who expresses these emotional trends but does not explain and understand them. And in contrast to the genuine trend of romanticism, he saw clearly that the social types and forms of community, and their modes of human self-realization—such as folkways, religion, and poetry—are correlated with definite social conditions and shift with them. These categories, however, are not historical but sociological. Repeatedly he emphasized that his concepts were general sociological concepts of transhistorical character. The manifestations of community and society may coexist in the same social structure. Even an individual institution like the family may be a combination of both elements. This is the reason for the ambiguity of these types of sociological concepts, which are at once both historical and transhistorical. In Max Weber's sociology, especially in the chapters on the types of domination, we have to examine carefully the methodological difficulties of this type of sociological conception. If one agrees with Tönnies, that life is historical in every moment and stratum of its process, then the introduction of sociological concepts transcending the realm of history presupposes some ideas on the continuity of human nature, ideas that cannot be empirical. Hence, Tönnies's sociological concepts are based upon the philosophical idea of the constancy of human nature within the shifting conditions of its strata.

Because his thinking grew from these presuppositions, he could regard the organic social relations in time (clan, family, nation) and in space (neighborhood, small cities) not only as primitive and historical but also as containing general permanent elements of human existence. Therefore, their destruction, or their stunted development, in the modern social structure and in rationalized industrial society is a question of their empirical forms, not of their essential character. In his different inquiries into the typical social forces within the community—mores, folkways, religion—he explained that their transformation into societal forms is a necessary and inevitable achievement of the rationalized willrelations that are the result of industrial society and of social conditions in the modern large cities.[12] This is more transformation than destruction. Nevertheless, Tönnies considered the dissolution and transformation of the ties of community to be a tragic necessity. But the logic of his philosophical presuppositions led him to believe that within the rational modern society new types of transrational social relations are growing. This modern society, in the logical consequences of its conditions, leads to socialism, whatever may be the concrete form of its realization. The process will destroy all the traditional types of organic social relations and their expressions in the intellectual and spiritual forms of life. There is indeed the strongest radical rationalism in his conviction that this process will dissolve the historical background of Western civilization. The Greek and Roman heritage and the Christian faith are in decline and will fall with the transition to socialism. The progressive power of enlightened scientific consciousness will destroy the transrational organic forms of devotion and creed and will create a scientific ethics as the spiritual basis of social life. This will be a synthesis between elements of community and of society. Also in the economic sphere of industrial society, there are growing social institutions, such as associations of producers and consumers, that combine the structural elements of community and society in a development toward new types of social organization. Therefore, the epoch of transition may produce a series of catastrophes that will shake Western civilization. In the long run, the realization of socialism will construct new types of common relationships because the new social order will transform the will-relations of man that are at the basis of the social behavior patterns.

Gabriel Marcel [1889–1973] is wrong in calling Tönnies's position a cultural pessimism.[13] It is rather the melancholy optimism of a passionate rationalist. But, in agreement with Herman Schmalenbach[14] and Gerhard Colm [1897–1968],[15] Marcel suggests an important problem. He sees clearly the limitations and boundaries of Tönnies's concept of community. Organic relations, such as the family, types of patriarchalism and religious attitudes based upon the experiences of natural devotion in the mother-relation, are not the only type of community. Spiritual ties create quite another type of community, which may be represented by the Platonic Academy, Epicurus's gardens, the early Christian communities, and some types of sects.

This development from community through society to a new community is not a sociological revival of the dialectics of Hegel and Marx. Tönnies understood the historical process as the evolution and development of reason, in combination and correlation with the organic and emotional elements of human nature. This is a way of slow progress, but it is a continuous growth toward the perfection of human life. Hence, his approach was neither dialectical nor romantic and can be compared only with the social philosophy of the seventeenth century law of nature. The transrational[16] is part of the unity of human nature and has to be understood. "Thinking man must be able to know the unconscious creative power in social and individual mind and find reason not only in formal discursive thinking."[17] This unity of reason, will, and nature and their complexity is the most characteristic trend in the thought of Tönnies.

There is another passage that points out clearly his comprehensive idea of reason and his critical conception of reason in society.

"The more we become free from mores and in mores, the more we need a conscious ethics, in other words a knowledge of what makes man genuine man: self-affirmation of reason. And therefore reason must cease to be an essentially analytical power. It must develop to the cheerful and vital healing force of the community. Then only will it be the supreme power of man."[18] This remark signifies clearly the basic position of Tönnies. Human nature as social existence may appear in different constellations and orders, but it is always one and essentially the same. Only from this presupposition do we get a full understanding of his individual achievement. He attempted to integrate the historical, economic, and psychological knowledge of the nineteenth century into a system of sociological concepts and categories that constitute the empirical realm of the social development of human nature. And he dissolved the pressure of institutions and organizations into concepts of social relationships—sociology as the dynamic and scientific type of a modern law of nature.

Here, the circle is closing. We may understand the causes of his solitude. The nineteenth century had broken the strength and vitality of the belief in a law of nature. It had developed two different trends of thinking: one scientific-positivistic and the other historical-romantic. They represented the growing tension and the antagonisms within the intellectual and spiritual structure of man. While the scientific type of thinking tried to analyze the complexity of life by abstracting and isolating the different strata of life and creating nominalistic entities, the historical way of thinking discovered only relativism and contingency. Neither approach was capable of a comprehensive understanding of the complexity of social existence, since neither contained any integrating principle. Neither of them allowed a genuine understanding of Tönnies.

The strong unity and completeness of his thinking were strange to his contemporaries. Nothing can prove this better than an analysis of his literary style. Although he had studied the social sciences and philosophy, his writing does not suggest the influence of anyone or of any definite type of scientific terminology. His writing is rich in new and imaginative words pointing out the creative power of his synthetic mind in uniting experience and thought. On the other hand, we find also strange and rational expressions comparable to those of the philosophers of the seventeenth century. Indeed, intellectually, he was a son of that century, representing the strongest tension between radical rationalism and a consciousness of the transrational powers in man. This passion for a scientific rationalism integrated all the elements of his inheritance. It is no accident that he was the descendant of Frisian farmers. The Frisians near the Danish border were almost the only German peasants who had never been serfs or served in manorial dependence. In his emphasis on the sociological structure of community, he tried to found an intellectual tradition for the permanent values implicit in these types of social behavior. This unity and tension between the highest standard of scientific rationalism and the knowledge of the transrational powers in the shaping of social ties created a rich understanding of the variety and the potentialities of social relationships, and suggests a general theory of social existence as a basis of the development of human nature.

Notes

1. *Reine und angewandte Soziologie, eine Festigabe für Ferdinand Tönnies* (Leipzig: Hans Buske, 1956).

2. Herman Schmalenbach, "Uber die Kategorie des Bundes," in *Die Dioskuren, Jahrbuch für Geisteswissenschaften* (Munich: 1922), vol. 1.

3. See Otto von Gierke, *Das deutsche Genossenschaftsrecht* (Berlin: 1868, 1873), vols. 1–2.

4. See *Revue Philosophique* (1889), vol. 3.

5. Pitirim Sorokin, *Contemporary Sociological Theories* (London: 1928), 491.

6. *Kritik der öffentlichen Meinung* (Berlin: 1922); *Fortschritt und soziale Entwicklung* (Kalsruhe: 1926); *Soziologische Studien und Kritiken* (Jena: 1924–28), vols. 1–3.

7. Works of Hobbes edited by Tönnies include: *The Elements of Law Natural and Politic* (London: 1889; Cambridge: 1928; German trans. Berlin: 1926); *Behemoth, or the Long Parliament* (London: 1889); "17 Briefe des Th. Hobbes," in *Archiv für die Geschichte der Philosophie,* vol. 3 (1890).

8. See F. Tönnies, *Hobbes, Leben und Lehre* (Stuttgart: 1896; 3rd ed. 1925); "Hobbes, Analekten," in *Archiv für Geschichte der Philosophie* (1904, 1906), vol. 17; "Hobbes' Naturrecht," in *Archiv für Rechts und Wirtschaftsphilosophie* (1912), vol. 5; "Die Lehre von den Volkaversammlungen und die Urversammlung in Hobbes Leviathan," in *Zeitschrift für die gesamte Staatswissenschaft* (1930), vol. 89.

9. R. Aron, *La Sociologie Allemande Contemporaine* (Paris: 1935), 20ff.

10. Tönnies did not quote Bachofen and gave no references to his books, but he seems to have known only *Das Mutterrecht*, not *Das lykische Volk und seine Bedeutung für die Entwicklung des Altertums* [1862] or *Versuch über die Gräbersymbolik der Alten* [1859].

11. *Gemeinschaft und Gesellschaft*, 208.

12. See *Die Sitte* (Frankfurt: 1909); *Fortschritt und soziale Entwicklung* (Karlsruhe: 1926); "Sitte und Freiheit," in *Gedächtnisgabe für Dunkmann* (Berlin: 1933).

13. Gabriel Marcel, *Etre et Avoir* (Paris: 1935), 352.

14. Schmalenbach, "Uber die Kategorie des Bundes."

15. Gerhard Colm, "Masse," in *Handworterbuch der Soziologie* (Stuttgart: 1931).

16. Christian Janentzky, in *Mystik und Rationalismus* (Leipzig: 1922), first used the term *transrational.*

17. *Die Sitte*, 92.

18. *Die Sitte*, 94.

16

Some Aspects of the Legacy of Durkheim

Of those thinkers who, in the history of sociology, have given new directions and perspectives to a discipline in the making, only Émile Durkheim [1858–1917] organized a school made up of the creative minds of a younger generation who were able to carry sociology forward. Vilfredo Pareto [1848–1923] contributed to depth sociology, Georg Simmel [1858–1918] to the epistemology of sociology, and Max Weber [1864–1920] to the development of sociology as comparative history—the ideas of these men were constructive and far-reaching, but they did not train students to continue and to expand their work.

Durkheim conceived of sociology as a new method, a scientific device for demonstrating the forces of attraction and coercion exerted by collective representations in all fields of thinking, feeling, and conduct. The method was revolutionary in that it rigorously applied scientific principles to the study of the concrete situation of man, and attempted to find rules that would enable sociologists to discover the laws of social behavior in typical situations found in life. The method found both enemies and enthusiastic disciples.

Published originally in a slightly different form in *Emile Durkheim, 1858-1917*, ed. Kurt H. Wolff (Columbus: Ohio State University Press, 1960), 247–66. Republished by permission from Frank Salomon.

The enemies fell into two groups: the first was composed of representatives of traditional social science—historians who relied on the guesswork of subjective interpretation, and psychologists who were concerned with the behavior of individuals. The second consisted of theologians and metaphysicians, who repudiated a science that rejected all ontological or spiritual assumptions to explain the natural process of human coexistence in social institutions. Among Durkheim's followers were students of philosophy who were attracted by a concrete theory and a philosophy of immanence; students of psychology who were convinced that the collective representations conceived by Durkheim provided the necessary complement to individual representations; and historians and social scientists who, in an age of mass societies, understood the value of discovering scientific rules, of setting up classifications of social phenomena, of developing quantitative methods, and of making morphological studies. These followers became members of a new school in sociology: the Durkheim School.

Durkheim's students were fascinated by his passionate belief in the efficiency of his method. They were attracted by his platonic love of finding higher truths in a search shared with his students: for Durkheim, dedication to his disciples was one with dedication to his cause. The common enterprise, Durkheim's students felt, was in the French humanistic tradition.

Durkheim hoped that his theoretical studies might help to raise human and social standards. He believed in scientific enlightenment. He knew of human suffering, of death and coercion; and he was grimly aware of the inertia of society that results from the false security of its prejudices. He believed in the potential blessings of solidarity, in spite of the trends of his time toward new patterns of despotism. He was convinced that science could give men courage to condition and control their world.

The work carried on by Durkheim with his students has left as its monuments *L'Année sociologique* and the many publications of his students. Our awareness of Durkheim's greatness increases when we examine his ideas as they were applied by his disciples. When we study his *Le suicide,* we should also consult *Les Causes de suicide* by Maurice Halbwachs [1877–1945].[1] In the thirty years between the two books, there had been improvements in the discipline of statistics and marked social and economic changes, but Halbwachs retained the general pattern of Durkheim's method. The reader of *Les règles de la méthod sociologique* and *Les forms élémentaires de la vie religieuse* should also study Marcel Mauss [1872–1950] and his theory of total sociology. Mauss presented his theory in an address on sociology and psychology, *Rapports réels et pratiques de la psychologie et de la sociologie* (1924), and in the book, *Essai sur le don: Forme et raison de l'échange dans les sociétés archaïques* (1923)[2]—one of the few great pieces in the field of total sociology.

Many remarkable men in the fields of economics and sociology have been students of Durkheim's; they have worked in the areas of social organization, legal and moral institutions, sociology of religion, statistics, technology, theory of civilization, social psychology, and cultural anthropology. In cooperating with the master, these men became the builders of the first series of *L'Année sociologique,* which, between 1896 and 1913, served to express Durkheim's spirit. The volumes of this periodical make exciting reading for the historian of ideas and for the student of sociology. For seventeen years, Durkheim and his group collected literature from all the fields that were concerned with the problems of man in his social aspects. The twelve volumes that resulted reflect the sociology of the time, containing analyses of the works of Lester F. Ward [1841–1913], Albion W. Small [1854–1926], Georg Simmel, and Ferdinand Tönnies [1855–1936]. The masters of the English and American schools of cultural anthropology were subjected to methodological and substantive critiques, and the German literature in the areas of economics, social history, moral statistics, and the social organization of the family was explored.

In compiling material for *L'Année sociologique*, Durkheim directed his students to do specialized research. He was convinced that the main task of the sociologist was to penetrate the diverse areas of social action and thought. He knew that methods do not develop in a vacuum and that problems entail their own specific methods according to the requirements of the fields in which they occur. For this reason, he urged his fellow workers to gain a thorough knowledge of specific areas. Marcel Mauss, Robert Hertz [1881–1915], and Henri Hubert [1872–1927] became experts in the large field of religion, where they made studies of cult, ritual, prayer, and dogma. In social economics, François Simiand [1873–1935] and Halbwachs specialized in making comparative studies of the family budgets of workers in Europe and the United States; Simiand also studied the sociological aspects of the setting of prices and the distribution of economic goods.

The Durkheim group used the literature in all of these fields as a testing ground for applying and verifying their method. From authors in the humanities and the social sciences, they learned what the substantive problems of their disciplines were, and they measured the value of their works according to the contributions they made to sociology. They found some whose ideas made it possible to form sociological hypotheses, and others who disregarded sociological methods entirely but who would have profited from applying them in their work. They were convinced that, unless these methods were used, no comprehensive analysis of social facts was possible; and in their critical evaluations, they stressed the problems of comparative methods.

Durkheim and other contributors to the *L'Année sociologique* were concerned with constructing classifications that were sufficiently flexible and dynamic to accommodate the infinite variety of human social situations. They remembered the dictum that Durkheim had expressed in the preface to the first volume of their periodical: Only a thorough acquaintance with the humanities, psychology, and the social sciences would enable sociologists to develop a general theory of civilization. They advanced the methods of social-functional and socialcausal analysis, although they were not always careful to distinguish their specific characteristics.

In 1908, Durkheim announced that in the future the periodical would appear only every third year. He pointed out that contributors had become so dedicated to their assignments that many of them had had to neglect their own work.

This was especially true of Marcel Mauss. Although Mauss directed the publication's section on religion, his articles also contributed a great deal to general theory. He worked constantly to devise new classifications for the study of religion and to reorganize the field. Thus, when new material on totemism appeared, he found it necessary to form a new subdivision. He also had some noteworthy ideas on the classification of myths. In addition, he wrote a number of illuminating pages on the sociological evolution of prayer from a collective to an individual phenomenon.

Mauss enjoyed a unique relation with Durkheim, who was his uncle as well as his master. As a young man, he worked with him on the final versions of *Le suicide* and *Les forms élémentaires de la vie religieuse.* The latter appeared at the same time as *Totemism and Exogamy* by Sir James Frazer [1854–1941],[3] and Durkheim and Mauss wrote a comparative analysis of the two studies, which showed the differences between the theories of totemism of the two men. This analysis was Durkheim's final statement concerning the relevance of totemism in explaining the social organization of the Australian tribes. In his most important books, Mauss often paid tribute to the inspiration that he had received from Durkheim, giving him the credit for the work that he himself did in sociology—work that turned a method of research into a theory of total sociology.

One article written jointly by Durkheim and Mauss in 1901 was of special importance to both of them. It is "*De quelques formes primitives de classification*,"[4] a contribution to the study of collective representations, and the foundation of a sociology of knowledge and religion. The authors explain that the patterns of logic that operate among the Australian tribes are the result of their having experienced the divisions of their own tribal organization. Durkheim and Mauss reject Lucien Lévy-Bruhl's [1857–1939] idea of prelogical thinking and develop a theory that demonstrates that logical patterns reflect social experiences. According to them, the Australians constructed concepts of genera and species from the social reality of phratries and clans. The modes of social cohesion, such as homogeneity and hierarchy, were transferred, in a logical sequence, to the categories of the mind. The bonds that united all beings were conceived of as social bonds.

The collective representations that give cohesion to society are, at the same time, collective affections. For this reason, logical and affective categories merge; value attitudes and logical procedures are intertwined. The Australians, for example, divide everything into sacred and profane, pure and impure. They conceive of a whole, for example, as a dual structure of positive and negative elements.

Collective representations are the basis for classifying the world, which is a totality of the divine and the demonic, and men, who are part of this totality. Man is by nature sociocentric: society is the center of all early conceptions of nature. The Sioux and Zuni Indians, the early Greeks, and others held that their land was the center of the world; they referred to other parts only in relation to themselves. The primary dualism of the social world—typified by the divisions into we and they, Greeks and barbarians, friends and enemies, and I and thou—is reflected in early conceptual systems. Durkheim and Mauss went so far as to assert that all diversities in primitive classifications could be explained on the basis of physiological differences.

This study by Durkheim and Mauss was the first effort ever made to conceive the social phenomenon as a totality in which the physiological, psychological, and social elements in the constitution of man in society are interdependent and interact with one another. The authors themselves noted that this discovery was the beginning of a new road—one that implied the possibility of error. Ultimately, it led to the idea of total sociology. For Mauss, it became the basis of his *Essai sur le don,* a masterpiece of analysis and synthesis in scientific sociology, in which he shows that exchange in primitive societies consists more frequently in reciprocal gifts than in economic transactions. Such gifts have a much more important function in archaic societies than in our own. Primitive exchange is a total social fact; at one and the same time, it has social and religious, magical and economic, utilitarian and sentimental, and legal and moral significance. In many of the societies found among the Indians of the American Northwest, and in many of those in Alaska, New Zealand, and Australia, the nobles or the whole tribe offered gifts to other groups on all solemn public and private occasions. Usually, gifts of equal value were exchanged simultaneously by both parties. Or, if the second group reciprocated later, the gifts they rendered had to be more precious than the ones they received earlier—in order to pay interest, as it were. These ceremonies had still other functions: to establish publicly the claim of a group or family to a title or privilege, and to surpass a rival in generosity or crush him under the burden of overwhelming obligations.

The goal of this exchange of gifts is social prestige rather than economic advantage. The leitmotiv of Mauss's work is that giving-receiving and rendering are the main patterns of behavior by which lasting human peace can be established and the possibilities of humaneness in the routine of economic or political institutions can be maintained. It is a universal pattern all over the world, one that transcends the artificial distinction between primitive and historical societies. Mauss gave proof that people everywhere are moved by the same desires for power, prestige, and social position, and by the fear of losing all three. For this reason, they offer gifts to one another, and it does not matter whether the giving is called presentation, potlatch, or contract. Mauss opens our eyes to the fact that in its everyday routine and on its great occasions—both public (the making of peace, the declaration of war, the punishing of an outlaw, the readmission of a repentant sinner) and private (birth, marriage, death)—the life of man is a series of rituals. The rituals in which gifts are exchanged are the bonds that make for the integration of the diverse interests, tensions, and affections that are indispensable factors in the coexistence of human beings with, for, or against one another. Rituals are more than habits since they are accompanied by the ambiguity of our affections. Gifts can be received and given with goodwill and friendship or with fear and resentment. They can be the expression of pride or humility, despair, or ambition. The German *sich revanchieren*, which means both "to return a gift or favor" and "to take revenge," preserves this ambiguity.[5]

Mauss did not share Durkheim's gloomy view of capitalist society. Rather, he saw in capitalism corporate elements that created mutual responsibilities for both management and labor, and transformed the revolutionary relationship between these classes into a variety of exchanges that were made in the spirit of giving, receiving, and rendering.

Essai sur le don found its counterpart in theory in the previously mentioned address on sociology and psychology that Mauss delivered in 1924, seven years after Durkheim's death. In this paper, he refers to specific Durkheimian investigations leading to a theory of the totality of social facts and the rules of total sociology. Mauss begins his speech by insisting on a point on which psychologists and sociologists agree: they share the attitude of the scientist and employ a method that is experimental and empirical but have different subject matters. Psychology is concerned with the individual conscience, sociology with the natural history of man in society and the manifestations of the *conscience collective*. However, both sciences are, according to Mauss, part of a larger complex that he calls anthropology—a combination of the sciences dealing with man as a living, conscious, and social being. It was Mauss's conviction that the cooperation of psychologists, biologists, and sociologists could create a sociology developed as a theory of the totality of social facts.

In logical sequence, the elements of total sociology are (1) social morphology, (2) mass phenomena, (3) social facts, and (4), collective representations, affections, and recollections. *Social morphology*—a term coined by Durkheim in 1900 to designate a classification that he added to a new division in social research—is the original sphere of the study of man in a social perspective. It deals with the relation between social behavior, collective representations and affections, and the substratum of group life. *Substratum* refers to the material and external conditions under which societies live. As they change, according to Durkheim's theory, so do intellectual, social, and emotional factors. Collectivities create specific modes of behavior and action in order to establish a sensible way of meeting and controlling their life conditions. In penetrating and organizing their substrata, they build up intelligible and subjectively meaningful social contexts.

Mauss pays particular attention to the substrata that are composed of climatic and geographic conditions, analyzing their presence or absence within particular political frontiers, and determining the effect they have on the size and density of the population and the system of communication that is used. And in his essay on the seasonal variations found in Eskimo societies, "*Essai sur les variations saisonnières des sociétés eskimos*,"[6] which he subtitled "Étude de morphologie sociale," he demonstrates the truth of the theory concerning the effect of the substratum on the way of life of the collectivity. The scientist, Mauss says, is not bound to apply quantitative methods only; the thorough qualitative analysis of phenomena can be equally evident and conclusive. Thus, in a paper that is as penetrating and comprehensive as the work on the gift, Mauss introduces the possibility of describing phenomena completely. Dwelling briefly on what is constant in Eskimo behavior throughout the year, Mauss analyzes the different substrata of the winter and summer settlements and the different ways of life that each presents: the religious and legal norms operative during the winter when the population is concentrated in a small area vary from those of the summer when the population is widely dispersed.

The second of Mauss's divisions of total sociology, mass phenomena, designates a subject matter that requires statistical treatment. The quantitative measurement of social traits is, indeed, fundamental to the scientific explanation of all societies, whether modern or archaic. It is concerned, among other things, with birth and mortality rates and the movement of populations—both under ordinary circumstances and under the pressure of war, famine, or revolution. Durkheim's *Le suicide* is a famous example and model of the use of statistical methods.

Social facts, the third division, deals with the total complex of such historical phenomena as traditions, mores, habits, rituals, language, religion, art, technology, philosophy, and poetry.

The last, but most important, division is the study of collective representations, affections, and recollections. The study consists of two parts: the collection and systematization of the ideas that constitute the collective representations, and the examination of the collective behavior patterns that correspond to these representations. Societies are united more closely by common ideas and values—economic, religious, or political—than by the pressures of the substratum that is studied by social morphology. Mauss states emphatically that the explanation of collective representations and affections is the task of the sociologist, not the psychologist; for the sociologist can penetrate to the deep layers of social cohesion that emerge from the density and intensity of the collective recollections and affections. This penetration is valuable to the sociological analysis of social and historical time, an analysis that is of importance to the political scientists and sociologists who study revolutions.

In constructing the rules of total sociology in this fourfold program, Mauss followed Durkheim's suggestions and expanded his investigations. In addition, he saw the significance of physiology for sociology, a consideration that Durkheim had ignored. Mauss's investigations concerning the techniques used in performing certain physical activities have provided new insights for the theoretical sociologist, the teacher of physical education, and the health officer. In his early life, Mauss had observed variations in the techniques used in swimming, and during the First World War, he had studied the various ways in which soldiers in different armies walked and marched. These observations prompted him to inquire into the extent to which collective norms produced such variations. He found that they were indeed conditioned by the social norms of the education promulgated by specific institutions, and that the techniques of marching, jumping, and running used by the different armies were the result of authoritarian decisions. His investigation uncovered further examples of collective education, such as girls educated in convents often walk with closed fists. In addition, he sought to determine the influence of motion pictures on the techniques of bodily activity. While convalescing in a hospital, he noticed that the nurses had a peculiar way of walking, which he could not account for until he realized that they were copying the manner of walking of American movie stars. Many other physical mannerisms can also be attributed to the influence of the motion picture.

The techniques of the body are socially conditioned habits; these habits produce our social nature (an idea first established by Michel de Montaigne [1533–1592]) and demonstrate the reality of the human being as a totality in which physiological, psychological, and sociological elements merge. Mauss defined a technique as a traditional, efficient act. Techniques form a part of magical, religious, and symbolic behavior. There can be no technique without a means of transmitting it, such as tradition.

Mauss and his disciples disagreed with Durkheim's definition of the relationship between the sociologist and the psychologist. Durkheim had been a student of Théodule-Armand Ribot [1839–1916] and Wilhelm Wundt [1832–1920], but he maintained that psychology could not contribute to the solution of the problems of the collectivity. Mauss, however, specified three ways in which the psychologist can be of value to the sociologist.

First, the psychologist's concept of mental vigor and weakness (this is related to tough and tender-mindedness of William James [1842–1910]) is implicit in the sociologist's idea of anomie. Mauss contributed a case study of anomie—or, more particularly, of thanatomania. Among the Maori, individuals have been known to abandon the will to live and subsequently to die, not because of any physical ailment or act of suicide, but simply because of the pressure of collective recriminations. Such a phenomenon presents a problem to the sociologist. But since it is centered in an individual's conscience, the psychologist can help the sociologist understand the social origins of the phenomenon.

Second, sociologists apply the category of psychosis, and they need the enlightenment that psychiatrists can provide concerning hallucinations, the frenzy of the vendetta, the amok (common among Polynesians and Malayans), and so on. Mauss had the opportunity of witnessing the collective hysteria that swept over Europe after 1933.

Third, the psychologist can help the sociologist in his study of the symbol-constructing activity of the mind. Mauss could not admit the validity of such a claim in its entirety, however, for he saw that the activities of the collective conscience are more symbolic than are those of the individual mind. Indeed, one of the characteristic features of the social fact is its symbolic aspect. Furthermore, the notion of the symbol is a sociological conception derived from the study of religion, law, language, and politics. Durkheim and his students demonstrated that one communicates through symbols. Therefore, although they are ambiguous in their meanings, symbols are easily identified with verities.

Mythical and moral symbols are the manifestations of the effects of the *conscience collective*. They permanently influence the behavior both of the group and of the individuals who compose it. Here, Mauss saw another meeting ground for the psychologist and the sociologist. And, in this case, Durkheim would not have objected, for he had explicitly stated that the individual, as part of the whole and in performing his social roles, retains various possibilities for realizing himself. Within the limits set by social coercion, human beings are astoundingly alert to loopholes that enable them to indulge their subjective interests. Most individuals are fifth columnists within the *conscience collective*.

The work of another of Durkheim's disciples, Maurice Halbwachs, demonstrates the lasting value and the constructive truth of Durkheim's greatest book, *Le suicide,* which appeared in 1896. Halbwachs published his own *Les causes du suicide* in 1930. A generation had elapsed between the two works, new material had been collected, and new refinements in statistical methods had been developed. But, in spite of all this, Durkheim's theses remained valid. Halbwachs verified and amended them but did not change their basic conceptions. Durkheim's book opened with some chapters on methodology that demonstrated that nonsociological factors were irrelevant to a sociological explanation of suicide rates. Halbwachs praised the sound methodology of the master, who had refused to be concerned with the subjective motivations of the individuals who committed suicide. Motives, he argued, are either subjective ideological constructs or arbitrary definitions laid down by the police or by coroners. He rejected any concern with them as unscientific.

According to Durkheim's fundamental conception, suicide and crime are normal social facts. They become pathological only when they increase at an accelerated tempo. Furthermore, they are subject to causal investigation, and there is a basic correlation between tendencies to suicide and other social patterns. Durkheim made the profound observation that every group and society has a specific scale of values founded on the evaluation of life and death. Military and commercial societies differ in the evaluations that they make, as do spiritual and secular societies, and industrial-urban and agricultural-preindustrial ones.

The social causes of suicidal tendencies can be derived from the diverse social roles that men play in the total social context. Men live in domestic, religious, professional, social, political, and occupational groupings that condition them positively and negatively. Durkheim showed that the suicide rate varies inversely with the degree to which these collective bodies are internally integrated. The more the rules of these groups disintegrate, the more the individual detaches himself from them. His goals and aspirations prevail over those of the group; the individual ego becomes stronger than the social ego.

Egoistic suicide results, then, from the excessive individualism or egoism that is caused by the deficient authority of a *conscience collective* that is disintegrating. For Durkheim, man is dual. He aspires to be safe, protected, and obedient, and is therefore willing to submit to the moral coercion exerted by society. At the same time, he desires to unfold his personality; thus, he revolts against the necessity of conforming with the collective imperatives. For this reason, societies are dual, as the individual human being is, and are both shelter and barracks, waiting room and prison. This duality emerges because civilized men are concerned with more than satisfying their organic needs. Moreover, the life of society is a process in which the vital forces are constantly being organized on behalf of social needs. The roles of art, science, morality, and religion, however, transcend the lowest level of social control and establish the higher level of social institutions. The influence of society is paramount in education, which is the socialization of man, the process by which society arouses the sentiments of sympathy and solidarity so as to fashion the young in its image and inculcate in them taken-for-granted beliefs and convictions concerning the good, the beautiful, and the true. Education is the socialization of man on the basis of the ideals of the older generations of society.

Durkheim's view of man is Machiavellian: man's greed, lusts, and needs are infinite, and they must be controlled. Niccolò Machiavelli [1469–1527] made the state the humanizing agency; Durkheim made it the moral authority of the *conscience collective*. Society must set the goal for the group and invent the modes of social relations by which human urges and passions are channeled and directed in a way that is favorable to the whole.

If society loses its regulating vitality, anomie arises. This state is further heightened by the passions that are unleashed when men are denied discipline and social authority. Such a situation promotes anomie suicide, which differs from egoistic suicide. The latter results from the release of radical self-centeredness that occurs when the social bonds and collective obligations have grown so weak they have lost the power to act as integrating forces. Anomic suicide, on the other hand, results when there are no social imperatives because there is no collective integration, a situation that leaves men suffering and forlorn.

Despite their differences, both egoistic and anomic suicides spring from the fact that society is not present in the necessary amounts in the individual egos. But this absence is not the same in the two cases. In egoistic suicide, the collective power is not sufficiently attractive and constructive to appeal to the vital and strong individual so that he is deprived of goals and directions. In the society in which there is a high incidence of anomic suicide, no creative strength comes from the collectivity. In the social roles he is supposed to perform, the individual does not receive moral direction and meaning from a constructive *conscience collective*, and men are exposed to passions within themselves that are not channeled by common goals and values. Egoistic and anomic suicides do not occur in the same human groups. Egoistic suicide prevails in the professional and intellectual worlds; anomic suicide prevails in the worlds of industry and finance, among workers and managers alike. Indeed, Durkheim saw a definite correlation between anomic suicide and the free capitalistic society with its grim and unregulated competition, its crises and depressions; for him, this kind of human tragedy expressed the moral vacuum of the contemporary economic and social world.

Before discussing Durkheim's third category of suicide—altruistic—it is important to understand his general definition of the phenomenon and the way in which Halbwachs modified it. Durkheim defined a suicide as a death that results—directly or indirectly—from an act accomplished by the victim who has full knowledge of what the result will be. Durkheim did not say that it is an act committed with the intention of killing oneself, and this was consistent with his belief that "motives" are not relevant for the scientist. Furthermore, the definition he did not choose would have excluded many acts, which he wished to include.

Halbwachs suggested a modified version. For him, a suicide is a death that results from an act committed by the victim with the intention of causing his own death. It is an act of which society disapproves, although the *conscience collective* does approve of certain suicides of expiation. This modification contains an implicit criticism of Durkheim's conception of altruistic suicide. According to Durkheim, this third type results from an individual's total identification with the commands of the collectivity, as when men die as heroes for their country in war, or permit themselves to be killed as sacrificial victims or as martyrs for their creeds when they have been forced to convert to the religion of a majority.

Halbwachs saw that Durkheim was victimized by his own definition, which made it possible to identify as suicides acts that are incompatible. For this reason, Halbwachs made a distinction between sacrifice and suicide. He defined sacrifice as a death that results from an act based on the decisions and duties emanating from the *conscience collective*. Such an act involves the volition of the sacrificial victim and his recognition of an obligation to the values of the collectivity: a human being who sacrifices himself for the sake of his platoon or becomes a martyr for his convictions meets death voluntarily because he is fulfilling his obligation to the collective institutions to which he belongs. Halbwachs reserves the term *suicide* to designate the voluntary act of a person emancipating himself from the bonds of the collectivity.

This distinction forced Halbwachs to reflect on the ambiguous attitudes that societies disclose in their judgments on death. They condemn suicide, but they strongly approve of it under certain circumstances. This means that, strictly speaking, there is no such thing as suicide as such: there are only types of suicide. Halbwachs distinguishes three: the expiatory, the imprecatory, and the disillusioned.

Expiatory suicide may result from a homicide or from sins committed against the social codes of honor in business or in the military or medical professions. The expiatory suicide kills himself in an act of self-condemnation and atonement. The imprecatory type, illustrated by Anna Karenina's suicide, is inspired by defiance of the collectivity. Here, an individual's killing herself is an act against society. Anna hates society's hypocrisy and collective judgment; she is disgusted with life. She kills herself in defiance of a group that has no understanding of the sufferings of a human being; she disputes the right of the collective conscience to act as a moral authority. In the case of the suicide that results from disillusionment, the cause is a profound disenchantment with the place of man in society, the consequence of the victim's not receiving from the collective structures the protection and guidance he needs. Halbwachs's critique of Durkheim's conception of altruistic suicide is valuable and constructive. In addition, Halbwachs's methods were more refined, for he applied microsociological devices that made Durkheim's broad generalizations specific. Durkheim had worked largely with national data, while Halbwachs made greater use of regional figures in drawing comparisons of the social facts in metropolitan, urban, and rural areas.

Halbwachs's reexamination of religion as a protective collective force confirmed Durkheim's thesis concerning the integrating power of Catholicism and the disintegrating tendency in Protestantism. Halbwachs's figures on Jewish suicides show a rapid increase all over Europe between 1891 and 1900; in Amsterdam, for instance, the Jewish suicide rate between 1905 and 1914 was the highest of all religious groups. In general, the suicide rates of various religious groups depend on the faith confessed, but they are also determined, in part, by social conditions. Thus, one must know whether a religious group is a majority or a minority, whether it is urban or rural, and whether it is politically conservative, liberal, or radical. For instance, there is a rather high suicide rate among Catholics when they are isolated and dispersed, but it becomes lower when they live in compact enclaves.

Halbwachs discovered an aspect of Catholic suicides that Durkheim had not realized: he found an exact correspondence between the number of mixed marriages and the suicide rate among Catholics. Mixed marriages are an index of Catholic disintegration; and in proportion to their increase, the Catholic suicide rate grows. Halbwachs refined Durkheim's thesis on Catholicism as an integrative force. Although the customs of Catholicism are religious customs, it is as customs that they are of interest to the sociologist; for it is as customs that they secure the unity of the group—through the authority of traditions and the traditions of authority. Catholicism is more than an ecclesiastical institution: it is a way of life, a pattern of civilization. Religious and traditionalist motives merge with the mores of the people; Catholic peasant societies are often identical in France, Italy, and the countries of Central Europe. Halbwachs concluded that it is not the religious unity of the Catholics, but the social cohesion produced by their traditions, habits, and customs, that explains why their suicide rate is lower than that of urban and Protestant milieus.

In this discussion, "rural" and "urban" refer not to geographic areas but to segments of the social structure. The high suicide rate among the urban population cannot be explained by assuming that city dwellers are more morbid; actually, native urban inhabitants are relatively secure. Rather, the high overall suicide rate of the city derives from the large number of maladjusted persons, who, after they have migrated from the country to the town or from the town to the metropolis, have found the ways of life and the patterns of work, sociability, and entertainment completely bewildering—a situation that produces anomie suicide.

One of the most impressive among Halbwachs's contributions is his reexamination of Durkheim's theory of the protective character of the family. Durkheim's thesis, he found, had remained valid: the husband is more protected than the wife, and the widower more than the widow. Halbwachs added the observation that as the number of children increases, the protective force exercised by the integrated family grows.

Halbwachs praised Durkheim for his keen analysis of the future of the family. Durkheim had foreseen that what had been the structure of the family for the last three hundred years was going to change because of changes in technology and morals. The technological revolution would free individual members of the family from the obligation to contribute to its maintenance; the disappearance of the moral and spiritual meaning of the family—together with its function as the model of sympathy, intimacy, and mutual responsibility—would come about, he predicted, with the transfer of allegiances and affections to the collective institutions of totalitarian societies.

Halbwachs accepted Durkheim's statement that the suicide rate is lower in time of war and political crisis, but he modified his analysis of the causes that explain this reduction. Durkheim believed that war and crisis stir the collective affections that unify and integrate otherwise antagonistic groups. Halbwachs did not reject this thesis but added his own observation that wars and crises produce a general simplification of all patterns of life. The limitations placed on all societal relationships and social intercourse by a common danger restrict the possibilities of suicide. When the shadow of death threatens the whole community, the tendency to suicide in the individual is reduced.

Although Durkheim's theory of anomic suicide refers specifically to the nineteenth century, it is confirmed by Halbwachs's analysis of the phenomenon in modern capitalist society; the analysis also substantiates Durkheim's prediction that economic institutions would undergo a transformation, and that, possibly, new patterns of anomie would emerge. Halbwachs points out, however, that Durkheim should have connected the higher suicide rate with the rapid industrialization that was taking place in Germany and France during the second half of the nineteenth century rather than with capitalism in general. Halbwachs makes a distinction between the industrial expansion and the financial expansion of Germany and France; he shows that, because it was new and revolutionary, it was the former that created maladjustment on all levels of society—a maladjustment that necessitated physiological, psychological, intellectual, and moral changes, and contributed to a rise in the suicide rate.

Halbwachs does well to stress the importance of the particular character of this period: the suicide rate decreased when dynamic capitalism became relatively stable before the First World War, and again following the postwar inflation. He corrects Durkheim when he observes that the suicide rate increases in the depression that follows an economic crisis rather than during the crisis itself. Durkheim's conviction was that capitalistic societies lack the regulatory powers of the *conscience collective*, and, for this reason, anomic suicide has become a feature of modern social pathology.

Halbwachs modifies Durkheim's prediction concerning the anomic state of modern economic societies; for, he maintains, as capitalism develops into a rationally planned society, capitalist and socialist elements merge. Therefore, it becomes possible to inject notions of government-planning and state interference into free economic institutions, so that governments are given the power to control crises and unemployment and to regulate segments of the economy. Halbwachs foresees the general trend to be toward a corporate capitalism that permits the use of socialist devices. Such a development would entail the reexamination of anomie and anomic suicide.

The new corporate state of society envisioned by Halbwachs is not, however, the corporate society in which Durkheim had seen the solution to the moral problem of capitalism. On the contrary, it is characterized by the tendency toward a new monopolistic capitalism, with all the political and moral implications of such a system. Halbwachs saw the trend of the economy moving toward a state of affairs which Durkheim could not have foreseen, but he did not realize that this new type of social organization, with its mammoth institutions and its total rationalization of social behavior, would create new patterns of anomie suicide, and that social stereotypes and the production of technological patterns of culture would throw surviving human beings into total anomie in a world that had become a vacuum ruled by the norms of anonymous efficiency.

Finally, to Halbwachs goes the credit for reconciling the sociologist's position on suicide with that of the psychiatrist—who too often assigned pathological suicides to himself and normal ones to the sociologist. Actually, the interaction of the two disciplines is indispensable for both theoretical and practical purposes.

Halbwachs saw that there is a reciprocal relationship between anomie and neurosis. All social catastrophes—such as loss of a loved one, economic failure, continuous lack of success, cultural and social displacement, exile, and disgrace—produce *déclassés*: men who are removed from their accustomed groups and are discriminated against by the codes of honor or the *conscience collective* of those groups. This feeling of being outside the social framework—a framework that has been taken for granted—produces a consciousness of isolation and loneliness; and men who become aware of solitude in a social vacuum are driven to suicide.

Durkheim did not see that because social facts cause anxieties and depressions it is necessary to use sociological method in psychiatry. Halbwachs and some of his contemporary psychiatrists did. Anarchy in the sphere of values and chaos in moral codes create anomie as a social condition of suicide, but the elements of depression and insecurity and other pathological features are never absent. Halbwachs held that no neurotic is adapted to his social environment, and that every mental illness is an element of social disequilibrium and must be explained by the interpenetration of social and organic causes.

One of the greatest French psychiatrists, Charles Blondel [1876–1939], was a sociologist because he was a psychiatrist. He wrote:

> What we call "will" exists merely by the fact that systems of collective imperatives are present in the individual conscience. When we do not conform in our conduct to the collective duties, our will has to justify our behavior before society. The very presence of collective representations suffices to turn our activities into acts of will. We human beings are within ourselves and outside ourselves. So are the reasons for the different patterns of suicide. They can be caused by external coercion and by psychic inner causes, the two most of the time being interdependent.[7]

This synthesizing procedure, which analyzes both the sociological aspects of neuroses and the pathological aspects of social catastrophes, marks genuine progress beyond Durkheim. It constitutes another of the achievements of his disciples in developing his method into a theory of the totality of social facts.

Notes

1. (Paris: Alcan, 1930).

2. *L'Année sociologique*, Nouvelle Série (1923–24), vol. 1. Translated as *The Gift* by Ian Cunnison (Glencoe, IL: Free Press, 1954).

3. (London: Macmillan, 1910) vols. 1–4.

4. *L'Année sociologique* (1901), 6:1–72.

5. [Mauss would have been fascinated by the extraordinarily complex obligations of *omiyage*, or gift-giving, in Japan. See Katherine Rupp, *Gift-Giving in Japan: Cash, Connections, Cosmologies* (Stanford, CA: Stanford University Press, 2003).—Eds.]

6. *L'Année sociologique* (1906), 9:39–132.

7. Maurice Halbwachs, *Les causes du suicide* (Paris: Alcan, 1950), 473.

17

Max Weber's Methodology

The writings of Max Weber [1864–1920], because of their unusual range, seem disparate and lacking in unity. His early treatises on the history of commercial and Roman agrarian law were followed by an analysis of contemporary problems of agrarian politics in East Germany. A passing interest in banking legislation and banking politics gave way in turn to active participation in the movements that centered around the opening of the *Evangelisch-Sozialer Kongress* and the early political activities of Friedrich Naumann [1860–1919]. After an illness that incapacitated Weber for five years, he turned his attention to an altogether new field of inquiry, and during the remainder of his life was preoccupied with the epistemological problems of the empirical historical and social sciences, slowly evolving the methodological principles of his formal system of sociology. At the same time, he began his historical works on the economic ethic of Protestantism, which were not designated as a "sociology of religion" until the final stages of composition. In the meantime, there had appeared in the third edition of the *Handwörterbuch der Staatswissenschaften* his article dealing with agrarian conditions in antiquity, in effect, a comprehensive analysis in sociological terms of

---

Published originally in a slightly different form in *Social Research* 1 (May 1934), 147–68. Republished by permission from *Social Research*.

the ancient world viewed from the perspective of the crucial social problems of the immediate present.

His various administrative and editorial connections in the scholarly world involved him in numerous occasional works, such as the report on the nature of the social system in primitive Germany, the methodological introduction to a joint research project sponsored by the Verein für Sozialpolitik on the problems of selection and adaptation (*Berufswahl und Berufsschicksal der Arbeiterschaff der geschlossenen Grossindustrie*), and, in connection with the latter, the work on the psychophysics of industrial labor. His essays on Prussian legislation in regard to entail [a predetermined order of succession of a property or office—Eds.] reveal his intense interest in those problems of East German colonization that he had dealt with in his youth. His activities as editor of the *Archiv für Sozialwissenschaft und Sozialpolitik* and his participation in the founding of the German *Gesellschaft für Soziologie* continually brought him to grips with new factual and methodological problems relating to the social sciences. In the period after 1908, he resumed his earlier studies in the field of religious sociology, enlarging the scope of his inquiry to include the Asiatic world religions and ancient Judaism. At the same time, as coeditor of a new collective work, the *Grundriss der Sozialökonomiki*, he sketched the preliminary outlines for a comprehensive sociological treatise on *Wirtschaft und Gesellschaft*. During the war, he wrote a series of political pamphlets and essays; he also contributed heavily to the discussion of the democratic and parliamentary features of the new German constitution.

Confronted with writings of such phenomenal range and diversity, the student of Max Weber's work is apt to be bewildered in his search for some underlying and integrating principle. Even among Weber's closest intellectual associates, there has been marked difference of opinion as to the essential trend and emphasis of his heterogeneous writings. Ernst Troeltsch [1865–1923], for example, in his "In Memoriam" tribute, declared that Weber, for all his impressive work as a scientific thinker, was at heart a statesman who had assumed the responsibilities of political leadership out of a sense of service to his countrymen. On the other hand, and with far more justification, Karl Jaspers [1883–1969] insisted that Weber was primarily a philosopher, in fact, the only philosopher of his age. Provided the term is understood in the sense in which it was used by the pre-Socratic schools in Greece, as the man who is swayed by an inner compulsion to grasp the meaning of life and to impart this secret to his fellow citizens, then Weber was unquestionably a philosopher: akin in spirit to the cryptic Heraclitus [c. 535–c. 475].

At the very outset of his career, Weber formulated the premises and objectives of his scientific work. His inaugural address, delivered at Freiburg in 1895 under the title "*Der Nationalstaat und die Volkswirtschaftspolitik*," offered a precise analysis of the state of science and politics at the moment when he first entered the lists as an active participant. Two years earlier, he had made a systematic study of the various types of agricultural labor existing in Germany, and the next year in connection with his research for the *Verein für Sozialpolitik* had analyzed the basic changes that were taking place among the agricultural laborers of East Elbe. The remarkable wealth of observation, no less than the penetrating interpretation, displayed in this analysis won the acclaim of Georg Friedrich Knapp [1842–1926]: "The predominant feeling aroused by this work is the sense that our knowledge is antiquated and that we must begin to learn all over again." Both pieces of research were combined in the inaugural address of 1895, which in addition extended the analysis to include the analogous situation in West Prussia.

According to Weber's analysis, the *Gutsherrschaften* [a form of manorial system developed in Northeast Germany, under which the peasants rendered services to the lord in return for their land—*Social Research* Eds.] of East Elbe had not benefited from the general transition to full capitalism (*Hochkapitalismus*). The cultivation of beets and the more widespread use of agricultural machinery were merely the technical manifestations of the radical economic transformation that with undiminishing force was disrupting the traditional rural system of agrarian labor hitherto prevailing among the *Instleute.* [Agricultural laborers on the large estates in the eastern provinces of Prussia. Engaged with their families for a long term of service, they are paid partly in money, partly in kind, and in addition are allowed to cultivate a piece of land belonging to the estate.—*Social Research* Eds.] These agricultural laborers, accustomed to identifying their own interests with the profits and prosperity accruing to the *Gutsherrschaft* economy, were being displaced, as a result of the shift to a money economy, by cheaper wage workers from Poland and Russia and in the process were reduced to a proletarian level. For the first time, there emerged a class antagonism between the owner of the manor and the agricultural laborer. Similarly, in West Prussia, the disappearance of the German day laborers from the more fertile estates was paralleled by an increase in the number of Poles to be found in the villages of less fertile estates.

Whether from an economic, a social, or a political point of view, this transformation was of primary significance. It not only revealed the penetration of rationalistic, capitalistic forms of enterprise into the rural economy, but at the same time furnished disturbing proof of the ability of comparatively backward groups like the migratory laborers from Poland to displace the more advanced Germans. It indicated further that the migration of the German peasants to the cities was inspired less by the allurements of urban civilization than by their own craving for independence. From the political angle, the transformation was doubly significant: the presence of large groups of Slavic immigrants was a distinct liability from the point of view of the military defense of eastern Germany; and in the second place, the position of dominance in Prussia was transferred into the hands of commercially minded entrepreneurs at a time when new forces and new methods were needed in the task of political renovation.

In interpreting the broader significance of this economic revolution in eastern Germany, Weber brought to bear a rich historical perspective. At a time when his intellectual contemporaries were evading the entire subject, he forcefully pointed out the tragedy implicit in the incomplete work of Otto von Bismarck [1815–1898]. While "the Iron Chancellor" had erected the framework of a new and unified nation-state, the foundations on which the political edifice rested had been undermined by the economic currents released in the course of the transition to *Hochkapitalismus*. And neither Bismarck nor the Prussian Junkers had been endowed with the insight or the political resourcefulness to cope with the new problem. Disheartened by the tragic situation confronting the nation, Weber ruminated on the question as to which social class was destined to assume the political leadership of the future. But as he turned successively to the "satiated" economic groups that comprised the upper minority, and then to the petty bourgeoisie, and finally to the proletariat, he was unable to detect in any of them even the rudiments of a capacity for political leadership:

> The disturbing element in the situation which confronts us is that while the bourgeois classes as bearers of the power interests of the nation seem to be withering, there is no evidence to indicate that the working classes are in any sense qualified to replace them. . . . In our cradles we were visited with the most grievous curse that history can impose upon a generation: the cruel fate of being political epigoni.

Weber's saturnine views on the state of contemporary affairs in Germany had a great deal to do with determining his premises regarding the proper content of political economy. In defining the scope and essential emphasis of the new discipline, which he designated as *Volkswirtschaftspolitik*, he maintained that the misery of the masses, however intense, is a less compelling consideration in determining the ultimate aim of *Volkswirtschaftspolitik* than is the responsibility felt toward history by the individual who sees his fellow countrymen in such a desperate state. For under such circumstances, the political education of the nation must claim precedence over all other aims that *Volkswirtschaftspolitik* or *Volkswirtschaftslehre* might set itself:

> Alternately in this discipline the technical economic problem of the production of goods, and the problem of the distribution of goods, that is to say the problem of social justice, have been played up as the true criteria of value . . . and above both has towered, time and again, the realization that a science dealing with man, and such is the case with political economy, must focus on the nature of man as bred out of the economic environment in which he lives.

Thus, the immediate political situation Weber experienced at the outset of his intellectual career was responsible for his selection of the criteria of value that should be observed in the analysis of economic and social-political activity. In his general approach, Weber set himself squarely against the historical school of national economy and the Socialists of the Chair (*Katheder-Sozialisten*), who maintained that it was possible to derive from the economy itself the norms necessary for the ordering of the social process. But however strongly Weber's intellectual system may have been conditioned by the broader situation of the moment in Germany, its epistemological foundations must be correlated with his own individual personality. For the peculiarity of his political economy lies in the fact that it is concerned not with laws of economics, not with *homo economicus*, but with the concrete personality of man as it manifests itself in particular historical situations. This type of approach is followed through not only in the various categories of political economy but also to an equal degree in the categories of all cultural and intellectual history, where it might prove most pertinent. Cultural history maximizes the objective impersonal forces at play and thus tends to blot out the individual except as a strand in a larger pattern of culture. Intellectual history is concerned with man only from its own specialized angle. But the science of society as formulated by Weber emphasized laying bare the qualitative existence of concrete historical individuals living under particular sets of economic and social conditions.

By *qualitative existence* Weber meant an existence that is capable of developing for itself some inner meaning and significance. Meaning and significance attach to an existence when the individual is accorded respect in the social world, or, on a more spiritual and intellectual plane, derives his sense of worthiness from the consciousness of being a participant in some *Sinnzusammenhang*—that is, in some purposive scheme of things. Without some kind of freedom, qualitative existence, for Weber, is impossible; since this conception of freedom with its obvious connotations from existential philosophy is the fundamental basis of Weber's sociology, certain metaphysical overtones are to be detected.

The particular form in which Weber worked out his science of society emphasized the interplay between this original metaphysical consciousness and the environmental forces with which it collides. In the modern setting, ideals of human freedom find themselves confronted with a capitalistic society, saturated with rationalism in all of its spheres. The clash between ideal standards and concrete realities posed the crucial question of Weber's sociological inquiries, namely, how man—that is, man conceived as molded by the passions and tensions of a lofty human soul—still finds a place for himself in the modern world. This is Weber's philosophical point of departure, as articulated in the inaugural address delivered at Freiburg in 1895 and as expressed time after time in his subsequent writings. It was of the utmost significance in the formulation of his interpretative sociology (*verstehende Soziologie*).

II

The existential philosophy that supplied Weber with his initial premises found its logically developed culmination in the body of works dealing with the theory of science. These constitute one of the most important inquiries into the problems of empiric cultural sciences during the final third of the nineteenth century in Germany. These works, which by 1900 had come to be accepted as the most authoritative statement in the field of epistemology, are indispensable to an understanding of Weber's sociology.

Along with Wilhelm Dilthey [1833–1911], Georg Simmel [1858–1918], Wilhelm Windelband [1848–1915], and Heinrich Rickert [1863–1936], Weber set out to transform the historical and social sciences into empiric, scientific disciplines. These scholars proceeded from quite different philosophical premises, but their undertakings had in common a lofty earnestness of purpose. From one point of view, they may be said to have emerged in response to the void caused by the collapse of the traditional metaphysical systems, particularly the Hegelian that had exerted an influence on the intellectual and moral sciences (*Geisteswissenschaften*), even in their formulation of concepts. From another point of view, they may be said to have arisen as a counteroffensive against the encroachments of the natural sciences. Scientific laws and mathematical relationships that had produced such fruitful results in the field of natural science were threatening to subject the *Geisteswissenschaften* to a methodological apparatus that was altogether alien and unsuited to types of inquiry where intellectual and moral values were involved. In the face of the widespread contention that the *Geisteswissenschaften* could not aspire to the status of real science, except in so far as they took over the methods of the natural sciences, Wilhelm Dilthey set himself the ambitious task of reconstituting the suspect disciplines on a new psychological basis compounded of experience and understanding (*Verstehen*) and of building them in strictly intellectual and moral terms, without recourse to irrelevancies borrowed from the natural sciences. In conception, Dilthey's pioneer efforts were titanic, propelled as they were by his personal sense of despair at the spectacle of spiritual and intellectual disintegration from which western European culture was suffering. In their total effect, however, they were abortive, in the sense that from Dilthey's philosophical premises, it was not feasible to derive a sure methodological foundation for the individual sciences that dealt with intellectual and moral relationships. Although on occasion Weber engaged in critical tilts with Dilthey and his school, he remained well outside their influence. He was far more indebted to Rickert, who in his systematic formulations as to the different methods pursued by the natural sciences and the *Geisteswissenschaften* in the building of concepts, supplied the key for much of Weber's own work of this type in the field of social sciences. This indebtedness Weber explicitly recognized when he said that he conceived his own task as that of proving the applicability of Rickert's theses to sociological inquiry.

The heated controversy over the epistemological foundations of science bulked as large in the social sciences as elsewhere. It was a particularly acrimonious point of controversy whether political economy was a natural science or a *Geisteswissenschaft*. Even the leaders of the historical school of economics insisted that it was their task to discover the natural laws of human activity without going beyond the economy itself, and from these laws to derive reality. Wilhelm Georg Friedrich Roscher [1817–1894], in his own peculiar way, had built his conceptual system with elements of positive Christian piety, an organismic theory of recurring cycles and certain extracts from Hegelian logic. Weber, in his scientific-logical writings, addressed the question whether historical and social scientific disciplines are properly classified as science. His works on Roscher and Karl Gustav Adolf Knies [1821–1898] pointed out those metaphysical elements in their concept building that stood in the way of a strictly empiric social science. According to Weber, in building their concepts, both of these outstanding exponents of the historical school of economics revealed unmistakable traces of the emanatistic logic of Hegel, and in the significance that they attached to certain ideas of free will and irrationality their metaphysical attachments became all too obvious. Weber's trenchant attack upon the metaphysical preconceptions of the historical school is of the utmost significance as revealing his initial position.[1] Citing examples from Paul Hinneberg [1862–1934], Friedrich Meinecke [1862–1954], and Heinrich von Treistschke [1834–1896], Weber observed:

> One encounters in them again and again the unpredictability of personal behavior, which is a consequence of freedom, interpreted, either explicitly or implicitly, as a peculiar dignity of man and therefore of history, while the creative significance of the personality in action is contrasted with the mechanical causality governing the processes of Nature. . . . At the bottom of these statements, all of which elevate the *ars ignorandi* caveat to the

> dignity of a central methodological principle, there is to be found the strange premise that the value of a science, or of its subject matter, corresponds to those very things we cannot know about it in the concrete or the general. If this were so the distinguishing characteristic of human behavior would be that it was incapable of being explained and, consequently, of being understood.[2]

He continued:

> The 'freer' the decision to act—that is, the more this decision is a response to its 'own' reflections rather than to 'external pressures or irresistible effects'—the more completely, *ceteris paribus*, the motivations involved in the decision may be fitted into the categories, end and means; so much the more adequate will be the rational analysis of these motivations and under given conditions their integration into a scheme of rational activity; all the greater therefore is the role which . . . monological knowledge plays, and all the more fixed is the relationship between the former and the means . . . but the greater the freedom of action—that is, the further removed from the processes of nature—the more there comes into play, finally, the conception of a personality that finds self-realization in the constant attunement of its inner being to certain ultimate values and life meanings; through the medium of an action these values and meanings are transformed into aims and purposes, and in the process this action becomes teleological and rational. Consequently there is less and less place for the romantic-naturalistic conception of personality which, proceeding in the opposite direction, searches out the ethos of the personality in the dank, fallow subsoil of human, or rather animal, life. From such romantic obscurantism,

> with its indiscriminate attempts to immure the freedom of the will in the dark recesses of the natural world, emanates that mystery of personality as invoked occasionally by Treitschke and more frequently by many of his fellow romantics. For the purposes of historical analysis human personality is not a mystery; on the contrary it is the one and only 'comprehensible' which can be explained. Under no circumstances—even where the possibility of rational explanation ceases—are human actions and conduct more irrational . . . than is each and every individual process as such. But these actions and conduct are raised far above the irrationality of the purely natural in all cases where rational interpretation is possible.[3]

These statements are thoroughly characteristic of the basic set of premises from which Weber proceeded in his scientific-logical studies. From the attack on the romantic irrationalism of German historiography emerged not only a definite conception of man but, at the same time, a sense as to what phases of the human personality are legitimate objects of scientific analysis and interpretation. The historian and the social scientist discover man in given objective situations, in which he plays either an active or a passive role. How he conducts himself is determined on the one hand by his interests, his sets of values, and his decisions; on the other, by the impersonal factors in the given situation. What he does and what he tolerates is built around his definite concrete evaluations and aims, be they on a material or an ideal plane. Therefore, since the behavior and conduct of the human being is oriented in terms of motives that lend themselves to explanation and comprehension, the personality, because it is inextricably set in this particular context of meanings and aims, becomes an object of rational inquiry.

This penetrating criticism of the epistemological principles of the historical school of economics could not have been made without a clearly formulated set of premises as to the boundaries and limitations of an empiric social science—that is, of a social science freed from metaphysical and dogmatic entanglements. Weber assumed at the outset that no individual science is capable of furnishing an authentic "copy" of reality. The utmost that can be accomplished by such sciences, either in the historical or the social disciplines, is, through reasoned thought, to bring order into the ceaseless flux of the real world. The principles of classification, by which this order is to be achieved, cannot, however, draw upon reality, but must be imposed by the scientist himself.

Where does the scientist who engages in such inquiries derive his methodological principles? Weber answers—from his existence as a participant in the culture. In so far as he feels that his own life has meaning—that is, if he conducts his life according to a set of ultimate values—he becomes interested in those elements of reality that have a bearing on these values. Thus, from the infinite manifold confronting him, particular features emerge as significant and calling for investigation. Moreover, according to Weber, "the set of values, to which the scientist relates the subjects of inquiry, may determine his conception (*Auffassung*) of an entire cultural epoch, not only establishing which phenomena are of value but also distinguishing between those that have significance and those that do not—between the 'important' and the 'unimportant.'"[4] Thus, for example, whereas Jacob Burckhardt [1818–1897], proceeding from the ideal conception of an aristocratic-aesthetic man, emphasized those tendencies in the Renaissance that served to substantiate his particular set of inner values, later historians threw their emphasis on those features of Renaissance culture that were equally characteristic of the Middle Ages.

From the very outset of his scholarly career, Weber held that in his evaluation of social structures the crucial consideration was the question of "the particular human type to which these structures, whether through external or internal (motive) selection, offered the optimal chance of gaining the ascendancy." With the aid of this practical-ethical criterion, he chose from the reality of his times, as well as from the historical processes that produced his times, the most significant elements "related to value" (*wertbezogen*), to use Rickert's terminology. These elements he found primarily in the forces of the capitalistic system and in the rationalism that pervaded all spheres of life. Of course, it is possible to imagine epochs in which these value relationships become utterly devoid of significance and disappear as fields of scientific inquiry, making way for some new or revived approach to reality. For in its flow to unknown ends, the stream of the historical-social world assumes ever new configurations, creating in turn new perspectives from which to examine the infinite multiplicity of motivation-patterns and the interweaving of man's efforts to order his life: ever new interrelationships are discovered that lie outside the ken of other epochs, whether of the past or the future.

Despite that, thus conceived, the starting point of knowledge is both subjective and ephemeral, empiric sciences of reality cannot, according to Weber, proceed from any other. What is required to make them sciences in the true sense of the word? "Only what is explained in terms of causality," replies Weber, "is scientifically worked out." All meaningful human activity and conduct can be causally explained. As already noted, meaning for Weber is "subjectively intended meaning" (*subjectiv gemeinter Sinn*), not objective, metaphysical meaning. Regarding the latter, the individual social sciences have nothing to say. Instead, they must understand meaning as being imposed on reality by man through his attempts to orient his life in terms of realizing those purposes, values, and aims that seem valuable to him. Reality, so interpreted, is the process of creating meaning, and the science of reality therefore is the understanding of such meaning patterns (*Sinnzusammenhang*). For a social science that aspires to be a science of reality, Weber prescribes three objectives: first, it must understand the peculiarities of the historical and social present; second, it must furnish an interpretation (*Wertinterpretation*) of the interrelationships between the component elements and of their significance for the culture; and, finally, it must understand, by a process of causal interpretation, why its essential elements have come about in the particular way they have rather than in some alternative way.[5]

To Weber, understanding is synonymous with the discovery of causal interrelationships, or in other words, with the imputation (*Zurechnung*) of concrete results to concrete causes. This is the essence of the scientific method and must be recognized as such even by those who have a radically different emotional and intellectual make up. For it is not essential to accept the particular values that happen to be assumed. The only sine qua non of the scientific approach is the rational acceptance of the truth that these premises, if true, must unfold along one line and only one line and must lead to one precise imputation and to no other.

This particular type of causal analysis constituted for Weber the essential characteristic of the social sciences. "The question of causality, where the individuality of a phenomenon is involved, is a question involving not laws, but concrete causal interrelationships; not a question of the category under which the phenomenon should be subsumed, but a question of the individual concatenation (*Konstellation*) which must have caused it: it is a question of imputation."[6] Social sciences are methodologically distinguished from the natural sciences. The end goal of knowledge in the natural sciences is the formulation of laws on the basis of classified facts. The social sciences are preoccupied with individual patterns of concatenation, and thus the general laws and norms of causal sequence are merely a means to understanding. As Weber points out, such general laws and norms are indispensable for concrete imputation in the understanding of reality. "Imputation cannot be understood without a knowledge of the regularity of causal interrelationships."[7]

Such regularities cannot be deduced from concepts. They are rules of experience that, given a certain set of conditions or objectives, construct in a rationally adequate manner a typical course of action. Practical activities of all kinds are undertaken on the presupposition that under a given set of circumstances certain causal sequences can be taken more or less for granted. The military chief of staff, for example, with the knowledge he possesses of the general strategic situation at the moment and of the objectives the enemy is aiming at, can visualize what course of action his antagonist must follow if he seeks to achieve these objectives. This same type of causal calculation is normally resorted to, likewise, in all political and economic pursuits as a means of anticipating a course of action.

Economic science, in the logical construction of its laws, affords the classic example of adequately erected causal interrelationships, which—under given conditions (such as a money economy) and given objectives (such as profit making)—can proceed in only one rational manner. "All economic laws are causal interrelationships expressed as rules which are adequate for the interrelationships."[8] In such cases, the category of objective possibility is valid; that is, by proceeding according to the rules of experience and by constructing these rules in the proper rational way, it is possible that events will transpire in conformity with the rules. These constructions are not hypotheses but merely aids toward forming hypotheses. They provide no copy of the real world, being technically constructed concepts, intended merely to serve as fixed points of reference for measuring the extent of the divergence therefrom of the individual imputations. Weber calls such conceptual constructs "ideal types."

In the social and historical sciences, these ideal types are the logical approaches to reality, in the sense that Weber conceives the function of the empiric sciences of reality as that of bringing order into the empiric world through the power of thought. The ideal type—as for example, city-economy, capitalism, imperialism, feudalism—is, to quote Weber, in the nature of "an ideal boundary concept, by reference to which reality is measured with a view to clarifying certain significant phases of its empiric makeup; an ideal concept with which reality is compared. Such concepts are creations, in which we construct interrelationships by drawing upon the category of objective possibility."[9]

Such "genetic concepts" are constructed from elements of reality in the intellectual and religious sphere as well as in the political and social, resulting in such ideal types as Christianity, liberalism, socialism, and the like. Although the construction of ideal types becomes progressively more difficult as the content of these concepts comes to coincide with the ideals and norms by which the investigator regulates his own personal conduct, they are not, however, to be dispensed with in the analysis of intellectual movements and religious trends. Their value as aids toward comprehending concrete causal relationships consists in the fact that, provided they are constructed purposefully, they serve to enhance the clarity and incisiveness with which individual causes are imputed. The actual motivations in a particular case and the individual processes of causation are far less elusive when the divergence in each instance is measured from a fictitious ideal type than when one relies on an immediate and direct interpretation.

The discovery of the ideal type opened the way to a strenuous offensive against conceptual realism in all its forms. It engendered an intense resistance against trying to derive an understanding of external reality through the reality of concepts. Scientific insight into the structure of the applied means and of the technical processes of understanding and into the precise delimitation between a concept of reality and reality itself requires a highly perfected scientific and intellectual discipline. At the same time, it requires a clear distinction between scientific construct and the subject of investigation. But such self-awareness depends also on an abandonment of all types of metaphysical, religious, and theological standards, and norms. Only rarely does one see such a clear and penetrating glimpse of a mind aware of the conditions, limitations, and potentialities under which it operates. And only a man of the extraordinary intellectual power and spiritual majesty of Max Weber would have had the capacity to articulate in enduring form such an instant of spiritual awareness. His struggles to free scientific methodology from value judgments throw a flood of light upon the intellectual milieu in which the new scientific theories were first evolved.

The social sciences from their earliest days, more than any other branch of science, had dealt with questions of practical politics and of organized social life. They were forced to pass judgment on measures of statecraft, legislative actions, and political decisions. The criteria that governed these judgments were not questioned so long as the aims of the state in whose services the economic sciences had originated were generally recognized and accepted. And when these sciences had abandoned their practical functions, the possibility of a dichotomy between value judgments and empiric analysis of reality was precluded by two sets of premises. The first held that, inasmuch as economic and social evolution proceeds according to the laws of nature, being and value are identical. The second held that inasmuch as a single principle of evolution governs economic reality, the genetic and the normative are one.[10]

The historical school of economics and the Socialists of the Chair were the first to try to discover immanent moral judgments in the process of economic unfolding and to establish in scientific terms a basis for the just ordering of social and economic institutions. Moreover, according to Gustav von Schmoller [1838–1917], there existed, despite national boundaries and the diversity of religious customs, a general agreement in all periods and among all peoples as to the nature of social justice. He was also inclined to assume the identity of ethical and cultural values. Against this naive saddling of the social sciences with ultimate values that their exponents professed to discover in and to deduce from science, Weber bluntly retorted that under no circumstances can the investigation of reality and the work of the sciences of reality substantiate ideals, evaluations, and norms in scientific terms.

With deadly earnestness, Weber repeatedly pointed out the extreme seriousness of the spiritual dilemma at hand:

> It is the fate of a cultural epoch which has eaten of the tree of knowledge to be aware that however completely we may investigate history we cannot read its real meaning, and that we must be content therefore to create our own sense of history; that our *Weltanschauung* can never be the product of the progressive knowledge of experience, and that thus the highest ideals and those which move us most deeply, work themselves out permanently only through conflict with rival ideals which are quite as sacred to other individuals as ours are to us.[11]

Time after time, he set out with the greatest vehemence to proclaim and bring about a complete divorce between the empiric sciences and practical ideals. "We know no ideals which can be demonstrated in scientific terms. To be sure, it is only the more arduous a task to draw them from one's own breast in a period of culture which is so subjective. But we have no fool's paradise and no streets of gold to offer, either in this world or the next, either in thought or in action; and it is a stigma of our dignity as men that the peace of our souls shall never be as great as the peace of him who dreams of such a paradise."[12]

The scientific labors involved in the rational knowledge, explanation, and understanding of nature and of society had drawn one after another of the realms of the divine order into the cold light of causal and mathematical analysis and had robbed the world of the security hitherto afforded by the idea of universal creation. This intellectual rationalization was accompanied by the disintegration of the Christian ethic that for almost two thousand years had been accepted throughout the Occident as the ultimate norm of human conduct. In its place, there appeared a multitude of value-claims and sets of norms: old scales of values crumbled and new ones were set up. The situation that Dilthey anticipated on his seventieth birthday had come to pass. Casting about sorrowfully for the intellectual means to transcend the dilemma, he asked, "Where are to be found the instruments for surmounting the spiritual chaos which threatens to engulf us?"

Weber would have replied that such instruments do not exist. His silence regarding the role of philosophy in his own age should most probably be interpreted as an indication of his belief that in such an intellectual dilemma the value of a philosophy that aspires to be more than epistemology is highly problematical. Empirical sciences, on the other hand, at such a juncture of intellectual history are in a particularly advantageous position—by reason of the fact that being free from all deeply rooted and axiomatic religious and metaphysical traditions they are conscious of the subjective nature of their evaluations—to gaze upon unadorned reality in a way denied to epochs that enjoy security and the sense of a meaning in life. Therefore, Weber was rightfully acclaimed as the philosopher of the time and his interpretative sociology as the empiric presentation and adequate expression of the prevailing metaphysical sterility and religious apathy. Following the empiric approach to reality, Weber perceived a manifold of values, discrete and mutually exclusive, at least in their significance. There are the values of life; erotic, political, and artistic values; the precepts of the Sermon on the Mount. All these sets of values are in a state of relentless strife with one another—as deadly as the conflict "between God and devil."

Weber repeatedly emphasized the tension between political and ethical decisions. In his inaugural address, he pointed out to the Socialists of the Chair that the man who is active in politics must place national ideals and realistic considerations of statecraft above personal ethical values; throughout his later writings, he revealed the divergence between norms of ethics and those of political activity. His investigations in the field of practical politics disclosed two contrasted types of ethical behavior: the one that emanates from inner convictions (*Gesinnungsethik*) and the one based on a sense of responsibility (*Verantwortungsethik*). In the case of the former, the individual is determined to realize his ethical ideals at any cost; loyalty in the service of these ultimate ideals is for him the criterion of his own integrity; nor is he given to asking himself whether perchance his behavior may not discredit the ideal or at least seriously delay its fulfillment. In the second type, the individual gauges the possible consequences of his action, ponders what effect it may have upon the ideal, and searches diligently for an opportunity to make the ideal operative: for him, success is an ever-relevant consideration. But the question of which of these alternative types of ethical behavior should be followed cannot be determined on scientific grounds, or indeed in any rational manner.

All human activity collides incessantly with ultimate decisions which in themselves cannot be carried through.

> In almost every single important decision by living beings, spheres of value cross and become interlaced. The leveling process of 'every-day life,' in the literal sense of that term, consists precisely in this, that the man who participates in it is not aware of this—in part psychologically, in part pragmatically conditioned—entanglement of mutually antagonistic values; and above all in the fact that he does not desire to be conscious that he is evading the choice between God and devil as well as his own final decision as to which of the colliding values is ruled over by the former, and which by the latter. Distasteful as it may be from the point of view of human self-assurance, the inevitable fruit of the tree of knowledge is nothing else than this: to be aware of these antagonisms and thus to be forced to see that every single important action no less than life in its entirety—provided it is not to drift along as a natural process but is to be consciously pursued—represents a concatenation of final decisions through which the soul, as conceived by Plato, chooses its own fate, that is to say selects the meaning of its existence and activity. Indeed the most egregious misapprehension that at recurring intervals has befallen the aims of those who have emphasized this collision of values is the characterization of such interpretations as 'relativism.' For a relativistic view of life proceeds from a diametrically opposite conception as to the relationships between the various spheres of value and to be carried through intelligently in logical form calls for a very particularly contrived type of organismic metaphysics.[13]

Nothing can show more clearly than this passage the meaning of the struggle that Weber carried on with such vehement intensity for the liberation of the sciences of reality from value judgments. The existential choice between God and devil is the only one that still ensures man a sense of dignity. But for Weber, a sense of dignity means man's consciousness of being, in the midst of intellectual and religious chaos, the one and only stage for an activity that through the decisions it makes imbues existence with an awareness of ultimate values. *We* confer meaning on life. Thus, as the truly disinherited sons of God, forced to struggle continuously in order to uphold this human dignity of ours, we find the guarantee of human existence only in the possibility of being able to determine our destiny through the agency of personality, which functions as a unit of practical decision. There is a kind of negative theology in this heroism. For the questions of why man proves true to himself, why these decisions between conflicting values are so important, remain obscure; and Weber veils the question in silence. The meaning of this silence must be conjectured with extreme caution. Even though the place of God remains vacant, all these decisions are in the last analysis meaningful only in so far as they serve absolute values.

Does science lose its value because its tasks are thus limited and because it must foreswear all pretensions to erecting norms of practical and ethical conduct? Tolstoy would have characterized a science thus limited as meaningless, since it would offer no guidance as to how we should live. In this respect, Weber's mind, accustomed to think of the sense of moral responsibility as governing activity, saw more clearly and deeply. A science of reality that deals with human activity may not be able, it is true, to prescribe what we should do, but it can make us more intelligently aware of what we want to do and, with particular ideals in mind, must want to do. For toward the understanding of human activity, science is capable of determining: first, the appropriateness of the means in relation to a given end; second, the adequacy of the ends in relation to a given concatenation of working interrelationships; and, finally, the unintended consequences and by-products of every human action or, in other words, the question as to what "the realization of a desired end will cost in terms of the presumably inevitable destruction of other values."[14]

If the sciences are in a position thus to stimulate self-awareness and intellectual discipline, they are serving, according to Weber, moral forces. For they intensify the realization that all activity and non-activity invariably entails an alignment on the side of certain particular values, a repudiation of others.[15] Furthermore, they may diffuse a clearer conception of what man must wish if he desires to realize particular ideals or, in other words, the consequences that the realization of the ideal may have in the form of byproducts that are often inconsistent with the ideals themselves. Thus, for instance, although socialism has set itself the ideal of establishing a realm of freedom, it may conceivably discover that the only means whereby it can realize, and at the same time perpetuate, the ideal of a homogeneous community is by a set of institutions involving a complete abnegation of freedom. The sciences can likewise throw light on the ultimate criteria of ideals and norms by which individuals are guided, and thus help us to live in more conscious attunement with those ideals. This consciousness is not an end in itself, however, but valuable only as a stimulus to action and decision. Therefore, in conclusion, the sciences may be said to be in the service of moral forces. Through the power of conscious responsibility, they are able to elevate decisions from the dank and gross levels of being to the plane where Jacob wrestles with the angel—that is to say, to the realm of ultimate self-expression of the human personality that lights up the deepest recesses of existence.

Notes

1. [See Max Weber, *Roscher and Knies: the logical problems of historical economics*, trans. and with an introduction by Guy Oakes (New York: Free Press, 1975).—Eds.]

2. Weber, Max, *Aufsätze zur Wissenschaftslehre* (Tübingen: 1925), 46.

3. Ibid., 132.

4. Ibid., 182.

5. Ibid., 170–71.

6. Ibid., 178.

7. Ibid., 179.

8. Ibid.

9. Ibid., 194.

10. Ibid., 148.

11. Ibid., 154.

12. Weber, Max, *Aufsätze zur Soziologie und Sozialpolitik* (Tübingen: 1924), 420.

13. *Aufsätze zur Wissenschaftslehre,* 469–70.

14. Ibid., 150.

15. Ibid., 150.

18

Max Weber's Sociology

I

In 1901, a pupil of Max Weber [1864–1920] demonstrated that the majority of industrial establishments in Baden were under the direction of Protestants. The Catholics, on the other hand, were but poorly represented among the industrial leaders in comparison with their percentage of the population.[1] This dissertation provided the external impetus to Max Weber's work in the sociology of religion, which revolves mainly around the problem of the relations between capitalism and evangelical Christianity.

The force of the ties between politics and religion had already become known to Max Weber from the cultural policy of the Prussian government. At the eighth Evangelical-social Congress, he had spoken on the "purely external and purely formal bureaucratic religious spirit" fostered in Prussia ever since Robert von Puttkamer [1828–1900]. Both contemporary political questions and Weber's universal historical knowledge impressed upon him the formative and determining influences of religion on the practical conduct of life. Was there a direct line between the drab and soberly rational everyday existence of capitalism and the forces of the Christian spirit? In his early investigations of agricultural conditions, Max Weber had

---

Published originally in a slightly different form in *Social Research* 2 (February 1935), 60–73. Republished by permission from *Social Research*.

already indicated the significance of the idea of "freedom" as one of the most powerful of the motivating factors of human activity, and he strongly emphasized the determining force of ideological factors together with economic, social, and political factors. The exposition of this principle continues the work of Karl Marx [1818–1883], while providing a fruitful and significant modification.

Unscrupulous striving for gain and greed for money, property, and economic goods existed at all times. Every historical epoch knew the irrational capitalism of adventurers, traders, and war profiteers. How was it, however, that the acquisition of money, in itself and for itself, came to be regarded as a moral duty? Such a conception would have appeared absurd to the aristocratic and feudal classes and degrading to any Greek or Roman freeman. How did the entrepreneur come to believe that his desire for profits was a moral obligation? In this connection, Martin Luther's [1483–1546] hostility to Catholic asceticism is of the greatest significance for all confessions of the Protestant churches. Luther's conception of "calling" (*Beruf*) attached a specific dignity to all secular and worldly activity and gave to all daily activity a moral and religiously divine sanctity. The monastery was demolished, but the whole world now became a monastery. Nevertheless, there is yet no connection between genuine Lutheranism and the capitalist spirit. The spirit of capitalism is to be understood only as a product of Calvin's gloomy doctrine of predestination and its resulting rules of life and conduct. In Calvin's Deus absconditus, only the terrible majesty of God is preserved without the characteristics of goodness, love and creation. Through His Majesty, all human souls, even before birth, are predestined without question either to heaven or to hell. This doctrine of predestination became the power that regulated the general everyday life of Calvinists. For there is only one single means whereby to assure one's self of the state of grace and that is through adherence to one's calling.

Unceasing devotion to work, the most minute and conscientious fulfilling of duty, restlessly successful activity for the glory of God—only these can lead to the certainty of belonging to the elect and the saved. Permeating the letters of Oliver Cromwell [1599–1658] is the motif that suffering obedience is more carnal and sinful than worldly activity. God demands from us activity, rational worldly constructions, and no moods or feelings. To the Puritan, accumulation of money served as a sign of grace. He is not to spend it for mere pleasure but rather for the glory of God, which means for new business enterprises. Like the medieval monasteries, the Puritan entrepreneurs could not escape from the inner logic of their position. The rational disciplining of life, the hostility to worldly and sensuous culture, the deepest mistrust of all those human ties that rest upon irrational feelings, all these served to force the occupational calling into the center of their life activity and made them look upon it as service of God. Since this logic demanded, however, that all profits in turn be used for more work, the accumulation of capital became almost an end in itself. Some time or other, the religious roots of this spirit would be torn away, but the accumulation of money, the calling, produced an autonomous and self-generating kind of activity. "The Puritan wanted to be an occupational being (*Berufsmensch*), we must be so." "The care for worldly goods was to be only like a thin coat on the shoulders of the pious and could be cast aside at any time. But this coat was destined to become a hard steel casing."[2] This represents the connection between the doctrine of predestination and worldly asceticism. This spirit together with its related doctrine of economic ethics became a condition for the development of that rational economic power that dominates modern life with increasing oppressiveness.

In an epoch that aimed to deduce all intellectual and spiritual relationships from material interests, this discovery of Max Weber's took on the greatest and most revolutionary significance. It spurred Weber to further research into the economic ethics of the great Asiatic world religions and Judaism. If Western Puritanism had provided a basis for the possibility of a rational industrial and economic organization, then the question arose whether the religious structures in Asia constituted a force that prevented the emergence of such economic forms of life. And it appeared that there were all kinds of ritualistic and religious restrictions that, despite highly significant commercial and finance-capitalistic forces, did not make possible the development of a continuously rational, industrial production system. The very religious tendencies of the Jews, which Weber brought forth in opposition to Werner Sombart's [1863–1941] interpretation of Jewish participation in modern capitalism, are in themselves proof of this thesis. The sanctified religious life of the Jews was never realized through or in their occupation but always outside their daily work, in prayer, in the study of the sacred literature, and in the ritual life—religious attitudes far removed from a worldly asceticism.

Whereas in these researches Max Weber revealed the influence of religious attitudes upon the economic activity of everyday life, in his continuation of these studies, especially in the section of his *Wirtschaft und Gesellschaft* dealing with sociology of religion, he showed the development of religious ideas within definite social groups and the influence of social conditions upon certain religious ideas and institutions. Max Weber thus described the relationship between Confucianism and the forms of life and consciousness of a literary bureaucracy and the social ethics of the older Islam as an expression of a warlike aristocracy. He discovered the significance of aristocratic and proletarian intellectual classes for the content of certain religions of salvation, and in this connection he disproved the theory of Friedrich Nietzsche [1844–1900] that the sources of these religions are to be found in the resentment of the pariahs. The intellectual classes of the nobility, who were the carriers of Buddhism, did not share in such resentment. Weber showed the peculiar significance of the Hebrew prophets for the continued existence of the Jews as a religious group, even after their political state had been destroyed, and he tied up the pariah existence of the Jews after the Exile with their religious consciousness. Despite the close connection of the spheres of religion with those of social life, the religious spontaneity of the former cannot be ultimately deduced from social relations. The content and character of religious ideas can be explained only from the internal laws of the religious sphere and religious needs. "Interests (material and ideal) and not ideas govern the immediate acts of man. But the 'world views' created by ideas have often served as switchmen to set the limits within which the dynamics of interests move activity."[3] The incomparable grandeur of the "economic ethics of the world religions," encompassing Protestantism and Judaism, Hinduism and Buddhism, Confucianism and Taoism, rests not only on the universal conception and the keen and illuminating power of Weber's ideas, but also particularly on the compactness and intensity of the sections on Puritanism and the ancient Hebrew prophets. One must go very far back in the literature of German cultural and intellectual history to find anything comparable. Wilhelm Dilthey's [1833–1911] justly famous *Weltanschauung und Analyse des Menschen seit Renaissance und Reformation* is, in comparison with Weber's work, lacking in clarity of formulation and pale in its description. Only the work of Leopold von Ranke [1795–1886] is as realistic and as intense as these works of Weber. Ranke's Christian humanism, however, was able to harmonize reality with the strained tension in his faith. All history ultimately rests peacefully in the hand of God; every epoch stands in immediate relation to God. The opposite view is found in Max Weber. His investigations showed him that not every epoch stood in this immediate relation to God. He knew that the force of the Christian charisma, which, through the religious heroism of the English sectarians, had revolutionized the entire life of the West, had disappeared. He knew that it was still manifest only in very limited circles and in individual souls. There was increasingly less room for religious charisma in the rationally standardized and rigid form of modern culture, in a time when the advance of rational sciences removed the magic spell from more and more aspects of organic and social life. The power of expression in his treatment of Puritan leaders and the prophets, such as John Bunyan [1628–1688] and Oliver Cromwell, George Fox [1624–1691] and John Milton [1608–1674], as well as the biblical prophets Isaiah and Jeremiah, bears witness to the influence on Max Weber of these heroes and agents of the divine pneuma with the greatness of their solitude and their calling. They were heroes in the literal sense of people whose lives were completely imbued with their calling.

In times of increasing rationalism and as a result of a growing lack of understanding for the greatness of this type of humanity there remained only the task to preserve at least the knowledge of this transforming power of religious charisma. The tension between the rational everyday life and the life of such religious heroes was not to be neglected but was rather to be sustained. Just because Weber knew what real religious charisma meant, he insisted that his own age was characterized by the reign of everyday life, and he looked with disgust at the need of contemporary intellectuals to mimic religious feeling.

> All this renders conditions unfavorable for the emergence of serious communal religious feeling carried by intellectuals. The need of literary and distinguished academic circles or coffee-house intellectuals for including

> 'religious' emotions among the collection of their sources of sensation and objects of discussion . . . might appear as a sign of widespread 'religious interest,' but it does not alter the fact that no new religion has ever emerged from such needs of intellectuals and their chatter and that fashion will also finally eradicate . . . this subject of conversation and journalism.[4]

No one fought more passionately than Max Weber for rational knowledge as opposed to all those kinds of sentimental, moralistic, and intellectualistic knowledge that served merely to secure peace of mind and were provisional in character. The best road to genuine knowledge was by way of radical doubt. Weber was deeply conscious, however, that there are problems that are beyond immediate scientific approach. Although human reason was able to penetrate deeply into the knowledge of life, there was still an impenetrable mystery that surrounded it all.[5] It was, however, a commandment of human existence to preserve this mystery. He knew that man's profoundest struggles, decisions, and evaluations lie beyond the realm of rational knowledge. They are the product of the totality of his existence. Just as Johann Wolfgang von Goethe [1749–1832] maintained a middle position between the forward pressure of knowledge and the calm reverence of the unsearchable, so Max Weber also knew the bounds between the world of knowledge and that of the unsearchable mystery of life. But unlike Goethe, there was no balanced harmony between the two in Weber. This radical tension between the two that is evident in the thought of Max Weber clearly reveals the intellectual and spiritual development of the nineteenth century. For Goethe, it was still possible to harmonize knowledge and faith within natural religion and pantheism. Weber could only recognize in knowledge and faith (or better perhaps, instead of faith, knowledge of the final superrational or irrational order) the extreme poles of modern human existence. To endure this tension and not break under it was the task that he set for the simple and sober heroism of modern man. The fulfilment of this demand under the conditions of modern life was possible only through unconditional service to a cause, to an impersonal ideal.

II

The foundation of the empirical sciences of reality on a theory of knowledge and the religio-sociological discovery of the significance of Puritanism for the origins of the capitalistic spirit provided the bases for the conception of Weber's most important sociological work. Another preparatory study, however, must be mentioned in this connection. The *Agrarverhältnisse im Altertum*[6] is an important part of Max Weber's work, and it is largely taken over in his *Wirtschaft und Gesellschaft.*[7] This study of agrarian relations is really a sociological investigation of the whole ancient social world and not only of agriculture. It considers what types of capitalism were developed in the ancient world and what hindrances there were to the emergence of a modern, rational, industrial capitalism. Through his knowledge of universal historical materials and through the keenness of his construction of ideal types, Weber developed the various forms of sociologically relevant types of cities: the military city, the aristocratic city, the guild city, the patrician city, the plebeian city, etc. And from the ideal type—feudalism—he developed various types of feudal aristocratic rule. He always adopted the viewpoint of attempting to explain through these instruments of knowledge the individual and historically different types of social structure and, above all, to bring out clearly the elements preventing or favoring the development of a rational industrial capitalism. This method also contributed a great deal toward the explanation of the decline of the ancient world. The very absence of a rational industrial capitalism and the supremacy of a commercial capitalism oriented purely on political chance, together with the increasing pacification of the world and the growing importance of a state military and bureaucracy with their resulting financial needs, must have brought about the most critical results—namely, the impossibility of finding a permanent source for the fiscal needs under the relatively underdeveloped rationality of the economic system. The state apparatus had become too extensive and costly to be supported by the social and economic forces of the Empire. Together with a series of quite different tendencies, these were the causes of a decisive political and economic transformation of the Empire.

Out of these three great phases of Weber's work—the methodological studies, the sociology of religion, and the sociology of ancient society—grew his last great work, *Wirtschaft und Gesellschaft*. This grandiose work of empirical sociology has remained a torso, externally because of the death of the author, yet also fragmentary and unfinishable in its very nature, like the process of historical life itself. For every form, and in a scientific sense this means every attempt at systematization, cannot do without dogmatic or metaphysical or philosophical-historical presuppositions. But Weber rejected these, as we have seen from his theoretical studies. Value judgments create the points of reference for the construction of sociological ideal types, but not for the combination of these into one comprehensive system. Every attack at Weber's lack of system, therefore, is meaningless, since Weber, by his fundamental theory of knowledge, rejected such a desire, and he repeatedly gave utterance to this view *expressis verbis*. In order to undermine this absence of system, therefore, it would be necessary to attack the logical foundations of his sociology, and not his sociology as such.

Another motive for the fragmentary form of this sociology is derived from the content that Weber gave to his sociology of understanding (*verstehende Soziologie*). He operates entirely without the concept of society. "Sociology is defined as a science which aims to understand clearly social behavior and thus give a causal explanation of its course and results."[8] Only human behavior is open to interpretation, and it matters not if this behavior is oriented around the attitudes of other human beings, social relations, or individually recognized commands and norms. Natural events can only be laid down as facts, but human behavior is capable of meaningful explanation. Only human behavior is determined by motives. These may be rational, purposeful, valuational, or emotional—and, therefore, from the "subjectively intended" meaning, intelligible. Social behavior, therefore, is human behavior related to the attitudes of other individuals. It may be unique or stereotyped, become integrated into social attitudes or remain amorphous, become institutionalized and assume a traditionalist character, or be organized into social forces. Sociology is interested in all those forms of the endless possibilities of human activities and relationships that reveal typical recurrences and present general empirically grounded developments. Sociological laws are possible only in the sense that they are conceptual formulations of such typical recurrences of human activity in the form of ideal types. Man occupies the central position in Weber's work because man is the bearer of all meaning. There is always the recurrent note that man can give meaning to his life only by his activity. For this reason, there are no institutions, or forces, or social forms that are not to be realized in human activity whether it be of purposes, values, or feelings. Thus, Weber's sociology destroys all the collectivistic concepts with which history and political science had operated and that always contained some latent dogmatic value judgments and presuppositions. Weber's destruction of conceptual realism in his ideal types parallels his destruction of collectivistic concepts in favor of sociological categories of man-to-man relations. Following from this, all values, norms, and moral commands exist, for this sociology, exclusively as maxims, ideas of value and ideas of norms, as chance that guides the activity of man. The category of chance plays a decisive role in Weber's sociology of understanding. It expresses the idea that with the knowledge of given conditions—that is, knowledge of the typical attitudes of definite human groups—only one particular course of action, and not another, is necessary for the attainment of the goal. Such an insight provides a certain assurance of success of individual activity in the field of the objectively possible. Such a category, therefore, is formal and technical in character. In a certain sense, it serves the variegated technique of life. Since life runs its course in various spheres and since economics and politics, religion and art, and science and technology each has its own orders that, in concrete historical situations, are swallowed up in a web of manifold motivations, an endless number of possible sociological categories and concepts exists. This is another reason for the fragmentary character of Max Weber's sociology.

Max Weber always protested that his sociological concepts and their casuistry did not represent an attempt to divide up reality into pigeon holes, as is so often the case in the works of formal sociology. It is an idle task to attempt to comprehend the endless stream of reality in such schematic arrangements. The aim of Weber's concepts is merely to present what sociological characteristics are revealed by any historical phenomenon.

The sociology of understanding, as an aid to the knowledge of concrete and individual relationships, became very fruitful and significant for the knowledge of the connections between the individual orders of life. Weber called his work "economics and the social orders and forces," and he sought to clarify their relations. In his theoretical studies, Weber pointed out that the sphere of economic life cannot be explained only in terms of immanent and internal development. Events in the political and religious spheres may often be more relevant to economics and may either further or retard tendencies in economic development. On the other hand, the structure and character of an economic order serve as conditions for political life and penetrate into the innermost forms of our personal life. Since he studied both the economic relevancy of all events of social life and how far economic forms served to create definite constellations and conditions for the political and social orders, his work reveals a characteristic fluidity of presentation without any point of equilibrium. Everywhere and always, the motifs are swallowed up in an endless sequence, and it is only the particularly chosen point of scientific interest that weaves together all the relevant links into one unified whole. The individual ideally typical constructions and the fundamental sociological categories of economic life are thus formed on the basis of the cultural significance of modern capitalism. Not through ideographic concepts, but through Weber's sociological ideal types, is it possible to understand unequivocally what were the conditions for the origins of capitalism in the West and what were the necessary conditions created by the modern state, modern bureaucracy, and the various forms of Western rationalism. Weber succeeds in developing the types of capitalistic orientation of industry and presenting the particular structure of modern rationalism oriented around chances of profits. For its origin and development, however, certain political and legal conditions were necessary. Weber takes up the monetary system and policy of the modern state as a condition for the modern economic order and the significance of political organizations for the economic system. In a corresponding way, his juridical sociology was concerned with the significance of the formal characteristics of modern law for capitalistic rationalism and, above all, with the importance of juristic rationalism for the peculiarities of the political and administrative structure of the modern European world. It is not only modern capitalism that is characteristic of the West. Rational science, classes, parties, cities, and the modern rationalistic structure of the state—all these are peculiar to the West. For this reason, the sociological categories in "*Typen der Herrschaft*" (Types of Ruling) in his juridical sociology and in chapters on sociology of religion in his *Wirtschaft und Gesellschaft* all serve to contrast the various typical forms and constructions of Western rationalism with the tendencies of rationalist thought in Asia, above all in India and China.

By extending the aims of knowledge beyond the confines of the relationships between economics and the great social forces of state, religion, and law, this sociology took on a most comprehensive aspect. It represents the first grand attempt to realize an empirical sociology of the forms of rationalism and its interacting influences on the emotional and irrational attitudes of Western man. His investigations into the sociology of religion also sufficiently demonstrated to him the enormous role of modern rationalism in the emergence of the reformed religions and how it continued its influence in Tridentine Catholicism and the Counter Reformation. Parallel with and in immediate relation with this rationalization of consciousness, however, came a deepening and an inward turn toward the irrational religious attitudes and also to the emotional life, such as never existed in the Middle Ages. Corresponding events occurred in political life in the legitimization of the power of sovereignty. The chapter on "Nation" is a most instructive example of the necessary increasing irrationality of the legitimacy of the state in mass democracies and the increasing depersonalized bureaucracy. Here are actual problems that will occupy the attention of several generations, for they are only indicated by Weber and need extended individual study.

Characteristically, these concepts developed by Weber proceed from a certain formal abstractness to a relatively concrete and individual fullness. The fundamental concepts of the first part of his sociology, especially, border closely on the categories of formal sociology, while the later sections, above all the fragments of the second and the third parts, reveal concepts with a strong historical and concrete content. To go into the various stages and forms of the concepts of ideal types in Weber would lead us too far afield here, and beyond the limits of a general introduction to his work. Only so much need be indicated, that wherever the sociological categories are developed in their purest form—such as "traditionalism," "charismatism," "secularization of the charisma"—they signify basic sociological phenomena, actual tendencies of activity that are structurally possible here or there or at any time. Tradition and charisma determined exclusively the motives of action in the prerationalist epochs. Tradition and custom are the ruling forces of routine daily life in all integrated epochs. The charisma of religions and political leaders and heroes, born out of need and enthusiasm, is the revolutionary force in such epochs.

The dominant role of these categories in the work of Weber is no mere accident. Tradition and economic daily life stand in polar position to charisma. Charisma as a sociological category signifies not a value judgment, but merely that quality of appearing as leader because of extraordinary achievements that must be legitimized by verification before his followers. The concept, therefore, is wholly independent of whether or not the individual is accorded "objective" greatness.

If our activity, however, gives meaning to history, then Weber must be rightly interpreted as maintaining that charisma, as "introduction of meaning" (*Einbruch von Sinn*), effects a revolutionary transformation and progress of man not only in the external institutions of the world, but also in the inner being of man. Reason also has worked as a revolutionary force, internally as intellectualization, externally as a transformation and reorganization of the entire order of living in the modern world. But this very new form of daily existence—no longer traditional, but dynamic, and oriented toward the rationalistic chances of modern economy, and increasingly rationally organized and institutionalized—makes all the more problematic the revolutionary power of charisma as one of the external forces of bringing human greatness into view. "The charismatic transfiguration of 'reason' is the final form which charisma has taken on its fateful road."[9] The prospect, like the general character of Weber's sociology, is one of somber character. It appears that the rationalistic existence of modern man completely crushes the possibilities for greatness and charismatic leadership.

Notes

1. Martin Offenbacher, *Konfession und soziale Schichtung* (Tübingen: Mohr Siebeck, 1901).

2. Max Weber, *Gesammelte Aufsätze zur Religionssoziologie,* 2nd ed. (Tübingen: Mohr Siebeck, 1922), 1:203.

3. Ibid., 252.

4. Max Weber, *Wirtschaft und Gesellschaft* (Tübingen: Mohr Siebeck, 1922), 296.

5. Marianne Weber, *Max Weber: ein Lebensbild* (Tübingen: J. C. B. Mohr, 1926), 340.

6. Contained in his *Gesammelte Aufsätze zur Sozial- und Wirtschaftsgeschichte* (Tübingen: Mohr Siebeck, 1924).

7. Cf. especially the chapter, "Die Stadt."

8. *Wirtschaft und Gesellschaft*, 1.

9. Ibid., 817.

19

Max Weber's Political Ideas

I

Max Weber always emphasized that he belonged to the historical school of political economy. He always accorded respectful treatment to Gustav von Schmoller [1838–1917], his teacher, even when he openly opposed him. At the same time, he also always pointed out the fundamental importance of the work of Karl Marx [1818–1883] for all modern social, economic, and sociological investigation. No one has analyzed the work of Marx more dispassionately, yet at the same time more critically, than Weber. There are, of course, many points of contact between Weber and Marx both in their thought and in their scientific understanding. They looked upon capitalism as a historical phenomenon of the modern world and not as a naturally given form of economic life or as a form of economic organization of long standing as described in the works of Karl Julius Beloch [1854–1929], Robert von Pöhlmann [1852–1914], and even Eduard Meyer [1855–1930]. These writers presented a modernized version of ancient history in which ancient industrial life is described as a capitalistic order with all the terminology of modern economy. For both Marx and Weber, the specifically modern character of our present economy was of the greatest scientific importance. They realized

---

Published originally in a slightly different form in *Social Research* 2 (August 1935), 368–84. Republished by permission from *Social Research*.

that this tremendous force of modern life had determined, in a far-reaching way, the fate of the Western world. In devoting themselves to the study of this subject, they were conscious of its bearing upon the picture of man that dominated their own standard of values and in this way determined their scientific interests. For both Weber and Marx, the existential point of departure for their scientific interests was a definite idea of man.

Despite very strong inner contacts, however, the works of Weber and Marx appear antagonistic to each other. For this, the different historical situations, intellectual and spiritual conditions of existence, and the characters of the two men are responsible. The powerful influence of the political revolutions of the first half of the nineteenth century is revealed in the works of Reinhold Niebuhr [1892–1971], Alexis de Tocqueville [1805–1859], and Jacob Burckhardt [1818–1897]. The structure of Marx's work, too, is inconceivable without taking into account the influence of the modern revolutions on his work. But this is not what makes Marx unique. What gives the work of Marx its characteristic importance is its combination of the sociological interpretation of revolution with Georg Hegel's [1770–1831] philosophy of history and its radical conclusions deduced from economic analysis of the world situation. Moreover, Marx represents the first great example of the interaction of revolutionary fanaticism with the striving for scientific knowledge. All previous revolutionary ideologists had oriented themselves around the eternal ideals of justice and divine order. Even in a secularized form, they still clung to the concepts of Christian natural law. Marx, for the first time, attempts to determine revolutionary developments from the spirit of scientific knowledge and thus makes them take on the character of necessity. This combination of scientific spirit with political and revolutionary pathos was extremely fruitful in positing the question: What makes men revolt? At the same time it also set up certain limitations to knowledge. In a dogmatic historical and social theory, reality can appear only in a distorted form.

Because of Marx's negative critique of social theories, he could never enter scientifically into all the manifold and unique aspects of reality and human institutions. In his view, no norms could be derived from the fundamental political assumptions of such theories. The "politicization" of scientific research, in which the work of Marx occupies a central position, came into being with the alliance of intellectual classes and unprivileged masses, who needed an intellectual orientation for their political aspirations. In a modern rational society, this could only be accomplished within the field of scientific research. The history of Western culture reveals the influence of this phenomenon in all fields of intellectual and literary activity. This is shown not only in the general decline in level but also in the change in importance attached to the concept of truth and in the ethos of intellectual and spiritual work. The path from Pierre-Joseph Proudhon [1809–1865] to Georges Sorel [1847–1922] indicates clearly enough the significance of this "politicization" of the spirit.

All the constructive elements in Weber's system stand in sharp contrast to the structure of the work of Marx. Precisely because Weber himself was most deeply a politically conscious individual, he always opposed most passionately the subordination of scientific learning to politics, particularly from the lecture platforms of universities. He was politically minded in a sense diametrically opposed to that of Marx. Marx was oriented toward a revolutionary utopia beyond all reality that, therefore, permitted only a partial knowledge of empirical reality. Max Weber's political thought was that of a Niccolò Machiavelli [1469–1527] or a Tocqueville. It was that of a practical statesman, faced with concrete tasks in concrete situations, whose activity is governed by the knowledge of the means whereby he can attain his goal. Weber's ideal types and the content of his sociology represent the fully conscious theoretical modes of thought and attitudes of a man possessed of political and social responsibilities, who is always confronted with concrete decisions and who is always forced to adapt the methods and aims of his activity to the constellation of the given historical situation.

A complete absence of illusion marks all great theoretical works on politics that were written by persons engaged in active political affairs as a sort of reflection upon their life activity, above all, such works as Machiavelli's *The Prince*, Tocqueville's *L'Ancien Régime et la Révolution*, and the *Mémoires* of Louis Duc de Saint-Simon [1675–1755]. Only the individual engaged in governing—the political technician—can come to view all the forces and motives of human activity as constellations of interests, whether they are of a material, class, or ideal nature. He sees all around him activity of individuals and groups of individuals motivated by the most realistic goals and often very irrational emotions that he must know how to direct and utilize. For him, all impulses of political and social activity, whether characterized by the noblest feelings or by the basest desires, are facts, free of value judgments. He must utilize them all in the same way, whenever he is confronted with them. The exercise of political power is the most perfect school for disillusionment from the world of human activity and for laying bare the motives by which human activity is directed.

In this sense, the inner structure of the work of Max Weber is political even though he actually never possessed political power. Few men were so equipped to possess and exercise such power, but fate denied him the realization of this decisive phase of his talent. But from the peculiar force of the theoretical realization of this political character there emerged a sociological work that takes its place beside the greatest political works, above all, beside that of Machiavelli. He who is only a technician or artist of politics takes a cynical and frivolous attitude toward the terrifying character of these insights into politics. Both Machiavelli and Weber, however, possessed such a passionate love for their city and their people, and such a complete inner identification with their destiny that they brought to bear all their devotion and self-sacrificing service morally to transcend this disenchantment of the universe that came to them from their knowledge of reality. Weber's pathos is national. The existence of his people and his nation is for him an absolute value for his own existence. Precisely because of this feeling he finds the age in which he is forced to live as one of epigones.

All political institutions, including that of the state, are, for Weber, nothing but a means to insure and increase the world power and position of Germany. His measure of the value of constitutional institutions consists in how far they are able to bring forth men with the qualities of leadership necessary for such a task. He also evaluates all political and social orders according to the human types they produce. His uncompromising struggle against the Germany of the prewar period rested upon the belief that the political and social institutions allowed for neither the emergence of political leaders nor for free and autonomous individuals of independent opinions. His bitter struggle against a legal administration that protected strikebreakers was prompted not by economic motives or particular sympathies but by a belief that such decisions trampled upon the sense of honor of the workers and desecrated their human rights and feelings. A state that, in the case of its army, fostered the cultivation of the spirit of camaraderie and honor would be unable to tolerate such a situation.

Marx and Weber differ in type of political attitude. This also involves quite different possibilities of scientific knowledge. Marx, with his revolutionary and fundamentally utopian position, was forced to be dogmatic and bound by his philosophy of history and thus shut himself off from an all-embracing and many-sided knowledge of reality. Weber, thanks to his keen theoretical soberness, on the one hand, and his profound theoretical consciousness of the vital political temperament within him, on the other, was able to achieve a universal comprehension of reality, the like of which had never been undertaken before him. In Weber, much more than in Nietzsche and Marx, and more than in Machiavelli precisely because Weber was more universal, the disenchantment of the world is completed.

As much as Weber recognized the positive influence of Marx, he, nevertheless, emphatically rejected his materialist philosophy of history and the one-sided character of his sociological interpretation. Precisely because he strove for a radical comprehension of reality, he found himself forced to distinguish as sharply between empirical and historico-philosophical elucidation and explanation as between interpretive and normative attitudes. A consideration of reality, without metaphysical, religious, or political dogmatism, revealed to him, however, that the chain of causes leads "at times from technical to economic and political fields and at times from political to religious and then economic fields. There is no point of equilibrium at any place. And that not infrequent version of historical materialism whereby the 'economic' factor represents something 'final' in the series of causes, this view is to my mind scientifically completely discredited."[1] Not even economic events as such can be explained by purely economic motives alone.[2] They are always codetermined by political, geographic, cultural, and religious causes. Weber repeatedly asserted his fundamental position in connection with the relation of religion and economics, particularly in the introduction to his sociology of religion.[3]

Weber's view of reality, therefore, forbade him to adhere to any philosophy of history. As a sociologist and as a scientist, he refused to speak of the "meaning" of historical development or to understand the meaning of world history. "It is . . . a fundamental fact of all history that the ultimate result of political activity often, nay regularly, stands in a completely inadequate and often even paradoxical relation to its original meanings."[4] As a grand example of such a paradox, he pointed to the ideals of piety of the Puritans that were directed toward a sanctification of personal life. The mundane asceticism and the church discipline of the sects developed, however, that type of the rationally acting "man of calling" without whom the economic spirit of capitalism—a world most distant from the spirit of God and one of calculation and coldness—would never have been possible. In the same paradoxical fashion, the human and fundamental right, springing from the deepest spiritual anguish of the sects struggling for liberty of conscience, created the "preparatory conditions for the free reign of capitalist utilization of property and human beings."[5]

The general tendencies of the historical process, moreover, revealed to him the influence of "chance" and its often-incalculable significance. The fulfilment of the prophecy of Isaiah on the salvation of Jerusalem, historically an "accident," created the impregnable foundation for the position of Jahweh and the prophets in Israel.[6] This observation of the "accidental" in the combination of series of historical causes always recurs in the work of Weber. This insight into the deep irrationality of history and economic life[7] left him speechless and prevented him from offering a rationalistic or intellectualistic interpretation of the historical process. If he had been a rationalist in the manner of the humanism of Voltaire [1694–1778], politics and history would have seemed to him nothing but a most ridiculous play of human stupidity and baseness. But Weber never drew such consequences from his view of history.

He constantly felt himself attracted to the poetic conceptions of reality found in Leo Tolstoy [1828–1910] and Fyodor Dostoyevsky [1821–1881]. Ever anew, he studied their works for the forms assumed by the various aspects and normative attitudes of history. Weber's plan to write a book on Tolstoy after the completion of his scientific work was never realized, so the following remarks are based merely on scattered references and expressions in his biography by Marianne Weber [1870–1954]. In *War and Peace*, above all, Tolstoy presented one of the grandest and most tragic epochs of modern history. In the pale light of his religiously colored presentation, the historical "heroes," Napoléon Bonaparte [1769–1821] and Mikhail Kututsov [1745–1813], Tsar Alexander I [1777–1825] and his courtiers, all appear as rouged actors in a tragedy of the Baroque. The world of history is but a transparent world of pretense in which human failing and earthly vanity are laid bare in all their emptiness. The marks of deepest earnestness that this picture of history revealed and by which the measure of Christian ethics was applied to the political and historical world appealed to Weber. But Weber could not identify himself with this Russian genius. In his very being, he was forced to reject such a disparagement of history. Although he never spoke of the meaning of history, he always spoke with pathos and emotion concerning the course of history. From the days of his inaugural address in Freiburg, he always spoke warningly and with exhortation and passion of a people's "responsibility before history." What could this formula mean to him?

From his observation of reality, Weber came to recognize conflict as the generator and master of all life, not only externally but also spiritually and inwardly. In his innermost being, Weber was militant and political. He was aware of all the diabolical forces that political activity necessarily engendered. He recognized that all forms of military and heroic life, their feeling of honor and dignity, are irreconcilably in conflict with the radicalism of the Christian ethics of brotherly love, as found in the Sermon on the Mount. Whoever subscribed to a life of this world's political order, or who joined the warrior class, must, therefore, transgress other values such as those of Christian ethics.

He saw this conflict clearly and had sufficient courage to endure it and not be overcome by the pressure of its tension. This spiritual conflict between two hostile orders of values, the decision for or against definite norms, the service that men assumed on behalf of one or the other system of values, all these gave man dignity and personality. This struggle alone makes existence meaningful. Life and history are nothing but stages of the realization of such services for values that men assumed only to give meaning to themselves. He found such heroism in history, irrespective of the systems of values to which men dedicated themselves. This applies to an individual as well as to a people. In the case of the latter, "responsibility before history" signifies keeping political power so available and strong that it is in the position to preserve, protect, and develop those values out of which and for which it lives. At the basis of this picture of history is a sort of negative theology of history.

All modern philosophy of history from Nicolas de Condorcet [1743–1794] to Georg Hegel [1770–1831] and Karl Marx [1818–1883] was a theory of progress and carried the function of providing a pseudoreligious legitimization of the course of history. After the destruction by modern natural science of the religious world picture and the religious disenchantment of nature as creation, the attempt was made to salvage the divine and the absolute as the principle of historical development and give to history a pathos and importance that neither antiquity nor Christianity ever recognized. "The necessity for the idea of progress appeared when the need arose to provide a secular and objective 'meaning' for the course of human destiny, stripped of its religious content."[8] Political, historical, and social scientific investigations have finally rendered it impossible for this form of philosophy of history to regard itself as a science. The divine element, first ejected from nature, now was taken out of the process of history. Weber's empirical sociology of understanding is at the opposite pole of every modern philosophy of history. The historical process has no apparent objective meaning, and one can speak of progress only in a technical sense or from the point of view of subjective values. But every realization of meaning stands in the service of superior forces. Weber, however, is silent regarding these.

The following might represent an adequate interpretation of what history meant for him and what he meant by what we have called negative philosophy of history: The place of God is empty and abandoned, but all know of Him. For His sake, the world becomes the world stage and the scene of all those struggles for the realization of meaning and the fashioning of meaningful lives. Even though we have lost His name we struggle amid the night and darkness of life for His return and for the coming of His kingdom. This, then, is the real meaning of history for both the individual and the life of nations—to be stages in this realization, in a final and highest sense.

II

This interpretation of the historico-theoretical presuppositions upon which Max Weber's sociology rests can be substantiated by an investigation of his idea of freedom. He measured reality with the following gauge: What human types become representative groups both from the viewpoint of the development of classes of political leaders and also from the viewpoint of "old and eternal human ideals"? Thus, he speaks vaguely, and only by allusion, of the passionate "urge to liberty" that pressed the proletarianized German peasants into the cities. This was a feeling that had nothing to do with the declining economic or political doctrine of liberalism, free competition, or laissez-faire economics. The concrete content of his conception of freedom is expressed more clearly in his attitude toward socialism than in these allusions. From his youth, Weber fought for the social and cultural uplifting of the working classes. He admired the proletarian movement so long as it possessed the strength to feel conscious of itself as a cultural movement. The way of radical opposition that it assumed, however, he considered dangerous and foolish. He considered the economic theories of Marxism outmoded as a result of social developments—in particular, the bureaucratization of industrial societies. He considered the class of peasants, petty bourgeoisie, officials, and ever increasing number of administrative workers as a great bar to a proletarian revolution in Central Europe. These political considerations, however, did not yet provide absolute criteria for evaluation. His scientific insight showed him the economic costs, in the sense of technical rationalization, of an ethically oriented socialism and how, therefore, the desired goals of higher standards of living and higher cultural levels might easily become converted into the opposite. Even these facts would perhaps not have prevented him from becoming a socialist had he only recognized the binding character of its ideals. This, however, he found impossible. Like no one in his epoch, he foresaw what human consequences a socialist community would entail and what the dominant human types in such a society would be.

At the *Verein für Sozialpolitik* in 1909, Weber ardently opposed the growing tendency toward plans for state socialist and municipal socialist organization. Because he saw that it was impossible to hold back the development of increased technical rationalization, he always felt it incumbent upon him to warn others about the significance of every new step in the direction of further intensive organization of society.

> This passion for bureaucratization . . . is a desperate one. . . . We are in the midst of a development in which the world will come to know of nothing further than such systematized individuals. The central problem, therefore,

> is not how we can more greatly further and hasten this process but rather what we have to set up against this machinery to keep a portion of humanity free from this parceling of the soul and from this supremacy of ideals of bureaucratic life.[9]

In the closing section of his agrarian history of antiquity, written shortly before this address, he makes this point even more clearly.

His intellectual passion was not directed against the thesis that the epoch of capitalism will at some time end. No one, not even a socialist, saw more clearly into the merciless and cruel struggle going on within the economic system of so-called peaceful competition. But he saw that in overcoming this social order, whether by revolutionary socialism or state intervention, society would only become more technically bureaucratized and socially mechanized and that man would become more and more of an administrator and functionary. This sort of future was simply intolerable in the light of his ideals.

For Weber, the human individual took on greatness and worth only in so far as he was able by conscious decisions to preserve his personality amidst the irrationality of the world and amidst the struggle between the forces and demons of the order of life. This was the meaning of liberty: the possibility of intellectual and spiritual struggle and the development therefrom of a spiritual and unadorned heroism that would in turn bring forth true humanity. However, the more the world became thoroughly and rationally organized and individuals assigned their position and function, the more likelihood there was that in a world so organized, the elements of spiritual dynamics—struggle and risk of the soul—would gradually die out and no longer be comprehended nor experienced. No one can, indeed, penetrate into the darkness of the future, but Weber spoke with painful anxiety of the men of the coming epochs.

> No one yet knows who will live in that future abode and if at the end of this enormous development new prophets might not arise or a powerful regeneration of old thoughts and ideals might not come about. Or else perhaps if none of these come to pass there might be a mechanical petrifaction embellished with a sort of convulsive attitude of self-importance. For these 'last men' of this cultural development the dictum would become realized: 'experts without spirit, sensualists without heart; with the false illusion that in this emptiness a stage of humanity never before realized has at last been attained.'[10]

This deep inner anxiety for the preservation of the values of moral and spiritual heroism and freedom as the only means of allowing for its realization also accounted for the profound inner emotion that Weber experienced as a result of the Russian Revolution of 1905. His "*Zur Beurteilung der gegenwärtigen politischen Entwicklung Russlands*" and his "*Russlands Übergang zum Scheinkonstitutionalismus*,"[11] despite their contemporary character, are still of fundamental importance for the problems of the sociology of the Russian intelligentsia. They also reveal clearly and plainly the place and meaning of Weber's idea of freedom. The struggle for the "inalienable rights of man" in the era of full capitalism is not liberalism but the desperate attempt to check the deadening centralization and bureaucratization by limiting and restricting them. These iron poles of increasing organization of state and private industries, with the accompanying increase of groups of state or private administrative officials, served only to convert this world into a new Egyptian bureaucratic state. The Russian Revolution occurs amid such conditions and, standing as it does at the point of intersection between the struggling rationalizing and liberating tendencies, it assumed the highest importance for Weber.

Those who live in constant anxiety that there might be too much democracy and individualism in the world and not enough authority, aristocracy and prestige of position or the like, may rest calmly. Only too well has history provided that the trees of democratic individualism do not grow to the sky. History, according to all experience, ever anew and inexorably produces aristocracy and authority, to which all who find this necessary, either for themselves or for 'the people,' can cling. If it is a question only of the 'material conditions' and the constellation of interests, 'created' either directly or indirectly by them, then any sober consideration must lead to the conclusion that all economic indications point in the direction of an increasing lack of freedom. It is altogether ridiculous to ascribe to this present day full capitalism, as it is now being imported into Russia and as it exists in America—to this 'inevitability' of our economic development—any elective affinity with 'democracy' or even with 'freedom' in any sense. The question is only how it is at all possible for all these things to exist permanently under its domination. They exist only when there is the determined will of a nation not to allow itself to be governed like a herd of sheep. We are 'individualists' and adherents of 'democratic institutions,' 'against the current' of material constellations. He who wants to be a weather vane for the general tendencies of future development will abandon these old fashioned ideals as soon as possible.[12]

But time urges us on 'to act as long as it is day.' Whatever inalienable spheres of personality and freedom will not be acquired now, in the course of the next generations

> while the economic and spiritual 'revolution,' the much abused 'anarchy' of production and the equally abused 'subjectivism' still remain unbroken, by the individual of the broad masses who becomes selfreliant through these and only through these, will perhaps never be acquired when the world comes to a full development and reaches a point of intellectual saturation. That is as far as we, with our weak eyes, are able to pierce through the impenetrable haze of the future of mankind. . . . 'Thousands of years must have passed before you came into life and many more thousands of years wait silently to see what you will begin to do with this life of yours.' This cry, which Carlyle's passionate faith in personality called to every new individual, can be applied, without exaggeration, to the present situation in the United States and to that of Russia, as it is in part now and as it will most probably be within another generation.[13]

This pathos for freedom reveals the deepest content of Max Weber's idea of man. To be a person, means to live a spiritual existence. This, in turn, signifies an indissolubility of will and spirit within the totality of man as a unit of decision. Only in freedom can man realize the intellectual and spiritual acts of autonomous decision, which are the primary constituents of his personality. Only the man who wrestles with the angel, who stands in daily need and danger of self-formation, can realize himself as man. It is not freedom from, but freedom for the realization of these values that constitutes man's service. This is the most onerous obligation and burden but also the only thing that gives man worth. It is the realm where human heroism is realized. Because Weber's thoughts and feelings were majestic, his idea of man could be nothing but majestic and exalted.

Weber's idea of man and freedom, therefore, was not related to any historical form of liberalism. For all political doctrines, arising out of concrete situations or in opposition to them, always, by necessity, rigidly place these situations in the foreground, and they never comprehend the totality of a given problem of political theory or social ethics. It is true that all existence appears only as concrete historical existence. But it is also true that the layers of this "historical existence" of intellectual and spiritual phenomena are, from the standpoint of the realization of ultimate principles and from that of the fundamental phenomena of man's moral existence, of varying density and purity. This is Weber's concern. It is a fundamental, heroic attitude toward the world. The struggle for freedom is an eternal form of human existence. It is a struggle for one of the forms of human perfection that is constantly being surrendered: a struggle for the self-molding and self-realization of personality. This form of life can find various concrete expressions in various historical situations: as prophet, Protestant, sectarian, mystic, revolutionary, or anarchist. But it always remains an eternal symbol of the spiritual apprehension of man. It alone enables man to cope with the tension of the demands of the spirit; it alone gives him strength to live without illusions concerning the course of the world and, yet, to give affirmation to life in order to be able to cope with it.

Alexis de Tocqueville called himself a *liberal d'une espèce nouvelle* almost one hundred years before Max Weber. He knew that the content of his conception of freedom, derived from the tension of existence, had nothing in common with contemporary doctrines and that he would remain solitary and alien to his epoch. The personalities and works of Weber and Tocqueville are alike in this respect and, for this reason, there is a common character to both their methods and their sociological insight into the spheres of politics. Above all, however, they stand together because both were men not of their times; although they could interpret their own age with understanding, they were men of greater stature than their age and, penetrating into the realm of history, they were able to perceive eternal and moral phenomena. For this reason, they remain solitary figures in time, but always new in every spiritual awakening. By their personalities and their work, they testify to an eternal element of human greatness. They can dispense with the approval and consent of their age, for they hand on the never extinguished torch of human existence. "They also serve, who only stand and wait," said John Milton [1608–1674], and he surely knew.

Weber found his ideals old fashioned in his times and felt himself surrounded by loneliness. Just as he could not adhere to the socialist movement, so he also rejected completely the youth movement centered in Stefan George [1868–1933]. Nevertheless, he had much in common with the poet in his criticism of the age. The cult of personality, negative self-reflection, uprooted thought without foundation, which destroys the deepest basis of human existence and runs its course in a vacuum—all these phenomena seemed also to Weber symptoms of disease and elements of spiritual and psychic decomposition. But he could see genuine salvation neither in the "Maximin cult" of the poet nor in the religious veneration accorded to George by his pupils. To him, as to his Puritans, every attempt to deify the earthly straying man was "idolatry" and a cowardly flight from individual responsibility in favor of absolutist authority. For his stern and heroic attitude, such a personal surrender of freedom and individual will for inner decision seemed a flight from the terrifying aspect of life. He always affirmed a personal attachment to a charismatic leadership, but never at the cost of a *sacrificium intellectus*. Therefore, to Weber, the harshness and severity of George's curse upon the entire age seemed merciless and unjust, quite apart from his criticism of George's romantic misunderstanding of both history and reality.

Weber must thus stand alone, revealed in his works. These, however, cannot provide us with either religious serenity or secure metaphysical shelter. There is no joyous promise either at the beginning or at the end of his work. The situation of his time hardly made this possible. But his existence and his work bear witness to something that, in the spiritual condition of the epoch, was more than any message. It was the fact that human greatness is not extinguished and that heroes are possible even in the gray and barren everyday existence of modern life. The figure of Weber and his work remain as a call to greatness and heroism. Not to a romantic irrational heroism that sacrifices itself amidst the delirium of self-decomposition, but a holy and sober heroism that grows out of the contradictions of life and out of the strength of knowledge of the suffering, greatness, and pangs of the spirit, and that can, without illusion, understand man's existence and activity and yet not become cynical. Only great moral power and an ever-flowing stream of human purity make it possible to bear the weight of the tremendous force of such disillusioning knowledge. This provided the secret source of strength of the man, which reverently we dare not touch.

Notes

1. *Aufsätze zur Soziologie und Sozialpolitik* (Tübingen: J. C. B. Mohr, 1924), 456.

2. *Aufsätze zur Wissenschaftslehre* (Tübingen: J. C. B. Mohr, 1925), 169.

3. *Aufsätze zur Religionssoziologie,* 2nd ed. (Tübingen: J. C. B. Mohr, 1922), 1:240ff.

4. *Gesammelte Politische Schriften* (Munich: Drei masken verlag, 1921), 437.

5. *Wirtschaft und Gesellschaft* (Tübingen: J. C. B. Mohr, 1924), 817.

6. *Wirtschaft und Gesellschaft*, 243.

7. Ibid., 60.

8. *Aufsätze zur Wissenschaftslehre*, 33.

9. *Aufsätze zur Soziologie und Sozialpolitik*, 414.

10. *Aufsätze zur Religionssoziologie*, 1:203ff.

11. *Archiv für Sozialwissenschaft und Sozialpolitik*, (Tübingen: J. C. B. Mohr, 1911–23), vol. 22, first supplement, and vol. 23, first supplement.

12. *Zur russischen Revolution von 1905*, vol. 10 of *Max Weber Gesamtausgabe* (Tübingen: J. C. B. Mohr), 348.

13. Ibid., 350.

20

The Place of Alfred Weber's *Kultursoziologie* in Social Thought

Alfred Weber [1868–1958], although influenced by the sociological work of Max Weber [1864–1920], takes a very personal approach to a sociological synthesis of the historical process.[1] *Kultursoziologie* is the outcome of twenty-five years of Alfred Weber's concentration on the subject.[2] Since he first formulated his sociological concept of culture,[3] his work has been a series of attempts to clarify the theoretical problems involved and to apply his theoretical tools to specific historical subjects.[4] These studies constitute the background for the present comprehensive work that tries to suggest a new sociological approach to the historical process.

The work comprehends the whole process of history, from primitive societies to the revolutionary movements taking place today in all spheres of life. After a general survey of primitive societies, he analyzes very carefully the social and historical structures of China and India and gives a sociological interpretation of the civilizations around the Mediterranean that influenced the origins of Greek thought and feeling. His analyses of ancient Persia, Babylonia, Egypt, Israel, and Greece show a high degree of intellectual understanding as well as an intuitive penetration of these cultures. The suggestive

---

Published originally in a slightly different form in *Social Research* 3 (November 1936), 494–500. Republished by permission from *Social Research.*

analysis of the Russian world reveals the continuity of its revolutionary evolution, and his description of the structural transformation of Japanese society and its interrelations with the Western world is an interesting attempt in the realm of sociological forecasts. And his interpretations of the Western past—the decline of Roman civilization, feudalism, the rise and growth of industrial society with all the implications involved—reveal Weber as a sociologist who has experienced the historical process as one stratum of our own present life.

The presentation of this universal process is not based upon any dogmatic presuppositions; hence, there is no attempt to find a unity in the evolution of mankind. The empirical analysis shows only different historical structures. Whatever the general trends of interrelationships in the economic, technical, or cultural spheres, the individual patterns of culture develop within their own gestalts. This presupposition of the structural character of the historical process is not theoretical or metaphysical but, like Gestalt psychology itself, is based on concrete and empirical observation. In fact, it was in opposition to the dogmatism of the first epoch of sociology that Alfred Weber's work developed. Sociology from Auguste Comte [1798–1857] to Herbert Spencer [1820–1903] was an attempt to synthesize empirical analyses of historical institutions with a metaphysical dogmatism concerning the dynamics of history—a philosophy of progress in different varieties. Alfred Weber's work attempts a new and different synthesis. He frees the historical process of metaphysical dogmatisms, but there is another metaphysical element in his own conception, radically different from that of the earlier sociological school. Repeatedly, he objects to the assumption that underlies the affirmations of this school concerning the meaning of the historical process as a whole—that is, the assumption that there is a hypostasis of one or another sphere of the historical process. What we must know is not the meaning of the historical process but the different types of human development and their revelation of the constant elements of human existence. Thus arises Weber's chief distinction between the social process (*Gesellschaftsprozess*), the process of civilization (*Zivilisationsprozess*), and the process of culture (*Kulturbewegung*).

Weber often emphasizes that his conceptions do not dissolve the unity of historical life into a sum of various abstractions. Instead, the abstractions signify the different forces that constitute social life as a whole. His fundamental sociological concepts are concerned with the three primary phenomena that constitute social life: order, domination, and meaning. These phenomena are realized in historical forms because life can only be thought of as historical. Within the historical forms of the general social attitudes, they are transhistorical because life is always transcending itself. Georg Simmel's [1858–1918] assertion that life is more life and more than life is at the basis of Weber's approach. In the *Pensées* of Blaise Pascal [1623–1662], we find the same idea, almost in the same formulation.

In terms of this threefold dynamics of life, social process has to be defined as the general social trend, at the basis of instincts and will-impulses, toward order, domination, and social integration in the economic and political sphere. In the evolution of this process, a limited variety of forms and types of social organization may be found that recur throughout history whenever the formal structure of the situation is the same or similar—for example, the general types of stabilization, disintegration, transformation, and crisis. The process of civilization, however, in contrast to this dynamics of will underlying the social process, is based upon the continuity and irreversible progress of reason. Civilization represents the human effort to conquer the world of nature and culture by means of intelligence in the spheres of technology, science, and planning. The role of reason in civilization was overemphasized by Comte and the positivists as the general denominator of the historical process; Karl Marx [1818–1883] combined it with the economic process as the primary force and dynamics of history. Social process and civilization together constitute the elements of circulation and progress that earlier sociological schools had developed. Culture, in distinction to social process and civilization, is based on the realization of spirit, on philosophical and emotional self-realization. Certainly, this too depends on the potentialities of development in a given moment. But at the same time, its responses reveal the creative power of human thought and soul. Hence, Weber emphasizes the spontaneity and creativeness that are inherent in culture. Whatever may be the limitations of human behavior patterns as they are revealed in the social process and in civilization, in culture they find freedom and spontaneity. Thus, there is no place in Weber's sociology for any kind of determinism, and he declares that it was in combating an economic and biological determinism that the idea of his *Kultursoziologie* arose.

This basis grounds any examination of the relationship between history and sociology in Weber's work. He recognized Wilhelm Dilthey's [1833–1911] radical insight into the historical character of life, but he approaches the historical world with general sociological concepts. Within the variety of historical experiences, he finds types of social behavior patterns, typical attitudes, and recurring situations of growth, revolution, and decline—typical patterns of conduct within the individual constellations of historical conditions. This interpretation of history as the indissoluble unity of general human attitudes and their particular realizations makes clear the title of Weber's book. *Kulturgeschichte als Kultursoziologie* means the conquering of isolated interpretations of historical causation and abstract sociological approaches. Universal sociological concepts are so abstract and empty that they have to be corrected by individual concepts adequate to the various historical realizations. Max Weber's work, especially the chapter on the types of domination in *Wirtschaft und Gesellschaft*, reveals the problematic character of sociological concepts applied to the material of history; Alfred Weber chooses the opposite method and presents his material historically and not systematically.

This endeavor expresses a new attitude of thinking, breaking through both the historicism and the sociologism of the past and revealing a new wealth of human experience and thought. Whatever the shifting powers in the process of history, they reveal in their particular character the constant elements of human existence. In the dynamics of the historical process, we are able to understand the development of the different functions of human nature that realizes itself only in historical situations. Alfred Weber's distinction between social process, civilization, and culture signifies the elasticity and tension of human life. Between the mechanical reactions of social responses and the spontaneity and creative power of mind, there are many interrelationships in the historical process. The merit of Alfred Weber is his emphasis on this interrelationship; here, we find the individual character of his work. It is a function of his approach to prepare the way for a science of man, the empirical part of a philosophy of existence.

Thus, we can understand the transhistorical and transsociological character of certain of Weber's concepts that attempt to create a new type of sociological ideas. The concept of primary constellation (*Anfangskonstellation*), for example, is to be interpreted as the coincidence of a series of conditions and situations that shape the character of a nation. Unfortunately, no Western language can adequately translate the admirable Greek term *kairos*, the creative power of a historical situation. Weber's term attempts a translation, although in a very limited sense. He gives many examples showing that a situation of crisis may shape the national character for centuries. Thus, the difference in the developments of magical cultures is determined by the historical moment when military strength was imposed on their peoples, and by the character of the conquerors. In the same way, we can discover in the different basic revolutions the elements that have shaped the national characters throughout the Western world. And Weber's *historical entelechy* is no metaphysical concept but a term signifying there are elements that cannot be dissolved, in spite of the different conditions and causations of a national character. Whatever the factors determining this national character, it becomes a power of its own, integrating the variable and constant elements into a social-shaping force.

Within the variety of historical institutions, the kaleidoscope of conditions can be analyzed; typical attitudes and structures can be discovered. With this combination of historical and sociological concepts, it is even possible to forecast those potentialities of human spontaneity and creativeness that have a chance to be developed or will be prevented by a given set of conditions. The limitations of sociological knowledge must be kept in mind, however. Every genuine sociological analysis deals with the topography of the conditions that make possible the development of human nature, but Weber knows very well the limitations of these empirical methods. The value of his approach is in its trend toward a very concrete analysis but with full consciousness of the metaphysical problems involved. Hence, it is symptomatic that we repeatedly find the term *immanent transcendence*, characterizing the dynamics of the historical and sociological process. It signifies the fact that spiritual and ultimate values are immanent within the process of history, not existing in a dualistic abstract realm beyond human life; they are interwoven in human conduct itself, and it is they that create man's unique power of transcending mechanical responses to the conditions of environment in the direction of a free and creative spirit. In Alfred Weber's new sociological approach, this is the philosophical background.

A review cannot examine the evidence for the different particular analyses in this book. Weber himself states the imperfection and imperfectibility of his undertaking and, particularly, the weakness of the interpretation of modern times. But the scientific heroism of his approach must be emphasized. Weber had the moral courage to finish this book, knowing very well its weaknesses and imperfections. He is an impressive example of the fact that there are situations in scientific thinking in which the work of pioneers is more fruitful than specialized perfection. As pioneers open the woods and break through the wilderness, so Weber pushes through the tangled mysteries of history with his sociological concepts, finding new perspectives on the intricacies of social causations and conditions.

This moral quality of the book is especially significant in an epoch of growing intellectual mechanization. And equally worthy of example is the discrimination that enables Weber to know the borders of empirical analysis and the starting point of ontological problems. Throughout the book, he does not leave the empirical method, but he knows very well that the mechanical responses represented by social actions are never able to explain the complexity of social dynamics. He is aware that his own empirical analysis is based upon and constantly recurs to a metaphysical position. His concept of immanent transcendence itself reveals his work to be the sociological and historical aspect of a philosophy of life and existence; hence, his work has to be correlated with this type of philosophy. Because he is so excellent a scholar, he reaches the intellectual discipline and modesty that are the characteristics of outstanding thinkers.

The shaken world of modern crisis produces ever anew types of thought that attempt through creative intelligence to integrate the variety of scientific experiences. It is a sociological law that situations of crisis and transformation give especial opportunity to develop such responses of the human mind, the only integrating force in the disintegrating world. There is today a danger that the spontaneity and the creative potentialities of human nature will be destroyed by the growing processes of mechanization and social planning, and this outstanding synthesis of Alfred Weber's is a positive response to that challenge. This approach to the problem of modern civilization and culture is distinctly European; it cannot be a natural American approach. The book is a representative document of one of the greatest epochs of transformation. It presents the unity and tension between the analytical and the synthetic qualities of modern thinking, combining the analytical achievements in the social sciences with the recognition of their borders, and the knowledge of the different historical structures with Weber's individual spontaneous imagination. This work matured not in twenty-five years but in twenty-five hundred; it has made the heritage of the Western past a living possession, not a pile of dead material. Even Weber's understanding of the constant and variable elements of social behavior patterns is not only an individual merit but is the achievement of two centuries of social and historical thought in the west, an achievement well worth preserving.

And it is no accident that within the same half decade other works were published, notably those by Arnold Toynbee [1889–1975][5] and Eugen Rosenstock-Huessy [1888–1973],[6] that represent the same trend of thinking and similar methods. All these works are alike in their attempts to free the sociological method from the abstract and isolating thought of positivism, and to combine the historical and the sociological approach in a new unity of social thinking. Toynbee's criticism of the categories of race and environment is based on his realization that the historical process can never be understood with such abstract denominators. His new categories, particularly "challenges and responses," are historical as well as sociological. The most important similarity between his work and Weber's is to be found in his challenge to any mechanical interpretation of the social process and in his emphasis on the spontaneous and creative vitality of man. Rosenstock-Huessy reveals the complex structure of revolution as a sociological phenomenon. He points out very clearly the interrelationship of the different strata in the dynamics of history and the unity of the constant and variable elements in the crisis of revolution.

Hence, we may say that Alfred Weber's work is an expression of the general revolt against the spirit of sociological positivism. It is an attempt to free sociology from the abstract rationalism of the social sciences and to discover new categories and methods capable of embracing the complex totality of life.

Notes

1. Cf. H. Becker's review of this book in *American Sociological Review* (April 1936), 1:310–15.

2. Alfred Weber, *Kulturgeschichte als Kultursoziologie* (Leiden: A. W. Sijthoff, 1935).

3. *Der soziologische Kulturbegriff, Verhandlungen des 2. Deutschen Soziologentages* (Tübingen: 1913). In this connection, cf. R. M. MacIver's distinction between culture and civilization as sociological concepts in *Modern State* (London: 1926), chapter 10; *Society* (New York: 1932), chapter 12.

4. "Prinzipielles zur Kultursoziologie," in *Archiv fur Sozialurissenschaft und Sozialpolitik* (1920–21), vol. 47; "Kultursoziologie" (Karlsruhe: 1927); "Kultursoziologie," in *Handworterbuch der Soziologie* (Stuttgart: 1931).

5. Arnold J. Toynbee, *A Study of History* (London: 1934), vols. 1–3; cf. M. Postan, review of Toynbee's *Study of History* in *Sociological Review* (January 1936), 28:50–63; Hilda D. Oakley, "Philosophic History and Prophecy," in *Philosophy* (July 1936), 11:186ff.; Hajo Holborn, "A New Study of History," in *Social Research* (February 1936), 3:105–8.

6. Eugen Rosenstock-Huessy, *Europäische Revolutionen* (Jena: 1931); *Revolution als politischer Begriff in der Neuzeit* (Breslau: 1931). [Rosenstock-Huessy's work was later published in English as *Out of Revolution: Autobiography of Western Man* (New York: Morrow, 1938).—Eds.]

21

Charles Péguy and the Calling of Israel

I

At last, a small volume of essays and poems by Charles Péguy [1873–1914] has been published in an English translation.[1] Charles Péguy is almost unknown in America. His works have received little attention in the English-speaking countries, where the intellectual and spiritual movements of modern France have not been considered as important as similar movements in Germany. The newly published translation introduces a thinker whose personality may become an image of spiritual heroism to the youth of postwar Europe.

Charles Péguy, born in Orléans, the town of Joan of Arc, was proud to have descended from a long line of workers and peasants. Because of his unusual intellectual gifts, he succeeded in getting the best scholarships in high school and college. He was an outstanding student at the École Normale Supérieure but did not take his degree. In 1899, he joined the Socialist Party and opened a Socialist bookshop. In the following year, however, he revolted against the party and from that time was completely independent of all formal allegiances and affiliations. He founded the *Cahiers de la Quinzaine*, a fortnightly in which he and a number of friends dealt with the

---

Published originally in a slightly different form in *Jewish Frontier* 10 (July 1943), 19–24. Republished by permission from Ameinu: Liberal Values, Progressive Israel.

philosophical, moral, and religious aspects of the social and political problems of the time. Most of his own writings appeared in this periodical. His influence grew steadily and spread beyond all party lines. Auguste-Maurice Barrès [1862–1923] and André Suarès [née Isaac Félix Suarès (1868–1948)] were as much affected by the power of Péguy as were Jacques Maritain [1882–1973] and Henri Bergson [1859–1941]. Emmanuel Mounier [1905–1950] and the social Catholics in France have gratefully acknowledged what they owe to Péguy. When the war broke out in 1914, he volunteered for the front. He was killed in action on September 5, 1914, the first day of the first Battle of the Marne. A short time before the war he wrote: "Blessed are those who died in great battles, stretched out on the ground in the face of God. Blessed are those who died in a just war. Blessed is the wheat that is ripe and the wheat that is gathered in sheaves."

What was the power that radiated from this man, and what is the significance of his work? Barrès once told how he had tried to persuade Péguy that it was right to use the established political and intellectual institutions to gain security for his own family and to extend the influence of his ideas. Péguy was indignant. He answered that his task could be performed only in the solitude of absolute independence. Like some of the Christian humanists of the sixteenth century, Péguy believed that there are moments in the history of man when people who have a vocation must renounce established social patterns and well-organized institutions in order to reestablish, in their very modes of living and thinking, the lost intensity of life. Desiderius Erasmus [1466–1536] called this vocation "the quest for Christian Liberty." Péguy's life and work were conceived in the tradition of this humanism. He cast the purity and power of his personality in the battle for freedom, challenging all social and ecclesiastical institutions. This eagerness to fight for the unity of the human personality and the uncompromising pursuit of this goal constitute the grandeur of his achievement. "We have never betrayed the spirit," was the guiding star of Péguy's life. He never ceased repeating that we shall be capable of experiencing the fullness of the spiritual and temporal life only if we have the purity and integrity to search for perfections qua perfections. He was puzzled when people spoke of his "philosophy." He was firmly convinced that his was a very humble task: to reestablish the innocence and the good conscience of common sense. Péguy believed that we are completely misled by our scientific type of education and have forgotten that all great and important verities are simple and unsophisticated. This was his vocation: to blend the social problems of the bourgeois world with the humanistic problem of reestablishing the dignity and completeness of the free man and citizen. Péguy was keenly aware that there is evil in the world, and he was convinced that man is sometimes capable of victory over it. Finally, he was certain that if we are to find remedies for our deficiencies and faults, we can find them only through our participation in a spiritual order. For three centuries, humanism and the religious spirit had been separated because of an artificial and pseudoscientific way of thinking. In his own life, he struggled again to merge these two major heritages of European civilization.

In the last decades of the nineteenth century, it was only natural for an independent-minded, sensitive young European to revolt against the established patterns of society. Most people labeled this negative attitude *socialism*, a term that covered many different ideas. Péguy's socialism certainly had little in common with Karl Marx's [1818–1883] Prussian conception of the class struggle. Péguy's socialism sprang from a pious devotion to the old-fashioned virtues of the common people, the workers, the peasants, and the craftsmen of France. They had inherited a faith in the dignity and honor of labor; they were proud of achieving perfection as a personal victory over brute matter. Poverty was their destiny. But it was a noble simplicity, a sober and clean way of life. This was an asceticism without rigor and compulsion; it was the wisdom of common sense and of moderation, an awareness of the essential purposes and possibilities of life. This was a pattern of life that came closest to the military ideal that Péguy cherished as another aspect of his positive belief in the "blessing of poverty." Comradeship and friendship, authority and obedience, discipline and courage, are best realized in the ascetic nobility of the soldier who is not confused and hampered by the temptations and seductions of the secular life of the modern bourgeoisie. The poor man and the soldier are the two dominating images of Péguy's socialism.

Péguy draws a sharp distinction between the poverty of his socialism and the misery of the worker in capitalist society. It is the modern capitalistic bourgeoisie that killed the ethos of labor that had made poverty a productive and positive virtue of the working people. The bourgeoisie transformed the productive worker into an object of exploitation, a servant of the all-powerful machine. This is misery, degrading and dehumanizing, because it eliminates honor, meaning, and personality from the life of the workers. The world of the modern bourgeoisie is the world of abstract money institutions. Money rules everything, Péguy repeats again and again. Avarice and venality are the psychological products of this world of moral disintegration. In the past, common bonds united patron and worker, manorial lord and peasant. They shared in some common work and in common responsibilities. Today, the common people are left alone, alone with the misery of an empty and meaningless life. The ruling classes no longer have any responsibilities and obligations toward the common people; there is no longer any unity among all groups of the community.

Most conspicuous is this breakdown of common ties and social obligations in the sphere of scholarship and learning. According to Péguy, the modern intellectuals constitute a class by themselves and are ruled by their vested interests. They have become technicians and experts, functionaries and employees. Gone is the old zeal of the learned to preserve and to carry on the moral and spiritual standards of society as a whole. Péguy's searching analyses of the position of the intellectual in the modem world present another aspect of his struggle for the socialism of the pure and decent life. Péguy is alarmed about the perspectives of the bourgeois world. The learned will become completely involved in the web of institutions that serve the economic and social interests of the ruling class. They will be hired in order to develop scientific devices for building up the most efficient and formidable institutions of power. They will establish the most advanced society history has ever known, but it will be a society in which we will know more and more about less and less. In the face of this danger, Péguy is determined to teach the young to rediscover the essentials, the "basic verities." This is the only way to bring back into existence man in his purity and intensity, in his dignity and humility, standing bareheaded under the thunders of God. Péguy is convinced that the establishment of socialism in this world deserves the full heroism of human integrity, but first, we must learn that socialism is not an end in itself. The secular salvation of a humanistic socialism is not enough if it is not simultaneously directed toward spiritual salvation.

II

Throughout his work, Péguy refers to the Dreyfus affair [1894–1906, after Captain Alfred Dreyfus (1859–1935)] as having opened his eyes to the incentives and motives of human action in the modem world. He often reiterates that it is a great privilege to live in times of such crises. They question and break the habits and patterns of an established society. Crises are the articulations of the historical process. They force men to face the fundamental issues and the basic decisions that seldom appear in their radical severity when obscured by the mechanisms of well-established habits and patterns of conduct. Crises test the vitality and strength of human institutions. Such institutions as states and churches will survive only when the belief in their positive value as a genuine way of life is not shaken by their failures and their unfulfilled promises. Péguy calls these beliefs *mystiques*, including under that term not only religious beliefs, but political and social beliefs as well. There is a socialist and democratic mystique just as there was a republican mystique and a Jewish and Christian mystique, in the Dreyfus affair. No institution can endure without such a mystique, the presence of which is understood by its members as a way of life, an integrating and vital power in building up human lives. For this very "mysticism," people have given and are giving their lives. Whether the "mysticism" refers to democracy or to religion does not matter. What matters only is that the belief is intelligible and reasonable, not irrational and arbitrary. All the institutions that now seem matter-of-fact and banal, like the ballot, free speech, and free worship, have been established by the anonymous heroism of unknown believers. This living spirit of democratic justice and of liberal purity constituted the mystique of the Dreyfus affair.

However, the creative power of mystique is killed by the vested interests of political and social institutions. In all spheres of life, the "mystical" beliefs are intertwined with the interests of the political, social, or ecclesiastical institutions. Principles and ideals, however lofty their aims, become involved in the conflicts and competitions of the secular world. That is what Péguy calls *politique*. All mystique ends in politique. Péguy experienced the operation of this cruel law in the Dreyfus affair. He broke with Jean Juarès [1859–1914] and the

Socialist Party when he felt that they betrayed the republican mystique and exploited their victory for spoils. As Péguy neatly put it: "Republican *mystique* means to die for democracy, *politique* to live off it."

III

If history is ruled by this dialectical movement of mystique and politique, one can find little meaning in those philosophies of history that are based on the concept of "progress." History is a human concern. Rise and decline, growth and decay, consummation and death, are natural categories of history. It is impossible to prove that the price we pay for our victories in eliminating obstacles is worthwhile. Péguy flatly refused to recognize the category of progress as a valid concept of history. There are Plato [c. 428–c. 348 BC], René Descartes [1596–1650], and Henri Bergson [1859–1941], but there is no progressive movement leading from one to another. What matters is not the fact of victory and conquest, but the unconditional devotion to truth, the heroic effort to reexamine time and again established concepts in the light of new experiences and the vision that makes it possible to grasp a variety of worlds in the diverse aspects of the universe. All political, social, and religious beliefs are subject to the law of decay, to the metamorphosis into "politics." Péguy's insistence on this law of history indicates his basic concern—the effort to realize the fullest and richest perfection of human potentialities in the unconditional and spontaneous pursuit of ideal goods. The true ideal goods are those that bring salvation from the evil that is part of and in the world. Salvation can be temporal, a revolution in the social and secular sphere. Péguy, however, was imbued with the messianic awareness that temporal salvation is meaningful only when referring to spiritual salvation. Péguy's socialism and republicanism are different aspects of the same ardent desire to work for remedying evil in the world. His vigorous effort was directed toward the clarification of this issue in the modern world. The temporal revolution of socialism is possible only as the secular aspect of the spiritual revolution. No humanist revolution can be effective without a spiritual renascence. The Kingdom of God will be realized fully in ourselves only in so far as we have succeeded to establish its reflection in the terrestrial city. From his youth, Péguy was preoccupied with the mystery and the destiny of Joan of Arc. For Péguy, Joan of Arc is the greatest saint because only she succeeded in connecting the two responsibilities of secular and spiritual salvation. The secular revolution is the humanistic effort. It can materialize only when carried on by the mysticism of justice as the norm of living equity among men. But justice cannot be comprehended except as flowing from the source of divine order. Throughout his work, Péguy returns to the problem of the interaction of grace and nature. Like Erasmus, he invites his followers to dare the highest efforts in order to become worthy of enjoying divine grace. Grace is not the result of an irrational Will of the Divinity. It comes into being in the cooperation between the highest devotion and abandonment of man to the divine and the embracing and blessing countermove of God.

In 1914, Péguy wrote: "The tree of grace and the tree of nature have intertwined their trunks in solemn knots; they have confounded their fraternal destiny to such extent that it is the same essence and the same being." This theory of grace makes it evident that humanistic heroism will be complete only when merged with the obligations imposed upon man participating in a spiritual order. In an unforgettable passage, Péguy points to the gap between Greek humanistic heroism and Jewish-Christian faith. Homer's heroes looked at their gods with an envy mixed with contempt—with envy because these gods had nothing to desire, with contempt because they missed the intensity of human lives with their tensions, victories, defeats, risks, and adventures. That is the superiority of the heroic effort over ready-made perfection without combat and effort. It is the great merit of the spiritual religions that they made possible the knowledge of the human world as referring to and materializing the potentialities of a spiritual universe. Because of this, they surpassed and superseded the credo of classical heroism. The vision of a spiritual universe made it possible to deepen the mood of expectation into a basic attitude of hope and the subjective feelings of sympathy into an objective and universal habitus of love. The striving for salvation and the recurrent clarification of the issues of redemption that are involved in this messianic longing are the criteria for man's intermediate position between the world of nature and the world of God. Péguy passionately presented the thesis that salvation is not a definite fact. It is a continuous process in which hope and faith support the never-ceasing efforts of man to establish salvation here and now. The true spiritual salvation can come only when the temporal salvation has made transparent the final and spiritual need for the Kingdom of God. In the final analysis, true humanism and true religion cannot be separated. For the final conquest of evil, God and man need each other in the mutual cooperation between heroic effort and embracing grace.

IV

The process of salvation is not yet completed. The mission of the saviors is only too often defeated by the inertia of man, caught in the web of the institutions he has created. However, where there is dire need, saviors will arise and again to take up the work of salvation. Here is the lasting place and the perennial function of the Hebrew religion in the scale of Péguy's catholicity. Time and again, the Jews have produced the prophets and the wise men who have forced their reluctant nation to recognize its wickedness and heed the call to temporal and spiritual salvation. Holiness is not enough if it remains in the sphere of personal perfection. What is at stake is the salvation of the whole community, of the whole city. Reference to the commands of the Eternal Being is necessary to any achievement in the secular world. There still is and will be evil and injustice in the world. They arouse our indignation and spur us to revolt because we live under the commandments of an eternal order. This was the vision of the Hebrew prophets and sages; even today, it remains the guiding star of Jewish destiny. No Gentile in the modern world has praised the Hebrews for this recurrent contribution to the salvation of man here and now as did Péguy in the forty pages of his *Notre Jeunesse,* in which he analyzed the elements that shared in the victory of the Dreyfus affair.

What is it that fascinates Péguy in the Hebrew religion? He is profoundly impressed by the paradoxical unity of unrest and patience, which he considered the unique quality of Jewish character. The Jews have been harassed for centuries; yet, they have survived. This is their secret and their lasting fascination for Péguy. Jewish history explains the constant patience of the Jews; they will always find life bearable and will try to convince others that it could be worse. They will examine all aspects of a situation until they find in it some meaning and positive value. This patience is full of a sublime melancholy; it is the sadness of a group that is invested with the dignity of suffering for the sake of God. But this patience is accompanied by a continuous unrest that springs from the presence of the eternal in their critical awareness of the wrongs of man. For Péguy, the Jews are unique human beings who have never been *completely* corrupted by the establishments of the world. They are always prepared to fold their tents and start on another forty-year sojourn in the desert. It is true that the average Jew is an average human being. The ambitions of the contemporary Jew are very modest:

> The whole policy of Israel is to make no noise in the world, to purchase peace with prudent silence. Israel wishes to be forgotten. It still has so many smarting bruises . . . not a square inch of its skin that does not smart with pain, that is not full of old bruises, old contusions, dull pain, the memory of dull pain, scars, wounds, lacerations from the East or from the West. This people bears its own battle scars and those of all the other races. . . . But the whole *mystique* of Israel demands that it should pursue its resounding and painful mission. Hence extraordinary lacerations, the most painful of inner antagonisms between *mystique* and *politique.* A people of merchants, and at the same time a people of prophets.

These reflections on the meaning of Jewish history and the mystery of the Jewish character lead to those unforgettable pages in which Péguy draws the portrait of his friend Bernard Lazare [1865–1903], the French Jewish writer who was in the forefront of the struggle for Dreyfus. The Dreyfus family treated Lazare like a professional advocate who is paid for his services, a kind of adviser in the shrewd tricks of politics. Reverently, Péguy searches for the words that will evoke the image of the beloved friend.

> I am going to paint the picture of Bernard Lazare. It cannot be denied that he had elements of saintliness. And when I speak of saintliness I am not guilty of speaking in metaphors. He had a gentleness, a goodness, a mystical tenderness, an evenness of disposition, an experience of bitterness and ingratitude, a perfect capacity to digest bitterness and ingratitude, a goodness that could not be outdone, a perfectly enlightened goodness of an unbe-

lievable profundity. He lived and died a martyr. He was a prophet. It was quite right that he should be buried prematurely in silence and neglect. In a calculated silence. In complete neglect.

He was dead before he died. And again, Israel pursued its eternal destiny in the most secular way. . . . I was his only friend during his last years. He had a genius for friendship, a mystical loyalty and attachment which is the heart of friendship. This was possible because he remained ever loyal to himself. Many *politiques* betray, devour, absorb their *mystiques.* It is rare enough that mystics do not betray themselves. Of course, his atheism was very sincere. He was a positivist, scientifically minded, intellectually modern in all respects. However, beneath all this was a heart sensitive to the faintest vibration of Jewish misery. His heart was bleeding in all the ghettos of the world—perhaps most in the broken, diffused ones like Paris—bleeding in Rumania, in Turkey, in Algeria, in America, in Hungary, wherever Jews are persecuted, that is, in a certain sense, everywhere. His heart was bleeding in the Orient and Occident. Our mighty ones did not see, did not like to see that he was the Prophet, the Jew, the leader; but the poorest Rumanian peddler knew it, felt his spiritual power. He was in a state of constant tension, in a state of tension that was imposed upon him by commandments more than fifty centuries old. He carried the load of a race and the weight of a world on his shoulders. His heart was devoured by fire, by the burning of his race; he was consumed by the flame of his people. A fire in his soul, a burning mind and the burning coal on the prophetic lips.

> I have never seen a Jew so disinterested, so indifferent to the law of retaliation. He did not intend to render precisely the good for the evil, but certainly the just for the unjust. . . . He had a secret, intimate sympathy with every manifestation of spiritual power. His hatred of the state and of the secular institutions of power correspond exactly to his love of and devotion to the power of the spiritual. He could not stand the fact that the temporal institutions interfered with the purity of the spiritual. What a paradox! The professional atheist who made the eternal Word re-echo with a power and sweetness that cannot be imagined. I still see him on his bed—the atheist trembling with the Word of God. In his very death the whole weight of his people rested on his shoulders. I have never seen a human being so burdened with an eternal responsibility. He felt himself as responsible for his people as we feel for our immediate family.

The image of this prophet in the guise of a journalist pervades the whole work of Péguy and appears where you would never expect it. In his reflections on Aloysius Gonzaga, S. J. [1568–1591], Péguy established the four elements of the human spirit in the modern world. They are the Greek, the French, the Christian, the Jewish.

> Let us be the heirs of the Hebrew way of life as far as we can, as far as we will and sometimes even a little bit more. Let us carry on the heritage of the ancient Jews in co-operation with the modern Jews, at least with some among the contemporary ones. A few of them are particularly qualified to represent the nobility, devotion and dignity of the temporal eternity of this incomparable race. . . . Let us learn that the temporal salvation of

> humanity demands an unaccountable price, that the survival of a race, that the secular and temporal survival of a race, that the indefatigable and continuous survival of a race through all the storms of the ages, that the maintenance of a race is an accomplishment and a task demanding the highest price, that the temporal and terrestrial immortality of a chosen group, that its maintenance and secular immortality is an end and a task requiring an immense price. I dedicate these paragraphs to Bernard Lazare whose memory I shall piously treasure and convey to future generations.

It would be erroneous to call these glowing pages "philosemitic" or to apply to them some other political label. They are, in a strict sense, philosophical. They suggest a mode of existence that is indispensable for the perpetual regeneration and the continuing salvation of the world. The Greeks and the Romans ceased to exist many centuries ago. Their spirit, the spirit of the secular city and of the *Pax Romana,* will live on as long as the classics remain an element of our educational tradition and are not confined to philologists and historians. In recurrent renascences, the classical tradition has reawakened in us the awareness of the interdependence of liberty and reminded us that we can enjoy the fruits of peace and justice only if we are willing to defend them with arms. If we are today capable of being republicans and citizens, it is because of the legacy of civic heroism that the ancients have bequeathed to the Western world. In the modern world, the French—the French above all—have carried on this tradition. Péguy has experienced the richness and fullness of his very existence as a product of the traditions of the classical world. As a Frenchman, he was able to blend the heritage of the classical past and the Christian faith with the regional virtues of the peasant and the worker. The Christian element is the invitation to bear the cross and the humility of the ultimate sacrifice; the Jewish element is the incorruptible thirst for God's justice in the secular world, the never-ending combat for the indissoluble unity of the spiritual and the temporal in human life.

These categories are by no means historical concepts. They represent the different elements and attitudes of the Eternal Presence in the human process of self-realization. For Péguy, there is no history in the sense that philosophers of the nineteenth century conceived it—i.e., history as a process in which an objective meaning of life becomes visible and understood. He recognizes the recurring dichotomy of mystique and politique. But always there is the Eternal Presence, the opportunity to transcend the historical situation, to grasp the eternal in the flux of time. The four categories of the Hebrew, the Christian, the French, and the Classic are the irreducible elements of Péguy's philosophy of the present. In Péguy's own highly unique way, he participated in the vigorous combat that William James [1842–1910] and Henri Bergson were waging against the determinism and materialism of their times and for the reestablishment of the character of the actual as dynamic, free, and creative.

Péguy is well aware that the passion to exhaust the meaning and purpose of human existence in scientific laws is motivated by a peculiarly modern yearning for security, tranquility, definiteness. It means all this on the largest scale in all spheres of life: the security of the status quo in politics, the economic security of the limited family, the illusion that modernity is the ultimate revelation of the meaning of history. All these trends were a denial of the four great elements of the Eternal Presence, each of them representing a specific mode of creative adventure and spiritual heroism in the process of time. Péguy wonders what will be the destiny of a world whose sole aim is to attain a sense of security as against the unrest in God of past ages. He hates this state of mind, this cheap peace for which we have relinquished that sense of immediacy without which life is, to Péguy, only a macabre ghost play.

The modernity that was the object of Charles Péguy's relentless criticism was a state of intellectual inertia, a fatigue of the mind that does not dare to hold together the spiritual and the temporal in the intensity of human concreteness. Péguy was convinced that this state of mind is destined to spread to all spheres of human endeavor. Security will become the supreme purpose of all—of every class of society; for this security, a heavy price will be paid. In the economic sphere, the fertility of the race will be sacrificed to the security of the childless family; in the emotional and psychic sphere of an individual's life, the real completely absorbing present will be sacrificed to the synthetic "moment" composed of the particles of the past; in morals, immediate personal choice and responsibility will be sacrificed to the social blueprint with its illusory promises of automatic bliss and virtue.

It would be misleading to classify Péguy as a philosopher, unless we admit that the biblical Job and Dante Alighieri [1265–1321], John Donne [1572–1631] and John Milton [1608–1674], are genuine philosophers. Péguy was a poet, a philosopher-poet, if poetry is understood in its original meaning, as an evocation of the essence of being. The central category of his philosophy was the reality of the present; the leading theme of his poetry was the Eternal Presence, as it is embodied in the four fundamental attitudes of the Christian and the Jewish faiths and classical and French humanism, all of which proclaim the paradoxical truth that "life is more life and more than life." In this flaming vision, the technical terminologies of philosophy and the sciences melt away. What remains is the pure image of man transcending the arbitrary boundaries of the social world he and his fathers have created. Péguy's voice is that of a modern intellectual who has never ceased to be a peasant, of a rooted Frenchman who is ever aware of the distant and diverse strains that have gone into the making of his small world. His words are not those of a litterateur. He speaks the language of a living man, reminiscing, reproving, discussing, and arguing. His friends and his enemies, his God and anti-Christ, are always present in his thinking and writing. When he addresses his spiritual ancestors, we know that the speaker is one of their companions. And when he rises to praise the Hebrew prophets and seers, we hear a voice in which their plaint and their passion still ring with ancient and undiminished magic and power.

Note

1. Charles Péguy, *Basic Verities*, trans. Ann and Julian Green (New York: Pantheon, 1943).

22

Methodological Reflections on the History of the German Jews in the Age of Emancipation

Recently, I had a most stimulating talk with Dr. Max Kreutzberger [1900–1978], the first director of the Leo Baeck Institute in New York City. We discussed the possibility of research on Rudolf Borchardt [1877–1945], the great German poet who abjured his Jewish ancestry;[1] the Jews in the Stefan George [1868–1933] circle;[2] Hugo von Hofmannsthal [1874–1929], the Austrian novelist, dramatist, poet, and librettist;[3] and Jewish studies of Johann Wolfgang Goethe [1749–1832].[4] I had met Borchardt forty-five years ago. I was fascinated at the idea of contributing a piece on this strange and prophetic man, whose perspectives were so deeply true and false at the same time. During my analysis of the Borchardt theme and the other topics that Dr. Kreutzberger and I had discussed, certain methodological questions arose as to the scientific validity of the results of such projects. So here I outline my thoughts on this matter and make certain proposals.

The emancipation of the Jews marked their entrance into the cultural, social, and economic processes of the diverse national civilizations. Social change of this sort requires thorough sociological and

Previously unpublished. Undated manuscript located in file on Albert Salomon, Leo Baeck Institute, New York, New York. Published by permission from Leo Baeck Institute.

social-psychological investigation. Sociologists, in particular, have developed a number of categories in the field of minority relations that are applicable to an analysis of the emancipation. These include the wide areas of maladjustment, conformism, identification, distance, marginality, and the notion of the stranger. In the field of psychology, however, it is more difficult to categorize the motivations of the emancipated Jews. Therefore, it is almost impossible to determine scientifically the influence of a Jewish heritage on individuals who have completely lost or abandoned their Jewish identification. Only in the case of intellectuals who express a Jewish consciousness can we make any correlation between their Jewishness and their contribution to German civilization. The thesis "once a Jew, always a Jew" has no scientific foundations whatsoever.

While the emancipation legally offered all Jews equal citizenship, only the high ranks of Jewish society gained social acceptance by the Christian community. As a result, this tiny Jewish elite felt that the Jewish people who were completely integrated into the national civilization should convert to the religion that was cemented into the foundations of all European cultures. The first stage of the emancipation is the movement away from the religious traditions and from the humble and joyful recollections of the ancestors. It is the age of submission to the so-called Christian civilizations by conversion. As a social phenomenon, the emancipation from the Jewish traditions to Protestant and Catholic Christianity means the will to total conformism. Throughout the last 150 years, this trend towards conformism remained one of the decisive manifestations of the emancipation. To many Jews, this procedure was logically and emotionally intelligible. They felt it necessary to convert as a symbol of gratitude for what German Kultur had contributed to their own professional and cultural existence.

Among the Jews who converted after the emancipation, we find two distinct types. First, we have the individuals who subjectively believed that the Christianity in their country and age, for example, the romantic Protestantism of Friedrich Schleiermacher [1768–1834], was the true religion. At the other extreme were the secular Jews who converted only for the sake of competing on an equal basis with their Christian colleagues. Their attitude was characterized by complete contempt for both Christianity and Judaism.

The trend away from Judaism after the emancipation is a universal pattern when Jews meet with other civilizations. The Greek, Arab, and German civilizations fascinated wealthy and educated Jews because they offered ways of life and possibilities of self-realization beyond the pale of a theocratic society. These cultures had philosophy and art, great tragedy and satirical comedy. They worshipped the heroic and sublime in spite of a deep pessimism about the meaning of human life. The rabbis despised the Greeks because they felt that these people had no charity, mercy, or chastity. But, on the other hand, the intellectual, educated Jews were attracted by the diversity of human possibilities of secular states.

Emancipation as an alienation from Judaism and conversion to Christian and national civilizations is the negative pattern of the secularization of the Jewish world. The authors mentioned earlier certainly have no place in the history of the positive Jewish emancipation. They would violently deny classifications as Jews, and rightly so. Men like Borchardt, Hofmannsthal, Friedrich Gundolf [1880–1931], and Ernst Kantorowicz [1895–1963] had no consciousness of being Jews. Jewishness is not rooted in a racial identity, but, instead, in an adherence to a common religious heritage. Consequently, it is mere speculation to infer a correlation between Jewish origins and the attitudes expressed in the works of assimilated Jews. There is no methodological principle that would permit the inclusion of these authors in the context of a history of the positive Jewish emancipation. However, there were many Jews whose religious origins were reflected in their contributions to German Kultur after the emancipation.

Between these two extremes, there are various marginal cases that lie between the categories of negative and positive emancipation. One of the most impressive cases of the creative interaction between Jewishness and Germanness is that of Hermann Cohen [1842–1918]. This great scholar can truly be called the only genuine philosopher in Germany at the end of the nineteenth century. Cohen lived by the principle that there is a basic affinity between the spirits of the Jewish prophets and the German spirit as embodied in the philosophy of Immanuel Kant [1724–1804]. He was never shaken in this conviction, in spite of the rapidly expanding anti-Semitism and the lowering moral standards in Germany, as it began to move toward a society dominated by the mob. His greatest Jewish book, *Die Religion der Vernunft aus den Quellen des Judentums*,[5] presents his pioneering work in the philosophy of "I and Thou" in terms that still carry the halo of Kant's categories.

What Kant had meant to Cohen, Georg Hegel [1770–1831], and Friedrich Hölderlin [1770–1843], Friedrich Nietzsche [1844–1900] meant to Franz Rosenzweig [1886–1929]. Rosenzweig differed sharply from Cohen in an important regard. For many years, he wrestled with the decision of converting to Christianity. His friend, Eugen Rosenstock-Huessy [1888–1973], a sociologist and social philosopher, was a Jewish convert to Protestant Christianity. Rosenstock-Huessy nearly succeeded in convincing Rosenzweig of the spiritual supremacy of the Christian religion. But Rosenzweig's final decision to continue in the tradition of Abraham, Isaac, and Jacob set a pattern for all forthcoming Jewish generations. After the example of Franz Rosenzweig, all of us Jews have had to pass through the experience of Jesus of

Nazareth as part of our spiritual heritage. Rosenzweig was as much a German as a Jewish philosopher, as is demonstrated by both his thought and his language. It is molded by Hölderlin and the young Hegel, by Nietzsche and Arthur Schopenhauer [1788–1860], instead of by the Luther Bible. And some of his observations about Goethe's religion are among the best interpretations of Goethe's thought.

Among the Zionist thinkers and scientists who were influenced by and made contributions to German learning, Ernst Akiba Simon [1899–1988] is perhaps the most moving and illuminating. No German Christian wrote interpretations as lucid, comprehensive, and true of the most German of Germans, the Brothers Grimm [Jacob (1785–1863) and Wilhelm (1786–1859)], as did Ernst Simon. Throughout his work, he demonstrated the constructive unity of Jewish and German learning and concerns.[6]

One can say the same about Martin Buber [1878–1965] and Gerhard (later, Gershom) Scholem [1897–1982]. Both had been imbued with the spirit of Christian and German mysticism before they discovered Kabbala and Chassidism and their relevance for a Jewish philosophy of religion.

In the field of poetry and literature, Franz Kafka [1883–1924], a Jewish poet whose main concern is the theological plight of human beings in the contemporary desert of remorseless bureaucracies and personal anonymity, became the voice of a suffering mankind. The *passio humana* is the leitmotiv of the great Jewish poets who are German writers. And, among the ideal images of the constructive unity of Jewish philosophy and German criticism, one must mention Walter Benjamin [1892–1940]. His work on Goethe is perhaps his most outstanding achievement since it is a critical appreciation of the greatest German poet.[7]

Being a Jew is an experience that refers to our total being. We cannot escape it by conversion in a secularized world. We are a tiny part in the sequence of the generations of our dead who have suffered persecutions, offenses, and humiliations. These dead form the deep layers of our existence. The Jewish cemeteries all over the world are our true country. We are part of many civilizations, and we are at home in Greece and Persia, in Rome and Egypt, as much as we are at home in Germany and America. But we are always ready to depart for the sake of our destiny—the integrity of the *passio humana*. We exist as Jews in order to affirm the chain of our collective recollections and to remember piously our ancestors. It is our existence to know the suffering of man in life and to love it.

Notes

1. [See Heinz Politzer, "Rudolf Borchardt, Poet of Assimilation: The Extreme Case of an Extreme Tendency," *Commentary*, January 1, 1950.—Eds.]

2. [See Ernest Kahn, "Jews in the Stefan George Circle," *The Leo Baeck Institute Yearbook* (1963), 8:171–83.—Eds.]

3. [Hugo von Hofmannsthal, *The Whole Difference: Selected Writings of Hugo von Hofmannsthal*, ed. J. D. McCarthy (Princeton, NJ: Princeton University Press, 2008).—Eds.]

4. [See, for instance, *Goethe in German-Jewish Culture*, eds. Klaus L. Berghahn and Jost Hermand (Rochester, NY: Camden House, 2001).—Eds.]

5. [(Leipzig: Fock, 1919).—Eds.]

6. [Ernst Simon, "Zur Jacob Grimms Sprache, Stil und Persönlichkeit," in *Deutsche Vierteljahrsschrift für Literaturwissenschaft und Geistesgeschichte* (1929), 7:515–59.—Eds.]

7. [Benjamin's essay on Goethe's 1809 *Die Wahlverwandtschaften* (The Elective Affinities) was first published in Hugo von Hofmannsthal, *Neue Deutsche Beiträge* (Munich: 1924–25). It is widely considered one of the seminal works of literary criticism of the twentieth century.—Eds.]

23

Eschatological Thinking in Western Civilization: Reflections on a Book

I

A doctoral dissertation rarely attracts an audience larger than that of experts in the particular field. In the case of Jacob Taubes [1923–1987], *Abendländische Eschatologie*,[1] however, both the name of the author and the topic will kindle the interest of scholars in many fields: theology, philosophy, the history of ideas, and the social sciences. Specifically, the philosopher who specializes in methodology and philosophy of history and the sociologist who is concerned with the problems of a sociology of knowledge and of religion will find the book rewarding in many respects.

The topic is a link in the chain of European self-interpretation. The self-interpretation of the West as a meaningful unity amid the variety of separate peoples is a persistent theme woven of historical and philosophical considerations. It has two distinct phases: one is prior to the national interpretations of European societies and extends from Montesquieu [1689–1755] to Jacob Burckhardt [1818–1897]; the second is postnationalistic and stretches from Johan Huizinga [1872–1945] to Paul Valéry [1871–1945] and to the young author of the book under discussion. Taubes's aim is to describe and to interpret the effect of eschatological thinking on all aspects of

---

Published originally in a slightly different form in *Social Research* 16 (March 1949), 90–98. Republished by permission from *Social Research*.

modern European thought and action. A learned and encyclopedic scholar, he is well aware that earlier thinkers have selected a variety of traits as constituting the European character in the process of history. He knows, of course, that for centuries the Catholic Church proclaimed that it had established the frontiers of Europe against the Mohammedan and Greek Orthodox religions. Within its confines, the church did develop a specific type of rationalism, blended of the intellectualism of its theology and the pragmatic rationalism of Roman imperialism. Taubes faithfully remembers that European thinkers from Montesquieu to Burckhardt and Valéry have insisted on the principle of freedom as the unique feature of European civilization in individual, social, political, and international relations. They stressed that the common attitude of the individual nations was a love of independence and a resistance to all kinds of social and political despotism.

There must, then, be special reasons that impelled the author to add a new perspective to the unceasing self-interpretation of Europe as a dynamic historical personality. The reasons are implicit in Taubes's own words. He chooses the topic and constructs the perspective as a Jew to whom being Jewish and European are the natural components of his existence—which distinguishes his work from the general contribution of Jews to European thinking. Most scientific and philosophical accomplishments by Jews have been produced by assimilated or assimilating persons and groups, who endeavored to identify themselves with liberal and radical movements in order to be completely absorbed in European civilization. Many assimilated Jews also joined revolutionary movements with which they identified their total existence. Uprooted French Jews turned to sociology as the philosophy of total progress to which they could transfer their old messianic hopes. In the meeting of such intellectual and emotional powers, they attempted to accomplish the self-redemption of industrial society.

In contrast to the assimilated Jews of Western civilizations, Taubes is sustained by the living spirit of Judaism. This existential attitude induced him to choose his theme. In dealing with eschatology, Taubes is able to demonstrate the historical productivity of a mode of thinking that was the legacy of his people to European civilization. The selection of the topic implies still another motive: a desire to bypass theological and ecclesiastical patterns of thinking. He is too well trained in sociological thinking not to see that all dogmatisms and systematized religious institutions, having compromised with intellectual and social powers in the world, have limited the expanding power of the total spiritual vision. Finally, he clings to the topic for methodological reasons. In the methodology of history, the adherents of idealism and realism have fought a rather sterile war. Taubes is conscious of the fact that the alternative between materialism and spiritualism is totally unsatisfactory. He rejects also the piecemeal relativism of Weber's interpretations. He sees that only total interpretation, which recognizes the lasting wholeness and interaction of the extremes of human thinking, will reconcile the conflicting methods.

For these reasons, Taubes deals with eschatological thinking. Eschatological thinking is radical. It goes to the roots of the whole; it is final and total. It is the first mode of thinking to offer the category of alienation. The God of Creation is alienated from the world that has liberated itself from its Creator and remains the sphere of evil under its demiurge. Only the ultimate and all-embracing actuality of God reunites the alienated world with His total being. Thus, the transcendent God remains alien and hidden from the world, which revolts and builds up the total power of negativity, a countercreation. It is the archetype of eschatological thinking that God will redeem the world in a final judgment of love and truth.

Taubes pursues the development, transformation, and renascences of eschatological thinking from the early Jewish and Gnostic sources to

Georg Hegel [1770–1831], Karl Marx [1818–1883], and Søren Kierkegaard [1813–1855]. Theologians of Jewish and Christian faith will be interested in the analysis of eschatological thinking in the preaching of Jesus, previously hinted at by Hermann Samuel Reimarus [1694–1768]. The historian of the church and the sociologist of knowledge will study attentively the description of the means employed by the Church Fathers and philosophers to reconcile the total and radical element of eschatological thinking with the relative and compromising theories of the church as established power. In this connection, Taubes stresses the authority of Saint Augustine of Hippo [354–430], who succeeded in integrating the totality of redemption with the church as *civitas coelestis*. The main part of the book deals with the renascences of eschatological thinking in the spiritual, philosophical, and social revolutions that thrust themselves in radical attitudes beyond the frontiers of academic and political institutions. Taubes sees the key positions in the development of modern history—the revolution of the Franciscan Spirituals (the Fratecelli), the unification of spiritual and social revolutions during the sixteenth century, the philosophical revolution of German idealism, and the total revolutions of the industrial worlds, all of which he cites as elements of negative spirituality. He demonstrates that eschatological thinking reappears in the open abyss of such radical situations and makes possible total interpretation. Taubes notes that Hegel proclaimed the end of the classical-Christian-national worlds of past history, and that Kierkegaard and Marx disclosed the hubris of Hegel's reconciliation in the contemplation of philosophy, reopening the perspective that might lead toward a new total interpretation of the whole. According to Taubes, their grandiose efforts might contribute to bringing into existence a new synthetic vision of the totality of life.

This investigation is carried on in a truly philosophical and historical spirit. The author's spirit is historical because he is concerned with the ways of thinking that recognize the meaningful evolution of mankind as the central theme of human understanding. He describes this pattern of thinking as modern, distinguishing it from the cyclical thinking that identifies the process of nature with that of history. Since Jewish and Christian thinking have developed the idea of the progress in salvation, history has become the lens that reveals the grandeur and misery of the human condition. History alone is the comprehensive study of the totality of human beings. Again and again, thinkers have recognized the primal relevance of history as the dynamic progress in the human enterprise, in which the opposite poles—such as creation and salvation, evil and redemption, or slavery and freedom—are intertwined and interact.

II

The thesis of the book is that the spiritual mode of thinking established by the Jewish prophets and Gnostic philosophers has set the pattern for the various types of eschatological thinking in Western civilization. The attentive reader will discern that in this wide field of investigation the author has succeeded in gaining some valuable new scientific insights.

First, he makes evident to all sociologists of knowledge that historical dialectics is in origin and structure eschatological thinking. This structure demonstrates the indivisible unity of monistic and dualistic principles. Eschatological thinking is the core of all types of historical dialectics that comprehend the philosophy of history as established by the Franciscan Spirituals, Hegel's philosophy of End-Time, and Marx's philosophy of total revolution. The varieties of spiritual experience can be explained as referring to the ambiguity of the term *kingdom of God on earth*, which permits the stressing of either secular or heavenly redemption. Taubes contends that the

Franciscan Spirituals put forth the idea that the final salvation is going to take place in the Here and Now, which suggests that spiritual and secular revolutions merge in the efforts of totally reconstructing the whole world.

Second, the author makes a thorough reexamination of the term *secularization.* He rejects the thesis that all atheistic and antireligious movements are necessarily antispiritual. If we take the idea of total history seriously, there will be periods that are estranged from the divine. Alienation, however, is a dialectical category that makes it possible to speak of negative spirituality in times of total revolution during which the secular redemption is the presupposition for total redemption. In this historical way of thinking, Taubes comes close to a thesis advocated enthusiastically by Georg Lukács [1885–1971] before he joined the Communist party. Lukács declared that total socialist revolution is indispensable. Only the realization of socialism will induce men to rediscover the infinite suffering and forlornness of the human being in the perfection of the social fabric. Then and only then, Lukács assumed, would the new-old eschatological vision come true again and reconstruct mankind as a redeemed universe. For this reason, the term *secularization* can only mean the total absence of any reference to a final meaning of history. The radical, satanic, and antireligious theories may have their place in a spiritual process of history.

Third, the author has rediscovered that the term *progress* is not limited to the intellectual and scientific movements. He articulates the spiritual connotation on the basis that the Franciscan Spirituals turned the process of salvation into a history of salvation taking place in the Here and Now.

Fourth, the author has innovated in describing the identical structure of the historical and philosophical thinking of Peter John of Olivi [1248–1298] and of Hegel. Both start from the Gospel of St.

John; both deal with the evolution of divine love or with the modifications of love, according to Hegel's terminology; both stress the actuality of the mind as becoming in history; both stress its dialectical movement which appears in certain stages of transition (Olivi's *ecclesia spiritualis* as the realization of the kingdom of God on earth is paralleled by Hegel's intellectual realm in the history of philosophy and by the kingdom of God in the philosophy of religion); both maintained the redeeming function of prophecy and of philosophy; both proclaimed themselves to be priests of the absolute and subject, respectively, to the Pope and the Prussian king; both practiced a relative conservatism in church and bourgeois society; both established an absolute radicalism in developing the idea of history as the self-realization of the spirit, as the fulfillment of the eternal gospel. Taubes has opened a great historical perspective by describing the identity and continuity of the eschatological mode of thinking in the rise and end of modernity. He indicates that spiritual historical thinking remains intact and is the living requirement beyond all theological and philosophical systems so long as the process of history is considered to be the unfolding of the range of human powers. This thesis permits the inclusion of one aspect of German idealism which opens the windows of rationalism onto the larger view of an eternal peace and a world of human reconciliation.

Fifth, a point of scientific progress is implied in this last discovery. Taubes has definitely settled the discussion on the origins of modernity in historical periodization. For almost fifty years, a conflict has raged between the students of Jacob Burckhardt [1818–1897] and those of Konrad Burdach [1859–1936] on this subject. Students of Burckhardt still assume that the Italian Renaissance—in all its aspects of emancipating rationalism, individualism, and secularized collective power—is the articulate break with the Middle Ages. Burdach, on the contrary, maintained that the beginnings of the modern time and of the true Renaissance lie in the rise of religious movements in the expanding urban centers, which led to the development of the mendicant orders. Taubes's articulate interpretation of the Franciscan Spirituals and of their role in the history of Western thinking decides the question finally in favor of Burdach. Taubes stresses, minutely, the relevance of the radical eschatological mode of thinking of the Franciscan Spirituals for all spheres of religious, political, and social action and thought. They ended the dualistic medieval thinking that separated the worldly and super worldly spheres. These radical spiritual pioneers were the first to establish the crucial idea of modern European thinking—namely, the indivisible unity of the spirit and of the world in the process of history. They nevertheless experienced the perversion, by others, of their spiritual radicalism into political propaganda against everything spiritual.

This phenomenon permits the author to derive a sixth thesis from the new and decisive stride toward the modern world. The spiritualization of the historical process brings with it a new radicalism and extremism in working out conflicts and antagonisms. Taubes is correct in assuming that, with such a radical change in outlook and perspective, the spirit of revolution and the revolution of the spirit are intertwined. He sees the new radicalism and extremism in all fields of thought and action because rulers and ruled, elite and opposition, refer their ideas and deeds to a frame of reference that gives a spiritual connotation to every thought and action. He is not, however, the victim of his own generalizations. He carefully excepts the lasting pattern of premodern rationalism, as practiced and taught by the institutions of the Catholic Church and by all organizations and relationships under its control. Taubes is well aware that the thesis of his book does not extend to the Catholic orbit, and states explicitly that the Catholic Church has always been conscious of the fact that all eschatological and spiritual movements question the very foundations of its existence. It has persecuted and exterminated them with inexorable logic. From the Franciscan Spirituals to the Spanish *Los Illuminados* and to the movement of Quietism, the church has gone on record as being violently antagonistic to the free and independent spirit. Indeed, secular revolutions in Catholic worlds still take on the pattern of the church and its hierarchy as the only image of total authority and control. Taubes is fully aware that the rational structure of power relations, as well as those of authority, superordination, obedience, gradation, and hierarchies is at the opposite pole of the leader-follower relations that arise from a communion united by the dedication to the spirit and its total requirements.

If this is so, Western eschatology is a marginal problem that comes into existence when authority, prestige, and the significance of established institutions—religious, political, social—are being questioned or exploded. In other words, eschatological thinking is by its very nature revolutionary: it has necessarily the perspective that reveals the deficiencies, corruptions, and degeneracies of all established regimes. It is not incidental that the author actually describes the eschatological element in German philosophical and social thinking. He gives an articulate presentation of the spiritual and social upheaval that reaches to the ultimate and stretches beyond all political and philosophical frontiers, and indicates the profound lack of equilibrium and rational moderation in German thought. The author feels that this is a constitutive element in the German world. Though he is familiar with the spiritual revolts and uprisings all over Europe at one time or another, he dismisses them as irrelevant to his purpose. He recognizes that a deep sense of anarchy predisposes the Germans to a radical insight into the evil and demonic character of the world and into the spiritual powers of reconciliation and salvation. With keen insight, Taubes states that all other nations brought up in the orbit of the Roman Empire (pagan or Christian) have established articulate structures of civilization within the frames of which individuals and groups feel secure and complete because they can always rely on the sober interference of reason. But for various historical reasons, the Germans never overcame the tribal narrowness and the imperial spiritualism. They were never able to construct between these extremes a civilized society. They remained open to all temptations of radical and extreme thinking and action. In the tension between the tribal primitivism and the universal spiritualism, the most wicked and the most sublime efforts were possible. They were able to visualize the most horrifying acts of corruption and degradation, and to convey at the same time, the sense of sublime renunciation as a presupposition of total salvation. Implicitly, the author describes the conditions that enabled the Germans, throughout their history, continuously to take the thrust into the absolute beyond all theological and ecclesiastical institutions, to leap into the realm of freedom beyond all political institutions. These conditions can be summarized briefly as the lack of political civilization and of an educated and enlightened society.

III

Contemporary Jews may wonder that a Jewish scholar should concentrate today on an interpretation of the German contribution to Western thought that presents their great spiritual possibilities and achievements fairly and objectively. Whatever the validity of such a response, the problem merits reflection. Here is a young, unassimilated Jewish scholar, completely secure and independent in his belonging to the flock of Israel, who writes a book that conveys to the reader the idea of the lasting adventure in spiritual thinking among the Germans. This effect does not imply any value judgment; it is the inevitable consequence of the author's theme and perspective.

Taubes deals with the structure of eschatological and apocalyptic thought and articulates the specific conditions under which it materializes. These conditions arise from prepolitical, loose, almost anarchical groups that fling their despair and fears, their insecurities and enthusiasms, into the lap of a divine ruler whom they declare their king. Such open societies cling to the idea of theocracy as prior to and beyond political institutions. This sociological statement, joined to the sociological reflections on the problematic character of German thought and culture, makes it possible to venture a conjecture. Taubes is compelled to dwell mainly on German attitudes in philosophy and action because the Germans were predestined to carry on the revolutionary and spiritual tradition founded by Jewish prophets and Gnostic philosophers. This indicates that there is a deep and hidden affinity between Jews and Germans, a common precivilized and postcivilized state of mind, which permits both to transcend the realm of worldly organization and to expand into the eschatological homeland, despite and because of the radical and extreme corruption in a state unprotected by a frame of civilization. There was one German who was fully aware of such a structural affinity between Jews and Germans—and that was Johann Wolfgang von Goethe [1749–1832]. It is indicative of Taubes's keen and passionate thinking that he is not perturbed by the implications of his scientific thinking.

It is necessary to note briefly the author's procedure and method. In such an adventure of ideas, a young scholar has to rely largely on interpretive studies. It is a characteristic feature of Taubes's position that he selects the most outstanding and progressive authors in the fields of Gnosis, Franciscan Spiritualism, Reformation, and Total Revolution with an unfailing sense of values. He is determined only by a burning desire for truth. For this reason, he praises the great scholarly achievements of the orthodox Lutheran, Karl Holl [1866–1926], as against the superficial and false imputations made by Ernst Troeltsch [1865–1923], whose religious attitude would be closer to Taubes than that of Holl. But Taubes remains superior to the overwhelming material he had to work through. He never commits himself to the conclusions of the authors whom he consults. He never loses his own perspective. He has his problem firmly in hand. This indicates the spontaneous and vital power of a superior and well-disciplined intelligence.

As to original sources, the author is well acquainted with the exegetical and historical literature on the respective parts of the Bible and of the Gospels. He knows Jewish and Christian mysticism. He is well versed in Hegel, Marx, and Kierkegaard.

It is desirable to state the scientific skills and the unwavering control of all methodological devices exhibited in this first book of a young scholar whose philosophical spontaneity is remarkable. But it would be unsatisfactory to end one's reflections on the book with so routine a check of its scientific standards. To make the evaluation complete, it must be added that the author has also a human sincerity and a humble dedication to that Jewish spiritual power that he made the theme of his investigation. There is a spark of the prophetic and philosophical genius of Israel in this book that describes its impact on Western thought and action. This work demonstrates anew that in all fields of history of ideas and of philosophy the quality of the author counts. There will never be an outstanding historian or philosopher who is not, in the sense of William James [1842–1910], capable of the varieties of human experience.

Note

1. Jakob Taubes, *Abendländische Eschatologie, Beiträge zur Soziologie und Sozialphilosophie*, ed. René König (Berne: A. Francke, 1947) [published in English as *Occidental Eschatology*, trans. David Ratmoko (Stanford, CA: Stanford University Press, 2009)—Eds.].

PART II
Syllabi

24

Origins of Sociology and Social Psychology (1947)

Annotated by Robert Jackall (2016)

I. Humanists and Educators

Machiavelli, Erasmus

II. Jurists and Statesmen: Science of Natural Law

Grotius, Hobbes, Pufendorf

III. Stoicism

Bacon, Charron, Montaigne, Spinoza, Descartes

Du Vair, Lipsius, Bishops Hall, Butler

IV. Francis Bacon: Statesman, Jurist, Philosopher

V. Mystical and social experiences contribute to Social Psychology

Francis de Sales, Ignatius of Loyola

Montaigne, Pascal, LaRochefoucauld, LaBruyere, Louis de Saint-Simon

---

Previously unpublished. Manuscript located in Publicity Office records, NS.030105, box 42, folder 8, The New School Archives and Special Collections, The New School, New York, New York. Published by permission from Frank Salomon.

VI. Variable mores and invariable human nature

History of Civilization and Sociology: Fontenelle, Bayle, Voltaire

VII. Universality of conditions, history, natural law

Montesquieu

VIII. Unity of Science: comparative method, historical relativism, political sociology, rise of positivism

Encyclopédie—D'Alembert, Diderot, and Holbach

IX. Genesis of Mind and Moral Sense

Locke, Shaftsbury, Mandeville

X. Unity of Sociology and Social Psychology

Scottish School

* * *

Introduction

Sociology is the science of society. It is indicative for the situation of modern learning that nobody is able to define "society." This is the reason why historians of sociology have no criteria for determining the discipline's origins and currents. Some begin the history of sociology with Plato, some with Comte, some with Confucius, some with Montesquieu. However, scrutiny of our contemporary situation yields criteria that make it possible to determine objectively the plan, scope, and function of sociology.

Contemporary trends are best illustrated by the work of Robert K. Merton [1910–2003]. He demonstrates the unification of sociological theory with techniques of social conduct that had been indicated and that ran in different directions for many decades. Merton, Robert M. MacIver [1882–1970], Robert Staughton Lynd [1892–1970], and Talcott Parsons [1902–1979] reunite the technical and theoretical problems of social studies.

Apart from this general trend, sociology as philosophy of total evolution still exists—mainly in the form of Spencerianism [after Herbert Spencer (1820–1903)] and Marxism [after Karl Marx (1818–1883)], often framed as Comtism [after Auguste Comte (1798–1857)] in Latin America. Sociology is taken for granted as method in all fields of history and the history of ideas. There are three common elements in these diverse manifestations of sociology.

First, there is the scientific principle that human conduct can be completely explained and understood from the analysis of its basic needs, desires, and goals. It is not necessary to take refuge in any transcendent or metaphysical principle. Second, there is the practical principle that human institutions could and should be improved. Third, there is the philosophical principle that these empirical studies offer to the student of human nature fundamental questions: What is man; what can he do; what can he accomplish? This stand makes it possible to see the unique situation in which sociology could come into existence.

The situation can, first, be determined negatively. It was the anti-Christian revolt under the impact of naturalistic Aristotle and of the rising independence of political power in lay societies. This lay spirit, even when remaining true to Christianism, revolted against Scholastic philosophies.

In positive terms, the situation is that of Renaissance and Humanism Men striving for a natural explanation of their social conditions.

They began to renounce the dualistic world picture of the Middle Ages. They favored a monistic world—the world of man as social universe. The best expression of the modern attitude is in the *Oratio De Hominis Dignitate* of Giovanni Pico della Mirandola [1463–1494]: "God said to Adam: 'I have put you into the center of the world so that you can easily look around you and inspect everything. I created you as a being neither celestial nor earthly, neither mortal nor immortal, so that you may be your own free creator and conqueror. You can degenerate into a beast or elevate yourself into a God-like being.'"

This discovery of man and society as an independent reality implied an experience and an attitude. The experience that united naturalistic and spiritualistic thinkers was the awareness of the increasing pressure of social institutions and of the precarious aspects of human freedom as emancipated from moral and spiritual values and subject to social and political requirements. The sociological attitude can be described as the consciousness that society is the destiny of man, a constructive or destructive fate that educates or destroys the individual. Experience, attitude, and scientific methods of analysis and imputation merge to bring about the origins of sociology and political science, economics, and social psychology.

The social sciences start neither as discipline nor as a new literary pattern of learning. The social thinkers use many literary patterns as developed by antiquity for social analyses and descriptions, such as dialogues, mock-eulogies, satires, essays, treatises on education, memoirs, and discourses, as well as dictionaries, encyclopedias, maxims, portraits, and characters, which they invent as modern forms for establishing truth about the real motives and impulses that make men act.

We must be aware that, on this question of origins, the idea of scientific truth was not as narrow as it is today. Nicolas Boileau-

Despréaux [1636–1711], in writing his *Satires*,[1] sincerely believed that he scientifically established truth about social behavior. Similarly, moralists like Jonathan Swift [1667–1745] or Samuel Richardson [1689–1761] were convinced that they recreated truth about men living in society.

The novel is the only literary form that resulted from the new sociological attitude. For this reason, no history of sociology could rightly neglect the relevance of the novel for knowledge of societal configurations under the conditions of the modern world. Social studies demonstrate from the beginning the inseparable unity of theory and of techniques for realizing and maintaining true principles and for clarifying the conditions that promote or prevent their actualization. Social studies refer to a philosophical frame of reference—namely, the practical improvement of institutions and of situations. It must be emphasized that this trend is deeply connected with the new printing press and its influence on human thought. For this reason, social studies have their own specific place and function in the rise of modern learning. They are intermediate between philosophy and politics. Philosophy is an eternal adventure in ideas that is carried on from philosopher to philosopher for enlarging the truth about the whole. Sociology and social studies strive for truth about the lasting changes of social process and conditions. Social thinkers are educators who strive to identify the techniques of behavior that permit men to adjust to and to live up to the standards of their respective societies.

For this reason, the historian of sociology must give ample attention to those writers who spread the gospel of good manners, from the Spanish Jesuit priest, Baltasar Gracián [1601–1658], to the mistress of etiquette, Emily Post [1872–1960]. The philosopher constructs ideals of the good life; the sociologist translates such abstract notions into the languages of social classes and ruling elites. The sociologist's notions come into existence where philosophical norms meet with the normative requirements of differently structured societies. Courtier, nobleman, and gentleman are sociological formulations of the philosophical notion of "the good." This intermediate place of social studies illuminates their function in society: they develop scientific tools and measuring rods for remedying and improving social conditions.

This indicates their historical origin from another angle. Such sciences of reform were needed in the political societies that could not rely any longer on patriarchal loyalties of a learned, rich, and powerful urban population. Such historical perspective makes it possible to shed light on the meaning of *society* in the origins of sociology. It is the social process beyond its political frame. This process implies all spontaneous and creative activities of human freedom, such as philosophy, art, science, poetry, moral courage, and spiritual independence. This science of society is one aspect of rising liberalism. It remains the frame of the social studies for the period we are dealing with in this course. Between 1489 and 1789, humanists, jurists, statesmen, educators, professors, intellectuals, and courtiers, freelance writers, and scientists contribute from the most diverse angles to build up an independent area of knowledge of human conduct in societal relations.

Sociology changes its character completely only after the French Revolution. It becomes a philosophy of total evolution; a science of industrial-technological progress and a philosophy of industrial revolution. The contemporary situation of sociology is closer to the period we are presenting here, at least in the Anglo-Saxon countries and in France. In Russia, revolutionary sociology is well established as social theology.

I. Humanists and Educators

Niccolò di Bernardo dei Machiavelli [1469–1527] and **Desiderius Erasmus** [1466–1536] share in the common experiences of the independent reality of social institutions. Both agree on the disastrous effect of ecclesiastical government on the religious and political reputation of the Church. The Holy Roman Empire is gone forever, and the national state is taken for granted. Machiavelli draws the conclusion that it is time to reconstruct the classical polis-state and to liberate the Italian states from the Church. Erasmus concludes that this is the last possibility for spiritualizing the secular world in order to remain true to Christian and classical social standards.

Both are humanists. Humanists are scholars and scientists who rediscover the ideals and realities of social life in classical philosophers, poets, and historians. They apply their scholarship, first, to editing these books scientifically; second, to establishing new-old standards of living and the educational techniques for their realization. Machiavelli revitalizes the ideal of the political order and the techniques of maintaining established governments.

Erasmus constructs the ideal of spiritual freedom—the ideal that harmonizes Christ and Epicurus. He uses a variety of former approaches for suggesting social reforms:

> 1. Analysis of social institutions. All of his essays on political and social institutions and societal relations—state, marriage, schools, business, church, monastery—describe the conditions that explain why people deviate and are frustrated in their ideal ends, the so-called *lex degenerandi.*
>
> 2. Scrutiny of the positive task of one individual versus institutions and illuminates the plight of the

> individual under the growing pressure of rational organizations. See his treatment of the Christian knight, the pragmatic mystic, and the priority of love over knowledge.
>
> 3. See the complex and ambiguous character of conduct and the interdependence of conscious-unconscious in *The Praise of Folly*.[2]

But Machiavelli is the real political philosopher and the greater sociologist of the two. His political philosophy implies certain sociological propositions without which there would be no philosophical politics. He explicitly stated that most of his theses are valid for the decisive social institutions: religion, state, and army. It can even be maintained that Machiavelli intended to establish sociology as a science that can predict the modes of social conduct by analyzing certain typical situations and studying human behavior in such behaviors in such situations. If we understand the mechanism of passions as responses to certain stimuli, we are able to predict conduct as required by specific situations. This has been neglected in Christian times. Renascence of political and historical classics helps to construct such a science, which contains principles and techniques of building a great state. It is the science of the statesman. Machiavelli's contributions to sociology are fourfold:

> 1. His theory of Challenge-Response is more philosophical and scientific than that of Arnold Toynbee. The relations between *Fortuna—Necessitas—Virtù* teach us how to accommodate change when we study the requirements of historical situations. *Virtù* is being superior to the experienced and understood stream of *Fortuna*. Understood necessities provoke

human possibilities: industry, goodness, justice, *virtù*. The Law of Renascences in hardening situations.

2. His theory of social change. The human character is identical all the time: man is never satisfied; he always desires new and more cupidity and ambition, which are his basic passions. The sequence of his desires is described as: power, health, security. These desires are expressions of insecurity and fear: interdependence between power—fear—external imperialism—domestic insecurity. Such desires determine the dynamics of social action. Desires can be manipulated by necessities, laws, and punishments.

3. Sociology of militarism (the art of war). Machiavelli set the patterns for all future discussions on this subject, including those by Adam Smith (on the sociological implications of mercenary or citizen armies). In addition, he elaborates technical problems of march-order, camping, tactics that are full of observations on the impact of the social structure of military bodies for the tactics to be applied. In spite of the negative criticism of Hans Delbrück [1848–1929],[3] it remains a pioneering book in the sociology of militarism.

4. Sociological theory of politics. The constituent elements of conspiracy and revolutions, complete with their technical aspects: size—scene—trust—action. The social conditions necessary for diverse

> types of government. The social and psychological requirements for maintaining a legitimate or an illegitimate government. The social presuppositions for social decomposition and the rise of tyranny. National character: products of different systems of education.

Machiavelli influenced all spheres of thinking and all strata of society: his impact on Bacon, Descartes, Hobbes, and Spinoza is well known. A sociological phenomenon is Machiavellianism as the theory and techniques of the Reason of State that became a popular topic for best sellers throughout the seventeenth century. Still more interesting is the fashion of Tacitismo, that is, to study the great Roman historian Cornelius Tacitus [56–120] as the textbook of Machiavellianism that contains all the weaknesses of human degradation and humiliation. Tacitismo has remarkable importance for raising the consciousness of what it meant for the intellectual, moral, and psychological standards of the ruled to live under a despotic regime.

[Here, Salomon included a draft of his essay, "Democracy and Religion in the Work of Erasmus," that is nearly identical to that presented as a separate chapter in this volume. The editors have removed the essay from this outline in the interests of efficiency.—Eds.]

II. Jurists and Statesmen: Science of Natural Law

Next to the humanistic educators who urged political independence and spiritual liberty, jurists and lawyers played a leading role in contributing to the field of sociology. They transformed the Christian theory of Natural Law into a secular science of Natural Law. This is the first systematic effort to establish a theory of the constitution of society.

Hugo Grotius [1583–1645] was a Dutch statesman, jurist, and historian. He nicely exemplifies the situation of transition between the spiritual and the secular Natural Law. God is the ultimate source of Natural Law. Holy Scripture and classical texts have the same validity for explaining universal legal norms. This definition of Natural Law is in harmony with that of the Spanish philosophers of Natural Law.[4] It says: "Jus naturale est dictamen rectae rationis iudicans actui alicui, ex eius convenientia ant disconvenientia cum ipsa natura rationale ac sociali in esse turpitudinem ant necessitate morale, ac consequenter ab autore Deo talem actum ant praecipiant vetari." ("Natural Law is the command of right reason that indicates the qualification of any action as degraded or necessary as in agreement or in disagreement with rational and social nature. Hence such action is either prescribed or forbidden by the commandments of God.")

In 1625, Grotius published *De Jure Belli ac Pacis.* This book stimulated the establishment of chairs of Natural Law and of the Law of Nations, where Natural Law was taught as a branch of Moral Philosophy. In 1661, Baron Samuel von Pufendorf held the first chair in the world in the Law of Nature and Nations at Heidelberg. Grotius's book was required reading. That treatise had suggested organizing the required courses in moral philosophy as follows: natural theology, natural law, ethics, and politics. In the reformed Scottish universities of the early eighteenth century, Adam Smith gratefully recognized his indebtedness to Grotius as setting the pattern for a science of the statesman. Grotius conceived of the book as *Ars naturalis et perpetuae jurisprudentiae.* It is a scientific discipline as evident in its demonstration as mathematics. It is Erasmian in spirit and purpose. It will reformulate the old Truth in terms of modern rationalistic-mathematical thinking. Like Erasmus, Grotius desires constructing *Res Christiana* in legal institutions. Grotius's spiritual position coincides with Neo-Stoicism. Modern Stoicism meant the immanence of divinity as creative reason in the universe of nature and society. Grotius supports all important theses with statements by Lucius Annaeus Seneca [4 BC–65 AD], Marcus Aurelius [121–180], and Marcus Tullius Cicero [106–43 BC] in order to demonstrate the universal validity of logos and *caritas*. This liberal and stoic spiritualism merged with the traditions of legal thinking. Together, these created a first system of societal relationships:

1. The notion of Socius is a conception of Roman Law

2. The notion of reciprocity is a conception of Roman Law

3. The notion of Society as the sum total of mutual relationships springs from Roman Law

   a. Give and take
   b. Superiority-subordination
   c. Equality among business partners, friends, members of groups, team workers
   d. Sympathetic agape and need for protection
   e. Kindness-sternness
   f. Cooperatives and equals
   g. Cooperatives as unequals

Natural Law to Grotius is the manifestation of human nature as innate right reason (*qua recta ratio insita*). This instinctive rationality for utilitarian ends is the characteristic trait of the human animal. Man desires social life "not of any and every sort, but peaceful, and organized according to the measure of his intelligence, with those who are of his own kind." The Stoics called this tendency sociableness. This means that Peace is the telos of human nature. Peace cannot be realized because of human corruption. Peace remains a lasting postulate of human social action.

Mutuality is composed of two elements: mutual needs and mutual sympathies. Maintenance of society (*custodia societatis*) is the one source of law and natural law. Natural Law's general principle is to live according to reason (nature). Its evident principles are private property and marriage. And granted marriage, adultery is inadmissible. A nonevident principle is that vengeance is bad.

There are two branches of Natural Law:

> *Social.* Self-preservation (of life-self-property); strict law enforced; security of individual in relations to socii. Pattern: contract. Social Natural Law in collective bodies; social consensus—associations of equals, hierarchies of inferior—superior. Agreements according to mutuality.
>
> *Humane.* Stratification of society, norms of justice that give every man what is due him, inherent in every man as a potential right. Established law v. Justice, legality v. morality.

Grotius identified *sources of civil law* in terms of basic types of societal relationships that correspond to natural requirements and reappear in all social branches: parents-children, husband-wife, guardian-ward, master-servant.

Grotius distinguishes between law proper and natural law, which includes a hierarchy of duties beyond the institutions of statutory law and customs. The dynamics of natural law comprehend the various spheres of normative rules from legality to morality, from things permissible to things good and better. There is a law of charity in natural law that was the common property of the pagan world, as manifested in Cicero and Seneca. Grotius intends to show the universality of human sympathies and of consensus as indicating the rational normativities of human nature.

Thomas Hobbes [1588–1679] was the founder of a secular science of Natural Law as a systematic theory of the elements that constitute society. In 1640, handwritten copies of his *Elements of Law, Natural and Politic* were circulated. A pirated copy was later published in 1650 without his permission. In the meantime, he wrote De Cive in 1642, published in Latin in a limited edition. Both of these works were important in his *Leviathan, or the Matter, Forme, and Power of a Common-wealth, Ecclesiasticall and Civill*, published in 1651.[5]

Hobbes created a new and scientific method, one that separated social from moral principles, one focused on human impulses and on an analysis of social institutions from a social-psychological standpoint. He argued that private property did not derive from nature, but from human conventions. This led to the question: Why do men want such artifice? Given a community of goods, there is a war of all against all. "Thus I had formed two certain postulates of human nature: (1) that of striving for private ownership; and (2) that of natural reason according to which everybody is anxious to escape violent death as the greatest natural evil. Starting from these principles, I believe that I have foreseen the necessity of fulfilling agreements, of keeping promises, that is, the elements of social duties." Thus, Hobbes disputes the hypothesis of the natural equality of men, pointing to the vanity, selfishness, and envy of individuals. In Hobbes's work, there is a conspicuous dilemma: Do affections or reason induce men to construct social institutions? In *De Cive*, I,[6] he argues that mutual fear of others is the real motive, a motive that is identified with reason. Only *Leviathan* clearly states that the State is a work of art. Its natural origins are agreement among citizens leading to an artificial patrimonial contract, a natural voluntary subjection to the majority leading to the artifice of government required by contract, and a coercive rule by a conqueror leading to a government acquired by force. The natural social relations between parents and children, and husbands and wives are characteristic of voluntary subjection and exemplify the hope of free men. The relationship between masters and servants is characteristic of coercive subjection because obedience is expected of servants. And Hobbes's Social Contract Theory includes a theory of social interpretation. A multitude of persons becomes a *personality* when a natural individual person represents the multivariety of men. The artificial unity of the representative creates the unity of the persons not represented. His view of the Social Contract is that men should subject themselves to an absolute sovereign power that represents them.

Samuel von Pufendorf [1632–1694] succeeds in connecting the positive elements of Grotius's Natural Law with Hobbes's scientific theory of human nature and of its laws. His work had a still wider influence on the Protestant universities than did the work of Grotius. His textbook for students was particularly important. This was *De Officio Homini et Civis, Juxta Legem Naturalem* (1682),[7] two volumes, a considerably shortened edition of his magnum opus, *De Jure Naturae et Gentium* (1672), 8 volumes.[8] In contrast to Grotius's work, Pufendorf's books are academic treatises, which should elaborate a science of the statesman and of the citizen. As academic treatises, they are much more theoretical than Grotius's book, which is imbued with the political disillusionment of the statesman and with the training of the practicing lawyer. Pufendorf mentions as his forerunners: Grotius, Hobbes, and John Selden [1584-1654]. He postulates a strictly scientific reform of law as indispensable after the progress that medicine, physics, and mathematics had accomplished. His violent criticism of Scholasticism and of Spanish philosophies of law indicates (1) the anti-Catholic resentment of Protestants;

(2) his philosophical ignorance, which Gottfried Leibniz [1646–1716] sharply criticizes; and (3) the complete diminution of the Christian Natural Law thinking from Protestant religion—what Thomas More had already practiced as logically necessary.

Most revealing is Pufendorf's preface to his *De Officio hominis et civis juxta legem naturalem libri duo* (1673). He distinguishes three sciences: (1) Natural Law common to all men, deriving its origin from reason alone; (2) Civil Law valid for the statutory law in the single states; and (3) Moral Theology, the dictates of which God has given in Holy Scriptures. The greatest difference between the first and third points lies in the fact that Natural Law is rooted only in this life and will make man a worthy member of society. Moral Theology trains the citizen of the Heavenly City. Hence, the precepts of Natural Law are directed to eternal conduct. Natural Law has to do with fallen man, an animal with many evil impulses and so commands aid for the poor, assistance to the unfortunate, care for widows and orphans, pardon for wrongs, and maintenance of peace. Hobbes founded his secular science of Natural Law on a naturalistic theory of man. Pufendorf adapted Hobbes's theory as the hypothesis of his system of social rights and duties, as the constituent elements of society. This system of Natural Law is interested in the independence of human rationality and in the dynamics of intelligent instincts. Both are moved by the impulse of *Socialitas* (the goal of society). This is the principle of Natural Law. It means that what serves *Socialitas* is lawful and what harms it is unlawful. For this reason, it is the *lex fundamentalis* of Natural Law that everyone should see to it that society's welfare be maintained and secured. Universal sociability is the norm, and all laws are merely correlates. Reason is sufficient to discover these in our hearts. The social duties of men are either absolute or conditional. There are only three absolute duties: (1) *Neminem laedere*, or do no one harm and make good any damage;

(2) to consider all others as by nature entitled to the same right; (3) to promote the well-being of fellow-men. There are six conditional duties, derived from: (1) agreements or engagements; (2) the use of language; (3) taking the oath; (4) acquisition of ownership and bona fide; (5) contracts and obligations; and (6) interpretation of laws and agreements. In the description of the state of nature and of the origins of state, Pufendorf closely follows Hobbes—with one important difference. He postulates two compacts: (1) pactum societatis and (2) pactum mutuum between ruler and subjects. Only through both does the state become a moral person. Like Hobbes, Pufendorf establishes a first sociological theory—a theory of the elements constituting social institutions. Within this theory, he classifies types of control and homogenous cooperation according to Grotius's scheme. He briefly touches on the problems of constitutional and international law.

Grotius's and Pufendorf's treatises were required readings in the classes on moral philosophy in which Moral Theology, Natural Law, Ethics, and Politics were the subdivisions, as implied in Grotius's work.

It is the merit of the Scottish philosophers in the second half of the eighteenth century to have turned the theories of Natural Law into sociological theories of human constitution under the influence of the empiricism and psychologism of John Locke and Shaftesbury and under the impact of the empirical rationalism of Montesquieu. They asserted that the science of the Statesman can be effective only when the professors are able to explain and to understand motives of social action and social conduct beyond the pale of legal institutions.

III. Stoicism

Philosophical Relevance

Roman Stoicism, as evinced by Seneca, Cicero, Epictetus [55–135], and Marcus Aurelius, became important to modern philosophers because:

1. Stoicism stressed first among the classical philosophies subjective consciousness.

2. It offers social and moral norms as essentials of natural law.

3. It emphasizes the primacy of moral and social conduct.

4. It is strictly *intellectualis* and rational with materialistic elements.

5. It suggests education for wisdom as potentially to all, actually to a few.

6. It presents a theory of passions and techniques for extirpating them.

7. It makes possible to know and to understand the process of nature and to adjust to it and to live according to nature.

8. It combines philosophy and religion.

Francis Bacon [1561–1626] refers frequently to Seneca, Cicero, Epictetus, Diogenes of Babylon or Seleucia [230–c. 150 BC], and Chrysippus [c. 279–c. 206 BC]. In his *Essays* (1597),[9] Bacon argues that all moral and social requirements are implied in the Law of

Nature. *Naturale est intellectus instinctus*, which includes the ultimate truth that conditions perception, induction, and conclusion. The consciousness of Natural Law is innate in man. Although it may be obscured, social consensus is its external sign. He sees the rule of Natural Law as an intersecting play of passions and their control, and he notes that affections can only be controlled by stronger affections. He transcends the Stoics, and he anticipates Hobbes. He saw Natural Law as a *social instinct*, linking the well-being of the individual to the commonweal and, at the same time, fortifying an individual's *self-preservation.* **Pierre Charron** [1541–1603], a close friend and disciple of **Michel de Montaigne** [1533–1592], stresses the independence of ethics from religion following Marcus Aurelius. Religion does not create morality. Passions are controlled by passions and by strength and density of Soul v. Fortune. One must learn to suspend judgment, pursue universal learning, become cosmopolitan, and retain an inner sense of superiority to the inevitable roles that one must play. The true Stoic is *l'honnête homme.*

Benedictus de Spinoza [1632–1677] believed that there exists a natural social impulse in man as well as a natural desire to have others rejoice in the good in which one rejoices. Here, he echoes Hobbes's *Leviathan* up to a point. But where Hobbes insists that fear of others underlies the origin of the state, Spinoza sees mutual aid as the justification of social institutions and the means of realizing human happiness. In the *Tractatus Theologico-Politicus* (1670),[10] he writes:

> The formation of society serves not only for defensive purpose, but is also very useful, and indeed, absolutely necessary, as rendering possible the division of labor. If men did not render mutual assistance to each other, no one would have either the skill or the time to provide for his own sustenance and preservation: for all men are

> equally apt for all work, and no one would be capable of preparing all that he individually stood in need of.[11]

And again, in the same treatise:

> [T]he object of government is not to change men from rational beings into beasts or puppets, but to enable them to develop their minds and bodies in security, and to employ their reason unshackled; neither showing hatred, anger, deceit, nor watched with the eyes of jealousy and injustice. In fact, the true aim of government is liberty.[12]

Spinoza was deeply influenced by Lucius Annaeus Seneca (the Younger) [4 BC–65 AD], especially by his *De Beneficiis*, Book IV. See for instance:

> (18.2) Taken one by one, what are we? The prey of animals, their victims, the choicest blood, and the easiest to come by. Other animals have enough strength to protect themselves, and those that were born to wander and lead isolated lives are armed. But man is covered with a delicate skin: he has neither powerful claws nor teeth to instill fear in others; naked and weak as he is, it is fellowship that protects him. God has granted two things that make this vulnerable creature the strongest of all: reason and fellowship. So the being that on its own was no match for anything is now the master of all things.
>
> (18.3) Fellowship has given him power over all animals; fellowship has conferred on this terrestrial creature control of another's sphere and ordered him to rule even by sea. It is this that has checked the incursions of disease, provided support for his old age, and given him comfort in his sufferings; it is this that makes us brave because we can call on it for help against Fortune.

> (18.4) Remove fellowship and you will destroy the unity of mankind on which our life depends. But you will remove it if you make ingratitude something to be avoided not for its own sake, but because it has something to fear: for how many there are who can safely be ungrateful! In fact, I call ungrateful anyone whose gratitude is caused by fear.[13]

Spinoza also invokes Cicero's *De Finibus Bonorum et Malorum*, Book III (65–66):

> And the fact that no one would choose to live in splendid isolation, however well supplied with pleasures, shows that we are born to join together and associate with one another and form natural communities. Indeed we are naturally driven to want to help as many people as possible, especially by teaching and handing on the principles of practical reason. It is hard to find anyone who does not pass on what they know to someone else. Thus we have a propensity for teaching as much as for learning.[14]

Spinoza postulates an organic conception of society with the analogy between the social organism and the individual, such as one finds in Marcus Aurelius, *Meditationes*, VII. Spinoza argued (Book IV, Proposition 54) that "Repentance is not a virtue, that is, it does not arise from reason; he who repents of his action is doubly unhappy or weak." Echoing Seneca again (*De Tranquillitate Animi*, 2, paragraph 8), he argues that fear and wavering of the mind come to men because they can neither rule nor obey their desires.

His Propositions 67–73 in Book IV of *Ethics* are written in the form of an apotheosis of the free man (*homo liber*) corresponding to the Stoics' apotheosis of the wise man. The Propositions are:

> P67. A free man thinks of death least of all things, and his wisdom is a meditation of life, not of death.
>
> P68. If men were born free, they would form no conception of good and evil so long as they were free.
>
> P69. The virtue of a free man is seen to be as great in avoiding dangers as in overcoming them.
>
> P70. The free man, who lives among the ignorant, strives, as far as he can, to avoid receiving favors from them.
>
> P71. Only free men are truly grateful to one another.
>
> P72. The free man never acts deceitfully, but always with good faith.
>
> P73. The man who is guided by reason is more free in a state where he lives under a system of laws than in solitude where [he] obeys only himself.[15]

The use of "free" as a description of the man who lives according to the guidance of reason is explained by Spinoza's use of the term *servitude* as a description of the "impotence of men to govern or restrain their emotions." (*Ethics*, IV, preface.)

Note on Proposition 69 on courage. Courage is caution: a free man chooses flight by the same courage or presence of mind as that by which he chooses battle. Here, Spinoza echoes Seneca, *Epistulae Morales*, 85, paragraphs 26 and 28.

Note on Proposition 70 on favors. Should favors be accepted from everybody? Here, Spinoza echoes Seneca *De Beneficiis*, II, 18, paragraphs 4–7.

Note on Proposition 71 on gratitude. Echoes Seneca *De Beneficiis,* II, 24.

Note on Proposition 72 on the virtues of honesty and good faith. These virtues are extolled in every copybook as fundamental elements of the free man. Is a man allowed to break faith in order to escape death? Spinoza's negative answer again reflects Seneca. *Fides* is the holiest good that may be in a man's heart. *Epistulae Morales,* 88, paragraph 29. Participation in the organized life of society (according to Seneca) was considered one of the characteristic virtues of the Wise Man. *De Otio,* III, 2.

Note on Proposition 73. A man who is guided by reason is freer in a state where he lives according to the common laws than he is in solitude where he obeys himself alone. One must seek remedies against emotions, which are diseases of the mind like desire (*cupiditas*), pleasure (*letitia*), pain (*tristitia*), and fear (*metum*).

René Descartes [1596–1650] is Stoic in his philosophical and moral attitude. His subjective intellectualism—his notions of innate ideas, superiority of mind, philosophical self-redemption by control of passions, and his theory of generosity—demonstrate his modern Stoicism. He is anti-Stoic because the Stoics do not develop scientific techniques needed to realize their principles. He evinces his position in his diverse approaches toward moral problems in *Discours de la méthode* (1637),[16] *Les passions de l'âme* (1649), and *Lettres sur la morale* (1643–1649), his 32 letters to Princess Elisabeth of Bohemia (he received 26 in exchange).

Stoicism as Intellectual and Social Fashion

1. Anti-Christian
   - Montaigne, Charron, Spinoza, Descartes upheld the self-redemption of the free and wise man

2. Christian Stoicism
   - Guillaume du Vair [1556–1621], Justus Lipsius [1547–1606], Bishop Joseph Hall [1574–1656], and Bishop Joseph Butler [1692–1752]
   - Aspects of Christian Stoicism:
     - How virtuous were the pagans, how un-Christian are we
     - Adjusting Christian ethics to modern rationalism and Panentheism
     - Reconciling the principles of Fortuna and Providence
     - Practical usefulness of theory of control of passions
3. Stoicism as attitude
   - Stoic principles among the writers of Essays and Characters
4. Stoicism as style
   - The chronology of the publication of Stoic writings over a period of 200 years is indicative of Stoicism as an intellectual and social fashion:

     1471. Cicero. Philosophical works at Venice. Introduced classical Stoicism to Europe
     1472. Diogenes Laërtius. *The Lives and Opinions of Eminent Philosophers.* Latin
     1475. Seneca. *Epistulae Morales*
     1493. Epictetus. *Manual.* Latin by Politian
     1509. Plutarch. *Moralia*
     1516. Pietro Pomponazzi [1462–1525]. *De Immoralitate Animae* (Stoicism—last stand of disillusioned intellectual)
     1528. Epictetus. *Manual.* Greek by Aldus
     1533. Diogenes Laërtius. *The Lives and Opinions of Eminent Philosophers.* Greek

1534. Cicero. *Three Books of Tullyas Offyces*, by Robert Whittington [1480–1553]

1544. Epictetus. *Manual*. French

1553. Cicero. *Three Books of Duties*. Translated by Nicolas Grimald [1519/20–1562]

1558. Marcus Aurelius. *Meditationes*

1567. Epictetus. *Manual*. Translated into English by James Sanford (flourished 1567)

1567. Epictetus. *Manual*. Translated into French

1575. Tacitus. Edited by Justus Lipsius

1578. Seneca. *De Clementia*. Translated into French

1581. Justus Lipsius. Commentary on Tacitus

1584. Justus Lipsius. *De Constantia*. More than 80 editions in 300 years

1585. Seneca. *De Ira*. Translated into French

1585. Guillaume du Vair. *Saincte Philosophie*

1587–8. Justus Lipsius. *Politicorum sive Civilis doctrinae libri sex*

1590. François de Malherbe [1555–1628]. *Bouquet de fleurs à Sénèque*

1592. Guillaume du Vair. *De la Philosophie morale des Stoiques*

1594. Guillaume du Vair. *De La Constance Et Consolation és Calamites Publiques*

1598. Seneca. *Les Oeuvres morales et meslees de Senecque*. Simon Goulart and Mathieu de Chalvet, editors

1598. Seneca. *Oeuvres morales* and Epictetus *Manual*. Translated into French

1601. William Cornwallis [1579–1614]. *Discourses upon Seneca the Tragedian*

1604. Justus Lipsius. *Manuductio ad Stoicam Philosophiam* and *Physiologia Stoicorum*
1605. Justus Lipsius. *Annaei Senecae Philosophi Opera, Quae Exstant Omnia, A Iusto Lipsio emendata, et Scholiis illustrate*
1609. Epictetus. *Manual.* Translated into French by the General of the Congregation of the Feuillants
1610. Epictetus. *Manual.* Translated into English by John Healey [d. 1610]
1611. Epictetus. Bishop Joseph Hall. *Epictetus in Six Decades*
1614. Seneca. The Workes Of Lvcius Annaevs Seneca, Both Morall And Naturall. Translated By Thomas Lodge [1558–1625]
1619. Seneca. *Works.* Translated into French par Mathieu de Chalvet [1528–1607], Président de Parlement de Toulouse
1627. Seneca. *Works.* Translated into French
1634. Marcus Aurelius. *Works.* Edited by Mericus Casanbonus von Oxford [1599–1671]. Latin
1643. Sir Thomas Browne [1605–1682]. *Religio Medici.*
1645. Edward Herbert of Cherbury [1583–1648]. *De Causis errorum: una cum tractatu de religione laici, et appendice ad sacerdotes, nec non quibusdam poematibus*
1646. Marin Le Roy Gomberville [1600–1674]. *La doctrine des moeurs; tirée de la philosophie des stoiques représentée en cent tableaux et expliquée en cent discours qui vient de loin* (for Louis XIV, then seven years old). *Les Quinti Horatii Flacci emblemata* (1607) *du peintre anversois Otto Van Veen*

1649. Descartes. *Discours de la méthode.* Translated into English
1651. Thomas Hobbes, *Leviathan.* English
1652. Jean-Louis Guez de Balzac [1597–1654]. *Le Socrate chrétien*
1653. Epictetus. *Manual.* Translated into French by mystic Desmants de Saint Sabin
1653. Justus Lipsius. *De Constantia.* 2nd edition.
1654. Justus Lipsius. *De Constantia.* 3rd edition.
1660. La Sure. *L'Esprit de Sénèque dédié a Touquet*
1663. Abbé d'Aubigny. *Macarie en la Reyne des isles fortunier, histoire allégorique, continuant la philosophie des Stoiques sous la crile de plusieurs aventures agréables en forme de roman*
1663. A. Legand. *Les caractères de l'homme sans passions selon les sentiments de Sénèque*
1663. George Mackenzie [1636/1638–1691]. *Religio Stoici*

IV. Francis Bacon: Statesman, Jurist, Philosopher

It is not enough to say that Francis Bacon takes up the naturalistic traditions as developed by Machiavelli and Hobbes. There are elements in his thinking and attitude toward life that do not occur in the past.

In all authors previously discussed, we find as hypotheses of their ideas some beliefs in the authority of the Classics or of Christianity, in the validity of a priori thinking, in the autonomy of theoretical and moral truth. All these thinkers were suspicious of the idea of progress or they admitted it only with strict reservations.

But Bacon challenged all previous traditions and standards. In spite of his cautious praise of the genius of the Ancients, he takes his stand on the side of the moderns. Advancement of learning is possible; that is, progress is possible. Progress implies optimism for the future. Learning is for Bacon knowledge about nature. He opposes nature to mind, matter to spirit, science to speculation, experiment to Aristotle, discoveries from the light of nature to the authority of the classics. *Antiquitas saeculi—juventus mundus.* New methods by Ancients untried and unknown. Bacon's goal: new methods by moderns will create a true universal natural philosophy. He proclaims knowledge for power and control of Nature, physical, human, and social. The goal of science is the utilitarian progress of conditions of living. He opposes the knowledge gained from senses, matter, and nature to the abstract deductions of mind and spirit. This radical criticism makes possible his contribution to a social-psychological theory of error and knowledge. There are four types of error:

> 1. *Idols of Tribe.* These mental characteristics are common to all. There is a proneness to suppose more regularity of order than actually exists; there is a tendency of mental presuppositions to bend all things into conformity with themselves. Influence of Will and Affections such as pride, hope, impatience, desires upon the mind: dullness, deception, and incompetence of senses.
>
> 2. *Idols of Care.* This refers to the bias that education and environment impose on the variable spirit of man.
>
> 3. *Idols of Theatre.* Being conditioned by classical idealistic and deductive philosophical dogmatism.
>
> 4. *Idols of Market.* This is the most troublesome form of error. This is the dispute over words—no faith in

> definition. Language does not impart to the mind a true and accurate picture of material reality.

Bacon's new method points toward a natural experimental history that may serve as the foundation of a true philosophy. Such a history would be a comprehensive interpretation of nature based on a comprehensive collection of experiments and observations.

Bacon divides such a Natural History into search for causes and operative production of effects. He is primarily concerned with the last division. In this connection, he develops his idea on the induction method. This has three distinctive features:

> 1. There are various intermediary stages of establishing general principles. His logic moves from particulars slowly and rises gradually to more abstract and more comprehensive generalizations.
>
> 2. A key feature of induction is his conception of form. He bases sciences on a purely physical foundation. The primary elements of nature: qualities of dense—rare; solid—fluid; hot—cold; heavy—light. Materialistic basis: bodies are not acted on but by other bodies (atomic theory, similar to Lucretius [99–55 BC] in *De Rerum Natura*). Matter rather than form draws his attention. Form—laws of movement of bodies—laws of absolute actuality. They govern and constitute any simple nature, such as heat, light, weight, in every kind of matter. Bacon believed that there are only a few forms of simple, or abstract, nature.
>
> 3. Its individualization by a rigid conception of rejection and exclusion. Bacon has influenced all

> ways of philosophical and practical thinking. His influence on Descartes's scientific attitude is obvious. Implicitly, his work has the greatest relevance for sociology.

The hypothesis of the *Essays* is and remains relevant for all types of sociological research as to distinguish inner goodness and external parading of goodness. What he calls Civil Knowledge would be a science in social institutions between socii. In his *Essays*, we have a variety of analyses of public attitudes that imply a theory of social conduct with a sequence of interest from security over prestige to power and wealth. Bacon calls himself anti-Ciceronian. Positively formulated, it means he feels himself closer to Machiavelli, Seneca, and Tacitus. In Bacon's work, the "Essay" has a specific function. It is the literary expression of a reflection on social conduct liberated from theological or metaphysical values. It is a consideration that does not refer to any system of social values as criteria for their good or bad qualifications. It is an attempt to construct an ideal type of situational behavior or of passion and to present it in such form as to raise the impression of a fragment of life that contains the whole in its unsystematic openness.

V. Mystical and social experiences contribute to Social Psychology

Bacon's essays and those by Jeremy Taylor [1613–1667], Thomas Traherne [1636–1674], and Henry Vaughan [1621–1695] have one element in common. They are all inspired by Seneca, the psychologist who experiences his solitude in a world of routine and of manipulated interests. Moderns understand such experiences. They understand Seneca's *Epistles* as the new literary pattern of the Essay. They define it as a form that permits them to regard and analyze from all angles a social-psychological phenomenon, to construct its ideal type and grasp a fragment of the stream of experience alike.

It is characteristic for the modern situation that Machiavelli joins Seneca all the time. However, mystical experiences deeply influenced introspection and psychological refinement. **Ignatius of Loyola** [1491–1556] and the modern Quietism contributed to creating new psychological insights. Loyola discovered the usefulness of mystical techniques for establishing complete control over Self and others by manipulating students who were striving for religious perfection. His technique should enable them to recognize their sins, to confess them, to begin a new life. His *Spiritual Exercises* were the first modern rule and regimentation of psychic training. In contrast to medieval usage, they required a relation between student and trainer, between soldier and officer. The military metaphors are valid because students were never informed about the sequence of the procedure or about the handbook of the *Spiritual Exercises*. No modern psychologist who wishes to train as elite has neglected to study the book and its new theory of asceticism, which neglects the physical asceticism of the past in favor of humiliating the mind and training total obedience.

Quietism is relevant to the social scientist through **Francis de Sales, Bishop of Geneva** [1567–1622], who made it fashionable. There are psychological and aesthetic elements in the poetry and philosophy of Saint Teresa of Ávila [1515–1582] and of Saint John of the Cross [1542–1591], founders of the Discalced Carmelites, that Saint Francis de Sales exploited for making religion attractive to the new society of an urban and learned court. He succeeded in cultivating a politeness and refinement of religious and societal relationships. The conscious enjoyment of such psychological processes induced the ladies in the salons to discover a new entertainment. This new game at parties was called "Portrait Writing."

La Carte de Tendre by Mademoiselle Madeleine de Scudéry [1607–1701] and *Les Précieuses ridicules* by Molière [Jean-Baptiste Poquelin, 1622–1673] describe the situation. *La Carte de Tendre* is as sophisticated an allegory of psychological types as Sales's manipulation of Calvary.[17]

Francis de Sales attempts to connect the Spiritual Humanism of Erasmus with the Spiritual Militarism of the Jesuits. That is why he was liked by Jesuits and Jansenists alike. His *Philotéa* or *Introduction à La Vie Dévote* was quickly translated into English and became a perennial best seller.[18] It raised the continuous reflection on psychological processes in ourselves and in our fellow-socii. His influence is still conspicuous in *Les Aventures De Télémaque* François Fénelon [1651–1715], in his tender sociability. Another mystical discovery, that of the "beautiful soul," influenced Shaftesbury and Francis Hutcheson. The notion derives from Saint Teresa; her mystical theology and poetry influenced social conduct and reflection on societal relations through various channels that made the mystical aloofness a fashionable psychological sensation. We should bear in mind that modern mysticism, in particular, Quietism, is different from medieval mysticism. Medieval mystics were speculative and philosophical in their procedure for attaining identification with the Divine. Modern Quietism applies new techniques for eliminating reason first and realizing the state of total love as complete emptiness and being open and ready for the appearance of the Divine in the vacuum. Such processes bring into existence what, finally, Fénelon called "paramour."

The struggle between Jacques-Bénigne Bossuet [1627–1704] and Fénelon regarding this problem anticipates in mystical terms the modern combat between the adherents of moral disinterestedness and hedonists or utilitarians. It is not incidental that naturalistic and mystical analyses of men's life in the world come to the same conclusion. The politician experiences the dynamics of interests in close combat for his own interests. The mystic experiences the dynamics of interests as temptation to be eradicated. Both come to the same conclusion as knowing and understanding human beings. Both are concerned with the "human condition," which is both sociological and psychological. All are influenced by Montaigne, who is at the borderline of our analysis because his topic is the Self, not Society and Self interrelated. However, he set the pattern, the perfect case of which we will see in the work of **Louis de Rouvroy, duc de Saint-Simon** [1675–1755], the dynamic analysis of characters as moving and being moved.

Blaise Pascal [1623–1662], who hated Montaigne and the modern fashion of Stoicism, repeats and recapitulates Montaigne in the passages that deal with the fallacies of social institutions as custom, procedure of law, social conventions, status, and prestige. The radical pessimism of Montaigne and Pascal is independent of mystical or political traditions—the awareness of the precarious situation of the thoughtful man in a world of rational institutions that spread uniformity and standardization. In many respects, **François de La Rochefoucauld** [1613–1680] is more pessimistic than Pascal. He elaborates in a variety of perspectives the thesis that our virtues are disguised vices and that self-love is the decisive passion that directs and fools men.

Les Caractères by **Jean de La Bruyère** [1645–1696] imitates Theophrastus [d. 287 BC] only at the surface. It advances the grim analysis of Pascal and La Rochefoucauld into the sphere of social institutions. La Bruyère's study is mainly concerned with the behavior patterns of a society that lives under a despotic regime. He studies the declining nobility's conduct, the attitude of the Parvenu, the diverse ways of being Christian under such conditions, the courtier, and the banker, both successful and bankrupt. He takes the categories of Court and

Town seriously as sociological categories; he discovers the "common people" as the very class that remains true to standards of human decency. Throughout the book, he scrutinizes the interdependence of attitudes of domination and of submission, the unity of encroaching on others and of being subservient. He comes to the conclusion that man is basically insecure in himself, a problem that Henri Bergson [1859–1941] took up in his last book.[19]

Memoirs became a source book of sociological and psychological insights since the defeated aristocrats of the French had gained leisure and time for reflecting on the causes of their defeat and of the victory of the absolute monarchy. Such memoirs are written by partisans, but they have scientific value. Jean François Paul de Gondi, Cardinal de Retz [1613–1679] and LaRochefoucauld have an intellectual superiority that makes it possible to present the two perspectives of victors and conquered alike.

The work of Saint-Simon is different and can claim scientific objectivity, although we know that his resentments have falsified his judgment in some rare cases of personal enemies. It was not a partisan book. It was not written for publication. It was not intended to be art or politics. It was supposed to be the true and comprehensive report on the events and happenings at the court during the reign of Louis XIV [1638–1715] and through the death of the Regent [Philippe II, Duke of Orléans from the death of Louis XIV in 1715 until 1723 when Louis XV ascended to the throne]. The *Mémoirs* became a great piece of sociological and psychological inquiry. Honoré de Balzac [1799–1850] understood it as "Human Comedy" of a historical society that he desired to remake for the bourgeois society of his own time. Valentin Louis Georges Eugène Marcel Proust [1871–1922] was thrilled by the psychological method that Saint-Simon had practiced prior to scientific psychology.

Saint-Simon's *Mémoirs* is one of the early cases of sociological-historical writings that demonstrate the scientific effectiveness of conservative thinkers for making accurate and correct sociological predictions. Conservative authors have the advantage over radical authors because they are able to consider all elements of social situations, including the positive sides of human conduct that never fail completely. In modern times, Edmund Burke [1729–1797], Alexis de Tocqueville [1805–1859], Prince Klemens von Metternich [1773–1859], and Jacob Burckhardt [1818–1897] succeeded in predicting the most shocking developments because their historical perspective permitted them to check the accounts of historical situations and make a balance sheet.

Saint-Simon was such a conservative thinker. He remained true to a romantic picture of the feudal monarchy that, he believed, had still existed in the early years of Louis XIII—a type of government where the king is the first among his peers and the feudal families are in charge of the administration of the country. The hypothesis for his analysis is the conviction that this feudal monarchy is gone. This historical insight with its normative implications made possible a comprehensive sociological description and analysis of an entire social world.

Saint-Simon states as his thesis that the Court is a social world of its own. It is not any longer the patriarchal home of the feudal ruler whose manorial lords are friends and fellows. The modern court is an abstract institution, a tremendous mechanism subject to its own laws. He emphasizes the thesis by presenting the exploited and desperate people of Paris and of the Provinces in revolt against taxation, starvation, and religious oppression at the fringes of his topic. François Fénelon and his loyal friends, Ambroise Chevreux [1728–1792] and Paul de Beauvilliers [1648–1714], appear at the borderline of the world of the Court as examples of sincere devotion to a sublime and universal cause. That world also portrays some libertines and adventurers as marginal cases of outlaws and of pathology.

The Court of modern absolute monarchy is a marketplace and exchange for bargaining positions for status and prestige. The King is supposed to be absolute. This remains a legal claim, not a social reality. Actually, the ministers decide the great issues, and they are shrewd enough to make the King believe that they only execute his sovereign will, while they keep him busy with details, such as design of uniforms, the organization of parades, and so on. Saint-Simon practices a true sociological method. He scrutinizes what the legal and constitutional institutions betray when seen in their social functioning. This approach, with the presupposition of his romantic and liberal conservatism, produces one of the most striking sociological analyses and predictions in prescientific times. Pursuing his ideas on the relative power of the absolute monarch, he investigates thoroughly the people who keep the wheels of government and administration moving. This is a genuinely sociological study on the rise of political bureaucracies. Ministers, intendants, and governors are described and scrutinized in their rise, service, and accomplishments. Such case studies, accumulated throughout the book, lead the author to definite conclusions. In sociological terms, this is not a monarchy any longer, supported by and claiming the cooperation of feudal lords. This is instead the rule of the "vile bourgeoisie." For ministers, governors, and even generals rise from the wealthy or poor middle classes because they have competence, skill, money, and moral stamina. In particular, the class of the "Nobility of Law" (*noblesse de la robe*) invades court and administration. The legal professionals have economic power, required training, and the will to attain the responsibility of political power. It is indicative for Saint-Simon's scientific objectivity that he never presents such cases in abstract generalizations. These men are "bourgeois." Among them are rascals, men of unscrupulous ambition, but there are also others qualified morally and technically who are devoted to the state and who subordinate their own interests to those of the body politic. They present moral qualifications and discipline that make their work irreproachable. Saint-Simon curses and praises at the same time.

He painted such background on purpose, to show the uprooted aristocracy of the Court. He describes them as a class of insecure actors. They parade prestige and power, but they betray economic poverty and social insecurity. They live off the arbitrary grace of the monarch, of his ministers, of the ruling pressure groups. They are chasing for jobs, for rents, for positions in order to gain security for all members of their class. Saint-Simon sees the external splendor and recognizes its lie. He analyzes the Fair of Vanity and Despair.

It is indicative of Saint-Simon that he understands the economic reasons for the plight of feudal society. He devotes some important analyses to cases of intermarriage between feudal and banker families. It is a characteristic of his superior humaneness that he is shocked by the moral cynicism of the feudal class and impressed by the dignified objections of the "bourgeois."

Saint-Simon analyses the Court as a social world of organized competition, a field of competitive intrigues and conspiracies. All these brilliant people are moving and moved by their interests. Interests can be reduced to two fundamental desires: power and wealth. They are interrelated with each other in a postfeudal world. Saint-Simon inaugurated a scientific procedure that we can label as a sociology of social structures and social institutions. From his pioneering clearing, we see the road to Balzac, Marx, Robert Staughton Lynd [1892–1970], and Thorstein Bunde Veblen [1857–1929]. The new method implies a sociological theory of revolution. Being a conservative radical, he is aware that revolutions do not result from a class alignment and the antagonisms between two classes. Revolutions arise when a status quo is attacked by the joint opposition of the oppressed and the deprived. Every regime establishes itself by depriving some groups of their status. They will be as revolutionary as are the exploited and oppressed. When the two antagonistic groups meet and merge, revolution will be possible.

There is still a third merit to Saint-Simon's work. He elaborated the pattern of portraits created in the salons under the inspiration of Mlle. de Scudéry to a social-psychological method. He refused to reduce characters of human persons to formulas or abstract conceptions. His characters are dynamic and moving. They move with the social process, which is moving and moved. Education, status, and prestige, social pressure, and a variety of changing conditions determine the moving kaleidoscope of human characters. There is the Duke of Anjou, educated as a playboy in order to thwart his developing political ambitions. Unexpectedly, he becomes king of Spain. His adjustment to the new situation is an element of his character. There are plenty of portraits that demonstrate the coexistence of most antagonistic traits on various levels of social contacts. There is Madame, both rude and tender, proud and helpless, of superior intelligence and of ridiculous naïveté. There is the in-depth analysis of the various reactions to the death of Monseigneur, a detailed description of what courtiers parade and betray, and an unforgettable description of the required masks of society. Proust was thrilled by such methods and praised them as those of an artist, a statement that needs correction. It is instead an effort toward *descriptive psychology* in the sense that Wilhelm Dilthey [1833–1911] used the term.

VI. Variable Mores and Invariable Human Nature

The Cartesian School exerted an indirect influence on social studies. They were suspicious of the scientific character of historical research, and they admitted only mathematical truth as evident and valid. However, they were able to state objectively the nature of human beings as dynamics of needs, desires, and passions. They assumed that the heart is in control of reason and directs it according to its wishes. This description of human nature is based on the analysis of societal relationships and of social conduct. The social nature of man remains identical although there are changes of mores, attitudes, conventions, and patterns of social ideals in the history of civilization. Among Cartesians, the theory of social variables and invariables led to scientific studies relevant for the rise of sociology.

Bernard Le Bovier de Fontenelle [1657–1757] takes the first strides toward scientific history that can establish objective truth when conscious of methodological tools such as selection according to interests, defining the structures of epochs and civilizations, and analyzing the minutest details that might have influenced the motives of agents. He was suspicious of general trends and of providential (final) causes. For him, history is not told but instead is explained and understood. It is history and sociology alike: sociology, because we can predict social conduct being aware of the sameness of the human heart and of its responses to certain conditions; history, because reason makes progress and changes institutions, mores, and standards.

Fontenelle lays the foundations for a sociology of knowledge by examining error in analyzing the causes that bring fables and myths into existence. His analysis of the origins of fables interprets the rise of myths and fables as efforts to explain the works of nature by prescientific tools. Here, he anticipates Comte's Law of Three Stages. [The Law of Three Stages proposes that society in general and each science goes through three stages: the theological stage, the metaphysical stage, and the positive stage.—Eds.]

In a more articulate and experienced analysis, Fontenelle lays the foundations for the sociology of primitive religions, developed in his *Histoire des Oracles*,[20] generally recognized as relevant for nineteenth-century anthropologists. Finally, his *Nouveaux Dialogues des Morts* [1683][21] implicitly present a sequence of interests that determine the life and action of human beings in history.

Pierre Bayle [1647–1706] contributed to the development of a positive sociology by opposing the all-embracing thirst for "facts" and all speculation and a priori thinking. He insisted on the use of the comparative method.

First, Bayle analyzes the structure of prejudice and superstition as mass phenomena. He sees their roots in human inertia, the desire for intellectual security in traditions and established authorities, in respect for taken-for-granted notions and, finally, in simple human credulity.

Second, Bayle looks at the structure of "miracles." His analysis here has a superficial affinity to that of Machiavelli, but it is different in method. He advises that one should not admit something as a miracle unless the facts of an incident are inexplicable by natural reason. He argues that "miracles" frequently result from desires and imagination.

Third, he analyzes the practice and theory of religion. He considers Christian society to be as wicked as pagan society. Atheist societies are capable of virtue, as seen in the work of Epicurus and, indeed, in the society of *Libertins* because of Bayle's own skepticism and advocacy of *hétérodoxie*.[22] Bayle applies methods of historical criticism carefully. He believed that objectivity was possible when the mind is liberated from personal animosities and particular partisan perspectives and subjective interests. He argued that political interests, not religious connections, caused civil wars. And so he advised religious toleration in a secular state, anticipating Montesquieu's *Lettres Persanes* [1721].[23]

Bayle analyzes the conditions of human nature, the constructive and destructive sides of the passions, and the idea of Original Sin and the Fall as both theological symbols and natural facts. He concludes that inner and moral theory is independent of theological-metaphysical speculations.

Bayle also concludes that there is unanimous recognition of the chief moral rules among civilized nations, established by his methods of observation and comparison. There is an autonomy of morals beyond theological doctrines, established by this historical/sociological method. Sociology reveals a regular sequence of human motives: interests, passions, ambitions, and lust for power. Passions themselves can be both good and bad and can lead to refinement and sensibility or to vices.

Bayle's most important works are:

- *Dictionnaire historique et critique* (Rotterdam: Leers, 1697; 2nd edition, 1702)
- *Pensées diverses sur la comète de 1680* (1681; Amsterdam, 1749), 4 volumes
- *Critique generale de l'histoire du Calvinisme du P. Maimbourg* (1682) (A Ville-Franche, Chez Pierre le Blanc, 1683), 2nd edition

Note: Lucien Lévy-Bruhl [1857–1939], a philosopher and anthropologist who specialized in the "primitive mind," takes over Fontenelle and Bayle for sociology in an article entitled "Les tendances générales de Bayle et de Fontenelle," that appeared in the *Revue d'Histoire de la Philosophie*, Volume 1, in both the January and March editions, 1927, 49–68.

François-Marie Arouet, nom de plume Voltaire [1694–1778] unified the special approaches developed by Fontenelle and Bayle and created a genuinely sociological history in his *Le Siècle de Louis XIV* [1751] and his *Essai sur les mœurs et l'esprit des nations* [1756]. Gotthold Ephraim Lessing [1729–1781] said of Voltaire's *Le Siècle de Louis XIV*: "No author has dared to make such a subject the topic of his research so far. For this reason the author of the book is entitled to boast: I first pioneered into virgin soil." Voltaire's work took a stride forward in detailed analysis of the social process. The motives and passions in the political sphere remain invariable. Only under certain circumstances do rulers arise who establish the security that makes possible the flowering of civilization, mores, and refinement. He avoids the grim reality of blood, tears, and despair that are embedded in the foundations of such security. His main intention is to describe the constructive faculties of societies beyond the pale of political institutions. Arts and crafts, science, philosophy, religion, sentimental refinement, and the high standards of societal relationships are his subject. He sees society as the very dynamics of history even as he sees the state, somewhat precariously, as indispensable for peace and security, even though it always misuses its power. He is interested as well in cultural cross-fertilization between civilizations, in the role of minorities in societies, in the influence of classes and of economic institutions, and in the place of ideas in the progress of history.

VII. Universality of conditions, history, natural law

The most important works of **Charles-Louis de Secondat, Baron de La Brède et de Montesquieu** [1689–1755] are *Lettres Persanes* (1721), *Considérations sur les causes de la grandeur des Romains et de leur decadence* (1734), and *De l'esprit des lois* (1758). The latter book is basic for sociology and for several of its different branches. All French sociologists, including Comte, Émile Durkheim [1858–1917], and Georges Gurvitch [1894–1965], have called Montesquieu the founder of French sociology. Among his contemporaries, Jean Le Rond d'Alembert [1717–1783] recognized the novelty of a purely empirical method for establishing the truth about the context of social institutions. Montesquieu takes for granted that there is justice prior to the positive law, that divine and natural laws pervade the whole. For his scientific and empirical method, he refrains from all speculation and understands the spiritual and moral ideas as elements of the human constitution in social action. This makes it possible to investigate social change, the dynamic context of social structures, and the general laws; that is, the tendencies coherent and necessary in themselves as ideal types that appear only in historical articulations. He does this empirically and objectively by explaining their developments in terms of the interaction of physical and moral causes. The invisible context is that man modifies nature; nature modifies man. Physical laws are invariable. Moral laws are flexible and dynamic and, ultimately, decisive. Moral laws create a general spirit of a society that leads to a specific ethos; that is, a prerational system of preferences and values that determine individual and social conduct. The term *ethos* was coined by Max Ferdinand Scheler [1874–1928], but Montesquieu discovered its decisive importance.

Montesquieu led the way to:

> 1. *Social morphology (ecology).* The study of the size, volume, and stratification of groups as well as the density of population as a function of the physical conditions of the soil, of the nature of the area, and of the climate and of all physical elements of environments.

2. *Structural sociology (historical sociology).* Montesquieu discovers the interdependence of all spheres of social action and of individual behavior. In the preface of the first edition of *De l'esprit des lois* (Geneve: Chez Barrillot & fils, 1748), he defines the book's title as indicating the interrelationships between the positive laws and the political forms of government, the mores, the climate, the population, the religion, commerce, and industrial forces. They create the context or structure within which the various societies develop according to the conditions established by the context. This is always a historical context. However, Montesquieu is still far away from recognizing history as a necessary evolution. It is the life of men in time. But the concatenations of conditions differ in each moment, and there is no general denominator for the whole process of history. Nor is there any general theory of progress. In these efforts toward a historical sociology, Montesquieu transforms the science of the Law of Nature into the empirical analysis of the varieties of social structures and of social attitudes. He opens the way for sociology as an empirical science that deals with the nature of man in time and space.

3. *Sociology of Religion.* Montesquieu anticipates the methodological devices of Max Weber [1864–1920] and Durkheim. First, he takes religion as a datum of social life. Second, he investigates its repercussions on mores and conduct.

4. *Sociology of Commerce.* Montesquieu establishes a general sociology of economic institutions in their interaction with all intellectual, moral, political, and legal institutions.

5. *Sociology of Mores.* Note Montesquieu's important suggestion to investigate the interrelationships between mores and the established civil, penal, and political laws. Frequently, laws are soft where the mores are strict, and vice versa.

6. *Sociology of Law.* Montesquieu examines the interaction between the constitutions and diverse types of civil, penal, and taxation laws, corresponding to the fundamental types of government. The analyses of these basic types of government are at the center of the book. They present the integrating power of three types of human rationality in shaping the organizations under which men can live in continuity and in order. Montesquieu is aware that his concepts are ideal types (in the sense that Max Weber developed them). He also sees that these fundamental institutions must be analyzed according to the elements that constitute their specific character. He calls it "nature." The second element of their existence is what makes them work and continuously function—that is, their "principle," or spirit. For example, in a *republic*—where people are both rulers and ruled, where judges and magistrates are elected, where laws are frugal and simple, and where penal laws are typically soft and

> lean toward rehabilitation—creative freedom is the kind of rationality that is extolled and the ethos of a republic is centered on virtue, a love of equality, the spirit of sacrifice, cooperation, and teamwork. In a *monarchy*, there is a ruler under a constitution, with intermediate powers possessed by courts, and checks and balances provided by the king's princes and lords who possess the "clemency of princes." The type of rationality in a monarchy is freedom under law, with an ethos focused on honor, *urbanitas*, and *humanitas*. In a *despotic regime*, one finds arbitrary domination, police, and widespread insecurity, accompanied by hypocrisy. Despotism is irrational, and its ethos is fear, terrorism, and the destruction of subjects' independence.

VIII. Unity of Science: comparative method, historical relativism, political sociology, rise of positivism

Between Montesquieu and the thinkers who established sociology proper in France—that is, Nicolas de Condorcet [1743–1794], Saint Simon, and Comte—the **Encyclopedists** present the universal spreading of a sociological spirit in many fields of research and among scholars of different philosophical convictions.

The *Encyclopédie* (1751–1765) was a summary of the state of positive knowledge in all fields with the intention of showing the growth of positive and empirical knowledge as over and against the theological and metaphysical dogmatisms. However, it was not revolutionary in a political or social sense, although it was resented and persecuted by the Jesuits, the Jansenists, the Court, and the Parliament. Its contributors came from all social strata, except the ruling elite. We find men who belong to the nobility of office and to the lower ranks of the clergy, professors, jurists, physicians, engineers, businessmen, industrialists, and intellectuals. They approach the problems of anthropology and of the origins of sociology with the instruments of a critical method in history and with the new tools of the sensualistic psychology of John Locke [1632–1704] and Étienne Bonnot de Condillac [1714–1780]. The readers were the general public, but especially the enlightened middle classes and the educated and urban elements of the nobility.

The Encyclopedists vigorously attacked the problems of the primitive societies in order to investigate the principle of the state of nature and the concept of the noble savage. They discarded the latter notion as incompatible with many facts, although they admitted that some reports pointed out that the primitive societies can share in the working of the Law of Nature and in its rational rules in intertribal relationships. They debunked the moral praise of the original goodness and excellence of the state of nature as proclaimed by Jean-Jacques Rousseau [1712–1778] as a political ideology. They used the comparative method successfully and made valuable suggestions in establishing conceptions of the universality of religious and moral attitudes. They reduced the varieties and differences of the universal tendencies to physical and historical conditions.

They introduced a sociological approach toward political institutions and clarified the issue of the best kind of government. In particular, they analyzed the different conditions of the political contract in the rise of the constitutional monarchy in France. In analyzing political and social institutions, they compared the institutions with their social meaning and the harmony or disharmony between them. They made the first scientific analyses of the problematic character of a military elite in a society that is no longer feudal. They hinted at the political function of urban industrial societies in the modern rational state. In all of these investigations, they established a sociological approach when postulating and questioning the functional character of institutions in a specific social structure. Their sociological approach focused on men's actual experiences in society, seen as a dynamic process over and against the hardening institutions of the state.

They found still another approach toward sociology in their psychological hypotheses. They took for granted that man consists of sensations and basic tendencies. For this reason, they eliminated the notion of the state of nature and postulated, as scientists, to start with investigating primitive societies because men never exist without some form of organization. They explained higher human activities such as philosophy and moral or political principles as the result of the basic needs of reason in society. They assumed that the group, the collectivity, is indispensable for the actualization of the intellectual and spiritual faculties that are inherent in human nature in potentialities. This thesis made possible the first strides toward a sociology of knowledge based on the process of learning, the traditions of reflection, and the progress of scientific thinking; the existence of institutions, philosophical schools, or monopolistic and esoteric organizations of sacred knowledge, such as the organizations in which priests educated their successors, appear as relevant for the life of reason. This approach made possible the first attempt at a sociological history of philosophy.

The interconnected effort to explain and understand human nature in action by historical, social, and psychological investigations ultimately made meaningless the traditional science of the Law of Nature. In the past, thinkers understood the science of the Law of Nature as describing the state of society in terms of reflex or of participation in a whole. Whether they called it universe or creation did not matter. New scientific methods, the study of external and internal conditions made it possible to explain human conduct and the varieties of behavioral patterns in terms of societal relationships in the development of the historical process. Empirical sociology, composed of social-psychological and historical methods, substitutes for the past science of social action. It carries on the same spirit of liberalism with the new means of scientific and positive methods.

- René Hubert, Article on Encyclopédie in the *Encyclopaedia of the Social Sciences*, editor-in-chief, Edwin R. A. Seligman, associate editor, Alvin Johnson (New York: Macmillan, c. 1930–35)
- René Hubert, *D'Holbach et ses amis* (Paris: A. Delpeuch, 1928)
- René Hubert, *Les Sciences Sociales Dans l'Encyclopédie: La philosophie de l'histoire et le problème des origines* (Paris: F. Alcan, 1923)
- John Morley, *Diderot and the Encyclopaedists*, 2 volumes (London: Chapman and Hall, 1878)
- Daniel Mornet, *La pensée française au XVIIIe siècle* (Paris: A. Colvin, 1926)
- Marius Roustan, *The Pioneers of the French Revolution* (London: Ernest Benn Ltd., 1926). Translated by Frederic Whyte. Original title: *Philosophes et la société française au XVIIIe siècle* (Lyon: A. Rey, imprimeur-éditeur: Librairie A. Picard et fils, 1926)

The diverse approaches in the Encyclopédie to find a substitute for the science of Natural Law in a psychological analysis of human incentives, in the investigations in social causation, and in the discovery of the historical process have finally created distinct sociological efforts, one of which is:

> Paul-Henry Thiry, Baron d'Holbach, *Système social, ou principes naturels de la morale et de la politique avec un examen de l'influence du gouvernement sur les moeurs* (Paris: Fayard, 1773).

Baron d'Holbach [1723–1789] wrote three hundred articles for the Encyclopédie on technology and sciences. His main work, *Système de la Nature; ou lois du monde physique & du monde moral* (A Londres, i.e. Amsterdam, 1777), was the most radical effort to reestablish a thorough materialistic system of absolute determinism. This philosophical position did not prevent his militant social liberalism. He was convinced that human happiness could only be established by cooperation in societal relationships. He attacked religion as disastrous to social ethics. The influence of religion was easily explained by two principles of psychology: (1) Sensation and Association—the beliefs that govern conduct are the product of education confirmed by habit, and (2) Utility. Man seeks his happiness, tries to avoid misfortune and, finding himself subject to the forces of nature, pictures nature as a divinity liable to human emotions. Science shows nature differently and provides the rational means to get rid of fear and to find happiness. The social system is based on the principle that the main human interest is social, that nature imposes on man social norms—that is, a social contract. Teaching the true social system will enlighten men about their true interests and make them cooperate for the common good. The Social Contract must become a political institution in order to transform the innate social norms into established laws that can be enforced. The rule of law restricts ruler and the people. The advantages of society—liberty, property, security—can be enjoyed only under the protection of laws. Civil laws reflect the social laws of nature and present the unity and the interdependent drives of liberty and self-restraint. Religious liberty is the natural result of the freedom of thinking. Political freedom can be established in all forms of government that are ruled by laws and a constitution. That means that despotism and revolution are both situations of anarchy and chaos for Baron d'Holbach. He suggested a science that would enlighten men on their utilitarian happiness in society. He called it the "Science de Moeurs." It is valid for princes and subjects, rich and poor, because it describes and analyzes the empirical reality of human behavior patterns as located in a specific frame of reference. This science will establish the invariables and variables of societal relationships without taking refuge in any dogmatism or metaphysical system. This suggestion anticipates Lucien Lévy-Bruhl's *La morale et la science des moeurs* (Paris: F. Alcan, 1903), in which the great anthropologist postulates an empirical sociological study of the diverse moral attitudes in their relationships to social structures.

IX. Genesis of Mind and Moral Sense

John Locke [1632–1704]. Locke did not contribute to social studies. But, indirectly, his empiricism and psychologism had tremendous repercussions in the rising social sciences. See, in particular, his *Essay Concerning Human Understanding (1690), Some Thoughts Concerning Education* (1693), and *Reasonableness of Christianity* (1695). His theoretical philosophy should lay the foundations to certain ethics. Since his work, all social studies are necessarily interconnected with epistemology, the basis of philosophy. Epistemology constructs the presuppositions for all social branches of action. It opens a road toward sociological investigations on the conditions of what men know or think they know—what we call today the sociology of knowledge. Locke's approach toward the genesis of our perceptions (psychological or rather psychogenetic) makes possible an analysis of our thinking processes. Locke's revolt against metaphysics and, in particular, against Descartes's innate ideas resulted in the most careful and cautious empiricism. This became the hallmark of the Scottish social sciences and most French studies from the Encyclopédie on. In particular, Locke's first stride toward psychology, his distinction between kinds of experience—sensation and reflection—and his analysis of the external and inner senses directed and determined Shaftesbury, Francis Hutcheson, and David Hume. In Locke's moral and educational writings, sociology as method prevails. Social conditions determine the articulate character of educational values, not different from Erasmus and Montaigne. In Locke's statements on morals and philosophy, he clearly conceives of the individual as socius whose personal well-being can be merely second to the standards and requirements of society.

Anthony Ashley-Cooper, 3rd Earl of Shaftesbury [1671–1713]. *Characteristicks of men, manners, opinions, times.* 3 volumes (London: John Derby, 1711). As a friend of Pierre Bayle, Shaftesbury continued and elaborated the idea of the complete independence of social and moral philosophies. He rejects theological efforts to hold ethics dependent on revelation, and he rejects Hobbes's efforts to find foundations of ethics in physiology or physics. Right, Virtue, and Goodness are valid in themselves. To know and realize them makes for human dignity and happiness. This is social eudaemonism—striving for and accomplishing the Good—is the highest pleasure and happiness. It is happiness because men fulfill the requirements of all embracing Nature. In striving for Right, Virtue, and Happiness, men adjust to the laws of nature. This is subordination under an understood context of Nature. Shaftesbury was influenced by the Stoics, by Spinoza, and by Giordano Bruno [1548–1600]. He believed in the harmony of the university, in the harmony and equilibrium of society, and in the pulchritude of the virtuous man. By harmony, he meant a unity of variety and a reconciliation of opposites. In presenting his philosophy in psychological terms, he appears as a student of

Locke's philosophy and psychology. By contrast, Hobbes had stated the original selfishness of human instincts.

Shaftesbury was partly influenced by **Richard Cumberland** [1632–1718] and his *De legibus naturæ disquisitio philosophica, in qua earum forma, summa capita, ordo, promulgatio, & obligatio è rerum natura investigantur; quinetiam elementa philosophiæ Hobbianæ, cum moralis tum civilis, considerantur & refutantur* (London: E. Flesher, 1672). Cumberland opposed Hobbes and made the benevolent, altruistic inclinations the foundations of social conduct. He considered these to be the counterweight to selfish passions and attempted to explain social process as a struggle between two complexes of drives. He agreed with Hobbes that man is egotistical by nature, but he insisted that man is also social. And he accepted Bacon's notion of psychological rules that guide inductive reasoning based on careful observation. But Cumberland thought that goodness was divinely created, whereas Shaftesbury saw it as original and substantive. Moreover, the two men disagreed about how men arrive at knowledge of the moral. Cumberland saw it as rational and intellectual, while Shaftesbury argued that men recognize the good by intuiting it.[24]

Shaftesbury saw man's selfish and social instincts as reconcilable, a harmony not based on prudence or on humility or subservience. Instead, he saw the reconciliation based on the constructive enthusiasm of human nature to achieve an identity of social and aesthetic perfection, a "moral taste." Shaftesbury made strides forward in psychological observations and intuitions. He laid the foundation for the sociology of sympathy and of intuition as practiced by the Scottish philosophers. He continued Locke's progress in the psychological analysis of passions. His analysis of the constructive and destructive types of enthusiasm and his description of the criteria for genuine enthusiasm are still valid and deserve a translation into modern psychological terminology. Further, he made remarkable progress when he coined the term *Moral Taste for Moral Sense*, a synthesis of Locke and of Stoic notions. It refers to the teleological character of our senses or instincts that lead us toward a well-balanced social and individual harmony as reflecting our being parts of a harmonious nature and universe. This universe is moving again and again for reestablishing its order and beauty. Man alone carries the responsibility for realizing the pattern of *kosmos* in self and society. In this frame of reference, Shaftesbury created the socio-psychological notions that led to the sociological doctrines that flourished in Scotland. In connection with his philosophy, the idea of "form" gains relevance for social studies as indicating a variety of societal relationships as variables or invariables in constituting the duration of societies. In particular, his conceptions of "Inner Form" and "Form of Truth" are relevant to sociological and psychological depth analysis of social institutions. They are important for all sociological analyses of poetry and of the arts. They make possible, at least, the question of what "form" means for and in the history of philosophy.

Bernard Mandeville [1670–1733]. *Fable of the Bees or Private Vices, Publick Benefits* (London: J. Roberts, 1714). Mandeville was a satirist who sharply opposed Shaftesbury's social optimism. In fact, he thought that social reality is exactly opposite from Shaftesbury's view of it. The invariable nature of man, he argued, is selfish, competitive, ambitious, and proud. Moreover, only these characteristics and attitudes make society move, make it prosperous and lasting. Mandeville used debunking psychology for explaining economic prosperity. His work influenced Adam Smith and, later, Friedrich Hayek [1899–1992].

X. Unity of Sociology and Social Psychology

The Scottish School made a synthetic effort to connect the methods of the modern sciences of physics and psychology with the traditions of the past science of the Law of Nature in order to establish a doctrine of liberalism based on the analysis and description of social man in action.

Historical Circumstances. In Scotland, the religious contests of the seventeenth century created a spirit of political and intellectual vigilance and alertness that made Glasgow and Edinburgh the intellectual centers of civilization. The power of the Presbyterian Church was exerted on behalf of the people against foreign domination. The educated classes were in continuous struggle against the reactionary Highlanders and conservative British of the Anglican Church. This intermediate position created a liberality of sentiment and a moderate and open-minded way of thinking that made possible the pioneering efforts and advances in creating a science of society. The Scottish Kirk had the highest appreciation for learning and created an unparalleled level of scholarship and intellectual curiosity.

Scientific Circumstances. Since the seventeenth century, all problems concerned with moral obligations were slowly shifted to the scientific investigations of psychology and of the conduct of man in his life situations. The general trend of British thought can be described as a struggle against two alignments. The first front was against the religious traditions. The scientific ethos did not accept principles and values imposed from an outer authority; the moderns tried to understand and explain social norms as inherent in social action. The second front was the revolt against Hobbes who had transformed the philosophy of the Law of Nature into a naturalistic philosophy of society. The first thinkers who revolted against Hobbes were the Cambridge Platonists who assumed original moral intentions in man. They advocated the Stoic conception of innate ideas and established the primacy of moral principles as the law of nature in the consensus of the peoples (*lex naturae in consensu gentium*). Most important were Henry More [1614–1687] and Ralph Cudworth [1617–1688], both fellows of Christ's College at Cambridge University. Others were Benjamin Whichcote [1609–1683], Peter Sterry [1613–1672], John Smith [1618–1652], Nathaniel Culverwell [1619–1651], and John Worthington [1618–1671], all of whom were fellows of Emmanuel College at Cambridge.

Richard Cumberland called benevolent inclinations the natural basis of moral conduct. He connected the modern scientific laws of association and of the mechanism of motivation with the idea of the antagonistic drives and the principle of the victory of the benevolent and good impulses. He opened the way for transforming the science of the Law of Nature into a science that explained the immanent morality of man as a requirement of his being a member of society.

Shaftesbury first assumed that moral values and judgments cannot be ascribed to rational reflection alone. He declared the positive and illuminating contribution of enthusiasm and sentiment to acts and judgments of moral and social character. Genuine virtue is the reconciliation of selfish and social drives in the constructive effort to realize a harmonious and complete personality in the social world. Man is capable of creative sociability because of his value sentiments.

Francis Hutcheson [1694–1746], professor of moral philosophy at the University of Glasgow, established the first system of moral philosophy on the basis of the *moral sense*. He coined the term and defined it as our determination to be pleased with the happiness of others. This moral sense works like a focusing conscience or the Stoic □γεμονικόν (*hêgemonikon*) to which all things are subjected. Hutcheson distinguished the natural good as connected with the approval of the moral sense. The moral sense refers human action to the specific functions that they have in the requirements of a given situation. It makes it possible to function as an impartial observer in the middle of one's action. It is the objective conscience in each human being. The moral good constitutes the existence of man as a social being. The distinction between natural and moral good is confused by the way in which Hutcheson identifies "moral sense" with benevolence.

David Hume [1711–1776] succeeded in clarifying the issue of the moral sense scientifically. He believed that the social scientist should proceed from experience and from the simple to the complex, from self-evident principles to demonstrated conclusions. He violently rejected the rationalism and naturalism of the past. His radical theoretical skepticism opened the avenues for the understanding and the intelligible character of human feeling that constitute societal relationships and the continuity of society. He started from a positive and critical analysis of Shaftesbury and Hutcheson. Both had insisted that the "other-regarding" impulses are a constitutive part of human nature. Both accepted the idea that the universality, the immediacy, and obligation of the moral judgment indicate the universality of a feeling of values. But they failed when they dissolved the interdependent and indivisible character of impulses and feelings and separated selfish and benevolent impulses. Hume argued that all impulses as such are value-neutral and can have positive and negative significances in different situations. In quest of an objective basis of morals and moral judgment, Hume looked for something common to all men in a "universal principle of the human frame." He called this principle "utility" or "sympathy." He defined it as the communication of sentiments from man to man and the openness to all impressions of agreeable and disagreeable human attitudes. This intersubjectivity between communicating individuals makes possible the objectivity of moral judgments and furnishes the logical solution of the problems of the "moral sense." The moral judgment preserves its basis in the feelings and thus remains in immediate contact with all the varieties of moral experience. At the same time, it is able to transcend subjectivity because it is not based merely on the isolated feelings of a particular individual, but on his feelings as they actually develop through his interaction with his fellow men. When a man makes a moral judgment, he must "depart from his private and particular situation and must choose a point of view common to him with others. He must move some universal principle of the human frame and touch a string to which all mankind has an accord." Neither self-love nor benevolence can be the basis of moral virtues and judgments. Sympathy and humanity alone are concerned with the universal utility of all humankind. All acts of approval or blame are based on the objective and universal principle of the welfare and utility of society. This means that there is an objective basis for the mutuality and intersubjectivity of human beings in social action. Man is by nature social, developing through and cooperating with society. He encroaches on others, but he practices self-restraint. Hume's idea of society as continuous intersubjectivity has historical continuity and becomes the object of a science of society that describes the reciprocity and the manifestations of the mutual relationships in all intellectual and social accomplishments on the basis of empirical methods of social causation. Hume suggested many sociological topics in his essays.

Adam Smith [1723–1790] started from Hume's principle of sympathy as establishing an objective basis for understanding social action. He developed Hume's suggestions systematically and elaborated a science of society that dealt with a variety of social experiences. Beginning in 1737, he attended the University of Glasgow where Francis Hutcheson was his teacher. He studied at Oxford University from 1740 to 1746 and then became a professor of logic at the University of Glasgow in 1750. In 1752, he was appointed to a chair in moral philosophy and began a friendship with Hume. He published *The Theory of Moral Sentiments* (London: A. Millar, 1759), an essay analyzing the principles by which men naturally judge the conduct and character of their neighbors and afterwards of themselves. The sixth edition of this book appeared in 1777 (Dublin: J. Beatty and C. Jackson, No. 32, Skinner-Row). And he published *An Inquiry into the nature and causes of the Wealth of Nations* (London: William Strahan and Thomas Cadell, 1776).

As professor of moral philosophy, he was required to lecture on natural theology, ethics, jurisprudence, and politics. *The Theory of Moral Sentiments* covers the lectures on ethics. *The Lectures on Jurisprudence*, originally titled *Lectures on Justice, Police, Revenue and Arms*, ed. E. Canaan (Oxford: Clarendon Press, 1896), covers the course on the Law of Nature. *The Wealth of Nations* covers the course on politics. All of these books are sociological insofar as they present moral, legal, and economic relationships as diverse aspects of the self-realization of man as a member of society. They indicate that the empirical investigation of social causation substitutes for the science of the Law of Nature. Societal relationships are the primary datum of human history. They are actually and logically prior to the artificial institutions of the political and legal establishments. There is a natural liberty, a natural justice, and natural common sense that would establish harmony and equilibrium as long as men do not violate the laws of justice and are left perfectly free to pursue their own interests their own way and to bring both their industry and capital into competition with those of any other man. Hence, all systems of accumulated power and of monopolies should be completely taken away. Between the world of absolutistic planning and the free economic system, the Scottish sociology comes into existence as the liberal eschatology of universal world citizenship of independent natural societies. The ideal of the nature of society as a dynamic harmony of competition and cooperation is the measuring rod for explaining and interpreting the social process as a deviation from the normative being of society. Utilitarian and teleological elements are intertwined in the foundations of the sociology of Adam Smith. The condition of moral merit is the promotion of the common good. Each human being strives for this end because every man desires praise and finally succeeds in evaluating the ends as meanings in themselves and to be loveable, not only be loved. In the third part of this ethics, Smith describes the rise of moral autonomy, the slow emancipation from social bonds and obligations of primitive societies to the individual conscience of the objective knowledge of moral values. He anticipates the research of Edvard Alexander Westermarck [1862–1939] on the origins of morals. See, in particular, *The Origin and Development of the Moral Ideas*, 2 volumes (London and New York: Macmillan and Co., 1906–08).

The Theory of Moral Sentiments deals with types of conduct in a variety of situations such as establishing societal relationships and maintaining the continuity of social organizations. Smith was particularly concerned about how the moral feelings of the ruled elements of a society affect the foundations of the social order. In all three of his books under discussion here, he focuses on this problem of consensus, precedence, and authority as a moral problem and his analysis is thoroughly sociological. Smith transformed the traditions of moral philosophy into an analysis of human conduct in social action so that the underlying moral issues appear as problems of attitudes in social relationships. It is a terrible social truth that the subjects of political control justify their situations by morally evaluating the qualities and attitudes of their rulers. Smith carefully analyzed this confusion of sentiments as a sociologist. Furthermore, he made the first sociological study of the social/moral ethos of different social groups. In particular, he analyzed the specific virtues, merits, and limitations of the urban middle classes and the respective qualities, both positive and negative, of the aristocratic societies of the courts. His analysis of the advantages and disadvantages of the division of labor is a model case of objective sociological research. In this context, he investigated the conditions of labor and the political and legal weaknesses of their situations. In all his efforts, he pointed out that the sociologist investigates the depth-situation of social spheres in all details and all strata. His analyses of the progress of the urban classes and the decline of rural structures make him the founder of rural and urban sociology. His analyses of militarism have the highest value for sociologists.

Outline of Adam Smith's important sociological work:

Topics

Consensus

Prestige

Reform

Revolution

Moral Sentiments

Book IV, Part 2, para. 2

Book VI, Part 2, para. 1

Jurisprudence

Part I, Chapter I, Part I

Wealth of Nations

Book V, Chapter I, Part 2

Militarism

Jurisprudence

Part IV

Wealth of Nations

Book V, Chapter I, Part 1

Social Change

Jurisprudence

Part I, Chapter I, paras. 2–16

Wealth of Nations

Book V, Chapter I, Part 3

Rural

Jurisprudence

Part II, Chapter 1, para. 16

Wealth of Nations

Book I, Chapter 2

Book III, Chapters 2 and 4

Urban

Jurisprudence

Part II, Chapter 2, para. 17

Wealth of Nations

Book III, Chapters 1, 3, 4

Book V, Chapter 1, Part 3

Labor

Jurisprudence

Part II, Chapter 2, para. 17

Wealth of Nations

Book I, Chapter 8

Book V, Chapter I, Part 3

Law

Jurisprudence

Part I, Chapter 2, paras. 1–4

Part I, Chapter 3, paras. 1–9

Wealth of Nations

Book I, Chapter 8

Book V, Chapter I, Part 3

Division of Labor

Jurisprudence
Part II, Chapter 2, paras. 3–6
Wealth of Nations
Book V, Chapter 1–3,
Book V, Chapter 1, Part 3, para. 2

Adam Ferguson [1723–1816] came from a family of ministers and took holy orders himself. He was chaplain in the army from 1745 to 1754. He was appointed to a chair in natural philosophy at the University of Edinburgh in 1759 and to a chair in moral philosophy there in 1764. He published *An Essay on the History of Civil Society* (London: Andrew Millar and Thomas Cadell, 1767); *Institutes of Moral Philosophy: For the Use of Students in the College of Edinburgh* (Edinburgh: Alexander Kinkaid & J. Bell, 1769), a book that went through many editions and was translated into many languages; *The History of the Progress and Termination of the Roman Republic*, 3 volumes (London: William Strahan & Thomas Cadell, 1783); and *Principles of Moral and Political Science* (Edinburgh: William Creech, 1792).

In contrast to Adam Smith, Ferguson was less optimistic about the workings of civil society as emancipated from power. So his contribution to sociology was more realistic in a comprehensive way:

1. He anticipated Max Weber's discussion of the methodological problems of social science. He studied the subjective elements in the use of documents and foreshadowed the critical method of Karl Paul Reinhold Niebuhr [1892–1971] in dealing with the mythological and religious foundations of primitive societies. He discovered the specific character of

sociological generalizations as presenting a rational construction of social reality in abstractions.

2. He used the suggestion of Thucydides and investigated the early history of the Greeks and Romans in light of anthropological discoveries. He described primitive society before the origin of property as a matriarchal group with free human relationships and evaluated the older men, the military youth, and the communion of the adult male members of the tribe. He gave the most comprehensive analysis of the character type of the warrior who, when outside the sphere of military action, was lazy and devoted to inertia, drinking, and gambling. He was the first to state that this was a sociological, not historical, condition. In dealing with primitive societies once the institution of property had emerged, he stressed the interdependence between types of government and legal structures.

3. He anticipated the problems of formal sociology with repeated efforts to emphasize the relevance of size (population, territory) for the character of social groupings. He was aware that the optimum of social organizations might depend on marginal situations.

4. He anticipated Arnold Toynbee [1889–1975] and his category of "challenge and response" with thorough investigations of the conditions of great social accomplishments. Virtues are indispensable for establishing and maintaining wealth, power, and continuous improvements. And virtues come into

existence only under conditions of danger, pressure, and conflict.

5. He developed the problems of the division of labor as interdependent with those of social stratification.

6. He discarded the organic theory of history as cycle and suggested a spiral theory that makes it possible to combine the unending continuity and interpenetration of civilizations with the categories of corruption and decay as sociological generalizations.

7. He prepared the way for the sociological analysis and description of historical processes and situations as the empirical science that made it possible to present the most comprehensive typology of human behavior patterns in social action as the self-realization of man. For this reason, he was eager to give an account of the advantages and disadvantages of progress in the diverse spheres of man as far as the completeness and happiness of man and society are concerned. In this respect, he anticipated the work of Burckhardt that connected sociology, history, and a doctrine of man.

8. He vigorously described the relevance of military virtues for perfect civil societies as the only guarantees for the maintenance and survival of progress in societies. He assumed that human perfection and social happiness were possible only if the political-philosophical and military-pragmatic virtues were not separated from each other.

9. He traced the first outline for a doctrine of man on the basis of empirical investigations and the elaboration of types of social behavior that are recurrent in different situations and show the identity of human nature in its dynamic adjustment to a variety of conditions. The inclinations of human nature remain the same. However, they look different in different situations such as those that call for courage or the adherence to honor, or to situations where luxury, corruption, or artificiality prevails. Ferguson's work points out more clearly than that of Adam Smith the transformation of the science of the Law of Nature into a sociology of the social and historical process with the philosophical intent to reestablish a scientific knowledge of man. This is because of his more violent temper in attacking the interdependence of the various strata of human beings in social action.

Bibliography:

Leslie Stephen, *History of English Thought in the Eighteenth Century*, 2 volumes (New York: G. P. Putnam's Sons, 1876)

Leslie Stephen, "Adam Smith," *Dictionary of National Biography*, 66 volumes (London: Smith, Elder & Co., 1885–1901)

James McCosh, *The Scottish Philosophy, biographical, expository, critical from Hutcheson to Hamilton* (London: Macmillan, 1875)

Richard Schüller, *Die klassische Nationalökonomie und ihre Gegner: zur Geschichte der Nationalökonomie und Social politik seit A. Smith* (Leipzig: Zentralantiquariat, 1976, originally published in 1895)

Albion W. Small, *Adam Smith and Modern Sociology: a study in the methodology of the social sciences* (Chicago: University of Chicago Press, 1907)

Albion W. Small, *Origins of Sociology* (Chicago: University of Chicago Press, 1924)

Dugald Stewart, *Collected Works*, 11 volumes. Volume 10, *Biographical memoirs of Adam Smith, William Robertson, Thomas Reid* (Edinburgh: T. Constable and Co., London: Hamilton, Adams & Co., 1854–60)

Glenn R. Morrow, *The Ethical and Economic Theories of Adam Smith* (New York: A. M. Kelley, 1969, reprint of 1923 edition)

Glenn R. Morrow, "The Significance of the Doctrine of Sympathy in Hume and Adam Smith," *The Philosophical Review*, Vol. 32, No 1 (January 1923), 60–78

Franklin Henry Giddings, *Studies in the Theory of Human Society* (New York: Macmillan Company, 1922)

Henry Laurie, *Scottish Philosophy in its National Development* (Glasgow: J. Maclehose, 1902)

William Christian Lehmann, *Adam Ferguson and the Beginnings of Modern Sociology* (New York: Columbia University Press, 1930)

Alfred North Whitehead, *Science and the Modern World: Lowell Lectures* (New York: Macmillan, 1925)

Georges Germain Lechartier, *David Hume: moraliste et sociologue* (Paris: F. Alcan, 1900)

Adam Smith, *An Inquiry into the Wealth of Nations*, ed. E. Cannan, 2nd edition, (London: Methuen, 1920)

Adam Smith, *Lectures on Justice, Police, Revenue and Arms*, ed. E. Cannan (Oxford: Clarendon Press, 1896)

Among Scottish scholars who established a science of society, Adam Smith strongly emphasized the economic aspects of societal relationships; Ferguson, the political and military foundations; and **John Millar** [1735–1801], the legal structures of the social constitutions. Together, they accomplished the complete transformation of the past science of the Law of Nature, which referred the life of man to a religious or cosmological frame of reference, into an empirical science of society that referred to the social and historical processes of man to an ideal society of independent and just human competitors. This science is an empirical science because it recognizes moral, political, and legal norms and values merely as impulses and intentions inherent in the human constitution and challenged by specific circumstances.

Millar attended Glasgow College and enjoyed the friendship and expectations of Adam Smith, David Hume, and Henry Home (Lord Kames) whose research on the history of manners and law largely determined Millar's own interests and investigations. Adam Smith and Lord Kames highly recommended Millar to become professor of law at Glasgow in 1761. His books on sociological problems are *The Origin of the Distinction of Ranks, or an inquiry into the circumstances which give rise to influence and authority in the different members of society*, 3rd edition (London: sold by J. Murray, Fleet Street, 1779, originally published in 1771) and *An Historical View of the English Government: from the settlement of the Saxons in Britain to the Accession of the house of Stewart* (London: A. Strahan and T. Cadell, 1787).

These books examine the functions of legal institutions in society and explain changes as enforced by processes in the development and progress of society. Millar analyzed not only the political institutions. He also described the fundamental changes in the legal status of women, servants, and children, because of the rise of urban and civilized societies. He applied the results of his findings in his militant struggle against the slave trade, in which he was joined by Francis Hutcheson, David Hume, Adam Smith, James Beattie, and Adam Ferguson.[25] The analyses in parts four and five of the Origin regarding the development of the urbanized patricians in Greece, Rome, America, and in all situations of colonization has become a model case of sociological description and explanation, followed by Guglielmo Ferrero [1871–1942] and Max Weber. The same praise can be extended to his analysis of the rise of the absolutistic regime that is correctly described as the result of the universal necessity for rationalizing the context of domestic and foreign policies. Here again, we find striking anticipation of Max Weber's famous presentation of the trends toward rationalization.

In his doctrine of man, he leaned heavily on Adam Smith's *Theory of Moral Sentiments* and suggested only slight corrections. He described the highest moral values as the effort toward establishing such self-control as to reduce our feelings to the level of the disinterested spectator. This complete self-objectification seems to him more valuable than utility or rectitude.

Conclusions. The Scottish School established the first science of society on the basis of psychology, moral philosophy, and the proud self-consciousness of an enlightened and urbanized middle-class society. They described the interdependent political, legal, economic, and biological strata in the causal context as referring to basic and constitutive impulses and intentions of man. They were aware that there is no blind historical necessity or evolution; there is instead acting and being acted upon, independence and dependence at the same time. They stated that progress and corruption could exist on all levels of the social process. They were eager to emphasize that they were mainly interested in one problem: the interpretation and the explanation of the dynamic kaleidoscope that we call "human being" that remains identical in a variety of situations. Happiness, striving for perfection, valor, honor, thoughtfulness, ambition, vanity, appear in all situations as many disguises, but they remain the same all the time. All the authors, however different their approaches may be, have this in common: they understand institutions in terms of societal relationships and societal relationships in terms of human desire and meaningful intentions.

For this reason, we may call this school a humanistic school of sociology because society is not imposed on the individuals as was suggested later on by Durkheim, but society is the free cooperation and competition of independent individuals under the protection and guidance of natural justice and natural common sense. Therefore, we may call this humanistic school of sociology a liberal and optimistic one. It has its analogy in the German School that was also a humanistic and liberal school, too, but in despair and pessimism. The Scottish School opened the way for an unbiased analysis of the social process as the interpenetration of human constellations rather than of institutions. It established an ideal of society as a frame of reference that is closest to the social implications of Gestalt psychology. It presents the sociology of moral sentiments as the sociological approach toward a theory of attitudes. This made possible and opened the road for sociologists like the radical empiricist M. Raul Frédéric Rauh [1861–1909] and Max Scheler [1874–1928], who promoted and developed the sociology of emotional attitudes. Finally, it used the historical processes as the material for a science of human behavior patterns and suggested and, in many respects, surpassed future historical sociology.

Notes

1. [*Satires et oeuvres de M. Boileau- Despréaux* (Londres: J. Nourse, 1776).—Eds.]

2. [*Moriae Encomium*. English from the Latin. 1509. Trans. White Kennett (London: G. Bickham, 173?).—Eds.]

3. [*Geschichte der Kriegskunst im Rahmen der politischen Geschichte*, 3 volumes (Berlin: G. Stilke, 1908–23).—Eds.]

4. [The most important of these was Francisco Suárez [1548–1617], a Spanish Jesuit priest. See, in particular, his *Tractatus De Legibus, Ac Deo Legislatore in Decem Libros Distributus, Utriusque Fori Hominibus Non Minus Utilis, Quam Necessarius* (Londini: Sumptibus J. Dunmore, T. Dring, B. Tooke & T. Sawbridge, 1679).—Eds.]

5. [(London: Printed for Andrew Crooke, at the Green Dragon in St. Paul's churchyard, 1651).—Eds.]

6. [Published in English as *Philosophical Rudiments Concerning Government and Society* (London: Printed by J. G. for R. Royston at the Angel in Ivie-lane, 1651).—Eds.]

7. [The English edition is *The Whole Duty of Man According to the Law of Nature* (London: Printed by Benj. Motte for Charles Harper, 1691).—Eds.]

8. [The English edition is *The Law of Nature and Nations*, 4th ed. (London: Printed for J. Walthoe et al., 1729).—Eds.]

9. [*Essayes: Religious Meditations. Places of perswasion and disswasion. Seene and Allowed.* (London: Printed by John Windet for Humfrey Hooper, 1597).—Eds.]

10. [Jan Rieuwertsz published Spinoza's treatise anonymously in Amsterdam to protect both himself and the author from Dutch authorities. Spinoza wrote the book in Latin, instead of Dutch, in an effort to avoid censorship.—Eds.]

11. [Spinoza, *Works*, Bohn ed. (London: G. Bell & Sons, 1916), 1:73.—Eds.]

12. [Spinoza, *Works*, Bohn ed., 1:259. See also, V. T. Thayer, "A Comparison of the Ethical Philosophies of Spinoza and Hobbes," *The Monist* (October 1922), 553–68.—Eds.]

13. [Lucius Annaeus Seneca, *On Benefits*. Series: *The Complete Works of Lucius Annaeus Seneca* Eds. Elizabeth Asmis, Shadi Bartsch, and Martha C. Nussbaum (Chicago: University of Chicago Press, 2011).—Eds.]

14. [Marcus Tullius Cicero, *De Finibus Bonorum et Malorum*, ed. Julia Annas, trans. Raphel Woolf (Cambridge, UK: Cambridge University Press, 2001).—Eds.]

15. [*The Essential Spinoza: Ethics and Related Writings* (Indianapolis, IN: Hackett Publishing Company, 2006).—Eds.]

16. [Published in English as *A Discourse of a Method for the Well Guiding of Reason, and the Discovery of the Truth in the Sciences* (London: Printed by Thomas Newcombe, 1649).—Eds.]

17. [See James S. Munro, Mademoiselle de Scudéry and The Carte de Tendre (Durham: University of Durham, 1986); Nicole Aronson, Mlle. de Scudéry ou Le Voyage Au Pays de Tendre (Paris: Librairie Fayard, 1986).—Eds.]

18. [See, for instance, *An introduction to a deuoute life composed in Frenche by the R. Father in God Francis Sales, Bishop of Geneua*, trans. I.Y. (Douai: Printed by G. Patté for John Heigham, 1613.—Eds.]

19. [Bergson's final published book was *La pensée et le mouvant*, a book of essays and lectures from 1903 to 1923. It was published in English as *The Creative Mind: An Introduction to Metaphysics* (New York: Philosophical Library, 1946).—Eds.]

20. [(Paris: G. De Luyne, 1687). The first English edition appeared a year later as *The History of Oracles, and the Cheats of the Pagan Priests, in two parts* (London: [s.n.], 1688).—Eds.]

21. [The first English version appeared the same year as *New Dialogues of the Dead: in three parts/dedicated to Lusian in Elysium;* made English by J. D. (London: Printed for D. Y., 1683).—Eds.]

22. [See Pierre Rétat, "Libertinage et hétérodoxie: Pierre Bayle in Aspects et contours du libertinage," *Dix-Septième Siècle Paris*, vol. 32, no. 2 (1980), 197–211.—Eds.]

23. [An early English edition is *Persian Letters*, trans. J. Ozell (1722).—Eds.]

24. [See Alexander Lyons (1867–1939), *Shaftesbury's Ethical Principle of Adaptation to Universal Harmony*. PhD Dissertation, New York University, 1909, 32–4.—Eds.]

25. [For a sharp critique of the practical efforts of these philosophers against the slave trade, see Glen Ian Doris, *The Scottish Enlightenment and the Politics of Abolition*, DPhil Thesis (University of Aberdeen, 2011). But see also Fred Ablondi, "Millar on Slavery," *Journal of Scottish Philosophy*, vol. 7, no. 2, 163–75.—Eds.]

25

An Introduction to Sociology for Students of the Social Sciences and of the Humanities: Balzac as Sociologist (1949–50)

I. Balzac's Thesis: The Human Comedy is a Historical-Sociological Treatise

A. His description implies the social function and the scientific significance of the social novel in a world of total revolution.

B. The Prefaces—Human Comedy, Girl with Golden Eyes, Ferragus, Facino Cane, Cousine Bette—indicate the specific place of his sociology between Bonald and Comte. In our historical perspective we recognize its affinity to Marx. We discover his influence on Max Weber, his anticipation of Simmel's microsociological method, of Lynd's analyses of Middletown and of Veblen's analysis of the dynamism of the technological and industrial society. The Human Comedy is a genuine piece of literature of sociology.

Previously unpublished. Manuscript located in New School faculty vertical files collection, NS.08.02.02, unprocessed collection, The New School Archives and Special Collections, The New School, New York, New York. Published by permission from Frank Salomon.

C. On the other hand, he states the scientific possibilities of a sociology of literature which explains and understands the changes in literary forms as resulting from social changes.

II. The Scientific Method

A. The microsociological analysis

1. Milieu: Father Goriot, The Old Girl, The Vicar of Tours
2. Environment: Marriage Contract, *La Muse du Département*
3. Worlds: Peasants, Government Clerks, Gobseck, Birotteau

B. The analysis of social structures

1. The structured world of the countryside: The Country Doctor
2. The structure of the intelligentsia: Treatises and *Scènes de la vie parisienne*
3. The structure of economic rackets: Gobseck, House Nucingen
4. The structure of bureaucracies: Government Clerks, Petty Bourgeois

C. The conception of ideal types

Balzac's character types are mainly cases of extreme and radical passions. This implies the methodological unification and generalization, which we call ideal types: Gaudissart, Deputy of Arcas, Z. Marcas, Princess of Cadignan, Esther, Vautrin, Nucingen, Gobseck, Goriot, Birotteau.

D. Phenomenological descriptions
   1. Gossip in a provincial town: The Old Girl, Grandet, Mirouet
   2. Social Control in Middletown: *La Rabouilleuse*
   3. Solitude in society: *La Muse du Département*

III. The Depth Strata of Society: Man within and without Society

A. The meaning of Balzac's classification of the Human Comedy

B. Society: the world of belonging to: Birotteau, Government Clerks

C. Society: the dynamics of advancement
   1. The ideals of social careers in the classes: Prefaces
   2. Economic progress:
      work: Birotteau, Gaudissaret, Séchard
      speculation: the bankers
      professional skills: Derville
   3. Social progress:
      push and pulls: Rastignac
      sex: Rubempre

D. Society: the matter of control: Rastignac, Gobseck, Vautrin

E. Society: the mutuality of controls and escapes: Rabouilleuse, Old Girl, Vicar of Tours, *La Muse du Département*

F. Society: the world to be escaped: *La Peau de Chagrin*

G. Society: the world to be renounced: Seamy Side of History

IV. Social Pathology

Anomie and Alienation:

A. The confusion of means-end relations: Nucingen, Gobseck, Goriot

B. The destructive effects of misplaced charity: Cousine Bette

C. The social perversions of marital relations: Treatise

D. The confusion between sex, love, passion: Cadignan, *La Duchesse de Langeais*

E. The outlaw: Vautrin

Should appear here and in the next chapter. He is alienated to the functional whole of a true society because he follows the same pattern of acquiring power for the sake of power which is cherished by the insiders of society who manipulate violence through the loopholes of law and conventions.

V. Marginality

A. The outlaw: Vautrin

B. The stranger: Gobseck, Marriage Contract

C. The strange outsider: *La Muse du Département*, Old Girl, Grandet, Cadignan, *Splendeurs* . . . etc.

D. The homecomer: Chabert, Bridau, Gilet, the officers of Napoleon

E. The adventurer: Rubempre

F. The gamblers: Young and Old Elite, *Splendeurs* . . .

G. The ballet: "Rate" and "*Marcheuses*," *Splendeurs* . . .

H. The police: secret, political, counterintelligence, criminal, commercial: *Splendeurs* . . . all volumes

VI. Social Change and Theory of History

A. Finance as the total determinism of the modern world

B. Merging of the economic and political revolution: total revolution

C. The transfer of the Napoleonic charismatism to all spheres of economic, social, personal conduct

A–C throughout the Human Comedy

D. The technological elements in the processes of revolution

1. Inventions: Gaudissart, Birotteau, Séchard
2. Rational administration: Government Clerks, offices of men of law
3. The new industrialism splits society into two classes, capital and labor, their conflict. The rise of the revolutionary proletariat as the revolt of the new barbarians: On the Workers, On Modern Government, Social Catechism . . .

VII. Social Control

A. The total control by money powers: all books

B. Technology in the distribution of social power

1. Administration as actual rulers: Physiology of Employee, Government Clerks
2. Public opinion and the manipulation of social values: mutual interdependence of intellectuals and elite: all books

3. Pressure groups:

   Camarilla: its analysis

   The law of the small numbers: on Modern Government, House Nucingen, Gobseck, Petty Bourgeois, Government Clerks

4. Traditions:
   a) Social conduct as ritual: *La Muse du Département*
   b) Stereotypes of duties, pleasures, hobbies: *La Muse du Département*, Old Girl, Vicar of Tours, Grandet, Miroust, *La Rabouilleuse*
   c) Gossip: same

5. Fashions:
   a) *La vie élégante*
   b) *La femme comme il faut*
   c) Matrimonial Requirements in bourgeoisie: three different treatises

VIII. Leisure Class

A. Leisure class and unleisurely wealth: all books Provincial and Parisian Life

B. Political monopolies and economic monopolies: Nucingen, Goriot, Gobseck

C. Leisure, sex, love: Cadignan, Women of Thirty, Goriot, *La Duchesse de Langeais*

D. Leisure, thought, poetry: Cadignan, *Splendeurs . . .*

E. Societal relations in a leisure class society: same

F. The vanishing of a true leisure class and the limitations of Veblen's approach: same

IX. Social Stratification

A. The principle of classification: independence, security.

B. Three classes: workers, thinkers, leisure

C. Laborless income: leisure class truly independent

D. Income through labor: dependencies and insecurity, from manual labor to the highest ranks of the professions and of the civil service. Detailed analyses in the Prefaces, in the Treatises on *Rentiers* and on *La vie élégante.*

X. Sex, Love, Marriage in various classes of Society

A. The rural traditions of sex and love: Peasants, Country Doctor

B. The petty bourgeoisie and the travelling salesman: Gaudissart

C. The respectable bourgeoisie in Paris and in the province: Birotteau, The Sufferings of the Inventor

D. The intellectuals and the game of love: *La Muse du Département*, *Splendeurs*

E. The traditionalistic groups: Antiques, Old Girl, Mirouet

F. The aristocratic elite: Cadignan, Woman of Thirty, Goriot, *Splendeurs*, *La Duchesse de Langeais*

XI. Intellectuals and Bohemians

A. Journalists as element in social control: Treatises on Elegance, Fashion, Government

B. Journalists as victims of the bourgeois spirit: *Splendeurs . . .*

C. Artists drawn into business: advertising: Gaudissart, Birotteau

D. Poets and writers, their dilemma: Cousine Bette, Cousin Pons, *Splendeurs . . .*

XII. The Rise of Bureaucracies and the Phenomenology of Offices

A. The social relations in the working of an administrative office
   1. The office boy
   2. The supernumeraries
   3. The cashier
   4. The clerk with tenure
   5. The lowest chief of bureau

B. The social relations in the administration
   1. Friends and enemies
   2. Gangs, competitive rackets
   3. Intrigues, advancement, careers
   4. Social role of wives of colleagues and of superiors
   5. Social role of the confessors for the ambitious
   6. Intermarriage as a problem of the career
   7. The part-time jobs and their repercussions for the career
   8. Grandeur and misery of the white collar worker

   For the whole chapter: Government Clerks, Petty Bourgeois, and *Physiologie de l'employe*

XIII. Urban Sociology

A. Middletown
   1. The market town: Grandet, Mirouet
   2. The administrative town: Old Girl
   3. The *rentier* town: *La Rabouilleuse*

B. Metropolitan area:
   1. The meeting between political and economic powers
   2. Relativity of open and closed groups
   3. Pride and prejudices
   4. Cynicism and fanaticism

      For B 1–4: *Scènes de la vie parisienne*

XIV. Rural Sociology

A. The country life as potential ideal

B. The peasants as revolutionary group

C. The military inventions: Peasants and Indians

   For A–C: Chouans, Peasants, Country Doctor

XV. Charity and Social Work

A. New devices: rehabilitation vs. charity

B. Renunciation and the elite: The Seamy Side of History

Note on the Editors

Duffy Graham is the author of *The Consciousness of the Litigator.*

Robert Jackall is Willmott Family Professor of Sociology and Public Affairs, Emeritus, at Williams College. He is the author of *Moral Mazes: The World of Corporate Managers* and *Street Stories: The World of Police Detectives*, among other books.

Robert Jackall and Duffy Graham are the editors of *From Joseph Bensman: Essays on Modern Society* (Newfound Press, 2014).

Index

www.ingramcontent.com/pod-product-compliance
Lightning Source LLC
Chambersburg PA
CBHW020328270326
41926CB00007B/92